THE CAMBRIDGE HANDBOOK OF THE LAW, ETHICS AND POLICY OF ARTIFICIAL INTELLIGENCE

This informative Handbook provides a comprehensive overview of the legal, ethical, and policy implications of artificial intelligence (AI) and algorithmic systems, with a focus on Europe. As these technologies continue to impact various aspects of our lives, it is crucial to understand and assess the challenges and opportunities they present. Drawing on contributions from experts in various disciplines, this book covers theoretical insights and practical examples of how AI systems are used in society today, as well as exploring the legal and policy instruments governing AI. The interdisciplinary approach of this book makes it an invaluable resource for anyone seeking to gain a deeper understanding of AI's impact on society and how it should be regulated. This title is also available as Open Access on Cambridge Core.

Nathalie A. Smuha is a legal scholar and philosopher at the KU Leuven Faculty of Law and Criminology, where she examines legal and ethical questions around AI and other digital technologies. Her research focuses particularly on AI's impact on human rights, democracy, and the rule of law. Professor Smuha is the academic coordinator of the KU Leuven Summer School on the Law, Ethics and Policy of AI and a member of the KU Leuven Institute for Artificial Intelligence and the Digital Society Institute. She is also the author of *Algorithmic Rule by Law: How Algorithmic Regulation in the Public Sector Erodes the Rule of Law* (2025).

The Cambridge Handbook of the Law, Ethics and Policy of Artificial Intelligence

Edited by

NATHALIE A. SMUHA

KU Leuven Faculty of Law and Criminology

CAMBRIDGE
UNIVERSITY PRESS

CAMBRIDGE
UNIVERSITY PRESS

Shaftesbury Road, Cambridge CB2 8EA, United Kingdom

One Liberty Plaza, 20th Floor, New York, NY 10006, USA

477 Williamstown Road, Port Melbourne, VIC 3207, Australia

314–321, 3rd Floor, Plot 3, Splendor Forum, Jasola District Centre, New Delhi – 110025, India

103 Penang Road, #05–06/07, Visioncrest Commercial, Singapore 238467

Cambridge University Press is part of Cambridge University Press & Assessment, a department of the University of Cambridge.

We share the University's mission to contribute to society through the pursuit of education, learning and research at the highest international levels of excellence.

www.cambridge.org
Information on this title: www.cambridge.org/9781009367813

DOI: 10.1017/9781009367783

When citing this work, please include a reference to the DOI 10.1017/9781009367783

First published 2025

A catalogue record for this publication is available from the British Library

A Cataloging-in-Publication data record for this book is available from the Library of Congress

ISBN 978-1-009-36781-3 Hardback

To the AI Summer School alumni

Contents

Figures and Tables

FIGURES

TABLES

Contributors

Imre Bárd is a postdoctoral researcher on the ethics team of the Dutch National Laboratory for AI in Education (NOLAI). He supports the responsible design and development of AI-driven solutions for primary and secondary schools. Imre's research interests include techno-moral change and the intersection of AI and democratic innovation. He holds a PhD in social research methodology from the London School of Economics, where he studied the social representation of neuroenhancement. He has an MSc in sociology from LSE and a degree in philosophy from the University of Vienna. Since 2022, Imre has been a contracted Trust and Safety analyst at OpenAI. Past engagements include academic and think tank projects on responsible innovation in neurotechnology, AI governance, and participatory AI development. Imre has been the (co-)recipient of grant funding from the European Commission, the Wellcome Trust, Google's Artists and Machines Intelligence Program, and the Survival and Flourishing Fund.

Duuk Baten is Responsible Tech Lead at SURF, the Dutch National Research and Education Network. With a background in the philosophy of science and technology from the University of Twente, Duuk has developed a strong passion for responsible innovation and public values in technology. As a core team member of the Dutch AI Coalition's Education working group, he actively contributes to shaping AI initiatives in the Dutch educational ecosystem. He served as an expert in the European Commission's AI in Education expert group, contributing to the creation of the European Commission ethical guidelines on the use of AI and data use in education. He has coauthored the insightful reports "Promises of AI in Education," "Responsible Tech: On Public Values and Emerging Technologies," and "The Impact of AI on the Modern Educational Institution."

Friso Bostoen is Assistant Professor of Competition Law and Digital Regulation at Tilburg University. Previously, he was Max Weber Fellow at the European University Institute. He holds degrees from KU Leuven (PhD and LLM) and Harvard University (LLM). Friso's research focuses on antitrust enforcement in digital markets. His work has resulted in numerous international publications, presentations, and awards (including the AdC Competition Policy Award 2019 and the Concurrences PhD Award 2022). In addition, Friso edits the *CoRe Blog* and hosts the *Monopoly Attack* podcast.

Stefan Buijsman is Associate Professor of the Philosophy of Technology at Delft University of Technology (TU Delft) and focuses on responsible AI. He has a background in the philosophy of mathematics, on which he did his PhD at Stockholm University, and his current research is primarily on the explainability and transparency of AI systems. Throughout his career, his approach has always been interdisciplinary; he conducts research both purely philosophically and in collaborations with cognitive scientists and computer scientists. He also manages the TU Delft Digital Ethics Centre, which broadly works on projects translating ethical requirements into (socio-)technical design requirements with stakeholders such as hospitals, the Dutch social benefit organizations, and the provincial governments.

Jan De Bruyne is Professor of IT Law at the KU Leuven and Head of the Centre for IT and IP Law (CiTiP). He teaches several courses on law and technology and is the Principal Investigator (PI) of many projects dealing with the legal and ethical aspects of technology. He successfully defended his PhD in September 2018 on a topic dealing with the liability of third-party certifiers. During his research, he became interested in liability for damage caused by AI systems. Jan De Bruyne was a postdoctoral researcher at the Ghent University Faculty of Law and Criminology working on robots and tort law from October 2018 to October 2020. He started working at CiTiP in October 2019 as a postdoctoral researcher on legal aspects of AI and as a senior researcher within the Flemish Knowledge Centre for Data & Society. From November 2020, he worked at CiTiP as a research expert on (tort) law and AI.

Tinne De Laet is a Full Professor at the Faculty of Engineering Science, KU Leuven. She obtained a doctoral degree in mechanical engineering in 2010 at KU Leuven, Belgium, supported by a scholarship from the Research Foundation – Flanders (FWO). She was a FWO postdoctoral researcher at KU Leuven from 2010 to 2013. In 2013, she obtained a tenure track position, focusing on engineering education and supporting and counselling of students, in particular during the transition from secondary to higher education. She is the Head of the Tutorial Services of Engineering Science, providing her with firsthand experience on the transition from secondary to higher education. Her research focuses on using learning analytics, explainable AI, academic advising, self-regulation in science, technology, engineering, and math (STEM), and study success of STEM students. She teaches courses in mechanics and AI and is driven to contribute to the advancement of education by multidisciplinary research combining AI and educational sciences, all with a strong ethical foundation.

Luc De Raedt is currently Director of Leuven.AI, the KU Leuven Institute for AI, Full Professor of Computer Science at KU Leuven, and Guest Professor at Örebro

University (Sweden) at the Center for Applied Autonomous Sensor Systems in the Wallenberg AI, Autonomous Systems and Software Program. He obtained his PhD in computer science from KU Leuven (1991). He was Full Professor and Chair of the Machine Learning and Natural Language Processing Lab at the Albert-Ludwigs-University Freiburg, Germany (1999–2006); and Head of the Lab for Declarative Languages and Artificial intelligence at KU Leuven from 2015 to 2019. His research interests are in AI, machine learning, and data mining, as well as their applications. He is well known for his contributions in the areas of learning and reasoning, in particular, for his contributions to statistical relational learning and probabilistic and inductive programming.

Pierre Dewitte is a researcher in law at the KU Leuven Centre for IT and IP Law (CiTiP), where he conducts interdisciplinary research on data protection by design, privacy engineering, smart cities, and algorithmic transparency. His main research track seeks to bridge the gap between software engineering practices and data protection regulations by creating a common conceptual framework for both disciplines and providing decision and trade-off support for technical and organizational mitigation strategies in the software development life cycle. He is also involved in multiple enforcement actions before the Belgian and Irish data protection authorities.

Lidia Dutkiewicz is a doctoral researcher at the KU Leuven Centre for IT and IP Law (CiTiP) – imec. In her PhD research, she analyses the regulation of online platforms from a freedom of expression perspective. She researches the phenomenon of the "platformization" of news and the impact of algorithmic content moderation on media freedom and media pluralism. She also works on the EU-funded AI4Media project, where she provides legal and ethical guidance on the use of AI in media. In the ALGEPI (understanding ALGorithmic gatekeepers to promote EPIstemic welfare) project, she investigates the power imbalance between platforms and media and the legal aspects of news recommender systems. Lidia also works as an ethics advisor in the vera.ai project. She is a coauthor of the EC report on the Pilot Project – Digital European Platform of Quality Content Providers (Media Data Space) and of a study on the national transposition of the Audiovisual Media Services Directive.

Gry Hasselbalch is an author and scholar with expertise in data and AI ethics and governance. She is the Cofounder and Director of academic research of the think tank DataEthics.eu, which has been active since 2015 in challenging the power of big tech companies. Gry holds a PhD in data ethics from the University of Copenhagen and has authored several influential books and reports, including *Data Ethics of Power: A Human Approach in the Big Data and AI Era* (2021), *Data Ethics: The New Competitive Advantage* (2016), and *Data Pollution & Power* (2022). She has played a crucial role in shaping core global policy documents and discussions, particularly on AI and data. Notably, she was a member of the EU's High-Level Expert Group on AI and Senior Key Expert (2018–20) for the EU's International Outreach for a Human-Centric Approach to Artificial Intelligence initiative (InTouchAI.eu, 2021–24).

Michael Klenk is a tenured Assistant Professor of ethics and philosophy of technology at TU Delft. He earned his PhD in philosophy from Utrecht University, graduating *cum laude*. With a focus on resolving foundational philosophical issues with practical implications, Klenk investigates the ethical dimensions of emerging technologies. His recent work centres on manipulation, particularly in online contexts. He coedited the *Philosophy of Online Manipulation* (2022) with Fleur Jongepier, and his work has appeared in journals such as the *American Philosophical Quarterly*, *Analysis*, *Synthese*, *Erkenntnis*, *Philosophy and Technology*, and *Ethics and Information Technology*.

Noémie Krack is a legal scholar at the KU Leuven Faculty of Law, Centre for IT and IP Law (CiTiP) – imec. Her work focuses on media law, AI, and the challenges that technology raises for fundamental rights. She works and has worked on several EU-funded projects (Horizon, 2020), including AI4Media and MediaFutures. Her latest research delves into content moderation, disinformation regulation, deepfakes, and the impact of generative AI on the media sector. She provides guest lectures in the media law class of the KU Leuven Master of Intellectual Property and ICT Law (LLM). She is also an editorial board member of the European AI Media Observatory.

Aleksandra Kuczerawy is Assistant Professor at the Centre for IT and IP Law (CiTiP) at KU Leuven University, where she leads the media law research group. Her research focus is on fundamental rights online with particular attention to freedom of expression, platform regulation, content moderation of illegal and harmful content, and AI in the context of new media technologies. She has worked on multiple European projects addressing the regulation of digital technologies in the areas of privacy and data protection, new media regulation, AI, and smart cities. She participated in the work of the Council of Europe committee of experts on internet intermediaries and the committee of experts on freedom of expression and digital technology. Since 2020, she has been a lecturer in media law at KU Leuven postgraduate programme. Aleksandra is the author of the book *Intermediary Liability and Freedom of Expression in the EU: From Concepts to Safeguards* (2018).

Katja Langenbucher is a Professor of Law at Goethe-University's House of Finance in Frankfurt, an affiliated Professor at Ecole de Droit de SciencesPo, a visiting faculty at Fordham Law School, and a global law Professor at New York University Law School (starting 2026). She has held visiting positions at Paris I, Vienna University of Economics and Business (Wirtschaftsuniversität Vienna), the London School of Economics, Columbia Law School, and PennLaw (Bok Visiting International Professorship). Katja has published extensively on corporate, banking, and securities law. Currently she is working on AI and how this impacts corporate and financial law. She is a member of the German BaFin's supervisory board, the German Federal Ministry of Finance's working group on capital markets law, and the Conseil d'administration of the Fondation Nationale de Sciences Politique. Katja was a member of the supervisory board of Postbank (2014–18) and of the EU Commission's High Level Forum on the Capital Market Union (2019–20).

Lode Lauwaert is Professor of Philosophy of Technology and Chair of Ethics and AI at KU Leuven.

Sylvia Martos Marquez holds a research master's degree in law from KU Leuven in 2023 and an advanced master's degree in tax law from the University of Antwerp.

Wannes Meert received his degrees of master of electrotechnical engineering, micro-electronics (2005), master of artificial intelligence (2006), and PhD in computer science (2011) from KU Leuven. He is Industrial Research Fund Research Manager in the Declarative Languages and Artificial Intelligence (DTAI) section at the Department of Computer Science, KU Leuven. His work is focused on applying machine learning and reasoning, AI, and anomaly detection technology to industrial application domains with various industrial and academic partners. This work has received a number of prizes (e.g., Intel Outstanding Researcher Award, EU Active and Assisted Living Smart Ageing Prize, Patient Room of the Future Award, and AAAI/IAAI Deployed Application Award).

Inge Molenaar is the Director of NOLAI and Professor of Education and Artificial Intelligence at the Behavioural Science Institute at Radboud University in the Netherlands. She has over twenty years' experience in technology-enhanced learning, taking multiple roles from entrepreneur to academic. Her research focuses on technology-empowered innovations to optimize human learning and teaching. The application of data, learning analytics, and AI in understanding how learning unfolds over time is central to her work. AI offers a powerful way to measure, understand, and design innovative learning scenarios. Dr. Molenaar envisions hybrid human–AI learning technologies that augment human intelligence with AI to empower learners and teachers in their quest to make education more efficient, effective, and responsive.

Vincent C. Müller is Alexander von Humboldt Professor for Philosophy and Ethics of AI and Director of the Centre for Philosophy and AI Research at FAU Erlangen-Nuremberg, as well as Visiting Professor at Eindhoven University of Technology, Turing Fellow at the Alan Turing Institute (London), President of the European Society for Cognitive Systems, and Chair of the euRobotics topics group on "ethical, legal and socio-economic issues." He was Professor at the Technical University of Eindhoven (2019–22) and at Anatolia College/American College of Thessaloniki (1998–2019), as well as James Martin Research Fellow at the University of Oxford

(2011–15) and Stanley J. Seeger Fellow at Princeton University (2005–06). Müller studied philosophy with cognitive science, linguistics, and history at the universities of Marburg, Hamburg, London, and Oxford. He works mainly on philosophical problems connected to AI, in both ethics and theoretical philosophy. Müller edits the *Oxford Handbook of the Philosophy of Artificial Intelligence* (forthcoming) and wrote the *Stanford Encyclopedia of Philosophy* article on the ethics of AI and robotics (2020). He has a book forthcoming with Oxford University Press (*Can Machines Think?*) and with Cambridge University Press (*Artificial Minds*) with G. Löhr.

Laurens Naudts is a postdoctoral researcher at the AI, Media and Democracy Lab and Institute for Information Law (University of Amsterdam) and an affiliated senior researcher at the KU Leuven Centre for IT and IP Law (CiTiP). He is working on the political philosophy and governance of AI, focusing on relational dynamics, social justice, and the protection of fundamental rights within a digitally mediated society. In his doctoral research, Laurens examined the concepts of equality and nondiscrimination and their function in the regulation of automated decision-making.

Ann-Katrien Oimann is a researcher and PhD candidate at the Royal Military Academy of Belgium in collaboration with the KU Leuven Institute of Philosophy. Her research focuses on the ethical implications of AI in military applications, specifically delving into the morality of the use of (semi-)autonomous weapon systems and the challenges of attributing moral responsibility. Broadly, her primary research interests lie at the intersection of the ethics, law, and policy related to AI in military technologies. She has a background in philosophy (MA and BA at KU Leuven) and law (LLM in intellectual property and ICT law) and was selected in 2022 to be in the third cohort of the two-year Europaeum Scholars training programme in European policy and leadership.

Wannes Ooms obtained a master's degree in law from KU Leuven and a master's in intellectual property and ICT law at the KU Leuven Brussels Campus. His thesis dealt with data protection and the right to freedom of expression and with the empirical study of data subject rights for news recommendation systems. He worked as an in-house legal counsel in the semiconductor industry for two years before joining the Centre for IT and IP Law (CiTiP) at the KU Leuven Faculty of Law as a researcher.

Aída Ponce Del Castillo holds a "Doctor Europaeus" PhD in law from the University of Valencia and a master's degree in bioethics. She is a senior researcher at the Brussels-based Foresight Unit of the European Trade Union Institute. Her research focuses on the legal, social, and regulatory issues of emerging technologies, in particular AI and data-driven technologies. She also conducts foresight projects. At the Organization for Economic Co-operation and Development (OECD), she is a member of the Working Party on Bio-, Nano- and Converging Technologies and of the OECD.AI expert group on policies for AI. Previously she worked as a corporate lawyer.

Nathalie A. Smuha is a legal scholar and philosopher at the KU Leuven Faculty of Law and Criminology, where she examines legal and ethical questions around AI and other digital technologies. Her research focuses particularly on AI's impact on human rights, democracy, and the rule of law. Professor Smuha is the academic coordinator of the KU Leuven Summer School on the Law, Ethics and Policy of AI and a member of the Leuven.AI Institute and the Digital Society Institute. Previously, she held visiting positions at the University of Chicago, New York University, and the University of Birmingham. Her work has been the recipient of several awards, and she is a sought-after speaker at academic conferences and events, being a regular advisor to governments and international organizations on AI policy. Professor Smuha is also the author of *Algorithmic Rule by Law: How Algorithmic Regulation in the Public Sector Erodes the Rule of Law* (2025).

Marthe Stevens is Assistant Professor at the Interdisciplinary Hub on Digitalization and Society and affiliated with the Department of Ethics and Political Philosophy at Radboud University. Marthe studies the ethical and societal impacts of new technological innovations, mainly in education and healthcare. She specializes in embedded ethics and seeks to integrate ethical thinking into innovation trajectories using insights from the philosophy of technology, science and technology studies, and critical data studies. Currently, she leads the ethics team of NOLAI. Previously, she worked on the Googlization of Health as a postdoctoral researcher in the European Research Council project "Digital Good" (PI Tamar Sharon). She holds a PhD from Erasmus University Rotterdam (2021), in which she studied what happens when promises surrounding big data and AI become drivers for concrete initiatives in healthcare.

Simon Taes has been a postdoctoral researcher at the Institute for Labour Law of KU Leuven since September 2018. In 2014, he obtained his master's degree in psychology at KU Leuven with distinction, with a specialization in labor and occupational psychology. This gave him the opportunity to gain knowledge regarding the implication of working conditions for workers and the research methodology in social sciences. In 2018, he obtained his master's degree in law (with a specialization in social and economic law) with distinction. During his studies, he also pursued a summer internship at the Public Prosecutor's Office of the Court of Appeal in Ghent. By assisting several Advocates General and Advocates for Labour, he gained experience in the enforcement of (social) law. With the combination of his expertise in labor psychology and labor law, he conducts research on the social implications of robotization and how labor law should address the legal challenges arising from these implications.

Evelyne Terryn is a Full Professor at the KU Leuven and teaches commercial law, company law, and consumer law. She studied law at KU Leuven (*summa cum laude*, 1997), King's College London (1996), and the University of Oxford. She obtained her PhD at KU Leuven in 2005 on the right of withdrawal as an instrument of consumer protection; it was awarded the Raymond Derine Prize for human sciences. She started her career as a lawyer with Cleary, Gottlieb Brussels (1998–99) and is of counsel at Roots advocaten Kortrijk. She is a coeditor-in-chief of *Tijdschrift voor Consumentenrecht* (DCCR) and a member of the editorial board of the Dutch *Tijdschrift voor Consumentenrecht & handelspraktijken* (TvC). She was a member of the Acquis group and of the European Consumer Law Group and the Consumer Law Enforcement Forum. Her research focuses on (European) consumer law and European contract law, with a special focus on sustainability and the circular economy. She is a coeditor of *Consumer Law: Ius Commune Casebook* (Hart, Oxford). She was a visiting Professor at the University of Amsterdam and the China EU School of Law (Beijing).

Peggy Valcke is a Full Professor of law and technology at KU Leuven's Faculty of Law and Criminology. She is an executive committee member at the Centre for IT and IP Law (CiTiP) and Leuven.AI and a PI at imec. She has taken up positions as a visiting and part-time Professor at Tilburg University, Bocconi University in Milan, the European University Institute in Florence, and Central European University (at that time) in Budapest. Since January 2024, she has been an executive board member at the Belgian Institute for Postal Services and Telecommunications. Peggy represents Belgium in CAI, the Council of Europe's Committee on Artificial Intelligence, which is tasked with negotiating a European Convention on AI, and previously served as elected vice chair of its predecessor committee, the Council of Europe's Ad Hoc Committee on AI (CAHAI). She is involved in several research projects on AI, including in the media sector (such as AI4Media) and was the Codirector of the Flemish Centre on Data & Society (which is part of the Action Plan Flanders on AI) from 2019 until 2023. She was an assessor in the Belgian Competition Authority and the Flemish Media Regulator between 2008 and 2023. In January 2024, she joined the executive board of the Belgian Institute for Postal Services and Telecommunications (BIPT – IBPT).

Rosamunde Van Brakel is an interdisciplinary social scientist who works as Assistant Professor at the Fundamental Rights Centre and as a postdoctoral researcher at the Research Group Crime & Society at the Free University of Brussels (Vrije Universiteit Brussel), where she teaches and coordinates the master's degree course on the legal, ethical and social issues of AI. She is an expert in surveillance and digital criminology. She has been studying the social, ethical, and legal consequences of (algorithmic) surveillance technologies in the public sector since 2006. Since finishing her PhD on algorithmic risk profiling systems in 2018, she has been conducting research on the democratic governance and harms of surveillance, criminal justice, and AI. She was an expert witness for the UK House of Lords Justice and Home Affairs Committee inquiry on new technologies and law enforcement in 2021 and for the EU Parliament Pegasus Inquiry in 2022.

Jeroen van den Hoven is University Professor and Full Professor of Ethics and Technology at TU Delft and the Editor-in-Chief of *Ethics and Information Technology*. He is currently Scientific Director of the Delft Design for Values Institute. He was the Founding Scientific Director of the 4TU.Centre for Ethics and Technology (2007–13). In 2009, he won the World Technology Award for Ethics and the International Federation for Information Processing prize for Information and Communication Technology (ICT) and Society for his work on ethics and ICT. Jeroen van den Hoven was the Founder, and until 2016 Programme Chair, of the program of the Dutch Research Council on responsible innovation. He is coeditor of *Designing in Ethics* (2017), with Seumas Miller and Thomas Pogge, and author of *Evil Online* (2018), with Dean Cocking. He is a permanent member of the European Group on Ethics to the European Commission. In 2017, he was made a knight of the Order of the Lion of the Netherlands.

Aimee Van Wynsberghe is the Alexander von Humboldt Professor for Applied Ethics of Artificial Intelligence at the University of Bonn in Germany. Aimee is the Director of the Institute for Science and Ethics and the Bonn Sustainable AI Lab. She is the Codirector of the Foundation for Responsible Robotics and a member of the European Commission's High-Level Expert Group on AI. She is a founding editor of the international peer-reviewed journal *AI & Ethics* and a member of the World Economic Forum's Global Futures Council on Artificial Intelligence and Humanity. She is the author of *Healthcare Robots: Ethics, Design, and Implementation* (2015) and is regularly interviewed by media outlets. In her work, Aimee seeks to uncover the ethical risks associated with emerging robotics and AI. Aimee's current research, funded by the Alexander von Humboldt Foundation, brings attention to the sustainability of AI by studying the hidden environmental costs of developing and using AI.

Jozefien Vanherpe is an Assistant Professor at the KU Leuven Centre for IT and IP Law (CiTiP) in Belgium. She studied law at KU Leuven and the University of Cambridge. After having worked as an attorney for several years, she successfully defended her PhD at KU Leuven in 2022. She teaches a range of courses on intellectual property law. In addition, she is a member of several international associations in the field of intellectual property law, including the International Association for the Protection of Intellectual Property, the International Literary and Artistic Association, the International Association for the Advancement of Teaching and Research in Intellectual Property, and the Benelux Association for Trademark and Design law.

Anton Vedder is Emeritus Professor of Technology, Law, and Ethics at the Faculty of Law and Criminology, KU Leuven. He is especially interested in the mutual relationships between technological developments and the conceptualization of basic moral and legal notions. His publications include articles and books on trust in eHealth, innovative technologies, care and enhancement and justice, privacy and profiling, privacy versus public security, ambient technology and autonomy and responsibility, quality of information and credibility of experts, legitimacy, trust, and technology adoption. He currently supervises PhD projects on ethics and law of automation of the workplace, the technological enhancement of emotions, cognitive enhancement of the judiciary, and the concept of accuracy in law. He is an active member of KU Leuven's Ethics Committee on "Dual Use, Military Use and Misuse of Research."

Griet Verhenneman is an Assistant Professor of privacy law at the Faculty of Law and Criminology at Ghent University. In her research, teaching, and service, Professor Verhenneman focuses on legal and ethical questions surrounding privacy, data (protection), and AI. Her work spans sector-specific research in healthcare and broader issues related to protecting sensitive data and vulnerable data subjects. She is a core member of the Metamedica and i4S steering committees. The Metamedica platform facilitates interdisciplinary academic research and integrated education in the fields of health law, health privacy law, and medical ethics. i4S (Smart Solutions for Secure Societies) is a multidisciplinary economic valorisation platform that brings together expertise from alpha, beta, and gamma disciplines around crime and security, technology, digitization, and privacy. Before joining Ghent University in 2023, she worked as a researcher and lecturer at the KU Leuven Centre for IT and IP Law and as a Data Protection Officer at the University Hospitals KU Leuven and the University Psychiatric Centre KU Leuven. Through her research and work in practice, she developed a particular interest in the legal and ethical aspects of eHealth. Today, Professor Verhenneman is a member of the Data Access Committee at the Ghent University Hospital and acts as an external expert for the Authorization and Advice service of the Belgian Data Protection Authority.

Karen Yeung joined Birmingham Law School and the University of Birmingham's School of Computer Science as Interdisciplinary Professorial Fellow in Law, Ethics and Informatics in January 2018. Her research has been at the forefront of understanding the challenges associated with the regulation and governance of emerging technologies. Over the course of more than twenty-five years, she has developed unique expertise in the regulation and governance of, and through, new and emerging technologies. Her ongoing work focuses on the legal, ethical, social, and democratic implications of a suite of technologies associated with automation and the "computational turn," including big data analytics, AI (including various forms of machine learning), distributed ledger technologies (including blockchain), and robotics.

Katerina Yordanova, a Bulgarian-qualified lawyer, has over ten years' experience in technology and human rights law. She is currently enriching her extensive practical and academic background as Senior Legal Expert at the KU Leuven Centre for IT and IP Law (CiTiP) and is engaged in a PhD focused on legal certainty in regulatory sandboxes for AI. Katerina's expertise covers data protection, cybersecurity, and the nexus between business, human rights, and technology regulation. She has a proven track record in legal research and consultancy for European and Belgian commercial projects, and is adept in contract drafting, IP advisory, and client representation in court. Additionally, Katerina brings educational depth in public international law from Sofia University, an advanced degree from KU Leuven, and a specialized postgraduate qualification from Cambridge University. As a lecturer and speaker at international forums, she disseminates her knowledge and contributes to the legal scholarship with published articles on diverse topics within her field.

Acknowledgments

The idea for this edited book first arose in the margin of the first edition of the KU Leuven Summer School on the Law, Ethics and Policy of Artificial Intelligence, which I organized in the summer of 2021. Since then, the course has taken place every year, bringing together people from various countries and disciplinary backgrounds to the small town of Leuven. When designing the program, I asked myself which type of course I would have loved to follow as a student, which made it evident from the get-go that the curriculum should be both interdisciplinary and comprehensive in providing an overview of AI's societal implications. Very soon, I was asked if there was a possibility to disseminate the content of the course more broadly as the demand to participate far exceeded the capacity, which led to the start of this open-source project.

A number of people were instrumental in making the Summer School (and hence this book) happen and are thus the first I wish to thank. *Sara Van Steyvoort* has been the best organizational assistant one could have wished for, in addition to being a fantastic colleague. *Sofia Devroe* took up the role of academic assistant during the Summer School's first edition, followed by *Victoria Hendrickx* who brilliantly took up the torch for the subsequent editions. Both of them were an absolute pleasure to work with, and their dedication, kindness, and wit have contributed immensely to the Summer School's success. None of this would have happened without *Geert Van Calster*, my then doctoral supervisor, who encouraged me to take up this slightly daunting task. In addition, I owe thanks to KU Leuven for enabling me to organize the Summer School, and to the many colleagues at the Faculty of Law, the Institute for AI, and elsewhere who supported this endeavor.

Next, I would like to thank all the authors who have contributed a chapter to this book, namely – in order of appearance – *Wannes Meert, Tinne De Laet, Luc De Raedt, Vincent C. Müller, Stefan Buijsman, Michael Klenk, Jeroen van den Hoven, Laurens Naudts, Anton Vedder, Lode Lauwaert, Ann-Katrien Oimann, Gry Hasselbalch, Aimee Van Wynsberghe, Pierre Dewitte, Jan De Bruyne, Wannes Ooms, Friso Bostoen, Evelyne Terryn, Sylvia Martos Marquez, Jozefien Vanherpe, Karen Yeung, Inge Molenaar, Duuk Baten, Imre Bárd, Marthe Stevens, Lidia Dutkiewicz,*

Noémie Krack, *Aleksandra Kuczerawy*, *Peggy Valcke*, *Griet Verhenneman*, *Katja Langenbucher*, *Aída Ponce Del Castillo*, *Simon Taes*, *Rosamunde Van Brakel*, and *Katerina Yordanova*. Most of them have also been guest lecturers at the Summer School, often for multiple years, and have consolidated the content of their lectures in their contributions. I am very grateful for their time and effort, and for the insights they have shared.

Most important of all, I wish to thank all the alumni of the AI Summer School, to whom this book is dedicated. When starting this program, I could never have imagined what an absolutely wonderful community it would become, full of intellectual curiosity, kindhearted generosity, and thoughtful support. Getting to know them has given me the best possible reason to be hopeful – amidst and despite the many concerns AI poses – that a brighter future is nevertheless achievable when individuals across countries and disciplines join forces to work on it together.

An Introduction to the Law, Ethics, and Policy of Artificial Intelligence

Nathalie A. Smuha

BEYOND THE AI HYPE

Artificial intelligence (AI) was founded as an academic discipline almost 70 years ago, when a conference took place at Dartmouth College. The proposal submitted by the conference conveners described the project as an attempt *"to find how to make machines use language, form abstractions and concepts, solve kinds of problems now reserved for humans, and improve themselves. We think that a significant advance can be made in one or more of these problems if a carefully selected group of scientists work on it together for a summer."*[1] Just a few years before the Dartmouth Conference, Alan Turing had already published a paper titled "*Computing Machinery and Intelligence*," in which he kickstarted not only a philosophical discussion on whether machines could *imitate* human thinking but also discussed the development of digital computing and "learning machines."[2]

Over the years, significant advances toward the achievement of those aims were made. Periods of great optimism (so-called "AI springs"), during which the technology knew rapid advancements and attracted elevated levels of funding, were followed by periods of pessimism in the technology's progress (so-called "AI winters"), during which interest and investment in the technology plummeted, with a low point in the 1990s. Gradually, the wider availability of data, advanced computing power, and significant research progress (especially in the subfield of machine learning) contributed to AI's latest boom. Interestingly, *"from 2010 to 2021, the total number of AI publications more than doubled, growing from 200,000 in 2010 to almost 500,000 in 2021."*[3]

[1] John McCarthy, Marvin Minsky, Nathaniel Rochester, and Claude Shannon, *Proposal for the Dartmouth Summer Research Project on Artificial Intelligence*, August 31, 1955.

[2] Alan Turing, "Computing machinery and intelligence" (1950) *Mind*, 59(236): 433–460.

[3] Nestor Maslej, Loredana Fattorini, Erik Brynjolfsson, John Etchemendy, Katrina Ligett, Terah Lyons, James Manyika, Helen Ngo, Juan Carlos Niebles, Vanessa Parli, Yoav Shoham, Russell Wald, Jack Clark, and Raymond Perrault, "The AI Index 2023 Annual Report," *AI Index Steering Committee, Institute for Human-Centered AI, Stanford University*, April 30, 2023.

The current AI spring is explained not only by the increased uptake and normalization of AI applications across virtually all sectors of the economy but also by the advent of generative AI and other applications which found their way to the public at large, resulting in a true "AI hype." One can only speculate about whether this hype will soon (or has already) hit its peak and an AI winter is coming, or whether more breakthroughs are underway.[4] There are, however, many more important questions to formulate and points to make, which are not always raised in many of the brief summaries about AI's hype – points that may be overlooked precisely because of our enthusiasm for the perceived benefits of this impressive technology. Let me focus on three aspects in particular that deserve our attention.

A Long History

First, it should be born in mind that the history of AI as a *concept* dates back at least to antiquity, where myths already existed about "automata" or self-operating machines displaying human behavior.[5] Hephaestus, the Greek god of artisans and blacksmiths, was for instance said to have created an artificial man of bronze, Talos, to protect Europa – a Phoenician princess after whom the European continent was named – against potential invaders and kidnappers. Moving from myth to reality, Ancient Greece also saw the birth of the Antikythera mechanism – a hand-powered mechanical model of the solar system developed around 200 BC and used to predict astronomical positions, often described as the first example of an analog computer.[6]

The human drive to transgress the boundaries of the natural and the artificial and to create "intelligent" machines by no means diminished in the Middle Ages. For instance, in 1206, Ismail al-Jazari, an Arab polymath from Mesopotamia who is described as the "father of robotics," wrote the *Book of Knowledge of Ingenious Mechanical Devices*, including detailed accounts of how to construct musical robot hands and drink-serving waitresses.[7] Scientists started experimenting with the creation of mechanical devices for a range of purposes, sometimes even purposely inflating the machine's capabilities and misleading audiences (like the example of the Automaton Chess Player or *the Mechanical Turk*, which was actually controlled by a human operator sitting inside it).[8]

[4] The hype's bubble is also increasingly being pierced, as AI developers not always able to deliver the technology's promises. See also Eric Siegel, "The AI hype cycle is distracting companies" (2023) *Harvard Business Review*, June 2, https://hbr.org/2023/06/the-ai-hype-cycle-is-distracting-companies.

[5] See for example Silvio A. Bedini, "The role of automata in the history of technology" (1964) *Technology and Culture*, 5(1): 24–42.

[6] See also John Hugh Seiradakis and M. G. Edmunds, "Our current knowledge of the Antikythera mechanism" (2018) *Nature Astronomy*, 2: 35–42.

[7] See for example Shahino Mah Abdullah, "Intelligent robots and the question of their legal rights: an Islamic perspective" (2018) *ICR Journal*, 9(3): 394–397.

[8] See also Elizabeth Stephens, "The mechanical Turk: a short history of 'artificial artificial intelligence'" (2022) *Cultural Studies*, 37(1): 65–87.

In sum, humans have been fascinated with artificial beings long before the Dartmouth Conference, which is also evidenced by literary works, from the Golems of Chełm and Prague to Mary Shelley's Frankenstein's Monster. The question is then: how can we avoid that this historical fascination does not make us overly focused on what AI *could* do instead of reflecting on what it *is* doing and what it *should be* doing in practice? For it is precisely within the gap between *is* and *should* that many problems around the technology's development and use can be situated, including the nonchalant, negligent, or even malicious launch of problematic AI applications, from which harmful consequences can ensue.

One of Many Technologies

Second, it must be noted that AI is but one of many technologies, and numerous other innovations have preceded its hype and discourse. The history of technology counts a long list of inventions that were heralded as groundbreaking and that transformed our societies to greater and lesser extents. AI is being treated as a shiny new toy, and is sometimes even compared with the discovery of fire, electricity, oil, or nuclear technology, which has led experts to debate whether these analogies are useful (or to claim that none of them makes much sense). Yet the fact that such analogies are being made in the first place should serve as a reminder that "*what has been will be again, what has been done will be done again; there is nothing new under the sun*."[9] Human beings have always sought to deploy (new) tools in ways that serve their purposes, in good, bad, and negligent ways – and this certainly applies to AI too, as it is developed and used by human beings.

Society has dealt with many other (powerful) inventions in the past, and there is a rich history of (failed and successful) governance practices that can be dug into to analyze which lessons to draw when it comes to AI – and how to govern human behavior in relation to AI. While it may be tempting to treat AI as an entirely novel and different phenomenon stemming from human ingenuity, this attitude not only feeds an excessive hype but also risks overlooking the ingenuity that humans have shown throughout history when it comes to setting up mechanisms and institutions to govern society. It is, furthermore, a convenient position for those actors who would prefer *not* to draw any lessons from past governance experiences, as some seek to avoid AI-related governance measures altogether.

The hype-fueled fixation on AI as fundamentally distinct from other technologies also has two other problematic corollaries. In first instance, it reinforces the narrative that AI is something elusive and inevitable, manifesting itself in society in a form that we cannot quite grasp, and that cannot properly be defined or understood. But discussing AI as something abstract, ephemeral and almost magical overlooks its very concrete – and governable – building blocks, from software code and

[9] Ecclesiastes, 1:9.

data-filled Excel sheets, to physical CPUs, motherboards and data centers, and of course the human beings creating and operating them. In addition, it also overlooks the fact that other technologies which may not fall under the contours of AI can lead to equally impactful and problematic consequences, and that the focus should hence lay not (merely) on the technology but rather on the values society cherishes and wishes to protect. The question is, hence, how to avoid the trap of treating AI as entirely novel, while at the same time being sufficiently mindful of the very concrete ways in which it can (adversely) affect society, and ensuring tailored governance mechanisms to counter potential harms.

Societal Impact

Third, as already alluded to above, there is an important societal dimension that needs to be considered within any AI history, as it does not stand separate from its technological dimension. Like all technologies, AI is inherently embedded in society, thus affecting and being affected by the broader environment in which it is designed, developed, and deployed – for better and for worse. The societal impact of Artificial Intelligence is of course more noticeable the more it is being implemented and used in a diversity of domains, which also explains the relatively recent surge of (academic and other) interest in AI ethics, in parallel with the technology's increased uptake. Yet AI's uptake is also enabled and furthered by the societal condition. These enabling factors pertain, inter alia, to society's belief in innovation as an almost absolute good, its technology-solutionist orientation, and its conception of "progress" as almost coinciding with technological advancement rather than also considering if and how these advancements translate into higher individual and societal welfare – for all. Yet if we shape technology and technology also shapes us, it is essential to ask how it can be ensured that this mutual shaping process takes place in a way that protects rather than undermines our legal, moral, and political standards.

The attentive reader will have noted that the three questions I formulated above are all variations of the same theme – one that lies at the heart of this book: given that AI systems are increasingly being developed and deployed in ways that impact our lives, what role do *law*, *ethics*, and *policy* play to govern this impact and to ensure that the core values of society are safeguarded? Answering this question requires a cross-disciplinary lens, as it is only by looking at it from different perspectives that AI's societal effects can be grasped.

To this end, in the summer of 2021, I convened the first edition of the Summer School on the Law, Ethics and Policy of Artificial Intelligence at the KU Leuven Faculty of Law and Criminology. This program brought together a multidisciplinary group of lecturers and participants to the city of Leuven for an intense deep dive into a range of topics related to the impact of AI on society, with a particular focus on Europe.

Many of the chapters of this book were born out of the rich exchanges and discussions that took place within the margin of the first and subsequent editions of the Summer School. The purpose of this book is to consolidate those insights and make them available to a wider readership.

BOOK OUTLINE

This book addresses the main challenges and opportunities of AI not only from a horizontal perspective (covering general areas in which the advent of the technology raises questions, such as philosophy, ethics, and various legal domains) but also from a vertical perspective (considering AI's implications in a range of sectors), with the aim of providing the reader a more holistic understanding of AI's impact across society. Just like in the program of the AI Summer School, the primary jurisdiction discussed in the chapters concerns Europe, and the underlying societal model that is taken for granted is one that seeks to protect human rights, democracy, and the rule of law – three core values of constitutional liberal democracies.

The book's focus not only lays on the latest wave of AI applications but also encompasses discussions of more traditional algorithmic systems that are equally able to raise challenges to societal values, and that should not be overlooked merely because we have become so accustomed to them that they are now considered too "traditional" to be called "AI." Each chapter is self-standing, yet many of the themes discussed therein are recurring, in particular the acknowledgment that more interdisciplinary research and cooperation on AI is needed. The book is divided into three parts, each focusing on a different angle.

Part I: AI, Ethics and Philosophy

The first part of this book starts by conceptualizing AI as a scientific discipline and setting out its technical foundations. In Chapter 1, Wannes Meert, Tinne De Laet, and Luc De Raedt provide a perspective from the field to describe machine learning and machine reasoning, two domains within the broader field of AI that are rapidly evolving. They distinguish different types of functions and techniques, and close with some reflections on what it means to build "trustworthy," "explainable," and "robust" AI, thereby also building a bridge between their technical discussion and the book's subsequent chapters, which discuss AI from a philosophical lens, with a particular focus on moral philosophy or ethics.

Chapter 2, written by Vincent C. Müller, offers a structured overview of the philosophy of AI. After describing a broader set of AI definitions beyond computer science, he introduces the concepts of intelligence and computation, as well as the main topics of artificial cognition, including perception, action, meaning, rational choice, free will, consciousness, and normativity. Through a better understanding of these topics, he argues, the philosophy of AI contributes to our understanding of the nature, prospects, and value of AI. At the same time, he also explains that these topics can be better understood by discussing AI, and thus suggests that "AI Philosophy" provides a new method for philosophy.

Next, Stefan Buijsman, Michael Klenk, and Jeroen van den Hoven dive into a subbranch of philosophy, ethics. In Chapter 3, they discuss the main ethical challenges raised by AI as a technology, as well as the potential methods to tackle those challenges. While they argue that ethical theories such as virtue ethics, consequentialism, and deontology are a helpful starting point, they believe these theories lack details for a more actionable and proactive "AI ethics." Instead, they propose that the best way forward is to consider design-approaches in the context of AI, such as "Design for Values," alongside interdisciplinary working methods. Their AI ethics overview paves the way for the next three chapters, which focus on a more specific ethical conundrum.

In Chapter 4, Laurens Naudts and Anton Vedder zoom in on the theme of AI and fairness. Taking as their point of departure one particular interpretation of fairness – namely fairness as non-arbitrariness – they analyze the distinction between procedural and substantive conceptions of fairness, as well as the relationship between fairness, justice, and equality. Subsequently, they distinguish distributive fairness approaches from socio-relational ones, and caution against the formalization of fairness by design as a form of techno-solutionism. Naudts and Vedder also emphasize that the design and regulation of fair AI systems is not an insular exercise, and that – beyond procedures and outcomes – sufficient attention must be paid to the social processes, structures, and relationships that inform and are co-shaped by the functioning of such systems.

Chapter 5 deals with another theme of ethical concern in the context of AI, namely moral responsibility. Lode Lauwaert and Ann-Katrien Oimann consider whether the use of autonomous AI causes a responsibility gap. After discussing how the notion of responsibility can be understood and what the responsibility gap is about, they explore in which ways it is sensible to assign responsibility to artificial systems and argue that their use does not necessarily lead to a responsibility gap. Moreover, they explain why, according to them, even if such a gap were to exist, it would not necessarily be problematic.

In the sixth and final chapter of this part, Gry Hasselbalch and Aimee Van Wynsberghe analyze the relationship between AI, power, and responsibility. They point out that AI has the potential to support solutions to counter sustainability concerns, while at the same time however also being unsustainable, given the high carbon emissions and the many ethical concerns it raises, from discrimination to surveillance and electoral micro-targeting. Making the plea that it is crucial to address the long-term sustainability of AI in light of its impact on our social, personal, and natural environments (also of future generations), they suggest a "sustainable" approach to AI. In Chapter 6, they hence argue that such an approach should be inclusive in time and space, meaning that the past, present, and future of human societies, as well as the planet and environment, are considered equally important to protect and secure, including the integration of all countries in economic and social changes.

Part II: AI, Law and Policy

The second part of this book deals with the law and policy of AI, which constitute important tools to govern the technology's impact on society and its ethical challenges. In Chapter 7, Pierre Dewitte discusses AI's impact on privacy and its relationship with data protection law, arguing that the large-scale processing of personal data that AI systems enable also puts a strain on individuals' fundamental rights and freedoms. The chapter focuses in particular on the General Data Protection Regulation (GDPR) and describes its position and role within the broader European data protection regulatory framework. After introducing some of the GDPR's key concepts, it draws attention to certain tension points between the characteristics inherent to most AI systems and the general principles outlined in the GDPR, such as lawfulness, transparency, purpose limitation, data minimization, and accountability.

Chapter 8 deals with extra-contractual or tort liability in the context of AI, an area that is increasingly on legislators' radar given that the technology's use will inevitably lead to damage. Jan De Bruyne and Wannes Ooms discuss the main challenges that arise in this context and highlight that national law remains of great importance to tackle them. Focusing on the procedural elements of tort liability, including disclosure requirements and rebuttable presumptions, they also illustrate how existing tort law concepts are challenged by AI's characteristics, and which regulatory answers are available.

Chapter 9 deals with another legal domain that is impacted by AI, namely competition law. Friso Bostoen explains how companies increasingly rely on AI systems for (strategic) decisions, and how their use can have procompetitive effects, for instance, by facilitating the undercutting of competitors or improving recommendations. Yet he also cautions for AI's distortive effects on competition, for instance, when used to collude or to exclude competitors. He then analyzes to what extent such anticompetitive algorithmic practices are already covered by EU competition law by examining their use to conclude horizontal and vertical agreements, as well as to foster exclusionary and exploitative conduct.

In Chapter 10, Evelyne Terryn and Sylvia Martos Marquez move from competition law to consumer protection law, which traditionally focuses on protecting consumers' autonomy and self-determination – both of which are affected by the growing use of AI. In their analysis, they provide an overview of the most relevant consumer protection instruments in the EU legal order which apply to the context of AI. Finally, through a case study on dark patterns, they illustrate the shortcomings of the current consumer protection framework and argue for better safeguards.

Chapter 11, written by Jozefien Vanherpe, delves into the interface of AI and intellectual property law. She discusses the extent to which AI technology can be protected, whether it can be qualified as an author or inventor, and who holds ownership of AI-assisted and AI-generated output. She also considers how liability is allocated for intellectual property right infringements taking place by or through the intervention of an AI system and concludes that – despite the apparent enthusiasm for the use of AI in practice – there is also a hesitancy to provide additional incentive creation through (new or adapted) intellectual property legislation in the AI sphere.

In Chapter 12, the final chapter of this part, Karen Yeung and I provide a critical analysis of the European Union's AI Act. This regulation not only seeks to establish a single European market for AI, but is also meant to address some of the most pressing risks that AI systems pose to the health, safety, and human rights of individuals. We however question whether the AI Act can translate its noble aspirations into meaningful and effective protection for people whose lives are affected by AI systems. Through a critical examination of the proposed conceptual vehicles and regulatory architecture upon which the AI Act relies, we argue there are good reasons for skepticism, as many of the AI Act's provisions delegate critical regulatory tasks to AI providers, without adequate oversight or redress mechanisms.

Part III: AI across Sectors

Having looked at AI from a horizontal perspective in the previous two parts, Part III of this book focuses on a number of sectoral domains in which AI systems are used, and analyzes their more context-specific effects. In Chapter 13, Inge Molenaar, Duuk Baten, Imre Bárd, and Marthe Stevens discuss the implications of AI in the field of education. After introducing multiple existing perspectives on the role of AI in education, with an emphasis on an augmentation-approach that supports human strengths, they distinguish between students-faced, teacher-faced, and administrative AI solutions and trace how AI ethics in education was taken up in international and European policies. They close with an example of how intelligent innovations in the field of education can be cocreated in collaboration with educational professionals, scientists, and companies, drawing on the example of the "Dutch value compass for the digital transformation of education."

Chapter 14 turns to the permeation of AI in the media sector. Lidia Dutkiewicz, Noémie Krack, Aleksandra Kuczerawy, and Peggy Valcke first discuss the opportunities of the use of AI in media content gathering and production, media content distribution, fact-checking, and content moderation. They then zoom into some of the risks that arise in the context of AI-driven media applications, such as the lack of data availability, the lack of transparency, the adverse impact on the right to freedom of expression, as well as threats to media freedom and pluralism online, and threats to media independence. They also offer an overview of the EU legal framework that aims to mitigate these risks, including the Digital Services Act, the European Media Freedom Act, and the AI Act.

In Chapter 15, Griet Verhenneman discusses the relationship between AI, healthcare data, and data protection law. She stresses that healthcare data are required not only for the research and development phases of AI but also for the establishment of evidence of compliance with legislation, such as the Medical Devices Regulation and the AI Act – which must occur without prejudice to other legal acts such as the GDPR. After introducing notions such as "real-world data," "evidence data," and "electronic health records," she discusses the role of healthcare data custodians and the impact of concepts like data ownership, patient autonomy, informed consent, and privacy and data protection-enhancing techniques in the context of AI healthcare applications.

Chapter 16, written by Katja Langenbucher, examines the role of AI in the financial world, where actors continuously process vast amounts of information, and increasingly do so with the aid of AI. To concretize the implications of this practice she describes AI scoring and creditworthiness assessments as an example of how AI systems are employed in financial services, which ethical challenges they raise, and how legal tools are balancing the advantages and challenges of this technology. Finally, she also looks ahead and cautions against AI-enabled scoring that ranges beyond the credit context, as it also extends toward people's social lives and facilitates novel forms of (unwarranted) control.

One area of increased control is the work sphere. In Chapter 17, Aída Ponce Del Castillo and Simon Taes provide an overview of the multifaceted aspects of AI and labor law, focusing on the profound questions arising in this intersection, from the impact on employment relationships, to the exercise of labor rights and social dialogue. After providing illustrations of common AI applications and discussing the use of automated decision-making and monitoring systems in the workplace, they also elucidate the most relevant rights and tools when it comes to the negotiation and implementation of AI in the workplace, as well as AI-related legislation with a work-oriented dimension.

Chapter 18, written by Rosamunde Van Brakel, introduces the use of AI in law enforcement and discusses the main legal, ethical, and social concerns this raises by focusing on one AI application in particular, namely predictive policing. In the last two decades, police forces in Europe and North America increasingly invested in such applications, of which she analyzes two types: predictive mapping and predictive identification. She discusses concerns around (the lack of information about) their effectiveness, as well as their impact on citizens and society.

In Chapter 19, I discuss the governance of algorithmic regulation in public administration – or the delegation of the application, execution, and enforcement of regulation to algorithmic systems. I contextualize public administrations' increased reliance on such digital technologies and discuss the ethical and legal conundrums that administrations face when outsourcing (part of) their tasks, from their impact on the rule of law and digital sovereignty, to their discriminatory and intrusive effects. I also offer an overview of the legal framework that governs this practice in Europe, covering constitutional and administrative law, as well as data protection law and AI-specific law, all of which ought to be considered when public administrations seek to deploy algorithmic regulation.

Chapter 20 is concerned with the intersection of AI and armed conflicts. Katerina Yordanova reflects on the widespread development and adoption of AI and other digital technologies in warfare and recognizes the potential that AI carries for improving the applicability of the basic principles of international humanitarian law, if used in an accountable and responsible way. At the same time, she questions whether international humanitarian law is at all up to the task of addressing the threats posed by these technologies. After a description of the system, principles, and internal logic of international humanitarian law, she evaluates the role of AI systems in (non-)international armed conflicts and discusses some of the policy developments in this field, with the aim of contributing to the discussion on ex-ante regulation of AI systems for military purposes.

Finally, I close this book by offering some concluding remarks, drawing on the richness of the insights provided by the chapter authors and pointing to a few gaps that this book leaves unaddressed, which merit further research in the future.

OPEN QUESTIONS

To conclude this introduction, I would like to set out a few open questions that scholars in the field are often confronted with when it comes to the governance of AI, and that the authors of this book's chapters also had to deal with when writing their contributions.

A first question to ask is which human behavior in the context of AI should be subjected to (new or updated) binding legal rules, and which behavior can be left to non-legal norms. Not all ethical imperatives are also enshrined in legislation, nor are all legal rules necessarily reflecting an ethical norm. That said, law and ethics are strongly connected with each other, though neither can substitute the other,[10] and both have an important function in the AI governance context. In addition, laws are typically implemented through – though often also guided and indirectly shaped by – (government) policy, despite the fact that policy should ideally be no more than a "servant of the formal rule of law" to avoid excesses.[11] Yet what should the contours of the respective functions of *law*, *ethics*, and *policy* be? Which role can and should they play in reigning in the societal effects of the development and deployment of AI?

[10] See also Nathalie A. Smuha, "The EU approach to ethics guidelines for trustworthy artificial intelligence" (2019) *Computer Law Review International*, 2(4): 101.

[11] Theodore J. Lowi, "Law vs. public policy: A critical exploration" (2003) *Cornell Journal of Law and Public Policy*, 12(3): 501.

Some academics have been fearful that reliance on ethics principles and non-binding policies and guidelines is merely a form of law-making procrastination and furthers the mistaken idea that self-regulation can be sufficient to counter the potential harms related to AI.[12] Yet in the European Union, the "Ethics Guidelines for Trustworthy AI" of the High Level Expert Group on AI – set up by the European Commission with a mandate to advise it on AI-related policy – were arguably an important propelling factor to subsequently move toward binding legislation in the form of the new AI Act, which is clearly inspired by those Guidelines as well as directly referring thereto.[13] More indirectly, the establishment of this Expert Group and its mandate has (perhaps unwittingly, but rightfully) launched a broader discussion on how democratic decision-making in the context of AI should be shaped, what the role of expertise and representation should be, and which institutions have and should have the power to suggest and adopt various normative instruments. An important take-away from that discussion is that law, ethics, and policy can complement and inform one another and are at their best when they act symbiotically rather than exclusionary. This does not mean that it is easy to make decisions about the extent of their respective role in AI-related matters, especially since those decisions can also be context- and sector-dependent. But it does imply that a normative framework for the governance of AI – and of any type of societal phenomenon – is best looked at from a more holistic perspective.

A second question pertains to the oft-made juxtaposition between protection and innovation. On the one hand, governments and stakeholders have been acknowledging the need to adopt and maintain adequate safeguards to protect individuals, collectives, and societies from AI's adverse effects. On the other hand, however, regulation is often also (implicitly or even explicitly) portrayed as an undermining factor of innovation. If regulators must hence balance the desire to protect their citizenry and to secure innovation, how can these seemingly contrasting aims be simultaneously achieved? How should this balance look like? Who should decide about this balance? And to which extent is the balance that is afforded by current AI governance frameworks effective in reaching either goal? These questions, while certainly not invalid, are not unique to AI and are often formulated overly simplistically.

Innovation is not an intrinsically valuable good. Rather, it is cherished because it can lead to findings that enhance individual and societal welfare, and has indeed

[12] See for example Ben Wagner, "Ethics as an escape from regulation. From 'ethics-washing' to ethics-shopping?" in Emre Bayamlioglu et al. (eds.), *Being Profiled* (Amsterdam University Press, 2019), 84–89; Karen Yeung et al., "AI governance by human rights–centered design, deliberation, and oversight: an end to ethics washing" in Markus D. Dubber, Frank Pasquale, and Sunit Das (eds.), *The Oxford Handbook of Ethics of AI* (Oxford University Press, 2020), 75–106.

[13] See in particular Recitals 7, 27, and 165 of the AI Act, or the Regulation of the European Parliament and of the Council laying down harmonized rules on AI and amending certain union legislative acts. Nathalie A. Smuha, "The Work of the High-Level Expert Group on AI as the Precursor of the AI Act" in Ceyhun Necati Pehlivan et al (eds), *AI Governance and Liability in Europe: A Primer* (Kluwer International Law, 2024).

been instrumental in doing so in significant ways. Yet not all innovations automatically and necessarily do so. It is hence legitimate to conclude, as a society, that certain types of innovation are not compatible with the values and principles that the society holds dear and wishes to preserve, or that the risk that those values will be undermined is too great to take. Regulation, in the broadest sense, can actually have the function of guiding innovators precisely toward initiatives that advance those values, and on which they should hence focus their efforts. After all, they are members of a society as well, by virtue of which they too will be adversely impacted if certain innovative applications actually undermine the very foundations of their social fabric – even if they are not always aware of it at the time of the application's development. In this sense, innovation and protection need not be antagonistic. But as noted elsewhere: *"as long as the dual issues of protection and innovation are juxtaposed rather than folded into each other, the uneasy balance between the two will most certainly be doomed."*[14]

A third question that continues leading to consternation is whether the law is ever able to "stay up to date" or even "catch up" with AI, given the reality of the technology's fast-paced development and constant evolution. Indeed, the creation of laws – and even of societal norms more generally – occurs at a very different speed, a discrepancy that is often highlighted.[15] A point in case is the European Union's path toward the AI Act, which started off with a proposal by the European Commission that did not mention generative AI. That particular technology was simply not yet on the radar of EU policymakers, despite its enormous boom less than two years later. This unpredictability of the technology's evolution is sometimes also used as an argument to hold off on any AI regulation for now, until we know better how it will look like and affect us in the future. At the same time, the deployment of AI is already causing serious harm today, and many examples exist in which its use facilitated the violation of rights – so how should society, and regulators in particular, align the urgent need for action with the incompleteness of the information they have about the actions that may be required?

Crucially, this is not a new question, but one that manifests itself with almost every innovation. Very often, the effects that the innovative technology will have – especially in the longer term, and at the level of society rather than solely at the level of individuals or groups[16] – will not be immediately known (and might never be fully known). Yet this knowledge gap should not stand in the way of regulatory

[14] Nathalie A. Smuha, "Europe's approach to AI governance: time for a vision," *Friends of Europe*, April 2, 2020, www.friendsofeurope.org/insights/europes-approach-to-ai-governance-time-for-a-vision/.

[15] See also for example Adam Satariano and Cecilia Kang, "How nations are losing a global race to tackle A.I.'s harms," *The New York Times*, December 6, 2023, www.nytimes.com/2023/12/06/technology/ai-regulation-policies.html. See also Nathalie A. Smuha, "From a 'race to AI' to a 'race to AI regulation': regulatory competition for artificial intelligence" (2021) *Law, Innovation and Technology*, 13(1): 80.

[16] Nathalie A. Smuha, "Beyond the individual: governing AI's societal harm" (2021) *Internet Policy Review*, 10(3): 10.

action, and it is precisely there that precautionary, principle-based, and risk-based approaches have a role to play.[17] Indeed, over time, numerous regulatory techniques have been developed to grapple with this problem, and the law's generality (which sometimes leads it to be accused of being overly broad and vague, yet also provides it with a level of flexibility and adaptivity to new situations) is an important factor in this respect.[18] Many Roman laws withstood the test of time for centuries, despite numerous innovations making their entry into society, so it would be dishonest to claim that laws always run behind technology. While the original question remains a critical one, the main focus should be on the quality of the law, rather than on the quality of its pace, as the former can supersede the problem of the latter. As part of the evaluation of the law's quality and effectiveness, it is hence also important to consider whether it adopts a technology-neutral rather than a technology-specific approach, and how narrow or broad its scope and definitions are.[19]

These are but a handful of questions that underlie the debate on the law, ethics, and policy of AI, none of which are easy to formulate an answer to. However, acknowledging this difficulty is already an essential assertion in and of itself, and it would be too much to ask from these disciplines to provide clear-cut answers. Human action and the motivations, manifestations, and consequences of that action are inherently complex. It is therefore not only pointless but also naïve to assume that, when it comes to governing human behavior in the context of AI – a technology that is able to reinforce the effects of human action in both positive and negative ways – simple solutions exist. I firmly believe that it is only through more nuance that we will achieve more understanding, and the world is in urgent need of both. This book aims to contribute to this purpose by portraying, in an introductory manner, the messiness of AI's impact on society in various contexts and by trying to make sense of the ways in which law, ethics, and policy contribute to its governance, in all its complexity.

[17] See also Karen Yeung and Sofia Ranchordas, *An Introduction to Law and Regulation*, 2nd ed. (Cambridge University Press, 2025).

[18] See H.L.A. Hart, *The Concept of Law*, 2nd ed. (Oxford University Press, 1994), 130.

[19] In the context of the AI Act, this is discussed extensively in Nathalie A. Smuha, *Algorithmic Rule by Law: How Algorithmic Regulation in the Public Sector Erodes the Rule of Law*, Chapter 5.4 (Cambridge University Press, 2025).

PART I

AI, Ethics and Philosophy

1

Artificial Intelligence

A Perspective from the Field

Wannes Meert, Tinne De Laet, and Luc De Raedt

1.1 INTRODUCTION

Since the early days of computers and programming, humankind has been fascinated by the question whether machines can be intelligent. This is the domain of artificial intelligence (AI),[1] a term first coined by John McCarthy when he organized the now legendary first summer project in Dartmouth in 1956. The field of AI seeks to answer this question by developing actual machines (robots or computers) that exhibit some kind of intelligent behavior.

Because intelligence encompasses many distinct aspects, one more complicated than the other, research toward AI is typically focused on one or only a few of these aspects. There exist many opinions and lengthy debates about how (artificial) intelligence should be defined. However, a reoccurring insight is that the capabilities of *learning* and *reasoning* are essential to achieve intelligence. While most practical AI systems rely on both learning and reasoning techniques, each of these techniques developed rather independently. One of the grand challenges of AI is achieving a truly integrated learning and reasoning mechanism.[2] The difference between both can be thought of in terms of "System I" and "System II" thinking, as coined in cognitive psychology.[3] System I thinking concerns our instincts, reflexes, or fast thinking. In AI we can relate this to the subdomain of *machine learning*, which aims to develop machines that learn patterns from data (e.g., do I see a traffic light). System II thinking concerns our more deliberate, multistep, logical, slow thinking. It relates to the subdomain of *reasoning* and focuses on knowledge and (logical or probabilistic) inference (e.g., do I need to stop in this traffic situation). In this chapter, we dive

[1] Luc De Raedt, "Over machines die leren" in Pieter d'Hoine and Bart Pattyn (eds), *Wetenschap in een veranderende wereld, Lessen voor de eenentwintigste eeuw* (Leuven University Press, 2020); Stuart Russell and Peter Norvig, *Artificial Intelligence: A Modern Approach, 4th* ed (Pearson, 2020).

[2] Luc De Raedt, Robin Manhaeve, Sebastijan Dumancic, Thomas Demeester, and Angelika Kimmig, "Neuro-symbolic = neural + logical + probabilistic" (2019) *Proceedings of the International Workshop on Neural-Symbolic Learning and Reasoning at IJCAI.*

[3] Daniel Kahneman, *Thinking, Fast and Slow* (Farrar, Straus and Giroux, 2013).

deeper into both machine learning and machine reasoning and describe why they matter and how they function.

1.2 WHAT IS MACHINE LEARNING?

To answer the question whether machines can learn and reason, we first need to define what is meant by a "machine" that can "learn" and "reason." For "machine learning" we go to the, within the domain generally accepted, definition of machine learning by Tom Mitchell. A machine is said to learn if its performance at the specific task improves with experience.[4] The term *machine* herein refers to a robot, a computer, or even a computer program. The machine needs to perform a given *task*, which is typically a task with a narrow scope such that the *performance* can be measured numerically. The more the machine performs the task and gets feedback on its performance, the more it is exposed to *experiences* and the better its performance. A more informal definition by Arthur Samuel, an American computer scientist, is[5] "computers that have the ability to learn without being explicitly programmed."[6]

One of the original, but still fascinating, examples of machine learning is a computer program (*the machine*) developed by Arthur Samuel to play checkers (*the task*). After playing multiple games (*the experience*), the program became a stronger player. This was measured by counting the number of games won or the ranking the program achieved in tournaments (*the performance*). This computer program was developed in the 1950s and 1960s and was one of the first demonstrations of AI. Already then, the program succeeded in winning against one of the best US checkers players. By the early 1990s, the checkers program Chinook, developed at the University of Alberta, outperformed all human players.[7] Nowadays, checkers is a "solved" game. This means that a computer program can play optimally, and the best result an opponent, human or machine, can achieve is to draw. Since then, we have observed AI conquer increasingly complicated games. Playing chess at a human level was reached when Deep Blue won against world chess champion Gary Kasparov in 1997. The game of Go, for which playing strategies were considered too difficult to be even represented in computer memory, was conquered when the program AlphaGo won against Lee Sedol in 2016.[8] And recently also games where not all information is available to a player can be played by AI at the same level as

4 Tom Mitchell, *Machine Learning* (McGraw Hill, 1997).

5 Arthur Samuel, "Some studies in machine learning using the game of checkers" (1959) *IBM Journal of Research and Development*, 3(3): 210–229.

6 Note that the "machine" requires programming to be created. The "without programming" refers to the machine adapting to a task it has not seen before and is thus not explicitly programmed for.

7 Schaeffer Jonathan, *One Jump Ahead: Challenging Human Supremacy in Checkers* (Springer, 1997).

8 David Silver et al., "Mastering the game of Go with deep neural networks and tree search" (2016) *Nature*, 589: 224.

top human players, such as the game of Stratego where DeepNash reached human expert level in 2022.[9]

Another ubiquitous example of learning machines are mail filters (*the machine*) that automatically remove unwanted emails, categorize mails into folders, or automatically forward the mail to the relevant person within an organization (*the task*). Since email is customized to individuals and dependent on one's context, mail handling should also be different from person to person and organization to organization. Therefore, mail filters ought to be adaptive, so that they can adapt to the needs and contexts of individual users. A user can correct undesired behavior or confirm desired behavior by moving and sorting emails manually, hereby indicating (lack) of *performance*. This feedback (*the experiences*) is used as examples from which the computer program can learn. Based on certain properties of those emails, such as sender, style, or word choice, the mail filter can learn to predict whether a new email is spam, needs to be deleted, moved, forwarded, or kept as is. Moreover, by analyzing the text and recognizing a question and intention, the mail filter can also learn to forward the mail to the person that previously answered a similar question successfully. The more examples or demonstrations are provided to the system, the more its performance improves.

A third example is a *recommender system* (*the machine*), which is used by shops to recommend certain products to their customers (*the task*). If, for example, it is observed that many of the customers who have watched Pulp Fiction by Quentin Tarantino also liked Kill Bill, this information can be used to recommend Kill Bill to customers that have watched Pulp Fiction. The *experience* is here the list of movies that customers have viewed (or rated), and the *performance* is measured by the revenue or customer retention, or customer satisfaction of the company.

These examples illustrate how machines need to process (digital) data to learn and thus perform machine learning. By analyzing previous experiences (e.g., games played, emails moved, and movies purchased), the system can extract relevant patterns and build models to improve the execution of their task according to the performance metric used. This also illustrates the inherent statistical nature of machine learning: It analyzes large datasets to identify patterns and then makes predictions, recommendations, or decisions based on those patterns. In that way, machine learning is also closely related to *data science*. Data science is a form of intelligent data analysis that allows us to reformat and merge data in order to extract novel and useful knowledge from large and possibly complex collections of data. Machine learning hence provides tools to conduct this analysis in a more intelligent and autonomous way. Machine learning allows machines to learn complicated tasks based on (large) datasets. While high performance is often achieved, it is not always easy to understand how the machine learning algorithm actually works and

[9] Julien Perolat et al., "Mastering the game of Stratego with model-free multiagent reinforcement learning" (2022) *Science*, 378(6623): 990–996.

to provide explanations for the output of the algorithm. This is what is referred to as a "black box."

1.3 WHAT IS MACHINE REASONING?

Machine learning has powered systems to identify spam emails, play advanced games, provide personalized recommendations, and chat like a human; the question remains whether these systems truly understand the concepts and the domain they are operating in. AI chatbots for instance generate dialogues that are human-like, but at the same time have been reported to invent facts and lack "reasoning" and "understanding." ChatGPT[10] will, when asked to provide a route description between two addresses, confidently construct a route that includes a turn from street A to street B without these streets even being connected in reality or propose a route that is far from being the fastest or safest. The model underlying current versions of ChatGPT does not "understand" the concept of streets and connections between streets, and it is not fast and safe. Similarly, a recommender engine could recommend a book on Ethics in AI based on the books that friends in my social network have bought without "understanding" the concept of Ethics and AI and how they are related to my interests. The statistical patterns exploited in machine learning can be perceived as showing some form of reasoning because these patterns originate from (human) reasoning processes. Sentences generated with ChatGPT look realistic because the underlying large language models are learned from a huge dataset of real sentences, or driving directions can be correct because guidebooks used as training data contain these directions. A slightly different question may however cause ChatGPT to provide a wrong answer because directions for a changed or previously unseen situation cannot always be constructed only from linguistic patterns.

This is where reasoning comes into the picture. Léon Bottou put forward a plausible definition of reasoning in 2011: "[the] algebraic manipulation of previously acquired knowledge in order to answer a new question."[11] Just like in Mitchell's definition, we can distinguish three elements. There is *knowledge* about the world that is represented, that knowledge can be used *to answer (multiple) questions*, and answering questions requires the manipulation of the available knowledge, a process that is often termed *inference*. A further characteristic of reasoning is that Bottou argues that his definition covers both logical and probabilistic reasoning, the two main paradigms in AI for representing and reasoning about knowledge.

Logical knowledge of a specific domain can be represented symbolically using rules, constraints, and facts. Subsequently, an inference engine can use deductive,

[10] https://chat.openai.com

[11] Léon Bottou. "From machine learning to machine reasoning: An essay" (2014) *Machine learning*, 94: 133–149.

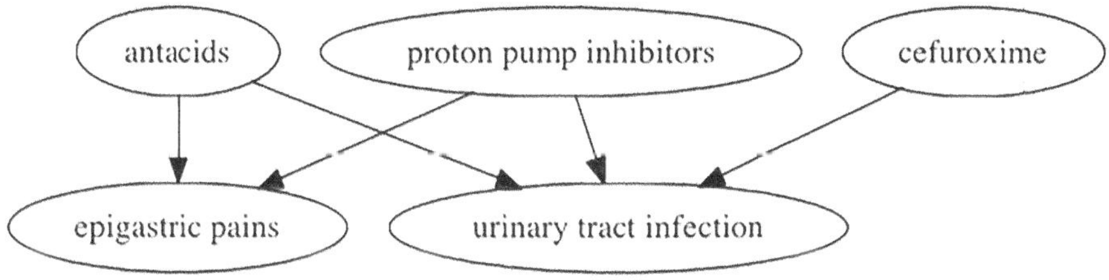

FIGURE 1.1 A (simple) Bayesian network to reason over the (joint) effects of two different medications that are commonly administered to patients suffering from epigastric pains because of pyrosis.

abductive, or inductive inference to derive answers to questions about that domain. The logical approach to machine reasoning is well suited for solving complex problems that require a thorough understanding of multistep reasoning on the knowledge base. It is of particular interest for domains where understanding is crucial and the stakes are high, as deductive reasoning will lead to sound conclusions, thus conclusions that logically follow from the knowledge base. For example, to explore and predict optimal payroll policies, one needs to reason over the clauses or rules present in the tax legislation.[12]

Probabilistic knowledge is often represented in graphical models.[13] These are graphical representations that represent not only the variables of interest but also the (in)dependencies between these variables. The variables are the nodes in the graphs and direct dependencies are specified using the edges (or arcs), and graphical models can be used to query the probability of some variables given that one knows the value of other variables.

Numerous contemporary expert systems are represented as graphical models. Expert systems are computer programs that mimic the decision-making ability of a human expert in a specific domain. Consider, for example, diagnosis in a medical domain such as predicting the preterm birth risk of pregnant women[14] or the impact of combining medication (see Figure 1.1).[15] The variables would then include the symptoms, the possible tests that can be carried out, and the diseases that the patient could suffer from. Probabilistic inference then corresponds to computing the answers to questions such as what is the probability that the patient has pneumonia, given a positive X-ray and coughing. Probabilistic inference can reason from causes

[12] Sebastijan Dumancic, Wannes Meert, Stijn Goethals, Tim Stuyckens, Jelle Huygen, and Koen Denies. "Automated reasoning and learning for automated payroll management" (2021) In *Proceedings of the AAAI Conference on Artificial Intelligence*, 35(17): 15107–15116.

[13] Daphne Koller and Nir Friedman, *Probabilistic Graphical Models: Principles and Techniques* (The MIT Press, 2009).

[14] Linda Woolery and Jerzy Grzymala-Busse, "Machine learning for an expert system to predict preterm birth risk" (1994) *Journal of the American Medical Informatics Association*, 1(6): 439–446.

[15] Steven Woudenberg, Linda van der Gaag, and Carin Rademaker, "An intercausal cancellation model for Bayesian-network engineering" (2015) *International Journal of Approximate Reasoning*, 63: 32–47.

to effects (here: diseases to symptoms) and from effects to causes (diagnostic reasoning) or, in general, draw conclusions about the probability of variables given that the outcome of other variables is known. Furthermore, one can use the (in)dependencies modeled in the graphical model to infer which tests are relevant in the light of what is already known about the patient. Or in the domain of robotics, machine reasoning is used to determine the optimal sequence of actions to complete a manipulation or manufacturing task. An example is CRAM (Cognitive Robot Abstract Machine), equipping autonomous robots performing everyday manipulation with lightweight reasoning mechanisms that can automatically infer control decisions rather than requiring the decisions to be preprogrammed.[16]

Logical and probabilistic knowledge can be created by knowledge experts encoding the domain knowledge elicited from domain experts, textbooks, and so on but can also be learned from data, hereby connecting the domain of reasoning to machine learning. Machine reasoning is, in contrast to machine learning, considered to be knowledge driven rather than data driven. It is also important to remark that logical and probabilistic inference naturally provides explanations for the answers to the questions it provides; therefore, machine reasoning is inherently explainable AI.

1.4 WHY MACHINE LEARNING AND REASONING?

The interest in machine learning and reasoning can be explained from different perspectives. First, the domain of AI has a general interest in developing intelligent systems, and it is this interest that spurred the development of machine learning and reasoning. Second, it is hoped that a better understanding of machine learning and reasoning can provide novel insights into human behavior and intelligence more generally. Third, from a computer science point of view, it is very useful to have machines that learn and reason autonomously as not everything can be explicitly programmed or as the task may require answering questions that are hard to anticipate.

In this chapter, we focus on the third perspective. Our world is rapidly digitizing and programming machines manually is in the best case a tedious task, and in the worst case a nearly impossible endeavor. Data analysis requires a lot of laborious effort, as it is nowadays far easier to generate data than it is to interpret data, as also reflected by the popular phrase: "We are drowning in data but starving for knowledge." As a result, machine learning and data mining are by now elementary tools in domains that deal with large amounts of data such as bio- and chem-informatics, medicine, computer linguistics, or prognostics. Increasingly, they are also finding

[16] Michael Beetz, Lorenz Mösenlechner, and Moritz Tenorth, "CRAM – A Cognitive Robot Abstract Machine for everyday manipulation in human environments," (2010) *In Proceedings of IEEE/RSJ International Conference on Intelligent Robots and Systems.*

their way into the analysis of data from social and economic sciences. Machine learning is also very useful to develop complex software that cannot be implemented manually. The mail filter mentioned earlier is a good example of this. It is impossible to write a custom computer program for each user or to write a new program every time a new type of message appears. We thus need computer programs that adapt automatically to their environment or user. Likewise, for complex control systems, such as autonomous cars or industrial machines, machine learning is essential. Whether it is to translate pixels into objects or a route into steering actions, it is not feasible to program all the subtleties that are required to successfully achieve this task. However, it is easy to provide ample examples of how this task can be carried out by gathering data while driving a car, or by annotating parts of the data.

In 2005, it was the first time that five teams succeeded in developing a car that could autonomously drive an entire predefined route over dust roads.[17] Translating all the measurements gathered from cameras, lasers, and sensors to steering would not have been possible if developers had to write down all computer code explicitly themselves. While there is still a significant work ahead to achieve a fully autonomous vehicle that safely operates in all possible environments and conditions, assisted driving and autonomous vehicles in constrained environments are nowadays operated daily thanks to advances in machine learning.

Machine reasoning is increasingly needed to support reasoning in complex domains, especially when the stakes are high, such as in health and robotics. When there is knowledge available about a particular domain and that knowledge can be used to flexibly answer multiple types of questions, it is much easier to infer the answer using a general-purpose reasoning technique than having to write programs for every type of question. So, machine reasoning allows us to reuse the same knowledge for multiple tasks. At the same time, when knowledge is already available, it does not make sense to still try to learn it from data. Consider applying the taxation rules in a particular country, we could directly encode this knowledge and it therefore does not make sense to try to learn these rules from tax declarations.

1.5 HOW DO MACHINE LEARNING AND REASONING WORK?

The examples in the introduction illustrate that the goal of machine learning is to make machines more intelligent, thus allowing them to achieve a higher performance in executing their tasks by learning from experiences. To this end, they typically use input data (e.g., pixels, measurements, and descriptions) and produce an output (e.g., a move, a classification, and a prediction). Translating the input to the output is typically achieved by learning a mathematical function, also referred to as the *machine learning model*. For the game of checkers, this is a function that

[17] Sebastian Thrun et al. "Stanley: The Robot That Won the DARPA Grand Challenge" (2007) *Springer Tracts in Advanced Robotics*, vol 36. Springer.

connects every possible game situation to a move. For mail filters, this is a function that takes an email and its metadata to output the categorization (spam or not). For recommender systems, the function links purchases of costumers to other products.

Within the domain of machine learning, we can distinguish different learning problems along two dimensions: (1) the type of function that needs to be learned and (2) the type of feedback or experiences that are available. While machine learning techniques typically cover multiple aspects of these dimensions, no technique covers all possible types of functions and feedback. Different methods exploit and sacrifice different properties or make different assumptions, resulting in a wide variety of machine learning techniques. Mapping the right technique to the right problem is already a challenge in itself.[18]

1.5.1 *Type of Function*

Before explaining how different types of functions used in machine learning differ, it is useful to first point out what they all have in common. As indicated earlier, machine learning requires the machine learning function, or model, to improve when given feedback, often in the form of examples or experiences. This requires a mechanism that can adapt our model based on the performance of the model output for a new example or experience. If, for instance, the prediction of an algorithm differs from what is observed by the human (e.g., the prediction *is a cat*, while the picture shows a dog), the predictive model should be corrected. Correcting the model means that we need to be able to compute how we should change the function to better map the input to the output for the available examples, thus, to better fit the available observations. Computing an output such as a prediction from an input is referred to as *forward inference*, while computing how our function should be changed is referred to as *backward inference*. All types of functions have in common that a technique exists that allows us to perform backward inference. We can relate this to human intelligence by means of philosopher Søren Kierkegaard's quote that says: "Life must be lived forward but can only be understood backwards."

We will provide more details for three commonly used types of functions: Symbolic functions, Bayesian functions, and Deep functions. For each of these functions, the domain of machine learning studies how to efficiently learn the function (e.g., how much data is required), which classes of functions can be learned tractably (thus in a reasonable time), whether the function can represent the problem domain sufficiently accurate (e.g., a linear function cannot represent an ellipse), and whether the learned function can be interpreted or adheres to certain properties (e.g., feature importance and fairness constraints). We explain these types based on

[18] When one tries to solve a machine learning problem using machine learning, this is referred to as meta-learning. See Luc De Raedt et al., "Elements of an automatic data scientist" (2018) In *Proceedings of Advances in Intelligent Data Analysis XVII*, Springer.

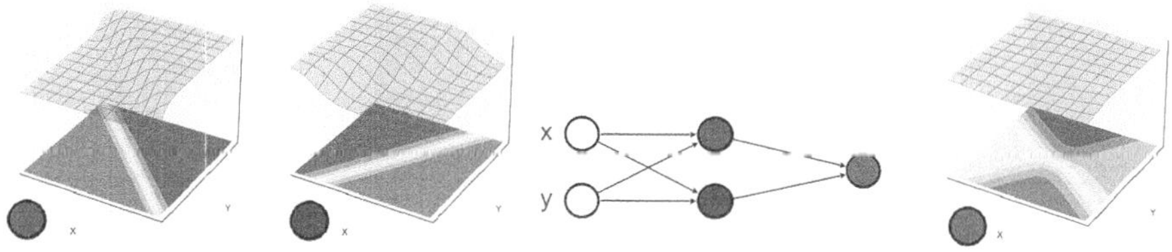

FIGURE 1.2 Each simple sigmoid function expresses a linear separation; together they form a more complicated function of two hyperbolas.

the supervised learning setting that will be introduced later. For now, it suffices to know that our feedback consists of observations that include a (target) label or an expected outcome (e.g., pictures with the label "cat" or "dog").

1.5.1.1 Deep Functions

With deep functions we refer to neural network architectures which, in their simplest form, are combinations of many small (nonlinear or piecewise linear) functions. We can represent this combination of small functions as a graph where each node is one function that takes as input the output of previous nodes. The nodes are organized in layers where nodes in one layer use the outputs of the nodes in the previous layer as input and send their outputs to the nodes in the next layer. The term "deep" refers to the use of many consecutive layers. Individually, these small functions cannot accurately represent the desired function. However, together these small functions can represent any continuous function. The resulting function can fit the data very closely. This is depicted in Figure 1.2 where two simple functions can only linearly separate two halves of a flat plane, while the combination of two such functions already provides a more complicated separation.

One way to think about this architecture is that nodes and layers introduce additional dimensions to look at the data and express chains of continuous transformations. Suppose we have a sheet of paper with two sets of points as depicted in Figure 1.3, and we want to learn a function that separates these two sets of points. We can now lift this piece of paper and introduce further dimensions in which we can rotate, stretch or twist the piece of paper.[19] This allows us to represent the data differently and ideally such that the points of the same group are close to each other and far away from the other group of points such that they are easier to distinguish (e.g., by a simple straight line). The analogy with a piece of paper does not hold completely when dealing with many layers, but we can intuitively still view it as stretching and twisting this paper until we find a combination of

[19] Note that all methods allow only a certain set of operations to allow for backward inference and thus not all possible operations. In the case of neural nets, for example, ripping the paper is an operation that is not supported.

FIGURE 1.3 A geometric interpretation of adding layers and nodes to a neural network.

transformations for which the points of each class or close to each other but far apart from the other class. If we find such a set of transformations, we have learned a function that can now be used to classify any point that we would draw on this piece of paper. In Figure 1.3, one can observe that all points close to the (dark gray) circles would be labeled as a circle (like the question mark) and similarly for the (light gray) squares.

Computing the outcome of this function from the inputs is called forward inference. To update the parameters that define what functions we will combine and how (e.g., amount of rotation, stretching or folding of the paper, and which combinations of transformations), we need to perform backward inference to decide in what direction we should slightly alter the parameters based on the observed performance (e.g., a wrong prediction). This algorithm is often a variation of what is called the backpropagation algorithm. This refers to the propagation of results backward through the functions and adapting the parameters slightly to compensate for errors and reinforce correct results in order to improve the performance of the task. In our example of the classification of squares and circles (Figure 1.3), the observed wrong classification of a point as a square instead of a circle will require us to adapt the parameters of the neural network.

1.5.1.2 Symbolic Functions

Symbolic functions that are used in machine learning are in line with logic-based reasoning. The advantage is that the learned symbolic functions are typically tractable and that rigorous proof techniques can be used to learn and analyze the function. The disadvantage is that they cannot easily cope with uncertainty or fit numerical data. While classical logic is based on *deductive* inference, machine learning uses *inductive* inference. For deductive inference, one starts from a set of premises from which conclusions are derived. If the premises are true, then this guarantees that the conclusions are also true. For example, IF we know that all swans are white, and we know there is a swan, THEN we know this swan will also be white. For inductive reasoning, we start from specific observations, and derive generic rules. For example, if we see two white swans, then we can derive a rule that all swans are white. Inductive inference does not guarantee, in contrast to classical deductive inference, that all conclusions are true if the premises are true. It is possible that the next swan we observe, in contrast to the two observed earlier and our deductively inferred symbolic rule, is a black swan. This means that inductive inference does not necessarily return universally true rules. Therefore, inductively inferred rules are often combined with statistical interpretations. In our example, the rule that all swans are white would only be true with a certain probability.

Another form of inference that is sometimes used is *abductive* reasoning. In this case, possible explanations for observations (or experiments) are generated. For example, if we know the following rule: "IF stung by mosquito AND mosquito carries malaria THEN malaria is transferred" and we know that someone has malaria, then there is a possible explanation, which states that the person is stung by a mosquito with malaria. There might be also other explanations. For example, that the person has received a blood transfusion with infected blood. Thus, also abductive inference does not offer guarantees about the correctness of the conclusion. But we can again associate probabilities with the possible explanations. This form of inference is important when building tests of theories and has been used by systems such as the Robot Scientist to select the most relevant experiments.[20] The goal of the Robot Scientist is to automate parts of the scientific method, notable the incremental design of a theory and to test hypotheses to (dis)prove this theory based on experiments. In the case of the Robot Scientist, an actual robot was built that operates in a microbiology laboratory. The robot starts from known theories about biological pathways for yeast. These known theories are altered on purpose to be incorrect, and the experiment was to verify whether the robot could retrieve the correct theories by autonomously designing experiments and executing these experiments in practice. When machine learning is not only learning from observations but also suggesting novel observations and asking for labels, this is called *active learning*.

1.5.1.3 Bayesian Functions

Some behaviors cannot be captured by logical if-then statements or by fitting a function because they are stochastic (e.g., rolling dice), thus the output or behavior of the system is uncertain. When learning the behavior of such systems, we need a function that can express and quantify stochasticity (e.g., the probability to get each side of a dice after a throw is 1/6). This can be expressed by a function using probability distributions. When dealing with multiple distributions that influence each other, one often uses Bayesian networks that model how different variables relate to each other probabilistically (Figure 1.1 shows a Bayesian network). These functions have as additional advantage that they allow us to easily incorporate domain knowledge and allow for insightful models (e.g., which variables influence or have a causal effect on another variable). For this type of function, we also need to perform

[20] Ross D. King, Jem Rowland, Wayne Aubrey, Maria Liakata, Magdalena Markham, Larisa N. Soldatova, Ken E. Whelan et al. "The robot scientist Adam." (2009) *Computer*, 42(8): 46–54.

forward and backward inference. In the forward direction these are conditional probabilities. In the spam example, forward inference entails calculating the probability that a mail spells your name correctly (*correct*) given that it is a spam email (spam): $P(correct \mid spam)$. For the backward direction we can use the rule of Bayes – therefore the name Bayesian networks – that tells us how to invert the reasoning: $P(spam \mid correct) = P(correct \mid spam)P(spam) / P(correct)$. For the example, if we know $P(correct \mid spam)$, that is, the probability that a spam email spells your name correctly, we can use Bayes rule to calculate $P(spam \mid correct)$, that is, the probability that a new mail with your name spelled correctly is a spam email.

Bayesian functions are most closely related to traditional statistics where one assumes that the type of distribution from which data is generated is known (e.g., a Gaussian or normal distribution) and then tries to identify the parameters of the distribution to fit the data. In machine learning, one can also start from the data and assume nothing is known about the distribution and thus needs to be learn as part of the machine learning. Furthermore, machine learning also does not require a generative view of the model – the model does not need to explain everything we observe. It suffices if it generates accurate predictions for our variable(s) of interest. However, finding this function is in both cases achieved by applying the laws of probability. Bayesian functions additionally suffer from limited expressional power: not all interactions between variables can be modeled with probability distributions alone.

1.5.2 *Type of Feedback*

The second dimension on which machine learning settings can be distinguished is based on the type of feedback that is available and is used in machine learning. The type of feedback is related to what kind of experience, examples, or observations we have access to. If the observation includes the complete feedback we are interested in directly, we refer to this as *supervised learning*. For example, supervised learning can take place if we have a set of pictures where each picture is already labeled as either "cat" or "dog," which is the information we ultimately want to retrieve when examining new unclassified pictures. For the spam example, it means we have a set of emails already classified as spam or not spam supplemented with the information regarding the correct spelling of our name in these emails. This is also the case when data exists about checkers or chess game situations that are labeled by grandmasters to indicate which next moves are good and bad. A second type of feedback is to learn from (delayed) rewards, also called *reinforcement learning*. This is the case, for example, when we want to learn which moves are good or bad in a game of checkers by actually playing the game. We only know at the end of a game whether it was won or lost and need to derive from that information which moves throughout the game were good or bad moves. A third type of feedback concerns the situation when we do not have direct feedback available, which is also referred to as *unsupervised learning*. For example, when we are seeking to identify good recommendations for movies, no direct labels of good or bad recommendations are available. Instead, we try to find patterns in the observations themselves. In this case, it concerns observations about which people watch which combinations of movies, based on which we can then identify sound recommendations for the future.

1.6 SUPERVISED LEARNING

As an example of a supervised learning technique, we discuss how *decision trees* can be derived from examples. Decision trees are useful for classification problems, which appear in numerous applications. The goal is to learn, in case of supervised learning, a function from a dataset with examples that are already categorized (or labeled) such that we can apply this function to predict the class of new, not yet classified examples. A good example concerns the classification of emails as spam or not spam.

Closely related with classification problems are regression problems where we want to predict a numerical value instead of a class. This is, for example, the case when the system is learning how to drive a car, and we want to predict the angle of the steering wheel and the desired speed that the car should maintain.

There is vast literature on supervised classification and regression tasks as it is the most studied problem in machine learning. The techniques cover all possible types of functions we have introduced before and combinations thereof. Here we use a simple but popular technique for classification that uses decision trees. In this example, we start from a table of examples, where each row is an example, and each column is an attribute (or feature) of an example. The class of each example can be found in a special column in that table. Take for example the table in Figure 1.4 containing (simplified) data about comic books. Each example expresses the properties of a comic book series: language, length, genre, and historical. The goal is to predict whether this customer would buy an album from a particular series. A decision tree is a tree-shaped structure where each node in the tree represents a decision

Title	Language	Length	Genre	Historical	Buy
Gaston	NL/FR	Strip	Humor	False	True
Calvin and Hobbes	USA	Strip	Humor	False	True
Spider-Man	USA	Album	Superhero	False	False
Tintin	NL/FR	Album	Humor	False	False
Asterix	NL/FR	Album	Humor	True	True
Kiekeboe	NL/FR	Album	Humor	False	True
Peanuts	USA	Strip	Humor	False	False
Le Petit Spirou	NL/FR	Strip	Humor	False	True
Thorgal	NL/FR	Album	Superhero	True	True
Lucky Luke	NL/FR	Album	Superhero	True	True

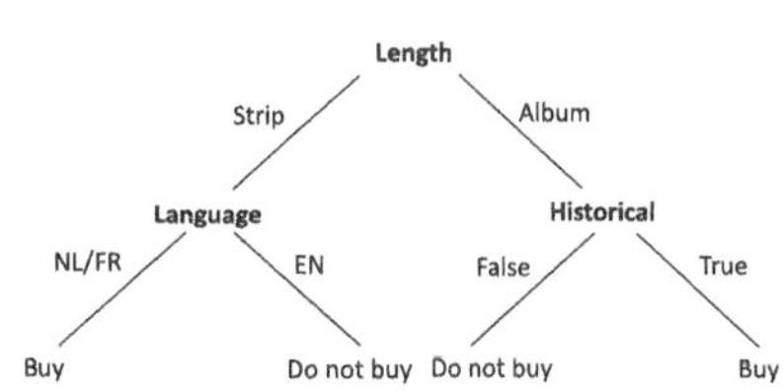

FIGURE 1.4 Table representing the dataset and the resulting decision tree

made based on the value of a particular attribute. The branches emerging from a node represent the possible outcomes based on the values of that attribute. The leaves of this tree represent the predicted classification, in this example buy or not buy. When a new example is given, we traverse the tree following the branch that corresponds to the value that the attribute has in the example. Suppose there exists a series that the customer has not yet bought, with attribute values (NL/FR, Strip, Humor, Historical). When we traverse the tree, we follow the left branch (Strip) for the top node that splits on length. The next node selects based on language and we follow the left branch (NL/FR) ending in the prediction that the customer will buy this new series.

The algorithm to learn a decision tree works as follows: we start with a single node and all available examples. Next, we estimate by means of a heuristic which attribute differentiates best between the different classes. A simple heuristic would be to choose the attribute where, if we split the examples based on the possible values for this attribute, this split is most similar to when we would have split the examples based on their class values (buy or not buy). Once the attribute is decided, we create a branch and a new node per value of that attribute. The examples are split over the branches according to their value for that attribute. In each node we check if this new node contains (almost) only once class. If this is the case, we stop and make the node a leaf with as class the majority class. If not, we repeat the procedure on this smaller set of examples.

An advantage of decision trees is that they are easy and fast to learn and that they often deliver accurate predictions, especially if multiple trees are learned in an ensemble where each tree of the ensemble "votes" for a particular classification outcome. The accuracy of the predictions can be estimated from the data and is crucial for a user to decide whether the model is good enough to be used. Furthermore, decision trees are interpretable by users, which increases the user's trust in the model. In general, their accuracy increases when more data is available and when the quality of this data increases. Defining what are good attributes for an observation, and being able to measure these, is one of the practical challenges that does not only apply for decision trees but for machine learning in general. Also, the heuristic that is used to decide which attribute to use first is central to the success of the method. Ideally, trees are compact by using the most informative attributes. Trying to achieve the most compact or simple tree aligns with the principle of parsimony from thirteenth-century philosopher William of Ockham. This is known as Ockham's Razor and states that when multiple, alternative theories all explain a given set of observations, then the best theory is the simplest theory that makes the smallest number of assumptions. Empirical research in machine learning has shown that applying this principle often leads to more accurate decision trees that generalize better to unseen data. This principle has also led to concrete mathematical theories such as minimum description length used in machine learning.

1.7 REINFORCEMENT LEARNING

Learning from rewards is used to decide which actions a system best takes given a certain situation. This technique was developed first by Arthur Samuel and has been further perfectioned since. We illustrate this technique using the Menace program developed by Donald Michie in 1961 to play the Tic-Tac-Toe game. While we illustrate this technique to learn from rewards using a game, these techniques are widely applied in industrial and scientific contexts (e.g., control strategies for elevators, robots, complex industrial processes, autonomous driving). Advances in this field are often showcased in games (e.g., checkers, chess, Go, Stratego) because these are controlled environments where performance is easily and objectively measured. Furthermore, it is a setting where human and machine performance are easily compared.

Tic-Tac-Toe is played on a board with three-by-three squares (see Figure 1.5: The Menace program playing Tic-Tac-Toe). There are two players, X and O, that play in turns. Player X can only put an X in an open square, and player O an O. The player that first succeeds in making a row, column, or diagonal that contains three identical letters wins the game. The task of the learning system is to decide which move to perform in any given situation on the board. The only feedback that is available is whether the game is eventually won or lost, not if a particular move is good or bad. For other strategy games such as checkers or chess, we can also devise rewards or penalties for winning or losing pieces on the board. Learning from rewards differs significantly from supervised learning for classification and regression problems because for every example, here a move, the category is not known. When learning from rewards, deriving whether an example (thus an individual move) is good or bad is part of the learning problem, as it must first be understood how credit is best assigned. This explains why learning from rewards is more difficult than supervised learning.

Donald Michie has developed Menace from the observation that there are only 287 relevant positions for the game of Tic-Tac-Toe if one considers symmetry of the board. Because Donald Michie did not have access to computers as we have now, he developed the "hardware" himself. This consisted of 287 match boxes, one for

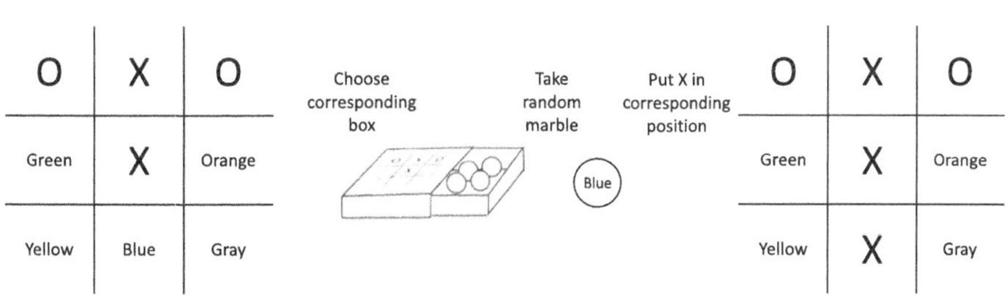

FIGURE 1.5 The Menace program playing Tic-Tac-Toe

each possible situation on the board. To represent each of the nine possible moves of player X – one for each open position on the board – he had many marbles in nine different colors. Each color represents one of the nine possible squares. These marbles were then divided equally over the match boxes, only excluding colors in those boxes representing a board situation where the move is not possible. Menace then decided on the move as follows:

a. Take the match box that represents the current situation on the board.
b. Randomly take a marble from the match box.
c. Play the move that corresponds to the color of the marble.

The Menace program thus represents a function that for every board situation and possible next moves returns a probability that this move should be played from this position. The probabilities are given by the relative number of marbles of a certain color in the corresponding match box. The learning then happens as follows. If the game is won by X, then for every match box from which one marble was taken, two marbles of that color are again added to these match boxes. If X loses the game, then no marbles are returned. The consequence of these actions is that the probability of winning moves in the relevant boxes (and thus board situations) is increased and that of losing moves is decreased. The more games that are played, the better the probabilities represent a good policy to follow to win a game. The rewards from which Menace learns are thus the won and lost games, where lost games are negative rewards or penalties.

When learning from rewards, it is important to find a good balance between exploration and exploitation. Exploration is important to explore the space of all possible strategies thoroughly, while exploitation is responsible for using the gained knowledge to improve performance. In the case of Menace, a stochastic strategy is used where a move is decided by randomly selecting a marble. Initially, the probability for any possible move in a particular situation is completely at random, which is important for exploration, as there are about an equal number of marbles for each (possible) color in each box. But after a while, the game converges to a good strategy when there are more marbles of colors that represent good moves, which is important for exploitation.

Today, learning from rewards does not use matchboxes anymore but still follows the same mathematical principles. These principles have been formalized as Markov Decision Processes and often a so-called Q-function $Q(s,a)$ is learned. Here $Q(s,a)$ represents the reward that is expected when an action a is taken in a state s. In the Tic-Tac-Toe example, the action is the next move a player takes and the state s is the current situation on the board. The Q-function is learned by using the famous Belmann equation, $Q(s,a) = R(s,a) + \gamma \max_{a'} Q(s',a')$, where $R(s,a)$ is the immediate reward received after taking action a in situation s, γ is a number between 0 and 1 that indicates how future rewards relate to the immediate reward (rewards obtained in the future are less valuable than an equal immediate reward), and s' the state that is reached after taking action a in situation s. The Q-function is also used to select the actions. The best action in a situation s is the action a for which $Q(s,a)$ is maximal. To illustrate Q-learning, consider again the Menace program. Each box can be considered as a state, and each color as an action that can be executed in that state. The Q-function then contains the probability of selecting a marble from that color in that box, and the best action is the one is that with the maximum probability (i.e., the color that occurs most in that box).

1.8 UNSUPERVISED LEARNING

For the third type of feedback, we look at learning *associations*. Here we have no labels or direct feedback available. This technique became popular as part of recommender systems used by online shops such as Amazon and streaming platforms such as Netflix. Such companies sell products such as books or movies and advise their customers by recommending products they might like. These recommendations are often based on their previous consuming behavior (e.g., products bought or movies watched). Such associations can be expressed as rules like:

IF X and Y are being consumed, THEN Z will also be consumed.

X, Y, and Z represent specific items such as books or movies. For example, X = Pulp Fiction, Y = Kill Bill, and Z = Django Unchained. Such associations are derived from transaction data gathered about customers. From this data frequently occurring subsets of items are derived. This is expressed as a frequency of the number of times this combination of items occurs together. A collection of items is considered frequent if their frequency is at least $x\%$, thus that it occurs in at least $x\%$ of all purchases. From these frequent collections, the associations are derived. Take for example a collection of items $\{X,Y,Z\}$ that is frequent since it appears in 15% of all purchases. In that case, we know that the collection $\{X,Y\}$ is also frequent and has a frequency of at least 15%. Say that the frequency of $\{X,Y\}$ is 20%, then we can assign some form of probability and build an association rule. The probability that Z will be consumed, if we know that X and Y have been consumed then:

$$\text{Frequency}(\{X,Y,Z\}) / \text{frequency}(\{X,Y\}) = 0.15 / 0.20 = 75\%$$

The information on frequent collections and associations allows us to recommend products (e.g., books or movies). If we want to suggest products that fit with product X and Y, we can simply look at all frequent collections $\{X,Y,Z\}$ and recommend products Z based on increasing frequency of the collections $\{X,Y,Z\}$.

Learning associations are useful in various situations, for instance, when analyzing customer information in a grocery store. When the products X and Y are often bought together, then we can strategically position product Z in the store. The store owner can put the products close to each other to make it easy for customers to buy this combination or to be reminded of also buying this product. Or the owner can put them far apart and hope the customer picks up some additional products when traversing from one end of the store to the other end.

Another form of unsupervised learning is clustering. For clustering, one inspects the properties of the given set of items and tries to group them such that similar items are in the same group and dissimilar items are in other groups. Once a set of clusters is found, one can recommend items based on the most nearby group. For example, in a database of legal documents, clustering of related documents can be used to simplify locating similar or more relevant documents.

1.9 REASONING

When considering reasoning, we often refer to knowledge as input to the system, as opposed to data for machine learning. Knowledge can be expressed in many ways, but logic and constraints are popular choices. We have already seen how logic can be used to express a function that is learned, but more deliberate, multi-step types of inference can be used when considering reasoning. As an example, consider a satisfiability problem, also known as a SAT problem. The goal of a SAT problem is to find, given a set of constraints, a solution that satisfies all these constraints. This type of problem is one of the most fundamental ones of computer science and AI. It is the prototypical hard computational problem and many other problems can be reduced to it. You also encounter SAT problems daily (e.g., suggesting a route to drive, which packages to pick up and when to deliver them, configuring a car). Say, we want to choose a restaurant with a group of people, and we know that Ann prefers Asian or Indian and is Vegan; Bob likes Italian or Asian, and if it is Vegan then he prefers Indian. Carry likes vegan or Indian but does not like Italian. We also know that Asian food includes Indian. We can express this knowledge using logic constraints:

$$(\text{Asian} \vee \text{Indian}) \wedge \text{Vegan} \wedge (\text{Italian} \vee \text{Asian}) \wedge (\text{Vegan} \rightarrow \text{Indian}) \wedge (\text{Vegan} \vee \text{Indian}) \wedge \neg\text{Italian} \wedge (\text{Indian} \rightarrow \text{Asian})$$

Observe that $\vee$ stands for OR (disjunction), and $\wedge$ for AND (conjunction). Furthermore, $A \rightarrow B$ stands for IF A THEN B (implication).

When feeding these constraints to a solver, the computer will tell you the solution is to choose Vegan.[21] Actually, the solution that the solver would find is Vegan, Indian, not Italian, and Asian. It is easy that starting from the solution Vegan, then we can also derive Indian, and from Indian, we can derive Asian. Furthermore, the conjunction also specifies that not Italian should be true. With

[21] A game based on SAT that illustrates the hardness of the problem can be found online: www.cril.univ-artois.fr/~roussel/satgame/satgame.php?level=3&lang=eng

these, all elements of the conjunction are satisfied, and thus this provides a solution to the SAT problem.

While we presented an example that required pure reasoning, the integration of learning and reasoning is required in practice. For the previous example, this is the case when we also want to learn preferences. Similarly, when choosing a route to drive, we want to consider learned patterns of traffic jams; or when supplying stores, we want to consider learned customer buying patterns.

1.10 TRUSTWORTHY AI

Models learned by machine learning techniques are typically evaluated based on their predictive performance (e.g., accuracy, f1-score, AUC, squared error) on a test set – a held-aside portion of the data that was not used for learning the model. A good value on these performance metrics indicates that the learned model can also predict other unseen (i.e., not used for learning) examples accurately. While such an evaluation is crucial, in practice it is not sufficient. We illustrate this with three examples. (1) If a model achieves 99% accuracy, what do we know about the 1% that is not predicted accurately? If our training data is biased, the mistakes might not be distributed equally over our population. A well-known example is facial recognition where the training data contained less data about people of color causing more mistakes to be made on this subpopulation.[22] (2) If groups of examples in our population are not covered by our training data, will the model still predict accurately? If you train a medical prediction model on adults – because consent is easier to obtain – the model cannot be trusted for children because their physiology is different.[23] Instead of incorrect predictions, more subtly this might lead to bias. If part of the population is not covered, say buildings in poor areas that are not yet digitized, should we then ignore such buildings in policies based on AI models? (3) Does our model conform to a set of given requirements? These can be legal requirements such as the prohibition to drive on the sidewalk, or ethical requirements such as fairness constraints.[24]

These questions are being tackled in the domain of trustworthy AI.[25] AI researchers have been trying to answer questions about the trustworthiness and interpretability of their models since the early days of AI. Especially when systems were deployed

[22] Joy Buolamwini and Timnit Gebru, "Gender shades: Intersectional accuracy disparities in commercial gender classification." (2018) *Machine Learning Research*, 81: 1–15.

[23] Dries Van der Plas et al., "A reject option for automated sleep stage scoring." (2021) In *Proceedings of the Workshop on Interpretable ML in Healthcare at the International Conference on Machine Learning (ICML)*.

[24] Laurens Devos, Wannes Meert, and Jesse Davis, "Versatile verification of tree ensembles" (2021) *In the Proceedings of the 38th International Conference on Machine Learning (ICML)*.

[25] The TAILOR Handbook of Trustworthy AI, https://tailor-network.eu/handbook/

in production like in the expert systems of the 1980s. But the recent explosion of deployed machine learning and reasoning systems together with the introduction of legislation such as the General Data Protection Regulation (GDPR) and the upcoming AI-act of the European Union has led to a renewed and much larger interest in all aspects related to trustworthy AI. Unfortunately, it is technically much more challenging to answer these questions as only forward and backward inference does not suffice. The field of trustworthy AI encompasses a few different questions that we will now discuss.

1.11 EXPLAINABLE AI (XAI)

When an AI model, that is, a function, translates input information into an output (e.g., a prediction or recommendation), knowing only the output may not be acceptable for all persons or in all situations. When making a decision based on machine learning output, it is important to understand at least the crucial parts that led to the output. his is important to achieve appropriate trust in the model when these decisions impact humans or for instance the yield or efficiency of a production process. This is also reflected in the motivation behind legislation such as the GDPR.[26] Often the need for explainability is driven by the realization that machine learning and reasoning models are prone to errors or bias. The training data might contain errors or bias that are replicated by the model, the model itself might have limitations in what it can express and induce errors or bias, inaccurate or even incorrect assumptions might have been made when modeling the problem, or there might simply be a programming error. On top of the mere output of a machine learning or reasoning algorithm, we thus need techniques to explain these outputs.

One can approach explaining AI models in two ways: only allowing white box models that can be inspected by looking at the model (e.g., a decision tree) or using and developing mechanisms to inspect black box models (e.g., neural networks). While the former is easier, there is also a trade-off with respect to accuracy.[27] We thus need to be able to obtain explainability of black box models. However, full interpretability of the internal mechanisms of the algorithms or up to the sensory inputs might not be required. We also do not need to explain how our eyes and brain exactly translate light beams into objects and shapes such as a traffic light to explain that we stopped because the traffic light is red. Explainability could in

[26] While explanations are mentioned in legislation such as GDPR, it is not a legal norm. Therefore, it is not clear to what level an explanation is required and opinions differ. See Andrew D. Selbst and Julia Powles, "Meaningful information and the right to explanation" (2017) *International Data Privacy Law*, 7(4); Sandra Wachter, Brent Mittelstadt, and Luciano Floridi, "Why a right to explanation of automated decision-making does not exist in the general data protection regulation" (2017) *International Data Privacy Law*, 7(2): https://iapp.org/news/a/is-there-a-right-to-explanation-for-machine-learning-in-the-gdpr/

[27] Note that this trade-off is not always accurately portrayed and (mis)used as an excuse to avoid responsibility. See https://hdsr.mitpress.mit.edu/pub/f9kuryi8/release/8

these cases focus on generating a global understanding of how outputs follow from particular inputs (e.g., in the most relevant or most prominent cases that occur). For particular cases though, full explainability or a white box model might be a requirement. For example, when applying legislation to a situation where we need to explain which clauses are used where and why.

There have been great advances in explaining black box models. Model-specific explainers are explainers that work only on a particular type of black box models, such as explainers for neural networks. As these explainers are developed for particular models, the known underlying function can be reverse-engineered to explain model outputs for individual examples. Model-agnostic explainers (e.g., LIME[28] and SHAP[29]) on the other hand can be applied to any black box model and therefore cannot rely on the internal structure of the model. Their broad applicability often comes at the cost of precision: they can only rely on the black box model's behavior between input and output and in contrast to the model-specific explainers cannot inspect the underlying function. Local explainers try to approximate the black box function around a given example and hereby generate the so-called "local explanations," thus explanations of the behavior of the black box model in the neighborhood of the given example. One possibility is to use feature importance as explanations as it indicates which features are most important to explain the output (e.g., to decide whether a loan gets approved or not the model based its decision for similar clients most importantly on the family income and secondly on the health of the family). Another way to explain decisions is to search for counterfactual examples[30] that give us, for example, the most similar example that would have received a different categorization (e.g., what should I minimally change to get my loan approved?). Besides local explanations one could ideally also provide global explanations that hold for all instances, also those not yet covered by the training data. Global explanations are in general more difficult to obtain.

1.12 ROBUSTNESS

Robustness is an assessment of whether our learned function meets the expected specifications. Its scope is broader than explanations in that it also requires certain guarantees to be met. A first aspect of robustness is to verify whether an

[28] Marco Tulio Ribeiro, Sameer Singh, and Carlos Guestrin. "Why should I trust you?": Explaining the predictions of any classifier (2016). In *Proceedings of the 22nd ACM SIGKDD International Conference on Knowledge Discovery and Data Mining (KDD '16)*. Association for Computing Machinery, New York, NY, USA, 1135–1144. https://doi.org/10.1145/2939672.2939778

[29] Scott M. Lundberg and Su-In Lee. "A unified approach to interpreting model predictions." (2017) In *Advances in Neural Information Processing Systems*.

[30] Riccardo Guidotti. "Counterfactual explanations and how to find them: Literature review and benchmarking. (2022) In *Data Mining and Knowledge Discovery*. https://doi.org/10.1007/s10618-022-00831-6

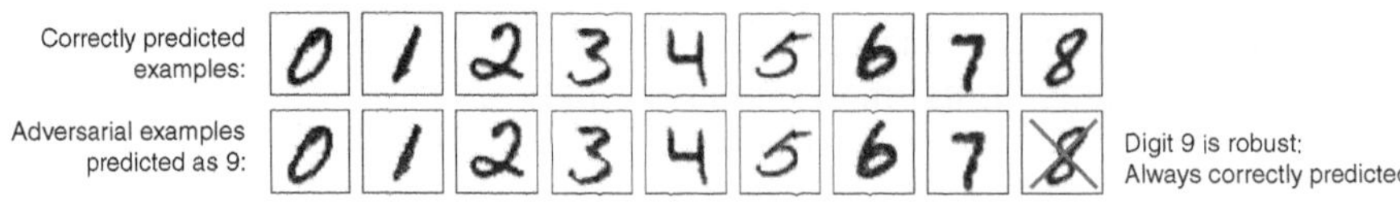

FIGURE 1.6 Adversarial examples for digits.[31]

adversarial example exists. An adversarial example is like a counterfactual example that flips the category, but one that is designed to deceive the model as a human would not observe a difference between the normal and the adversarial example (see Figure 1.6). For example, if by changing a few pixels in an image, changes that are meaningless to a human observer, the learned function can be convinced to change the predicted category (e.g., a picture that is clearly a stop sign for a human observer but deceives the model to be classified as a speed limit sign). A second popular analysis is about data privacy: does the learned function leak information about individual data examples (e.g., a patient)? A final aspect is that of fairness, sometimes also considered separately from robustness. It is vaguer by nature as it can differ for cultural or generational reasons. In general, it is an unjust advantage for one side. Remember the facial recognition example where the algorithm's goal to optimize accuracy disadvantages people of color because they are a minority group in the data. Another example of fairness can be found in reinforcement learning where actions should not block something or somebody. A traffic light that never allows one to pass or an elevator that never stops on the third floor (because in our training data nobody was ever on the third floor) is considered unfair and to be avoided.

Robustness thus entails testing strategies to verify whether the AI system does what is expected under stress, when being deceived, and when confronted with anomalous or rare situations. This is also mentioned in the White Paper on Artificial Intelligence: A European approach to excellence and trust.[32] Offering such guarantees, however, is also the topic of many research projects since proving that the function adheres to certain statements or constraints is in many cases computationally intractable and only possible by approximation.

1.13 CONCLUSIONS

Machine learning and machine reasoning are domains within the larger field of AI and computer sciences that are still growing and evolving rapidly. AI studies how one can develop a machine that can learn from observations and what fundamental laws guide this process. There is consensus about the nature of machine learning,

[31] Laurens Devos, Wannes Meert, and Jesse Davis, "Versatile verification of tree ensembles." (2021) *International Conference on Machine Learning (ICML)*.

[32] European Commission, "White Paper on Artificial Intelligence: A European approach to excellence and trust" (2020), https://ec.europa.eu/info/publications/white-paper-artificial-intelligence-european-approach-excellence-and-trust_en.

in that it can be formalized as learning of functions. There is also consensus that machine reasoning enables the exploitation of knowledge to infer answers to a wide range of queries. However, for now, there is neither a known set of universal laws that govern all AI and machine learning and reasoning, nor do we understand how machine learning and reasoning can be fully integrated. Therefore, many different approaches and techniques exist that push forward our insights and available technology. Despite the work ahead there are already many practical learning and reasoning systems and exciting applications that are being deployed and influence our daily life.

2

Philosophy of AI

A Structured Overview

Vincent C. Müller

2.1 TOPIC AND METHOD

2.1.1 *Artificial Intelligence*

The term *Artificial Intelligence* became popular after the 1956 "Dartmouth Summer Research Project on Artificial Intelligence," which stated its aims as follows:

> The study is to proceed on the basis of the conjecture that every aspect of learning or any other feature of intelligence can in principle be so precisely described that a machine can be made to simulate it.[1]

This is the ambitious research program that human intelligence or cognition can be understood or modeled as rule-based computation over symbolic representation, so these models can be tested by running them on different (artificial) computational hardware. If successful, the computers running those models would display artificial intelligence. Artificial intelligence and cognitive science are two sides of the same coin. This program is usually called *Classical AI*:[2]

a) AI is a research program to create computer-based agents that have intelligence.

The terms *Strong AI* and *Weak AI* as introduced by John Searle stand in the same tradition. *Strong AI* refers to the idea that: "the appropriately programmed computer really is a mind, in the sense that computers given the right programs can be literally said to understand and have other cognitive states." *Weak AI* is means that AI merely simulates mental states. In this weak sense "the principal value of the computer in the study of the mind is that it gives us a very powerful tool."[3]

1 John McCarthy et al., "A proposal for the Dartmouth Summer Research Project on Artificial Intelligence" (1955), www-formal.stanford.edu/jmc/history/dartmouth/dartmouth.html, accessed October 1, 2006.

2 As a sample: Eric Dietrich, "Philosophy of artificial intelligence" *The Encyclopedia of Cognitive Science* 203. The classic historical survey is Margaret A. Boden, *Mind as Machine: A History of Cognitive Science* (Oxford University Press, 2006).

3 John R. Searle, "Minds, brains and programs" (1980) *Behavioral and Brain Sciences*, 3(3): 417–424.

On the other hand, the term "AI" is often used in computer science in a sense that I would like to call *Technical AI*:

b) AI is a set of computer-science methods for perception, modelling, planning, and action (search, logic programming, probabilistic reasoning, expert systems, optimization, control engineering, neuromorphic engineering, machine learning (ML), etc.).[4]

There is also a minority in AI that calls for the discipline to focus on the ambitions of (a), while maintaining current methodology under (b), usually under the name of *Artificial General Intelligence* (AGI).[5]

This existence of the two traditions (classical and technical) occasionally leads to suggestions that we should not use the term "AI," because it implies strong claims that stem from the research program (a) but have very little to do with the actual work under (b). Perhaps we should rather talk about "ML" or "decision-support machines," or just "automation" (as the 1973 Lighthill Report suggested).[6] In the following we will clarify the notion of "intelligence" and it will emerge that there is a reasonably coherent research program of AI that unifies the two traditions: The *creation of intelligent behavior through computing machines.*

These two traditions now require a footnote: Both were largely developed under the notion of *classical AI*, so what has changed with the move to ML? Machine learning is a traditional computational (connectivist) method in neural networks that does not use representations.[7] Since ca. 2015, with the advent of massive computing power and massive data for deep neural networks, the performance of ML systems in areas such as translation, text production, speech recognition, games, visual recognition, and autonomous driving has improved dramatically, so that it is superior to humans in some cases. Machine learning is now the standard method in AI. What does this change mean for the future of the discipline? The honest answer is: We do not know yet. Just like any method, ML has its limits, but these limits are less restrictive than was thought for many years because the systems exhibit a nonlinear improvement – with more data they may suddenly improve significantly. Its

4 Stuart Russell, *Human Compatible: Artificial Intelligence and the Problem of Control* (Viking, 2019); Stuart Russell and Peter Norvig, *Artificial Intelligence: A Modern Approach* (4th ed., Prentice Hall, 2020); Günther Görz, Ute Schmid, and Tanya Braun, *Handbuch der Künstlichen Intelligenz* (5th ed., De Gruyter, 2020); Judea Pearl and Dana Mackenzie, *The Book of Why: The New Science of Cause and Effect* (Basic Books, 2018).

5 AGI conferences have been organized since 2008.

6 James Lighthill, *Artificial Intelligence: A General Survey* (Science Research Council, 1973).

7 Frank Rosenblatt, "The Perceptron: a perceiving and recognizing automaton (Project PARA)" Vol. 85, Issues 460–461 of Report (Cornell Aeronautical Laboratory, 1957); Yann LeCun, Yoshua Bengio, and Geoffrey Hinton, "Deep learning" (2015) *Nature*, 521: 436–444; James Garson and Cameron Buckner, "Connectionism" in Edward N. Zalta (ed.), *Stanford Encyclopedia of Philosophy* (CSLI, Stanford, 2019), https://plato.stanford.edu/entries/connectionism/; Cameron J. Buckner, *From Deep Learning to Rational Machines: What the History of Philosophy Can Teach Us about the Future of Artificial Intelligence* (Oxford University Press, 2024).

weaknesses (e.g., overfitting, causal reasoning, reliability, relevance, and black box) may be quite close to those of human rational choice, especially if "predictive processing" is the correct theory of the human mind (Sections 2.4 and 2.6).

2.1.2 *Philosophy of AI and Philosophy*

One way to understand the philosophy of AI is that it mainly deals with three Kantian questions: What is AI? What can AI do? What should AI be? One major part of the philosophy of AI is the *ethics* of AI but we will not discuss this field here, because there is a separate entry on "Ethics of AI" in the present CUP handbook.[8]

Traditionally, the philosophy of AI deals with a few selected points where philosophers have found something to say about AI, for example, about the thesis that cognition is computation, or that computers can have meaningful symbols.[9] Reviewing these points and the relevant authors (Turing, Wiener, Dreyfus, Dennett, Searle, …) would result in a fragmented discussion that never achieves a picture of the overall project. It would be like writing an old-style human history through a few "heroes." Also, in this perspective, the philosophy of AI is separated from its cousin, the philosophy of cognitive science, which in turn is closely connected to the philosophy of mind.[10]

In this chapter we use a different approach: We look at *components of an intelligent system*, as they present themselves in philosophy, cognitive science, and AI. One way to consider such components is that there are relatively simple animals that can do relatively simple things, and then we can move "up" to more complicated animals that can do those simple things, and more. As a schematic example, a *fly* will continue to bump into the glass many times to get to the light; a *cobra* will understand that there is an obstacle here and try to avoid it; a *cat* might remember that there was an obstacle there the last time and take another path right away; a *chimpanzee* might realize that the glass can be broken with a stone; a *human* might find the key and unlock the glass door … or else take the window to get out.

[8] See Chapter 3 of this book. See also: Vincent C. Müller, "Ethics of artificial intelligence and robotics" in Edward N. Zalta (ed.), *Stanford Encyclopedia of Philosophy*, (CSLI, Stanford University, 2020), https://plato.stanford.edu/entries/ethics-ai/; Vincent C. Müller, *Can Machines Think? Fundamental Problems of Artificial Intelligence* (Oxford University Press, forthcoming).

[9] There are very few surveys and no recent ones. See Jack B. Copeland, *Artificial Intelligence: A Philosophical Introduction* (Blackwell, 1993); Dietrich Matt Carter, *Minds and Computers: An Introduction to the Philosophy of Artificial Intelligence* (Edinburgh University Press, 2007); Luciano Floridi (ed.) *The Blackwell Guide to the Philosophy of Computing and Information* (Blackwell, 2003); Luciano Floridi, *The Philosophy of Information* (Oxford University Press, 2011). Some of what philosophers had to say can be seen as undermining the project of AI, compare Eric Dietrich et al., *Great Philosophical Objections to Artificial Intelligence: The History and Legacy of the AI Wars* (Bloomsbury Academic, 2021).

[10] Eric Margolis, Richard Samuels, and Stephen Stich (eds.), *The Oxford Handbook of Philosophy of Cognitive Science* (Oxford University Press, 2012).

To engage in the philosophy of AI properly, we will thus need a wide range of philosophy: philosophy of mind, epistemology, language, value, culture, society, …

Furthermore, in our approach, the philosophy of AI is not just "applied philosophy"; it is not that we have a solution ready in the philosopher's toolbox and "apply" it to solve issues in AI. The philosophical understanding itself *changes* when looking at the case of AI: It becomes less anthropocentric, less focused on our own human case. A deeper look at concepts must be normatively guided by the *function* these concepts serve, and that function can be understood better when we consider both the natural cases *and* the case of actual and possible AI. This chapter is thus also a "proof of concept" for doing philosophy through the conceptual analysis of AI: I call this *AI philosophy*.

I thus propose to turn the question from its head onto its feet, as Marx would have said: If we want to understand AI, we have to understand ourselves; and if we want to understand ourselves, we have to understand AI!

2.2 INTELLIGENCE

2.2.1 *The Turing Test*

"I propose to consider the question 'Can Machines Think?'" Alan Turing wrote at the outset of his paper in the leading philosophical journal *Mind*.[11] This was 1950, Turing was one of the founding fathers of computers, and many readers of the paper would not even have heard of such machines, since there were only half a dozen universal computers in the world (Z3, Z4, ENIAC, SSEM, Harvard Mark III, and Manchester Mark I).[12] Turing moves swiftly to declare that searching for a definition of "thinking" would be futile and proposes to replace his initial question by the question whether a machine could successfully play an "imitation game." This game has come to be known as the "Turing Test": A human interrogator is connected to another human and a machine via "teleprinting," and if the interrogator cannot tell the machine from the human by holding a conversation, then we shall say the machine is "thinking." At the end of the paper he returns to the issue of whether machines can think and says: "I believe that at the end of the century the use of words and general educated opinion will have altered so much that one will be able to speak of machines thinking without expecting to be contradicted."[13] So, Turing proposes to replace our everyday term of "thinking" by an operationally defined term, a term for which we can test with some procedure that has a measurable outcome.

Turing's proposal to replace the definition of thinking by an operational definition that relies exclusively on behavior fits with the intellectual climate of the time

[11] Alan Turing, "Computing machinery and intelligence" LIX Mind 433.

[12] Anonymous, "Digital computing newsletter" (1950) 2 Office of Naval Research, Mathematical Sciences Division, Washington DC 1.

[13] Turing 442.

where behaviorism became a dominant force: In psychology, behaviorism is a *methodological* proposal that psychology should become a proper scientific discipline by relying on testable observation and experiment, rather than on subjective introspection. Given that the mind of others is a "black box," psychology should become the science of stimulus and behavioral response, of an input–output relation. Early analytic philosophy led to *reductionist behaviorism*; so if the meaning of a term is its "verification conditions," then a mental term such as "pain" just *means* the person is disposed to behaving a certain way.

Is the Turing Test via observable behavior a useful definition of intelligence? Can it "replace" our talk of intelligence? It is clear that there will be intelligent beings that will not pass this test, for example, humans or animals that cannot type. So I think it is fair to say that Turing very likely only intended the passing of the test as being sufficient for having intelligence and not as necessary. So, if a system passes that test, does it have to be intelligent? This depends on whether you think intelligence is just intelligent behavior, or whether you think for the attribution of intelligence we also need to look at internal structure.

2.2.2 *What Is Intelligence?*

Intuitively, intelligence is an ability that underlies intelligent action. Which action is intelligent depends on the goals that are pursued, and on the success in achieving them – think of the animal cases mentioned earlier. Success will depend not only on the agent but also on the conditions in which it operates, so a system with fewer options how to achieve a goal (e.g., find food) is less intelligent. In this vein, a classical definition is: "Intelligence measures an agent's ability to achieve goals in a wide range of environments."[14] Here intelligence is the *ability to flexibly pursue goals*, where flexibility is explained with the help of different environments. This notion of intelligence from AI is an *instrumental* and normative notion of intelligence, in the tradition of classical decision theory, which says that a rational agent should always try to maximize expected utility (see Section 2.6).[15]

If AI philosophy understands intelligence as relative to an environment, then to achieve more intelligence, one can change the agent or change the environment. Humans have done both on a huge scale through what is known as "culture": Not only have we generated a sophisticated learning system for humans (to change the agent), we have also physically shaped the world such that we can pursue our goals in it; for example, to travel, we have generated roads, cars with steering wheels,

[14] Shane Legg and Marcus Hutter, "Universal intelligence: A definition of machine intelligence" (2007) *Minds and Machines*, 17(4): 391–444, 402.

[15] See, for example, Herbert A. Simon, "A behavioral model of rational choice" (1955) *Quarterly Journal of Economics*, 69(1): 99–118; Johanna Thoma, "Decision theory" in Richard Pettigrew and Jonathan Weisberg (eds), *The Open Handbook of Formal Epistemology* (PhilPapers, 2019), see also the neo-behaviorist proposal in Dimitri Coelho Mollo, "Intelligent Behaviour" [2022] Erkenntnis.

maps, road signs, digital route planning, and AI systems. We now do the same for AI systems; both the learning system, and the change of the environment (cars with computer interfaces, GPS, etc.). By changing the environment, we will also change our cognition and our lives – perhaps in ways that turn out to be to our detriment.

In Sections 2.4–2.9, we will look at the main components of an intelligent system; but before that we discuss the mechanism used in AI: computation.

2.3 COMPUTATION

2.3.1 *The Notion of Computation*

The machines on which AI systems run are "computers," so it will be important for our task to find out what a computer is and what it can do, in principle. A related question is whether human intelligence is wholly or partially due to computation – if it is wholly due to computation, as classical AI had assumed, then it appears possible to recreate this computation on an artificial computing device.

In order to understand what a computer is, it is useful to remind ourselves of the history of computing machines – I say "machines" because before ca. 1945, the word "computer" was a term for a human who has a certain profession, for someone who does computations. These computations, for example, the multiplication of two large numbers, are done through a mechanical step-by-step procedure that will lead to a result once carried out completely. Such procedures are called "algorithms." In 1936, in response to Gödel's challenge of the "Entscheidungsproblem," Alan Turing suggested that the notion of "computing something" could be explained by "what a certain type of machine can do" (just like he proposed to operationalize the notion of intelligence in the "Turing Test"). Turing sketched what such a machine would look like, with an infinitely long tape for memory, a head that can read from and write symbols to that tape. These states on the tape are always specific discrete states, such that each state is of a type from a finite list (symbols, numbers,...), so for example it either is the letter "V" or the letter "C," not a bit of each. In other words, the machine is "digital" (not analog).[16] Then there is one crucial addition: In the "universal" version of the machine, one can *change* what the computer does through further input. In other words, the machine is *programable* to perform a certain algorithm, and it stores that program in its memory.[17] Such a computer is a universal

[16] Nicholas Negroponte, *Being digital* (Vintage, 1995); see also John Haugeland, *Artificial intelligence: The very idea* (MIT Press, 1985) 57; Vincent C. Müller, "What is a digital state?" in Mark J. Bishop and Yasemin J. Erden (eds), *The Scandal of Computation – What Is Computation? – AISB Convention 2013* (AISB, 2013), www.aisb.org.uk/asibpublications/convention-proceedings.

[17] Alan Turing, "On computable numbers, with an application to the Entscheidungsproblem" 2 Proceedings of the London Mathematical Society 230 Kurt Gödel, "Über formal unentscheidbare Sätze der Principia Mathematica und verwandter Systeme I" 38 Monatshefte für Mathematik und Physik 173. The original program outlined in David Hilbert, "Mathematische Probleme" [Springer] Nachrichten von der Königlichen Gesellschaft der Wissenschaften zu Göttingen, Math-Phys Klasse

computer, that is, it can compute any algorithm. It should be mentioned that wider notions of computation have been suggested, for example, analog computing and hypercomputing.[18]

There is also the question whether computation is a real property of physical systems, or whether it is rather a useful way of describing these. Searle has said: "The electrical state transitions are intrinsic to the machine, but the computation is in the eye of the beholder."[19] If we take an anti-realist account of computation, then the situation changes radically.

The exact same computation can be performed on different physical computers, and it can have a different semantics. There are thus three levels of description that are particularly relevant for a given computer: (a) The *physical level* of the actual "realization" of the computer, (b) the *syntactic level* of the algorithm computed, and (c) the *symbolic level* of content, of what is computed.

Physically, a computing machine can be built out of anything and use any kind of property of the physical world (cogs and wheels, relays, DNA, quantum states, etc.). This can be seen as using a physical system to encode a formal system.[20] Actually, all universal computers have been made with large sets of switches. A switch has two states (open/closed), so the resulting computing machines work on two states (on/off, 0/1), they are *binary* – this is a design decision. Binary switches can easily be combined to form "logic gates" that operate on input in the form of the logical connectives in Boolean logic (which is also two-valued): NOT, AND, OR, and so on. If such switches are in a state that can be *syntactically* understood as 1010110, then *semantically*, this could (on current ASCII/ANSI conventions) represent the letter "V," the number "86," a shade of light gray, a shade of green, and so on.

2.3.2 *Computationalism*

As we have seen, the notion that computation is the cause of intelligence in natural systems, for example, humans, and can be used to model and reproduce this intelligence is a basic assumption of classical AI. This view is often coupled with (and

253. See, for example, Jack B. Copeland, Carl J Posy, and Oron Shagrir, *Computability: Turing, Gödel, Church, and Beyond* (MIT Press, 2013).

[18] Hava T. Siegelmann, "Computation beyond the Turing limit" *Science* 545; *Neural Networks and Analog Computation: Beyond the Turing Limit* (Birkhäuser, 1997); Oron Shagrir, *The Nature of Physical Computation* (Oxford University Press, 2022); Gualtiero Piccinini, "Computation in physical systems" (2010) *Stanford Encyclopedia of Philosophy*, https://plato.stanford.edu/entries/computation-physicalsystems/.

[19] John R. Searle, *Mind: A Brief Introduction* (Oxford University Press, 2004); Gordana Dodig-Crnkovic and Vincent C. Müller, "A dialogue concerning two world systems: Info-computational vs. mechanistic" in Gordana Dodig-Crnkovic and Mark Burgin (eds), *Information and Computation: Essays on Scientific and Philosophical Understanding of Foundations of Information and Computation* (World Scientific, 2011), https://worldscientific.com/worldscibooks/10.1142/7637#t=aboutBook.

[20] Clare Horsman et al., "When does a physical system compute?" (2014) *Proceedings of the Royal Society A: Mathematical, Physical and Engineering Science*, 470(2169): 1–25.

motivated by) the view that human mental states are functional states and that these functional states are that of a computer: "machine functionalism." This thesis is often assumed as a matter of course in the cognitive sciences and neuroscience, but it is also the subject of significant criticism in recent decades.[21] The main sources for this view are an enthusiasm for the universal technology of digital computation, and early neuroscientific evidence indicated that human neurons (in the brain and body) are also somewhat binary, that is, either they send a signal to other neurons, they "fire," or they don't. Some authors defend the *Physical Symbol System Hypothesis*, which is computationalism, plus the contention that only computers can be intelligent.[22]

2.4 PERCEPTION AND ACTION

2.4.1 *Passive Perception*

You may be surprised to find that the heading of this chapter combines perception and action in one. We can learn from AI and cognitive science that the main function of perception is to allow action; indeed that perception *is* a kind of action. The traditional understanding of perception in philosophy is *passive* perception, watching ourselves watching the world in what Dan Dennett has called the *Cartesian Theatre*: It is as though I had a little human sitting inside my head, listening to the outside world through our ears, and watching the outside world through our eyes.[23] That notion is absurd, particularly because it would require there to be yet another little human sitting in the head of that little human. And yet, a good deal of the discussion of human perception in the philosophical literature really does treat perception as though it were something that happens to me when inside.

For example, there is the 2D–3D problem in vision, the problem of how I can generate the visual experience of a 3D world through a 2D sensing system (the retina, a 2D sheet that covers our eyeballs from the inside). There must be a way of processing the visual information in the retina, the optical nerve and the optical processing centers of the brain that generates this 3D experience. Not really.[24]

[21] Marcin Miłkowski, "Objections to computationalism: A survey" *Roczniki Filozoficzne*, LXVI: 1; Shimon Edelman, *Computing the Mind: How the Mind Really Works* (Oxford University Press, 2008), for the discussion Stevan Harnad, "The symbol grounding problem" *Physica D*, 42: 335; Matthias Scheutz (ed) *Computationalism: New Directions* (Cambridge University Press, 2002); Oron Shagrir, "Two dogmas of computationalism" *Minds and Machines*, 7: 321; Francisco J. Varela, Evan Thompson, and Eleanor Rosch, *The Embodied Mind: Cognitive Science and Human Experience* (MIT Press, 1991).

[22] Allen Newell and Herbert A. Simon, "Computer science as empirical inquiry: Symbols and search" *Communications of the ACM*, 19(3): 113–126, 116; cf. Boden 1419ff.

[23] Dennett D. C., *Consciousness Explained* (Little, Brown & Co., 1991), 107.

[24] For an introduction to vision, see Kevin J. O'Regan, *Why Red Doesn't Sound Like a Bell: Understanding the Feel of Consciousness* (Oxford University Press, 2011), chapters 1–5.

2.4.2 *Active Perception*

Actually, the 3D impression is generated by an interaction between me and the world (in the case of vision it involves movement of my eyes and my body). It is better to think of perception along with the lines of the sense of touch: Touching is something that I *do*, so that I can find out the softness of an object, the texture of its surface, its temperature, its weight, its flexibility, and so on. I do this by acting and then perceiving the change of sensory input. This is called a perception-action-loop: I do something, that changes the world, and that changes the perception that I have.

It will be useful to stress that this occurs with perception of my own body as well. I only know that I have a hand because my visual sensation of the hand, the proprioception, and the sense of touch are in agreement. When that is not the case it is fairly easy to make me feel that a rubber hand is my own hand – this is known as the "rubber hand illusion." Also, if a prosthetic hand is suitably connected to the nervous system of a human, then the perception-action-loop can be closed again, and the human will feel this as their own hand.

2.4.3 *Predictive Processing and Embodiment*

This view of perception has recently led to a theory of the "predictive brain": What the brain does is not to passively wait for input, but it is *always on* to actively participate in the action-perception-loop. It generates *predictions* what the sensory input will be, given my actions, and then it matches the predictions with the actual sensory input. The difference between the two is something that we try to minimize, which is called the "free energy principle."[25]

In this tradition, the perception of a natural agent or AI system is something that is intimately connected to the physical interaction of the body of the agent with the environment; perception is thus a component of embodied cognition. A useful slogan in this context is "4E cognition," which says that cognition is *embodied*; it is *embedded* in an environment with other agents; it is *enactive* rather than passive; and it is *extended*, that is, not just inside the head.[26] One aspect that is closely connected to 4E cognition is the question whether cognition in humans is

[25] Andy Clark, "Whatever next? Predictive brains, situated agents, and the future of cognitive science." *Behavioral and Brain Sciences*, 36: 181; Andy Clark, *Surfing Uncertainty: Prediction, Action, and the Embodied Mind* (Oxford University Press, 2016); Karl J. Friston, "The free-energy principle: A unified brain theory?" *Nature Reviews Neuroscience*, 11: 127.

[26] Andy Clark, *Natural Born Cyborgs: Minds, Technologies, and the Future of Human Intelligence* (Oxford University Press, 2003); Andy Clark and David J. Chalmers, "The extended mind" *Analysis*, 58: 7; Albert Newen, Shaun Gallagher, and Leon De Bruin, "4E Cognition: Historical roots, key concepts, and central issues" in Albert Newen, Leon De Bruin, and Shaun Gallagher (eds), *The Oxford Handbook of 4E Cognition* (Oxford Academic, Oxford University Press, 2018), pp. 3–16, https://doi.org/10.1093/oxfordhb/9780198735410.013.1, accessed June 29, 2023.

fundamentally representational, and whether cognition in AI has to be representational (see Section 2.5).

Embodied cognition is sometimes presented as an empirical thesis about actual cognition (especially in humans) or as a thesis on the suitable design of AI systems, and sometimes as an analysis of what cognition is and has to be. In the latter understanding, non-embodied AI would necessarily miss certain features of cognition.[27]

2.5 MEANING AND REPRESENTATION

2.5.1 *The Chinese Room Argument*

As we saw earlier, classical AI was founded on the assumption that the appropriately programmed computer really *is* a mind – this is what John Searle called *strong AI*. In his famous paper "Minds, Brains and Programs," Searle presented a thought experiment of the "Chinese Room."[28] The Chinese Room is a computer, constructed as follows: There is a closed room in which John Searle sits and has a large book that provides him with a computer program, with algorithms, on how to process the input and provide output. Unknown to him, the input that he gets is Chinese writing, and the output that he provides are sensible answers or comments about that linguistic input. This output, so the assumption, is indistinguishable from the output of a competent Chinese speaker. And yet Searle in the room understands no Chinese and will learn no Chinese from the input that he gets. Therefore, Searle concludes, *computation is not sufficient for understanding*. There can be no strong AI.

In the course of his discussion of the Chinese room argument, Searle looks at several replies: The *systems reply* accepts that Searle has shown that no amount of simple manipulation of the person in the room will enable that person to understand Chinese, but objects that perhaps symbol manipulation will enable *the wider system*, of which the person is a component, to understand Chinese. So perhaps there is a part-whole fallacy here? This reply raises the question, why one might think that the whole system has properties that the algorithmic processor does not have.

One way to answer this challenge, and change the system, is the *robot reply*, which grants that the whole system, as described, will not understand Chinese because it is missing something that Chinese speakers have, namely a causal connection between the words and the world. So, we would need to add sensors and actuators to this computer, that would take care of the necessary causal connection. Searle responds to this suggestion by saying input from sensors would be "just more

[27] Hubert L. Dreyfus, *What Computers Still Can't Do: A Critique of Artificial Reason* (2nd ed, MIT Press, 1992, 1972); Rolf Pfeifer and Josh Bongard, *How the Body Shapes the Way We Think: A New View of Intelligence* (MIT Press, 2007).

[28] Searle, "Minds, brains and programs."

Chinese" to Searle in the room; it would not provide any further understanding, in fact Searle would have no idea that the input is from a sensor.[29]

2.5.2 *Reconstruction*

I think it is best to view the core of the Chinese room argument as an extension of Searle's remark:

> No one would suppose that we could produce milk and sugar by running a computer simulation of the formal sequences in lactation and photosynthesis, but where the mind is concerned many people are willing to believe in such a miracle.[30]

Accordingly, the argument that remains can be reconstructed as:

a. If a system does only syntactical manipulation, it will not acquire meaning.
b. A computer does only syntactical manipulation.
→
c. A computer will not acquire meaning.

In Searle's terminology, a computer has *only syntax* and *no semantics*; the symbols in a computer lack the intentionality (directedness) that human language use has. He summarizes his position at the end of the paper:

> "Could a machine think?" The answer is, obviously, yes. We are precisely such machines. [...] But could something think, understand, and so on solely in virtue of being a computer with the right sort of program? [...] the answer is no.[31]

2.5.3 *Computing, Syntax, and Causal Powers*

Reconstructing the argument in this way, the question is whether the premises are true. Several people have argued that premise 2 is false, because one can only understand what a computer does as responding to the program as meaningful.[32] I happen to think that this is a mistake, the computer does not *follow* these rules, it is just constructed in such a way that it *acts according to* these rules, if its states are suitably

[29] David Cole, "The Chinese room argument" (2020), http://plato.stanford.edu/entries/chinese-room/,; John Preston and Mark Bishop (eds), *Views into the Chinese Room: New Essays on Searle and Artificial Intelligence* (Oxford University Press, 2002).

[30] Searle, 'Minds, brains and programs' 424.

[31] Ibid.

[32] John McCarthy, "John Searle's Chinese room argument" (2007), www-formal.stanford.edu/jmc/chinese.html, accessed June 10, 2007; John Haugeland, "Syntax, semantics, physics" in John Preston and Mark Bishop (eds), *Views into the Chinese Room: New Essays on Searle and Artificial Intelligence* (Oxford University Press, 2002) 385; Margaret A. Boden, *Computer Models of the Mind: Computational Approaches in Theoretical Psychology* (Cambridge University Press, 1988) 97.

interpreted by an observer.[33] Having said that, any actual computer, any physical realization of an abstract algorithm processor, *does* have causal powers, it does more than syntactic manipulation. For example, it may be able to turn the lights on or off.

The Chinese room argument has moved the attention in the philosophy of language away from convention and logic toward the conditions for a speaker to mean what they say (speakers' meaning), or to mean anything at all (have intentionality); in particular, it left us with the discussion on the role of *representation* in cognition, and the role of computation over representations.[34]

2.6 RATIONAL CHOICE

2.6.1 *Normative Decision Theory: MEU*

A rational agent will perceive the environment, find out which options for action exist, and then take the best decision. This is what decision theory is about. It is a normative theory on how a rational agent *should* act, given the knowledge they have – not a descriptive theory of how rational agents *will* actually act.

So how should a rational agent decide which is the best possible action? They evaluate the possible outcomes of each choice and then select the one that is best, meaning the one that has the highest subjective utility, that is, utility as seen by the particular agent. It should be noted that rational choice in this sense is not necessarily egoistic, it could well be that the agent puts a high utility on the happiness of someone else, and thus rationally chooses a course of action that maximizes overall utility through the happiness of that other person. In actual situations, the agent typically does not know what the outcomes of particular choices will be, so they act under uncertainty. To overcome this problem, the rational agent selects the action with *maximum expected utility* (MEU), where the value of a choice equals the utility of the outcome multiplied by the probability of that outcome occurring. This thought can be explained with the expected utility of certain gambles or lotteries. In more complicated decision cases the rationality of a certain choice depends on subsequent choices of *other agents*. These kinds of cases are often described with the help of "games" played with other agents. In such games it is often a successful strategy to cooperate with other agents in order to maximize subjective utility.

In artificial intelligence it is common to perceive of AI agents as rational agents in the sense described. For example, Stuart Russell says: "In short, a rational agent acts so as to maximise expected utility. It's hard to over-state the importance of this conclusion. In many ways, artificial intelligence has been mainly about working out the details of how to build rational machines."[35]

[33] Ludwig Wittgenstein, "Philosophische Untersuchungen" in *Schriften I* (Suhrkamp, 1980, 1953) §82.

[34] John R. Searle, "Intentionality and its place in nature" in *Consciousness and Language* (Cambridge University Press, 2002, 1984); Searle, *Mind: A brief introduction*.

[35] Russell 23.

2.6.2 *Resources and Rational Agency*

It is not the case that a rational agent *will* always choose the perfect option. The main reason is that such an agent must deal with the fact that their resources are limited, in particular, data storage and time (most choices are time-critical). The question is thus not only what the best choice is, but how many resources I should spend on optimizing my choice; when should I stop optimizing and start acting? This phenomenon is called *bounded rationality*, *bounded optimality*, and in cognitive science, it calls for *resource rational* analysis.[36] Furthermore, there is no set of discrete options from which to choose, and a rational agent needs to reflect on the goals to pursue (see Section 2.9).

The point that agents (natural or artificial) will have to deal with limited resources when making choices, has tremendous importance for the understanding of cognition. It is often not fully appreciated in philosophy – even the literature about the limits of rational choice seems to think that there is something "wrong" with using heuristics that are biased, being "nudged" by the environment, or using the environment for "extended" or "situated" cognition.[37] But it would be irrational to aim for perfect cognitive procedures, not to mention for cognitive procedures that would not be influenced by the environment.

2.6.3 *The Frame Problem(s)*

The original frame problem for classical AI was how to *update a belief system* after an action, without stating all the things that have *not* changed; this requires a logic where conclusions can change if a premise is added – a non-monotonic logic.[38] Beyond this more technical problem, there is a philosophical problem of updating beliefs after action, popularized by Dennett, which asks how to find out what is relevant, how wide the frame should be cast for *relevance*.

[36] Simon 99. Gregory Wheeler, "Bounded rationality" in Edward N. Zalta (ed), *The Stanford Encyclopedia of Philosophy*, vol Fall 2020 Edition (CSLI, 2020), https://plato.stanford.edu/archives/fall2020/entries/bounded-rationality/; Stuart Russell, "Rationality and intelligence: A brief update" in Vincent C. Müller (ed), *Fundamental Issues of Artificial Intelligence* (Springer, 2016) 16ff; Falk Lieder and Thomas L. Griffiths, "Resource-rational analysis: Understanding human cognition as the optimal use of limited computational resources" (Cambridge University Press) 43; *Behavioral and Brain Sciences*, e1.

[37] Daniel Kahneman and Amos Tversky, "Prospect theory: An analysis of decision under risk" *Econometrica*, 47: 263; Daniel Kahnemann, *Thinking Fast and Slow* (Macmillan, 2011); Richard H. Thaler and Cass Sunstein, *Nudge: Improving Decisions about Health, Wealth and Happiness* (Penguin, 2008) vs. David Kirsh, "Problem solving and situated cognition" in P. Robbins and M. Aydede (eds), *The Cambridge Handbook of Situated Cognition* (Cambridge University Press, 2009).

[38] Murray Shanahan, "The frame problem" in Edward N. Zalta (ed), *Stanford Encyclopedia of Philosophy*, vol Spring 2016 edition (CSLI, Stanford University, 2016), https://plato.stanford.edu/archives/spr2016/entries/frame-problem/.

As Shanahan says "relevance is holistic, open-ended, and context-sensitive" but logical inference is not.[39]

There is a very general version of the frame problem, expressed by Jerry Fodor, who says, the frame problem really is: "Hamlet's problem: when to stop thinking." He continues by saying that "modular cognitive processing is *ipso facto* irrational [...] by attending to less than all the evidence that is relevant and available."[40] Fodor sets the challenge that in order to perform a logical inference, especially an abduction, one needs to have decided what is relevant. However, he seems to underestimate that one cannot attend to *all* that is relevant and available (rationality is bounded). It is currently unclear whether the frame problem can be formulated without dubious assumptions about rationality. Similar concerns apply to the claims that Gödel has shown deep limitations of AI systems.[41] Overall, there may be more to intelligence than instrumental rationality.

2.6.4 *Creativity*

Choices that involve *creativity* are often invoked as something special, not merely mechanical, and thus inaccessible to a mere machine. The notion of "creation" has significant impact in our societal practice particularly when that creation is protected by intellectual property rights – and AI systems *have* created or cocreated music, painting, and text. It is not clear that there is a notion of creativity that would provide an argument against machine creativity. Such a notion would have to combine two aspects that seem to be in tension: On the one hand, creativity seems to imply causation that includes acquiring knowledge and techniques (think of J. S. Bach composing a new cantata), on the other hand, creativity is supposed to be a non-caused, non-predictable, spark of insight. It appears unclear whether such a notion of creativity can, or indeed should, be formulated.[42] Perhaps a plausible account is that creativity involves moving between different spaces of relevance, as in the frame problem.

39 Daniel C. Dennett, "Cognitive wheels: The frame problem of AI" in Christopher Hookway (ed), *Minds, Machines, and Evolution: Philosophical Studies* (Cambridge University Press, 1984).

40 Jerry A. Fodor, "Modules, frames, fridgeons, sleeping dogs, and the music of the spheres" in J. L. Garfield (ed), *Modularity in Knowledge Representation and Natural-Language Understanding* (The MIT Press, 1987) 140f; Dan Sperber and Deirdre Wilson, "Fodor's frame problem and relevance theory" *Behavioral and Brain Sciences*, 19: 530.

41 J. R. Lucas, "Minds, machines and Gödel: A retrospect" in Peter J. R. Millican and Andy Clark (eds), *Machines and Thought* (Oxford University Press, 1996); Peter Koellner, "On the question of whether the mind can be mechanized, I: From Gödel to Penrose" *Journal of Philosophy*, 115: 337; Peter Koellner, "On the question of whether the mind can be mechanized, II: Penrose's new argument" *Journal of Philosophy*, 115: 453.

42 Margaret A. Boden, "Creativity and artificial intelligence: A contradiction in terms?" in Elliot Samuel Paul and Scott Barry Kaufman (eds), *The Philosophy of Creativity: New Essays* (Oxford University Press, 2014), 224–244, https://philpapers.org/archive/PAUTPO-3.pdf; Simon Colton and Geraint A. Wiggins, *Computational Creativity: The Final Frontier?* (Montpelier, 2012); Martha Halina, "Insightful artificial intelligence" *Mind and Language*, 36: 315.

2.7 FREE WILL AND CREATIVITY

2.7.1 *Determinism, Compatibilism*

The problem that usually goes under the heading of "free will" is how physical beings like humans or AI systems can have something like free will. The traditional division for possible positions in the space of free will can be put in terms of a decision tree. The first choice is whether *determinism* is true, that is, the thesis that all events are caused. The second choice is whether *incompatibilism* is true, that is, the thesis that if determinism is true, then there is no free will.

The position known as *hard determinism* says that determinism is indeed true, and if determinism is true then there is no such thing as free will – this is the conclusion that most of its opponents try to avoid. The position known as *libertarianism* (not the political view) agrees that incompatibilism is true, but adds that determinism is not, so we are free. The position known as *compatibilism* says that determinism and free will are compatible and thus it may well be that determinism is true *and* humans have free will (and it usually adds that this is actually the case).

This results in a little matrix of positions:

	Incompatibilism	Compatibilism
Determinism	Hard Determinism	Optimistic/Pessimistic Compatibilism
Non-Determinism	Libertarianism	[Not a popular option]

2.7.2 *Compatibilism and Responsibility in AI*

In a first approximation, when I say I did something freely, it means that it was *up to me* that I was *in control*. That notion of control can be cashed out by saying I could have done otherwise than I did, specifically I could have done otherwise if I had *decided* otherwise. To this we could add that I would have decided otherwise if I had had other *preferences* or *knowledge* (e.g., I would not have eaten those meatballs if I had a preference against eating pork, and if I had known that they contain pork). Such a notion of freedom thus involves an *epistemic condition* and a *control condition*.

So, I act freely if I do as I choose according to the preferences that I have (my subjective utility). But why do I have these preferences? As Aristotle already knew, they are not under my voluntary control, I could not just *decide* to have other preferences and then have them. However, as Harry Frankfurt has pointed out, I can have *second-order* preferences or desires, that is, I can prefer to have other preferences than the ones I actually have (I could want not to have a preference for those meatballs, for example). The notion that I can overrule my preferences with rational thought is what Frankfurt calls the *will*, and it is his condition for being a person.

In a first approximation one can thus say, *to act freely is to act as I choose, to choose as I will, and to will as I rationally decide to prefer.*[43]

The upshot of this debate is that the function of a notion of free will for agency in AI or humans is to allow personal *responsibility*, not to determine *causation*. The real question is: What are the conditions such that an agent is *responsible* for their actions and *deserves* being praised or blamed for them. This is independent of the freedom from causal determination; that kind of freedom we do not get, and we do not need.[44]

There is a further debate between "optimists" and "pessimists" whether humans actually do fulfil those conditions (in particular whether they can truly cause their preferences) and can thus properly be said to be responsible for their actions and *deserve* praise or blame – and accordingly whether reward or punishment should have mainly forward-looking reasons.[45] In the AI case, an absence of responsibility has relevance for their status as moral agents, for the existence of "responsibility gaps," and for what kinds of decisions we should leave to systems that cannot be held responsible.[46]

2.8 CONSCIOUSNESS

2.8.1 *Awareness and Phenomenal Consciousness*

In a first approximation, it is useful to distinguish two types of consciousness: *Awareness* and *phenomenal consciousness*. Awareness is the notion that a system has cognitive states on a base level (e.g., it senses heat) and on a meta level, it has states where it is aware of the states on the object level. This awareness, or access, involves the ability to remember and use the cognitive states on the base level. This is the notion of "conscious" that is opposed to "unconscious" or "subconscious" – and it appears feasible for a multi-layered AI system.

Awareness is often, but not necessarily, connected to a specific way that the cognitive state at the base level *feels* to the subject – this is what philosophers call *phenomenal consciousness*, or how things *seem* to me (Greek *phaínetai*). This notion

43 Harry Frankfurt, "Freedom of the will and the concept of a person" *The Journal of Philosophy*, LXVIII: 5; Daniel C. Dennett, *Elbow Room: The Varieties of Free Will Worth Wanting* (Cambridge, Mass. ed, MIT Press, 1984).

44 Chapter 6 of this book by Lode Lauwaert and Ann-Katrien Oimann delves further into the subject of AI and responsibility.

45 Galen Strawson, "Free will" (2011) *Routledge Encyclopedia of Philosophy, Taylor and Francis*, doi:10.4324/9780415249126-V014-2, www.rep.routledge.com/articles/thematic/free-will/; Thomas Pink, *Free Will: A Very Short Introduction* (Oxford University Press, 2004); Alfred R. Mele, *Free Will and Luck* (Oxford University Press, 2006); Daniel C. Dennett and Gregg D. Caruso, "Just deserts" *Aeon*.

46 Thomas W. Simpson and Vincent C. Müller, "Just war and robots' killings" *The Philosophical Quarterly*, 66: 302; Rob Sparrow, "Killer robots" *Journal of Applied Philosophy*, 24: 62; Vincent C. Müller, "Is it time for robot rights? Moral status in artificial entities" *Ethics & Information Technology*, 23: 579.

of consciousness is probably best explained with the help of two classical philosophical thought experiments: the bat, and the color scientist.

If you and I go out to have the same ice cream, then I can still not know what the ice cream tastes like to you, and I would not know that even if I knew everything about the ice cream, you, your brain, and your taste buds. Somehow, *what it is like* for you is something epistemically inaccessible to me, I can never know it, even if I know everything about the physical world. In the same way, I can never know what it is like to be a bat.[47]

A similar point about what we cannot know in principle is made by Frank Jackson in the article "What Mary didn't know."[48] In his thought experiment, Mary is supposed to be a person who has never seen anything with color in her life, and yet she is a perfect color scientist, she knows everything there is to know about color. One day, she gets out of her black and white environment and sees color for the first time. It appears that she learns something new at that point.

The argument that is suggested here seems to favor an argument for a mental-physical *dualism* of *substances* or at least *properties*: I can know all the physics, and I cannot know all the phenomenal experience, therefore, phenomenal experience is not part of physics. If dualism is true, then it may appear that we cannot hope to generate phenomenal consciousness with the right physical technology, such as AI. In the form of *substance dualism*, as Descartes and much of religious thought had assumed, dualism is now unpopular since most philosophers assume physicalism, that "everything is physical."

Various arguments against the reduction of mental to physical *properties* have been brought out, so it is probably fair to say that *property dualism* has a substantial following. This is often combined with substance monism in some version of "supervenience of the mental on the physical," that is, the thesis that two entities with the same physical properties must have the same mental properties. Some philosophers have challenged this relation between property dualism and the possibility of artificial consciousness. David Chalmers has argued that "the physical structure of the world – the exact distribution of particles, fields, and forces in spacetime – is logically consistent with the absence of consciousness, so the presence of consciousness is a further fact about our world." Despite this remark, he supports computationalism: "… strong artificial intelligence is true: there is a class of programs such that any implementation of a program in that class is conscious."[49]

47 Thomas Nagel, "What is it like to be a bat?" *Philosophical Review*, 83: 435; Thomas Nagel, *What Does It All Mean? A Very Short Introduction to Philosophy* (Oxford University Press, 1987), chapter 3.

48 Frank Jackson, "What Mary didn't know" *Journal of Philosophy*, 83: 291.

49 David J. Chalmers and John R. Searle, "'Consciousness and the philosophers': An exchange" (1997) *The New York Review of Books*, www.nybooks.com/articles/1997/05/15/consciousness-and-the-philosophers-an-exchange/; David J. Chalmers, "Précis of the Conscious Mind" (1999) *Philosophy and Phenomenological Research*, LIX(2): 435–438, 436; Donald Davidson, "Mental events" in L. Foster and J. Swanson (eds), *Experience and Theory* (Amherst, MA: University of Massachusetts Press, 1970).

What matters for the function of consciousness in AI or natural agents is not the discussion about dualisms, but rather why phenomenal consciousness in humans is the way it is, how one could tell whether a system is conscious, and whether there could be a human who is physically just like me, but without consciousness (a "philosophical zombie").[50]

2.8.2 *The Self*

Personal identity in humans is mainly relevant because it is a condition for allocating responsibility (see Section 2.7): In order to allocate blame or praise, there has to be a sense in which I am *the same person* as the one who performed the action in question. We have a sense that there is a life in the past that is mine, and only mine – how this is possible is known as the "persistence question." The standard criteria for me being the same person as that little boy in the photograph are my *memory* of being that boy, and the *continuity of my body* over time. Humans tend to think that *memory* or *conscious experience*, or *mental content* are the criteria for personal identity, which is why we think we can imagine surviving our death, or living in a different body.[51]

So, what is a "part" of that persistent self? Philosophical phantasies and neurological rarities[52] aside, there is now no doubt what is "part of me" and what is not – I continuously work on maintaining that personal identity by checking that the various senses are in agreement, for example, I try to reach for the door handle, I see my hand touching the handle, I can feel it ... and then I can see the door opening and feel my hand going forward. This is very different from a computer: The components of the standard Von Neumann architecture (input-system, storage, random-access memory, processor, output-system) can be in the same box or miles apart, they can even be split into more components (e.g., some off-board processing of intensive tasks) or stored in spaces such as the "cloud" that are not defined through physical location. And that is only the hardware, the software faces similar issues, so a persistent and delineated self is not an easy task for an AI system. It is not clear that there is a function for a self in AI, which would have repercussions for attributing moral agency and even patiency.

2.9 NORMATIVITY

Let us return briefly to the issues of rational choice and responsibility. Stuart Russell said that "AI has adopted the standard model: we build optimising machines, we

[50] O'Regan.

[51] Thomas Metzinger, *The Ego Tunnel: The Science of the Mind and the Myth of the Self* (Basic Books, 2009); Eric Olsen, "Personal identity" (2023) *Stanford Encyclopedia of Philosophy*, https://plato.stanford.edu/entries/identity-personal/.

[52] See, for example, "The man who fell out of bed" in Oliver Sacks, *The Man Who Mistook His Wife for a Hat, and Other Clinical Tales* (New York: Summit Books, 1985) or the view of humans as superorganisms, based on the human microbiome.

feed objectives into them, and off they go."[53] On that understanding, AI is a tool, and we need to provide the objectives or goals for it. Artificial intelligence has only *instrumental intelligence* on how to reach given goals. However, *general intelligence* also involves a metacognitive reflection on which goals are relevant to my action now (food or shelter?) and a reflection on which goals one should pursue.[54] One of the open questions is whether a nonliving system can have "real goals" in the sense required for choice and responsibility, for example, of goals that have subjective value to the system, and that the system recognizes as important after reflection. Without such reflection on goals, AI systems would not be moral agents and there could be no "machine ethics" that deserves the name. Similar considerations apply to other forms of normative reflection, for example, in aesthetics and politics. This discussion in AI philosophy seems to show that there is a function for normative reflection in humans or AI as an elementary part of the cognitive system.

[53] Russell, *Human Compatible: Artificial Intelligence and the Problem of Control*, 172.

[54] Vincent C. Müller and Michael Cannon, "Existential risk from AI and orthogonality: Can we have it both ways?" *Ratio*, 35: 25.

3

Ethics of AI

Toward a "Design for Values" Approach

Stefan Buijsman, Michael Klenk, and Jeroen van den Hoven

3.1 INTRODUCTION

Artificial intelligence can (help) make decisions and can steer actions of (autonomous) agents. Now that it gets better and better at performing these tasks, in large part due to breakthroughs in deep learning (see Chapter 1 of this Handbook), there is an increasing adoption of the technology in society. AI is used to support fraud detection, credit risk assessments, education, healthcare diagnostics, recruitment, autonomous driving, and much more. Actions and decisions in these areas have a high impact on individuals, and therefore AI becomes more and more impactful every day. Fraud detection supported by AI has already led to a national scandal in the Netherlands, where widespread discrimination (partly by an AI system) led to the fall of the government.[1] Similarly, healthcare insurance companies using AI to estimate the severity of people's illness seriously discriminated against black patients. A correlation between race and healthcare spending in the data caused the AI system to give lower risk scores to black patients, leading to lower reimbursements for black patients even when their condition was worse.[2] The use of AI systems to conduct first-round interviews in recruitment has led to more opacity in the process, harming job seekers' autonomy.[3] Self-driving cars can be hard to keep under meaningful human control,[4] leading to situations where the driver cannot effectively intervene and even

1 Heikkilä, M. "Dutch scandal serves as a warning for Europe over risks of using algorithms" (2022) *Politico*, March 29. www.politico.eu/article/dutch-scandal-serves-as-a-warning-for-europe-over-risks-of-using-algorithms/

2 Ledford, H. "Millions of black people affected by racial bias in health-care algorithms" (2019) *Nature*, 574(7780): 608–609.

3 Aizenberg, E. and Van Den Hoven, J. "Designing for human rights in AI." (2020) *Big Data & Society*, 7(2): 2053951720949566.

4 Heikoop, D. D., Hagenzieker, M., Mecacci, G., Calvert, S., Santoni De Sio, F., and van Arem, B. "Human behaviour with automated driving systems: A quantitative framework for meaningful human control" (2019) *Theoretical Issues in Ergonomics Science*, 20(6): 711–730.

situations where nobody may be accountable for accidents.[5,6] In all of these cases, AI is part of a socio-technical system where the new technologies interact with social elements (operators, affected persons, managers, and more). As we will see, ethical challenges emerge both at the level of technology and at the level of the new socio-technical systems. This wide range of ethical challenges associated with the adoption of AI is discussed further in Section 3.2.

At the same time, many of these issues are already well known. They come up in the context of AI because it gets integrated into high-impact processes, but the processes were in many cases already present without AI. For instance, discrimination has been studied extensively, as have complementary notions of justice and fairness. Autonomy, control, and responsibility have likewise received extensive philosophical attention. We also shouldn't forget about the long tradition of normative ethical theories, such as virtue ethics, deontology, and consequentialism, which have all reflected on what makes an action the right one to take. AI and the attention it gets provides a new spotlight on perennial moral issues, some of which are novel and have not been encountered by humanity before and some of which are new instances of familiar problems. We discuss the main normative ethical accounts that may apply to AI in Section 3.3, along with their applicability to the ethical challenges raised earlier.

As we argue, the general ethical theories of the past are helpful but at the same time often lack the specificity needed to tackle the issues raised by new technologies. Instead of applying highly abstract traditional ethical theories such as Aristotle's account of Virtue, Mill's principle of utility, or Kant's Categorical Imperative, straightforwardly to particular AI issues it is often more helpful to utilize mid-level normative ethical theories, which are less abstract, more testable and which focus on technology, interactions between people, organizations, and institutions. Examples of mid-level ethical theories are Rawls' theory of justice,[7] Pettit's account of freedom in terms of non-domination,[8] or Klenk's account of manipulation,[9] which could be construed as broadly Kantian, Amartya Sen and Martha Nussbaum's capability approach,[10] which can be construed as broadly Aristotelian, and Posner's economic theory of law,[11] which is broadly utilitarian. These theories already address a specific

[5] Santoni de Sio, F. and Mecacci, G. "Four responsibility gaps with artificial intelligence: Why they matter and how to address them" (2021) *Philosophy & Technology*, 34: 1057–1084.

[6] On the so-called responsibility gap, see also Chapter 6 of this book.

[7] Rawls, J., *Justice as Fairness: A Restatement* (Harvard University Press, 2001).

[8] Pettit, P. *A Theory of Freedom: from the Psychology to the Politics of Agency* (Oxford University Press, 2001).

[9] Klenk, M. "Digital well-being and manipulation online" in C. Burr and L. Floridi (eds.), *Ethics of Digital Well-Being: A Multidisciplinary Perspective* (Cham: Springer, 2020), pp. 81–100. https://doi.org/10.1007/978-3-030-50585-1_4

[10] Robeyns, I. "The capability approach: A theoretical survey" (2005) *Journal of Human Development*, 6(1): 93–117.

[11] Posner, R. A. *Economic Analysis of Law* (Aspen Publishing, 2014).

set of moral questions in their social, psychological, economic, or social context. They also point to the empirical research that needs to be done in order to apply the theory sensibly. A meticulous understanding of the field to which ethical theory is being applied is essential and part of (applied) ethics itself. We need to know what the properties of artificially intelligent agents are, how they differ from human agents; we need to establish what the meaning and scope is of the notion of, for example, "personal data," what the morally relevant properties of virtual reality are. These are all examples of preparing the ground conceptually before we can start to apply normative ethical considerations.

We then need to ensure that normative ethical theories and the consideration to which they give rise are recognized and incorporated in technology design. This is where design approaches to ethics come in (Value-sensitive design,[12] Design for Values[13] and others). Ethics needs to be present when and where it can make a difference and in the form that increases the chances of making a difference. We discuss these approaches in Section 3.4, along with the way in which they relate to the ethical theories from Section 3.3. These new methods are needed to realize the responsible development and use of artificial intelligence, and require close cooperation between philosophy and other disciplines.

3.2 PROMINENT ETHICAL CHALLENGES

Artificial intelligence differs from other technologies in at least two ways. First, AI systems can have a greater degree of agency than other technologies.[14] AI systems can, in principle, make decisions on their own and act in dynamic fashion, responding to the environment they find themselves in. Whether they can *act* and *make decisions* is a matter of dispute, but what we can say in any case is that they can initiate courses of events that would not have occurred without their initiating it. A self-driving car is thus very different from a typical car, even though both are technological artifacts. While a car can automatically perform certain actions (e.g., prevent the brakes from locking when the car has to stop abruptly), these systems lack the more advanced agency that a self-driving car has when it takes us from A to B without further instructions from the driver.

Second, AI systems have a higher degree of epistemic opacity than other technical systems.[15] While most people may not understand how a car engine works,

[12] Umbrello, S. and De Bellis, A. F. "A value-sensitive design approach to intelligent agents" in Roman V. Yampolskiy (eds.), *Artificial Intelligence Safety and Security* (Chapman & Hall/CRC, 2018), 395–409.

[13] Van den Hoven, J., Vermaas, P., and van de Poel, I. eds.), *Handbook of Ethics, Values, and Technological Design: Sources, Theory, Values and Application Domains* (Dordrecht: Springer Netherlands, 2015).

[14] List, C. "Group agency and artificial intelligence" (2021) *Philosophy & Technology*, 34(4): 1213–1242.

[15] Durán, J. M. and Jongsma, K. R. "Who is afraid of black box algorithms? On the epistemological and ethical basis of trust in medical AI" (2021) *Journal of Medical Ethics*, 47(5): 329–335.

there are engineers who can explain exactly why the engine behaves the way it does. They are also able to provide clear explanations of why an engine fails under certain conditions and can to a great extent anticipate these situations. In the case of AI systems – and in particular for deep learning systems – we do not know why the systems give us these individual outputs rather than other ones.[16,17] Computer scientists do understand how these systems work generally speaking and can explain general features of their behavior such as why convolutional neural networks are well suited for computer vision tasks, whereas recurrent neural networks are better for natural language processing. However, for individual outputs of a specific AI system, we do not have explanations available as to why the AI generates this specific output (e.g., why it classifies someone as a fraudster, or rejects a job candidate). Likewise, it is difficult to anticipate the output of AI systems on new inputs,[18] which is exacerbated by the fact that small changes to the input of a system can have big effects on the output.[19]

These two features of AI systems make it difficult to develop, deploy, and use them responsibly. They have more agency than other technologies, which exacerbates the challenge – though we should be clear that AI systems do not have *moral* agency (and, for example, developments of artificial moral agents are still far from achieving this goal[20]), and thus should not be anthropomorphized and cannot bear responsibility for results of their outputs.[21] In addition, even its developers struggle to anticipate (due to the opacity) what the AI system will output and why. As a result, familiar ethical problems that arise out of irresponsible or misaligned action are repeated and exacerbated by the speed, scale, and opacity that come with AI systems. It makes it difficult to work with them responsibly in the wider socio-technical system in which AI is embedded, and also complicates efforts to ensure that AI systems realize ethical values[22] as we cannot easily verify if their behavior is aligned with these values (also known as the alignment problem[23]). It is a pressing issue to find ways to embed these values despite the difficulties that AI systems present us with.

[16] Arrieta, A. B., Díaz-Rodríguez, N., Del Ser, J., Bennetot, A., Tabik, S., Barbado, A., … and Herrera, F. "Explainable artificial intelligence (XAI): Concepts, taxonomies, opportunities and challenges toward responsible AI" (2020) *Information Fusion*, 58: 82–115.

[17] Buijsman, S. "Defining explanation and explanatory depth in XAI" (2022) *Minds and Machines*, 32(3): 563–584.

[18] van der Waa, J., Nieuwburg, E., Cremers, A., and Neerincx, M. "Evaluating XAI: A comparison of rule-based and example-based explanations" (2021) *Artificial Intelligence*, 291: 103404.

[19] Akhtar, N. and Mian, A. "Threat of adversarial attacks on deep learning in computer vision: A survey" (2018) *IEEE Access*, 6: 14410–14430.

[20] Cervantes, J. A., López, S., Rodríguez, L. F., Cervantes, S., Cervantes, F., and Ramos, F. "Artificial moral agents: A survey of the current status" (2020) *Science and Engineering Ethics*, 26: 501–532.

[21] In this regard, see also Chapter 6 of this book.

[22] Van de Poel, I. "Embedding values in artificial intelligence (AI) systems" (2020) *Minds and Machines*, 30(3): 385–409.

[23] Gabriel, I. "Artificial intelligence, values, and alignment" (2020) *Minds and Machines*, 30(3): 411–437.

This brings us to the ethical challenges that we face when developing and using AI systems. There have already been a number of attempts to systematize these in the literature. Mittelstadt et al.[24] group them into epistemic concerns (inconclusive evidence, inscrutable evidence and misguided evidence) and normative concerns (unfair outcomes and transformative effects) in addition to issues of traceability/ responsibility. Floridi et al.[25] use categories from bioethics to group AI ethics principles into five categories. There are principles of beneficence (promoting well-being and sustainability), nonmaleficence (encompassing privacy and security), autonomy, justice, and explicability. The inclusion of explicability as an ethical principle is contested,[26] but is not unusual in such overviews. For example, Kazim and Koshiyama[27] use the headings human well-being, safety, privacy, transparency, fairness, and accountability, which again include opacity as an ethical challenge. Huang et al.,[28] in an even more extensive overview, again include it as an ethical challenge at the societal level (together with, for example, fairness and controllability), as opposed to challenges at the individual (autonomy, privacy, and safety) and environmental (sustainability) level. In addition to these, there are myriad ethics guidelines and principles from organizations and states, such as the statement of the European Group on Ethics (European Group on Ethics in Science and New Technologies, "Artificial Intelligence, Robotics and 'Autonomous' Systems") and EU High-Level Expert Group's guidelines that mention human oversight, technical robustness and safety, privacy, transparency, diversity and fairness, societal, and environmental well-being and accountability. Recent work suggests that all these guidelines do converge on similar terminology (transparency, justice and fairness, non-maleficence, responsibility, and privacy) on a higher level but that at the same time there are very different interpretations of these terms once you look at the details.[29]

Given these different interpretations, it helps to look in a little more detail at the different ethical challenges posed by AI. Such an examination will show that, while overviews are certainly helpful starting points, they can also obscure the relevance of socio-technical systems to, and context-specificity of, the ethical challenges that AI systems can raise. Consider, first of all, the case of generative natural language

24 Mittelstadt, B. D., Allo, P., Taddeo, M., Wachter, S., and Floridi, L. "The ethics of algorithms: Mapping the debate" (2016) *Big Data & Society*, 3(2): 2053951716679679.

25 Floridi, L., Cowls, J., Beltrametti, M., Chatila, R., Chazerand, P., Dignum, V., ... and Vayena, E. "AI4People – An ethical framework for a good AI society: Opportunities, risks, principles, and recommendations" (2018) *Minds and Machines*, 28: 689–707.

26 Cortese, J. F. N. B., Cozman, F. G., Lucca-Silveira, M. P., and Bechara, A. F. "Should explainability be a fifth ethical principle in AI ethics?" (2022) *AI and Ethics*, 1–12.

27 Kazim, E. and Koshiyama, A. S. "A high-level overview of AI ethics" (2021) *Patterns*, 2(9): 100314.

28 Huang, C., Zhang, Z., Mao, B. and Yao, X. "An overview of artificial intelligence ethics" (2022) *IEEE Transactions on Artificial Intelligence*, 4(4): 799–819.

29 Jobin, A., Ienca, M., and Vayena, E. "The global landscape of AI ethics guidelines" (2019) *Nature Machine Intelligence*, 1(9): 389–399.

processing of which ChatGPT is a recent and famous example. Algorithms such as ChatGPT can generate text based on prompts, such as to compose an email, generate ideas for marketing slogans, or even summarize research papers.[30] Along with many (potential) benefits, such systems also raise ethical questions because of the content that they generate.

There are prominent issues of bias, as the text that such algorithms generate is often discriminatory.[31] Privacy can be a challenge, as these algorithms can also remember personal information that they have seen as part of the training data and – at least under certain conditions – can as a result output social security numbers, bank details, and other personal information.[32] Sustainability is also an issue, as ChatGPT and other Large Language Models require massive amounts of energy to be trained.[33] But in addition to all of these ethical challenges that are naturally derived from the overviews there are more specific issues. ChatGPT and other generative algorithms may produce outputs that heavily draw on the work of specific individuals without giving credit to them, raising questions of plagiarism.[34] The possibility to use such algorithms to help write essays or formulate answers to exam questions has also been raised, as ChatGPT already performs reasonably well on a range of university exams.[35,36] One may also wonder how such algorithms end up being used in corporate settings, and whether this will replace part of the writing staff that we have. Issues about the future of work[37] are thus quickly connected to the rapidly improving language models. Finally, large language models can produce highly personalized influence at a massive scale and their outputs can be used to mediate communication between people

30 Tabone, W. and de Winter, J. "Using ChatGPT for Human–Computer Interaction Research: A Primer" (2023) www.researchgate.net/profile/Wilbert-Tabone/publication/367284084_Using_ChatGPT_for_Human-Computer_Interaction_Research_A_Primer/links/63ca6066e922c50e99abb2c8/Using-ChatGPT-for-Human-Computer-Interaction-Research-A-Primer.pdf

31 Hovy, D. and Prabhumoye, S. "Five sources of bias in natural language processing" (2021) *Language and Linguistics Compass*, 15(8): e12432.

32 Carlini, N., Liu, C., Erlingsson, Ú., Kos, J., and Song, D. "The secret sharer: Evaluating and testing unintended memorization in neural networks" (2019, August) in *USENIX Security Symposium* (Vol. 267).

33 Bender, E. M., Gebru, T., McMillan-Major, A., and Mitchell, S. "On the dangers of stochastic parrots: Can language models be too big?" (2021, March) in *Proceedings of the 2021 ACM Conference on Fairness, Accountability, and Transparency* (pp. 610–623).

34 Lee, J., Le, T., Chen, J., and Lee, D. "Do language models plagiarize?" (2022) arXiv preprint arXiv:2203.07618.

35 Choi, J. H., Hickman, K. E., Monahan, A., and Schwarcz, D. "ChatGPT goes to law school" (2023) Available at SSRN. doi:https://papers.ssrn.com/sol3/papers.cfm?abstract_id=4335905

36 Gilson, A., Safranek, C., Huang, T., Socrates, V., Chi, L., Taylor, R. A., and Chartash, D. "How well does ChatGPT do when taking the medical licensing exams? The implications of large language models for medical education and knowledge assessment" (2022) *medRxiv*, 2022–12. doi:https://doi.org/10.1101/2022.12.23.22283901

37 Wang, W. and Siau, K. "Artificial intelligence, machine learning, automation, robotics, future of work and future of humanity: A review and research agenda" (2019) *Journal of Database Management (JDM)*, 30(1): 61–79.

(augmented many-to-many communication[38]); they raise a peculiar risk of manipulation at scale. The ethical issues surrounding manipulation are certainly related to issues of autonomy. For example, manipulation may be of ethical relevance insofar as it negatively impacts people's autonomy and well-being.[39] At the same time, manipulation does not necessarily impact autonomy, but instead raises ethical issues all on its own; issues that may well be aggravated in their scope and importance by the use of large language models.[40,41] This illustrates our main point in this section, namely that general frameworks offer a good start, but that they are insufficient as comprehensive accounts of the ethical issues of AI.

A second and very different example is that of credit scoring algorithms that help to decide whether someone qualifies for a bank loan. A recent review shows that the more complex deep learning systems are more accurate at this task than simpler statistical models,[42] so we can expect that AI is used more and more by banks for credit scoring. While this may lead to a larger amount of loans being granted, because the risk per loan is lower (as a result of more accurate risk assessments), there are of course also a number of ethical considerations to take into account that stem from the function of distributing finance to individuals. Starting off again with bias, there is a good chance of unfairness in the distribution of loans. AI systems may offer proportionally fewer loans to minorities[43] and are often also less accurate for these groups.[44] This can be a case of discrimination, and a range of statistical fairness metrics[45] has been developed to capture this. This particular case brings with it different challenges, as fairness measures rely on access to group membership (e.g., race or gender) in order to work, raising privacy issues.[46] Optimizing for fairness can also drastically reduce the accuracy of an AI system, leading to conflicts

38 Cappuccio, M. L., Sandis, C., and Wyatt, A. "Online manipulation and agential risk" in M. Klenk and F. Jongepier (eds.), *The Philosophy of Online Manipulation* (New York, NY: Routledge, 2022), pp. 72–90.

39 Klenk, 2020.

40 Klenk, M. and Hancock, J. "Autonomy and online manipulation" (2019) *Internet Policy Review*. Retrieved from https://policyreview.info/articles/news/autonomy-and-online-manipulation/1431

41 Klenk, M. and Jongepier, F. (eds.). *The Philosophy of Online Manipulation* (New York, NY: Routledge, 2022).

42 Dastile, X., Celik, T., and Potsane, M. "Statistical and machine learning models in credit scoring: A systematic literature survey" (2020) *Applied Soft Computing*, 91: 106263.

43 Zou, L. and Khern-am-nuai, W. "AI and housing discrimination: The case of mortgage applications" (2022) *AI and Ethics*, 1–11.

44 Liu, L. T., Dean, S., Rolf, E., Simchowitz, M., and Hardt, M. "Delayed impact of fair machine learning." (2018, July) in *International Conference on Machine Learning*, pp. 3150–3158. PMLR.

45 Mitchell, S., Potash, E., Barocas, S., D'Amour, A., and Lum, K. "Algorithmic fairness: Choices, assumptions, and definitions" (2021) *Annual Review of Statistics and Its Application*, 8: 141–163.

46 Alves, G., Bernier, F., Couceiro, M., Makhlouf, K., Palamidessi, C., and Zhioua, S. "Survey on fairness notions and related tensions" (2022) *EURO Journal on Decision Processes*, 11, 100033, arXiv preprint arXiv:2209.13012.

with their reliability.[47] From a more socio-technical lens, there are questions of how bank personnel will interact with these models and rely on them, raising questions of meaningful human control, responsibility, and trust in these systems. The decisions made can also have serious impacts for decision subjects, requiring close attention to their contestability[48] and institutional mechanisms to correct mistakes.

Third, and lastly, we can consider an AI system that the government uses to detect fraud among social benefits applications. Anomaly detection is an important subfield of artificial intelligence.[49] Along with other AI techniques, it can be used to more accurately find deviant cases. Yeung describes how New Public Management in the Public Sector is being replaced by what she calls New Public Analytics.[50] Such decisions by government agencies have a major impact on potentially very vulnerable parts of the population, and so come with a host of ethical challenges. There is, again, bias that might arise in the decision-making where a system may disproportionately (and unjustifiably) classify individuals from one group as fraudsters – as actually happened in the Dutch childcare allowance affair.[51] Decisions about biases here are likely to be made differently than in the bank case, because we consider individuals to have a right to social benefits if they need them, whereas there is no such right to a bank loan. Some other challenges, such as those to privacy and reliability, are similar, though again different choices will likely be made due to the different decisions resulting from the socio-technical system. At the same time, new challenges arise around the legitimacy of the decision being made. As the distribution of social benefits is a decision that hinges on political power, it is subject to the acceptability of how that power is exercised. In an extreme case, as with the social benefits affair, mistakes here can lead to the resignation of the government.[52] Standards of justice and transparency, like other standards such as those of contestability/algorithmic recourse,[53] are thus different depending on the context.

What we hope to show with these three examples is that the different classifications of ethical challenges and taxonomies of moral values in the literature are certainly valid. They show up throughout the different applications of AI systems

47 Wang, Y., Wang, X., Beutel, A., Prost, F., Chen, J., and Chi, E. H. "Understanding and improving fairness-accuracy trade-offs in multi-task learning" (2021, August) in *Proceedings of the 27th ACM SIGKDD Conference on Knowledge Discovery & Data Mining*, pp. 1748–1757.

48 Henin, C. and Le Métayer, D. "Beyond explainability: justifiability and contestability of algorithmic decision systems" (2021) *AI & SOCIETY*, 1–14.

49 Pang, G., Shen, C., Cao, L., and Hengel, A. V. D. "Deep learning for anomaly detection: A review" (2021) *ACM Computing Surveys (CSUR)*, 54(2): 1–38.

50 Yeung, K. "The new public analytics as an emerging paradigm in public sector administration" (2023) *Tilburg Law Review*, 27(2): 1–32.

51 Heikkilä, 2022.

52 Ten Seldam, B. and Brenninkmeijer, A. "The Dutch benefits scandal: A cautionary tale for algorithmic enforcement" (2021) *EU Law Enforcement*, April 30, 2021, https://eulawenforcement.com/?p=7941.

53 Venkatasubramanian, S. and Alfano, M. "The philosophical basis of algorithmic recourse" (2020) in *Proceedings of the 2020 Conference on Fairness, Accountability, and Transparency*, 284–293.

and to some extent they present overarching problems that may have solutions that apply across domains. We already saw this for bias across the different cases. Another example comes from innovations in synthetic data, which present general solutions to the trade-off between privacy and (statistical) fairness by generating datasets with the attributes needed to test for fairness, but for fake people.[54] However, even when the solution is domain-general, the task of determining when such a synthetic dataset is relevantly similar to the real world is a highly context-specific issue. It needs to capture the relevant patterns in the world. For social benefits, this includes correlations between gender, nationality, and race with one's job situation and job application behavior, whereas for a bank, patterns related to people's financial position and payment behavior are crucial. This means that synthetic datasets cannot easily be reused and care must be taken to include the context. Even then, recent criticisms have raised doubts that synthetic data do not fully preserve privacy,[55] and thus may not be the innovative solution that we hope for. Overviews are therefore helpful to remind ourselves of commonly occurring ethical challenges, but they should not be taken as definitive lists, nor should they tempt us into easily transferring answers to ethical questions from one domain to another.

Finally, we pointed already to the socio-technical nature of many of the ethical challenges. This deserves a little more discussion, as the overviews of ethical challenges can often seem to focus more narrowly on the technical aspects of AI systems themselves,[56] leaving out the many people that interact with them and the institutions of which they are a part. Bias can come back into the decision-making if operators can overrule an AI system, and reliability may suffer if operators do not appropriately rely on AI systems.[57] Values such as safety and security are likewise just as dependent on the people and regulations surrounding AI systems as they are on the technologies themselves. Without appropriate design of these surroundings we may also end up with a situation where operators lack meaningful human control, leading to gaps in accountability.[58] The list goes on, as contestability, manipulation and legitimacy also in many ways depend on the interplays of socio-technical elements rather than the AI models themselves. Responsible AI thus often involves changes to the socio-technical system in which AI is embedded. In short, even though the field is called "AI ethics" it should concern itself with more than just the AI models in a strict sense. It is just as much about the people interacting with

[54] Nikolenko, S. I. *Synthetic Data for Deep Learning* (2021) Springer Nature, Vol. 174: Springer Optimization and Its Applications (SOIA).

[55] Stadler, T., Oprisanu, B., and Troncoso, C. "Synthetic data–anonymisation groundhog day" (2022) in *31st USENIX Security Symposium (USENIX Security 22)*, pp. 1451–1468.

[56] Selbst, A. D., Boyd, D., Friedler, S. A., Venkatasubramanian, S., and Vertesi, J. "Fairness and abstraction in sociotechnical systems" (2019, January) in *Proceedings of the Conference on Fairness, Accountability, and Transparency*, pp. 59–68.

[57] Schemmer, M., Hemmer, P., Kühl, N., Benz, C., and Satzger, G. "Should I follow AI-based advice? Measuring appropriate reliance in human-AI decision-making" (2022) arXiv preprint arXiv:2204.06916.

[58] Santoni de Sio and Mecacci, 2021.

AI and the institutions and norms in which AI is employed. With that said, the next question is how we can deal with the challenges that AI presents us with.

3.3 MAIN ETHICAL THEORIES AND THEIR APPLICATION TO AI

The first place to look when one wants to tackle these ethical challenges is the vast philosophical literature centered around the main ethical theories. We have millennia of thinking on the grounds of right and wrong action. Therefore, since the problems that AI raises typically involve familiar ethical values, it would be wise to benefit from these traditions. To start with, the most influential types of normative ethical theories are virtue ethics, deontology, and consequentialism. Normative ethical theories are attempts to formulate and justify general principles – normative laws or principles if you will[59] – about the grounds of right and wrong (there are, of course, exceptions to this way of seeing normative ethics[60]). Insofar as the development, deployment, and use of AI systems involves actions just like any other human activity, the use of AI falls under the scope of ethical theories: it can be done in right or wrong fashion, and normative ethical theories are supposed to tell just *why* what was done was right or wrong. In the context of AI, however, the goal is often not understanding (*why* is something right or wrong?) but action-guidance: what should be done, in a specific context? Partly for that reason, normative ethical theories may be understood or used as decision aids that should resolve concrete decision problems or imply clear design guidelines. When normative ethical theories are (mis-)understood in that way, when they are construed as a decisional algorithm, for example, when scholars aim to derive ethical precepts for self-driving cars from normative theories and different takes on the trolley problem, it is unsurprising that the result is disappointment in a rich and real world setting. At the same time, there is a pressing need to find concrete and justifiable answers to the problems posed by AI and we can use all the help we can get. We therefore aim to not only highlight the three main ethical theories here the history of ethics has handed down to us but also point to the many additional discussions in ethics and philosophy that promise insights that are more readily applicable to practice and that can be integrated in responsible policymaking, professional reflection, and societal debates. Here the ethical traditions in normative ethical theory are like "sensitizing concepts."[61] that draw our attention to particular aspects

[59] Berker, Selim. "The explanatory ambitions of moral principles" 2019 *Noûs*, 53: 904–36.

[60] Dancy, Jonathan, "Moral particularism," in Edward N. Zalta (ed.), *The Stanford Encyclopedia of Philosophy* (Winter 2017 Edition), https://plato.stanford.edu/archives/win2017/entries/moral-particularism/.

[61] Zerubavel, Eviatar, "Toward a concept-driven sociology: Sensitizing concepts and the prepared mind" in Wayne H. Brekhus, Thomas DeGloma, and William Ryan Force (eds), *The Oxford Handbook of Symbolic Interactionism* (online ed., Oxford Academic, April 14, 2021), https://doi.org/10.1093/oxfordhb/9780190082161.013.10

of complex situations. Following Thomas Nagel, we could say that these theoretical perspectives each champion one particular type of value at the expense of other types. Some take agent relative perspectives into account, but others disregard the individual's perspective and consider the agent's place in a social network or champion a universalistic perspective.

The focus of virtue ethics is on the character traits of agents. Virtue ethicists seek to answer the question of "how ought one to live" by describing the positive character traits – virtues – that one ought to cultivate. Virtue ethicists have no problem talking about right or wrong actions, however, for the right action is the action that a virtuous person would take. How this is worked out precisely differs, and in modern contexts, one can see a difference between, for example, Slote who holds that one's actual motivations and dispositions matter and that if those are good/virtuous then the action was good.[62] On the other hand, Zagzebski thinks that one's actual motives are irrelevant, and that what matters is whether it matches the actions of a hypothetical/ideal virtuous person.[63] In yet another version, Swanton holds that virtues have a target at which they aim[64]: for example, courage aims to handle danger and generosity aims to share resources. An action is good if it contributes to the targets of these virtues (either strictly by being the best action to promote the different targets, or less strictly as one that does so well enough). In each case, virtues or "excellences" are the central point of analysis and the right action in a certain situation depends somehow on how it relates to the relevant virtues, linking what is right to do to what someone is motivated to do.

This is quite different from consequentialism, though consequentialists can also talk about virtues in the sense that a virtue is a disposition that often leads to outcomes that maximize well-being. Virtues can be acknowledged, but are subsumed under the guiding principle that the right action is the one that maximizes (some understanding of) well-being.[65] There are then differences on whether the consequences that matter are the actual consequences or the consequences that were foreseeable/intended,[66] whether one focuses on individual acts or rules,[67] and on what consequences matter (e.g., pleasure, preference satisfaction, or a pluralist notion of well-being[68]). Whichever version of consequentialism one picks, however, it is consequences that matter and there will be a principle that the right action leads to the best consequences.

62 Slote, M. *Morals from Motives* (Oxford University Press, 2001).

63 Zagzebski, L. *Divine Motivation Theory* (New York: Cambridge University Press, 2004).

64 Swanton, C. *Virtue Ethics: A Pluralistic View* (Oxford University Press, 2003).

65 Sinnott-Armstrong, W. "Consequentialism" in Edward N. Zalta and Uri Nodelman (eds.), *The Stanford Encyclopedia of Philosophy* (2022) https://plato.stanford.edu/archives/win2022/entries/consequentialism/.

66 Feldman, F. "Actual utility, the objection from impracticality, and the move to expected utility" (2006) *Philosophical Studies*, 129: 49–79.

67 Emmons, D. C. "Act vs. rule-utilitarianism" (1973) *Mind*, 82(326): 226–33.

68 Mulgan, T. *Understanding Utilitarianism* (Routledge, 2014).

The third general view on ethics, namely deontology, looks at norms instead. So, rather than grounding right action in its consequences, what is most important for these theories is whether actions meet moral norms or principles.[69] A guiding idea here is that we cannot predict the consequences of our actions, but we can make sure that we ourselves act in ways that satisfy the moral laws. There are, again, many different ways in which this core tenet has been developed. Agent-centered theories focus on the obligations and permissions that agents have when performing actions.[70] There may be an obligation to tell the truth, for example, or an obligation not to kill another human being. Vice versa, patient-centered theories look not at the obligations of the agent but at the rights of everyone else.[71,72] There is a right to not be killed that limits the purview of morally permissible actions. Closer to the topic of this chapter, we may also think of, for example, a right to privacy that should be respected unless someone chooses to give up that right in a specific situation.

All three accounts can be used to contribute to AI ethics, though it is important to remember that they are conflicting and thus cannot be used interchangeably (though they can be complementary). A philosophically informed perspective on AI ethics will need to take a stand on how these theories are understood, but for here we will merely highlight some of the ways they might be applied. First, we can look at the practices and character of the developers and deployers of artificial intelligence through the lens of virtue ethics. What virtues should be instilled in those who develop and use AI? How can the education of engineers contribute to this, to instill core virtues such as awareness of the social context of technology and a commitment to public good[73] and sensitivity to the needs of others? It can also help us to look at the decision procedure that led to the implemented AI system. Was this conducted in a virtuous way? Did a range of stakeholders have a meaningful say in critical design choices, as would be in line with value sensitive design and participatory design approaches?[74] While it is typically difficult to determine what a fully virtuous agent would do, and virtue ethics may not help us to guide specific trade-offs that have to be made, looking at the motivations and goals of the people involved in realizing an AI system can nevertheless help.

The same goes for consequentialism. It's important to consider the consequences of developing an AI system, just as it is important for those involved in the operation

69 Alexander, L. and Moore, M. "Deontological ethics" in Edward N. Zalta (ed.), *The Stanford Encyclopedia of Philosophy* (Winter 2021 Edition), https://plato.stanford.edu/archives/win2021/entries/ethics-deontological/.

70 Kamm, F. M. *Intricate Ethics: Rights, Responsibilities, and Permissible Harm* (Oxford University Press, 2007).

71 Nozick, R. *Anarchy, State and Utopia* (New York: Basic Books, 1974).

72 Vallentyne, P. and Steiner, H. (eds.). *Left-Libertarianism and Its Critics* (Houndmills: Palgrave, 2000).

73 Harris, C. E. "The good engineer: Giving virtue its due in engineering ethics" (2008) *Science and Engineering Ethics*, 14: 153–164.

74 Liao, Q. V. and Muller, M. "Enabling value sensitive AI systems through participatory design fictions" (2019) arXiv preprint arXiv:1912.07381.

of the system to consider the consequences of the individual decisions made once the AI is up and running. Important as it is, it is also difficult to anticipate consequences beforehand and often the more we can still shape the workings of a technology (in the early design stages), the less we know about the impacts it will have.[75] There are, of course, options to redesign technologies and make changes as the impacts start to emerge, and consequentialism rightly draws our attention to the consequences of using AI. The point we want to make here, rather, is that in practice the overall motto to optimize the impact of an AI system is often not enough to help steer design during the development phase.

Deontology is no different in this respect. It can help to look at our obligations as well as at the rights of those who are impacted by AI systems, but deontology as it is found in the literature is too coarse-grained to be of practical assistance. We often do not exactly know what our moral obligations are on these theories, or how to weigh *prima facie* duties and rights to arrive at what we should do, all things considered. The right to privacy of one person might be overruled by someone else's right not to be killed, for example, and deontological theories typically do not give the detailed guidance needed to decide to what extent one right may be waived in favor of another. In short, we need to supplement the main ethical theories with more detailed accounts that apply to more specific concerns raised by emerging technologies.

These are readily available for a wide range of values. When we start with questions of bias and fairness, there is a vast debate on distributive justice, with for example Rawls' Justice as Fairness[76] as a substantive theory of how benefits and harms should be distributed.[77] Currently, these philosophical theories are largely disconnected from the fairness debate in the computer science/AI Ethics literature,[78] but there are some first attempts to develop connections between the two.[79] The same goes for other values, where for example the philosophical work on (scientific) explanation can be used to better understand and perhaps improve the explainability of machine learning systems.[80,81] Philosophical views on responsibility and control have also already been developed in the context of AI, specifically linked to the concept of meaningful human control over autonomous technology.[82] More attention has also

75 Genus, A. and Stirling, A. "Collingridge and the dilemma of control: Towards responsible and accountable innovation" (2018) *Research Policy*, 47(1): 61–69.

76 Rawls, 2001.

77 See also the discussion of Rawls in Chapter 5 of this book.

78 Kuppler, M., Kern, C., Bach, R. L., and Kreuter, F. "Distributive justice and fairness metrics in automated decision-making: How much overlap is there?" (2021) arXiv preprint arXiv:2105.01441.

79 Barsotti, F. and Koçer, R. G. "MinMax fairness: From Rawlsian Theory of Justice to solution for algorithmic bias" (2022) *AI & SOCIETY*, 1–14.

80 Beisbart, C. and Räz, T. "Philosophy of science at sea: Clarifying the interpretability of machine learning" (2022) *Philosophy Compass*, 17(6): e12830.

81 Buijsman, 2022.

82 Santoni de Sio, F. and Van den Hoven, J. "Meaningful human control over autonomous systems: A philosophical account" (2018) *Frontiers in Robotics and AI*, 5: 15.

been paid to the ethics of influence, notably the nature and ethics of manipulation, which can inform the design and deployment of AI-mediated influence, such as (hyper-)nudges.[83,84] None of these are general theories of ethics, but the more detailed understanding of important (ethical) values that they provide are nevertheless useful when trying to responsibly design and use AI systems. Even then, however, we need an idea of how we go from the philosophical, conceptual, analysis to the design of a specific AI system. For that, the (relatively recent) design approaches to (AI) ethics are crucial. They require input from all the different parts of philosophy mentioned in this section, but add to that a methodology to make these ethical reflections actionable in the design and use of AI.

3.4 DESIGN-APPROACHES TO AI ETHICS

In response to these challenges the ethics of technology has switched, since the 1980s[85] to a constructive approach of integrating ethical aspects already in the design stage of technology. Frameworks such as value-sensitive design[86] and design for values,[87] coupled with methods such as participatory design[88] have led the way in doing precisely this. Here we will highlight the design for values approach, but note that there are close ties with other design approaches to ethics of technology and design for values is not privileged among these. It shares with other frameworks the starting point that technologies are not value neutral, but instead embed or embody particular values.[89] For example, biases can be (intentionally or unintentionally) replicated in technologies, whether it is in the design of park benches with middle armrests to make sleeping on them impossible or in biased AI systems. The same holds for other values, as the design of an engine will strike a balance between cost-effectiveness and sustainability or content moderation at a social media platform realizes values of the decision-makers. The challenge is to ensure that the relevant values are embedded in AI systems and the socio-technical systems of which they are a part. This entails three different challenges: identifying the relevant values, embedding them in systems, and assessing whether these efforts were successful.

When identifying values, it is commonly held important to consider values of all stakeholders, both those directly interacting with the AI system and those indirectly

[83] Klenk and Jongepier, 2022.

[84] Yeung, K. "'Hypernudge': Big Data as a mode of regulation by design" (2017) *Information, Communication & Society*, 20(1): 118–136.

[85] Friedman, B., Kahn, P., and Borning, A. "Value sensitive design: Theory and methods" (2002) *University of Washington Technical Report*, 2: 12.

[86] Umbrello and De Bellis, 2018.

[87] van den Hoven et al., 2015.

[88] Spinuzzi, C. "The methodology of participatory design" (2005) *Technical Communication*, 52(2): 163–174.

[89] Van de Poel, 2020.

affected by its use.[90] This requires the active involvement of (representatives of) different stakeholder groups, to elicit the different values that are important to them. At the same time, it comes with a challenge. Design approaches to AI ethics require that values of a technology's stakeholders (bottom-up) are weighed up against values derived from theoretical and normative frameworks (top-down). Just because people think that, for example, autonomy is valuable does not imply that it is valuable. To go from the empirical work identifying values of stakeholders to a normative take on technologies requires a justification that will likely make recourse to one of the normative ethical approaches discussed earlier. Engaging stakeholders is thus important, because it often highlights aspects of technologies that one would otherwise miss, but not sufficient. The fact that a solution or application would be *de facto accepted* by stakeholders, does not imply that it would be (therefore) also *morally acceptable*. Moral acceptability needs to be independently established, a good understanding of the arguments and reasons that all directly and indirectly affected parties bring to the table is a good starting point, but not the end of the story. We should aim at a situation where technology is accepted, because it is morally acceptable, and that if technologies are not accepted, that is because they are not acceptable.

Here the ethical and more broadly philosophical theories touched upon in the previous section can help. They are needed for two reasons: first, to justify and ground the elicited values in a normative framework, the way, for example, accounts of fairness, responsibility, and even normative takes on the value of explainability[91] can justify the relevance of certain values. Here, it also helps to consider the main ethical theories as championing specific values (per Nagel), be they agent-relative, focused on social relations or universalistic. For these sets of values, these theories help to justify their relevance. Second, they help in the follow-up from the identification of values to their implementation. Saying that an AI system should respect autonomy is not enough, as we need to know what that entails for the concrete system at issue.

As different conceptualizations of these values often lead to different designs of technologies, it is necessary to both assess different conceptions and develop new conceptions. This work can be fruitfully linked to the methods of conceptual engineering[92] and can often draw on the existing conceptions in extant philosophical accounts. Whether those are used or new conceptions are developed, one needs to make the steps from values to norms, and then from norms to design requirements.[93]

[90] Friedman, B., Hendry, D. G., and Borning, A. "A survey of value sensitive design methods" (2017) *Foundations and Trends® in Human–Computer Interaction*, 11(2): 63–125.

[91] Cortese et al., 2022.

[92] Veluwenkamp, H. and van den Hoven, J. "Design for values and conceptual engineering" (2023) *Ethics and Information Technology*, 25(1): 1–12.

[93] Van de Poel, I. "Translating values into design requirements" (2013) *Philosophy and Engineering: Reflections on Practice, Principles and Process*, 253–66.

To give a concrete example, one may start from the value of privacy. There are various aspects to privacy, which can be captured in the conceptual engineering step to norms. Here things such as mitigating risks of personal harm, preventing biased decision-making, and protecting people's freedom to choose are all aspects that emerge from a philosophical analysis of privacy[94] and can act as norms in the current framework. For they, in turn, can be linked to specific design requirements. When mitigating risks, one can look at specific technologies such as coarse graining[95] or differential privacy[96] that aim to minimize how identifiable individuals are, thus reducing their risks for personal harm. Likewise, socio-technical measures against mass surveillance can support the norm for protecting people's freedom to choose, by preventing a situation where their choices are impacted by the knowledge that every action is stored somewhere.

For the actual implementation of values there are a number of additional challenges to consider. Most prominently is the fact that conflicts can occur between different design requirements, which is more often referred to as value conflicts or trade-offs.[97] These already came up in passing in the cases discussed in Section 3.2, such as conflicts between accuracy and fairness or between privacy and fairness. If we want to use statistical fairness measures to promote equal treatment of, for example, men and women, then they need datasets labeled with gender, thus reducing privacy. Likewise, it turns out that when optimizing an AI system for conformity with a statistical fairness measure its accuracy is (greatly) reduced.[98] Such conflicts can be approached in a number of ways[99]: (1) maximizing the score among alternative solutions to the conflict, assuming that there is a way to rank them; (2) satisficing among alternatives, finding one that is good enough on all the different values; (3) respecifying design requirements to ones that still fit the relevant norms but no longer conflict; and (4) innovating, as with synthetic data and the privacy/fairness conflict, to allow for a way to meet all the original design requirements. All of these are easier said than done, but highlight different strategies for dealing with the fact that often we have to balance competing *prima facie* (ethical) requirements on AI systems.

Another problem is that recent work has drawn attention to the possibility of changing values. Perceptions of values certainly change over time. That is, people's

94 Moore, A. D. "Privacy: its meaning and value" (2003) *American Philosophical Quarterly*, 40(3): 215–27.

95 Gedik, B. and Liu, L. "Protecting location privacy with personalized k-anonymity: Architecture and algorithms" (2007) *IEEE Transactions on Mobile Computing*, 7(1): 1–18.

96 Dwork, C. "Differential privacy" in *Automata, Languages and Programming: 33rd International Colloquium*, ICALP 2006, Venice, Italy, July 10–14, 2006, Proceedings, Part II 33 (pp. 1–12). Springer Berlin Heidelberg.

97 Van de Poel, I. "Conflicting values in design for values," *Handbook of Ethics, Values, and Technological Design: Sources, Theory, Values and Application Domains* (2015), 89–116.

98 Kozodoi, N., Jacob, J. and Lessmann, S. "Fairness in credit scoring: Assessment, implementation and profit implications" (2022) *European Journal of Operational Research*, 297(3): 1083–1094.

99 Van de Poel, 2015.

interpretation of what it means for a technology to be sustainable (to adhere to or embody that value) may change over time and people may begin to value things that they did not value before: sustainability is a case in point. That means that, even if people's perceptions of values are correctly identified at the beginning of a design project, they may change, and insofar as people's perceptions of values matter (see above), the possibility of value change represents another methodological challenge for design for value approaches. Actively designing for this scenario, by including adaptability, flexibility and robustness[100] is thus a good practice. We may not be able to anticipate value changes, just as it is hard to predict more generally the impact of an AI system before it is used, but that is no reason not to try to do everything in our power to realize systems that are as responsible as possible.

Because we cannot predict everything, and because values may change over time, it is also important to assess the AI systems once they are in use – and to keep doing so over time. Did the envisaged design requirements indeed manage to realize the identified values? Were values missed during the design phase that now emerge as relevant – the way Uber found out that surge pricing during emergencies is ethically wrong (because it privileges the rich who can then still afford to flee the site of an attack) only after this first happened in 2014.[101] And are there no unintended effects that we failed to predict? All of these questions are important, and first attempts to systematically raise them can be found in the emerging frameworks for ethics-based auditing[102] as well as in the EU AI Act's call for continuous monitoring of AI systems. In these cases, too, the translation from values to design requirements can help. Design requirements should be sufficiently concrete to be both implementable and verifiable, specifying for example a degree of privacy in terms of k-anonymity (how many people have the same attributes in an anonymized dataset) or fairness in terms of a statistical measure. These can then guide the assessment afterward, though we have to be careful that the initial specification of the values may be wrong. Optimizing for the wrong fairness measure can, for example, have serious negative long-term consequences for vulnerable groups[103] and these should not be missed due to an exclusive focus on the earlier chosen fairness measure during the assessment.

In all three stages (identification, implementation, and assessment), we should not forget the observations from Section 3.2: we should design more than just the technical AI systems and what implications values have will differ from context to context. The problem of Uber's algorithm raising prices whenever demand

[100] Van de Poel, I. "Design for value change" (2021) *Ethics and Information Technology*, 23(1): 27–31.

[101] Sullivan, W. "Uber backtracks after jacking up prices during Sydney hostage crisis" (2014) *Washington Post*, December 15, 2014, www.washingtonpost.com/news/morning-mix/wp/2014/12/15/uber-backtracks-after-jacking-up-prices-during-syndey-hostage-crisis/

[102] Mökander, J. and Floridi, L. "Ethics-based auditing to develop trustworthy AI" (2021) *Minds and Machines*, 31(2): 323–27.

[103] Liu et al., 2018.

increases regardless of the cause for that demand was ultimately not solved in the AI system, but by adding on a control room where a human operator can turn off the algorithm in emergencies. Response times were an issue initially,[104] but it shows that solutions need not be purely technical. Likewise, an insurance company in New Zealand automated its claims processing and massively improved efficiency while maintaining explainability when it counts, by automatically paying out every claim that the AI approved but sending any potential rejections to humans for a full manual review.[105] In this case, almost 95% of applications get accepted almost instantaneously, while every rejected application still comes with a clear motivation and an easily identifiable person who is accountable should a mistake have been made. A combination that would be hard to achieve using AI alone is instead managed through the design of the wider socio-technical system. Of course, this will not work in every context. Crucial to this case is that the organization knew that fraudulent claims are relatively rare and that the costs of false positives are thus manageable compared to the saving in manpower and evaluation time. In other situations, or in other sectors such as healthcare (imagine automatically giving someone a diagnosis and only manually checking when the AI system indicates that you do not have a certain illness) different designs will be needed.

To sum up, design approaches to AI ethics focus on the identification of values, the translation of these values into design requirements, and the assessment of technologies in the light of values. This leads to a proactive approach to ethics, ideally engaging designers of these systems in the ethical deliberation and guiding important choices underlying the resulting systems. It is an approach that aims to fill in the oft-noted gap between ethical principles and practical development.[106] With the increasing adoption of AI, it becomes ever more pressing to fill this gap, and thus to work on the translation from ethical values to design requirements. Principles are not enough[107] and ethics should find its way into design. Not only are designs value laden as we discussed earlier, but values are design consequential. In times where everything is designed, commitment to particular values implies that one is bent on exploring opportunities to realize these values – when and where appropriate – in technology and design that can make a difference. We therefore think that we can only tackle the challenges of AI ethics by combining normative ethical theories, and

[104] Cox, J. "London terror attack: Uber slammed for being slow to turn off 'surge pricing' after rampage" (2017) *Independent*, June 4, 2017, www.independent.co.uk/news/uk/home-news/london-terror-attack-uber-criticised-surge-pricing-after-london-bridge-black-cab-a7772246.html

[105] Zerilli, J., Knott, A., Maclaurin, J., and Gavaghan, C. "Algorithmic decision-making and the control problem" (2019) *Minds and Machines*, 29: 555–78.

[106] Georgieva, I., Lazo, C., Timan, T., and van Veenstra, A. F. "From AI ethics principles to data science practice: A reflection and a gap analysis based on recent frameworks and practical experience" (2022) *AI and Ethics*, 2(4): 697–711.

[107] Mittelstadt, B. "Principles alone cannot guarantee ethical AI" (2019). *Nature Machine Intelligence*, 1(11): 501–07.

detailed philosophical accounts of different values, with a design approach.[108] Such an approach additionally requires a range of interdisciplinary, and often transdisciplinary, collaborations. Philosophy alone cannot solve the problems of AI ethics, but it has an important role to play.

3.5 CONCLUSION

Artificial intelligence poses a host of ethical challenges. These come from the use of AI systems to take actions and support decision-making and are exacerbated by our limited ability to steer and predict the outputs of AI systems (at least the machine learning kind). AI thus raises familiar problems, of bias, privacy, autonomy, accountability, and more, in a new setting. This can be both a challenge, as we have to find new ways of ensuring the ethical design of decision-making procedures, and an opportunity to create even more responsible (socio-technical) systems. Thanks to the developments of AI we now have fairness metrics that can be used just as easily outside of the AI context, though we have to be careful in light of their limitations (see also Chapter 4 of this Handbook).[109] Ethics can be made more actionable, but this requires renewed efforts in philosophy as well as strong interdisciplinary collaborations.

Existing philosophical theories, starting with the main ethical theories of virtue ethics, consequentialism and deontology, are a good starting point. They can provide the normative framework needed to determine which values are relevant and what requirements are normatively justified. More detailed accounts, such as those of privacy, responsibility, distributive justice, and explanation, are also needed to take the first step from values that have been identified to conceptualizations of them in terms of norms and policies or business rules. Often, we cannot get started on bridging the gap from values and norms to (concrete) design requirements before we have done the conceptual engineering work that yields a first specification of these values. After that design approaches to AI ethics kick in, helping guide us through the process of identifying values for a specific case, and then specifying them in requirements that can finally be used to assess AI systems and the broader socio-technical system in which they have been embedded.

While we have highlighted these steps here from a philosophical perspective, they require strong interdisciplinary collaborations. Identifying values in practical contexts is best done in collaboration with empirical sciences, determining not only people's preferences but also potential impacts of AI systems. Formulating design requirements requires a close interaction with the actual designers of these systems

108 van den Hoven, J., Miller, S., and Pogge, T. (eds.). *Designing in Ethics* (Cambridge University Press, 2017). doi:10.1017/9780511844317.

109 Carey, A. N. and Wu, X. "The statistical fairness field guide: Perspectives from social and formal sciences" (2023) *AI and Ethics*, 3(1): 1–23.

(both technical and socio-technical), relating the conceptions of values to technological, legal, and institutional possibilities and innovations. Finally, assessment again relies heavily on an empirical understanding of the actual effects of socio-technical (and AI) systems. To responsibly develop and use AI, we have to be proactive in integrating ethics into the design of these systems.

4

Fairness and Artificial Intelligence

Laurens Naudts and Anton Vedder

4.1 INTRODUCTION

Within the increasing corpus of ethics codes regarding the responsible use of AI, the notion of fairness is often heralded as one of the leading principles. Although omnipresent within the AI governance debate, fairness remains an elusive concept. Often left unspecified and undefined, it is typically grouped together with the notion of justice. Following a mapping of AI policy documents commissioned by the Council of Europe, researchers found that the notions of justice and fairness show "the least variation, hence the highest degree of cross-geographical and cross-cultural stability."[1] Yet, once we attempt to interpret these notions concretely, we soon find that they are perhaps best referred to as essentially contested concepts: over the years, they have sparked constant debate among scholars and policymakers regarding their appropriate usage and position.[2] Even when some shared understanding concerning their meaning can be found on an abstract level, people may still disagree on their actual relation and realization. For instance, fairness and justice are often interpreted as demanding some type of equality. Yet equality, too, has been the subject of extensive discussions.

In this chapter, we aim to clear up some of the uncertainties surrounding these three concepts. Our goal, however, is not to put forward an exhaustive overview of the literature, nor to promote a decisive view of what these concepts should entail. Instead, we want to increase scholars' sensibilities as to the role these concepts can perform in the debate on AI and the (normative) considerations that come with that role. Taking one particular interpretation of fairness as our point of departure (fairness as nonarbitrariness), we first investigate the distinction and relationship

[1] In addition to the notion of privacy. Isaac Ben-Israel et al., "Towards regulation of AI systems: Global perspectives on the development of a legal framework on artificial intelligence systems based on the Council of Europe's Standards on Human Rights, Democracy and the Rule of Law" (Council of Europe, 2020) 2020/16 50, https://rm.coe.int/prems-107320-gbr-2018-compli-cahai-couv-texte-a4-bat-web/1680a0c17a.

[2] W. B. Gallie, "IX.—Essentially contested concepts" (1956) *Proceedings of the Aristotelian Society*, 56: 167.

between procedural and substantive conceptions of fairness (Section 4.2). We build upon this distinction to further analyze the relationship between fairness, justice, and equality (Section 4.3). We start with an exploration of Rawls' conception of justice as fairness, a theoretical framework that is both procedural and substantively egalitarian in nature. This analysis forms a stepping stone for the discussion of two distinct approaches toward justice and fairness. In particular, Rawls' outcome-oriented or distributive approach is critiqued from a relational perspective. In parallel, throughout both sections, we pay attention to the challenges these conceptions may face in light of technological innovations. In the final step, we consider the limitations of techno-solutionism and attempts to formalize fairness by design in particular (Section 4.4), before concluding (Section 4.5).

4.2 CONCEPTIONS OF FAIRNESS: PROCEDURAL AND SUBSTANTIVE

In our digital society, public and private actors increasingly rely on AI systems for the purposes of knowledge creation and application. In this function, data-driven technologies guide, streamline, and/or automate a host of decision-making processes. Given their ubiquity, these systems actively co-mediate people's living environment. Unsurprisingly then, it is expected for these systems to operate in correspondence to people's sense of social justice, which we understand here as their views on how a society should be structured, including the treatment, as well as the social and economic affordances citizens are owed.

Regarding the rules and normative concepts used to reflect upon the ideal structuring of society, a distinction can generally be made between procedural notions or rules and substantive ones. Though this distinction may be confusing and is equally subject to debate, substantive notions and rules directly refer to a particular political or normative goal or outcome a judgment or decision should effectuate.[3] Conversely, procedural concepts and rules describe *how* judgments and decisions in society should be made rather than prescribing *what* those judgments and decisions should ultimately be. Procedural notions thus appear seemingly normatively empty: they simply call for certain procedural constraints in making a policy, judgment, or decision, such as the consistency or the impartial application of a rule. In the following sections, we elaborate on the position fairness typically holds in these discussions. First, we discuss fairness understood as a purely procedural constraint (Section 4.2.1), and second, how perceptions of fairness are often informed by a particular substantive, normative outlook (Section 4.2.2). Finally, we illustrate how procedural constraints that are often claimed to be neutral nonetheless tend to reflect a specific normative position as well (Section 4.2.3).

[3] See, for instance: Christine M. Korsgaard, "Self-constitution in the ethics of Plato and Kant" in Christine M. Korsgaard (ed.), *The Constitution of Agency: Essays on Practical Reason and Moral Psychology* (Oxford University Press, 2008), 106–107, https://doi.org/10.1093/acprof:oso/9780199552733.003.0004, accessed February 15, 2023.

4.2.1 *Fairness as a Procedural Constraint*

Fairness can be viewed as a property or set of properties of processes, that is, particular standards that a decision making procedure or structure should meet.[4] Suppose a government and company want to explore the virtues of automation. A government wants to streamline the distribution of welfare benefits and a company seeks the same with its hiring process. Understood as a procedural value, fairness should teach us something about the conditions under which (a) the initial welfare or hiring policy was decided upon and (b) how that policy will be translated and applied to individuals by means of an automated procedure. A common approach to fairness in this regard is to view it as a demand for nonarbitrariness: a procedure is unfair when it arbitrarily favors or advantages one person or group or situation over others, or arbitrarily favors the claims of some over those of others.[5] In their analysis of AI-driven decision-making procedures, Creel and Hellmann evaluate three different, yet overlapping, understandings that could be given to the notion of arbitrariness, which we will also use here as a springboard for our discussion.[6]

First, one could argue that a decision is arbitrary when it is unpredictable. Under this view, AI-driven procedures would be fair only when their outcome is reasonably foreseeable and predictable for decision subjects. Yet, even in the case a hiring or welfare algorithm would be rendered explicable and reasonably foreseeable, would we still call it fair when its reasoning process placed underrepresented and marginalized communities at a disproportionate disadvantage?

Second, the arbitrariness of a process may lie in the fact that it was "unconstrained by ex-ante rules."[7] An automated system should not have the capacity to set aside the predefined rules it was designed to operate under. Likewise, government case workers or HR personnel acting as a human in the loop should not use their discretionary power to discard automated decisions to favor unemployed family members. Instead, they should maintain impartiality. Once a given ruleset has been put in place, it creates the legitimate expectation among individuals that those rules will be consistently applied. Without consistency, the system would also become unpredictable. Yet, when seen in isolation, most AI-driven applications operate on some

4 T. M. Scanlon, "Rights, Goals, and Fairness" 85.

5 See, for example: Scanlon (n 4); Jonathan Wolff, "Fairness, respect, and the egalitarian ethos" (1998) *Philosophy & Public Affairs*, 27: 97; Christopher McMahon, *Reasonableness and Fairness: A Historical Theory* (1st ed., Cambridge University Press, 2016), www.cambridge.org/core/product/identifier/9781316819340/type/book, accessed January 31, 2023.

6 Creel and Hellmann do not necessarily position these three understandings as the sole interpretations that could be given to the notion of arbitrariness. Kathleen Creel and Deborah Hellman, "The algorithmic leviathan: Arbitrariness, fairness, and opportunity in algorithmic decision-making systems" (2022) *Canadian Journal of Philosophy*, 52: 26, 34, 37–38. For their analysis of these definitions, and their limitations in light of AI-driven decision-making, reference can be made to the aforementioned work.

7 Creel and Hellman (n 6).

predefined ruleset or instructions.[8] Even in the case of neural networks, unless some form of randomization is involved, there is some method to their madness. In fact, one of AI's boons is its ability to streamline the application of decision-making procedures uniformly and consistently. However, the same observation would apply: would we consider decisions fair when they are applied in a consistent, rule-bound, and reproducible manner, even when they place certain people or groups at a disproportionate social or economic disadvantage?

Finally, one could argue that arbitrariness is synonymous with irrationality.[9] Fairness as rationality partly corresponds to the principle of formal equal treatment found within the law.[10] Fairness as rationality mandates decision-makers to provide a rational and reasonable justification or motivation for the decisions they make. Historically, the principle of equal treatment was applied as a similar procedural and institutional benchmark toward good governance: whenever a policy, decision, or action creates a distinction between a (group of) people or situations, that differentiation had to be reasonably justified. Without such justification, a differentiating measure was seen as being in violation of the procedural postulate that "like situations should be treated alike."[11] This precept could be read as the instruction to apply rules consistently and predictably. However, where a differentiating measure is concerned, the like-cases axiom is often used to question not only the application of a rule but also that rule's content: did the decision-maker consider the differences between individuals, groups, or situations that were relevant or pertinent?[12] Yet, this conception might be too easily satisfied by AI-driven decisions. Indeed, is it often not the entire purpose of AI-driven analytics to find relevant points of distinction that can guide a decision? As observed by Wachter: "Since data science mainly focuses on correlation and not causation [...] it can seemingly make any data point or attribute appear relevant."[13] However, those correlations can generate significant exclusionary harm: they can make the difference between a person's eligibility or disqualification for a welfare benefit or job position. Moreover, due to the scale and uniformity at which AI can be rolled out, such decisions do not affect single individuals but large groups of people. Perhaps then, we should also be guided by the

8 Ibid., 28–29.

9 Ibid., 28.

10 H. L. A. Hart, *The Concept of Law* (Clarendon Press, 1961); Stefan Sottiaux, "Het Gelijkheidsbeginsel: Langs Oude Paden En Nieuwe Wegen (Artikel, 2008) [WorldCat.Org]" (2008) *Rechtskundig Weekblad*, 72: 690.

11 See among others: Stefan Sottiaux, "Het Gelijkheidsbeginsel : Langs Oude Paden En Nieuwe Wegen (Artikel, 2008) [WorldCat.Org]" (2008) *Rechtskundig Weekblad*, 72: 690. Christopher McCrudden and Haris Kountouros, "Human Rights and European Equality Law," in *Equality Law in an Enlarged European Union: Understanding the Article 13 Directives*, ed. Helen Meenan (Cambridge University Press, 2007), 73–116, https://doi.org/10.1017/CBO9780511493898.004.

12 Creel and Hellman (n 6).

13 Sandra Wachter, "The theory of artificial immutability: protecting algorithmic groups under anti-discrimination law" (2022) *SSRN Electronic Journal*, 20, www.ssrn.com/abstract=4099100, accessed May 27, 2022.

disadvantage a system will likely produce and not only by whether the differences relied upon to guide a procedure appear rational or nonarbitrary.[14]

Through our analysis of the notion of nonarbitrariness, a series of standards have been identified that could affect the fairness of a given decision-making procedure. In particular, fairness can refer to the need to motivate or justify a particular policy, rule, or decision, and to ensure the predictable and consistent application of a rule, that is, without partiality and favoritism. In principle, those standards can also be imposed on the rules governing the decision-making process itself. For example, when a law is designed or agreed upon, it should be informed by a plurality of voices rather than be the expression of a dominant majority. In other words, it should not arbitrarily exclude certain groups from having their say regarding a particular policy, judgment, or decision. Likewise, it was shown how those standards could also be rephrased as being an expression of the procedural axiom that "like cases ought to be treated alike." Given this definition, we might also understand why fairness is linked to other institutional safeguards, such as transparency, participation, and contestability. These procedural mechanisms enable citizens to gauge whether or not a given procedure was followed in a correct and consistent fashion and whether the justification provided took stock of those elements of the case deemed pertinent.

4.2.2 *Toward a Substantive Understanding of Fairness*

As the above analysis hints, certain standards imposed by a purely procedural understanding of fairness could be easily met where AI is relied upon to justify, guide, and apply decision-making rules. As any decision-making procedure can be seemingly justified on the basis of AI analytics, should we then deem every decision fair?

In the AI governance debate, the notion of fairness is seldom used purely procedurally. The presence of procedural safeguards, like a motivation, is typically considered a necessary but often an insufficient condition for fairness. When we criticize a decision and its underlying procedure, we usually look beyond its procedural components. People's fairness judgments might draw from their views on social justice: they consider the context in which a decision is made, the goals it aims to materialize and the (likely) disadvantage it may cause for those involved. In this context, Hart has argued that justice and fairness seemingly comprise two parts: "a uniform or constant feature, summarized in the precept 'Treat like cases alike' and a shifting or varying criterion used in determining when, for any given purpose,

[14] Of course, differences will play a role in our evaluation of decision-making procedures. We need to assess whether characteristics were reasonable or sensible in light of the task at hand. The point made, however, is that it might not be the only thing that should take up our attention. Wachter, for instance, argues that AI-guided decisions and procedures should be based on empirically coherent information that has a proven connection or an intuitive link to the procedure at hand Wachter (n 13). See also: Sandra Wachter and Brent Mittelstadt, "A right to reasonable inferences: Re-thinking data protection law in the age of big data and AI" (2019) *Columbia Business Law Review*, 2019: 494.

cases are alike or different."[15] This varying criterion entails a particular political or moral outlook, a standard we use to evaluate whether a specific policy or rule contributes to the desired structuring of society.

For example, we could invoke a substantive notion of equality that a procedure should maintain or achieve. We might say that AI-driven procedures should not bar oppressed social groups from meaningfully engaging with their social environment or exercising meaningful control and agency over the conditions that govern their lives.[16] In so doing, we could also consider the exclusionary harm algorithms might introduce. Hiring and welfare programs, for instance, affect what Creel and Hellman refer to as "realms of opportunities:" the outcomes of these decisions give people more choices and access to alternative life paths.[17] In deciding upon eligibility criteria for a welfare benefit or job opportunity, we should then carefully consider whether the chosen parameters risk reflecting or perpetuating histories of disadvantage. From a data protection perspective, fairness might represent decision-makers' obligation to collect and process all data they use transparently.[18] Needless to say, articulating one's normative outlook is one thing. Translating those views into the making, structuring, and application of a rule is another. While a normative perspective might support us in the initial design of a decision-making procedure, the latter's ability to realize a set of predefined goals will often only show in practice. In that regard, the normative standard relied upon, and its procedural implementation should remain subject to corrections and criticisms.[19]

Of course, purely procedural constraints could maintain their value regardless of one's particular moral outlook: whether a society is structured alongside utilitarian or egalitarian principles, in both cases, consistency and predictability of a rule's application benefit and respects people's legitimate expectations. Given this intrinsic value, we might not want to discard the application of an established procedure outright as soon as the outcomes they produce conflict with our normative goals and ambitions.[20] The point, however, is that once a substantive or normative position has been taken, it can be used to scrutinize existing procedures where they fail to meet the desired normative outcome. Or, positively put, procedural constraints

[15] See also: Peter Westen, "The empty idea of equality" (1982) *Harvard Law Review*, 95: 537; Hart (n 10) 159–160.

[16] Iris Marion Young, *Justice and the Politics of Difference* (Princeton University Press, 1990); Naudts, *Fair or Unfair Differentiation? Reconsidering the Concept of Equality for the Regulation of Algorithmically Guided Decision-Making* (Doctoral Dissertation). (2023).

[17] Creel and Hellman (n 6) 22.

[18] Damian Clifford and Jef Ausloos, "Data protection and the role of fairness" (2018) *Yearbook of European Law*, 37: 130.

[19] See also: Westen (n 15); Hart (n 10) 159–160.

[20] On this point, see also: Christine M. Korsgaard, "Self-Constitution in the Ethics of Plato and Kant" in Christine M. Korsgaard (ed), *The Constitution of Agency: Essays on Practical Reason and Moral Psychology* (Oxford University Press, 2008) 106–108, https://doi.org/10.1093/acprof:oso/9780199552733.003.0004, accessed 15 February 2023.

can now be modeled to better enable the realization of the specific substantive goals we wanted to realize. For example, we may argue that the more an AI application threatens to interfere with people's life choices, the more institutional safeguards we need to facilitate our review and evaluation of the techniques and procedures AI decision-makers employ and the normative values they have incorporated into their systems.[21] The relationship between procedural and substantive fairness mechanisms is, therefore, a reciprocal one.

4.2.3 *The Myth of Impartiality*

Earlier we said that procedural fairness notions appear normatively empty. For example, the belief that a given rule should not arbitrarily favor one group over others might be seen as a call toward impartiality. If a decision-making process must be impartial to be fair, does this not exclude the decision-making process of being informed by a substantive, and hence, partial normative outlook? Even though the opposite may sometimes be claimed, efforts to remain impartial are not as neutral as they appear at first sight.[22] For one, suppose an algorithmic system automates the imposition of traffic fines for speeding. Following a simple rule of logic, any person driving over the speed limit allocated to a given area must be handed the same fine. The system is impartial in the sense that without exception it will consistently apply the rules as they were written regardless of those who were at the wheel. It will not act more favorably toward politicians speeding than ordinary citizens for instance. At the same time, impartiality thus understood excludes the system from taking into account contextual factors that could favor leniency, as might be the case when a person violates the speed limit as they are rushing to the hospital to visit a sick relative. Second, in decision-making contexts made in relation to the distribution of publicly prized goods, such as job and welfare allocation, certain traits, such as a person's gender or ethnicity, are often identified as arbitrary. Consequently, any disadvantageous treatment on the basis of those characteristics is judged to be unfair. The designation of these characteristics as arbitrary, however, is not neutral either: it represents a so-called color-blind approach toward policy and decision-making. Such an approach might intuitively appear as a useful strategy in the pursuit of socially egalitarian goals, and it can be. For instance, in a hiring context, there is typically no reason to assume that a person's social background, ethnicity, or gender will affect their ability to perform a given job. At the same time, this color-blind mode of thinking can be critiqued for its tendency to favor merit-based criteria as the most appropriate differentiating metric instead. Under this view, criteria reflecting merit are (wrongfully) believed

[21] Creel and Hellman (n 6). See also: Jeremy Waldron, *One Another's Equals: The Basis of Human Equality* (Belknap Press: Harvard University Press, 2017).

[22] See also: Takis Tridimas, *The General Principles of EU Law* (2nd ed., Oxford University Press, 2006), p. 62.

to be most objective and least biased.[23] In automating a hiring decision, designers may need to define what a "good employee" is, and they will look for technical definitions and classifications that further specify who such an employee may be. As observed by Young, such specifications are not scientifically objective, nor neutrally determined, but instead "they concern whether the person evaluated supports and internalizes specific values, follows implicit or explicit social rules of behavior, supports social purposes, or exhibits specific traits or character, behavior, or temperament that the [decision-maker] finds desirable."[24] Moreover, a person's social context and culture have a considerable influence on the way they discover, experience, and develop their talents, motivations, and preferences.[25] Where a person has had fewer opportunities to attain or develop a talent or skill due to their specific social condition, their chance of success is more limited than those who could.[26] A mechanical interpretation of fairness as impartiality obscures the differences that exist between people and their relationship with social context and group affinities: individual identities are discarded and rendered abstract in favor of "impartial" or "universal" criteria. The blind approach risks decontextualizing the disadvantage certain groups face due to their possession of, or association with, a given characteristic. Though neutral at first glance, the criteria chosen might therefore ultimately favor the dominant majority disadvantaging those minorities a color-blind approach was supposed to protect in the first place. At the same time, it also underestimates how certain characteristics are often a valuable component of one's identity.[27] Rather than render differences between people, such as their gender or ethnicity, invisible, differences could instead be accommodated and harnessed to eliminate the (social and distributive) disadvantage attached to them.[28] For example, a person's gender or ethnicity may become a relevant and nonarbitrary criterion if we want to redress the historical disadvantage faced by certain social groups by imposing positive or affirmative action measures on AI developers.

[23] Young (n 16) 201. See also: Michael J. Sandel, *The Tyranny of Merit: What's Become of the Common Good?* (Penguin Books, 2021).

[24] Young (n 16) 204.

[25] In this sense, Rawls observes, the principle of fair opportunity can only be imperfectly carried out: "the extent to which natural capacities develop and reach fruition is affected by all kinds of social conditions and class attitudes." John Rawls, *A Theory of Justice* (Harvard University Press (Belknap Press, 1971), p. 74.

[26] Richard J. Arneson, "Against Rawlsian equality of opportunity" (1999) *Philosophical Studies: An International Journal for Philosophy in the Analytic Tradition*, 93: 77.

[27] See also: Sandra Fredman, "Substantive equality revisited" (2016) *International Journal of Constitutional Law*, 14: 712; Sandra Fredman, "Providing equality: Substantive equality and the positive duty to provide" (2005) *South African Journal on Human Rights*, 21: 163.

[28] This is also a criticism that can be leveled against "fairness-by-unawareness" design metrics. These metrics construct fairness as achieved when certain characteristics are not explicitly used in a prediction process. Fredman, "Substantive equality revisited" (n 27) 720. See also: Naudts (n 16).

4.3 JUSTICE, FAIRNESS, AND EQUALITY

In the previous section, we illustrated how a procedural understanding of fairness is often combined with a more substantive political or normative outlook. This outlook we might find in political philosophy, and theories of social justice in particular. In developing a theory of social justice, one investigates the relationship between the structure of society and the interests of its citizens.[29] The interplay and alignment between the legal, economic, and civil aspects of social life determine the social position as well as the burdens and benefits that the members of a given society will carry. A position will be taken as to how society can be structured so it best accommodates the interests of its citizens. Of course, different structures will affect people in different ways, and scholars have long theorized as to what structure would suit society the best. Egalitarian theories for instance denote the idea that people should enjoy (substantive) equality of some sort.[30] This may include the recognition of individuals as social equals in the relationships they maintain, or their ability to enjoy equal opportunities in their access to certain benefits. In order to explain the intricate relationship that exists between the notions of justice, fairness, and equality as a normative and political outlook, John Rawls is a good place to start.

4.3.1 *Justice as Fairness*

In his book *A Theory of Justice*, Rawls defines justice as fairness.[31] For Rawls, the subject of justice is the basic structure of society. These institutions are the political constitution and the principal economic and social arrangements. They determine people's life prospects: their duties and rights, the burdens, and benefits they carry. In our digital society, AI applications are technological artifacts that co-mediate the basic structure of society: they affect the options we are presented (e.g., recommender systems), the relationships we enter into (e.g., AI-driven social media), and/or the opportunities we have access to (e.g., hiring and welfare algorithms).[32] While AI-driven applications must adhere to the demands of justice, the concept of fairness is, however, fundamental to arrive at a proper conception of justice.[33] More specifically, Rawls argues that the principles of justice can only arise out of an agreement made under fair conditions: "A practice will strike the parties as fair if none feels

[29] Philip Pettit, *Judging Justice. An Introduction to Contemporary Political Philosophy* (Routledge & Kegan Paul, 1980).

[30] See also Richard Arneson, "Egalitarianism" in Edward N. Zalta (ed.), *The Stanford Encyclopedia of Philosophy* (Summer 2013, Metaphysics Research Lab, Stanford University, 2013), https://plato.stanford.edu/archives/sum2013/entries/egalitarianism/, accessed February 8, 2023.

[31] Rawls, *A Theory of Justice* (n 25).

[32] Iason Gabriel, "Towards a theory of justice for artificial intelligence" (2022) *Daedalus*, 151: 12.

[33] John Rawls, "Justice as fairness" (1958) *The Philosophical Review*, 67: 164, 178.

that, by participating in it, they or any of the others are taken advantage of, or forced to give in to claims which they do not regard as legitimate."[34] It is this position of initial equality, where free and rational persons choose what course of action best suits the structure of society, from which principles of justice may arise.[35] Put differently, fairness does not directly inform the regulation, design, and development of AI, the principles of justice do so, but these principles are chosen from a fair bargaining position. While fairness could thus be perceived as a procedural decision-making constraint, the principles that follow from this position are substantive. And as the principles of justice are substantive in nature, Rawls argues, justice as fairness is not procedurally neutral either.

One major concern Rawls had was the deep inequalities that arise between people due to the different social positions they are born into, the differences in their natural talents and abilities, and the differences in the luck they have over the course of their life.[36] The basic structure of society favors certain starting positions over others, and the principles of justice should correct as much as possible for the inequalities people may incur as a result thereof. Rawls' intuitive understanding regarding the emergence of entrenched social inequality, which AI applications tend to reinforce, could therefore function as a solid basis for AI governance.[37]

In his A *Theory of Justice*, Rawls proposes (among others) the difference principle, which stipulates that once a society has been able to realize basic equal liberties to all and fair equality of opportunity in social and economic areas of life, social and economic inequalities can only be justified when they are to the benefit of those least advantaged within society. As AI applications not only take over social inequality but also have a tendency to reinforce and perpetuate the historical disadvantage faced by marginalized or otherwise oppressed communities, the difference principle could encourage regulators and decision-makers, when a comparison is made between alternative regulatory and design options, to choose for those policy or design options that are most likely to benefit the least advantaged within society. In this context, one could contend that justice should not only mitigate

[34] Ibid. Fairness is guaranteed as a result of the fair conditions under which people are able to reach an agreement regarding the principles of justice. They are the outcome of an original agreement in a suitably defined initial situation. The participants of this initial situation – or the original position – decide upon the principles that will govern their association. While the participants are rational and in the pursuit of their own interests, they are also each other's equals. They view themselves and each other as a source of legitimate claims. In addition, the parties that partake in this hypothetical original position are situated behind a veil of ignorance. No participant knows their place in society, their natural talents. They do not know the details of their life. From this position, they are to derive the appropriate principles of justice. Rawls, A *Theory of Justice* (n 25) chapter 3, The Original Position, and p. 119.

[35] Rawls, A *Theory of Justice* (n 25) 11.

[36] Rawls, A *Theory of Justice* (n 25).

[37] See also: Gabriel (n 32) 10; Jamie Grace, "'AI theory of justice': Using Rawlsian approaches to better legislate on machine learning in government" (2020) *SSRN Electronic Journal*, www.ssrn.com/abstract=3588256, accessed August 10, 2022.

and avoid the replication of social and economic injustice but also pursue more ambitious transformative goals.[38] AI should be positively harnessed to break down institutional barriers that bar those least advantaged from participating in social and economic life.[39]

4.3.2 *Distributive Accounts of Fairness*

Like conceptions of fairness, people's understanding of what justice is, and requires, is subject to dispute. Rawls' understanding of justice for instance is distributive in nature. His principles of justice govern the distribution of the so-called primary goods: basic rights and liberties; freedom of movement and free choice of occupation against a background of diverse opportunities; powers and prerogatives of offices and positions of authorities and responsibility; income and wealth; and the social bases of self-respect.[40] These primary goods are what "free and equal persons need as citizens."[41] A distributive approach toward fairness may also be found in the work of Hart, who considered fairness to be a notion relevant (among others) to the way classes of people are treated when some burden or disadvantage must be *distributed* among them. In this regard, unfairness is a property not only of a procedure but also of the shares produced by that procedure.[42] Characteristic of the distributive paradigm is that it formulates questions of justice as questions of distribution. In general terms, purely distributive-oriented theories argue that any advantage and disadvantage within society can be explained in terms of people's possession of, or access to, certain material (e.g., wealth and income) or nonmaterial goods (e.g., opportunities and social positions).[43] Likewise, social and economic inequalities can be evaluated in light of the theory's proposed or desired distribution of those goods it has identified as "justice-relevant."[44] Inequality between people can be

[38] Gabriel (n 32) 9–10. See also: Virginia Eubanks, *Automating Inequality: How High-Tech Tools Profile, Police and Punish the Poor* (Macmillan Publishers, 2018); Caroline Criado Perez, *Invisible Women: Exposing Data Bias in a World Designed for Men* (1st ed., Chatto & Windus, 2019); Safiya Umoja Noble, *Algorithms of Oppression: How Search Engines Reinforce Racism* (New York University Press, 2018), www.degruyter.com/document/doi/10.18574/9781479833641/html, accessed December 8, 2021.

[39] See also: Gabriel (n 32) 9–10.

[40] John Rawls, *Justice as Fairness: A Restatement* (Kelly Erin ed., Belknap Press: Harvard University Press, 2001), pp. 58–59.

[41] John Rawls, "The basic liberties and their priority" in Sterling M. Mcmurrin (ed.) (1981), p. 89; Rawls, *Justice as Fairness: A Restatement* (n 40) 60.

[42] An additional area of social life where fairness is mandated is the situation where a person has been done some injury and must be compensated. Hart (n 10) 159.

[43] Young (n 16) 8.

[44] Thomas Pogge, "Relational conceptions of justice: Responsibilities for health outcomes" in Sudhir Anand, Fabienne Peter, and Amartya Sen (eds), *Public Health, Ethics, and Equity* (Oxford University Press, 2004), p. 147; Christian Schemmel, "Distributive and relational equality": (2011) *Politics, Philosophy & Economics* 127, http://journals.sagepub.com/doi/10.1177/1470594X11416774, accessed August 4, 2020.

justified as long as it contributes to the desired state of affairs. If it does not, however, mechanisms of redistribution must be introduced to accommodate unjustified disadvantages.[45]

Distributive notions of fairness have an intuitive appeal as AI-driven decisions are often deployed in areas that can constrain people in their access to publicly prized goods, such as education, credit, or welfare benefits.[46] Hence, when fairness is to become integrated into technological applications, the tendency may be for design solutions to focus on the distributive shares algorithms produce and, conversely, to correct AI applications when they fail to provide the desired outcome.[47]

4.3.3 *Relational Accounts of Fairness*

Though issues of distribution are important, relational scholars have critiqued the dominance of the distributive paradigm as the normative lens through which questions of injustice are framed.[48] They believe additional emphasis must be placed on the relationships people hold and how people ought to treat one another as part of the relationships they maintain with others, such as their peers, institutions, and corporations. Distributive views on fairness might be concerned with transforming social structures, institutions, and relations, but their reason for doing so lies in the outcomes these changes would produce.[49] Moreover, as Young explains, certain phenomena such as rights, opportunities, and power are better explained as a

45 Thomas W. Pogge, "Three problems with Contractarian-Consequentialist ways of assessing social institutions" (1995) *Social Philosophy and Policy*, 12: 241. Young (n 16) 24–25.

46 Reuben Binns, "Fairness in machine learning: Lessons from political philosophy" (2018) *Proceedings of Machine Learning Research*.

47 Atoosa Kasirzadeh, "Algorithmic fairness and structural injustice: Insights from feminist political philosophy" (2022) *Proceedings of the 2022 AAAI/ACM Conference on AI, Ethics, and Society*, http://arxiv.org/abs/2206.00945, accessed February 3, 2023; Pratik Gajane and Mykola Pechenizkiy, "On formalizing fairness in prediction with machine learning" (2017) arXiv:1710.03184 [cs, stat], http://arxiv.org/abs/1710.03184, accessed July 23, 2018; presented during the 5th Workshop on Fairness, Accountability, and Transparency in Machine Learning (Stockholm, 2018).

48 Young (n 16); Carina Fourie, Fabian Schuppert, and Ivo Walliman-Helmer (eds), *Social Equality: On What It Means to Be Equals* (Oxford University Press, 2015). For a relational perspective on AI, see: Abeba Birhane, "Algorithmic injustice: A relational ethics approach" (2021) *Patterns*, 2: 100205; Salomé Viljoen, "A relational theory of data governance" (2021) *The Yale Law Journal*, 82; Kasirzadeh (n 47); Virginia Dignum, "Responsible Artificial Intelligence: Recommendations and Lessons Learned," in *Responsible AI in Africa: Challenges and Opportunities*, ed. Damian Okaibedi Eke, Kutoma Wakunuma, and Simisola Akintoye (Cham: Springer International Publishing, 2023), 195–214, https://doi.org/10.1007/978-3-031-08215-3_9; Virginia Dignum, "Relational artificial intelligence" (2022) arXiv:2202.07446 [cs], http://arxiv.org/abs/2202.07446, accessed February 17, 2022; Naudts (n 16); Laurens Naudts, "The Digital Faces of Oppression and Domination: A Relational and Egalitarian Perspective on the Data-driven Society and its Regulation." In *Proceedings of the 2024 ACM Conference on Fairness, Accountability, and Transparency (FAccT '24)*. Association for Computing Machinery, New York, NY, USA (2024), 701–12. https://doi.org/10.1145/3630106.3658934.

49 Schemmel (n 44); Pogge (n 44).

function of social processes, rather than thing-like items that are subject to distribution.[50] Likewise, inequality cannot solely be explained or evaluated in terms of people's access to certain goods. Instead, inequality arises and exists, and hence is formed, within the various relationships people maintain. For example, people cannot participate as social equals and have an equal say in political decision-making processes when prejudicial world views negatively stereotype them. They might have "equal political liberties" on paper, but not in practice.

When fairness not only mandates "impartial treatment" in relation to distributive ideals but also requires a specific type of relational treatment, the concept's normative reach goes even further.[51] AI applications are inherently relational. On the one hand, decision-makers hold a position of power over decision-subjects, and hence, relational fairness could constrain the type of actions and behaviors AI developers may impose onto decision-subjects. At the same time, data-driven applications, when applied onto people, divide the population into broad, but nonetheless consequential categories based upon generalized statements concerning similarities people allegedly share.[52] Relational approaches toward fairness will specify the conditions under which people should be treated as part of and within AI procedures.

Take for instance the relational injustice of cultural imperialism. According to Young, cultural imperialism involves the social practice in which a (dominant) group's experience and culture is universalized and established as the norm.[53] A group or actor is able to universalize their world views when they have access to the most important "means of interpretation and communication."[54] The process of cultural imperialism stereotypes and marks out the perspectives and lived experiences of those who do not belong to the universal or dominant group as an "Other."[55] Because AI-applications constitute a modern means of interpretation and communication in our digital society, they in turn afford power to those who hold control

[50] Young (n 16) 25–31.

[51] See, for example: Schemmel (n 44); John Baker, "Conceptions and dimensions of social equality" in Carina Fourie, Fabian Schuppert, and Ivo Walliman-Helmer (eds), *Social Equality: On What It Means to Be Equals* (Oxford University Press, 2015); Marie Garrau and Cécile Laborde, "Relational equality, non-domination, and vulnerability" in Carina Fourie, Fabian Schuppert, and Ivo Walliman-Helmer (eds), *Social Equality: On What It Means to Be Equals* (Oxford University Press, 2015).

[52] See also: Viljoen (n 48).

[53] Young (n 16) 59. See also: María C. Lugones and Elizabeth V. Spelman, "Have we got a theory for you! Feminist theory, cultural imperialism and the demand for 'the woman's voice'" (1983) *Women's Studies International Forum*, 6: 573; For a more in-depth application of this notion onto AI, as well as Young's other "faces of oppression," see also: Laurens Naudts, The Digital Faces of Oppression and Domination: A Relational and Egalitarian Perspective on the Data-driven Society and its Regulation. In *Proceedings of the 2024 ACM Conference on Fairness, Accountability, and Transparency (FAccT '24)*. Association for Computing Machinery, New York, NY, USA (2024), 701–12. https://doi.org/10.1145/3630106.3658934.

[54] Nancy Fraser, "Talking about needs: Interpretive contests as political conflicts in welfare-state societies" (1989) *Ethics*, 99: 291; Nancy Fraser, "Toward a discourse ethic of solidarity" (1985) *PRAXIS International*, 5: 425.

[55] Young (n 16) 59. See also: WEB Du Bois, *The Souls of Black Folk* (Oxford University Press, 2007).

over AI: AI-driven technologies can discover and/or apply (new) knowledge and give those with access to them the opportunity to interpret and structure society. They give those in power the capacity to shape the world in accordance with their perspective, experiences, and meanings and to encode and naturalize a specific ordering of the world.[56] For example, in the field of computer vision methods are sought to understand the visual world via recognition systems. In order to do so AI must be trained on the basis of vast amounts of images or other pictorial material. To be of any use; however, these images must be classified as to what they contain. Though certain classification acts seemingly appear devoid of risk (e.g., does a picture contain a motorbike), others are not.[57] Computer vision systems that look to define and classify socially constructed categories, such as gender, race, and sexuality, tend to wrongfully present these categories as universal and detectable, often to the detriment of those not captured by the universal rule.[58] Facial recognition systems and body scanners at airports that have been built based on the gender binary risk treating trans-, non-binary, and gender nonconforming persons as nonrecognizable human beings.[59] In a similar vein, algorithmic systems may incorporate stereotyped beliefs concerning a given group. This was the case in the Netherlands, where certain risk scoring algorithms used during the evaluation of childcare benefit applications operated on the prejudicial assumption that ethnic minorities and people living in poverty were more

[56] The notion classification is used here in a broad sense. It not only refers to the ways in which an algorithmic decision-making process may group together individuals. It also refers to instances where data are classified or labelled in a training set. Kate Crawford, *Atlas of AI: Power, Politics, and the Planetary Costs of Artificial Intelligence* (Yale University Press, 2021) 128 and 139, https://doi.org/10.12987/9780300252392; Kate Crawford and Trevor Paglen, "Excavating AI: The politics of images in machine learning training sets" (*Excavating AI*, September 19, 2019), www.excavating.ai, accessed February 7, 2020.

[57] On the role of power in image data sets, see also the work by Milagros Miceli et al.: Milagros Miceli et al., "Documenting computer vision datasets: An invitation to reflexive data practices," *Proceedings of the 2021 ACM Conference on Fairness, Accountability, and Transparency* (ACM, 2021), https://dl.acm.org/doi/10.1145/3442188.3445880, accessed March 10, 2021; Milagros Miceli, Julian Posada, and Tianling Yang, "Studying up machine learning data: Why talk about bias when we mean power?" (2021) arXiv:2109.08131 [cs], http://arxiv.org/abs/2109.08131, accessed October 4, 2021; Milagros Miceli, "AI's symbolic power: Classification in the age of automation" (2019); Milagros Miceli and Julian Posada, "A question of power: How task instructions shape training data" (2020) *Symposium on Biases in Human Computation and Crowdsourcing* (BHCC2020, November 11, 2020), https://sites.google.com/sheffield.ac.uk/bhcc-2020/program?authuser=0; Milagros Miceli, Martin Schuessler, and Tianling Yang, "Between subjectivity and imposition: Power dynamics in data annotation for computer vision" (2020) *Proceedings of the ACM on Human-Computer Interaction*, 4: 1.

[58] Crawford (n 56) 144. See also: Miceli et al. (n 57); Miceli and Posada, "A question of power: How task instructions shape training data" (n 57); Milagros Miceli and Julian Posada, "Wisdom for the crowd: Discoursive power in annotation instructions for computer vision" (arXiv, May 23, 2021), http://arxiv.org/abs/2105.10990, accessed August 29, 2022.

[59] Lucas Waldron and Medina Brenda, "TSA's body scanners are gender binary. Humans are not." (*ProPublica*), www.propublica.org/article/tsa-transgender-travelers-scanners-invasive-searches-often-wait-on-the-other-side?token=7bjY-MRzWk5Ed4DCZRvFVYwt2HBrAFXd, accessed February 7, 2022. See also: Os Keyes, "The misgendering machines: Trans/HCI implications of automatic gender recognition" (2018) *Proceedings of the ACM on Human-Computer Interaction*, 2: 1.

likely to commit fraud.[60] The same holds true for highly subjective target variables, such as the specification of the "ideal employee" in hiring algorithms. As aforementioned, technical specifications may gain an aura of objectivity once they become incorporated within a decision-making chain and larger social ecosystem.[61]

Under a relational view, these acts, and regardless of the outcomes they may produce, are unjust because they impose representational harms onto people: they generalize, misrepresent, and deindividualize persons. From a relational perspective, these decisions may be unjustified because they interfere with people's capacity to learn, develop, exercise, and express skills, capacities, and experiences in socially meaningful and recognized ways (self-development) and their capacity to exercise control over, and participate in determining, their own options, choices, and the conditions of their actions (capacity to self-determination).[62] They do so however, not by depriving a particular good to people, but by rendering the experiences and voices of certain (groups of) people invisible and unheard. Unlike outcome-focused definitions of justice, whose violation may appear as more immediate and apparent, these representational or relational harms are less observable due to the opacity and complexity of AI.[63]

If we also focus on the way AI-developers treat people as part of AI procedures, a relational understanding of fairness will give additional guidance as to the way these applications can be structured. For instance, procedural safeguards could be implemented to facilitate people's ability to exercise self-control and self-development when they are likely to be affected by AI. This may be achieved by promoting diversity and inclusion within the development, deployment, and monitoring of decision-making systems as to ensure AI-developers are confronted by a plurality of views and the lived experiences of others, rather than socially dominant conventions.[64] Given the power they hold, AI-developers should carefully consider their normative assumptions.[65] Procedural safeguards may attempt to equalize power asymmetries within the digital environment and help those affected by AI to regain, or have increased, control over those structures that govern and shape their choices and options in socially meaningful and recognized ways. The relational lens

60 "Xenophobic machines: Discrimination through unregulated use of algorithms in the Dutch childcare benefits scandal." (Amnesty International, 2021), www.amnesty.nl/content/uploads/2021/10/20211014_FINAL_Xenophobic-Machines.pdf?x42580; "Dutch childcare benefit scandal an urgent wake-up call to ban racist algorithms" (*Amnesty International*, October 25, 2021), www.amnesty.org/en/latest/news/2021/10/xenophobic-machines-dutch-child-benefit-scandal/, accessed August 15, 2022; Jan Kleinnijenhuis, "Hoe de Belastingdienst lage inkomens profileerde in de jacht op fraude" (*Trouw*, November 22, 2021), www.trouw.nl/gs-bbb66add, accessed November 23, 2021.

61 Crawford (n 56) chapter 4, Classification.

62 For an application of both notions onto AI, see also Naudts (n 16 and 48), drawing from the work of Young (n 16).

63 Solon Barocas, Moritz Hardt, and Arvind Narayanan, "Fairness and machine learning" 253, chapter Introduction.

64 See also Naudts (n 48).

65 See, for instance: Miceli et al. (n 57).

may contribute to the democratization of modern means of interpretation and communication to realize the transformative potential of technologies.

4.4 LIMITATIONS OF TECHNO SOLUTIONISM

From a technical perspective, computer scientists have explored more formalized approaches toward fairness. These efforts attempt to abstract and embed a given fairness notion into the design of a computational procedure. The goal is to develop a "reasoning" and "learning" processes that will operate in such a way that the ultimate outcome of these systems corresponds to what was defined beforehand as fair.[66] While these approaches are laudable, it is also important to understand their limitations. Hence, they should not be seen as the only solution toward the realization of fairness in the AI-environment.

4.4.1 *Choosing Fairness*

During the development of AI systems, a choice must be made as to the fairness metric that will be incorporated. Since fairness is a concept subject to debate, there has been an influx of various fairness metrics.[67] Yet, as should be clear from previous sections, defining fairness is a value-laden and consequential exercise. And even though there is room for certain fairness conceptions to complement or enrich one another, others might conflict. In other words, trade-offs will need to be made in deciding what type of fairness will be integrated, if the technical and mathematical formalization thereof would already be possible in the first place.[68]

Wachter and others distinguish between bias preserving and bias transforming metrics and support the latter to achieve substantive equality, such as fair equality of opportunity and the ability to redress disadvantage faced by historically oppressed social groups.[69] Bias-preserving metrics tend to lock in historical bias present within society and cannot effectuate social change.[70] In related research, Abu-Elyounes

[66] Laurens Naudts, "Towards accountability: The articulation and formalization of fairness in machine learning" (2018) *SSRN Electronic Journal*, www.ssrn.com/abstract=3298847, accessed July 30, 2020.

[67] Gajane and Pechenizkiy (n 47); Doaa Abu Elyounes, "Contextual fairness: A legal and policy analysis of algorithmic fairness" (September 1, 2019), https://papers.ssrn.com/abstract=3478296, accessed February 5, 2023; Sandra Wachter, Brent Mittelstadt, and Chris Russell, "Bias preservation in machine learning: The legality of fairness metrics under EU non-discrimination law" (Social Science Research Network, 2021) *SSRN Scholarly Paper* 3792772, https://papers.ssrn.com/abstract=3792772, accessed April 28, 2022.

[68] Jon Kleinberg, Sendhil Mullainathan, and Manish Raghavan, "Inherent trade-offs in the fair determination of risk scores" (2016) arXiv:1609.05807 [cs, stat], http://arxiv.org/abs/1609.05807, accessed October 11, 2020. See also Section 1.4.2 The Limitations of Abstraction.

[69] Wachter, Mittelstadt, and Russell (n 67).

[70] Ibid.

suggested that different fairness metrics can be linked to different legal mechanisms.[71] Roughly speaking, she makes a distinction between individual fairness, group fairness, and causal reasoning fairness metrics. The first aim to achieve fairness toward the individual regardless of their group affiliation and is closely associated with the ideal of generating equal opportunity. Group fairness notions aim to achieve fairness to the group an individual belongs to, which is more likely to be considered as positive or affirmative action. Finally, due process may be realized through causal reasoning notions that emphasize the close relationship between attributes of relevance and outcomes.[72] This correspondence between fairness metrics and the law could affect system developers and policymakers' design choices.[73] For example, affirmative action measures can be politically divisive. The law might mandate decision-makers to implement positive action measures but limit their obligation to do so only for specific social groups and within areas such as employment or education because they are deemed critical for people's social and economic participation. Thus, the law might (indirectly) specify which fairness metrics are technologically fit for purpose in which policy domains.

Regardless of technical and legal constraints, formalized approaches may still be too narrowly construed in terms of their *inspiration*. For instance, Kasirzadeh has observed how "most mathematical metrics of algorithmic fairness are inherently rooted in a distributive conception of justice."[74] More specifically, "theories or principles of social justice are often translated into the distribution of material (such as employment opportunities) or computational (such as predictive performance) goods across the different social groups or individuals known to be affected by algorithmic outputs."[75] In other words, when outcome-based approaches are given too much revery, we may discard the relational aspects of AI-systems. In addition, and historically speaking, machine learnings efforts arose out of researchers' attempts to realize discrimination-aware data mining or machine learning.[76] In this regard, the notion of fairness has often been closely entwined with more substantive interpretations of equality and nondiscrimination law. This often results in the identification of certain "sensitive attributes" or "protected characteristics," such as gender

[71] Doaa Abu-Elyounes, "Contextual fairness: A legal and policy analysis of algorithmic fairness" (2020) *University of Illinois Journal of Law, Technology & Policy*, 2020: 1, 5.

[72] Abu Elyounes (n 67).

[73] Ibid. See also: Agathe Balayn and Seda Gurses, "Beyond debiasing: Regulating AI and its inequalities." (EDRi, 2021).

[74] Kasirzadeh (n 47) 4.

[75] Ibid.

[76] Binns (n 46). Bettina Berendt and Sören Preibusch, "Better decision support through exploratory discrimination-aware data mining: Foundations and empirical evidence" (2014) *Artificial Intelligence and Law*, 22: 175; Bettina Berendt and Sören Preibusch, "Toward accountable discrimination-aware data mining: The importance of keeping the human in the loop—and under the looking glass" (2017) *Big Data*, 5: 135; Dino Pedreschi Salvatore Ruggieri and Franco Turini, "Discrimination-aware data mining," 9.

or ethnicity. The underlying idea would be that fairness and equality are realized as soon as the outcome of a given AI-system does not disproportionately disadvantage individuals because of their membership of a socially salient group. For instance, one could design a hiring process so the success rate of an application procedure should be (roughly) the same between men and women when individuals share the same qualifications. Even though these approaches aspire to mitigate disadvantage experienced by underrepresented groups, they may do so following a (distributive), single-axis and difference-based nondiscrimination paradigm. This could be problematic for a two-fold reason. First, intersectional theorists have convincingly demonstrated the limitations of nondiscrimination laws' single-attribute focus.[77] Following an intersectional approach, discrimination must also be evaluated considering the complexity of people's identities, whereby particular attention must be paid to the struggles and lived experiences of those who carry multiple burdens. For instance, Buolamwini and Gebru demonstrated how the misclassification rate in commercial gender classification systems is the highest for darker-skinned females.[78] Second, the relational and distributive harms generated by AI-driven applications are not only faced by socially salient groups. For instance, suppose a credit scoring algorithm links an applicant's trustworthiness to a person's keystrokes during their online file application. Suppose our goal is to achieve fair equality of opportunity or equal social standing for all. Should we not scrutinize any interference therewith, and not only when the interference is based upon people's membership of socially salient groups?[79]

Yet, in our attempt to articulate and formalize fairness, Birhane and others rightfully point out that we should be wary of overly and uncontestedly relying on white, Western ontologies to the detriment and exclusion of marginalized philosophies and systems of ethics.[80] More specifically, attention should also be paid to streams of philosophy that are grounded "in down-to-earth problems and [...] strive to challenge underlying oppressive social structures and uneven power dynamics," such as Black Feminism, Critical Theory, and Care Ethics and other non-Western and feminist philosophies.[81] Hence, questions regarding fairness and justice of AI

77 Kimberle Crenshaw, "Demarginalizing the intersection of race and sex: A black feminist critique of antidiscrimination doctrine, feminist theory and antiracist politics" (1989) *University of Chicago Legal Forum*, 1989: 31; Kimberle Crenshaw, "Mapping the margins: Intersectionality, identity politics, and violence against women of color" (1991) *Stanford Law Review*, 43: 1241.

78 Joy Buolamwini and Timnit Gebru, "Gender shades: Intersectional accuracy disparities in commercial gender classification," 15.

79 That is not to say that our approach in tackling the harms faced by socially oppressed and non-oppressed groups should be identical. Indeed, in our attempt to protect the interests of both groups, we may need to distinguish in the protective measures we envisage to accommodate their respective needs and struggles. Naudts (n 16). See also: Wachter (n 13).

80 Abeba Birhane et al., "The forgotten margins of AI ethics," *2022 ACM Conference on Fairness, Accountability, and Transparency* (ACM, 2022), https://dl.acm.org/doi/10.1145/3531146.3533157, accessed February 2, 2023.

81 Ibid., 949–50.

systems must be informed by the lived experiences of those they affect, rather than rendered into a purely abstract theoretical exercise of reflection or technological incorporation.

4.4.2 *Disadvantages of Abstraction*

If fairness is constructed toward the realization of a given outcome by design, they run the risk of oversimplifying the demands of fairness as found within theories of justice or the law. Fairness should not be turned into a simplified procedural notion the realization of which can be achieved solely via the technological procedures that underlie decision-making systems. While fairness can be used to specify the technical components underlying a decision-making process and their impact, it could also offer broader guidance regarding the procedural, substantive, and contextual questions that surround their deployment. Suppose a system must be rendered explicable. Though technology can help us in doing so, individual mechanisms of redress via personal interaction may enable people to better understand the concrete impact AI has had on their life. Moreover, when fairness is seen as a technical notion that governs the functioning of one individual or isolated AI-system only, the evaluation of their functioning may become decontextualized from the social environment in which these systems are embedded and from which they draw, as well as their interconnection with other AI-applications.[82] Taking a relational perspective as a normative point of departure, the wider social structures in which these systems are developed, embedded, and deployed, become an essential component for their overall evaluation. For example, fairness metrics are often seen as a strategy to counter systemic bias within data sets.[83] Large datasets, such as CommonCrawl, used for training high-profile AI applications are built from information mined from the world wide web. Once incorporated into technology, subtle forms of racism and sexism, as well as more overt toxic and hateful opinions shared by people on bulletin boards and fora, risk being further normalized by these systems. As Birhane correctly notes: "Although datasets are often part of the problem, this commonly held belief relegates deeply rooted societal and historical injustices, nuanced power asymmetries, and structural inequalities to mere datasets. The implication is that if one can 'fix' a certain dataset, the deeper problems disappear."[84] Computational approaches might wrongfully assume complex (social) issues can be formulated in terms of problem/solution. Yet this, she believes, paints an overly simplistic picture of the matter at hand: "Not only are subjects of study that do not lend themselves

[82] See, for instance: Andrew D. Selbst et al., "Fairness and abstraction in sociotechnical systems," *Proceedings of the Conference on Fairness, Accountability, and Transparency* (Association for Computing Machinery 2019), https://doi.org/10.1145/3287560.3287598, accessed February 2, 2023.

[83] Balayn and Gurses (n 73).

[84] Birhane (n 48) 6.

to this formulation discarded, but also, this tradition rests on a misconception that injustice, ethics, and bias are relatively static things that we can solve once and for all."[85] As AI systems operate under background conditions of structural injustice, efforts to render AI fairer are fruitless if not accompanied by genuine efforts to dismantle existing social and representational injustice.[86] Fairness thus requires us to view the bigger picture, where people's relationships and codependencies become part of the discussion. Such efforts should equally extend to the labor conditions that make the development and deployment of AI systems possible. For instance, in early January 2023, reports emerged how OpenAI, the company behind ChatGPT, outsourced the labeling of data as harmful to Kenyan data workers as part of their efforts to reduce users' exposure to toxic-generated content. For little money, data workers have to expose themselves to sexually graphic, violent, and hateful imagery under taxing labor conditions.[87] This begs the question: can we truly call a system fair once it has been rid of its internal biases knowing this was achieved through exploitative labor structures, which rather than the exception, appear to be standard practice?[88]

Finally, one should be careful as to which actors are given the discretionary authority to decide how fairness should be given shape alongside the AI value-chain. For example, the EU AI Act, which governs the use of (high-risk) AI systems, affords considerable power to the providers of those systems as well as (opaque) standardization bodies.[89] Without the public at large, including civil society and academia, having access to meaningful procedural mechanisms, such as the ability to contest, control, or exert influence over the normative assumptions and technical metrics that will be incorporated into AI-systems, the power to choose and define what is fair will be predominantly decided upon by industry actors. This discretion may, in the

85 Ibid.

86 See also: Annette Zimmermann and Chad Lee-Stronach, "Proceed with caution" (2021) *Canadian Journal of Philosophy*, 1.

87 Billy Perrigo, "The $2 per hour workers who made ChatGPT safer" (2023) *Time*, January 18, https://time.com/6247678/openai-chatgpt-kenya-workers/, accessed July 5, 2023.

88 Milagros Miceli and Julian Posada. 2022. The Data-Production Dispositif. Proc. ACM Hum.-Comput. Interact. 6, CSCW2, Article 460 (November 2022), 37 pages. https://doi.org/10.1145/3555561

89 See among others, Article 16 (Obligations of Providers of High-Risk AI Systems), as well as Article 40 (Harmonised Standards and Standardisation Deliverables), read in conjunction with Section 2 (Requirements for High-Risk Systems) of the AI Act. Regulation (EU) 2024/1689 of the European Parliament and of the Council of 13 June 2024 laying down harmonised rules on artificial intelligence and amending Regulations (EC) No 300/2008, (EU) No 167/2013, (EU) No 168/2013, (EU) 2018/858, (EU) 2018/1139 and (EU) 2019/2144 and Directives 2014/90/EU, (EU) 2016/797 and (EU) 2020/1828 (Artificial Intelligence Act)Text with EEA relevance. See also: Nathalie A Smuha et al., "How the EU can achieve legally trustworthy AI: A response to the European Commission's Proposal for an Artificial Intelligence Act" (August 5, 2021) <https://papers.ssrn.com/abstract=3899991> accessed July 21, 2023; Johann Laux, Sandra Wachter, and Brent Mittelstadt, 'Three Pathways for Standardisation and Ethical Disclosure by Default under the European Union Artificial Intelligence Act', *Computer Law & Security Review* 53 (1 July 2024): 105957, https://doi.org/10.1016/j.clsr.2024.105957.

words of Barocas, lead to situations "in which the work done by socially conscious computer scientists working in the service of traditional civil rights goals, which was really meant to be empowering, suddenly becomes something that potentially fits in quite nicely with the existing interests of companies."[90] In other words, it could give those in control of AI the ability to pursue economic interests under the veneer of fairness.[91] In this regard, Sax has argued how the regulation of AI, and the choices made therein, may not only draw inspiration from liberal and deliberative approaches to democracy, but could also consider a more agonistic perspective. While the former try to look for rational consensus among political and ideological conflict through rational and procedural means, agonism questions the ability to solve such conflicts: "from an agonistic perspective, pluralism should be respected and promoted not by designing procedures that help generate consensus, but by always and continuously accommodating spaces and means for the contestation of consensus(-like) positions, actors, and procedures."[92]

4.5 CONCLUSION

The notion of fairness is deep and complex. This chapter could only scratch the surface. This chapter demonstrated how a purely procedural conceptualization of fairness completely detached from the political and normative ideals a society wishes to achieve, is difficult to maintain. In this regard, the moral aspirations a society may have regarding the responsible design and development of AI-systems, and the values AI-developers should respect and incorporate, should be clearly articulated first. When we have succeeded in doing so, we can then start investigating how we could best translate those ideals into procedural principles, policies, and concrete rules that can facilitate the realization of those goals.[93] In this context, we argued that as part of this articulation process, we should not only be focused on

90 Solon Barocas, "Machine learning is a co-opting machine" (*Public Books*, June 18, 2019), www.publicbooks.org/machine-learning-is-a-co-opting-machine/, accessed February 15, 2023.

91 Ben Wagner, "Ethics as an escape from regulation. From 'ethics-washing' to ethics-shopping?" in Emre Bayamlioglu et al. (eds), *BEING PROFILED* (Amsterdam University Press, 2019), www.degruyter.com/view/books/9789048550180/9789048550180-016/9789048550180-016.xml, accessed August 26, 2020; Luciano Floridi, "Translating principles into practices of digital ethics: Five risks of being unethical" (2019) *Philosophy & Technology*, 32: 185; Elettra Bietti, "From ethics washing to ethics bashing: A view on tech ethics from within moral philosophy," *Proceedings of the 2020 Conference on Fairness, Accountability, and Transparency* (Association for Computing Machinery, 2020), https://doi.org/10.1145/3351095.3372860.

92 Marijn Sax, "Algorithmic news diversity and democratic theory: Adding agonism to the mix" (2022) *Digital Journalism*, 10: 1650, 1651. In it, the author draws on the work of political theorist Chantal Mouffe.

93 See also: Wibren van der Burg, "The morality of aspiration: A neglected dimension of law and morality" in Willem Witteveen J. and Wibren van der Burg (eds), *Rediscovering Fuller: Essays on Implicit Law and Institutional Design* (Amsterdam University Press, 2009).

how AI-systems interfere with the distributive shares or outcomes people hold. In addition, we should also pay attention to the relational dynamics AI systems impose and their interference into social processes, structures, and relationships. Moreover, in so doing, we should be informed by the lived experiences of the people that those AI systems threaten to affect the most.

Seeking fairness is an exercise that cannot be performed within, or as part of, the design phase only. Technology may assist in mitigating the societal risks AI systems threaten to impose, but it is not a panacea thereto. The realization of fair AI requires a holistic response; one that incorporates the knowledge of various disciplines, including computer and social sciences, political philosophy, ethics, and the law, and where value-laden decisions are meaningfully informed and open to contestation by a plurality of voices and experiences.

5

Moral Responsibility and Autonomous Technologies

Does AI Face a Responsibility Gap?

Lode Lauwaert and Ann-Katrien Oimann

5.1 INTRODUCTION

There are several ethical conundrums associated with the development and use of AI. Questions around the avoidance of bias, the protection of privacy, and the risks associated with opacity are three examples, which are discussed in several chapters of this book. However, society's increased reliance on autonomous systems also raises questions around responsibility, and more specifically the question whether a so-called responsibility gap exists. When autonomous systems make a mistake, is it unjustified to hold anyone responsible for it?[1] In recent years, several philosophers have answered in the affirmative – we think primarily of Andreas Matthias and Robert Sparrow. If, for example, a self-driving car hits someone, in their opinion, no one can be held responsible. The argument we put forward in this chapter is twofold. First, there does not necessarily exist a responsibility gap in the context of AI systems and second, even if there would be, this is not necessarily a problem.

We proceed as follows. First, we provide some conceptual background by discussing respectively what autonomous systems are, how the notion of responsibility can be understood, and what the responsibility gap is about. Second, we explore to which extent it could make sense to assign responsibility to artificial systems. Third, we argue that the use of autonomous system does not necessarily lead to a responsibility gap. In the fourth and last section of this chapter, we set out why the responsibility gap is not necessarily problematic and provide some concluding remarks.

5.2 CONCEPTUAL CLARIFICATIONS

In the section, we first discuss what autonomous systems are. Next, we explain the concept of responsibility and what the responsibility gap is about. Finally, we describe how the responsibility gap differs from related issues.

[1] By "AI" in this text, we mean "autonomous AI."

5.2.1 *Autonomous Systems*

Before we turn to responsibility, let us begin with a brief exploration of AI systems, which are discussed in more details in the second chapter of this book. One of the most controversial examples are autonomous weapons systems or the so-called "killer robots,"[2] designed to kill without human intervention. It is to date unclear to which extent such technology currently already exists in fully autonomous form, yet the use of AI in warfare (which is also discussed in Chapter 20 of this book) is on the rise. For instance, a report by the UN Panel of Experts on Libya of 2020 mentions the system Kargu-2, a drone which may have hunted down and attacked retreating soldiers without any data connectivity between the operator and the system.[3] Unsurprisingly, the propensity toward ever greater autonomy in weapon systems is also accompanied by much speculation, debate, and protest.

For another example of an AI system, one can think of Sony's 1999 robot dog AIBO, a type of toy that can act as a substitute for a pet, which is capable of learning. The robot dog learns to respond to specific phrases of its "owner," or learns to adapt its originally programmed walking motion to the specific shape of the owner's house. AI systems are, however, not necessarily embedded in hardware. Consider, for instance, a software-based AI system that is capable of detecting lung cancer based on a pattern analysis of radiographic images, which can be especially useful in poorer regions where there are not enough radiologists. Amazon's Mechanical Turk platform is also a good example, as the software autonomously allocates tasks to suitable workers who subscribed to the platform, and subsequently handles their payment in case it – autonomously – verified that the task was adequately carried out. The uptake of AI systems is on the rise in all societal domains, which also means that questions around responsibility arise in various contexts.

5.2.2 *Notions of Responsibility*

The term "responsibility" can be interpreted in several ways. When we say "I am responsible," we can mean more than one thing by it. In general, a distinction can be made between three meanings: causal responsibility, moral responsibility, and role responsibility.[4] We will discuss each in turn.

2 See among others: video Slaughterbots of 2017 by the Future of Life Institute and AI expert Stuart Russell, open letters in 2015 and 2017 by renowned technology experts to raise awareness among the general public around the dangers associated with the technology, The Campaign to Stop Killer Robots calling for a new international treaty.

3 UN Security Council, Final report of the Panel of Experts on Libya established pursuant to Security Council resolution 1973 (2011), S/2021/229, 8 March 2021, https://documents.un.org/doc/undoc/gen/n21/037/72/pdf/n2103772.pdf?token=DtEs8GLFoOLY8vGG39&fe=true

4 These terms already make it clear that we are not concerned here with the domain of the law and are therefore not talking about liability or legal responsibility. For a good overview of the different kinds of responsibility, see Nicole A. Vincent, "A Structured Taxonomy of Responsibility Concepts" in

Suppose a scientist works in a laboratory and uses a glass tube that contains toxic substances that if released would result in the death of many colleagues. Normally the scientist is careful, but a fly in the eye causes her to stumble. The result is that the glass tube breaks and the toxins are released, causing deaths. Asked who is responsible for the havoc, some will answer that it is the scientist. They then understand "responsibility" in a well-defined sense, namely in a causal sense. They mean that the scientist is (causally) responsible because she plays a role in the course of events leading to the undesirable result.

Let us make a slight modification. Say the same scientist works in exactly the same context with exactly the same toxic substances, but now also belongs to a terrorist group and wants the colleagues to die, and therefore deliberately drops the glass tube, resulting in several people dying. We will again hold the scientist responsible, but the content of this responsibility is clearly different from the first kind of responsibility. Without the scientist's morally wrong act, the colleagues would still be alive, and so the scientist is the cause of the colleagues' deaths. So, while the scientist is certainly causally responsible, in this case she will also be morally responsible.

Moral responsibility usually refers to one person, although it can also be about a group or organization. That person is then held responsible for something. Often this "something" is undesirable, such as death, but you can also be held responsible for good things, such as saving people. If a person is morally responsible, it means that others can respond to that person in a certain way: praise or reward when it comes to desirable things; disapproval or punishment when it comes to bad things. In addition, if one were to decide to punish or to reward, it would also mean that it is morally right to punish or reward that person. In other words, there would be good reasons to punish or reward that particular person, and not someone else. Note that moral responsibility does not necessarily involve punishment or reward. It only means that someone is the rightful *candidate* for such a response, that punishment or reward *may* follow. So, I may be responsible for something undesirable, but what happened was not so bad that I should be punished.

The third form, role responsibility, refers to the duties that come with a role or position. Parents are responsible in this sense because they must ensure their children grow up in a safe environment, just as it is the role responsibility of a teacher to ensure a safe learning environment for students. When revisiting the earlier example of the scientist, we can also discuss her responsibility without referring to her role in a chain of events (causal responsibility) or to the practice of punishment and reward (moral responsibility). Those who believe that the scientist is responsible may in fact refer to her duty to watch over the safety of the building, to ensure that the room is properly sealed, or to verify that the glass tubes she uses do not have any cracks.

Nicole Vincent, Ibo van de Poel, and Jeroen van den Hoven (eds), *Moral Responsibility. Library of Ethics and Applied Philosophy* (Dordrecht Springer, 2011) who develops a taxonomy of responsibility concepts inspired by H. L. A Hart's illustration of the drunken ship captain.

These three types of responsibilities are related. The preceding paragraphs make it clear that a person can be causally responsible without being responsible in a moral sense. We typically do not condemn the scientist who trips over a shoelace. Conversely, though, moral responsibility always rests on causal responsibility. We do not hold someone morally responsible if they are in no way part of the process that led to the (un)desired result. That causal involvement, by the way, should be interpreted in a broad sense. Suppose the scientist is following an order. The person who gave the order is then not only causally but also morally responsible, despite not having committed the murder itself. Finally, role responsibility is always accompanied by moral responsibility. If, for example, as a scientist it is your duty to ensure that the laboratory is safe, it follows at least that you are a candidate for moral disapproval or punishment if it turns out that you have not done your duty adequately, or that you can be praised or rewarded if you have met the expectations that come with your role.

5.2.3 *Responsibility Gap*

Autonomous systems lead to a responsibility gap, some claim.[5] But what does one understand by "responsibility" here? Clearly, one is not talking about causal responsibility in this context. AI systems are normally created by humans (we say "normally" because there already exist AI systems that design other AI systems). Therefore, if one would claim that no humans are involved in the creation of AI systems, this would come down to a problematic view of technology.

The responsibility gap is also not about the third form of responsibility namely role responsibility. That argument refers to the duty of engineers, not so much to create more sustainability or well-being, but to make things that have as little undesirable effect on moral values as possible, and thus to think about such possible effects in advance. Since there is no reason why this should not apply to the developers of autonomous systems, the responsibility gap does not mean that developers and users of AI systems have no special duties attached to them. On the contrary, such technology precisely affirms the importance of moral duties. Because the decision-making power is being transferred to that technology, and because it is often impossible to predict exactly what decision will be made, the developers of AI systems must think even more carefully than other tech designers about the possible

[5] See among others: Roos De Jong, "The retribution-gap and responsibility-loci related to robots and automated technologies: A reply to Nyholm" (2020) *Science and Engineering Ethics*, 26; Robert Sparrow, "Killer robots" (2007) *Journal of Applied Philosophy*, 24; Andreas Matthias, "The responsibility gap: Ascribing responsibility for the actions of learning automata" (2004) *Ethics and Information Technology*, 6. The term was first used by Andreas Matthias with respect to autonomous machines (2004) and was later applied to autonomous weapon systems by Robert Sparrow (2007). For a recent overview of the discussion on autonomous weapons, see: Ann-Katrien Oimann, "The responsibility gap and LAWS: A critical mapping of the debate" (2023) *Philosophy & Technology*, 36.

undesirable effects that may result from the algorithms' decisions in, for example, the legal or medical world.[6]

The thesis of the so-called responsibility gap is thus concerned with moral responsibility. It can be clarified as follows: in the case of mistakes made by autonomous AI, despite a possible spontaneous tendency to punish someone, that tendency has no suitable purpose as there is no candidate for punishment.

5.2.4 *Related but Different Issues*

Before we examine whether the thesis of the responsibility gap holds water, it is useful to briefly touch upon the difference between the alleged problem of the responsibility gap and two other problems. The first problem is reminiscent of a particular view of God and the second is the so-called problem of many hands.

Imagine strolling through the city on a sunny afternoon and stepping in chewing gum. You feel it immediately: with every step, your shoe sticks a little to the ground and your mood changes, the sunny afternoon is gone (at least for a while) and you are looking for a culprit. However, the person who left the gum on the ground is long gone. There is definitely someone causally responsible here: someone dropped the gum at some point. And the causally responsible person is also morally responsible. You're not supposed to leave gum, and if you do it anyway, then you're ignoring your civic duty and you're justified in being reprimanded. However, the annoying thing about the situation is that it is not possible to detect the morally responsible person.

The problem in this example is that you do not know who the morally responsible person is, even though there is a responsible person. This is reminiscent of the relationship between man and God as described in the Old Testament. God created the world, but has subsequently distanced Himself so far from His creation that it is impossible for man to perceive Him. In the case of the responsibility gap the problem is of a different nature. Here it is not an epistemic problem, but an ontological problem. The difficulty is not that I do not know who is responsible; the problem is that there is no one morally responsible for the errors caused by an autonomous system, so the lack of knowledge cannot be the problem here.

The second problem that deviates from the responsibility gap is the problem of many hands.[7] This term is used to describe situations where many actors have contributed to an action that has caused harm and it is unclear how responsibility

[6] See in this regard also Hans Jonas' study *Das Prinzip Vernatwortung* (1979), which is one of the first major works on the ethics of technology. Jonas suggested that in a modern world, the effects of technology are not so uncertain that designers need to think about the consequences even more so than before.

[7] The expression "many hands" was reportedly first used by Dennis Thompson, "Moral responsibility and public officials: The problem of many hands" (1980) *American Political Science Review*, 74 and later applied to computer technology by Helen Nissenbaum, "Accountability in a computerized society" (1996) *Science and Engineering Ethics*, 2.

should be allocated. It is often used with respect to new technologies such as AI systems because a large number of actors are involved in their development and use, but the problem also occurs in nontechnical areas such as climate change.

To illustrate this problem, we turn to the disaster of the Herald of Free Enterprise, the boat that capsized on March 6, 1987, resulting in the deaths of nearly 200 people. An investigation revealed that water had flowed into the boat. As a result, the already unstable cargo began to shift to one side. This displacement eventually caused the ferry to disappear under the waves just outside the port of Zeebrugge in Belgium. This fatal outcome was not the result of just one cause. Several things led to the boat capsizing. Doors had been left open, the ship was not stable in the first place, the bulkheads that had been placed on the car deck were not watertight, there were no lights in the captain's cabin, and so on. Needless to say, this implies that several people were involved: the assistant boatman who had gone to sleep and left the doors open; the person who had not checked whether the doors were closed; and finally, the designers of the boat who had not fitted it with lights.

There are so many people involved in this case that not only one person can be held responsible. But this differs from saying that no one is responsible. The case is not an example of an ontological problem; there is no lack of moral responsibility in the case of the capsized ferry. Indeed, there are multiple individuals who are morally responsible. There is, however, an epistemic problem. The problem is that there are so many hands involved that it is very difficult (if not impossible) to know exactly who is responsible for what and to what extent each person involved is responsible. In the case of the Herald of Free Enterprise, many knots had to be untangled in terms of moral responsibility, but that is different from claiming that the use of a technology is associated with a responsibility gap.

5.3 CAN AI BE MORALLY RESPONSIBLE?

Is it true that there is no moral responsibility for mistakes made by an AI system? There is an answer to that question that is often either not taken seriously or overlooked, namely the possibility of AI systems being responsible themselves.[8] To be clear, we refer here to moral responsibility and not the causal type of responsibility. After all, autonomous technologies very often play a causal role in a chain of events with an (un)desirable outcome. Our question is: is it utter nonsense to see an AI system as the object of punishment and reward, praise, and indignation?

One of the sub-domains of philosophy is philosophical anthropology. A central question in that domain is whether there are properties that separate humans from, say, plants and nonhuman animals, as well as from artificial entities. In that context,

[8] An author like Joanna Bryson explicitly rejects this option, emphasizing that autonomous systems are essentially nonexistent and should be viewed as nothing more than tools: Joanna Bryson, "Robots should be slaves" in Yorick Wilks (ed), *Close Engagements with Artificial Companions: Key Social, Psychological, Ethical and Design Issues* (John Benjamins Publishing Company, 2010).

one can think, for instance, of the ability to play and communicate, to suffer psychologically or to get gray hair. However, it is almost impossible not to consider responsibility here. After all, today, we only attribute that moral responsibility to human beings. Sure, there are some exceptions to this rule. For instance, we do not hold people with mental disabilities or disorders responsible for a number of things. And we also punish and reward animals that are not humans. But moral responsibility is something we currently reserve exclusively for humans, and thus do not attribute to artifacts.

Part of the reason we do not hold artificial entities responsible has to do with what responsibility entails. We recall that a morally responsible person is the justifiable target of moral reactions such as punishment and reward, anger and indignation. Those reactions do not necessarily follow, but if they follow then the responsible person is the one who is justifiably the subject of such a reaction. But that presupposes the possibility of some form of sensation, the ability to be affected in the broad sense, whether on a mental or physical level. There is no point in designating someone as responsible if that person cannot be affected by the moral reactions of others. But where do we draw the line? Of course, the ability to experience pain or pleasure in the broad sense of the word is not sufficient to be morally responsible. This is evident from our dealings with nonhuman animals: dogs can experience pain and pleasure, but we do not hold them responsible when they tip a vase with their tail. However, the ability to be physically or mentally affected by another's reaction is a necessary condition. And since artifacts such as autonomous technologies do not currently have that ability, it would be downright absurd to hold them responsible for what they do.

On the other hand, moral practices are not necessarily fixed forever. They can change over the course of history. Think about the allocation of legal rights. At the end of the eighteenth century, people were still arguing against women's rights based on the following argument: if we grant rights to women, then we must also grant rights to animals. The concealed assumption was that animal rights are unthinkable. Meanwhile, it is completely immoral to deny women rights that are equal to those of men. One can also think of the example of the robot Sophia who was granted citizenship of Saudi Arabia in 2017. If throughout history more and more people have been granted rights, and if other moral practices have changed over time, why couldn't there be a change when it comes to moral responsibility? At the time of writing, we cannot hold artifacts responsible; but might it be possible in the future?

That question only makes sense if it is not excluded that robots in the future may be affected on a physical or mental level, and they may later experience pain or pleasure in some way. If that ability can never exist, then it is out of the question that our moral attitudes will change, then we will never hold AI systems morally responsible. And exactly that, some say, is the most realistic scenario: we will never praise technology because it will never be capable of sensation on a physical or mental level.

Much can be said about that assertion. We will limit ourselves to a brief response to the following thought experiment that is sometimes given to support that claim.

Suppose a robot that looks like a human falls down the stairs and reacts as humans normally do by providing the output that usually follows the feeling of pain: yelling, crying, and so on. Is the robot in pain? Someone may react to the robot's fall, for example, because it is a human reflex to react to signs of pain. However, one is unlikely to respond because the robot is in pain. Although the robot does show signs of pain, there is no pain, just as computer programs such as Google Translate and DeepL do not really understand the sentence that they can nevertheless translate perfectly.

AI can produce things that indicate pain in humans, but those signals, in the case of the software, are not in themselves a sufficient reason to conclude that the technology is in pain. However, we cannot conclude at this point that AI systems will never be able to experience pain nor exclude that machines will never be able to be affected mentally. Indeed, next to software, technologies usually consist of hardware as well and the latter might be a reason not to immediately cast aside the possibility of pain.[9] Why?

Like all physiological systems of a human body, the nervous system is made up of cells, mainly neurons, which constantly interact. This causal link ensures that incoming signals lead to the sensation of pain. Now, suppose that you are beaten up, and that for 60 minutes, you are actually in pain, but that science has advanced to the point where the neurons can be replaced by a prosthesis, microchips, for example, without it making any difference otherwise. The chips are made on a slice of silicon – but other than that, those artificial entities do exactly the same thing as the neurons: they send signals to other cells and provide sensation. Well, imagine that, during one month and step by step, a scientist replaces every cell with a microchip so that your body is no longer only made up of cells but also of chips. Is it still utter nonsense to claim that robots might one day be able to feel pain?

To avoid confusion, we would like to stress the following: we are not claiming that intelligent systems will one day be able to feel pain, that robots will one day resemble us – us, humans – in terms of sensation. At most, the last thought experiment was meant to indicate that it is perhaps a bit short-sighted to simply brush this option aside as nonsense. Furthermore, if it does turn out that AI systems can experience pain, we will not automatically hold them morally responsible for the things they do. The reason is that the ability to feel pain is not enough to be held responsible. Our relationships with nonhuman animals, for example, demonstrate

9 Debates about embodied information are discussed for many years in philosophy of mind. In this regard, see, among others: Daniel Dennett, *Consciousness Explained* (Little Brown, 1992); John Rogers Searle, "Minds, brains, and programs" (1980) *The Behavioral and Brain Sciences*, 3: 417–57; Hubert Dreyfus, *What Computers Can't Do: The Limits of Artificial Intelligence* (Harper & Row, 1972); Alan Turing, "Computer Machinery and Intelligence" in Edward A. Feigenbaum and Julian Feldman (eds), *Computers and Thought* (McGraw-Hill, 1963).

this, as we pointed out earlier. Suppose, however, that all conditions are met (we will explain the conditions in the next section), would that immediately imply that we will see AI systems as candidates for punishment and reward? Attributing responsibility exclusively to humans is an age-old moral practice, which is why this may not change any time soon. At the same time, history shows that moral practices are not necessarily eternal, and that the time-honored practice of attributing rights only to humans is only gradually changing in favor of animals that are not humans. That alone is a reason to suspect that ascribing moral responsibility to robots may not become a reality in the near future, even if robots could be affected physically or mentally by reward or punishment.

5.4 THERE IS NO RESPONSIBILITY GAP

So we must return to the central question: do AI systems create a responsibility gap? Technologies themselves cannot be held morally responsible today, but does the same apply to the people behind the technology?

There is reason to suspect that you can hold people morally responsible for mistakes made by an AI system. Consider an army officer who engages a child soldier. The child is given a weapon to fight the enemy. But in the end, the child kills innocent civilians, thus committing a war crime. Perhaps not many people would say that the child is responsible for the civilian casualties, but in all likelihood we would believe that at least someone is responsible, that is, the officer. However, is there a difference between this case and the use of, for example, autonomous weapons? If so, is that difference relevant? Of course, child soldiers are human beings, robots are not. In both cases, however, a person undertakes an action knowing that undesirable situations may follow and that one can no longer control them. If the officer is morally responsible, why shouldn't the same apply to those who decide to use autonomous AI systems? Are autonomous weapons and other autonomous AI systems something exceptional in that regard?

At the same time, there is also reason to be skeptical about the possibility of assigning moral responsibility. Suppose you are a soldier and kill a terror suspect. If you used a classic weapon that functions as it should, a 9-mm pistol for example, then without a doubt you are entirely – or at least to a large extent – responsible for the death of the suspect. Suppose, however, that you want to kill the same person, and you only have a semiautomatic drone. You are in a room far away from the war zone where the suspect is, and you give the drone all the information about the person you are looking for. The drone is able to scout the area itself, and when the technology indicates that the search process is over, you can assess the result of the search and then decide whether or not the drone should fire. Based on the information you gathered, you give the order to fire. But what actually happens? The person killed is not the terror suspect and was therefore killed by mistake. That mistake has everything to do with a manufacturing error, which led to a defect in the drone's operating. Of course, that does not imply that you are in no way morally responsible for the death of the suspect. So, there is no responsibility gap, but probably most people would feel justified in saying that you are less responsible than if you used a 9-mm pistol. This has to do with the fact that the decision to fire is based on information that comes not from yourself but from the drone, information that incidentally happens to be incorrect.

For many, the decrease in the soldier's causal role through technology is accompanied by a decrease in responsibility. The siphoning off of an activity – the acquisition of information –implies, not that humans are not responsible, but that they are responsible to a lesser degree. This fuels the suspicion that devolving all decisions onto AI systems leads to the so-called responsibility gap. But is that suspicion correct? If not, why? These questions bring us to the heart of the analysis of the issue of moral responsibility and AI.

5.4.1 *Conditions for Responsibility*

Our thesis is that reliance on autonomous technologies does not imply that we can never hold anyone responsible for their mistakes. To argue this, we must consider whether the classical conditions for responsibility are also met. We already referred to the capacity for sensation in the broad sense of the word, but what other conditions must be fulfilled for someone to be held responsible? Classically, these are three sufficient conditions for moral responsibility: causal responsibility, autonomy, and knowledge.

It goes without saying that moral responsibility presupposes causal responsibility. Someone who is not involved at all in the creation of the (undesirable) result of an action cannot be held morally responsible for that result. In the context of AI systems, several people meet this condition: the programmer, the manufacturer, and the user. However, this does not mean that we have undermined the responsibility gap theorem. Not every (causal) involvement is associated with moral responsibility. Recall the example of the scientist in the laboratory we discussed earlier: we do hold the scientist responsible, but only in a causal sense.

Thus, more is needed. Moral responsibility also requires autonomy. This concept can be understood in at least two ways. First, "autonomy" can be interpreted in a negative way. In that case, it means that the one who is autonomous in that respect can function completely independently, without human intervention. For our reasoning, only the second, positive form is relevant. This variant means that you can weigh things against each other, and that you can make your own decision based on that. However, the fact that you are able to deliberate and decide is not sufficient to be held morally responsible. For example, you may make the justifiable decision to kill the king, but when the king is killed, you are not necessarily responsible for it, for example, because someone else does it just before you pull the trigger and independently of your decision. You are only responsible if your deliberate decision is at the root of the murder, that is, if there is a causal link between the autonomy and the act.

Knowledge is the final condition. You can only be held morally responsible if you have the necessary relevant knowledge.[10] One who does not know that an action is wrong cannot be responsible for it. Furthermore, if the consequences of an act are unforeseeable, then you cannot be punished either. Note that, the absence of knowledge does not necessarily exonerate you. If you may not know certain things while you should have known them, and the lack of knowledge leads to an undesirable result, then you are still morally responsible for that result. For example, if a driver runs a red light and causes an accident as a result, then the driver is still responsible for the accident, even if it turns out that she was unaware of the prohibition against running a red light. After all, it is your duty as a citizen and car driver – read: your role responsibility – to be aware of that rule.[11]

5.4.2 *Control as Requirement*

So, whoever is involved in the use of a technology, whoever makes the well-considered decision to use that technology, and whoever is aware of the necessary relevant consequences of that technology, they can all be held morally responsible for everything that goes wrong with the technology. At least that is what the classical analysis of responsibility implies. So why do authors such as Matthias and Sparrow nevertheless conclude that there are responsibility gaps?

They point to an additional condition that must be met. Once an action or certain course of events has been set in motion, they believe you must have control over it. So even if you are causally involved, for example, because you have made the decision that the action or course of events should take place, while you can do nothing else about it at the time it was initiated, it would be unfair to punish you when it all results in an undesirable outcome. They argue that, since AI systems can function completely independently, in such a way that you cannot influence their decisions due to their high degree of autonomy and capacity for self-learning, you cannot hold anyone responsible for the consequences.

10 According to an ordinary conception of responsibility attribution, it is only fitting to hold someone responsible if the agent can foresee that the device will or is likely to create a certain kind of outcome. This is usually termed the epistemic condition and many philosophers agree that such a requirement is a necessary condition for moral responsibility. See among others: John Martin Fischer and Neal A. Tognazzini, "The truth about tracing" (2009) *Noûs*, 43; John Martin Fischer and Mark Ravizza, *Responsibility and Control: A Theory of Moral Responsibility* (Cambridge University Press, 2000); Michael J. Zimmerman, "Moral responsibility and ignorance" (1997) *Ethics*, 107.

11 The epistemic condition often relies on a *tracing* strategy and plays an important role in many theories of responsibility. It is used in cases where an agent is blameworthy for the harm caused based on the ground that her responsibility can be traced back to previous acts of the agent when she did meet the conditions to fulfill on moral responsibility. See for example: John Martin Fischer and Neal A. Tognazzini, "The truth about tracing" (2009) *Noûs*, 43.

If you are held responsible for an action, it usually means that you have control. As CEO, I am responsible for my company's poor numbers because I could have made different decisions that benefited the company more. Conversely, I have no control over a large number of factors and thus bear no responsibility for them. For example, I have no control over the weather conditions, nor do I bear any responsibility for the consequences of good or bad weather. Thus, responsibility is often accompanied by control, just as the absence of control is usually accompanied by the absence of responsibility. Yet we argue that it is false to say that you must have control over an initiated action or course of events to be held responsible, and that not having control takes away your responsibility. This is demonstrated by the following.

Imagine you are driving and after a few minutes, you have an epileptic seizure that causes you to lose control of the wheel and to seriously injure a cyclist. It is not certain that you will be punished, let alone receive a severe sentence, but perhaps few, if any, will hold you responsible for the cyclist's injury, in spite of your lack of control of the car's steering wheel. This is mainly the case because you possess all the relevant knowledge. You do not know that a seizure will occur within a few minutes, but as someone with epilepsy you do know that there is a risk of a seizure and that it may be accompanied by an accident. Furthermore, you are autonomous (in a positive sense). You are able to weigh up the desire to drive somewhere by yourself against the risk of an attack, and to decide on that basis. Finally, you purposefully get in the car. As a result, you are causally connected to the undesirable consequence in a way that sufficiently grounds moral responsibility. After all, if you decide knowing that it may lead to undesirable consequences, then you are justified in considering yourself a candidate for punishment at the time the undesirable consequence actually occurs. Again, it is not certain that punishment will follow, but those who take a risk are responsible for that risk, and thus can be punished when it turns out that the undesirable consequence actually occurs.

We can conclude from the above that not having control does not absolve moral responsibility. Therefore, we do not believe that AI systems are associated with a responsibility gap due to a lack of control over the technology. However, we cannot conclude from the foregoing that the idea of a responsibility gap in the case of autonomous AI is incorrect and that in all cases someone is responsible for the errors caused by that technology. After all, perhaps situations might occur in which the other conditions for moral responsibility are not met, thus still leading us to conclude that the use of autonomous AI goes hand in hand with a responsibility gap.

5.4.3 *Is Someone Responsible?*

To prove that it is not true that no one can ever be held responsible, we invoke some previously cited examples: a civilian is killed by an autonomous weapon and a self-driving car hits a cyclist.

To begin with, it is important to note that both dramatic accidents are the result of a long chain of events that stretch from the demand for production, through the search for funding, and finally to the programming and use. If we are looking for a culprit, we might be able to identify several people – one could think of the designer or producer, for example – but the most obvious culprit is the user: the commander who decides to deploy an autonomous weapon during a conflict, or the occupant of the autonomous car. It is justified to put them forward as candidates for punishment for the following reasons, just as the epilepsy patient is responsible for the cyclist's injury.

First of all, both are aware of the context of the use and of the possible undesirable consequences. They do not know whether or not an accident will happen, let alone where and when exactly. After all, autonomous cars and weapons are (mainly) based on machine learning, which means that it is not (always) possible to predict what decision will be made. But the kinds of accidents that can happen are not unlimited. Killing civilians and destroying their homes (autonomous weapons) and hitting a cyclist or crashing into a group of people (self-driving car) are dramatic but foreseeable; as a user, you know such things can happen. And if you don't know, that is a failure from your part: you should know. It is your duty, your role responsibility, to consider the possible negative consequences of the things you use.

Second, both commander and owner are sufficiently autonomous. They are able to weigh up the advantages and disadvantages: the chance of fewer deaths in their own ranks and war crimes (autonomous weapons), the chance of being able to work while on the move and traffic casualties (self-driving car).

Third, if, based on these considerations, the decision is made to effectively pursue the use of autonomous cars and weapons, while knowing that it may bring undesirable consequences, then it is justifiable to hold both the commander and owner responsible for deliberately allowing the undesirable anticipated consequences to occur. Those who take risks accept responsibility for that risk; they accept that they may be penalized in the event that the unwanted, unforeseen consequence actually occurs.

Thus, in terms of responsibility, the use of AI systems is consistent with an existing moral practice. Just as you can hold people responsible for using nonautonomous technologies, people are also responsible for things over which they have no control but with which they are connected in a relevant way. So not only does the autonomy of technology not erase the role responsibility of the user; it does not absolve moral responsibility either. The path the system takes to decide may be completely opaque to the user, but the system does not create a responsibility gap.

Those who disagree must either demonstrate what is wrong with the existing moral practice in which we ascribe responsibility to people or demonstrate the relevant difference between moral responsibility in the case of autonomous systems and everyday moral practice. Of course, there are differences between using an autonomous system on the one hand and driving a car as a patient on the other. The question, however, is whether those differences matter when it comes to moral responsibility.

To be clear, our claim here is only that the absence of control does not necessarily lead to a gap. The thesis we put forward is not that there can never be a gap in the case of AI. The reason is that the third, epistemic condition must be met. There is no gap if the consequences are and should be foreseen (and if there is autonomy and a causal link). In contrast, there may be a gap in case the consequences are unforeseeable (or in case one of the other conditions is not met).

5.5 IS A RESPONSIBILITY GAP PROBLEMATIC?

We think there are good reasons to believe that at least someone is responsible when autonomous AI makes mistakes – maybe there is even collective responsibility[12] – since it is sufficient to identify one responsible person to undermine the thesis of a responsibility gap (assuming the other conditions are met). However, suppose that our analysis goes wrong in several places, and that you really cannot hold anyone responsible for the damage caused by the toy robot AIBO, Google's self-driving car, Amazon's recruitment system, or the autonomous weapon system. In that case, would that make an argument for the conclusion that ethics is being disrupted by autonomous systems? In other words, would this gap also be morally problematic? To answer that question, we look at two explanations for the existence of the practice of responsibility. The first has to do with prevention; the second points to the symbolic meaning of punishment.

Someone robs a bank, a soldier kills a civilian, and a car driver ignores a red light: these are all examples of undesirable situations that we, as a society, do not want to happen. To prevent this, to ensure that the norm is not infringed again later, something like the imputation of responsibility was created, a moral practice based on the psychological mechanism of classical conditioning. After a violation, a person is held responsible and is a candidate for unpleasant treatment, with the goal of preventing the violation from happening again in the future.

That goal, prevention, must obviously be there, and it is clear that the means – punishing the responsible party – is often sufficient to achieve the goal. Yet prevention is not necessarily related to punishment; punishing the person responsible is not necessary for the purpose of prevention. There are ways other than punishment to ensure that the same mistake is not made again. You can teach people to follow the rules, for example, by giving them extra explanations and setting a good example. It is possible that undesirable situations will not occur in the future without moral responsibility. This appears to be exactly the case in the context of AI.

Take an algorithm that ignores all women's cover letters, or the Amazon Mechanical Turk platform that wrongfully blocks your account, preventing you

[12] It is debated whether collective entities can be qualified as group agents that can be held morally responsible. See: Neta C. Crawford "Organizational responsibility" in *Accountability for Killing: Moral Responsibility for Collateral Damage in America's Post-9/11 Wars* (Oxford University Press, 2013); Christian List, "Group agency and artificial intelligence" (2021) *Philosophy & Technology*, 34.

from accepting jobs. To prevent such a morally problematic event from occurring again in the future, it is natural that the AI system is tinkered with by someone with sufficient technical knowledge, such as the programmer. It is quite possible that the system has so many layers that the designer cannot see the problem and therefore cannot fix it. But it is also possible that the programmer can successfully intervene, to the extent that the AI system will not make that mistake in future. In that case, the technical work is sufficient for preventing the problem, and further, for the purpose of prevention, you don't need anyone to be a candidate for punishment – we raise again that this is the definition of moral responsibility. In other words, if the goal is purely preventive in nature, then the solely technical intervention of the designer can suffice and thus the alleged absence of moral responsibility is not a problem.

There is another purpose that is often cited to justify the imputation of responsibility. That purpose has a symbolic character. Namely, it is about respecting the dignity of a human being. Is that goal, too, related to the designation of a candidate for punishment? In light of that objective, would a responsibility gap be a problem?

In a liberal democracy, everyone has moral standing. Whatever your characteristics are and regardless of what you do, you have moral standing due to the mere fact of being a human, and that counts for everyone. That value is only substantial insofar as legal rights are attached to that value. The principle that every human being has moral value implies that you have rights and that others have duties toward you. Among other things, you have the right to education and employment, and others may not intentionally hurt or insult you without good reason. It is permitted for an employer to decide not to hire you on the basis of relevant criteria, but it flagrantly violates your status as a being with moral standing if they belittle or ridicule you during a job interview without good reason.

Imagine the latter happens. This is a problem, because it is a denial of the fact that you have moral standing. Well, the practice of imputing moral responsibility is at least in part a response to such a problem. Something undesirable takes place – a person's dignity is violated – and in response someone is punished, or at least that person is designated as a candidate for punishment. Punishment here means that a person is hurt and experiences an unpleasant sensation, something that you do not wish for. Now the purpose of that punishment, that unpleasant experience, is to underscore that the violation of dignity was a moral wrong, and thus to affirm the dignity of the victim. The punishment does not heal the wound or undo the error, but it has symbolic importance. It cuts through the denial of the moral status that was inherent to the crime.

The affirmation of moral value is clearly a good, and a goal that can be realized by means of punishment. However, it is questionable whether that goal can be achieved exclusively by these means. Suppose an autonomous weapon kills a soldier. Suppose, moreover, that it is true, contrary to what we have just argued, that no one can be held responsible for this death. Does that mean that the moral value of the soldier can no longer be emphasized? It is true that assigning responsibility expresses the idea that the value of the soldier is taken seriously. Moreover, it is undoubtedly desirable that, out of respect for the value of individual, someone should be designated as a candidate for punishment. However, the claim that responsibility is necessary for the recognition of dignity is false. One can also do justice to the deceased without holding anyone responsible. Perhaps the most obvious example of this is a funeral. After all, the significance of this ritual lies primarily in the fact that it underscores that the deceased has intrinsic value.

To be clear, we are not claiming that ascribing moral responsibility is a meaningless practice. Nor do we mean to say that, if the use of AI led to a gap, the impossibility of holding someone responsible would never be a problem. Our point is that prevention and respect are not in themselves sufficient reasons to conclude that a responsibility gap in the context of AI is a moral tragedy.[13]

5.6 CONCLUSION

AI offers many opportunities, but also comes with (potential) problems – many of which are discussed in the various chapters of this handbook. In this contribution, we focused on the relationship between AI and moral responsibility, and make two arguments. First, the use of autonomous AI does not necessarily involve a responsibility gap. Second, even if this were the case, we argued why that is not necessarily morally problematic.

[13] This manuscript is based partly on: Lode Lauwaert, *Wij robots: Een filosofische blik op technologie en artificiële intelligentie* (LannooCampus, 2021); Lode Lauwaert, "Artificial intelligence and responsibility" (2021) *AI & Society*; Lode Lauwaert, "Artificiële intelligentie en normatieve ethiek: Wie is verantwoordelijk voor de misdaden van LAWS?" (2019) *Algemeen Nederlands tijdschrift voor wijsbegeerte*.

6

Artificial Intelligence, Power and Sustainability*

Gry Hasselbalch and Aimee Van Wynsberghe

6.1 INTRODUCTION

Artificial intelligence (AI) has the potential to address several issues related to sustainable development. It can be used to predict the environmental impact of certain actions, to optimize resource use and streamline production processes. However, AI is also unsustainable in numerous ways, both environmentally and socially. From an environmental perspective, both the training of AI algorithms and the processing and storing of the data used to train AI systems result in heavy carbon emissions, not to mention the mineral extraction, water and land usage that is associated with the technology's development. From a social perspective, AI to date has worked to maintain discriminatory impacts on minorities and vulnerable demographics resulting from nonrepresentative and biased training data sets. It has also been used to carry out invisible surveillance practices or to influence democratic elections through microtargeting. These issues highlight the need to address the long-term sustainability of AI, and to avoid getting caught up in the hype, power dynamics, and competition surrounding this technology.

In this chapter we outline the *ethical dilemma of sustainable AI*, centering on AI as a technology that can help tackle some of the biggest challenges of an evolving global sustainable development agenda, while at the same time in and by itself may adversely impact our social, personal, and natural environments now and for future generations.

In the first part of the chapter, AI is discussed against the background of the global sustainable development agenda. We then continue to discuss AI for sustainability

* Thank you to the Data Pollution & Power Group at the Bonn Sustainable AI Lab for empowering discussions: Carolina Aguerre, Larissa Bolte, Jenny Brennan, Signe Daugbjerg, Lynn H. Kaack, Federica Lucivero, Pak-Hang Wong, and Sebnem Yardimci-Geyikci. A portion of this work has been funded through the Alexander von Humboldt Foundation through the professorship of Prof. Dr. Aimee van Wynsberghe.

and the sustainability of AI,[1] which includes a view on the physical infrastructure of AI and what this means in terms of the exploitation of people and the planet. Here, we also use the example of "data pollution" to examine the sustainability of AI from multiple angles.[2] In the last part of the chapter, we explore the ethical implications of AI on sustainability. Here, we apply a "data ethics of power"[3] as an analytical tool that can help further explore the power dynamics that shape the ethical implications of AI for the sustainable development agenda and its goals.

6.2 AI AND THE GLOBAL SUSTAINABLE DEVELOPMENT AGENDA

Public and policy discourse around AI is often characterized by hype and technological determinism. Companies are increasingly marketing their big data initiatives as "AI" projects[4] and AI has gained significant strategic importance in geopolitics as a symbol of regions' and countries' competitive advantages in the world. However, in all of this, it is important to remember that AI is a human technology with far-reaching consequences for our environment and future societies. Consequently, the ethical implications of AI must be considered integral to the ongoing global public and policy agenda on sustainable development. Here, the socio-technical constitution of AI necessitates reflection on its sustainability in our present and a new narrative about the role it plays in our common futures.[5] The "sustainable" approach is one that is inclusive in both time and space; where the past, present, and future of human societies, the planet, and environment are considered equally important to protect and secure, as is the integration of all countries in economic and social change.[6] Furthermore, our use of the concept "sustainable" demands we ask what practices in the current development and use of AI we want to maintain and alternatively what practices we want to repair and/or change.

AI technologies are today widely recognized as having the potential to help achieve sustainability goals such as those outlined in the EU's Green Deal[7] and

1 Aimee van Wynsberghe, "Sustainable AI: AI for sustainability and the sustainability of AI" (2021) *AI and Ethics*, 1: 213, 218.

2 Gry Hasselbalch, "Data pollution & power: A white paper for a global sustainable development agenda on AI" (2022), www.datapollution.eu/, accessed June 27, 2023.

3 Gry Hasselbalch, *Data Ethics of Power. A Human Approach in the Big Data and AI Era* (Edward Elgar, 2021).

4 Madeleine C Elish and Danah Boyd, "Situating methods in the magic of big data and artificial intelligence" (2018) *Communication Monographs*, 85: 57.

5 Francesco Lapenta, *Our Common AI Future* (JCU Future and Innovation, 2021).

6 As outlined throughout the "Brundtland report"/World Commission on Environment and Development, "Our Common Future," https://sustainabledevelopment.un.org/content/documents/5987our-common-future.pdf, accessed June 6, 2023.

7 Council of the European Union, *European Green Deal*, accessed July 19, 2024: www.consilium.europa.eu/en/policies/green-deal/

the UN's Sustainable Development goals.[8] Indeed, AI can be deployed for climate action by turning raw data into actionable information. For example, AI systems can analyze satellite images and identify deforestation or help improve predictions with forecasts of solar power generation to balance electrical grids. In cities, AI can be used for smart waste management, to measure air pollution, or to reduce energy use in city lighting.[9]

However, the ethical implications of AI are also intertwined with the sustainability of our social, personal, and natural environments. As described before, AI's impacts on those environments come in many shapes and forms, such as carbon footprints,[10] biased or "oppressive" search algorithms,[11] or the use of AI systems for microtargeting voters on social media.[12] It is hence becoming increasingly evident that – if AI is in and by itself an unsustainable technology – it cannot help us reach the sustainable development goals that have been defined and refined over decades by multiple stakeholders.

Awareness of the double edge of technological progress and the role of humans in the environment has long been a central part of the global political agenda of collaborative sustainable action. The United Nations Conference on the Human Environment, held in Stockholm in 1972, was the first global conference to recognize the impact of science and technology on the environment and emphasize the need for global collaboration and action stating. As the report from the conference states:

> In the long and tortuous evolution of the human race on this planet, a stage has been reached when, through the rapid acceleration of science and technology, man has acquired the power to transform his environment in countless ways and on an unprecedented scale.[13]

This report also coined the term "Environmentally Sound Technologies" (ESTs) to refer to technologies or technological systems that can help reduce

[8] United Nations, "The future we want outcome document" (United Nations Conference on Sustainable Development, Rio de Janeiro, Brazil, 2012).

[9] Global Partnership on AI Report, "Climate change and AI. Recommendations for government action" (November 2021), GPAI, www.gpai.ai/projects/climate-change-and-ai.pdf, accessed June 6, 2023, 18–19.

[10] Alan Winfield, "Energy and exploitation: AIs dirty secrets" (June 28, 2019), https://alanwinfield.blogspot.com/2019/06/energy-and-exploitation-ais-dirty.html, accessed June 27, 2023.
Lynn H Kaack et al., "Aligning artificial intelligence with climate change mitigation" (2022) *Nature Climate Change*, 12: 518.

[11] As described in Safiya U Noble, *Algorithms of Oppression: How Search Engines Reinforce Racism* (NYU Press, 2018).
Tolga Bolukbasi et al., "Man is to computer programmer as woman is to homemaker? Debiasing word embeddings" (30th Conference on Neural Information Processing Systems, Barcelona, 2016).

[12] As described in Christopher Wylie, *Mindf*ck: Cambridge Analytica and the Plot to Break America* (Random House, 2019).

[13] Report of the United Nations Conference on the Human Environment, Stockholm, June 5–16, 1972, 3. Quoted in Gry Hasselbalch, "Data pollution & power: A white paper for a global sustainable development agenda on AI" (2022), www.datapollution.eu/, accessed June 27, 2023.

environmental pollution while being sustainable in their design, implementation, and adoption.

The Brundtland report *Our Common Future*,[14] published in 1987 by the United Nations, further developed the direction for the sustainable development agenda. It drew attention to the fact that global environmental problems are primarily the result of the poverty of the Global South and the unsustainable consumption and production in the Global North. Thus, the report emphasized that while risks of cross-border technology use are shared globally, the activities that give rise to the risks as well as the benefits received from the use of these technologies are concentrated in a few countries.

At the United Nations Conference on Environment and Development (UNCED) held in Brazil in 1992, also known as the *Earth Summit*, the "Agenda 21 Action Plan" was created calling on governments and other influential stakeholders to implement a variety of strategies to achieve sustainable development in the twenty-first century. The plan reiterated the importance of developing and transferring ESTs: *"Environmentally sound technologies protect the environment, are less polluting, use all resources in a more sustainable manner, recycle more of their wastes and products, and handle residual wastes in a more acceptable manner than the technologies for which they were substitutes."*[15]

In a subsequent step, the United Nations Member States adopted the 17 Sustainable Development Goals (SDGs) in 2015 as part of the UN 2030 Agenda for Sustainable Development. The goals are set to achieve a balance between economic, social, and environmental sustainability and address issues such as climate change, healthcare and education, inequality, and economic growth.[16] They also emphasized the need for ESTs to achieve these goals and stressed the importance of adopting environmentally sound development strategies and technologies.[17]

If we look at how the global policy agenda on AI and sustainability has developed in tandem with the sustainable development agenda, the intersection of AI and sustainability become clear. Hasselbalch[18] has illustrated how a focus on AI and sustainability is the result of a recognition of the ethical and social implications of AI combined with a long-standing focus on the environmental impact of science and

[14] World Commission on Environment and Development, *Our Common Future* (1987), https://sustainabledevelopment.un.org/content/documents/5987our-common-future.pdf, accessed June 27, 2023.

[15] United Nations, "Agenda 21" (United Nations Conference on Environment & Development, Rio de Janeiro, June 3–14, 1992).

[16] United Nations, "Transforming our world: The 2030 agenda for sustainable development" (March 22–24, 2023), https://sdgs.un.org/2030agenda, accessed June 6, 2023.

[17] UN Environment Programme, "Environmentally sound technologies," www.unep.org/regions/asia-and-pacific/regional-initiatives/supporting-resource-efficiency/environmentally-sound, accessed June 6, 2023. Quoted in Gry Hasselbalch, "Data pollution & power: A white paper for a global sustainable development agenda on AI" (2022), www.datapollution.eu/, accessed June 27, 2023.

[18] Ibid., Hasselbalch, 2022, 36–49.

technology in a global and increasingly inclusive sustainable development agenda. In this context, the growing awareness of AI's potential to support sustainable development goals is discussed in several AI policies, strategies, research efforts, and investments in green transitions and circular economies around the world.[19]

In this regard, the European Union (EU) has been taking a particularly prominent role in establishing policies and regulations for the responsible and sustainable development of AI. In 2018, the European Commission for instance established the High-Level Group on AI (HLEG),[20] as part of its *European AI Strategy*, tasked with the development of ethics guidelines as well as policy and investment recommendations for AI within the EU. The group was composed of 52 individual experts and representatives from various stakeholder groups. The HLEG developed seven key requirements that AI systems should meet in order to be considered trustworthy. One of these requirements specifically emphasized "societal and environmental well-being":

> AI systems should benefit all human beings, including future generations. It must hence be ensured that they are sustainable and environmentally friendly. Moreover, they should take into account the environment, including other living beings, and their social and societal impact should be carefully considered.[21]

The establishment of the HLEG on AI and the publication of its ethics guidelines and requirements illustrate a growing awareness in the EU of the environmental impact of AI on society and the natural environment. The EU's Green Deal presented in 2019 highlighted several environmental considerations related to AI and emphasized that the principles of sustainability must be a fundamental starting point for not only the development of AI technologies but also the creation of a digital society.

Furthermore, the European Commission's *Communication on Fostering a European approach to artificial intelligence*[22] and its revised Coordinated Plan on AI emphasized the European Green Deal's encouragement to use AI to achieve its objectives and establish leadership in environmental and climate change related sectors. This includes activities aimed at developing trustworthy (values-based with

[19] See, for example, The EU's Green Deal (Ibid. Council of the European Union) and AI Strategy (https://digital-strategy.ec.europa.eu/en/policies/european-approach-artificial-intelligence accessed July 19, 2024) and AI for SDGs Canada, www.ai4sdgs.org/, accessed June 6, 2023;
United Nations, "The United Nation's Resource Guide on Artificial Intelligence (AI) Strategies, June 2021," https://sdgs.un.org/sites/default/files/2021-06/Resource%20Guide%20on%20AI%20Strategies_June%202021.pdf, accessed June 6, 2023.

[20] The authors of this chapter were members of the HLEG.

[21] European Commission, "Ethics guidelines for trustworthy AI" (HLEG A, 2019), https://digital-strategy.ec.europa.eu/en/library/ethics-guidelines-trustworthy-ai, accessed June 6, 2023.

[22] European Commission, "Communication on fostering a European approach to artificial intelligence" (April 21, 2021), https://digital-strategy.ec.europa.eu/en/library/communication-fostering-european-approach-artificial-intelligence, accessed June 6, 2023.

a "culture by design" approach[23]) AI systems, as well as an environmentally sound AI socio-technical infrastructure for the EU. For example, the European Commission's proposal on the world's first comprehensive AI legislation lays down a uniform legal framework for the development, marketing and use of AI according to Union values based on the categorization of risks posed by AI systems to the fundamental rights and safety of citizens. In early 2023, the European Parliament suggested adding further transparency requirements on AI's environmental impact to the proposal. Moreover, the coordinated plan on AI also focuses on creating a "green deal data space" and seeks to incorporate environmental concerns in international coordination and cooperation on AI.

6.3 AI FOR SUSTAINABILITY AND THE SUSTAINABILITY OF AI

In 2019, van Wynsberghe argued that the field of AI ethics has neglected the value of sustainability in its discourse on AI. Instead, at the time, this field was concentrated on case studies and particular applications that allowed industry and academics to ignore the larger systemic issues related to the design, development, and use of AI. Sustainable AI, as van Wynsberghe proposed, forces one to take a step back from individual applications and to see the bigger picture, including the physical infrastructure of AI and what this means in terms of the exploitation of people and the planet. Van Wynsberghe defines Sustainable AI as "*a movement to foster change in the entire lifecycle of AI products (i.e. idea generation, training, re-tuning, implementation, governance) towards greater ecological integrity and social justice*."[24] She also outlines two branches of sustainable AI: "AI for sustainability" (for achieving the global sustainable agenda) and the "sustainability of AI" (measuring the environmental impact of making and using AI). There are numerous examples of the former, as AI is increasingly used to accelerate efforts to mitigate the climate crisis (think, for instance, of initiatives around "AI for Good," and "AI for the sustainable development goals"). However, relatively little is done for the latter, namely, to measure and decrease the environmental impact of making and using AI. To be sure, the sustainability *of* AI is not just a technical problem and cannot be reduced to measuring the carbon emissions from training AI algorithms. Rather, it is about fostering a deeper understanding of AI as exacerbating and reinforcing patterns of discrimination across borders. Those working in the mines to extract minerals and metals that are used to develop AI are voiceless in the AI discourse. Those whose backyards are filled with mountains of electronic waste from the disposal of the physical infrastructure underpinning AI are also voiceless in the AI debate.

[23] Gry Hasselbalch, "Culture by design: A data interest analysis of the European AI policy agenda" (2020) *First Monday*, 25, https://firstmonday.org/ojs/index.php/fm/article/view/10861/10010, accessed June 27, 2023.

[24] Aimee van Wynsberghe, "Sustainable AI: AI for sustainability and the sustainability of AI" (2021) *AI and Ethics*, 1: 213.

Sustainable AI is meant to be a lens through which to uncover ethical problems and power asymmetries that one can only see when one begins from a discussion of environmental consequences. Thus, sustainable AI is meant to bring the hidden, vulnerable demographics who bear the burden of the cost of making and using AI to the fore and to show that the environmental consequences of AI also shed light on systemic social injustices that demand immediate attention.

The environmental and social injustices resulting from the making and using of AI inevitably raises the question: what is it that we, as a society, want to sustain? When sustainability carries with it a connotation of maintenance and to continue something, is sustainable AI then just about maintaining the environmental practices that give rise to such social injustices? Or, is it also possible to suggest that sustainable AI carries with it the possibility to open a dialogue on how to repair and transform such injustices?[25]

6.3.1 *Examining the Sustainability of AI: Data Pollution*

Taking an interest in sustainability and AI is simultaneously a tangible and an intangible endeavor. As Sætra[26] has emphasized, many of AI's ethical implications as well as impacts on society and nature (positive and negative) are intangible and potential, meaning that they cannot be empirically verified or observed. At the same time, many of its impacts are also visible, tangible, and even measurable. Understanding the ethical implications of AI in the context of a global sustainability agenda should hence involve both a philosophical analysis and an ethical analysis about its intangible and potential impacts and their role in our personal, social, and natural environments, as well as a sociological and technological analyses of the tangible impacts of AI's very concrete technology design, adoption, and development.

One way of examining the sustainability of AI from multiple angles is to explore the sustainability of the data of AI, often associated with concerns around "data pollution," as discussed further below.[27] Since the mid-1990s, societies have transformed through processes of "datafication,"[28] converting everything into data configurations. This process has enabled a wide range of new technological capabilities and applications, including the currently most practical application of the *idea* of AI (conceptualized as a machine that mimics human intelligence in one form or another), namely machine learning (ML). ML is a method used

[25] Taylor Stone and Aimee van Wynsberghe, "Repairing AI" in Mark Young and Mark Coeckelbergh (eds), *Maintenance and Philosophy of Technology: Keeping Things Going* (1st ed, Routledge, 2024).

[26] Henrik S Sætra, *AI for the Sustainable Development Goals* (1st ed, CRC Press, 2022), 5.

[27] This approach has been taken by Hasselbalch and the University of Bonn's *Data Pollution and Power Group*: www.datapollution.eu. See also Gry Hasselbalch, "Data pollution & power: A white paper for a global sustainable development agenda on AI" (2022), www.datapollution.eu/, accessed June 27, 2023.

[28] Viktor Mayer-Schönberger and Kenneth Cukier, *Big Data: A Revolution that Will Transform How We Live, Work and Think* (John Murray, 2013), 15.

to autonomously or semiautonomously make sense of big data generated in the areas such as health care, transportation, finance, and communication. As datafication continues to expand and evolve as the fuel of AI/ML models, its ethical implications become more apparent as well. Hasselbalch[29] has argued that AI can be seen as an extension of "Big Data Socio-Technical Infrastructures" (BDSTIs) that are institutionalized in IT practices and regulatory frameworks. "Artificial Intelligence Socio-Technical Infrastructures" (AISTIs) are then an evolution of BDSTIs, with added components that allow for real-time sensing, learning, and autonomy.

In turn, the term "data pollution" can then be considered a discursive response to the implications of BDSTI and AISTI in society. It is used as a catch-all metaphor to describe the adverse impacts that the generation, storing, handling, and processing of digital data has on our natural environment, social environment, and personal environment.[30] As an unsustainable handling, distribution, and generation of data resources,[31] data pollution due diligence in a business setting, for example, will hence imply managing the adverse effects and risks of what could be described as the data exhaust of big data.

Firstly, the data pollution of AI has been understood as a *tangible* impact, that is, as "data-driven unsustainability"[32] with environmental effects on the natural environment. For example, a famous study by Strubell et al. found that training (including tuning and experimentation) a large AI model for natural language processing, such as machine translation, uses seven times more carbon than an average human in one year.[33] The environmental impact of digital technologies such as AI is not limited to just the data they use, but also includes the disposal of information and communication technology and other effects that may be harder to identify (such as consumers' energy consumption when making use of digital services).[34]

Secondly, data pollution is also described as the more *intangible* impacts of big data on our social and personal environments. Originally, the term was used to illustrate mainly the privacy implications for citizens of the big data economy

[29] Ibid. Hasselbalch, 2021.

[30] Gry Hasselbalch "Data pollution & power: A white paper for a global sustainable development agenda on AI" (2022), www.datapollution.eu/, accessed June 27, 2023.

[31] Dennis D Hirsch and Jonathan King, "Big data sustainability: An environmental management systems analogy" (2016) *Washington and Lee Law Review*, 72, http://dx.doi.org/10.2139/ssrn.2716785, accessed June 27, 2023; Omri Ben-Shahar, "Data pollution" (2019) *Journal of Legal Analysis*, 11: 104.

[32] Federica Lucivero et al., "Data-driven unsustainability? An interdisciplinary perspective on governing the environmental impacts of a data-driven society" (2020), Available at SSRN, http://dx.doi.org/10.2139/ssrn.3631331, accessed June 27, 2023.

[33] Alan Winfield, "Energy and exploitation: AIs dirty secrets" (June 28, 2019), https://alanwinfield.blogspot.com/2019/06/energy-and-exploitation-ais-dirty.html, accessed June 27, 2023. Emma Strubell, Ananya Ganesh, and Andrew McCallum, "Energy and policy considerations for deep learning in NLP" (2019) Cornell University, https://arxiv.org/abs/1906.02243, accessed June 27, 2023.

[34] Federica Lucivero, "Big data, big waste? A reflection on the environmental sustainability of big data Initiatives" (2019) *Science and Engineering Ethics*, 26: 1009.

and the datafication of individual lives and societies. Schneier has emphasized the effects of the massive collection and processing of big data by companies and governments alike on people's right to privacy by stating that *"this tidal wave of data is the pollution problem of the information age. All information processes produce it."*[35] Furthermore, Hirsch and King have deployed the term "data pollution" as analogous to the "negative externalities" of big data as used in business management.[36] They argue that when managing negative impacts of big data, such as data spills, privacy violations, and discrimination, businesses can learn from the strategies adopted to mitigate traditional forms of pollution and environmental impacts. Conversely, Ben-Shahar[37] has introduced data pollution in the legal field as a way to *"rethink the harms of the data economy"*[38] to manage the negative externalities of big data with an *"environmental law for data protection."*[39] He, however, also recognizes that harmful data exhaust is not only disrupting the privacy and data protection rights of individuals but that it adversely affects an entire digital ecosystem of social institutions and public interests.[40] The scope of "data pollution" hence evolved over time and expanded into a more holistic approach to the adverse effects of the big data economy. In this way, the term is also a testimony to the rising awareness of what is at stake in a big data society, including a disruption of the power balances in society, across multiple environments. As argued by Hasselbalch and Tranberg in their 2016 book on data ethics: *"The effects of data practices without ethics can be manifold – unjust treatment, discrimination and unequal opportunities. But privacy is at its core. It's the needle on the gauge of society's power balance."*[41]

6.3.2 *AI as Infrastructure*

Let us be clear that we are not speaking of isolated events when we discuss AI, ML, and the data practices necessary to train and use these algorithms. Rather, we are talking about a massive infrastructure of algorithms used for business models of large tech companies as well as for the infrastructure to power startups and the like. And this infrastructure has internalized the exploitation of people and the planet. A key issue is here that the material constitution of AI and data is often

35 Bruce Schneier, "The future of privacy" (2006), www.schneier.com/blog/archives/2006/03/the_future_of_p.html, accessed June 27, 2023.

36 Dennis D Hirsch and Jonathan H King, "Big data sustainability: An environmental management systems analogy" (2016) *Washington and Lee Law Review Online*, 72(3): 406–419. https://scholarlycommons.law.wlu.edu/wlulr-online/vol72/iss3/4/, accessed June 27, 2023.

37 Omri Ben-Shahar, "Data pollution" (2019) *Journal of Legal Analysis*, 11: 104.

38 Ibid., 104.

39 Ibid., 104.

40 Ibid., 105.

41 Gry Hasselbalch and Pernille Tranberg, *Data Ethics. The New Competitive Advantage* (1st ed, Publishare, 2016), 183.

ignored, or we are oblivious to it. The idea that data is "stored on the cloud," for example, invokes a symbolic reference to the data being stored "somewhere out there" and not in massive data centers around the world requiring large amounts of land and water.

AI not only uses existing infrastructures to function, such as power grids and water supply chains, but it is also used to enhance existing infrastructures. Google famously used the algorithm created by DeepMind to conserve electricity in their data centers. In addition, Robbins and van Wynsberghe have shown how AI itself ought to be conceptualized as an infrastructure in so far as it is embedded, transparent, visible upon breakdown, and modular.[42]

Understanding AI as infrastructure demands that we question the building blocks of said infrastructure and the practices in place that maintain the functioning of said infrastructure. Without careful consideration, we run the risk of lock-in, not only in the sense of carbon emissions, but also in the sense of the power asymmetries that are maintained, the kinds of discrimination that run through our society, the forms of data collection underpinning the development and use of algorithms, and so on. In other words, "*…the choices we make now regarding our new AI-augmented infrastructure not only relate to the carbon emissions that it will have; but also relate to the creation of constraints that will prevent us from changing course if that infrastructure is found to be unsustainable.*"[43]

As raised earlier, the domain of sustainable AI aims not only at addressing unsustainable environmental practices at the root of AI production, but it also asks the question of what we, society, wish to maintain. What practices of data collection and of data sovereignty do we want to pass on to future generations? Alternatively, what practices, both environmental and social, require a transformative kind of repair to better align with our societal values?

6.4 ANALYZING AI AND SUSTAINABILITY WITH A DATA ETHICS OF POWER

Exploring AI's sustainability implies understanding AI in context; that is, a conception of AI as socio-technical infrastructure created and directed by humans in social, economic, political, and historical contexts with impacts in the present as well as for future generations. Thus, AISTIs, as explored by Hasselbalch,[44] also represent power dynamics among various actors at the local, regional, and global levels. This is because they are human-made spaces evolving from the very negotiation and

[42] Scott Robbins and Aimee van Wynsberghe, "Our new artificial intelligence infrastructure: Becoming locked into an unsustainable future" (2022) *Sustainability*, 14(8): 4829, www.mdpi.com/2071-1050/14/8/4829, accessed June 27, 2023.

[43] Ibid., 6.

[44] Gry Hasselbalch, *Data Ethics of Power. A Human Approach in the Big Data and AI Era* (Edward Elgar, 2021).

tension between different societal interests and aspirations.[45] An ethical analysis of AI and sustainability therefore necessitates an exploration of these power dynamics that are transformed, impacted, and even produced by AI in natural, social, and personal environments. We can here consider AISTIs as "socio-technical infrastructures of power,"[46] infrastructures of *empowerment* and *disempowerment*, and ask questions such as whose or what interest and values does the core infrastructure serve? For example, which "data interests"[47] are embedded in the data design? Which interests and values conflict with each other, and how are these conflicts resolved in, for example, AI policies or standards?

Hasselbalch's "data ethics of power" is an applied ethics approach concerned with making the power dynamics of the big data society and the conditions of their negotiation visible in order to point to design, business, policy, and social and cultural processes that support a human(-centric) distribution of power.[48] When taking a "data ethics of power" approach, the ethical challenges of AI and sustainability are considered from the point of view of power dynamics, with the aim of making these power dynamics visible and imagining alternative realities in design, culture, policy, and regulation. The assumption is that the ethical implications of AI are linked with architectures of powers. Thus, the identification of – and our response to – these ethical implications are simultaneously enabled and inhibited by structural power dynamics.

A comprehensive understanding of the power dynamics that shape and are shaped by AISTIs of power and their effect on sustainable development requires a multilevel examination of a "data ethics of power" that takes into account perspectives on the micro, meso, and macro levels.[49] This means, as Misa describes it, that we take into consideration different levels in the interaction between humans, technology,

[45] Susan L Star and Geoffrey C Bowker, "How to infrastructure?" in Leah A Lievrouw and Sonia Livingstone (eds), *Handbook of New Media. Social Shaping and Social Consequences of ICTs* (SAGE Publications, 2006);
Geoffrey C Bowker, "Toward information infrastructure studies: Ways of knowing in a networked environment" in Jeremy Hunsinger et al. (eds), *International Handbook of Internet Research* (Springer Netherlands, 2010);
Penelope Harvey, Casper Jensen, and Asturo Morita (eds), *Infrastructures and Social Complexity: A Companion* (Routledge, 2017).

[46] Gry Hasselbalch, *Data Ethics of Power. A Human Approach in the Big Data and AI Era* (Edward Elgar, 2021), 11.

[47] Gry Hasselbalch, "A framework for a data interest analysis of artificial intelligence" (2021) 26 First Monday, https://doi.org/10.5210/fm.v26i7.11091, accessed August 21, 2023.

[48] Gry Hasselbalch, "Making sense of data ethics. The powers behind the data ethics debate in European policymaking" (2019) *Internet Policy Review*, 8(2) https://policyreview.info/articles/analysis/making-sense-data-ethics-powers-behind-data-ethics-debate-european-policymaking, accessed June 27, 2023.

[49] Thomas J Misa, "How machines make history, and how historians (and others) help them to do so" (1988) *Science, Technology, and Human Values*, 13: 308;
Thomas J Misa, "Theories of technological change: Parameters and purposes" (1992) *Science, Technology and Human Values*, 17: 3; Thomas J Misa, "Findings follow framings: Navigating the empirical turn" (2009) *Synthese*, 168: 357.

and the social and material world we live in.[50] In addition, as Edwards describes it, we should also consider "scales of time"[51] when grasping larger patterns of technological systems' development and adoption in society on a historical scale, while also looking at their specific life cycles.[52] This approach allows for a more holistic understanding of the complex design, political, organizational, and cultural contexts of power of these technological developments. The objective of this approach is to avoid reductive analyses of complex socio-technical developments either focusing on the ethical implications of designers and engineers' choices in micro contexts of interaction with technology or, on the other hand, reducing ethical implications to outcomes of larger macroeconomic or ideological patterns only. A narrow focus on ethical dilemmas in the micro contexts of design will steal attention from the wider social conditions and power dynamics, while an analysis constrained to macro structural power dynamics will fail to grasp individual nuances and factors by making sense of them only in terms of these larger societal dynamics. A "multi-level analysis"[53] hence has an interest in the micro, meso, and macro levels of social organization and space, which also includes looking beyond the here and now into the future, so as to ensure intergenerational justice.

The three levels of analysis of power dynamics (micro, meso, and macro) in time and space are, as argued by Hasselbalch,[54] central to the delineation of the ethical implications of AI and its sustainability. Let us concretize how these lenses can foster our understanding of what is at stake.

First, on the micro level, ethical implications are identified in the contexts and power dynamics of the very design of an AI system. Ethical dilemmas pertaining to issues of sustainability can be identified in the design of AI and a core component of a sustainable approach to AI would be to design AI systems differently. What are the barriers and enablers on a micro design level for achieving sustainable AI? Think, for example, about an AI systems developer in Argentina who depends on the cloud infrastructure from one of the big cloud providers Amazon or Microsoft, which locks in her choices.

Second, on the meso level, we have institutions, companies, governments, and intergovernmental organizations that are implementing institutionalized requirements, such as international standards and laws on, for example, data protection. While doing so, interests, values, and cultural contexts (such as specific cultures of

[50] Thomas J Misa, "How machines make history, and how historians (and others) help them to do so" (1988) *Science, Technology, and Human Values*, 13: 308.

[51] Paul N Edwards, "Infrastructure and modernity: Scales of force, time, and social organization in the history of sociotechnical systems" in Thomas J Misa, Philip Brey, and Andrew Feenberg (eds), *Modernity and Technology* (MIT Press, 2002).

[52] Ibid.

[53] Misa, Findings follow framings.

[54] Gry Hasselbalch, "Data pollution & power: A white paper for a global sustainable development agenda on AI" (2022), www.datapollution.eu/, accessed June 27, 2023.

innovation) are negotiated, and some interests will take precedence in the implementation of these requirements. What are the barriers and enablers on an institutional, organizational, and governmental levels for tackling ethical implications and achieving sustainable AI? Think for example about a social media company in Silicon Valley with a big data business model implementing the requirements of the EU Data Protection Regulation for European users of the platform.

Lastly, socio-technical systems such as AISTIs need what Hughes has famously referred to as a "technological momentum"[55] in society to evolve and consolidate. A technological momentum will most often be preceded by sociotechnical change that take the form of negotiations of interests. A macro-level analysis could therefore consider the increasing awareness of the sustainability of AI on the geopolitical agenda and how different societal interests are being negotiated, expressed in cultures, norms, and histories on macro scales of time. This analysis would thus seek to understand the power dynamics of the geopolitical battle between different approaches to data and AI. What are the barriers and enablers on a historical and geopolitical scale for achieving sustainable AI data? Think for example about the conflicts between different legal systems, or between different political and business "narratives" that shape the development of global shared governance frameworks between UN member states.

6.5 CONCLUSION

The public and policy discourse surrounding AI is frequently marked by excessive optimism and technological determinism. Most big data business endeavors are today promoted as "AI," and AI has acquired a crucial significance in geopolitics as a representation of nations' and regions' superiority in the global arena. However, it is crucial to acknowledge that AI is a human-created technology with significant effects on our environment and on future societies. The field of sustainable AI is focused on addressing the unsustainable environmental practices in AI development, but not only that. It also asks us to consider the societal goals for AI's role in future societies. This involves examining and shaping the design and use of AI, as well as the policy practices that we want to pass down to future generations.

In this chapter we brought together the concepts of sustainable AI with a "data ethics of power." The public discourse on AI is increasingly recognizing the importance of both frameworks, and yet not enough is done to systematically mitigate the concerns they identify. Thus, we addressed the ethical quandary of using AI for sustainability, as it presents opportunities both for addressing sustainable development challenges and for causing harm to the environment and society. By discussing the

[55] Thomas P Hughes, "The evolution of large technological systems" in Wiebe E Bijker, Thomas P Hughes, and Trevor Pinch (eds), *The Social Construction of Technological Systems* (MIT Press, 1987).

concept of AI for sustainability within the context of a global sustainable development agenda, we aimed to shed light on the power dynamics that shape AI and its impact on sustainable development goals. We argued that exploring the powers that shape the "data pollution" of AI can help to make the social and ethical implications of AI more tangible. It is our hope that, by considering AI through a more holistic lens, its adverse effects both in the present and in the future can be more effectively mitigated.

PART II

AI, Law and Policy

7

AI Meets the GDPR

Navigating the Impact of Data Protection on AI Systems

Pierre Dewitte

7.1 INTRODUCTION

To state that artificial intelligence ("AI") has seen drastic improvements since the age of expert systems is rather euphemistic at a time when language models have become so powerful they could have authored this piece – hint, they didn't. If, conceptually speaking, AI systems refer to the ability of a software to mimic the features of human-like reasoning, most are used to draw predictions from data through the use of a trained model, that is, an algorithm able to detect patterns in data it has never encountered before. When such models are used to derive information relating to individuals, personal data are likely involved somewhere in the process, whether at the training or deployment stage. This can certainly result in many benefits for those individuals. However, as abundantly illustrated throughout this book, the link between personal information and natural persons also exposes them to real-life adverse consequences such as social exclusion, discrimination, identity theft or reputational damage, all the while directly contributing to the opacification of the decision-making processes that impact their daily lives. For all these reasons, specific legal guarantees have been adopted at various levels to minimize these risks by regulating the processing of personal data and equipping individuals with the appropriate tools to understand and challenge the output of AI systems.

In Europe, the General Data Protection Regulation ("GDPR")[1] is the flagship piece of legislation in that regard, designed to ensure both the protection of natural persons and the free movement of personal data. Reconciling the intrinsic characteristics of AI systems with the principles and rules contained therein is a delicate exercise, though. For two reasons. First, the GDPR has been conceived as a technology-neutral instrument comprised of voluntarily open-ended provisions meant to carry their normative values regardless of the technological environment

[1] Regulation 2016/679 of the European Parliament and of the Council of April 27, 2016 on the protection of natural persons with regard to the processing of personal data and on the free movement of such data, and repealing Directive 95/46/EC (General Data Protection Regulation) [2016] OJ L119/1 ELI: http://data.europa.eu/eli/reg/2016/679/oj.

they are applied in.[2] Such is the tradeoff necessary to ensure resilience and future-proofness when technological progresses have largely outpaced the capacity of regulators to keep up with the unbridled rhythm of innovation.[3] In turn, navigating that ecosystem comprised of multiple layers of regulation designed to reconcile flexibility and legal certainty can prove particularly daunting. Second, AI systems have grown more and more complex, to the point where the opacity of their reasoning process has become a common ground for concern.[4] This reinforces the need for interdisciplinary collaboration, as the proper understanding of their functioning is essential for the correct application of the law. In short, regulating the processing of personal data in AI systems requires to interpret and apply a malleable regulatory framework to increasingly complex technological constructs. This, in itself, is a balancing act between protecting individuals' fundamental rights and guaranteeing a healthy environment for innovation to thrive.

The purpose of this chapter is not to provide a comprehensive overview of the implications of the GDPR for AI systems. Nor is it to propose concrete solutions to specific problems arising in that context.[5] Rather, it aims to walk the reader though the core concepts of EU data protection law, and highlight the main tensions between its principles and the functioning of AI systems. With that goal in mind, Section 7.2 first sketches the broader picture of the European privacy and data protection regulatory framework, and clarifies the focus for the remainder of this chapter. Section 7.3 then proceeds to delineate the scope of application of the GDPR and its relevance for AI systems. Finally, Section 7.4 breaks down the main friction

[2] This is recalled in Recital 15 GDPR: "In order to prevent creating a serious risk of circumvention, the protection of natural persons should be technologically neutral and should not depend on the techniques used."

[3] This is most commonly referred to as the "pacing problem" of the law. See Roger Brownsword, *Rights, Regulation, and the Technological Revolution* (Oxford University Press, 2008); Larry Downes, *The Laws of Disruption: Harnessing the New Forces That Govern Life and Business in the Digital Age* (Basic Books, 2009); Gary E Marchant, "The growing gap between emerging technologies and the law" in Gary E Marchant, Braden R Allenby, and Joseph R Herkert (eds), *The Growing Gap Between Emerging Technologies and Legal-Ethical Oversight*, vol. 7 (Springer Netherlands, 2011) 20–22, http://link.springer.com/10.1007/978-94-007-1356-7_2, accessed December 4, 2019.

[4] For instance, in the context of predictive policing, where algorithms are used to assess the likelihood of defendants becoming recidivists. See ProPublica's analysis of the COMPAS algorithm used by US courts: Julia Angwin, Jeff Larson, Surya Mattu and Lauren Kirchner, "Machine Bias – There's Software Used Across the Country to Predict Future Criminals. And It's Biased against Blacks" *ProPublica* (May 23, 2016), www.propublica.org/article/machine-bias-risk-assessments-in-criminal-sentencing, accessed January 14, 2023. Their calculation is also available on GitHub at the following address: https://github.com/propublica/compas-analysis.

[5] For that, I redirect the reader to dedicated reference manuscripts and studies such as, among many others: Dara Hallinan, Ronald Leenes, and Paul De Hert (eds), *Data Protection and Privacy: Data Protection and Artificial Intelligence* (Hart Publishing, 2021); Giovanni Sartor and Francesca Lagioia, "The impact of the general data protection regulation (GDPR) on artificial intelligence" (European Parliamentary Research Service, 2020) Think Tank: European Parliament, Study, www.europarl.europa.eu/thinktank/en/document/EPRS_STU(2020)641530, accessed January 11, 2023.

points between the former and the latter and illustrates each of these with examples of concrete data protection challenges raised by AI systems in practice.

7.2 SETTING THE SCENE – THE SOURCES OF PRIVACY AND DATA PROTECTION LAW IN EUROPE

While the GDPR is the usual suspect when discussing European data protection law, it is but one piece of a broader regulatory puzzle. Before delving into its content, it is therefore crucial to understand its position and role within that larger ecosystem. Not only will this help clarify the different sources of privacy and data protection law, but it will also equip the reader with keys to understand the interaction between these texts. The goal of this section is hence to contextualize the GDPR in order to highlight its position within the hierarchy of legal norms.

In Europe, two coexisting legal systems regulate the processing of personal data.[6] First, that of the Council of Europe ("CoE") through Article 8 of the European Convention on Human Rights ("ECHR")[7] as interpreted by the European Court of Human Rights ("ECtHR").[8] Second, that of the European Union ("EU") through Articles 7 and 8 of the Charter of Fundamental Rights of the European Union ("CFREU")[9] as interpreted by the Court of Justice of the European Union ("CJEU").[10] While these systems differ in scope and functioning, the protection afforded to personal data is largely aligned as the case law from both Courts influence each other.[11] National legislation constitutes an extra layer of privacy and data protection law, bringing the amount of regulatory silos up to three (see Figure 7.1).

[6] Juliane Kokott and Christoph Sobotta, "The distinction between privacy and data protection in the jurisprudence of the CJEU and the ECtHR" (2013) *International Data Privacy Law*, 3: 222, 222–223. See, for further information on these two systems: European Union Agency for Fundamental Rights and Council of Europe, *Handbook on European Data Protection Law – 2018 Edition* (2018), https://fra.europa.eu/en/publication/2018/handbook-european-data-protection-law-2018-edition, accessed January 16, 2023.

[7] Convention for the Protection of Human Rights and Fundamental Freedoms (European Convention on Human Rights, as amended by Protocols n° 11, 14, and 15 and supplemented by Protocols n° 6, 7, 12, 13, and 16).

[8] An overview of the jurisprudence of the ECtHR on Article 8 is available here: Registry of the European Court of Human Rights, "Guide on Article 8 of the European Convention on Human Rights. Right to respect for private and family life, home and correspondence" (April 9, 2024), https://ks.echr.coe.int/documents/d/echr-ks/guide_art_8_eng, accessed July 30, 2024.

[9] Charter of Fundamental Rights of the European Union, O.J.E.U., December 18, 2000, C 364/01.

[10] See, for an overview of the main relevant cases: Research and Documentation Directorate, "Fact Sheet: Protection of Personal Data" (Court of Justice of the European Union, 2021), https://curia.europa.eu/jcms/upload/docs/application/pdf/2018-10/fiche_thematique_-_donnees_personnelles_-_en.pdf, accessed January 16, 2023.

[11] More specifically, Article 52(3) CFREU states that "*in so far as this Charter contains rights which correspond to rights guaranteed by the Convention for the Protection of Human Rights and Fundamental Freedoms, the meaning and scope of those rights shall be the same as those laid down by the said Convention.*"

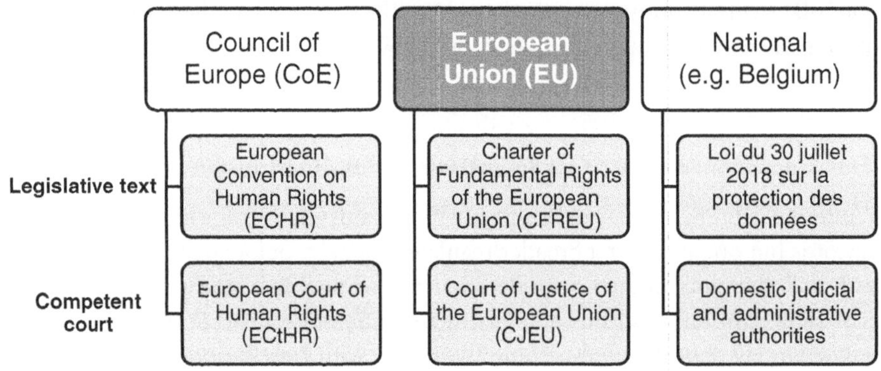

FIGURE 7.1 A fundamental rights perspective on the sources of privacy and data protection law

For the purpose of this chapter, let's zoom in on the EU legal order, comprised of primary and secondary legislation. While the former sets the foundational principles and objectives of the EU, the latter breaks them down into actionable rules that can then be directly applied or transposed by Member States into national law. This is further supplemented by "soft law" instruments issued by a wide variety of bodies to help interpret the provisions of EU. While these are not strictly binding, they often have quasi-legislative authority.[12] As illustrated in Figure 7.2, the GDPR is only *a* piece of secondary EU law meant to protect all data subjects' fundamental rights – including but not limited to privacy and data protection – when it comes to the processing of their personal data. As illustrated in the following sections, the Guidelines issued by the Article 29 Working Party ("WP29") and its successor the European Data Protection Board ("EDPB") are particularly helpful when fleshing out the scope and substance of the rules contained in the GDPR.[13] While all three of the silos detailed above impact – to a certain extent – the processing of personal data by AI systems, the remainder of this chapter focuses exclusively on the EU legal order, more specifically on the GDPR and its accompanying soft law instruments.

[12] See, for an overview of the GDPR soft law ecosystem and its limitations: Athena Christofi, Pierre Dewitte, and Charlotte Ducuing, "Erosion by standardisation: Is ISO/IEC 29134:2017 on privacy impact assessment up to (GDPR) standard?" in Maria Tzanou (ed), *Personal Data Protection and Legal Developments in the European Union* (IGI Global, 2020) 145–148, http://services.igi-global.com/resolvedoi/resolve.aspx?doi=10.4018/978-1-5225-9489-5, accessed January 16, 2023.

[13] The Article 29 Working Party (WP29) and its successor the European Data Protection Board (EDPB) are independent EU bodies composed of representative from national supervisory authorities tasked with ensuring the consistent interpretation of the GDPR throughout the Union. More specifically, the Board now plays a central role in the cooperation and consistency mechanism outlined in Chapter VII GDPR by issuing the so-called "binding decisions" in cases where national supervisory authorities disagree on substance of a draft decision (Article 65(1)a GDPR). The duties of the Board are detailed in Article 70 GDPR.

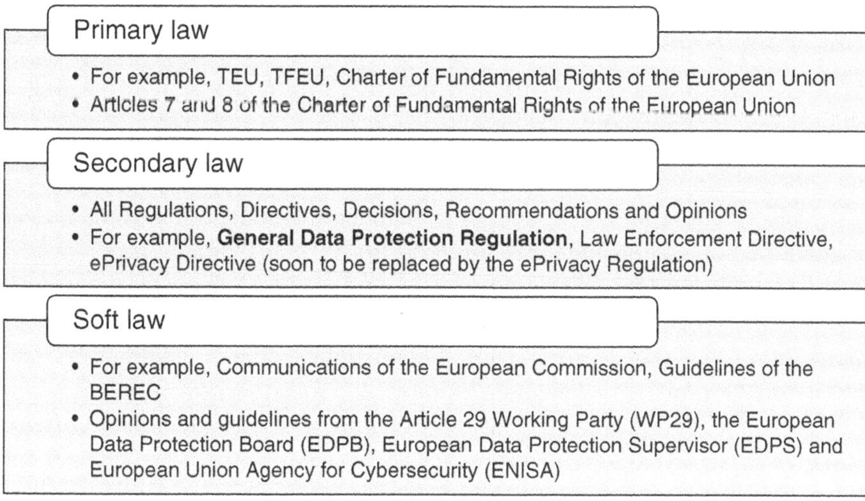

FIGURE 7.2 The EU legal order – general and data protection specific

7.3 OF PERSONAL DATA, CONTROLLERS AND PROCESSORS – THE APPLICABILITY OF THE GDPR TO AI SYSTEMS

As hinted at earlier, the GDPR is likely to come into play when AI systems are trained and used to make predictions about natural persons. Turning that intuition into a certainty nonetheless requires a careful analysis of its precise scope of application. In fact, this is the very first reflex anyone should adopt when confronted to *any* piece of legislation, as it typically only regulates certain types of activities (i.e., its "material scope") by imposing rules on certain categories of actors (i.e., its "personal scope"). Should the situation at hand fall outside the remit of the law, there is simply no need to delve into its content. Before discussing the concrete impact of the GDPR on AI systems in Section 7.4, it is therefore crucial to clarify whether (Section 7.3.1) and to whom it applies (Section 7.3.2).

7.3.1 *Material Scope of Application – The Processing of Personal Data*

7.3.1.1 The Notion of Personal Data and the Legal Test of Identifiability

Article 2(1) GDPR limits the applicability of the Regulation "to the processing of personal data wholly or partly by automated means." Equally important, Article 4(1) defines the concept of personal data as "any information relating to an identified or identifiable natural person." The reference to "any information" implies that the qualification as personal data is nature-, content-, and format-agnostic,[14] while

[14] See the examples in: Lee A Bygrave and Luca Tosoni, "Article 4(1). Personal data" in Christopher Kuner et al. (eds), *The EU General Data Protection Regulation (GDPR): A Commentary* (Oxford University Press, 2020) 109–110, https://doi.org/10.1093/oso/9780198826491.003.0007, accessed January 17, 2023.

"relating to" must be read as "linked to a particular person."[15] As such, the notion of personal data is not restricted to "information that is sensitive or private, but encompasses all kinds of information, not only objective but also subjective, in the form of opinions or assessments."[16] The term "natural persons," then, refers to human beings, thereby excluding information relating to legal entities, deceased persons, and unborn children from the scope of protection of the Regulation.[17]

The pivotal – and most controversial – element of that definition is the notion of "identified or identifiable." According to the WP29's Opinion 4/2007, a person is "identified" when "within a group of persons, he or she is 'distinguished' from all other members of the group." This can be the case when that piece of information is associated with a name, but any other indirect identifier or combination thereof, such as a telephone number or a social security number, might also lead to the identification of that individual. A person is "identifiable" when, "although he or she has not been identified yet, it is possible to do so."[18] "To determine whether a natural person is identifiable," states Recital 26 GDPR, "account should be taken of all the means reasonably likely to be used, such as singling out, either by the controller or by another person to identify the natural person directly or indirectly." In turn, "to ascertain whether means are reasonably likely to be used to identify the natural person, account should be taken of all objective factors, such as the costs of and the amount of time required for identification, taking into consideration the available technology at the time of the processing and technological developments." This makes the qualification of "personal data" a dynamic, context-sensitive assessment that calls for a case-by-case analysis of the reidentification potential.

Such an assessment was conducted by the CJEU in the *Breyer* case,[19] in which it held that a dynamic IP address collected by a content provider was to be considered as a piece of personal data, even though that provider was not able, by itself, to link the IP address back to a particular individual. German law indeed allowed content providers, in the context of criminal proceedings following cyberattacks for instance, to obtain from the internet service provider the information

[15] C-434/16 *Nowak* [2017] ECLI:EU:C:2017:994, para 35.

[16] Ibid., para 34. In that case, the CJEU held that the written answers submitted by a candidate at a professional examination as well as any comments made by an examiner with respect to those answers constitute personal data, within the meaning of Article 4(1) GDPR.

[17] On post-mortem privacy, see: Edina Harbinja, "Post-mortem privacy 2.0: Theory, law, and technology" (2017) *International Review of Law, Computers & Technology*, 31: 26. The author offers a deeper analysis of these issues in her doctoral thesis: Edina Harbinja, "Legal Aspects of Transmission of Digital Assets on Death" (University of Strathclyde, Law School, 2017), https://scholar.archive.org/work/owjux2fhlbbjnkiar2tfiowkki/access/wayback/https://stax.strath.ac.uk/downloads/pz50gw38v, accessed May 16, 2023.

[18] Article 29 Working Party, "Opinion 4/2007 on the concept of personal data" 12, https://ec.europa.eu/justice/article-29/documentation/opinion-recommendation/files/2007/wp136_en.pdf, accessed January 16, 2023.

[19] C-582/14, *Patrick Breyer v Bundesrepublik Deutschland* [2016] ECLI:EU:C:2016:779, para 49.

necessary to turn that dynamic IP address back to its static form, and therefore link it to an individual user. That means of reidentification was considered "reasonably likely" to be used, thereby falling under the scope of Article 4(1) read in combination with Recital 26 GDPR. On the contrary, that likelihood test would not have been met if such reidentification was "prohibited by law or practically impossible on account of the fact that it requires disproportionate efforts in terms of time, cost, and workforce, so that the risk of identification appears in reality to be insignificant."[20] By investigating the actual means of reidentification at the disposal of the content provider to reidentify the data subject to whom the dynamic IP address belonged, the Court embraced a "risk-based" approach to the notion of personal data, as widely supported in legal literature and discussed in Section 7.4.3.[21]

Data for which the likelihood of reidentification falls below that "reasonable" threshold are considered "anonymous" and are not subject to the GDPR. Lowering the risk of reidentification to meet the GDPR standard of anonymity is no small feat, however, and depends on multiple factors such as the size and diversity of the dataset, the categories of information it contains, and the effectiveness of the techniques applied to reduce the chances of reidentification.[22] For instance, swapping names for randomly generated number-based identifiers might not be sufficient to reasonably exclude the risk of reidentification if the dataset at stake is limited to the employees of a company paired with specific categories of data such as hobbies, gender, or device fingerprints. In that case, singling someone out, linking two records, or deducing the value of an attribute based on other attributes – in this example, the name of a person based on a unique combination of the gender and hobbies – remains possible. For the same reason, hashing the license plate of a car entering a parking before storing it into the payment system, even when the hash function used is strictly nonreversible, might not reasonably shield the driver from reidentification if the hash value is stored alongside other information such as the time of arrival or departure, which might later be combined with unblurred CCTV

20 Ibid., para 46.

21 Michèle Finck and Frank Pallas, "They who must not be identified – distinguishing personal from nonpersonal data under the GDPR" (2020) *International Data Privacy Law*, 10(11): 34–36; Daniel Groos and Evert-Ben van Veen, "Anonymised data and the rule of law" (2020) *European Data Protection Law Review*, 6(498): 5; Sophie Stalla-Bourdillon, "Anonymising personal data: Where do we stand now?" (2019) *Privacy & Data Protection*, 19(3): 3–5.

22 For examples of anonymization techniques and their robustness, see Article 29 Working Party, "Opinion 05/2014 on Anonymisation Techniques," 11–19, https://ec.europa.eu/justice/article-29/documentation/opinion-recommendation/files/2014/wp216_en.pdf, accessed January 16, 2023. It is worth noting that these guidelines, which have been abundantly criticized in legal literature for their extremely strict understanding of anonymization, are being revised as the time of writing. See Finck and Pallas (n 21) 15; Sophie Stalla-Bourdillon, "Anonymous data v. personal data – false debate: An EU perspective on anonymization, pseudonymization and personal data" (2016) *Wisconsin International Law Journal*, 34(384): 306–320.

footages to retrieve the actual plate number.[23] These techniques are therefore considered as "pseudonymization" rather than "anonymization,"[24] with the resulting "pseudonymized data" falling under the scope of the GDPR in the same way as regular personal data. As detailed in Section 7.4.3, pseudonymization techniques nonetheless play a critical role as mitigation strategies in the risk-based ecosystem of the Regulation.[25]

7.3.1.2 The Processing of Personal Data in AI Systems

AI systems, and more specifically machine learning algorithms, process data at different stages, each of which is likely to involve information that qualifies as personal data. The first of these is the training stage, if the target and predictor variables are sufficiently granular to allow a third party to reidentify the individuals included in the training dataset.[26] This could be the case, for instance, when training a model to detect tax fraud based on taxpayers' basic demographic data, current occupation, life history, income, or previous tax returns, the intimate nature of which increases the risk of reidentification. Anonymization – or pseudonymization, depending on the residual risk – techniques can be used to randomize variables by adding noise (e.g., replacing the exact income of each taxpayer by a different yet comparable amount) or permutating some of them (e.g., randomly swapping the occupation of two taxpayers).[27] Generalization techniques such as *k*-anonymity (i.e., ensuring that the dataset contains at least *k*-records of taxpayers with identical predictors by decreasing their granularity, such as replacing the exact age with a range) or *l*-diversity

[23] Agencia Española de Protección de Datos and European Data Protection Supervisor, "Introduction to the hash function as a personal data pseudonymisation technique" (October 2019), https://edps.europa.eu/sites/default/files/publication/19-10-30_aepd-edps_paper_hash_final_en.pdf, accessed January 16, 2023.

[24] Defined in Article 4(5) GDPR as "the processing of personal data in such a manner that the personal data can no longer be attributed to a specific data subject without the use of additional information, provided that such additional information is kept separately and is subject to technical and organizational measures to ensure that the personal data are not attributed to an identified or identifiable natural person."

[25] For an overview of the state of the art on pseudonymization, see European Union Agency for Cybersecurity, "Data pseudonymisation: Advanced techniques and use cases," www.enisa.europa.eu/publications/data-pseudonymisation-advanced-techniques-and-use-cases, accessed January 16, 2023.

[26] The target variable being the variable that the model, once trained, will be able to predict, and the predictor variables being the information on the basis of which the model will ground its prediction. For a simplified overview of the functioning of supervised and unsupervised machine learning, see Datatilsynet, "Artificial intelligence and privacy," 7–14, www.datatilsynet.no/globalassets/global/english/ai-and-privacy.pdf, accessed January 11, 2023.

[27] The Information Commissioner's Office, UK's supervisory authority, provides a solid introduction to anonymization techniques in: Information Commissioner's Office, "Anonymisation: Managing data protection risk code of practice." See also: Information Commissioner's Office, "Big data, artificial intelligence, machine learning and data protection," paras 130–138, https://ico.org.uk/media/for-organisations/documents/2013559/big-data-ai-ml-and-data-protection.pdf, accessed January 18, 2023.

(i.e., extending *k*-anonymity to make sure that the variables in each set of *k*-records have at least *l*-different values) are also widely used in practice. Synthetic data, namely artificial data that do not relate to real individuals but are produced using generative modeling, can serve as an alternative to actual, real-life personal data to train machine learning models.[28] Yet, doing so is only a workaround, as the underlying generative model also needs to be trained on personal data. Plus, the generated data might reveal information about the natural persons who were included in the training dataset in cases where one or more specific variable stand out.

Second, a trained machine learning model might leak some of the personal data included in the training dataset. Some models might be susceptible to model inversion or membership inference attacks, which respectively allow an entity that already knows some of the characteristics of the individuals who were part of the training dataset to infer the value of other variables simply by observing the functioning of the said model, or to deduce whether a specific individual was part of that training dataset.[29] Other models might leak by design.[30] The qualification of trained models as personal – even if pseudonymized – data means that the GDPR will regulate their use, as the mere sharing of these models with third parties, for instance, will be considered as a "processing" of personal data within the meaning of Article 4(2) GDPR.

As detailed in Section 7.3.1.1, the criteria used for the identifiability test of Article 4(1) lead to a broad understanding of the notion of personal data; so much so that the GDPR has been coined as the "law of everything."[31] This is especially true when it comes to the role of "the available technology" in assessing the risk of reidentification, the progress of which increases the possibility that a technique considered as proper anonymization at time t is reverted and downgraded to a mere pseudonymizations method at time $t + 1$.[32] Many allegedly anonymous datasets have already been reidentified using data that were not available at the time of their

[28] For an overview of generative (adversarial) modeling, see Fida K Dankar and Mahmoud Ibrahim, "Fake it till you make it: Guidelines for effective synthetic data generation" (2021) *Applied Sciences*, 11(2158): 3–5. For a real-life example of a generative adversarial network, check the website, https://thispersondoesnotexist.com/.

[29] Michael Veale, Reuben Binns, and Lilian Edwards, "Algorithms that remember: Model inversion attacks and data protection law" (2018) *Philosophical Transactions of the Royal Society A: Mathematical, Physical and Engineering Sciences*, 376: 20180083.

[30] Such as support vector machines and *k*-nearest neighbors algorithms, as mentioned and explained in: Information Commissioner's Office, "Guidance on AI and Data Protection," 58, https://ico.org.uk/for-organisations/guide-to-data-protection/key-dp-themes/guidance-on-artificial-intelligence-and-data-protection/, accessed January 11, 2023.

[31] Nadezhda Purtova, "The law of everything. Broad concept of personal data and future of EU data protection law" (2018) *Law, Innovation and Technology*, 10: 40.

[32] Authors have even suggested that the current technological progress implies that 99.98% of Americans would be correctly reidentified in any dataset using 15 demographic attributes. See: Luc Rocher, Julien M Hendrickx, and Yves-Alexandre de Montjoye, "Estimating the success of re-identifications in incomplete datasets using generative models" (2019) *Nature Communications*, 10: 1.

release, or by more powerful computational means.[33] This mostly happens through linkage attacks, which consist in linking an anonymous dataset with auxiliary information readily available from other sources, and looking for matches between the variables contained in both datasets. AI makes these types of attacks much easier to perform, and paves the way for even more efficient reidentification techniques.[34]

7.3.2 *Personal Scope of Application – Controllers and Processors*

7.3.2.1 The Controller–Processor Dichotomy and the Notion of Joint Control

Now that Section 7.3.1 has clarified *what* the GDPR applies to, it is crucial to determine *who* bears the burden of compliance.[35] "Controllers" are the primary addressees of the Regulation, and are responsible to comply with virtually all the principles and rules it contains. Article 4(7) defines the controller as "the natural or legal person that, alone or jointly with others, determines the purposes and means of the processing of personal data." The EDPB provides much needed clarifications on how to interpret these notions.[36] First, the reference to "natural or legal person" – in contrast with a mere reference to the former in Article 4(1) GDPR – implies that both individuals and legal entities can qualify as controllers. The capacity to "determine" then refers to "the controller's influence over the processing, by virtue of an exercise of decision making power." That influence can either stem from a legal designation, such as when national law specifically appoints a tax authority as the controller for the processing of the personal data necessary to calculate citizens' tax returns, or follow from a factual analysis. In the latter case, the EPBD emphasizes that the notion of controller is a "functional concept" meant to "allocate responsibilities according to the actual roles of the parties." It is therefore necessary to look past any existing

[33] Two examples are worth a mention. First, the linkage attack performed on mobility data that suggests that four spatiotemporal points are enough to uniquely identify 95% of individuals. See: Yves-Alexandre de Montjoye et al., "Unique in the crowd: The privacy bounds of human mobility" (2013) *Scientific Reports*, 3(1): 2. Second, the reidentification attack performed on Netflix's user ratings dataset that uncovered that six ratings are sufficient to reidentify 84% of individuals. See: Arvind Narayanan and Vitaly Shmatikov, "How to break anonymity of the Netflix Prize dataset" (arXiv, November 22, 2007) 12, http://arxiv.org/abs/cs/0610105, accessed January 18, 2023.

[34] See, for instance: Stefan Vamosi, Thomas Reutterer, and Michael Platzer, "A deep recurrent neural network approach to learn sequence similarities for user-identification" (2022) *Decision Support Systems*, 155: 113718.

[35] See, for more a more detailed overview of the allocation of responsibilities under the GDPR, the seminal work of Brendan Van Alsenoy, *Data Protection Law in the EU: Roles, Responsibilities and Liability*, vol 6 (Intersentia, 2019), www.larcier-intersentia.com/en/data-protection-law-the-eu-roles-responsibilities-liability-9781780688282.html, accessed January 16, 2023.

[36] European Data Protection Board, "Guidelines 07/2020 on the concepts of controller and processor in the GDPR" (July 2021), https://edpb.europa.eu/our-work-tools/our-documents/guidelines/guidelines-072020-concepts-controller-and-processor-gdpr_en, accessed January 17, 2023. For the remainder of Section 3.2.1, reference is made to these guidelines. The notion of controller is covered in paras 15–45, that of joint control in paras 46–72 and that of processor in paras 73–84.

formal designation – in a contract, for instance – and to analyze the factual elements or circumstances indicating a decisive influence over the processing.

Next, the "purposes" and "means" relate, respectively, to the "why's" and "how's" of the processing. An entity must exert influence over both those elements to qualify as a controller, although there is a margin of maneuver to delegate certain "non-essential means" without shifting the burden of control. This would be the case, for instance, for the "practical aspects of implementation." For example, a company that decides to store a backup copy of its customers' data on a cloud platform remains the controller for that processing even though it does not determine the type of hardware used for the storage, nor the transfer protocol, the security measures or the redundancy settings. On the contrary, decisions pertaining to the type of personal data processed, their retention period, the potential recipients to whom they will be disclosed, and the categories of data subjects they concern typically fall within the exclusive remit of the controller; any delegation of these aspects to another actor would turn that entity into a (joint) controller in its own right.

Finally, the wording "alone or jointly with others" hints at the possibility for two or more entities to be considered as joint controllers. According to the EDPB, the overarching criterion for joint controllership to exist is "the joint participation of two or more entities in the determination of the purposes and means of a processing operation." This is the case when the entities at stake adopt "common" or "converging" decisions. Common decisions, on the one hand, involve "a common intention." Converging decisions, on the other, "complement each other and are necessary for the processing to take place in such a manner that they have a tangible impact on the determination of the purposes and the means of the processing." Another indication is "whether the processing would not be possible without both parties' participation in the sense that the processing by each party is inseparable, i.e. inextricably linked." The CJEU has, for instance, recognized a situation of joint controllership between a religious community and its members for the processing of the personal data collected in the course of door-to-door preaching, as the former "organized, coordinated and encouraged" the said activities despite the latter being actually in charge of the processing.[37] The Court held a similar reasoning with regard to Facebook and the administrator of a fan page, as creating such a page "gives Facebook the opportunity" to place cookies on visitors' computer that can be used to both "improve its system of advertising" and to "enable the fan page administrator to obtain statistics from the visit of the page."[38] Lastly, the Court also considered Facebook and Fashion ID, an online clothing retailer that had embedded Facebook's "Like" plugin on its page, as joint controllers for the collection and transmission of the visitors' IP address and unique browser string, since both entities

[37] Case C-25/17 *Tietosuojavaltuutettu* [2018] ECLI:EU:C:2018:551, paras 70–75.

[38] Case C-210/16 *Wirtschaftsakademie Schleswig-Holstein GmbH* [2018] ECLI:EU:C:2018:388, paras 25–44.

benefitted from that processing. Facebook, because it could use the collected data for its own commercial purpose. And Fashion ID, because the presence of a "Like" button would contribute to increasing the publicity of its goods.[39]

Next to "controllers," "processors" also fall within the scope of the GDPR. These are entities distinct from the controller that process personal data on its behalf (Article 4(8) GDPR). This is typically the case for, say, a call center that processes prospects' phone numbers in the context of a telemarketing campaign organized by another company. The requirement to be a separate entity implies that internal departments, or employees acting under the direct authority of their employer, will – at least in the vast majority of cases – not qualify as processors. Besides, processors can only process personal data upon the documented instructions and for the benefit of the controller. Should a processor go beyond the boundaries set by the controller and process personal data for its own benefit, it will be considered as a separate controller for the portion of the processing that oversteps the original controller's instructions. If the said call center decides, for instance, to reuse the phone numbers it has obtained from the controller to conduct its own marketing campaign or to sell it to third parties, it will be considered as a controller for those activities. Compared to controllers, processors must only comply with a subset of the rules listed in the GDPR, such as the obligation keep a record of processing activities (Article 30(2)), to cooperate with national supervisory authorities (Article 31), to ensure adequate security (Article 32), to notify data breaches to controllers (Article 33(2)), and to appoint a Data Protection Officer (DPO) when certain conditions are met (Article 44).

7.3.2.2 The Allocation of Responsibilities in AI Systems

The CJEU has repeatedly emphasized the importance to ensure, through a broad definition of the concept of controller, the "effective and complete protection of data subjects."[40] The same goes for the notion of joint control, which the Court now seems to have extended to any actor that has made the processing possible by contributing to it.[41] In the context of complex processing operations involving multiple actors intervening at different stages of the processing chain, such as the ones at stake in AI systems, an overly broad interpretation of the notion of joint control might lead to situations where everyone is considered as a joint controller.[42] Properly allocating responsibilities is therefore essential, as the qualification of each

39 Case C-40-17 *Fashion ID* [2019] ECLI:EU:C:2019:629, paras 64–85.

40 Case C-131/12 *Google Spain* [2014] ECLI:EU:C:2014:317, para 34; Case C-210-16 (n 38), para 28; Case C-25/17 (n 37), para 21; ibid., para 66.

41 See, on that note, the remark of Advocate General Bobek in his Opinion on the Fashion ID case. Case C-40/17 (n 39), Opinion of Advocate General Bobek, ECLI:EU:C:2018:1039, para 74.

42 Concerns have been voiced by, for instance: Jiahong Chen et al., "Who is responsible for data processing in smart homes? Reconsidering joint controllership and the household exemption" (2020)

party will drastically impact the scope of their compliance duties. Doing so requires the adoption of a "phase-oriented" approach, by slicing complex sets of processing operations into smaller bundles that pursue an identical overarching purpose before proceeding with the qualification of the actors involved.[43] Machine learning models, for instance, are the products of different activities ranging from the gathering and cleaning of training datasets, to the actual training of the model and its later use to make inferences in concrete scenarios. The actors involved do not necessarily exert the same degree of influence over all these aspects. As a result, their qualification might differ depending on the processing operation at stake. This makes it particularly important to circumscribe the relevant processing activities before applying the criteria detailed in Section 7.3.2.1.[44]

Let's illustrate the above by breaking down the processing operations typically involved in machine learning, starting with the collection and further use of the training datasets. Company X might specialize in the in-house development and commercialization of trained machine learning models. When doing so, it determines why the training datasets are processed (i.e., to train their model with the view of monetizing it) as well as the essential and nonessential means of the processing (e.g., which personal data are included in the training dataset and the technical implementation of the training process). It will therefore be considered as the sole controller for the processing of the training datasets. Company X might also decide to collaborate with Company Y, the latter providing the training dataset in exchange for the right to use the model once trained. This could be considered as converging decisions leading to a situation of joint controllership between Companies X and Y. Looking at the inference stage, then, Company X might decide to offer its trained model to Company Z, a bank, that will use it to predict the risk of default before granting loans. By doing so, Company Z determines the purposes for which it processes its clients' personal data (i.e., calculating the risk of default), as well as the essential means of the processing (e.g., the granularity of the data fed to the model). As a result, Company Z will be considered as the sole controller for the processing of its customers' data, regardless of whether Company X retains a degree of influence over how the algorithm works under the hood. Company X could also be considered as a processor in case it computes the risk score on behalf of Company Z using its own hardware and software infrastructure. This is a common scenario in the context of software- or platform-as-a-service cloud-based solutions.

International Data Privacy Law, 10: 279; Christopher Millard, "At this rate, everyone will be a [joint] controller of personal data!" (2019) *International Data Privacy Law*, 9: 217.

43 René Mahieu and Joris van Hoboken, "Fashion-ID: Introducing a phase-oriented approach to data protection?" (*European Law Blog*, September 30, 2019), https://europeanlawblog.eu/2019/09/30/fashion-id-introducing-a-phase-oriented-approach-to-data-protection/, accessed January 19, 2023.

44 See, for more examples, the ICO Guidance on AI and data protection, more specifically under the section "How should we understand controller/processor relationships in AI?" Information Commissioner's Office, "Guidance on AI and Data Protection" (n 30) 23–27.

7.4 AI SYSTEMS MEET THE GDPR – OVERVIEW AND FRICTION POINTS

Controllers – and, to a certain extent, processors – that process personal in the context of the development and/or use of AI systems must comply with the foundational principles detailed in Article 5 GDPR, namely lawfulness, fairness, transparency, purpose limitation, data minimization, accuracy, storage limitation, integrity and confidentiality, and accountability. These are the pillars around which the rest of the Regulation is articulated. While AI systems are not, *per se*, incompatible with the GDPR, reconciling their functioning with the rules of the Regulation is somewhat of a balancing act. The following sections aim at flagging the most pressing tensions by contrasting some of the characteristics of AI systems against the guarantees laid down in Article 5 GDPR.

7.4.1 *The Versatility of AI Systems v. the Necessity and Compatibility Tests*

7.4.1.1 Lawfulness and Purpose Limitation at the Heart of the GDPR

In order to prevent function creep, Article 5(1)a introduces the principle of "lawfulness," which requires controllers to justify their processing operations using one of the six lawful grounds listed in Article 6. These include not only the consent of the data subject – often erroneously perceived as the only option – but also the alternatives such as the "performance of a contract" or the "legitimate interests of the controller." Relying on any of these lawful grounds (except for consent) requires the controller to assess and demonstrate that the processing at stake is "objectively necessary" to achieve the substance of that lawful ground. In other words, there is no other, less-intrusive way to meet that objective. As recently illustrated by the Irish regulator's decision in the Meta Ireland case,[45] the processing of Facebook and Instagram users' personal data for the purpose of delivering targeted advertising is not, for instance, objectively necessary to fulfil the essence of the contractual relationship between these platforms and their users.[46] As a result, the processing cannot be based on Article 6(1)b, and it has to rely on another lawful ground. Consent, on the other hand, must be "freely given, specific, informed and unambiguous," thereby undermining its validity when obtained in a scenario that involves

[45] Full decision still to be published; see: www.dataprotection.ie/en/news-media/data-protection-commission-announces-conclusion-two-inquiries-meta-ireland, accessed January 23, 2023.

[46] See, for other examples: European Data Protection Board, "Guidelines 2/2019 on the processing of personal data under Article 6(1)(b) GDPR in the context of the provision of online services to data subjects," paras 23–29, https://edpb.europa.eu/sites/edpb/files/files/file1/edpb_guidelines-art_6-1-b-adopted_after_public_consultation_en.pdf, accessed January 17, 2023.

unbalanced power or information asymmetries, such as when given by an employee to its employer.[47]

With that same objective in mind, Article 5(1)b lays down the principle of "purpose limitation," according to which personal data shall be "collected for specified, explicit and legitimate purposes and not further processed in a manner that is incompatible with those purposes."[48] In practice, this requires controllers to, first, determine the exact reasons why personal data are collected and, then, assess the compatibility of every subsequent processing activity in light of the purposes that were specified at the collection stage. Doing so requires to take into account various criteria such as, for instance, the context in which the personal data have been collected and the reasonable expectations of the data subjects.[49] While compatible further processing can rely on the same lawful ground used to justify the collection, incompatible processing must specify a new legal basis. Reusing a postal address originally collected to deliver goods purchased online for marketing purposes is a straightforward example of an incompatible further processing. The purposes specified during the collection also serve as the basis to assess the amount of personal data collected (i.e., "data minimization"), the steps that must be taken to ensure their correctness (i.e., "accuracy") and their retention period (i.e., "storage limitation").

Lawfulness and purpose limitation are strongly interconnected, as the purposes specified for the collection will influence the outcome of both the necessity test required when selecting the appropriate lawful ground – with the exception of consent, for which the purposes delimit what can and cannot be done with the data – and the compatibility assessment that must be conducted prior to each further processing. Ensuring compliance with these principles therefore calls for a separate analysis of each "personal data – purpose(s) – lawful ground" triad, acting as a single, indissociable whole (see Figure 7.3).

Severing the link between these three elements would empty Articles 5(1)a and 5(1)b from their substance and render any necessity or compatibility assessment meaningless. Whether a webshop can rely on its legitimate interests (Article 6(1)f) to profile its users and offers targeted recommendations, for instance, heavily depends on the actual personal data used to tailor their experience, and therefore the intrusiveness of the processing.[50]

[47] European Data Protection Board, "Guidelines 05/2020 on Consent under Regulation 2016/679," paras 13–54, https://edpb.europa.eu/sites/edpb/files/files/file1/edpb_guidelines_202005_consent_en.pdf, accessed January 15, 2023.

[48] For a thorough overview of that principle, see: Article 29 Working Party, "Opinion 03/2013 on purpose limitation," https://ec.europa.eu/justice/article-29/documentation/opinion-recommendation/files/2013/wp203_en.pdf, accessed January 16, 2023.

[49] Recital 50 GDPR also highlights the relevance of other criteria such as "the nature of the personal data, the consequences of the intended further processing for data subjects, and the existence of appropriate safeguards in both the original and intended further processing operations."

[50] More examples can be found in Annex 2 of: Article 29 Working Party, "Opinion 06/2014 on the notion of legitimate interests of the data controller under Article 7 of Directive 95/46/EC," www.dataprotection.ro/servlet/ViewDocument?id=1086, accessed January 14, 2023.

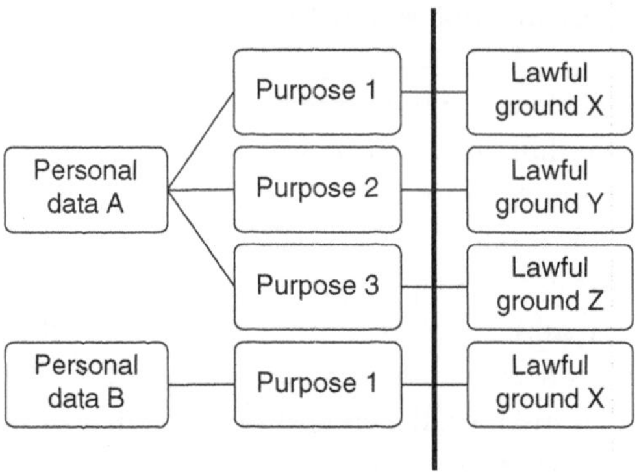

FIGURE 7.3 Lawfulness and purpose limitation, combined

7.4.1.2 Necessity and Compatibility in AI Systems

While complying with the principles of lawfulness and purpose limitation is already a challenge in itself, the very nature of AI systems spices it up even more. The training of machine learning models, for example, often involves the reuse, as training datasets, of personal data originally collected for completely unrelated purposes. While it is still unclear whether scraping publicly accessible personal data should be regarded as *a further processing* activity subject to the compatibility assessment pursuant to Articles 6(1)b and 6(4) GDPR, or as a *new collection* for which the said entity would automatically need to rely on a *different* lawful ground than the one used to legitimize the original collection, this raises the issue of function creep and loss over one's personal data. The case of Clearview AI is a particularly telling example. Back in 2020, the company started to scrape the internet, including social media platforms, to gather images and videos to train its facial recognition software and offer its clients – among which law enforcement authorities – a search engine designed to look up individuals on the basis of another picture. After multiple complaints and a surge in media attention, Clearview was fined by the Italian,[51] Greek,[52] French,[53]

[51] Garante per la protezione dei dati personali, Ordinanza ingiunzione nei confronti di Clearview AI [2022], www.gpdp.it/web/guest/home/docweb/-/docweb-display/docweb/9751362, accessed January 24, 2023.

[52] Αρχή προστασίας δεδομένων προσωπικού χαρακτήρα, Επιβολή προστίμου στην εταιρεία Clearview AI, Inc [2022], www.dpa.gr/el/enimerwtiko/prakseisArxis/epiboli-prostimoy-stin-etaireia-clearview-ai-inc, accessed January 24, 2023.

[53] Commission nationale de l'informatique et des libertés, Délibération de la formation restreinte n° SAN-2022-019 du octobre 17, 2022 concernant la société Clearview AI [2022], www.legifrance.gouv.fr/cnil/id/CNILTEXT000046444859, accessed January 24, 2023. See also, more recently, the 5.2 million penalty payment issued by the CNIL against Clearview AI for non-compliance with the above-mentioned injunction: Commission nationale de l'informatique et des libertés, Délibération de la formation restreinte n° SAN-2023-005 du 17 avril 2023 concernant la société Clearview AI [2023], www.legifrance.gouv.fr/cnil/id/CNILTEXT000047527412, accessed June 15, 2023.

and UK[54] regulators for having processed these images without a valid lawful ground. The Austrian regulator issued a similar decision, if not paired with a fine.[55] As detailed in Section 7.4.1.1, the fact that these images are *publicly accessible* does not, indeed, mean that they are *freely reusable* for any purpose. All five authorities noted the particularly intrusive nature of the processing at stake, the amount of individuals included in the database, and the absence of any relationship between Clearview AI and the data subjects who could therefore not reasonably expect their biometric data to be repurposed for the training of a facial recognition algorithm.

The training of Large Language Models ("LLMs") such as OpenAI's GPT-4 or EleutherAI's GPT-J raises similar concerns, which the Garante recently flagged in its decision to temporarily ban[56] – then conditionally reauthorize –[57] ChatGPT on the Italian territory.[58] This even prompted the EDPB to set up a dedicated task force to "foster cooperation and to exchange information on possible enforcement actions conducted by data protection authorities."[59] Along the same lines, but looking at the

[54] Information Commissioner's Office, Monetary Penalty Notice to Clearview AI Inc of May 26, 2022 [2022], https://ico.org.uk/media/action-weve-taken/mpns/4020436/clearview-ai-inc-mpn-20220518.pdf, accessed June 15, 2023; see also, for the order to stop obtaining and using the personal data of UK residents that is publicly available on the internet, and to delete the data of UK residents from its systems: Information Commissioner's Office, Enforcement Notice to Clearview AI Inc. of May 26, 2022 [2022], https://ico.org.uk/media/action-weve-taken/enforcement-notices/4020437/clearview-ai-inc-en-20220518.pdf, accessed June 15, 2023.

[55] Datenschutzbehörde, Decision of May 9, 2023 against Clearview AI [2023], https://noyb.eu/sites/default/files/2023-05/Clearview%20Decision%20Redacted.pdf.

[56] Garante per la protezione dei dati personali, Provvedimento del 30 marzo 2023 [9870832] [2023], www.garanteprivacy.it/web/guest/home/docweb/-/docweb-display/docweb/9870832, accessed June 15, 2023. An earlier decision issued against Luka Inc., the company behind Replika, also questioned the lawful ground applicable in the context of companion chatbots. See: Garante per la protezione dei dati personali, Provvedimento del 2 febbraio 2023 [9852214] [2023], www.garanteprivacy.it/web/guest/home/docweb/-/docweb-display/docweb/9852214, accessed June 15, 2023.

[57] Garante per la protezione dei dati personali, ChatGPT: Garante privacy, limitazione provvisoria sospesa se OpenAI adotterà le misure richieste. L'Autorità ha dato tempo allá società fino al 30 aprile per mettersi in regola [2023], www.garanteprivacy.it/home/docweb/-/docweb-display/docweb/9874751, accessed June 15, 2023; ChatGPT: OpenAI riapre la piattaforma in italia garantendo più trasparenza e più diritti a utenti e non utenti europei, www.gpdp.it/home/docweb/-/docweb-display/docweb/9881490. For an overview of the new controls added by ChatGPT following the Garante's ban, see the dedicated Help Centre Article on OpenAI's website: https://help.openai.com/en/articles/7842364-how-chatgpt-and-our-language-models-are-developed, accessed June 15, 2023. Yet, OpenAI did not offer any solution to remedy the unlawfulness of the processing of the personal data contained in the dataset used to train ChatGPT.

[58] It is also worth noting that OpenAI now faces a class action in California for a breach of both data protection and copyright law. See: Gerrit De Vynck, "ChatGPT maker OpenAI faces a lawsuit over how it used people's data" (2023) *Washington Post* (June 28), www.washingtonpost.com/technology/2023/06/28/openai-chatgpt-lawsuit-class-action/, accessed July 4, 2023.

[59] The EDPB announced the creation of the task force back in April 2023. See: www.edpb.europa.eu/news/news/2023/edpb-resolves-dispute-transfers-meta-and-creates-task-force-chat-gpt. In May 2024, it published a meager interim report documenting the results of the said taskforce that "reflect[s] the common denominator agreed by the Supervisory Authorities in their interpretation of the applicable provisions of the GDPR in relation to the matters that are within the scope of their investigation."

inference rather than the training phase, relying on algorithmic systems to draw predictions might not always be proportional – or even necessary – to achieve a certain objective. Think about an obligation to wear a smart watch to dynamically adjust a health insurance premium, for instance.

As hinted at earlier, the principle of "data minimization" requires to limit the amount of personal data processed to what is objectively necessary to achieve the purposes that have been specified at the collection stage (Article 5(1)c GDPR). At first glance, this seems to clash with the vast amount of data often used to train and tap into the potential of AI systems. It is therefore essential to reverse the "collect first, think after" mindset by laying down the objectives that the AI system is supposed to achieve *before* harvesting the data used to train or fuel its predictive capabilities. Doing so, however, is not always realistic when such systems are designed outside any concrete application area and are meant to evolve over time. Certain techniques can nonetheless help reduce their impact on individuals' privacy. At the training stage, pseudonymization methods such as generalization and randomization – both discussed in Section 7.3.1.2 – remain pertinent. Standard feature selection methods can also assist controllers in pruning their training datasets from variables that are of little added-value in the development of their model.[60] In addition, federated machine learning, which relies on the training, sharing and aggregation of "local" models, is a viable alternative to the centralization of training datasets in the hands of a single entity, and reduces the risks associated with their duplication.[61] At the inference stage, running the machine learning model on the device itself rather than hosting it on the cloud is also an option to cut on the need to share personal data with a central entity.[62]

7.4.2 *The Complexity of AI Systems v. Transparency and Explainability*

7.4.2.1 Ex-ante and Ex-post Transparency Mechanisms

As a general principle, transparency percolates through the entire Regulation and plays a critical role in an increasingly datified society. As noted in Recital 39 GDPR,

See: European Data Protection Board, "Report of the Work Undertaken by the ChatGPT Taskforce," www.edpb.europa.eu/system/files/2024-05/edpb_20240523_report_chatgpt_taskforce_en.pdf. Looking beyond the EU, ChatGPT is also on the radar of the Office of the Privacy Commissioner of Canada. See: Office of the Privacy Commissioner of Canada, Announcement of April 4, 2023, www.priv.gc.ca/en/opc-news/news-and-announcements/2023/an_230404/, accessed June 15, 2023.

60 For an overview of these methods: Jason Brownlee, "How to choose a feature selection method for machine learning" (MachineLearningMastery.com, November 26, 2019), https://machinelearningmastery.com/feature-selection-with-real-and-categorical-data/, accessed January 25, 2023.

61 Stephanie Rossello, Luis Muñoz-González, and Roberto Díaz Morales, "Data protection by design in AI? The case of federated learning" (2021) *Computerrecht: Tijdschrift voor Informatica, Telecommunicatie en Recht*, 3: 273.

62 For other relevant examples of minimization techniques that can be deployed at the inference stage, see: Information Commissioner's Office, "Guidance on AI and Data Protection" (n 30) 66–68.

"it should be transparent to natural persons that personal data concerning them are collected, used, consulted or otherwise processed and to what extent the personal data are or will be processed." To meet that objective, Articles 13 and 14 detail the full list of information controllers must provide to data subjects. It includes, among others, the contact details of the controller and its representative, the purposes and legal basis of the processing, the categories of personal data concerned, any recipient, and information on how to exercise their rights.[63] Article 12 then obliges controllers to communicate that information in a "concise, transparent, intelligible and easily accessible way, using clear and plain language," in particular for information addressed to children. This requires them to tailor the way they substantiate transparency to their audience by adapting the tone and language to the targeted group. Beyond making complex environments observable, this form of *ex-ante* transparency also pursues an instrumental goal by enabling other prerogatives.[64] As pointed out in literature, "neither rectification or erasure [...] nor blocking or objecting to the processing of personal data seems easy or even possible unless the data subject knows exactly what data [are being processed] and how."[65] Articles 13 and 14 therefore ensure that data subjects are equipped with the necessary information to later exercise their rights.

In this regard, Articles 15 to 22 complement Articles 13 and 14 by granting data subjects an arsenal of prerogatives they can use to regain control or balance information asymmetries. These include the right to access, to rectify, to erase, restrict, and move one's data, as well as the right to challenge and to object to certain types of automated decision-making processes. More specifically, Article 15 grants data subjects the right to request a confirmation that personal data concerning them are being processed, more information on the relevant processing operations and a copy of the personal data involved. As a form of *ex-post* transparency mechanism, it allows data subjects to look beyond what is provided in a typical privacy policy and obtain an additional, individualized layer of transparency. Compared to the information provided in the context of Articles 13 and 14, controllers should, when answering an access request, tailor the information provided to the data subject's specific situation. This would involve sharing the recipients to whom their personal data have *actually* been disclosed, or the sources from which these have *actually* been obtained – a point of information that might not always be clear at the time

[63] For a detailed overview of Articles 12, 13, and 14 GDPR, see: Article 29 Working Party, "Guidelines on Transparency under Regulation 2016/679," https://ec.europa.eu/newsroom/article29/redirection/document/51025, accessed January 16, 2023.

[64] Laurens Naudts, Pierre Dewitte, and Jef Ausloos, "Meaningful transparency through data rights: A multidimensional analysis" (2022) *Research Handbook on EU Data Protection Law* 530, 540.

[65] Jef Ausloos and Pierre Dewitte, "Shattering one-way mirrors – data subject access rights in practice" (2018) *International Data Privacy Law*, 8: 7, https://academic.oup.com/idpl/advance-article/doi/10.1093/idpl/ipy001/4922871, accessed May 16, 2023. See also the many references therein.

the privacy policy is drafted.[66] By allowing data subjects to verify controllers' practices, Article 15 paves the way for further remedial actions, should it be necessary. It is therefore regarded as one of the cornerstones of data protection law, and is one of the few guarantees explicitly acknowledged in Article 8 CFREU.

7.4.2.2 Algorithmic Transparency – And Explainability?

AI systems are increasingly used to make or support decisions concerning individuals based on their personal data. Fields of applications range from predictive policing to hiring strategies and healthcare, but all share a certain degree of opacity as well as the potential to adversely affect the data subjects concerned. The GDPR seeks to address these risks through a patchwork of provisions regulating what Article 22(1) defines as "decisions based solely on automated processing, including profiling, which produce legal effects concerning [the data subject] or similarly significantly affect him or her." This would typically include, according to Recital 71, the "automatic refusal of an online credit applications" or "e-recruiting practices without any form of human intervention." Based *solely*, in this case, suggests that the decision must not necessarily be *taken* by an automated system for it to fall within the scope of Article 22(1). The routine usage of a predictive system by a person who is not in a position to exercise any influence or meaningful oversight over its outcome would, for instance, also fall under Article 22(1).[67] While fabricating human involvement is certainly not a viable way out, national data protection authorities are still refining the precise contours of that notion.[68]

Controllers that rely on such automated decision-making must inform data subjects about their existence, and provide them with "meaningful information about the logic involved," as well as their "significance and the envisaged consequences." This results from the combined reading of Articles 13(2)f, 14(2)g, and 15(1)h. Additionally, Article 22(3) and Recital 71 grant data subjects the right to obtain human intervention, express their point of view, contest the decision and – allegedly – obtain an explanation of the decision reached. Over the last few years, these provisions have fueled a lively debate as to the existence of a so-called "right to

[66] The fact that the elements listed in Article 15 partially overlap with the ones listed in Articles 13 and 14 does not mean that the controller can always answer an access request by recycling elements from its privacy policy or record of processing. See: European Data Protection Board, "Guidelines 01/2022 on data subject rights – right of access," para 111, https://edpb.europa.eu/our-work-tools/our-documents/guidelines/guidelines-012022-data-subject-rights-right-access_en, accessed January 16, 2023.

[67] Article 29 Working Party, "Guidelines on data protection impact assessment (DPIA) and determining whether processing is 'likely to result in a high risk' for the purposes of regulation 2016/679" 21, https://ec.europa.eu/newsroom/document.cfm?doc_id=47711, accessed January 25, 2022.

[68] See, for the interpretation proposed by national supervisory authorities across Europe: Sebastião Barros Vale and Gabriela Zanfir-Fortuna, "Automated decision-making under the GDPR: Practical cases from courts and data protection authorities" (Future of Privacy Forum, 2022), https://fpf.org/wp-content/uploads/2022/05/FPF-ADM-Report-R2-singles.pdf, accessed January 11, 2023.

explanation" that would allow data subjects to enquire about how a *specific* decision was reached rather than only about the overall *functioning* of the underlying system.[69] Regardless of these controversies, it is commonly agreed that controllers should avoid "complex mathematical explanations" and rather focus on concrete elements such as "the categories of data that have been or will be used in the profiling or decision-making process; why these categories are considered pertinent; how the profile is built, including any statistics used in the analysis; why this profile is relevant and how it is used for a decision concerning the data subject."[70] The "right" explanation will therefore strongly depend on the sector and audience at stake.[71] A media outlet that decides to offer users a personalized news feed might, for instance, need to explain the actual characteristics taken into account by its recommender system, as well as their weight in the decision-making process and how past behavior has led the system to take a specific editorial decision.[72]

7.4.3 *The Dynamicity of AI v. the Risk-Based Approach*

7.4.3.1 Accountability, Responsibility, Data Protection by Design and DPIAs

Compared to its predecessor,[73] one of the main objectives of the GDPR was to move away from compliance as a mere ticking-the-box exercise – or window dressing[74] – by incentivizing controllers to take up a more proactive role in the

[69] See, among others: Bryce Goodman and Seth Flaxman, "European Union Regulations on algorithmic decision-making and a 'right to explanation'" (2017) *AI Magazine*, 38, http://arxiv.org/abs/1606.08813; Sandra Wachter, Brent Mittelstadt, and Luciano Floridi, "Why a right to explanation of automated decision-making does not exist in the general data protection regulation" (2017) *International Data Privacy Law*, 7: 76; Gianclaudio Malgieri and Giovanni Comandé, "Why a right to legibility of automated decision-making exists in the general data protection regulation" (2017) *International Data Privacy Law*, 7: 243.

[70] See Annex 1 of Article 29 Working Party, "WP29, guidelines on DPIA" (n 67) 31.

[71] The British regulator has provided a solid overview of the different types of explanations controllers could provide. See, more specifically, the Section "What goes into an explanation" from the Information Commissioner's Office and Alan Turing Institute, "Explaining decisions made with AI," https://ico.org.uk/media/for-organisations/guide-to-data-protection/key-dp-themes/explaining-decisions-made-with-artificial-intelligence-1-0.pdf, accessed January 25, 2023.

[72] Max van Drunen, Natali Helberger, and Mariella Bastian, "Know your algorithm: What media organizations need to explain to their users about news personalization" (2019) *International Data Privacy Law*, 9: 220.

[73] Directive 95/46/EC of the European Parliament and of the Council of 24 October 1995 on the protection of individuals with regard to the processing of personal data and on the free movement of such data [1995] OJ L281/31 ELI: http://data.europa.eu/eli/dir/1995/46/oj.

[74] The EDPS indeed noted that "in the past, privacy and data protection have been perceived by many organisations as an issue mainly related to legal compliance, often confined to the mere formal process of issuing long privacy policies covering any potential eventuality and reacting to incidents in order to minimise the damage to their own interests." See: European Data Protection Supervisor, "Opinion 5/2018 – Preliminary Opinion on Privacy by Design," para 13, https://edps.europa.eu/sites/edp/files/publication/18-05-31_preliminary_opinion_on_privacy_by_design_en_0.pdf, accessed January 15, 2023.

implementation of appropriate measures to protect individuals' rights and freedoms. This led to the abolition of the antique, paternalistic obligation for controllers to notify their processing operations to national regulators in favor of a more flexible approach articulated around the obligation to maintain a record of processing activities (Article 30), to notify data breaches to competent authorities and the affected data subjects (Articles 33 and 34) and to consult the former in cases where a data protection impact assessment ("DPIA") indicates that the processing would result in a high risk in the absence of measures taken by the controller to mitigate the risk (Article 36). The underlying idea was to responsibilize controllers by shifting the burden of analyzing and mitigating the risks to data subject's rights and freedoms onto them. Known as the "risk-based approach," it ensures both the flexibility and scalability needed for the underlying rules to remain pertinent in a wide variety of scenarios. As noted in legal literature, the risk-based approach "provides a way to carry out the shift to accountability that underlies much of the data protection reform, using the notion of risk as a reference point in light of which we can assess whether the organisational and technical measures taken by the controller offer a sufficient level of protection."[75]

The combined reading of Articles 5(2) ("accountability"), 24(1) ("responsibility"), and 25(1) ("data protection by design") now requires controllers to take into account the state of the art, the cost of implementation, and the nature, scope, context, and purposes as well as the risks posed by the processing. They should implement, both at the time of determination of the means for processing and at the time of the processing itself, appropriate technical and organizational measures to ensure and demonstrate compliance with the Regulation. In other words, they must act responsibly as of the design stage, and throughout the entire data processing lifecycle. Data protection-specific risks are usually addressed in a DPIA, which should at least provide a detailed description of the relevant processing activities, an assessment of their necessity and proportionality, as well as an inventory of the risks and corresponding mitigation strategies (see Figure 7.4).[76] While Article 35(1) obliges controllers to conduct a DPIA for processing activities that are "likely to result in a high risk for rights and freedoms of natural persons," such an exercise, even if succinct, is also considered as best practice for all controllers regardless of the level of risk.[77]

[75] Claudia Quelle, 'Enhancing Compliance under the General Data Protection Regulation: The Risky Upshot of the Accountability- and Risk-Based Approach' (2018) 9 *European Journal of Risk Regulation* 502, 505.

[76] See, for a detailed overview of the steps involved in a DPIA: Article 35(7) GDPR and Annex 2 of the Article 29 Working Party, "WP29, Guidelines on DPIA" (n 67).

[77] European Data Protection Board, "Guidelines 4/2019 on Article 25 Data Protection by Design and by Default," para 32, https://edpb.europa.eu/sites/edpb/files/files/file1/edpb_guidelines_201904_dataprotection_by_design_and_by_default_v2.0_en.pdf, accessed May 3, 2022.

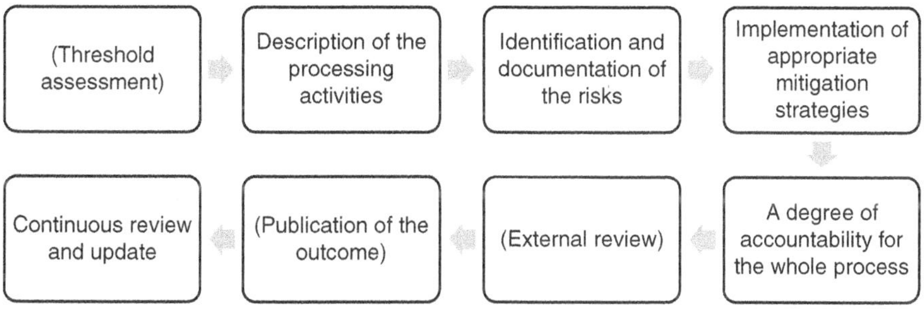

FIGURE 7.4 Overview of the main steps of a Data Protection Impact Assessment

7.4.3.2 From DPIAs to AIAs, and the Rise of Algorithmic Governance

The development and use of AI systems are often considered as processing likely to result in a "high risk," for which a DPIA is therefore mandatory. In fact, Article 35(3) GDPR, read in combination with the Guidelines from the WP29 on the matter,[78] extends that obligation to any processing that involves, among others, the evaluation, scoring or systematic monitoring of individuals, the processing of data on a large scale, the matching or combining of datasets or the innovative use or application of new technological or organizational solutions. All these attributes are, in most cases, inherent to AI systems and therefore exacerbate the risks for individuals' fundamental rights and freedoms. Among these is, for instance, the right not to be discriminated. This is best illustrated by the Dutch "Toeslagenaffaire," following which the national regulator fined the Tax Administration for having unlawfully created erroneous risk profiles using a machine learning algorithm in an attempt to detect and prevent child care benefits fraud, which led to the exclusion of thousands of alleged fraudsters from social protection.[79] Recent research has also uncovered the risk of bias in predictive policing and offensive speech detection systems, both vulnerable to imbalanced training datasets, and susceptible to reflect past discrimination.[80]

Addressing these risks requires more than just complying with the principles of lawfulness, purpose limitation, and data minimization. It also goes beyond the provision of explanations, however accessible and accurate these may be. In fact, that issue largely exceeds the boundaries of the GDPR itself which, as hinted in Section 7.3, is but one regulatory angle among many others. The AI Act is, for

78 Article 29 Working Party, "WP29, Guidelines on DPIA" (n 67) 9–12.

79 Autoriteit Persoonsgegevens, "Boete Belastingdienst voor zwarte lijst FSV" April 12, 2022, https://autoriteitpersoonsgegevens.nl/nl/nieuws/boete-belastingdienst-voor-zwarte-lijst-fsv, accessed January 25, 2023.

80 Competition and Market Authority and others, "Auditing algorithms: The existing landscape, role of regulators and future outlook" (Digital Regulation Cooperation Forum) Findings from the DRCF Algorithmic Processing workstream – Spring 2022, www.gov.uk/government/publications/findings-from-the-drcf-algorithmic-processing-workstream-spring-2022/auditing-algorithms-the-existing-landscape-role-of-regulators-and-future-outlook, accessed January 26, 2023.

instance, a case in point.[81] More generally, this book is a testimony to the diversity of the regulatory frameworks applicable to AI systems. This calls for a drastic rethinking of how AI systems are designed and deployed to mitigate their adversarial impact on society. This has led to the development of *Algorithmic* – rather than *Data Protection* – Impact Assessments ("AIAs"), conceived as broader risk management approaches that integrate but are not limited to data protection concerns.[82] While these assessments can assist controllers in developing their own technology, they are also relevant for controllers relying on off-the-shelf AI solutions offered by third parties, who are increasingly resorting to auditing and regular testing to ensure that these products comply with all applicable legislation. All in all, the recent surge in awareness of AI's risks has laid the groundwork for the rise of a form of algorithmic accountability.[83] Far from an isolated legal exercise, however, identifying and mitigating the risks associated with the use of AI systems is, by nature, an interdisciplinary exercise. Likewise, proper solutions will mostly follow from the research conducted in fora that bridge the gap between these different domains, such as the explainable AI ("XAI") and human–computer interaction ("HCI") communities.

7.5 CONCLUSION

As pointed out from the get go, this chapter serves as an entry point into the intersection of AI and data protection law, and strives to orient the reader toward the most authoritative sources on each of the subjects it touches upon. It is hence but a curated selection of the most relevant data protection principles and rules articulated around the most salient characteristics of AI systems. Certain important issues therefore had to be left out, among which the obligation to ensure a level of security appropriate to the risks at stake, the rules applicable to special categories of personal data, the exercise of data subjects rights, the role of certification mechanisms and codes of conduct, or the safeguards surrounding the transfers of personal data to third countries. Specific sources on these issues are, however, plentiful.

There is no doubt that AI systems, and the large-scale processing of personal data that is often associated with their development and use, has put a strain on individuals' fundamental rights and freedoms. The goal of this chapter was to highlight the

[81] Regulation (EU) 2024/1689 of the European Parliament and of the Council of 13 June 2024 laying down harmonised rules on artificial intelligence and amending Regulations (EC) No 300/2008, (EU) No 167/2013, (EU) No 168/2013, (EU) 2018/858, (EU) 2018/1139 and (EU) 2019/2144 and Directives 2014/90/EU, (EU) 2016/797 and (EU) 2020/1828 (Artificial Intelligence Act) (Text with EEA relevance) [2024] OJ L144/1 ELI: http://data.europa.eu/eli/reg/2024/1689/oj.

[82] See, for a use case in the healthcare sector: Lara Groves, "Algorithmic impact assessment: A case study in healthcare" (Ada Lovelace Institute, 2022), www.adalovelaceinstitute.org/report/algorithmic-impact-assessment-case-study-healthcare/, accessed January 26, 2023.

[83] Christian Katzenbach and Lena Ulbricht, "Algorithmic governance" (2019) *Internet Policy Review*, 8(4), https://policyreview.info/concepts/algorithmic-governance, accessed January 26, 2023.

role of the GDPR in mitigating these risks by clarifying its position and function within the broader EU regulatory ecosystem. It also aimed to equip the reader with the main concepts necessary to decipher the complexity of its material and personal scope of application. More importantly, it ambitioned to debunk the myth according to which the applicability of the GDPR to AI systems would inevitably curtail their deployment, or curb innovation altogether. As illustrated throughout this contribution, tensions do exist. But the open-ended nature of Article 5, paired with the interpretation power granted to European and national supervisory authorities, provide the flexibility needed to adapt the GDPR to a wide range of scenarios. As with all legislation that aims to balance competing interests, the key mostly – if not entirely – lies in ensuring the necessity and proportionality of the interferences of the rights at stake. For that to happen, it is crucial that all stakeholders are aware of both the risks raised by AI systems for the fundamental rights to privacy and data protection, and of the solutions that can be deployed to mitigate these concerns and hence guarantee an appropriate level of protection for all the individuals involved.

8

Tort Liability and Artificial Intelligence

Some Challenges and (Regulatory) Responses

Jan De Bruyne and Wannes Ooms

8.1 INTRODUCTION

Artificial intelligence (AI) is becoming increasingly important in our daily lives and so is academic research on its impact on various legal domains.[1] One of the fields that has attracted much attention is extra-contractual or tort liability. That is because AI will inevitably cause damage, for instance, following certain actions/decisions (e.g., an automated robot vacuum not recognizing a human and eventually harming them) or when it provides incorrect information that results in harm (e.g., when AI used in construction leads to the collapse of a building that hurts a bystander). Reference can also be made to accidents involving autonomous vehicles.[2] The autopilot of a Tesla car, for instance, was not able to distinguish a white tractor-trailer crossing the road from the bright sky above, leading to a fatal crash.[3] A self-driving Uber car hit a pedestrian in Arizona. The woman later died in the hospital.[4] These – and many other – examples show that accidents may happen despite optimizing national and supranational safety rules for AI. This is when questions of liability become significant.[5] The importance of liability and AI systems has already been

[1] See, for example, Ronald Leenes et al., "Regulatory challenges of robotics: some guidelines for addressing legal and ethical issues" (2017) *Law, Innovation and Technology*, 9(1): 2; Marcelo Corrales, Mark Fenwick, and Nikolaus Forgó, *Robotics, AI and the Future of Law* (Springer, 2018); Jacob Turner, *Robot Rules: Regulating Artificial Intelligence* (Springer, 2018); Martin Ebers and Susana Navas (eds), *Algorithms and Law* (Cambridge University Press, 2020); Matt Hervey and Matthew Lavy, *The Law of Artificial Intelligence* (Sweet & Maxwell, 2021); Jan De Bruyne and Cedric Vanleenhove, *Artificial Intelligence and the Law* (Intersentia, 2023).

[2] See, for example, Jan De Bruyne and Jochen Tanghe, "Liability for damage caused by autonomous vehicles: a Belgian perspective" (2017) *Journal of European Tort Law*, 8(3): 324.

[3] The Tesla Team, "A Tragic Loss" (June 30, 2016) *Tesla.com*, www.teslamotors.com/blog/tragic-loss, accessed February 16, 2023.

[4] Sam Levin and Julia Carrie, "Self-driving Uber kills Arizona woman in first fatal crash involving pedestrian" *The Guardian* (March 19, 2018), www.theguardian.com/technology/2018/mar/19/uber-self-driving-car-kills-woman-arizona-tempe, accessed February 16, 2023.

[5] European Commission, "Report on the safety and liability implications of Artificial Intelligence, the Internet of Things and robotics" COM(2020) 64 final.

mentioned in several documents issued by the European Union (EU). The White Paper on Artificial Intelligence, for instance, stresses that the main risks related to the use of AI concern the application of rules designed to protect fundamental rights as well as safety and liability-related issues.[6] Scholars have also concluded that "[l] iability certainly represents one of the most relevant and recurring themes"[7] when it comes to AI systems. Extra-contractual liability also encompasses many fundamental questions and problems that arise in the context of AI and liability.

Both academic research[8] and policy initiatives[9] have already addressed many pressing issues in this legal domain. Instead of discussing the impact of AI on different (tort) liability regimes or issues of legal personality for AI systems,[10] we will touch

6 European Commission, "White Paper on Artificial Intelligence – A European approach to excellence and trust" COM(2020) 65 final.

7 E. Palmerini et al., "RoboLaw: Towards a European framework for robotics regulation" (2016) *Robotics and Autonomous Systems*, 86: 78–85, 83.

8 See, for example, the many contributions in Sebastian Lohsse, Reiner Schulze, and Dirk Staudenmayer (eds), *Liability for Artificial Intelligence and the Internet of Things* (Hart Publishing, 2019); Mihailis Diamantis, "Vicarious liability for AI" (2021) *U Iowa Legal Studies*, 27: Research Paper; Anna Beckers and Gunther Teubner, *Three Liability Regimes for Artificial Intelligence: Algorithmic Actants, Hybrids, Crowds* (Bloomsbury Publishing, 2021); Jan De Bruyne, Elias Van Gool and Thomas Gils, "Tort law and damage caused by AI systems" in Jan De Bruyne and Cedric Vanleenhove (eds), *Artificial Intelligence and the Law* (Intersentia, 2023); Mark A. Geistfeld et al., *Civil Liability for Artificial Intelligence and Software* (Walter de Gruyter GmbH & Co KG, 2022); Philipp Hacker, "The European AI liability directives – Critique of a half-hearted approach and lessons for the future" (2023) *Computer Law & Security Review*, 51:1–17; Jan De Bruyne, Orian Dheu and Charlotte Ducuing, "The European Commission's approach to extra-contractual liability and AI – An evaluation of the AI liability directive and the revised product liability directive" (2023) *Computer Law & Security Review* 51: 1–19; Orian Dheu, and Jan De Bruyne, "Artificial Intelligence and Tort Law: A 'Multi-faceted' Reality" *European Review of Private Law*, 31: 261–298 with further references. It should be noted that research has also been done on the contractual liability of AI (e.g., Hervé Jacquemin and Jean-Benoit Hubin, "Aspects contractuels et de responsabilité civile en matière d'intelligence artificielle" in Hervé Jacquemin and Alexandre De Streel (eds), *L'intelligence artificielle et le droit* (Larcier, 2017) 77; Martin Ebers, Cristina Poncibo, and Mimi Zou (eds), *Contracting and Contract Law in the Age of Artificial Intelligence* (Bloomsbury Publishing, 2021); Jan De Bruyne and Maarten Herbosch, "Artificiële intelligentie, aansprakelijkheid en contractenrecht. Enkele aandachtspunten voor bedrijfsjuristen" in IBJ, *Artificiële intelligentie door de ogen van de bedrijfsjurist / L'intelligence artificielle à travers les yeux des juristes d'entreprise* (Larcier, 2022) 45.

9 See, for example, European Parliament, "Report with recommendations to the Commission on Civil Law Rules on Robotics" (2017) 2015/2103(INL); European Parliament, "Report with recommendations to the Commission on a civil liability regime for artificial intelligence" (2020) 2020/2014(INL); Expert Group on Liability and New Technologies – New Technologies Formation, "Liability for artificial intelligence and other emerging digital technologies" (Publications Office of the European Union, 2019); COM(2020) 64 final (n 5). The European Commission adopted two proposals containing liability rules for AI and providing some guidance on many of these issues. One proposal revises the Product Liability Directive (see n 24) and another one introduces an extra-contractual civil liability regime for AI systems (see n 23).

10 See on this topic, for example, Joanna J. Bryson, Mihailis E. Diamantis, and Thomas D. Grant, "Of, for, and by the people: The legal lacuna of synthetic persons" (2017) *Artificial Intelligence and Law*, 25: 273; Mark Fenwick and Stefan Wrbka, "AI and legal personhood" in Larry A. DiMatteo, Cristina Poncibò, and Michael Cannarsa (eds.) *The Cambridge Handbook of Artificial Intelligence: Global Perspectives on Law and Ethics* (Cambridge University Press, 2022) 288–303.

upon some of the main challenges and proposed solutions at the EU and national level. More specifically, we will illustrate the remaining importance of national law (Section 8.2) and procedural elements (Section 8.3). We will then focus on the problematic qualification and application of certain tort law concepts in an AI-context (Section 8.4). The most important findings are summarized in the chapter's conclusion (Section 8.5).[11]

8.2 THE REMAINING IMPORTANCE OF NATIONAL LAW FOR AI-RELATED LIABILITY

In the recent years, several initiatives with regard to liability for damage involving AI have been taken or discussed at the EU level. Without going into detail, we will provide a high-level overview to give the reader the necessary background to understand some of the issues that we will discuss later.[12]

The European Parliament (EP) issued its first report on civil law rules for robots in 2017. It urged the European Commission (EC) to consider a legislative instrument that would deal with the liability for damage caused by autonomous systems and robots, thereby evaluating the feasibility of a strict liability or a risk management approach.[13] This was followed by a report issued by an Expert Group set up by the EC on the "Liability for artificial intelligence and other emerging digital technologies" in November 2019. The report explored the main liability challenges posed to current tort law by AI. It concluded that liability regimes "in force in member states ensure at least basic protection of victims whose damage is caused by the operation of such new technologies."[14] However, the specific characteristics of AI systems, such as their complexity, self-learning abilities, opacity, and limited predictability,

[11] It should be noted that this chapter is based on a presentation given at the KU Leuven Summer School on the Law, Ethics and Policy of AI from 2021 to 2024. As such, it aims to be introductory and understandable to readers with a nonlegal background as well. This chapter also builds upon previous work. See, for example, De Bruyne, Van Gool, and Gils, "Tort law and damage" (n 8); Jan De Bruyne, Elias Van Gool, and Amber Boes, "Wat bracht 2022 en wat brengt de toekomst op het vlak van artificiële intelligentie en buitencontractuele aansprakelijkheid?" in Thierry Vansweevelt and Britt Weyts (eds), *Recente ontwikkelingen in het aansprakelijkheids- en verzekeringsrecht* (Intersentia, 2022); Jan De Bruyne and Orian Dheu, "Liability for damage caused by artificial intelligence – Some food for thought and current proposals" in Phillip Morgan (ed.), *Tort Liability and Autonomous Systems Accidents Common and Civil Law Perspectives* (Edward Elgar Publishing, 2024); De Bruyne Dheu, "Artificial Intelligence and Tort Law: A 'Multi-faceted' Reality" (n 8); De Bruyne, Dheu and Ducuing, "The European Commission's approach to extra-contractual liability and AI – An evaluation of the AI liability directive and the revised product liability directive" (n 8).

[12] See extensively: De Bruyne and Dheu, "Liability for damage caused by artificial intelligence – Some food for thought and current proposals" (n 11).

[13] European Parliament, "Civil Law Rules on Robotics" (n 9). Note that several reports have also been published upon request by European institutions (e.g., Andrea Bertolini, "Artificial intelligence and civil liability" (Report for the European Parliament JURI Committee, 2020)).

[14] Expert Group on Liability and New Technologies – New Technologies Formation, "Liability for artificial intelligence" (n 9).

may make it more difficult to offer victims a claim for compensation in all cases where this seems justified. The report also stressed that the allocation of liability may be unfair or inefficient. It contains several recommendations to remedy potential gaps in EU and national liability regimes.[15] The EC subsequently issued a White Paper on AI in 2020. It had two main building blocks, namely an "ecosystem of trust" and an "ecosystem of excellence."[16] More importantly, the White Paper was accompanied by a report on safety and liability. The report identified several points that needed further attention, such as clarifying the scope of the product liability directive (PLD) or assessing procedural aspects (e.g., identifying the liable person, proving the conditions for a liability claim or accessing the AI system to substantiate the claim).[17] In October 2020, the EP adopted a resolution with recommendations to the EC on a civil liability regime for AI. It favors strict liability for operators of high-risk AI systems and fault-based liability for operators of low-risk AI systems,[18] with a reversal of the burden of proof.[19] In April 2021, the EC issued its draft AI Act, which entered into force in August 2024 after a long legislative procedure.[20] The AI Act adheres to a risk-based approach. While certain AI systems are prohibited, several additional requirements apply for placing high-risk AI systems on the market. The AI Act also imposes obligations upon several parties, such as providers and users of high-risk AI systems.[21] Those obligations will be important to assess the potential liability of such parties, for instance, when determining whether an operator or user committed a fault (i.e., violation of a specific legal norm or negligence).[22] More importantly, the EC published two proposals in September 2022 that aim to adapt (tort) liability rules to the digital age, the circular economy, and the impact of the global value chain. The "AI Liability Directive" contains rules on the disclosure of information and the alleviation of the burden of proof in relation to damage caused

[15] Ibid.; Andrea Bertolini and Francesca Episcopo, "The Expert Group's Report on Liability for Artificial Intelligence and Other Emerging Digital Technologies: A critical assessment," (2021) *European Journal of Risk Regulation*, 12(3): 644.

[16] COM(2020) 65 final (n 6).

[17] COM(2020) 64 final (n 5).

[18] Under the law of evidence, the default rule is that each party has to prove its claims and contentions (*actori incumbit probatio*). The claimant/victim would thus have to prove that a fault of the operator or provider caused the damage they suffered. In some cases, however, this burden can be reversed to other parties, such as the operator, producer, or provider of the AI system. See extensively Section 8.3.

[19] European Parliament, "European Parliament resolution of 20 October 2020 with recommendations to the Commission on a civil liability regime for artificial intelligence" (2020) 2020/2014(INL) art 4 (1).

[20] The AI Act is extensively discussed in Chapter 12 of this book authored by Nathalie A. Smuha and Karen Yeung, "The European Union's AI Act: beyond motherhood and apple pie?" For the original proposal of the AI Act, see Commission, "Proposal for a regulation of the European Parliament and of the Council laying down harmonised rules on artificial intelligence (Artificial Intelligence Act) and amending certain Union legislative acts" COM(2021) 206 final.

[21] Regulation (EU) 2024/1689 of 13 June 2024 laying down harmonised rules on artificial intelligence and amending Regulations (EC) No 300/2008, (EU) No 167/2013, (EU) No 168/2013, (EU) 2018/858, (EU) 2018/1139 and (EU) 2019/2144 and Directives 2014/90/EU, (EU) 2016/797 and (EU) 2020/1828 art 16–27.

[22] De Bruyne, Van Gool and Gils, 'Tort Law and Damage' (n 8) 407–408.

by AI systems.[23] The "revised Product Liability Directive" substantially modifies the current product liability regime by including software within its scope, integrating new circumstances to assess the product's defectiveness and introducing provisions regarding presumptions of defectiveness and causation.[24]

These evolutions show that much is happening at the EU level regarding liability for damage involving AI. The problem, however, is that the European liability landscape is rather heterogeneous. With the exception of the (revised) PLD and the newly proposed AI Liability Directive, contractual and extra-contractual liability frameworks are usually national. While initiatives are thus taken at the EU level, national law remains the most important source when it comes to tort liability and AI. Several of these proposals and initiatives discussed in the previous paragraph contain provisions and concepts that refer to national law or that rely on the national courts for their interpretation.[25] According to Article 8 of the EP Resolution, for instance, the operator will not be liable if he or she can prove that the harm or damage was *caused* without his or her fault, relying on either of the following grounds: (a) the AI system was activated without his or her knowledge while all *reasonable and necessary measures* to avoid such activation outside of the operator's control were taken or (b) *due diligence* was observed by performing all the following actions: selecting a suitable AI system for the right task and skills, putting the AI system duly into operation, monitoring the activities, and maintaining the operational reliability by regularly installing all available updates.[26] The AI Liability Directive also relies on concepts that will eventually have to be explained and interpreted by judges. National courts will, for instance, need to limit the disclosure of evidence to that which is *necessary* and *proportionate* to support a potential claim or a claim for damages.[27] It also relies on national law to determine the scope and definition of "fault" and "causal link."[28] The revised PLD includes different notions that will have to be interpreted, explained, and refined by national judges as well according to their legal tradition. These concepts, for instance, include "reasonably foreseeable," "substantial," "relevant," "proportionate," and "necessary."[29] The definitions provided by courts may vary from one jurisdiction

[23] Commission, "Proposal for a Directive of the European Parliament and of the Council on adapting non-contractual civil liability rules to artificial intelligence" COM(2022) 496 final (hereafter referred to as "AI Liability Directive").

[24] Commission, "Proposal for a Directive of the European Parliament and of the Council on liability for defective products" COM(2022) 495 final (hereafter referred to as "revised PLD").

[25] De Bruyne and Dheu, "Liability for damage caused by artificial intelligence – Some food for thought and current proposals" (n 11) referring to the "tort law dilemma."

[26] European Parliament, "Recommendations on a civil liability regime for artificial intelligence" (n 19).

[27] AI Liability Directive, art 3.4. See for an extensive analysis: Hacker, "The European AI liability directives – Critique of a half-hearted approach and lessons for the future" (n 8).

[28] AI Liability Directive, art 4.1.

[29] Dheu, De Bruyne and, Ducuing, "The European Commission's approach to extra-contractual liability and AI – An evaluation of the AI liability directive and the revised product liability directive" (n 8) 7.

to another, which does give some flexibility to Member States, but may create legal fragmentation as well.[30]

8.3 PROCEDURAL ELEMENTS

A "general, worldwide accepted rule"[31] in the law of evidence is that each party has to prove its claims and contentions (*actori incumbit probatio*).[32] The application of this procedural rule can be challenging when accidents involve AI systems. Such systems are not always easily understandable and interpretable but can come in forms of "black boxes" that evolve through self-learning. Several actors are also involved in the AI life cycle (e.g., the developers of the software, the producer of the hardware, owners of the AI product, suppliers of data, public authorities, or the users of the product). Victims are therefore confronted with the increasingly daunting task of trying to identify and prove AI systems as their source of harm.[33] Moreover, injured parties, especially if they are natural persons, do not always have the needed knowledge on the specific AI system or access to the necessary information to build a case in court.[34] Under the Product Liability Directive, the burden of proof is high as well. A victim has to prove that the product *caused* the damage because it is *defective*, implying that it did not provide the safety one is legitimately entitled to expect.[35] It is also uncertain what exactly constitutes a defect of an advanced AI system. For instance, if an AI diagnosis tool delivers a wrong diagnosis, "there is no obvious malfunctioning that could be the basis for a presumption that the algorithm was defective."[36] It may thus be difficult and costly for consumers to prove the defect when they have no expertise in the field, especially when the computer program is

[30] Ibid.

[31] Ivo Giesen, "The burden of proof and other procedural devices in tort law" in Helmut Koziol and Barbara C. Steiniger (eds), *European Tort Law 2008* (Springer, 2009) 50.

[32] Mojtaba Kazazi, *Burden of Proof and Related Issues: A Study on Evidence Before International Tribunals* (Martinus Nijhoff Publishers, 1996). See, for example, art 8.4, para 1, Civil Code (Wet 13 April 2019 tot invoering van een Burgerlijk Wetboek en tot invoeging van boek 8 'Bewijs' in dat Wetboek, *BS* May 14, 2019, 46353.); art 870 Judicial Code.

[33] Expert Group on Liability and New Technologies – New Technologies Formation, "Liability for artificial intelligence" (n 9) 32–33. Also see: AI Liability Directive, recitals (3)–(7); Dheu, De Bruyne, "Artificial Intelligence and Tort Law: A 'Multi-faceted' Reality" (n 8).

[34] COM(2020) 65 final (n 6) 13; Expert Group on Liability and New Technologies – New Technologies Formation, "Liability for artificial intelligence" (n 9) 35 and 51.

[35] Council Directive 85/374/EEC of July 25, 1985 on the approximation of the laws, regulations and administrative provisions of the Member States concerning liability for defective products [1985] OJ L 210 (further referred to as the "PLD"). See in general: Bernhard Koch et al., "Response of the European Law Institute to the Public Consultation on Civil Liability – Adapting Liability Rules to the Digital Age and Artificial Intelligence" (2022) *Journal of European Tort Law*, 13: 43–46.

[36] Jean-Sébastien Borghetti, "How can artificial intelligence be defective?" in Sebastian Lohsse, Reiner Schulze, and Dirk Staudenmayer (eds), *Liability for Artificial Intelligence and the Internet of Things* (Hart Publishing, 2019) 67 (as referred to in Miriam Buiten, Alexandre de Streel, and Martin Peitz, "EU liability rules for the age of artificial intelligence" (2021) SSRN https://papers.ssrn.com/sol3/papers.cfm?abstract_id=3817520 accessed February 22, 2023 34–35).

complex and not readable *ex post*.[37] An additional hurdle is that the elements of a claim in tort law are governed by national law. An example is the requirement of causation including procedural questions such as the standard of proof or the laws and practice of evidence.[38]

In sum, persons who have suffered harm may not have effective access to the evidence that is necessary to build a case in court and may have less effective redress possibilities compared to situations in which the damage is caused by "traditional" products.[39] It is, however, important that victims of accidents involving AI systems are not confronted with a lower level of protection compared to other products and services for which they would get compensation under national law. Otherwise, societal acceptance of those AI systems and other emerging technologies could be hampered and a hesitance to use them could be the result.[40]

To remedy this "vulnerable" or "weak" position, procedural mechanisms, and solutions have been proposed and discussed in academic scholarship.[41] One can think of disclosure requirements. Article 3 of the AI Liability Directive, for instance, contains several provisions on the disclosure of evidence. A court may, upon the request of a (potential) claimant, order the disclosure of relevant evidence about a specific high-risk AI system that is suspected of having caused damage. Such requests for evidence may be addressed to inter alia the provider of an AI system, a person subject to the provider's obligations or its user.[42] Several requirements must be fulfilled by the (potential) claimant before the court can order the disclosure of evidence.[43] National courts also need to limit the disclosure of evidence to what is necessary and proportionate to support a potential claim or an actual claim for damages.[44] To that end, the legitimate interests of all

37 Also see revised PLD, recitals (30)–(31) ("Injured persons, are, however, often at a significant disadvantage compared to manufacturers in terms of access to, and understanding of, information on how a product was produced and how it operates. This asymmetry of information can undermine the fair apportionment of risk, in particular in cases involving technical or scientific complexity").

38 Koch et al., "Response of the European Law Institute" (n 35) 44–46 and 57–58. Similarity in the context of the PLD: Daily Wuyts, "The product liability directive – more than two decades of defective products in Europe" (2014) *Journal of European Tort Law*, 5(1): 1–34.

39 COM(2020) 65 final (n 6) 13 Also see: Buiten, de Streel, and Peitz, "EU Liability Rules"(n 36) 24–38.

40 COM(2020) 64 final (n 5) 13; De Bruyne, Van Gool, and Gils, "Tort Law and Damage" (n 8) 396–397.

41 See, for example, Gerhard Wagner, "Robot Liability" in Sebastian Lohsse, Reiner Schulze, and Dirk Staudenmayer (eds), *Liability for Artificial Intelligence and the Internet of Things* (Hart Publishing, 2019) 47; Charlotte de Meeus, "The product liability directive at the age of the digital industrial revolution: Fit for innovation?" (2019) *Journal of European Consumer and Market Law*, 8(4): 149–154, 152; Christian Twigg-Flesner, "Guiding principles for updating the product liability directive for the digital age (Pilot ELI Innovation Paper)" (2021) ELI Innovation Paper Series, *SSRN*, 9–10, https://papers.ssrn.com/sol3/papers.cfm?abstract_id=3770796, accessed February 22, 2023; Koch et al., "Response of the European law institute" (n 35) 44. See extensively with further references: Dheu and De Bruyne, "Artificial Intelligence and Tort Law: A 'Multi-faceted' Reality" (n 8).

42 AI Liability Directive, art 3.1, first para.

43 Ibid. art 3.1 and 3.2.

44 Ibid. art 3.4, first para.

parties – including providers and user – as well as the protection of confidential information should be taken into account.[45] The revised PLD contains similar provisions. Article 8 allows Member States' courts to require the defendant to disclose to the injured person – the claimant – relevant evidence that is at its disposal. The claimant must, however, present facts and evidence that are sufficient to support the plausibility of the claim for compensation.[46] Moreover, the disclosed evidence can be limited to what is necessary and proportionate to support a claim.[47]

Several policy initiatives also propose a reversal of the burden of proof. The Expert Group on Liability and New Technologies, for instance, proposes that "where the damage is of a kind that safety rules were meant to avoid, failure to comply with such safety rules, should lead to a reversal of the burden of proving (a) causation, and/or (b) fault, and/or (c) the existence of a defect."[48] It adds that if "it is proven that an emerging digital technology caused harm, and liability therefore is conditional upon a person's intent or negligence, the burden of proving fault should be reversed if disproportionate difficulties and costs of establishing the relevant standard of care and of proving their violation justify it."[49] The burden of proving causation may also be alleviated in light of the challenges of emerging digital technologies if a balancing of the listed factors warrants doing so (e.g., the likelihood that the technology at least contributed to the harm or the kind and degree of harm potentially and actually caused).[50] It has already been mentioned that the Resolution issued by the EP in October 2020 also contains a reversal of the burden of proof regarding fault-based liability for operators of low-risk AI systems.[51]

In addition to working with a reversal of the burden of proof, one can also rely on rebuttable presumptions. In this regard, both the AI Liability Directive and the revised PLD are important. Article 4.1 of the AI Liability Directive, for instance, introduces a rebuttable presumption of a "causal link between the fault of the defendant and the output produced by the AI system or the failure of the AI system to produce an output." However, this presumption only applies when three conditions are met. First, the fault of the defendant has to be proven by the claimant according to the applicable EU law or national rules, or presumed by the court following Article 3.5 of the AI Liability Directive. Such a fault can be established, for example, "for non-compliance with a duty of care pursuant

45 Ibid. art 3.4, second para.
46 Revised PLD, art 8.1.
47 Ibid. art 8.2.
48 Expert Group on Liability and New Technologies – New Technologies Formation, "Liability for artificial intelligence" (n 9) 7 and 48.
49 Ibid. 8 and 52.
50 Ibid. 8 and 49–50.
51 European Parliament, "recommendations to the Commission on a civil liability regime for artificial intelligence" (n 9) art 8.

to the AI Act."[52] Second, it can be considered reasonably likely, based on the circumstances of the case, that the fault has influenced the output produced by the AI system or the failure of the AI system to produce an output. Third, the claimant needs to demonstrate that the output produced by the AI system or the failure of the AI system to produce an output gave rise to the damage. The defendant, however, has the right to rebut the presumption of causality.[53] Moreover, in the case of a claim for damages concerning a high-risk AI system, the court is not required to apply the presumption when the defendant demonstrates that sufficient evidence and expertise is reasonably accessible for the claimant to prove the causal link.[54]

The revised PLD also introduces presumptions of defectiveness and causality that apply under certain conditions. Such conditions include the defendant's failure to disclose relevant evidence, when the claimant provides evidence that the product does not comply with mandatory safety requirements set in EU or national law, or when the claimant establishes that the damage was caused by an "obvious malfunction" of the product during normal use or under ordinary circumstances. Article 9.3 also provides a presumption of causality when "it has been established that the product is defective and the damage caused is of a kind typically consistent with the defect in question." In other words, Article 9 contains two specific presumptions, one of the product's defectiveness and one related to the causal link between the defectiveness of the product and the damage. In addition, Article 9.4 contains a more general presumption. Where a national court decides that "the claimant faces excessive difficulties, due to the technical or scientific complexity, to prove the product's defectiveness or the causal link between its defectiveness and the damage" (or both), the defectiveness of the product or causal link between its defectiveness and the damage (or both) are presumed when certain conditions are met. The claimant must demonstrate, based on "sufficiently relevant evidence," that the "product contributed to the damage"[55] and that it is "likely that the product was defective or that its defectiveness is a likely cause of the damage, or both."[56] The defendant, however, has the right "to contest the existence of excessive difficulties" or the mentioned likelihood.[57] Of course, the defendant is allowed to rebut any of these presumptions as well.[58]

[52] AI Liability Directive, 13 and art 4.1 (a).

[53] Ibid. art 4.4.

[54] Ibid. art 4.5. See for an extensive analysis: Jan De Bruyne, Orian Dheu and Charlotte Ducuing, "The European Commission's approach to extra-contractual liability and AI – An evaluation of the AI liability directive and the revised product liability directive" (n 8).

[55] Revised PLD, art 9.4 (a).

[56] Ibid. art 9.4 (b).

[57] Ibid. art 9.4, second para.

[58] Ibid. art 9.5. See for an extensive analysis: De Bruyne, Dheu and Ducuing, "The European Commission's approach to extra-contractual liability and AI – An evaluation of the AI liability directive and the revised product liability directive" (n 8).

8.4 PROBLEMATIC QUALIFICATION OF CERTAIN TORT LAW CONCEPTS

The previous parts focused on more general evolutions regarding AI and liability. The application of "traditional" tort law concepts also risks to become challenging in AI context. Regulatory answers will need to be found to remedy the gaps that could potentially arise. We will illustrate this with two notions used in the Product Liability Directive, namely "product" (part 8.4.1) and "defect" (part 8.4.2). We will also show that the introduction of certain concepts in (new) supranational AI-specific liability legislation can be challenging due to the remaining importance of national law. More specifically, we will discuss the requirement of "fault" in the proposed AI Liability Directive (part 8.4.3).

8.4.1 *Software as a Product?*

Article 1 of the Product Liability Directive stipulates that the producer is liable for damage caused by a defect in the product. Technology and industry, however, have evolved drastically over the last decades. The division between products and services is no longer as clear-cut as it was. Producing products and providing services are increasingly intertwined.[59] In this regard, the question arises whether software is a product or instead is provided as a service, and thus falling outside the scope of the PLD.[60] Software and AI systems merit specific attention in respect of product liability. Software is essential to the functioning of a large number of products and affects their safety. It is integrated into products but it can also be supplied separately to enable the use of the product as intended. Neither a computer nor a smartphone would be of particular use without software. The question whether stand-alone software can be qualified as a product within the meaning of the Product Liability Directive or implementing national legislation has already attracted a lot of attention, both in academic scholarship[61] and in policy initiatives.[62] That is because software is a collection of data and instructions that is imperceptible to the human eye.[63]

59 See, for example, Bert Keirsbilck, Evelyne Terryn, and Elias Van Gool, "Consumentenbescherming bij *servitisation* en product-dienst-systemen (PDS)" (2019) Tijdschrift voor Privaatrecht 817; De Bruyne, Van Gool, and Gils, "Tort law and damage" (n 8) 417.

60 See, for example, Bertolini, "Artificial intelligence and civil liability" (n 13) 57.

61 See, for example, Duncan Fairgrieve and Eleonora Rajneri, "Is software a product under the product liability directive?" (2019) *Zeitschrift für Internationales Wirtschaftsrecht*, 24; Koch et al., "Response of the European Law Institute" (n 35) 34–36.

62 Previously, several EU policy documents already favored a broad interpretation of the notion of a product (e.g., Expert Group on Liability and New Technologies – New Technologies Formation, "Liability for artificial intelligence" (n 9) 42–43; COM(2020) 64 final (n 5) 14).

63 De Bruyne, Van Gool, and Gils, "Tort law and damage" (n 8) 418.

Unclarity remains as to whether software is (im)movable and/or a (in)tangible good.[64] The Belgian Product Liability Act – implementing the PLD – stipulates that the regime only concerns tangible goods.[65] Although the Belgian Court of Cassation and/or the European Court of Justice have not yet ruled on the matter, the revised PLD specifically qualifies software and digital manufacturing files as products.[66] The inclusion of software is rather surprising, yet essential.[67] Recital (13) of the revised PLD states that it should not apply to "free and open-source software developed or supplied outside the course of a commercial activity" in order not to hamper innovation or research. However, where software is supplied in exchange for a price or personal data is provided in the course of a commercial activity (i.e., for other purposes than exclusively improving the security, compatibility or interoperability of the software), the Directive should apply.[68] Regardless of the qualification of software, the victim of an accident involving an AI system may have a claim against the producer of a product incorporating software such as an autonomous vehicle, a robot used for surgery or a household robot. Software steering the operations of a tangible product could be considered as a part or component of that product.[69] This means that an autonomous vehicle or material robot used for surgery would be considered as a product in the sense of the Product Liability Directive and can be defective if the software system it uses is not functioning properly.[70]

8.4.2 *"Defective" Product*

Liability under the Product Liability Directive requires a "defect" in the product. A product is defective when it does not provide the safety that a person is entitled to expect, taking all circumstances into account (the so-called "consumer expectations

[64] See extensively: De Bruyne, Van Gool, and Gils, "Tort law and damage" (n 8) 417–421 with further references.

[65] Art. 2 Act 25 February 1991 concerning liability for defective products, *BS* 22 March 1991. Also see Dimitri Verhoeven, "Productveiligheid en productaansprakelijkheid: krachtlijnen en toekomstperspectieven" in Reinhard Steennot and Gert Straetmans (eds), *Wetboek economisch recht en de bescherming van de consument* (Intersentia, 2015) 198; Jacquemin and Hubin, "Aspects contractuels" (n 8) 129–130.

[66] Revised PLD, art 4 (1).

[67] See, for example, Jochen Tanghe and Jan De Bruyne, "Software aan het stuur. Aansprakelijkheid voor schade veroorzaakt door autonome motorrijtuigen" in Thierry Vansweevelt and Britt Weyts (eds), *Nieuwe risico's in het aansprakelijkheids- en verzekeringsrecht* (Intersentia, 2018) 56–57; Buiten, de Streel, and Peitz, "EU liability rules" (n 36) 51; Twigg-Flesner, "Guiding principles" (n 41) 5; Koch et al., "Response of the European Law Institute" (n 35) 34–36.

[68] AI Liability Directive, recital 13. See extensively De Bruyne, Dheu and Ducuing, "The European Commission's approach to extra-contractual liability and AI – An evaluation of the AI liability directive and the revised product liability directive" (n 8) 11–13.

[69] COM(2020) 64 final (n 5) 13–14.

[70] De Bruyne and Tanghe, "Liability for damage caused by autonomous vehicles" (n 2) 357.

test" as opposed to the "risk utility test").[71] This does not refer to the expectations of a particular person but to the expectations of the general public[72] or the target audience.[73] Several elements can be used to determine the legitimate expectations regarding the use of AI systems. These include the presentation of the product, the normal or reasonably foreseeable use of it and the moment in time when the product was put into circulation.[74] This enumeration of criteria, however, is not exhaustive as other factors may play a role as well.[75] Especially the criterion of the presentation of the product is important for manufacturers of autonomous vehicles or medical robots. That is because they often tend to market their products explicitly as safer than existing alternatives. The presentation of the product may on the other hand also provide an opportunity for manufacturers of AI systems to reduce their liability risk through appropriate warnings and user information. Nevertheless, it remains uncertain how technically detailed or accessible such information should be.[76] The revised PLD also refers to the legitimate safety expectations.[77] A product is deemed defective if it fails to "provide the safety which the public at large is entitled to expect, taking all circumstances into account."[78] The non-exhaustive list of such circumstances that allow to assess the product's defectiveness is expanded and also includes "the effect on the product of any ability to continue to learn after deployment."[79] It should, however, be noted that the product cannot be considered defective for the sole reason that a better product, including updates or upgrades to a product, is already or subsequently placed on the market or put into service.[80]

71 Product Liability Directive, art 6.

72 Product Liability Directive, recital 6. Bocken argues that it concerns the consumer as part of a group (Hubert Bocken, "Buitencontractuele aansprakelijkheid voor gebrekkige producten" in Hubert Bocken et al., (ed), *Bijzondere overeenkomsten* (Postuniversitaire cyclus Willy Delva 34, Wolters Kluwer, 2008–2009) 367).

73 Cass 26 September 2003 Arr.Cass. 2003 1765 RW 2004–05 22 annotation by Britt Weyts; Court of Appeal Antwerp 13 April 2005 RW 2008–09 803; Court of Appeal Antwerp 28 October 2009 TBBR 2011 381 annotation by Dimitri Verhoeven; Hubert Bocken and Ingrid Boone with cooperation by Marc Kruithof, *Inleiding tot het schadevergoedingsrecht: buitencontractueel aansprakelijkheidsrecht en andere schadevergoedingsstelsels* (Die Keure, 2014) 196; Jacquemin and Hubin, "Aspects contractuels" (n 8) 131.

74 Product Liability Directive, art 6, first para.

75 Bocken and Boone, *Inleiding tot het schadevergoedingsrecht* (n 73) 196; Marc Kruithof, "Wie is aansprakelijk voor schade veroorzaakt door onveilige producten?: de toepassing van de artikelen 1382, 1384 lid 1, en 1645 BW herbekeken in het licht van het – door het Hof van Justitie sterk beperkte – aanvullend karakter voorzien in artikel 13 Wet Productaansprakelijkheid" in Ignace Claeys and Reinhard Steennot (eds), *Aansprakelijkheid, veiligheid en kwaliteit* (Postuniversitaire cyclus Willy Delva 40, Wolters Kluwer, 2015) 148, fn 18.

76 De Bruyne, Van Gool, and Gils, "Tort law and damage" (n 8) 422 with further references.

77 De Bruyne, Dheu, and Ducuing, "The European Commission's approach to extra-contractual liability and AI – An evaluation of the AI liability directive and the revised product liability directive" (n 8) 13–14.

78 Revised PLD, art 6.1.

79 Ibid.

80 Revised PLD, art 6.2.

That being said, the criterion of legitimate expectations remains very vague (and problematic[81]). It gives judges a wide margin of appreciation.[82] As a consequence, it is difficult to predict how this criterion will and should be applied in the context of AI systems.[83] The safety expectations will be very high for AI systems used in high-risk contexts such as healthcare or mobility.[84] At the same time, however, the concrete application of this test remains difficult for AI systems because of their novelty, the complexity to compare these systems with human or technological alternatives and the characteristics of autonomy and opacity.[85] The interconnectivity of products and systems also makes it hard to identify the defect. Sophisticated AI systems with self-learning capabilities also raise the question of whether unpredictable deviations in the decision-making process can be treated as defects. Even if they constitute a defect, the state-of-the-art defense[86] may eventually apply. The complexity and the opacity of emerging digital technologies such as AI systems further complicate the chance for the victim to discover and prove the defect and/or causation.[87] In addition, there is some uncertainty on how and to what extent the Product Liability Directive applies in the case of certain types of defects, for example, those resulting from weaknesses in the cybersecurity of the product.[88] It has already been mentioned that the revised PLD establishes a presumption of defectiveness under certain conditions to remedy these challenges.[89]

8.4.3 *The Concept of Fault in the AI Liability Directive*

In addition to the challenging application of "traditional" existing tort law concepts in an AI context, the introduction of new legislation in this field may also contain notions that are unclear. This unclarity could affect legal certainty, especially considering the remaining importance of national law. We will illustrate this with the requirement of "fault" as proposed in the AI Liability Directive.

81 Bertolini, "Artificial intelligence and civil liability" (n 13) 57.

82 Bocken, "Buitencontractuele aansprakelijkheid" (n 72) 368; Thierry Vansweevelt and Britt Weyts, *Handboek Buitencontractueel Aansprakelijkheidsrecht* (Intersentia, 2009) 515.

83 See extensively: Borghetti, "How can artificial intelligence" (n 36) 63–76.

84 De Bruyne and Tanghe, "Liability for damage caused by autonomous vehicles" (n 2) 362. See also: Thomas Malengreau, "Automatisation de la conduite: quelles responsabilités en droit belge? (Première partie)" (2019) *RGAR*, 5: 15578, no 27.

85 See: Borghetti, "How can artificial intelligence" (n 36) 68–69; De Bruyne and Tanghe, "Liability for damage caused by autonomous vehicles" (n 2) 358–362.

86 Under this defense, the producer will not be held liable if he or she proves that the state of scientific and technical knowledge at the time when he or she put the product into circulation was not such as to enable the existence of the defect to be discovered (Product Liability Directive, art 7, e).

87 Expert Group on Liability and New Technologies – New Technologies Formation, "Liability for artificial intelligence" (n 9) 28.

88 COM(2020) 65 final (n 6) 13.

89 See the discussion *supra* in part 3.

It has already been mentioned that Article 4.1 of the AI Liability Directive contains a rebuttable presumption of a "causal link between the fault of the defendant and the output produced by the AI system or the failure of the AI system to produce an output." The *fault* of the defendant has to be proven by the claimant according to the applicable EU law or national rules. Such a fault can be established, for example, "for non-compliance with a duty of care pursuant to the AI Act."[90] The relationship between the notions of "fault" and "duty of care" under the AI Liability Directive, and especially in Article 4, is unclear and raises interpretation issues.[91] The AI Liability Directive uses the concept of "duty of care" at several occasions. Considering that tort law is still to a large extent national, the reliance on the concept of "duty of care" in supranational legislation is rather surprising. A "duty of care" is defined as "a required standard of conduct, set by national or Union law, in order to avoid damage to legal interests recognized at national or Union law level, including life, physical integrity, property and the protection of fundamental rights."[92] It refers to how a reasonable person should act in a specific situation, which also "ensure[s] the safe operation of AI systems in order to prevent damage to recognized legal interests."[93] In addition to the fact that the content of a duty of care will ultimately have to be determined by judges, a more conceptual issue arises as well. That is because the existence of a *generally applicable positive duty* of care has already been contested, for instance, in Belgium. Kruithof concludes that case law and scholarship commonly agree that no breach of a "pre-existing" duty is required for a fault to be established. As noted by Kruithof, what is usually referred to as the generally required level or the duty of care, "is therefore more properly qualified not as a legal duty or obligation, but merely a standard of behavior serving as the yardstick for judging whether an act is negligent or not for purposes of establishing liability."[94] However, Article 4.1 (a) seems to equate the "fault" with the noncompliance with a duty of care, thereby implicitly endorsing the view that the duty of care consists in a standalone obligation. This does not necessarily fit well in some national tort law frameworks, and may thus cause interpretation issues and fragmentation.[95]

Article 1.3 (d) of the AI Liability Directive mentions that the Directive will not affect "how fault is defined, other than in respect of what is provided for in Articles 3 and 4." A fault under Belgian law (and by extension other jurisdictions) consists

[90] AI Liability Directive, 13 and art 4.1 (a).

[91] See extensively: De Bruyne, Dheu, and Ducuing, "The European Commission's approach to extra-contractual liability and AI – An evaluation of the AI liability directive and the revised product liability directive" (n 8) 7–9.

[92] AI Liability Directive, art 2 (9).

[93] AI Liability Directive, recital 24.

[94] Marc Kruithof, *Tort Law in Belgium* (Kluwer Law International, 2018) 47 with references.

[95] See extensively: De Bruyne, Dheu, and Ducuing, "The European Commission's approach to extra-contractual liability and AI – An evaluation of the AI liability directive and the revised product liability directive" (n 8) 8–9.

of both a subjective component and an objective component. The (currently still applicable) subjective component requires that the fault can be attributed to the free will of the person who has committed it ("imputability"), and that this person generally possesses the capacity to control and to assess the consequences of his or her conduct ("culpability").[96] This subjective element does, however, not seem to be covered by the AI Liability Directive. This raises the question whether the notion of "fault," as referred to in the Articles 3 and 4, *requires* such a subjective element to be present and/or *allows* for national law to require this. The minimal harmonization provision of Article 1.4 does not answer this question.[97] The objective component of a fault refers to the wrongful behavior in itself. Belgian law traditionally recognizes two types of wrongdoings, namely a violation of a specific legal rule of conduct[98] and the breach of a standard of care.[99] Under Belgian law, a violation of a standard of care requires that it was reasonably foreseeable for the defendant that his or her conduct could result in some kind of damage.[100] This means that a provider of a high-risk AI system would commit a fault when he or she could reasonable foresee that a violation of a duty of care following provisions of the AI Act would result in damage. However, it is unclear whether the notion of a "duty of care" as relied upon in the AI Liability Directive also includes this requirement of foreseeability or, instead, whether it is left to national (case) law to determine the additional modalities under which a violation of a "duty of care" can be established.[101]

8.5 CONCLUDING REMARKS AND TAKEAWAYS

We focused on different challenges that arise in tort law for damage involving AI. The chapter started by illustrating the remaining importance of national law for the interpretation and application of tort law concepts in an AI context. There will be an increasing number of cases in which the role of AI systems in causing damage, and especially the interaction between humans and machines, will have to be assessed. Therefore, a judge must have an understanding on how AI works and the risks it entails. As such, it should be ensured that judges – especially in the field of

[96] See, for example, Court of Cassation 3 October 1994 (1984) Arr.Cass. 807; (1996–1997) RW 1227; Geert Jocqué, "Bewustzijn en subjectieve verwijtbaarheid" in Hubert Bocken, *XXXIIIste Postuniversitaire cyclus Willy Delva 2006–2007* (Intersentia, 2007) 1–101; Vansweevelt and Weyts, *Handboek* (n 82) 147–148; Kruithof, *Tort Law* (n 94) 53–56.

[97] De Bruyne, Dheu, and Ducuing, "The European Commission's approach to extra-contractual liability and AI – An evaluation of the AI liability directive and the revised product liability directive" (n 8) 9.

[98] See, for example, Cass 3 October 1994 Arr.Cass. 1994 807; Cass 10 April 2014 Arr.Cass. 2014 962.

[99] See, for example, Cass 25 November 2002 Arr.Cass. 2002 2543; Bocken and Boone, *Inleiding tot het schadevergoedingsrecht* (n 73) 90–92.

[100] Kruithof, *Tort Law* (n 94) 49 with references; Vansweevelt and Weyts, *Handboek* (n 82) 134–137.

[101] De Bruyne, Dheu, and Ducuing, "The European Commission's approach to extra-contractual liability and AI – An evaluation of the AI liability directive and the revised product liability directive" (n 8) 9.

tort law – have the required digital capacity. We also emphasized the importance of procedural elements in claims involving AI systems. Although the newly proposed EU frameworks introduce disclosure requirements and rebuttable presumptions, it remains to be seen how these will be applied in practice, especially considering the many unclarities these proposals still entail. The significant amount of discretion that judges have in interpreting the requirements and concepts used in these new procedural solutions may result in various and differing applications throughout the Member States. While these different interpretations might be interesting case studies, they will not necessarily contribute to the increased legal certainty that the procedural solutions aim to achieve. We also illustrated how AI has an impact on "traditional" and newly proposed tort law concepts. From a more general perspective, we believe that interdisciplinarity – for instance through policy prototyping[102] – will become increasingly important to remedy regulatory gaps and to devise new "rules" on AI and tort law.

[102] See, for example, Thomas Gils, Frederic Heymans, and Wannes Ooms (Knowledge Centre Data & Society), "From Policy To Practice: Prototyping The EU AI Act's Transparency Requirements," January 2024, https://papers.ssrn.com/sol3/papers.cfm?abstract_id=4714345, accessed August 2, 2024.

9

Artificial Intelligence and Competition Law

Friso Bostoen

9.1 INTRODUCTION

Algorithmic competition issues have been in the public eye for some time.[1] In 2017, for example, *The Economist* warned: "Price-bots can collude against consumers."[2] Press attention was fueled by Ezrachi and Stucke's *Virtual Competition*, a well-received book on the perils of the algorithm-driven economy.[3] For quite some time, however, academic and press interest outpaced the reality on the ground.[4] Price algorithms had been used to fix prices, but the collusive schemes were relatively low-tech (overseen by sellers themselves) and the consumer harm seemingly limited (some buyers of Justin Bieber posters overpaid).[5] As such, the AI and competition law literature was called "the closest ever our field came to science-fiction."[6] More recently, that has started to change – with an increase in science, and a decrease in fiction. New economic models show that sellers cannot just use pricing algorithms to collude – algorithms can actually supplant human decision-makers and learn to charge supracompetitive prices autonomously.[7] Meanwhile, in the real world, pricing

[1] Generative AI applications fall outside the scope of this chapter, as it is updated until January 31, 2023. For more recent developments on the intersection of competition law and generative AI, see Friso Bostoen and Anouk van der Veer, "Regulating competition in generative AI: A matter of trajectory, timing and tools" (2024) *Concurrences*, 2-2024: 27–33.

[2] "Price-bots can collude against consumers" *The Economist* (May 6, 2017), www.economist.com/finance-and-economics/2017/05/06/price-bots-can-collude-against-consumers.

[3] Ariel Ezrachi and Maurice Stucke, *Virtual Competition: The Promise and Perils of the Algorithm-Driven Economy* (Harvard University Press, 2016). For an update, see Ariel Ezrachi and Maurice Stucke, "Sustainable and unchallenged algorithmic tacit collusion" (2020) *Northwestern Journal of Technology and Intellectual Property*, 17: 217.

[4] See Thibault Schrepel, "Here's why algorithms are NOT (really) a thing" *Concurrentialiste* (May 2017) www.networklawreview.org/algorithms-based-practices-antitrust/.

[5] The case often referred to concerned Amazon sellers fixing the price of celebrity posters, which sparked enforcement in the US and the UK. See Competition and Markets Authority (CMA), Case 50223, *Online sales of posters and frames*, August 12, 2016.

[6] Nicolas Petit, "Antitrust and artificial intelligence: A research agenda" (2017) *Journal of European Competition Law & Practice*, 8(6): 361–362, 361.

[7] Emilio Calvano et al., "Artificial intelligence, algorithmic pricing, and collusion" (2020) *American Economic Review*, 110: 3267.

algorithms became even more common and potentially pernicious, affecting markets as essential as real estate.[8]

The topic of AI and competition law is thus ripe for reexamination, for which this chapter lays the groundwork. The chapter only deals with *substantive* competition law (and related areas of law), not with more *institutional* questions like enforcement, which deserve a separate treatment. Section 9.2 starts with the end-goal of competition law, that is, consumer welfare, and how algorithms and the increasing availability of data may affect that welfare. Section 9.3 dives into the main algorithmic competition issues, starting with restrictive agreements, both horizontal and vertical (Section 9.3.1), and moving on to abuse of dominance, both exclusionary and exploitative (Section 9.3.2). The guiding question is whether EU competition rules are up to the task of remedying these issues. Section 9.4 concludes with an agenda for future research.

Before we jump in, a note on terminology. The careful reader will have noticed that, despite the "AI" in the title, I generally refer to "algorithms." An algorithm is simply a set of steps to be carried out in a specific way.[9] This "specific way" can be pen and paper, but algorithms truly show their potential when executed by computers that are programmed to do so. At that point, we enter the "computational" realm, but when can we refer to AI? The problem is that AI is somewhat of a nebulous concept. In the oft-quoted words of the late Larry Tesler: "AI is whatever hasn't been done yet" (the so-called "AI Effect").[10] Machine learning (ML) is a more useful term, referring to situations where the computer (machine) *itself* extracts the algorithm for the task that underlies the data.[11] Thus, with ML, "it is not the programmers anymore but the data itself that defines what to do next."[12] In what follows, I continue to refer to algorithms to capture its various uses and manifestations. For a more extensive discussion of the technological aspects of AI, see Chapter 1 of this book.

9.2 CONSUMER WELFARE, DATA, AND ALGORITHMS

The goal of EU competition law has always been to prevent distortions of competition, in other words, to protect competition.[13] But protecting competition is a means

[8] Heather Vogell, "Rent going up? One company's algorithm could be why" *ProPublica* (October 15, 2022), www.propublica.org/article/yieldstar-rent-increase-realpage-rent.

[9] Panos Louridas, *Algorithms* (MIT Press, 2020), Chapter 1.

[10] On his CV (Section "Adages & Coinages"), Larry Tesler corrects the record: "What I actually said was: 'Intelligence is whatever machines haven't done yet,'" see, www.nomodes.com/Larry_Tesler_Consulting/Adages_and_Coinages.html.

[11] Ethem Alpaydin, *Machine Learning* (MIT Press, 2021) 17–18. Alpaydin argues that ML is a requirement for AI (see 18–22) and defines AI as computers doing things, which – if done by humans – would be said to require intelligence (while stressing the problem that AI definitions tend to be human-centric).

[12] Ibid., 12.

[13] See the various references to "distort[ions of] normal competition" in the Treaty establishing the European Coal and Steel Community (1951); more recently, see the Consolidated version of the

to an end. As the General Court put it: "the ultimate purpose of the rules that seek to ensure that competition is not distorted in the internal market is to increase the well-being of consumers."[14] Competition, and thus consumer welfare, has different parameters, in particular price, choice, quality or innovation.[15] A practice's impact on those parameters often determines its (il)legality.

Algorithmic competition can affect the parameters of competition. At the outset, though, it is important to understand that algorithms need input – that is, data – to transform into output. When it comes to competition, the most relevant type of data is price data. Such data used to be hidden from view, requiring effort to collect (e.g., frequenting competitors' stores). Nowadays, price transparency has become the norm, at least in business-to-consumer (B2C) settings, so at the retail level.[16] Prices tend to be available online (e.g., on the seller's website). And digital platforms, including price comparison websites (PCWs), aggregate prices of different sellers in one place.

The effects of price transparency are ambiguous, as the European Commission (EC) found in its E-Commerce Sector Inquiry.[17] The fact that consumers can easily compare prices online leads to increased price competition between sellers.[18] At the same time, price transparency also allows firms to monitor each other's prices, often algorithmically.[19] In a vertical relation between supplier and distributor, the supplier can more easily spot deviations from the retail price it recommended – and perhaps ask retailers for adjustment. In a horizontal relation between competitors, it has become common for firms to automatically adjust their prices to those of competitors.[20] In this case, the effects can go two ways. As EU Commissioner Vestager noted: "the effect of an algorithm depends very much on how you set it up."[21] You can use an algorithm to undercut your rivals, which is a boon for consumers. Or you can use algorithms to increase prices, which harms consumers.

Both types of algorithms (undercutting and increasing) feature in the story of *The Making of a Fly*, a book that ended up being priced at over $23 million on

Treaty on European Union – Protocol (No 27) on the internal market and competition [2008] OJ C115/309 ("the internal market as set out in Article 3 [TFEU] includes a system ensuring that competition is not distorted").

14 Joined Cases T-213/01 and T-214/01 *Österreichische Postsparkasse* v *Commission* EU:T:2006:151, para 115.

15 Case C-413/14 P *Intel* v *Commission* EU:C:2017:632, para 134.

16 In business-to-business (B2B) settings, prices are often individually negotiated, or in any case not made public.

17 EC, "Final report on the E-Commerce Sector Inquiry" (Staff Working Document) COM (2017) 229.

18 Ibid., para 12. The EC adds, however, that increased price competition may negatively affect competition on parameters other than price, such as quality and innovation.

19 Ibid., para 13.

20 Ibid. ("Two thirds of [retailers] use automatic software programmes that adjust their own prices based on the observed prices of competitors.").

21 Margrethe Vestager, "Algorithms and competition" (Bundeskartellamt 18th Conference on Competition, Berlin, March 16, 2017).

Amazon. What happened? Two sellers of the book relied on pricing algorithms, with one systematically undercutting the other (but only just), and the other systematically charging a price 27% higher than the other. An upward price spiral ensued, resulting in the book's absurd price. In many other instances, however, the effects are less absurd and more harmful. Various studies have examined petrol prices, which are increasingly transparent.[22] In Chile, the government even obliged petrol station owners to post their prices on a public website. After the website's introduction in 2012, coordination by petrol station owners increased their margins by 9%, at the expense of consumers.[23] A similar result can be reached in the absence of such radical transparency. A study of German petrol stations found that adoption of algorithmic pricing also increased their margins by 9%.[24] Companies such as A2i specialize in providing such pricing software.[25]

Algorithms can create competition issues beyond coordination on a supracompetitive price point. They can also be at the basis of unilateral conduct, of which two types are worth highlighting. First, algorithms allow for personalized pricing.[26] The input here is not pricing data from competitors but rather personal data from consumers. If personal data allows the seller to infer the consumers' *exact* willingness to pay, they can *perfectly* price discriminate, although this scenario is theoretical for now. The impact of price discrimination is not straightforward: while some consumers pay more than they otherwise would, it can also allow firms to serve consumers they otherwise would not.[27] Second, algorithms are widely used for non-pricing purposes, in particular for ranking.[28] Indeed, digital platforms have sprung up to bring order to the boundless internet (e.g., Google Search for websites, Amazon Marketplace for products). Given the platforms' power over consumer choice, a tweak of their ranking algorithm can marginalize one firm while bringing fortune to another. As long as tweaks are made in the interests of consumers, they are not

22 Petrol prices are displayed prominently, so even in the past, they could be collected by driving by petrol stations. Meanwhile, specific apps have sprung up to compare petrol prices. Navigation apps such as Google's Waze also provide information on the prices charged by petrol stations.

23 Fernando Luco, "Who benefits from information disclosure? The case of retail gasoline" (2019) *American Economic Journal: Microeconomics*, 11: 277 (due to differences in search behavior, low-income consumers were more affected than high-income consumers).

24 Stephanie Assad et al., "Algorithmic pricing and competition: Empirical evidence from the German retail gasoline market" (2020) CESifo Working Paper No. 8521 (the 9% increase was found in non-monopoly markets; in duopoly markets, the authors found that margins do not change when only one of the two stations adopts, but increase by 28% when both do).

25 See Sam Schechner, "Why do gas station prices constantly change? Blame the algorithm" *The Wall Street Journal* (May 8, 2017), www.wsj.com/articles/why-do-gas-station-prices-constantly-change-blame-the-algorithm-1494262674.

26 CMA, "Algorithms: How they can reduce competition and harm consumers" (Report) 2021, 2.9–2.20.

27 An important question is whether *total* output increases, see Hal Varian, "Price discrimination" in Richard Schmalensee and Robert Willig (eds), *Handbook of Industrial Organization – Volume I* (Elsevier, 1989) 597.

28 See Michael Schrage, *Recommendation Engines* (MIT Press, 2020).

problematic. But if tweaks are made simply to give prominence to the platform's own products ("self-preferencing"), consumers may suffer the consequences.

9.3 ALGORITHMIC COMPETITION ISSUES

Competition law protects competition, thus guaranteeing consumer welfare, via specific rules. I focus on two provisions: the prohibitions of restrictive agreements (Article 101 TFEU) and of abuse of dominance (Article 102 TFEU).[29] The next sections examine these prohibitions, and the extent to which they substantively cover algorithmic competition issues.

9.3.1 *Restrictive Agreements*

Restrictive agreements come in two types: they are *horizontal* when entered into between competitors ("collusion") and *vertical* when entered into between firms at different levels of the supply chain (e.g., supplier and distributor). An agreement does not require a contract; more informal types of understanding between parties ("concerted practices") also fall under Article 101 TFEU.[30] To be illegal, the common understanding must have the object or effect of restricting competition. According to the case law, "by object" restrictions are those types of coordination that "can be regarded, by their very nature, as being harmful to the proper functioning of normal competition."[31] Given that such coordination reveals, in itself, a sufficient degree of harm to competition, it is not necessary to assess its effects.[32] "By effect" restrictions do require such an assessment. In general, horizontal agreements are more likely to fall into the "by object" category (price-fixing being the typical example), while vertical agreements are more likely to be categorized as "by effect" (e.g., recommending retail prices). Let us look at horizontal and vertical agreements in turn.

9.3.1.1 Horizontal Agreements

There are two crucial aspects to every horizontal price-fixing agreement or "cartel": the moment of their formation and their period of stability (i.e., when no cartelist

[29] The merger control regime is also important, but algorithmic competition issues have not played an important role there yet. For a primer, see Ai Deng and Cristián Hernández, "Algorithmic pricing in horizontal merger review: An initial assessment" (2022) *Antitrust*, 36(2): 36–41.

[30] See Case C-8/08 *T-Mobile Netherlands* v *Nederlandse Mededingingsautoriteit* EU:C:2009:343, para 23 ("the definitions of 'agreement' … and 'concerted practice' are intended, from a subjective point of view, to catch forms of collusion having the same nature which are distinguishable from each other only by their intensity and the forms in which they manifest themselves").

[31] Case C-345/14 *Maxima Latvija* v *Konkurences padome* EU:C:2015:784, para 18.

[32] Ibid., para 20.

deviates from the arrangement). In the physical world, cartel formation and stability face challenges.[33] It can be difficult for cartelists to reach a common understanding on the terms of the cartel (in particular the price charged), and coordination in any case requires contact (e.g., meeting in a hotel in Hawaii). Once an agreement is reached, the cartelists have to abide by it even while having an incentive to cheat (deviating from the agreement, e.g., by charging a lower price). Such cheating returns a payoff: in the period before detection, the cheating firm can win market/profit share from its co-cartelists (after detection, all cartelists revert to the competitive price level). The longer the period before detection, the greater the payoff and thus the incentive to cheat.

In a digital world, cartel formation and stability may face fewer difficulties.[34] Cartel formation does not require contact when algorithms *themselves* reach a collusive equilibrium. When given the objective to maximize profits (in itself not objectionable), an ML algorithm may figure out that charging a supracompetitive price, together with other firms deploying similar algorithms, satisfies that objective. And whether or not there is still an agreement at the basis of the cartel, subsequent stability is greater. Price transparency and monitoring algorithms allow for quicker detection of deviations from the cartel agreement.[35] As a result, the expected payoff from cheating is lower, meaning there is less of an incentive to do so.[36] When a third party algorithmically sets prices for different sellers (e.g., Uber for its drivers), deviation even becomes impossible. In these different ways, algorithmic pricing makes cartels more robust. Moreover, competition authorities may have more trouble detecting cartels, given that there is not necessarily a paper trail.

In short, digitization – in particular price transparency and the widespread use of algorithms to monitor/set prices – does not make cartels less likely or durable. Taking a closer look at algorithmically assisted price coordination, it is useful to distinguish three scenarios.[37] First, firms may explicitly agree on prices and use algorithms to (help) implement that agreement. Second, firms may use the same pricing

[33] This has been well documented in the case of the lysine cartel, where an executive from one of the firms served as FBI informant, making up to 300 audio and video recordings of cartel-related meetings. The picture that emerges is one of constant distrust between the cartelists. See John Connor, "'Our customers are our enemies': The Lysine Cartel of 1992–1995" (2001) *Review of Industrial Organization*, 18: 5.

[34] Salil Mehra, "Antitrust and the robo-seller: Competition in the time of algorithms" (2016) *Minnesota Law Review*, 100: 1323–1375, 1348–49.

[35] Note that quicker detection of deviations only works at the retail (B2C) level, where prices tend to be transparent. In addition to quicker detection of deviations, the use of algorithms also reduces the chance of errors and accidental deviations. See CMA, "Pricing algorithms" (Economic Working Paper) 2018, paras 5.7–5.11.

[36] E-commerce Sector Inquiry (n 17), para 33.

[37] These three scenarios are in line with Autorité de la concurrence and Bundeskartellamt, "Algorithms and competition" (Report) 2019, 26–60 and Autoridade da Concorrência, "Digital ecosystems, big data and algorithms" (Issues Paper) 2019, paras 243–275.

algorithm provided by a third party, which results in price coordination without explicit agreement between them. Third, firms may instruct distinct pricing algorithms to maximize profits, which results in a collusive equilibrium/supracompetitive prices. With each subsequent scenario, the existence of an agreement becomes less clear; in the absence of it, Article 101 TFEU does not apply. Let us test each scenario against the legal framework.

The first scenario, in which *sellers algorithmically implement a prior agreement*, does not raise difficult questions. The *Posters* case, referenced in the introduction, offers a model.[38] Two British sellers of posters, Trod and GB, agreed to stop undercutting each other on Amazon Marketplace. Given the difficulty of manually adjusting prices on a daily basis, the sellers implemented their cartel agreement via re-pricing software (widely available from third parties).[39] In practice, GB programmed its software to undercut other sellers but match the price charged by Trod *if* there were no cheaper competing offers. Trod configured its software with "compete rules" but put GB on an "ignore list" so that the rules it had programmed to undercut competitors did not apply to GB. Still, humans were still very much in the loop, as evidenced by emails in which employees complained about apparent noncompliance with the arrangement, in particular when the software did not seem to be working properly.[40] The UK Competition and Markets Authority had no trouble establishing agreement, which fixed prices and was thus restrictive "by object."

In this first scenario, the use of technology does not expose a legal vacuum; competition law is up to the task. But what if there was no preexisting price-fixing agreement? In that case, the sellers would simply be using repricing software to undercut other sellers *and* each other. At first sight, that situation appears perfectly competitive: undercutting competitors is the essence of competition – if that happens effectively and rapidly, all the better. The reality is more complex. Brown has studied the economics of pricing algorithms, finding that they change the nature of the pricing game.[41] The logic is this: once a firm commits to respond to whatever price its competitors charge, those competitors internalize that expected

38 CMA, *Posters* (n 5). For the equivalent U.S. case, see U.S. District Court for the Northern District of California, Case 3:15-cr-00419-WHO, *United States* v *Daniel Aston*, August 11, 2016. The U.S. Department of Justice (DOJ) pursued a similar case earlier, see U.S. District Court for the Northern District of California, Case3:15-cr-00201-WHO, *United States* v *David Topkins*, April 30, 2015. Both U.S. cases ended with a plea agreement.

39 On the availability and operation of such software, see Autoridade da Concorrência, "Digital ecosystems" (n 37), paras 208–221.

40 See, for example, CMA, *Posters* (n 5), para 3.83, quoting a message from a Trod employee to a GB employee: "nearly all posters you are undercutting, so presume your software is broken, so had to remove you from ignore list. Let me know when repaired."

41 Zach Brown, "Competition in pricing algorithms" (2021) NBER Working Paper 28860, including both formal and empirical analysis. See also Autorité de la concurrence and Bundeskartellamt, "Algorithms" (n 37), 43–44.

reaction, which conditions their pricing (they are more reluctant to decrease prices in the first place).[42] In short, even relatively simple pricing algorithms can soften competition. This is in line with the aforementioned study of algorithmic petrol station pricing in Germany.[43]

The second scenario, in which *sellers rely on a common algorithm to set their prices*, becomes more difficult but not impossible to fit within Article 101 TFEU. There are two sub-scenarios to distinguish. First, the sellers may be suppliers via an online platform that algorithmically sets the price for them. This setting is not common as platforms generally leave their suppliers free to set a price but Uber, which sets prices for all of its drivers, provides an example.[44] Second, sellers may use the same "off-the-shelf" pricing software offered by a third party. The U.S. firm RealPage, for example, offers its YieldShare pricing software to a large number of landlords.[45] It relies not on public information (e.g., real estate listings) but on private information (actual rent charged) and even promotes communication between landlords through groups.[46] In either sub-scenario, there is not necessarily communication between the different sellers, be they Uber drivers or landlords. Rather, the coordination originates from a third party, the pricing algorithm provider. Such scenarios can be classified as "hub-and-spoke" cartels, where the hub refers to the algorithm provider and the spokes are the sellers following its pricing guidance.[47]

The guiding EU case on this second scenario is *Eturas*.[48] The case concerned the Lithuanian firm Eturas, operator of the travel booking platform E-TURAS. At one

[42] The commitment needs to be credible. Brown argues that investments of a high-technology firm in the frequency and automation of its price-setting make its commitment credible. Note that the logic is similar to that of price-matching guarantees.

[43] The mechanism is similar but not equal to that of the German petrol stations studied in Assad et al., "Algorithmic pricing and competition" (n 24). In a duopoly setting, Assad et al. find evidence for price effects only when both firms adopt superior pricing technology, which suggests that the mechanism in their setting is collusion or symmetric commitment.

[44] On Uber's pricing, see www.uber.com/us/en/marketplace/pricing/. Note that other platforms do offer pricing tools: Airbnb, for example, offers "Smart Pricing," which automatically adapts hosts' nightly prices to demand, see, www.airbnb.co.uk/help/article/1168.

[45] Vogell, "Rent going up?" (n 8).

[46] For a similar example, see Daniel Mândrescu, "When algorithmic pricing meets concerted practices – the case of Partneo" *CoRe Blog* (June 7, 2018), www.lexxion.eu/coreblogpost/when-algorithmic-pricing-meets-concerted-practices-the-case-of-partneo/ (on a pricing algorithm for auto parts, including allegations of clandestine meetings between certain auto makers).

[47] Advocate General Spuznar already suggested the hub-and-spoke qualification for Uber in Case C-434/15 *Asociación Profesional Elite Taxi* v *Uber Systems Spain* EU:C:2017:364, para 62 and footnote 23. Another potential qualification is that of cartel facilitator, as in Case C-194/14 P *AC-Treuhand* v *Commission* EU:C:2015:717, but that qualification appears more suited to firms (such as consultancies) that operate on a completely different market.

[48] Case C-74/14 *Eturas t. Lietuvos Respublikos konkurencijos taryba* EU:C:2016:42. Similar cases have been pursued at the national level, see, for example, Comisión Nacional de los Mercados y la Competencia, "The CNMC fines several companies EUR 1.25 million for imposing minimum commissions in the real estate brokerage market" (press release, December 9, 2021),

point, Eturas messaged the travel agencies using its platforms that discounts would be automatically reduced to 3% "to normalise the conditions of competition."[49] In a preliminary reference, the European Court of Justice (ECJ) was asked whether the use of a "common computerized information system" to set prices could constitute a concerted practice between travel agencies under Article 101 TFEU.[50] The ECJ started from the foundation of cartel law, namely that every economic operator must *independently* determine their conduct on the market, which precludes any direct *or indirect* contact between operators so as to influence each other's conduct.[51] Even *passive* modes of participation can infringe Article 101 TFEU.[52] But the burden of proof is on the competition authority, and the presumption of innocence precludes the authority from inferring from the mere dispatch of a message that travel agencies were also aware of that message.[53] Other objective and consistent indicia may justify a rebuttable presumption that the travel agencies were aware of the message.[54] In that case, the authority can conclude the travel agencies tacitly assented to a common anticompetitive practice.[55] That presumption too must be rebuttable, including by (i) public distancing, or a clear and express objection to Eturas; (ii) reporting to the administrative authorities; or (iii) systematic application of a discount exceeding the cap.[56]

With this legal framework in mind, we can return to the case studies introduced earlier. With regard to RealPage's YieldShare, it bears mentioning that the algorithm does not impose but suggests a price, which landlords can deviate from (although very few do). Nevertheless, the U.S. Department of Justice (DOJ) has opened an investigation.[57] The fact that RealPage also brings landlords into direct contact with each other may help the DOJ's case. Uber has been subject to investigations around the globe, including the U.S. and Brazil, although no infringement was finally established.[58] In the EU, there has not been a case, although *Eturas*

www.cnmc.es/expedientes/s000320 (concerning a real estate platform that imposed minimum commissions of 4% on agencies).

49 Case C-74/14 *Eturas* (n 48), para 10.

50 Ibid., para 25.

51 Ibid., para 27, referencing Case C-8/08 *T-Mobile* (n 30), paras 32–33.

52 Case C-74/14 *Eturas* (n 48), para 28.

53 Ibid., para 39.

54 Ibid., paras 40–41. Travel agencies can rebut the presumption "for example by proving that they did not receive that message or that they did not look at the section in question or did not look at it until some time had passed since that dispatch."

55 Ibid., paras 42 and 44. Note that an illegal concerted practice requires not only concertation but also "subsequent conduct on the market and a relationship of cause and effect between the two," see C-286/13 P *Dole Food* v *Commission* EU:C:2015:184, para 126.

56 Case C-74/14 *Eturas* (n 48), paras 46–49.

57 Heather Vogell, "Department of Justice opens investigation into real estate tech company accused of collusion with landlords" *ProPublica* (November 23, 2022), www.propublica.org/article/yieldstar-realpage-rent-doj-investigation-antitrust.

58 U.S. District Court for the Southern District of New York, Case 15 Civ. 9796, *Spencer Meyer* v *Travis Kalanick*, March 31, 2016 (the judge believed there to be a hub-and-spoke cartel but Uber managed to move the case to arbitration). CADE, Technical Note No. 26/2018/CGAA4/SGA1/CADE, *Public*

could support a finding of infringement: drivers are aware of Uber's common price-setting system and can thus be presumed to participate in a concerted practice.[59] That is not the end of it though, as infringements of Article 101(1) TFEU can be justified under Article 101(3) TFEU if they come with countervailing efficiencies, allow consumers a fair share of the benefit, are proportional, and do not eliminate competition.[60] Uber might meet those criteria: its control over pricing is indispensable to the functioning of its efficient ride-hailing system (which reduces empty cars and waiting times), and that system comes with significant consumer benefits (such as convenience and lower prices). In its *Webtaxi* decision on a platform that operates like Uber, the Luxembourgish competition authority exempted the use of a common pricing algorithm based on this reasoning.[61]

To conclude, this second scenario of sellers relying on a common price-setting algorithm, provided by either a platform or a third party, can still be addressed by EU competition law, even though it sits at the boundary of it. And if a common pricing algorithm is essential to a business model that benefits consumers, it may be justified.

The third scenario, in which *sellers' use of distinct pricing algorithms results in a collusive equilibrium*, may escape the grasp of Article 101 TFEU. The mechanism is the following: sellers instruct their ML algorithms to maximize profits, after which the algorithms figure out that coordination on a supracompetitive price best attains that objective. These algorithms tend to use "reinforcement learning" and more specifically "Q-learning": the algorithms interact with their environment (including the algorithms of competing sellers) and, through trial and error, learn the optimal pricing policy.[62] Modeling by Salcedo showed "how pricing algorithms not only facilitate collusion but inevitably lead to it," albeit under very strong assumptions.[63] More recently, Calvano et al. took an experimental approach, letting pricing algorithms interact in a simulated marketplace.[64] These Q-learning algorithms systematically learned to adopt collusive strategies, including the punishment of deviations

Ministry of the State of São Paulo v Uber do Brasil Tecnologia (the authority did not find sufficient concertation between drivers; simply accepting Uber's terms and conditions did not suffice).

59 In addition to concertation, there is also subsequent conduct, that is, drivers follow Uber's pricing (they cannot deviate from it).

60 See further EC, Guidelines on the application of Article 81(3) of the Treaty (Communication) OJ C101/97.

61 Conseil de la Concurrence Grand-Duché de Luxembourg, Case 2018-FO-01, *Webtaxi*, June 7, 2018. The authority found the pricing restriction proportional given that it was indispensable to realize the efficiencies and there was no less restrictive way of doing so. Competition was not eliminated because Webtaxi represented only a quarter of Luxembourg cabs.

62 On reinforcement and Q-learning in a pricing context, see Ashwin Ittoo and Nicolas Petit, "Algorithmic pricing agents and tacit collusion: A technological perspective" in Hervé Jacquemin and Alexandre de Streel (eds), *L'Intelligence Artificielle et le Droit* (Larcier, 2017) 247–256.

63 Bruno Salcedo, "Pricing algorithms and collusion" (2015), available at https://brunosalcedo.com/docs/collusion.pdf.

64 Calvano et al., "Artificial intelligence" (n 7).

from the collusive equilibrium. That collusive equilibrium was typically below the monopoly level but substantially above the competitive level. In the end, while these theoretical and experimental results are cause for concern, it remains an open question to what extent autonomous price coordination can arise in real market conditions.[65]

Nevertheless, it is worth asking whether EU competition law is up to the task if/when the third scenario of autonomously coordinating pricing algorithms materializes. The problem is in fact an old one.[66] In oligopolistic markets (with few players), there is no need for *explicit* collusion to set prices at a supracompetitive level; high interdependence and mutual awareness may suffice to reach that result. Such *tacit* collusion, while societally harmful, is beyond the reach of competition law (the so-called "oligopoly problem"). Tacit collusion is thought to occur rarely given the specific market conditions it requires but some worry that, through the use of algorithms, it "could become sustainable in a wider range of circumstances possibly expanding the oligopoly problem to non-oligopolistic market structures."[67] To understand the scope of the problem, let us take a closer look at the EU case law.

In case of autonomous algorithmic collusion, there is no agreement. Might there be a concerted practice? The ECJ has defined a concerted practice as "a form of coordination between undertakings by which, without it having reached the stage where an agreement properly so called has been concluded, practical cooperation between them is knowingly substituted for the risks of competition."[68] This goes back to the requirement that economic operators *independently* determine their conduct on the market.[69] The difficulty is that, while this requirement strictly precludes direct or indirect contact between economic operators so as to influence each other's conduct, it "does not deprive economic operators of the right to adapt themselves intelligently to the existing and anticipated conduct of their competitors."[70] Therefore, conscious parallelism – even though potentially as harmful as a cartel – does not meet the concertation threshold of Article 101 TFEU. Indeed, "parallel conduct cannot be regarded as furnishing proof of concertation unless concertation constitutes the only plausible explanation for such conduct."[71] Discarding every other plausible explanation for parallelism is

[65] See Autorité de la concurrence and Bundeskartellamt, "Algorithms" (n 37), 45–52 for a discussion of the assumptions underlying the research of Calvano et al. and other experimental studies.

[66] See Richard Posner, "Oligopoly and the antitrust laws: A suggested approach" (1968) *Stanford Law Review*, 21: 1562.

[67] Organisation for Economic Co-operation and Development (OECD), "Algorithms and collusion: Competition policy in the digital age" (Background Note) 2017, 35–36.

[68] Case 48–69 *Imperial Chemical Industries (ICI)* v *Commission* EU:C:1972:70, para 64.

[69] Case C-74/14 *Eturas* (n 48), para 27; Case C-8/08 *T-Mobile* (n 30), paras 32–33.

[70] Joined cases 40–48, 50, 54–56, 111, 113 and 114–73 *Suiker Unie* v *Commission* EU:C:1975:174, para 174.

[71] Joined cases C-89/85, C-104/85, C-114/85, C-116/85, C-117/85 and C-125/85 to C-129/85 A. *Ahlström Osakeyhtiö* v *Commission ('Wood Pulp II')* EU:C:1993:120, para 71. Earlier case law was less strict, see

a Herculean task with little chance of success. The furthest the EC has taken the concept of concertation is in *Container Shipping*.[72] The case concerned shipping companies that regularly announced their intended future price increases, doing so 3–5 weeks beforehand, which allowed for customer testing *and* competitor alignment. According to the EC, this could be "a strategy for reaching a common understanding about the terms of coordination" and thus a concerted practice.[73]

Truly autonomous collusion can escape the legal framework in a way that tacit collusion has always done. In this sense, it is a twist on the unsolved oligopoly problem. Even the price signaling theory of *Container Shipping*, already at the outer boundary of Article 101 TFEU, hardly seems to capture autonomous collusion. If/when autonomous pricing agents are widely deployed, however, it may pose a *bigger* problem than the oligopoly one we know. Scholars have made suggestions on how to adapt the legal framework to fill the regulatory gap, but few of proposed rules are legally, economically and technologically sound *and* administrable by competition authorities and judges.[74]

9.3.1.2 Vertical Agreements

When discussing horizontal agreements, I only referenced the nature of the restrictions in passing, given that price-fixing is the quintessential "by object" restriction. Vertical agreements require more careful examination. An important distinction exists between *recommended* resale prices, which are presumptively legal, and *fixed* resale prices ("resale price maintenance" or RPM), which are presumptively illegal as "by object" restrictions.[75] The difference between the two can be small, especially when a supplier uses carrots (e.g., reimbursing promotional costs) or sticks (e.g., withholding supply) to turn a recommendation into more of an obligation.

Case 48–69 *ICI* (n 68), para 66 ("Although parallel behaviour may not by itself be identified with a concerted practice, it may however amount to strong evidence of such a practice if it leads to conditions of competition which do not correspond to the normal conditions of the market").

[72] *Container Shipping* (Case AT.39850) Commission Decision of 7 July 2016. Note that the case ended with commitments so there is no final decision, let alone a judgment confirming it.

[73] Ibid., paras 45–47.

[74] For a well-considered proposal, situated in the U.S. context, see Joseph Harrington, 'Developing competition law for collusion by autonomous artificial agents' (2018) *Journal of Competition Law & Economics*, 14: 331, in particular Section 6.

[75] Case 243/83 *Binon* EU:C:1985:284, para 44 and Case 27/87 *Louis Erauw-Jacquery* v *La Hesbignonne* EU:C:1988:183, para 15. RPM constitutes a "hardcore" restriction under Commission Regulation (EU) 2022/720 on the application of Article 101(3) of the Treaty on the Functioning of the European Union to categories of vertical agreements and concerted practices [2022] OJ L134/4, art 4(a). See further EC, "Guidelines on vertical restraints" (Communication) OJ C248/1, paras 185–201. Note that *maximum* prices are treated similarly to recommended resale prices and *minimum* resale prices similarly to RPM.

Algorithmic monitoring/pricing can play a role in this process. It can even exacerbate the anticompetitive effects of RPM.

In the wake of its E-Commerce Sector Inquiry, the EC started a number of investigations into online RPM. In four decisions, the EC imposed more than €110 million in fines on consumer electronics suppliers Asus, Denon & Marantz, Philips, and Pioneer.[76] These suppliers restricted the ability of online retailers to price kitchen appliances, notebooks, hi-fi products, and so on. Although the prices were often "recommendations" in name, the suppliers intervened in case of deviation, including through threats or sanctions. The online context held dual relevance. First, suppliers used monitoring software to effectively detect deviations by retailers and to intervene swiftly when prices decreased. Second, many retailers used algorithms to automatically adjust their prices to other retailers. Given that automatic adjustment, the restrictions that suppliers imposed on low-pricing retailers had a wider impact on overall prices than they would have had in an offline context.

There is also renewed interest in RPM at the national level. The Authority for Consumers & Markets (ACM) fined Samsung some €40 million for RPM of television sets.[77] Samsung took advantage of the greater transparency offered by web shops and PCWs to monitor prices through so-called "spider software,"[78] and confronted retailers that deviated from its price "recommendations." Retailers also used "spiders" to adjust their prices (often downward) to those of competitors. Samsung regularly asked retailers to disable their spiders so that they would not automatically switch along to lower online prices. The ACM, like the EC, classified these practices as anticompetitive "by object." Thus, while the methods of RPM may evolve, the traditional legal analysis remains applicable.

9.3.2 *Abuse of Dominance*

Abusive conduct comes in two types: it is *exclusionary* when it indirectly harms consumers by foreclosing competitors from the market and *exploitative* when it directly harms consumers, for example, by charging excessive prices. I discuss the main algorithmic concern under each category of abuse, that is, discriminatory ranking and personalized pricing, respectively. While I focus on abusive conduct, remember that such conduct only infringes Article 102 TFEU if the firm in question is also in a dominant position.

[76] *Asus* (Case AT.40465) Commission Decision of 24 July 2018, *Denon & Marantz* (Case AT.40469) Commission Decision of 24 July 2018, *Philips* (Case AT.40181) Commission Decision of 24 July 2018, and *Pioneer* (Case AT.40182) Commission Decision of 24 July 2018. For an overview, see EC, "Commission fines four consumer electronics manufacturers for fixing online resale prices" (press release, July 24, 2018) IP/18/4601.

[77] Authority for Consumers & Markets (ACM), Case ACM/20/040569, *Samsung*, September 14, 2021.

[78] Spider software crawls the web to collect price data from different sources.

9.3.2.1 Exclusion

Given the abundance of online options (of goods, videos, webpages, etc.), curation is key. The role of curator is assumed by platforms, which rank the options for consumers; think, for example, of Amazon Marketplace, TikTok, and Google Search. Consumers trust that a platform has their best interests in mind, which is generally the case, and thus tend to rely on their ranking without much further thought. This gives the platform significant power over consumer choice, which can be abused. A risk of skewed rankings exists particularly when the platform does not only intermediate between suppliers and consumers, but also offers its own options. In that case, the platform may want to favor its own offering through choice architecture ("self-preferencing").[79]

The landmark case in this area is *Google Search (Shopping)*.[80] At the heart of the abusive conduct was Google's Panda algorithm, which demoted third-party comparison shopping services (CSS) in the search results, while Google's own CSS was displayed prominently on top. Even the most highly ranked non-Google CSS appeared on average only on page four of the search results. This had a significant impact on visibility, given that users tend to focus on the first 3–5 results, with the first 10 results accounting for 95% of user clicks.[81] Skewed rankings distort the competitive process by excluding competitors and can harm consumers, especially when the promoted results are not the most qualitative ones.[82]

Google was only the first of many cases of algorithmic exclusion.[83] Amazon has also been on the radar of competition authorities, with a variety of cases regarding the way it ranks products (and in particular, selects the winner of its "Buy Box").[84] It is also under investigation for its "algorithmic control of price setting by third-party

[79] On choice architecture, see CMA, "Online choice architecture: How digital design can harm competition and consumers" (Discussion Paper) 2022. Ranking (paras 4.35–4.41) is only one aspect of choice architecture, defaults (paras 4.27–4.34) are another powerful tool.

[80] *Google Search (Shopping)* (Case AT.39740) Commission Decision of 27 June 2017, confirmed in Case T-612/17 *Google and Alphabet* v *Commission* EU:T:2021:763. For a discussion, see Friso Bostoen, "The General Court's Google Shopping judgment: Finetuning the legal qualifications and tests for platform abuse" (2022) *Journal of European Competition Law & Practice*, 13: 75.

[81] *Google Search (Shopping)* (n 80), paras 454–461. See also CMA, "Online search: Consumer and firm behaviour" (Literature Review) 2017.

[82] This appeared to be the case. By way of illustration, one Google executive wrote that Froogle (then the name of Google's CSS) "simply doesn't work," see *Google Search (Shopping)* (n 80), para 490.

[83] Ranking is but one method of algorithmic exclusion. For a discussion of other methods (including defaults), see Thomas Cheng and Julian Nowag, "Algorithmic predation and exclusion" (2023) *University of Pennsylvania Journal of Business Law*, 25: 41.

[84] Amazon does not only promote its own products but also those of third-party sellers that use its "Fulfilled by Amazon" logistics service. See EC, "Commission accepts commitments by Amazon barring it from using marketplace seller data, and ensuring equal access to Buy Box and Prime" (press release, December 20, 2022) IP/22/7777 and AGCM, "Amazon fined over € 1,128 billion for abusing its dominant position" (press release, December 9, 2021), https://en.agcm.it/en/media/press-releases/2021/12/A528.

sellers," which "can make it difficult for end customers to find offers by sellers or even lead to these offers being no longer visible at all."[85]

EU legislators considered the issue of discriminatory ranking serious enough to justify the adoption of *ex ante* regulation to complement *ex post* competition law. The Digital Markets Act (DMA) prohibits "gatekeepers" from self-preferencing in ranking, obliging them to apply "transparent, fair and non-discriminatory conditions to such ranking."[86] Earlier instruments, like the Consumer Rights Directive (CRD)[87] and the Platform-to-Business (P2B) Regulation,[88] already mandated transparency in ranking.[89]

9.3.2.2 Exploitation

Price discrimination, and more specifically personalized pricing, is of particular concern in algorithmically driven markets. *Dynamic* pricing, that is, firms adapting prices to market conditions (essentially, supply and demand) has long existed. Think for example of airlines changing prices over time (as captured by the saying that "the best way to ruin your flight is to ask your neighbor what they paid"). With *personalized* pricing, prices are tailored to the characteristics of the consumers in question (e.g., location and previous purchase behavior) so as to approach their willingness to pay. Authorities have put limits to such personalized pricing. Following action by the ACM, for example, the e-commerce platform Wish decided to stop using personalized pricing.[90]

85 Bundeskartellamt, "Extension of ongoing proceedings against Amazon to also include an examination pursuant to Section 19a of the German Competition Act" (press release, November 14, 2022), www.bundeskartellamt.de/SharedDocs/Meldung/EN/Pressemitteilungen/2022/14_11_2022_Amazon_19a.html.

86 Regulation (EU) 2022/1925 of the European Parliament and of the Council on contestable and fair markets in the digital sector (Digital Markets Act) [2022] OJ L265/1, art 6(5). Other provisions are also relevant from a choice architecture point of view, see, for example, arts 6(3)–(4) on defaults. "Gatekeepers" are defined in art 3.

87 Directive 2011/83/EU of the European Parliament and of the Council on consumer rights [2011] OJ L304/64 (as amended by Directive (EU) 2019/2161 of the European Parliament and of the Council as regards the better enforcement and modernisation of Union consumer protection rules [2019] OJ L328/7), art 6a(1)(a). See further EC, "Guidance on the interpretation and application of Directive 2011/83/EU" (Notice) [2021] OJ C525/1, Section 3.4.1.

88 Regulation (EU) 2019/1150 of the European Parliament and of the Council on promoting fairness and transparency for business users of online intermediation services [2019] OJ L186/57, art 5. See further EC, "Guidelines on ranking transparency pursuant to Regulation (EU) 2019/1150" (Notice) [2020] OJ C424/1.

89 Regulation (EU) 2022/2065 of the European Parliament and of the Council on a Single Market for Digital Services (Digital Services Act) [2022] OJ L277/1 also regulates recommender systems, see, for example, art 27 on transparency.

90 ACM, "Following ACM actions, Wish bans fake discounts and blocks personalized pricing" (press release, July 26, 2022), www.acm.nl/en/publications/following-acm-actions-wish-bans-fake-discounts-and-blocks-personalized-pricing.

The ACM did not intervene based on competition law.[91] Article 102(a) TFEU prohibits excessive prices, but personalized prices are not necessarily excessive as such, and competition authorities are in any case reluctant to intervene directly in price-setting. Price discrimination, explicitly prohibited by Article 102 TFEU(c), may seem like a more fitting option, but that provision is targeted at discrimination between firms rather than between consumers.[92] Another limitation is that Article 102 TFEU requires dominance, and most firms engaged in personalized pricing do not have market power. While competition law is not an effective tool to deal with personalized pricing, other branches of law have more to say on the matter.[93]

First, personalization is based on data, and the General Data Protection Regulation (GDPR) regulates the collection and processing of such data.[94] The DMA adds further limits for gatekeepers.[95] Various other laws – including the Unfair Commercial Practices Directive (UCPD),[96] the CRD,[97] and the P2B Regulation[98] – also apply to personalized pricing but are largely restricted to transparency obligations. The recent Digital Services Act (DSA)[99] and AI Act[100] go a step further with provisions targeted at algorithms, although their applicability to personalized pricing is yet to be determined.

Despite different anecdotes on personalized pricing (e.g., by Uber), there is no empirical evidence of widespread personalized pricing.[101] One limiting factor may be the reputational costs a firm incurs when its personalized pricing is publicized, given how consumers tend to view such practices as unfair. In addition, the technological capability to effectively personalize prices is sometimes

[91] Rather, the ACM referenced the CRD (n 87), discussed further *infra*.

[92] Article 102(c) TFEU prohibits "applying dissimilar conditions to equivalent transactions with other trading parties, thereby placing them at a competitive disadvantage." Given that the list of potential abuses is non-exhaustive, this framing of price discrimination is not necessarily limiting.

[93] See OECD, "Personalised pricing in the digital era" (note by the European Union) DAF/COMP/WD(2018)128, 9–12.

[94] Regulation (EU) 2016/679 of the European Parliament and of the Council on the protection of natural persons with regard to the processing of personal data and on the free movement of such data (General Data Protection Regulation) OJ L119/1. See further Richard Steppe, "Online price discrimination and personal data: A general data protection regulation perspective" (2017) *Computer Law & Security Review*, 33: 768.

[95] Digital Markets Act (n 86), art 6(a) on data collection, combination and cross-use.

[96] Directive 2005/29/EC of the European Parliament and of the Council concerning unfair business-to-consumer commercial practices in the internal market (Unfair Commercial Practices Directive) [2005] OJ L149/22. A personalized price may, for example, be "aggressive" or an exertion of "undue influence" under arts 8–9, see further EC, "Guidance on the interpretation and application of Directive 2005/29/EC" (Notice) OJ C526/1, Section 4.2.8.

[97] CRD (n 87), art 6(1)(ea). See further CRD Guidance (n 87), Section 3.3.1.

[98] P2B Regulation (n 87), arts 7 and 9.

[99] DSA (n 89).

[100] Regulation (EU) 2024/1689 of the European Parliament and of the Council laying down harmonised rules on artificial intelligence (Artificial Intelligence Act).

[101] CMA, "Pricing algorithms" (n 35), paras 2.13–2.20.

overstated.[102] It would be good, however, to have a clear view of the fragmented regulatory framework for when the day of widespread personalized pricing does arrive.

9.4 CONCLUSION

Rather than revisiting interim conclusions, I end with a research agenda. This chapter has set out the state of the art on AI and competition, at least on the *substantive* side. Algorithms also pose risks – and opportunities – on the *institutional* (enforcement) side. Competition authority heads have vowed that they "will not tolerate anticompetitive conduct, whether it occurs in a smoke-filled room or over the Internet using complex pricing algorithms."[103] While this elegant one-liner is a common-sense policy statement, the difficult question is "how?". Substantive issues aside, algorithmic anticompetitive conduct can be more difficult to detect and deter. Compliance *by design* is key. Just like the ML models that have become world-class at playing Go and Texas Hold'em have the rules of those games baked in, firms deploying algorithms should think about programming them with the rules of economic rivalry, that is, competition law. At the same time, competition authorities will have to build out their algorithmic detection capabilities.[104] They may even want to go a step further and intervene algorithmically – or, in the words of the *Economist* article this chapter started with: "Trustbusters might have to fight algorithms with algorithms."[105]

Returning to substantive questions, the following would benefit from further research:

- Theoretical and experimental research shows that autonomous algorithmic collusion is a possibility. To what extent are those results transferable to real market conditions? Do new developments in AI increase the possibility of algorithmic collusion?
- Autonomous algorithmic collusion presents a regulatory gap, at least if such collusion exits the lab and enters the outside world. Which rule(s) would optimally address this gap, meaning they are legally, economically, and technologically sound *and* administrable by competition authorities and judges?

[102] See Axel Gautier, Ashwin Ittoo, and Pieter Van Cleynenbreugel, "AI algorithms, price discrimination and collusion: A technological, economic and legal perspective" (2020) *European Journal of Law and Economics*, 50: 405.

[103] DOJ, "Former E-Commerce executive charged with price fixing in the antitrust division's first online marketplace prosecution" (press release, April 6, 2015), www.justice.gov/opa/pr/former-e-commerce-executive-charged-price-fixing-antitrust-divisions-first-online-marketplace. See similarly Vestager, "Algorithms and competition" (n 21) ("companies can't escape responsibility for collusion by hiding behind a computer program").

[104] See Joseph Harrington and David Imhof, "Cartel screening and machine learning" (2022) *Stanford Computational Antitrust*, 2: 133.

[105] "Price-bots can collude against consumers" (n 2).

- Algorithmic exclusion (ranking) and algorithmic exploitation (personalized pricing) are regulated to varying degrees by different instruments, including competition law, the DMA, the DSA, the P2B Regulation, the CRD, the UCPD and the AI Act. How do these instruments fit together – do they exhibit overlap? A lot of instruments are centered around transparency – is that approach effective given the bounded rationality of consumers?

The enforcement questions (relating, e.g., to compliance by design) are no less pressing and difficult. Even more so than the substantive questions, they will require collaboration between lawyers and computer scientists.

10

AI and Consumer Protection

An Introduction

Evelyne Terryn and Sylvia Martos Marquez

10.1 INTRODUCTION

AI brings risks but also opportunities for consumers. For instance, AI can help consumers to optimize their energy use, detect fraud with their credit cards, simplify or select relevant information or translate. Risks do however also exist, for instance, in the form of biased erroneous information and advice or manipulation into choices that do not serve consumers best interests. Also when it comes to consumer *law*, which traditionally focuses on protecting consumers' autonomy and self-determination, the increased use of AI poses major challenges, which will be the focal point of this chapter.

We start by setting out how AI systems can affect consumers in both positive and negative ways (Section 10.2). Next, we explain how the fundamental underpinnings and basic concepts of consumer law are challenged by AI's ubiquity, and we caution against a silo approach to the application of this legal domain in the context of AI (Section 10.3). Subsequently, we provide a brief overview of some of the most relevant consumer protection instruments in the EU and discuss how they apply to AI systems (Section 10.4). Finally, we illustrate the shortcomings of the current consumer protection law framework more concretely by taking dark patterns as a case study (Section 10.5). We conclude that additional regulation is needed to protect consumers against AI's risks (Section 10.6).

10.2 CHALLENGES AND OPPORTUNITIES OF AI FOR CONSUMERS

The combination of AI and data offers traders a vast range of new opportunities in their relationship with consumers. Economic operators may use, among other techniques, *machine learning* algorithms, a specialized subdiscipline of AI, to analyze large datasets. These algorithms process extensive examples of desired and interesting behavior, known as the "training data," to generate computer-readable data-learned knowledge. This knowledge can then be used to optimize various processes.[1] The (personal) data of consumers thus becomes a valuable source of information for companies.[2] Moreover, with the increasing adoption of the Internet of Things and advances in Big Data, the accuracy and amount of information obtained about individual consumers and their behavior is only expected to increase.[3] In an ideal situation consumers know which input (data set) was employed by the market operator to train the algorithm, which learning algorithm was applied and which assignment the machine was trained for.[4] However, market operators using AI often fail to disclose this information to consumers.[5] In addition, consumers also often face the so-called "*black box*" or "inexplicability" problem with data-driven AI, which means that the exact reasoning that led to the *output*, the final decision as presented to humans, remains unknown.[6] Collectively, this contributes to an asymmetry of information between businesses and consumers with market players collecting a huge amount of personal data on consumers.[7] In addition, consumers often remain unaware that pricing, or advertising have been tailored to their supposed preferences, thus creating an enormous potential to exploit the inherent weaknesses in the consumers' ability to understand that they are being persuaded.[8] Another major challenge, next to the consumer's inability to understand business behavior, is that automated decisions of algorithmic decision-making can lead to biased or discriminatory results, as the training data may not be neutral (selected by a human and thus perpetuating human biases) and may contain outdated data, data reflecting consumer's behavioral biases or existing social biases against a minority.[9] This could lead directly to consumers receiving biased and erroneous advice and information.

[1] Agnieszka Jabłonowska, Anna Maria Nowak, Giovanni Sartor, Hans-W Micklitz, Maciej Kuziemski, and Pałka Przemysław (EUI working papers), "Consumer law and artificial intelligence: Challenges to the EU consumer law and policy stemming from the business' use of artificial intelligence – final report of the ARTSY project" (2018), https://ssrn.com/abstract=3228051, accessed December 23, 2022, 7; Martin Ebers "Liability for AI & consumer law" (2021) *JIPITEC*, 12: 206.

[2] Jabłonowska a.o., "Consumer law and AI" 5 and 36.

[3] Jabłonowska a.o., "Consumer law and AI" 49.

[4] Jablonowska a.o., "Consumer law and AI" 5.

[5] CMA, "Online platforms and digital advertising: Market study final report" (July 1, 2020), www.gov.uk/cma-cases/online-platforms-and-digital-advertising-market-study#final-report, accessed December 23, 2022.16; Jablonowska a.o., "Consumer law and AI," 5.

[6] Ebers, "Liability for AI & consumer law" 208; Giovani Sartor, "Artificial intelligence: Challenges for EU citizens and consumers" (January 2019), www.europarl.europa.eu/RegData/etudes/BRIE/2019/631043/IPOL_BRI(2019)631043_EN.pdf, accessed December 23, 2022, 5.

[7] European Commission, DG Justice and Consumers, Francisco Lupiáñez-Villanueva, Alba Boluda, Francesco Bogliacino et al., "Behavioural study on unfair commercial practices in the digital environment: Dark patterns and manipulative personalisation: final report" (2022) *Publications Office of the European Union*, https://data.europa.eu/doi/10.2838/859030. 73; Ebers, "Liability AI-consumer law" 208.

[8] EC, "Behavioural study" 103.

[9] Ebers, "Liability for AI & consumer law" 212; CMA, "Digital advertising" 64; Brent Mittelstadt, Johann Laux, and Sandra Wachter, "Neutralizing online behavioural advertising: Algorithmic targeting with market power as an unfair commercial practice" (2021) *Common Market Law Review*, 58: 719.

In addition, AI brings significant risks of influencing consumers into making choices that do not serve their best interests.[10] The ability to predict the reactions of consumers allows businesses to trigger the desired behavior of consumers, potentially making use of consumer biases,[11] for instance through choice architecture. Ranging from the color of the "buy" button on online shopping stores to the position of a default payment method – the choice in design architecture can be based on algorithms that define how choices are presented to consumers in order to influence them.[12]

Economic operators may furthermore influence or manipulate consumers by restricting the information or offers they can access and thus their options and this for purely economic goals.[13] Clustering techniques are used to analyze consumer behavior to classify them into meaningful categories and treat them differently.[14] This personalization can occur in different forms, including the "choice architecture," the offers that are presented to consumers or in the form of different prices for the same product for different categories of consumers.[15] AI systems may also be used to determine and offer consumers the reserve price – the highest price they are able or willing to pay for a good or service.[16]

Although AI entails risks, it also provides opportunities for consumers, in various sectors. Think of AI applications in healthcare (e.g., through mental health chatbots, diagnostics[17]), legal services (e.g., cheaper legal advice), finance and insurance services (e.g., fraud prevention), information services (e.g., machine translation, selection of more relevant content), and energy services (e.g., optimization of energy use through "smart homes"), to name but a few.[18] Personalized offers by traders and vendors could (at least in theory) also assist consumers to overcome undesirable information overload. An example of a consumer empowering technology in the legal sector is CLAUDETTE. This online system detects potentially unfair clauses in online contracts and privacy policies, to empower the weaker contract party.[19]

[10] OECD, "Dark commercial patterns, OECD digital economy papers" (2022) No.336 *OECD Publishing* 9.

[11] Sartor, "AI: challenges for EU citizens and consumers" 14.

[12] OECD, "Dark commercial patterns" 12; CMA, 'Algorithms: how they can reduce competition and harm consumers' (January 19, 2021), www.gov.uk/government/publications/algorithms-how-they-can-reduce-competition-and-harm-consumers/algorithms-how-they-can-reduce-competition-and-harm-consumers, accessed December 23, 2022.

[13] Sartor, "AI: challenges for EU citizens and consumers" 3.

[14] CMA, "Algorithms – how they can harm consumers"; Iqbal H. Sarker, "Machine learning: Algorithms, real-world applications and research directions" (2021) *SN Computer Science*: 160.

[15] CMA, "Algorithms – how they can harm consumers."

[16] Sartor, "AI: Challenges for EU citizens and consumers" 18.

[17] Ahbimanyu S. Ahuja, "The impact of artificial intelligence in medicine on the future role of physician" (2019) *PeerJ* 12; Louise I. T. Lee, Radha S. Ayyalaraju, Rakesh Ganatra, and Senthooran Kanthasamy, "The current state of artificial intelligence in medical imaging and nuclear medicine" (2019) *BJR Open* 5.

[18] For more examples, Jablonowska a.o., "Consumer law and AI" 19 et seq.

[19] Jablonowska a.o., "Consumer law and AI" 33.

10.3 CHALLENGES OF AI FOR CONSUMER LAW

Section 10.2 illustrated how AI systems can both positively and negatively affect consumers. However, the digital transformation in general and AI specifically also raises challenges to consumer law. The fundamental underpinnings and concepts of consumer law are increasingly put under pressure, and these new technologies also pose enormous challenges in terms of enforcement. Furthermore, because of the different types of concerns that AI systems raise in this context, these challenges make it clear that consumer law cannot be seen or enforced in isolation from data protection or competition law. These aspects are briefly discussed in Sections 10.3.1–10.3.3.

10.3.1 *Challenges to the Fundamental Underpinnings of Consumer Law*

Historically, the emergence of consumer law is linked to the development of a consumer society. In fact, this legal domain has been referred to as a *"reflection of the consumer society in the legal sphere."*[20] The need for legal rules to protect those who consume, was indeed felt more urgently when consumption, above the level of basic needs, became an important aspect of life in society.[21] The trend to attach increasing importance to consumption had been ongoing for several centuries,[22] but the increasing affluence, the changing nature of the way business was conducted, and the massification of consumption, all contributed to a body of consumer protection rules being adopted, mainly from the 1950s.[23] More consumption was thought to equal more consumer welfare and more happiness. Consumer protection law in Europe first emerged at national level.[24] It was only from the 1970s on that European institutions started to develop an interest in consumer protection and that the first consumer protection programs followed.[25] The first binding instruments were adopted in the 1980s, and consisted mostly of minimum harmonization instruments. This means that member states are allowed to maintain or adopt more

[20] Geraint Howells, Ian Ramsay, and Thomas Wilhelmsson, "Consumer law in its international dimension" in G. Howells and T. Wilhelmsson (eds), *Handbook of Research in International Consumer Law*, 2nd ed (Edward Elgar Publishing, 2018), 4.

[21] Howells, Ramsay, and Wilhelmsson, "Consumer law in its international dimension" 4.

[22] Frank Trentmann, *Empire of Things: How We Became a World of Consumers, from the Fifteenth Century to the Twenty-First* (HarperCollins, 2016).

[23] Howells, Ramsay, and Wilhelmsson, "Consumer law in its international dimension," 4–6.

[24] On the emergence of consumer law in the EU, see more elaborately H.-W. Micklitz et al. (eds), *The Fathers and Mothers of Consumer Law and Policy in Europe: The Foundational Years 1950–1980* (2019), EUI, https://cadmus.eui.eu/handle/1814/63766, accessed February 22, 2023.

[25] Council Resolution of 14 April 1975 on a preliminary programme of the European Economic Community for a consumer protection and information policy [1975] OJ C 92/1; Council Resolution of 19 May 1981 on a second programme of the European Economic Community for a consumer protection and information policy [1981] OJ C133/1; See, in more detail, Ludwig Krämer, "European Commission" in Micklitz, *The Fathers and Mothers of Consumer Law*, 26 ff.

protective provisions, as long as the minimum standards imposed by the harmonization instrument are respected. From 2000 onwards, the shift to maximum harmonization in the European consumer protection instruments reduced the scope for a national consumer (protection) policy.

While originally the protection of a weaker consumer was central in many national regimes, the focus in European consumer law came to be on the rational consumer whose right to self-determination (private autonomy) on a market must be guaranteed.[26] This right to self-determination can be understood as the right to make choices in the (internal) market according to one's own preferences[27] thereby furthering the realization of the internal market.[28] This focus on self-determination presupposes a consumer capable of making choices and enjoying the widest possible options to choose from.[29] EU consumer law could thus be described as the guardian of the economic rights of the nonprofessional player in the (internal) market. Private autonomy and contractual freedom should in principle suffice to protect these economic rights and to guarantee a bargain in accordance with one's own preferences, but consumer law acknowledges that the preconditions for such a bargain might be absent, especially due to information asymmetries between professional and nonprofessional players.[30] Information was and is therefore used as the main corrective mechanism in EU consumer law.[31] Further reaching intervention – for example, by regulating the content of contracts – implies a greater intrusion into private autonomy and is therefore only a subsidiary protection mechanism.[32]

AI and the far-reaching possibilities of personalization and manipulation it entails, especially when used in combination with personal data, now challenges the assumption of the rational consumer with its "own" preferences even more fundamentally. The efficiency of information as a means of protection had already been questioned before the advent of new technologies,[33] but the additional

26 See also H.-W. Micklitz, "Squaring the circle? Reconciling consumer law and the circular economy" (2019) *EuCML* 229, pointing out that the protective element faded into the background when the EU took over consumer policy in the aftermath of the Single European Act.

27 On the omnipresent risk of manipulation of such interests and preferences, see Cass Sunstein, "Fifty shades of manipulation" (2016) *Journal of Marketing Behavior*, 213: 32.

28 Most EU consumer legislation indeed tends to be based on internal market justifications, see Howells, Ramsay, and Wilhelmsson, "Consumer law in its international dimension," 9. See also the legal basis used for most consumer protective directives: Art 114 TFEU rather than Art 169 TFEU.

29 Howells, Ramsay, and Wilhelmsson, "Consumer law in its international dimension," 35.

30 Ugo Mattei and Alessandra Quarta, *The Turning Point in Private Law* (Elgar Edward Publishing, 2019) 95.

31 On the information paradigm that plays a central role in EU consumer policy, see among others: Norbert Reich and H.-W. Micklitz, "Economic law, consumer interests and EU integration" in Norbert Reich et al. (eds), *European Consumer Law* (Intersentia, 2014) 1, 21; Steven Weatherill, *EU Consumer Law and Policy* (Edward Elgar Publishing, 2013) ch 4.

32 In this sense, see Josef Drexl, *Die wirtschaftliche Selbstbestimmung des Verbrauchers* (Mohr Siebeck, 1998).

33 See among others for insights from behavioral sciences, Geneviève Helleringer and Anne-Lise Sibony (2017) "European consumer protection through the behavioral lens" *Columbia Journal of European Law*, 23(3): 607–646.

complexity of AI leaves no doubt that the mere provision of information will not be a solution to the ever increasing information asymmetry and risk of manipulation. The emergence of an "attention economy" whereby companies strive to retain consumers' attention in order to generate revenue based on advertising and data gathering, furthermore also makes clear that "more consumption is more consumer welfare" is an illusion.[34] The traditional underpinnings of consumer law therefore need revisiting.

10.3.2 *Challenges to the Basic Concepts of Consumer Law*

European consumer law uses the abstract concept of the "average" consumer as a benchmark.[35] This is a "reasonably well informed and reasonably observant and circumspect" consumer;[36] a person who is "reasonably critical [...], conscious and circumspect in his or her market behaviour."[37] This benchmark, as interpreted by the Court of Justice of the European Union, has been criticized for not taking into account cognitive biases and limitations of the consumers and for allowing companies to engage in exploitative behavior.[38] AI now creates exponential possibilities to exploit these cognitive biases and the need to realign the consumer benchmark with the realities of consumer behavior is therefore even more urgent. There is furthermore some, but only limited, attention to the vulnerable consumer in EU consumer law.[39] Thus, the Unfair Commercial Practices Directive, for example, allows to assess a practice from the perspective of the average member of a group of vulnerable consumers even if the practice was directed to a wider group, if the trader could reasonably foresee that the practice would distort the behavior of vulnerable consumers.[40] The characteristics the UCPD identifies to define vulnerability (such as mental or physical infirmity, age, or credulity) are however not particularly helpful nor exhaustive in a digital context. Interestingly, however, the Commission Guidance does stress that vulnerability is not a static concept, but a dynamic and

34 The same remark can be made from a sustainability perspective.

35 Most prominently in the UCPD, see arts. 5–9 and Recital 18 UCPD. See, however, also the case law with regard to the UCTD, where the benchmark of the average consumer is invoked to determine the transparency of contract terms, for example, Case C-348/14 *Bucura*, para. 66; Case C-26/13 *Kásler and Káslerné Rábai*, para. 73–74.

36 Recital 18 UCPD and see Case C-210/96 *Gut Springenheide and Tusky* [1998] ECR I-4657, para 3.

37 Commission Notice – Guidance on the interpretation and application of Directive 2005/29/EC of the European Parliament and of the Council concerning unfair business-to-consumer commercial practices in the internal market ("Guidance UCPD"), C/2021/9320, point 2.5.

38 See, for example, Jason Cohen, "Bringing down the average: The case for a less sophisticated reasonableness standard in US and EU consumer law" (2019) *Loyola Consumer Law Review*, 32:1, p. 2; Rossella Incardona, Cristina Poncibò, "The average consumer, the unfair commercial practices directive, and the cognitive revolution" (2007) *Journal of Consumer Policy*, 30: 36.

39 See, for criticism on this point, among others. Martijn Hesselink, "EU private law injustices" (2022) *Yearbook of European Law*, 1: 22–23.

40 Art. 5(3) UCPD. The concrete application of these benchmarks is discussed in more detail below (Section 5 Dark patterns).

situational concept[41] and that the characteristics mentioned in the directive are indicative and non-exhaustive.[42] The literature has however rightly argued that a reinterpretation of the concept of vulnerability will not be sufficient to better protect consumers in a digital context. It is submitted that in digital marketplaces, most, if not all consumers are potentially vulnerable; digitally vulnerable and susceptible *"to (the exploitation of) power imbalances that are the result of increasing automation of commerce, datafied consumer-seller relations and the very architecture of digital marketplaces."*[43] AI and digitalization thus create a structural vulnerability that requires a further reaching intervention than just to reinterpret vulnerability.[44] More attention to tackling the sources of digital vulnerability and to the architecture of digital marketplaces is hence definitely necessary.[45]

10.3.3 *Challenges to the Silo Approach to Consumer Law*

Consumer law has developed in parallel with competition law and data protection law but, certainly in digital markets, it is artificial – also in terms of enforcement – to strictly separate these areas of the law.[46] The use of AI often involves the use of (personal) consumer data and concentration in digital markets creates a risk of abuses of personal data also to the detriment of consumers. Indeed, there are numerous and frequent instances where the same conduct will be covered simultaneously by consumer law, competition law, and data protection law.[47] The German Facebook case of the Bundesgerichtshof[48] is just one example where competition law (abuse of dominant position) was successfully invoked also to guarantee consumer's choice in the data they want to share and in the level of personalization of the services provided.[49] There is certainly a need for more convergence and a

[41] So a consumer can be vulnerable in one situation but not in another, see Guidance UCPD, points 2.6 and 4.2.7.

[42] Guidance UCPD, points 2.6 and 4.2.7.

[43] Natali Helberger, Orla Lynskey, H.-W. Micklitz, Peter Rott, Marijn Sax, and Joanna Strycharz, "EU Consumer Protection 2.0. Structural asymmetries in digital consumer markets," (March 2021), www.beuc.eu/sites/default/files/publications/beuc-x-2021-018_eu_consumer_protection_2.0.pdf, p. 5.

[44] For recommendations on further reaching interventions, among others in the form of additional prohibited practices; reversal of the burden of proof for the fairness of data exploitation strategies and the concretization of legal benchmarks, see Helberger et al., "Structural asymmetries" 79.

[45] See in the same sense Helberger et al., "Structural asymmetries."

[46] For a plea to move away from a silo approach, see Christof Koolen, "Consumer protection in the age of artificial intelligence: Breaking down the silo mentality between consumer, competition and data," to be published in ERPL 2023; similarly: Wolfgang Kerber, "Digital markets, data, and privacy: Competition law, consumer law and data protection" (2016) *Journal of Intellectual Property Law & Practice*, 865–866.

[47] Opinion of Advocate General AG J. Richard de la Tour, Case C-319/20 *Meta Platforms Ireland*, para. 81.

[48] Decision of BGH of 23 June 2020, KVR 69/19.

[49] The case involved the use of data collected on and off Facebook to provide Facebook consumers with personalized services. It was held that consumers had no choice to refuse such personalized

complementary application of these legal domains, rather than artificially dividing them, especially when it comes to enforcement. The case law allowing consumer protection organizations to bring representative actions on the basis of consumer law (namely unfair practices or unfair contract terms), also for infringements of data protection legislation, is therefore certainly to be welcomed.[50]

10.4 OVERVIEW OF RELEVANT CONSUMER PROTECTION INSTRUMENTS

The mentioned challenges of course do not imply that AI currently operates in a legal vacuum and that there is no protection in place. The existing consumer law instruments provide some safeguards, both when AI is used in advertising or in a precontractual stage, and when it is the actual subject matter of a consumer contract (e.g., as part of a smart product). The current instruments are however not well adapted to AI, as will be illustrated by the brief overview of the most relevant instruments below.[51] An exercise is ongoing to potentially adapt several of these instruments[52] and make them fit for the digital age.[53] In addition, several new acts were adopted or proposed in the digital sphere that also have an impact on consumer protection and AI.

10.4.1 *The Unfair Commercial Practices Directive*

The UCPD is a maximum harmonization instrument that regulates unfair commercial practices occurring before, during and after a B2C transaction. It has a broad scope of application and the combination of open norms and a blacklist of practices that are prohibited in all circumstances allows it to tackle a wide range of unfair business practices, also when these practices result from the use of AI.[54] Practices are unfair, according to the general norm, if they are contrary to the requirements

services and the collection of off-Facebook data as this was only possible by completely giving up access to Facebook services. See for a more detailed analysis, Marco Loos and Joasia Luzak, Study of the European Parliament. Update the unfair contract terms directive for digital services (2021), www.europarl.europa.eu/RegData/etudes/STUD/2021/676006/IPOL_STU(2021)676006_EN.pdf, 31–32.

[50] Case C-319/20 *Meta Platforms Ireland*.

[51] Extra-contractual liability is not covered in this contribution, and we refer to the contribution of Jan De Bruyne and Wannes Ooms in Chapter 8 of this book.

[52] Concretely: The Unfair Commercial Practices Directive 2005/29/EC ("UCPD"); the Consumer Rights Directive 2011/83/EU; the Unfair Contract Terms Directive 93/13/EEC ("UCTD").

[53] European Commission, "Digital fairness – fitness check of EU consumer law," https://ec.europa.eu/info/law/better-regulation/have-your-say/initiatives/13413-Digital-fairness-fitness-check-on-EU-consumer-law_en.

[54] Giovanni Sartor, IMCO committee study, "New aspects and challenges in consumer protection: Digital services and artificial intelligence," 2020, pp. 36–37; Guidance UCPD, point 4.2.7.

of "professional diligence and are likely to materially distort the economic behaviour of the average consumer."[55] The UCPD furthermore prohibits misleading and aggressive practices. Misleading practices are actions or omissions that deceive or are likely to deceive and cause the average consumer to make a transactional decision they would not have taken otherwise.[56] Aggressive practices are practices that entail the use of coercion or undue influence which significantly impairs the average consumer's freedom of choice and causes them to make a transactional decision they would not have taken otherwise.[57]

The open norms definitely offer some potential to combat the use of AI to manipulate consumers, either using the general norm or the prohibition of misleading or aggressive practices.[58] However, the exact application and interpretation of these open norms makes the outcome of such cases uncertain.[59] When exactly does the use of AI amount to "undue influence," how is the concept of the "average consumer" to be used in a digital context; when exactly does personalized advertising become misleading. We make these problems more concrete in our analysis of dark patterns below (Section 10.5). More guidance on the application of these open norms could make the application to AI-based practices easier.[60] Additional blacklisted practices could also provide more legal certainty.

10.4.2 *Consumer Rights Directive*

The CRD – also a maximum harmonization directive[61] – regulates the information traders must provide to consumers when contracting, both for on premises contracts and for distance and doorstep contracts. In addition, it regulates the right of withdrawal from the contract. The precontractual information requirements are extensive and they include an obligation to provide information about the main characteristics and total price of goods or services; about the functionality and interoperability of digital content and digital services, and the duration and conditions for termination of the contract.[62] However, as Ebers mentions, these obligations are

[55] Art. 5 (2) UCPD. See for the (limited) possibilities to take the vulnerable consumer as a benchmark, above point 10.3.3 and below point 10.5.2.

[56] Arts. 6–7 UCPD.

[57] Art. 8 UCPD.

[58] See, for example, the analysis of Johann Laux, Brent Mittelstadt, and Sandra Wachter, "Neutralizing online behavioural advertising: Algorithmic targeting with market power as an unfair commercial practice" (2021) *Common Market Law Review*, 58.

[59] See also the conclusion of the European Commission, DG for Justice and Consumers, Francisco Lupiáñez-Villanueva, Alba Boluda, Francesco Bogliacino et al., "Behavioural study on unfair commercial practices in the digital environment: Dark patterns and manipulative personalisation: final report," Publications Office of the European Union, 2022, https://data.europa.eu/doi/10.2838/859030.

[60] Sartor, "Digital services and artificial intelligence," 2020, 36–37.

[61] With limited exceptions, inter alia, with regard to information obligations for on premises contracts, see art. 5 CRD.

[62] See arts. 5 and 6 CRD, as amended by the Modernization Directive.

formulated quite generally, making it difficult to concretize their application to AI systems.[63] The Modernization directive[64] – adopted to "modernize" a number of EU consumer protection directives in view of the development of digital tools[65] – introduced a new information obligation for personal pricing.[66] Art. 6 (1) (ea) of the modernized CRD now requires the consumer to be informed that the price was personalized on the basis of automated decision-making. There is however no obligation to reveal the algorithm used nor its methodology; neither is there an obligation to reveal how the price was adjusted for a particular consumer.[67] This additional information obligation has therefore been criticized for being too narrow as it hinders the finding of price discrimination.[68]

10.4.3 *Unfair Contract Terms Directive*

The UCTD in essence requires contract terms to be drafted in plain, intelligible language and the terms must not cause a significant imbalance in the parties' rights and obligations, to the detriment of the consumer[69] Contract terms that do not comply with these requirements can be declared unfair and therefore nonbinding.[70] The directive has a very broad scope of application and applies to (not individually negotiated) clauses in contracts between sellers/suppliers and consumers "in all sectors of economic activity."[71] It does not require that the consumer provides monetary consideration for a good or service. Contracts whereby the consumer "pays" with personal data or whereby the consideration provided consists in consumer generated content and profiling are also covered.[72] It is furthermore a minimum harmonization directive, so stricter national rules can still apply.[73]

The UCTD can help consumers to combat unfair clauses (e.g., exoneration clauses, terms on conflict resolution, terms on personalization of the service,

[63] Ebers, "Liability for AI & consumer law," 210.

[64] Directive (EU) 2019/2161 of the European Parliament and of the Council of 27 November 2019 amending Council Directive 93/13/EEC and Directives 98/6/EC, 2005/29/EC and 2011/83/EU of the European Parliament and of the Council as regards the better enforcement and modernisation of Union consumer protection rules, OJ L 328, 18.12.2019.

[65] Recital 17 Modernization directive.

[66] The directive had to be implemented by November 28, 2021. The implementing provisions had to be applied from May 28, 2022 (art. 7 Modernization directive).

[67] Loos and Luzak, "Unfair contract terms for digital services," 30.

[68] Ibid., see also critical Agustin Reyna, "The price is (not) right: The perils of personalisation in the digital economy," *InformaConnect*, January 4, 2019, https://informaconnect.com/the-price-is-not-right-the-perils-of-personalisation-in-the-digital-economy/.

[69] Art. 3 (1) UCTD.

[70] Art. 6 UCTD.

[71] Cases C-74/15 *Dumitru Tarcău* and C-534/15 *Dumitraş*.

[72] Commission notice – Guidance on the interpretation and application of Council Directive 93/13/EEC on unfair terms in consumer contracts, *OJ* C 323, 27.9.2019, pp. 4–92, point 1.2.1.2.

[73] Art. 8 UCTD.

terms contradicting the GDPR)[74] in contracts with businesses that use AI. It could also be used to combat untransparent personalized pricing whereby AI is used. In principle, the UCTD does not allow for judges to control the unfairness of core contract terms (clauses that determine the main subject matter of the contract), nor does it allow to check the adequacy of price and remuneration.[75] This is however only the case if these clauses are transparent.[76] The UCTD could furthermore also be invoked if AI has been used to personalize contract terms without disclosure to the consumer.[77] Unfair terms do not bind the consumer and may even lead to the whole contract being void if the contract cannot continue to exist without the unfair term.[78]

10.4.4 *Consumer Sales Directive and Digital Content and Services Directive*

When AI is the subject matter of the contract, the new Consumer Sales Directive 2019/771 ("CSD") and Digital Content and Services Directive 2019/770 ("DCSD"), provide the consumer with remedies in case the AI application fails. The CSD will apply when the digital element – provided under the sales contract – is thus incorporated or connected with the good that the absence of the digital element would prevent the good from performing its function.[79] If this is not the case, the DCSD will apply. Both directives provide for a similar – but not identical – regime that determines the requirements for conformity and the remedies in case of nonconformity. These remedies include specific performance (repair or replacement in case of a good with digital elements), price reduction and termination. Damages caused by a defect in an AI application continue to be governed by national law. The directives also provide for an update obligation (including security updates) for the seller of goods with digital elements and for the trader providing digital content or services.[80]

74 For a detailed analysis on the possibilities and shortcomings of the UCTD in a digital context, see: Loos and Luzak, "Unfair contract terms for digital services."

75 Art. 4 (2) UCTD.

76 Art. 4(2) UCTD.

77 See Loos and Luzak, "Unfair contract terms for digital services," 31. The authors propose to introduce a presumption of unfairness, implying that that personalized prices and terms are discriminatory and therefore unfair.

78 Art. 6(1) UCTD.

79 Art. 2(5) and art. 3(3) CSD.

80 For a detailed analysis, see Piia Kalamees, "Goods with digital elements and the seller's updating obligation" (2021) *JIPITEC*, 12: 131; Hugh Beale, "Digital content directive and rules for contracts on continuous supply" (2021) *JIPITEC*, 12: 96.

10.4.5 *Digital Markets Act and Digital Services Act*

The Digital Markets Act ("DMA"), which applies as of May 2, 2023[81] aims to maintain an open and fair online environment for businesses users and end users by regulating the behavior of large online platforms, known as "gatekeepers," which have significant influence in the digital market and act as intermediaries between businesses and customers.[82] Examples of such gatekeepers are Google, Meta, and Amazon. The regulation has only an indirect impact on the use of AI, as it aims to prevent these gatekeepers from engaging in unfair practices, which give them significant power and control over access to content and services.[83] Such practices may involve the use of biased or discriminatory AI algorithms. The regulation imposes obligations on gatekeepers such as providing the ability for users to uninstall default software applications on the operating system of the gatekeeper,[84] a ban on self-preferencing,[85] and the obligation to provide data on advertising performance and ad pricing.[86] The DMA certainly provides for additional consumer protection, but it does so indirectly, by mainly regulating the relationship between platforms and business users and by creating more transparency. Consumer rights are not central in the DMA and this is also apparent from the lack of involvement of consumers and consumer organizations in the DMA's enforcement.[87]

The Digital Services Act ("DSA"),[88] which applies as of February 17, 2024,[89] establishes a harmonized set of rules on the provision on online intermediary services and aims to ensure a safe, predictable, and trustworthy online environment.[90] The regulation mainly affects online intermediaries (including online platforms), such as online marketplaces, online social networks, online travel and accommodation platforms, content-sharing platforms, and app stores.[91] It introduces additional transparency obligations, including advertising

[81] Art. 54 Regulation (EU) 2022/1925 of the European Parliament and of the Council of 14 September 2022 on contestable and fair markets in the digital sector and amending Directives (EU) 2019/1937 and (EU) 2020/1828 (Digital Markets Act) [2022] OJ L265/1. Note that article e 3(6) and (7) and Articles 40, 46, 47, 48, 49, and 50 shall apply from November 1, 2022 and article 42 and Article 43 shall apply from June 25, 2023.

[82] Recitals 2, 4, and 34 DMA.

[83] Recitals 6 and 15 DMA.

[84] Art. 6 (3) DMA.

[85] Art. 6(5) DMA.

[86] Art. 5 (9) and art. 6(8) DMA.

[87] Rupprecht Podszun, 'The Digital Markets Act: What's in It for Consumers?', *EuCML* 2022, 3–5.

[88] Regulation (EU) 2022/2065 of the European Parliament and of the Council of 19 October 2022 on a Single Market for Digital Services and amending Directive 2000/31/EC (Digital Services Act) [2022] OJ L277/1.

[89] Article 93 DSA. However, Article 24(2), (3), and (6), Article 33(3) to (6), Article 37(7), Article 40(13), Article 43 and Sections 4, 5, and 6 of Chapter IV shall apply from November 16, 2022.

[90] Art. 1 DSA.

[91] European Commission, "The Digital Services Act package" (November 24, 2022), https://digital-strategy.ec.europa.eu/en/policies/digital-services-act-package, accessed on December 24, 2022.

transparency requirements for online platforms[92] and a ban on targeted advertisement of minors based on profiling[93] as well as a ban on targeted advertising based on profiling using special categories of personal data, such as religious belief or sexual orientation.[94] It also introduces recommender system transparency for providers of online platforms.[95] The regulation furthermore obliges very large online platforms to carry out a risk assessment of their services and systems, including their algorithmic systems.[96]

10.4.6 *Artificial Intelligence Act*

The Artificial Intelligence Act ("AI Act") Act, adopted June 13, 2024, provides harmonized rules for "the placing on the market, the putting into service and the use of AI systems in the Union."[97] It uses a risk-based methodology to classify certain uses of AI systems as entailing a low, high, or unacceptable risk.[98] AI practices that pose an unacceptable risk are prohibited, including subliminal techniques that distort behavior and cause significant harm.[99] The regulation foresees penalties for noncompliance[100] and establishes a cooperation mechanism at European level (the so-called European Artificial Intelligence Board), composed of representatives from the Member States and the Commission, to ensure enforcement of the provisions of the AI Act across Europe.[101] Concerns have been expressed whether the AI Act is adequate to also tackle consumer protection concerns. It has been argued that the list of "high-risk" applications and the list of forbidden AI practices does not cover all problematic AI applications or practices for consumers.[102] Furthermore, the sole focus on public enforcement and the lack of appropriate individual rights

[92] Art. 26 DSA; see also art. 39 DSA for additional transparency obligations for very large online platforms.
[93] Art. 28(2) DSA.
[94] Art. 26(3).
[95] Art. 3(s) and art. 27 DSA.
[96] Art. 34 DSA. For a discussion of this risk assessment requirement, see also Chapter 14 of this book on AI and Media by Lidia Dutkiewicz, Noémie Krack, Aleksandra Kuczerawy, and Peggy Valcke.
[97] Art 1(a) "Regulation (EU) 2024/1689 of the European Parliament and the council of 13 June 2024 laying down harmonised rules on artificial intelligence and amending Regulations" (Artificial Intelligence Act) ("AI Act").
[98] Explanatory memorandum, AI Act Proposal COM (2021) 206 final, 12; Recital 26 AI Act.
[99] Art. 5(1) (a) AI Act.
[100] Art. 99 AI Act.
[101] Art. 65 AI Act.
[102] See BEUC, Position Paper on the AI Act. Regulating AI to protect the consumer, www.beuc.eu/sites/default/files/publications/beuc-x-2021-088_regulating_ai_to_protect_the_consumer.pdf. See in this regard also Nathalie A. Smuha, Emma Ahmed-Rengers, Adam Harkens, Wenlong Li, James MacLaren, Riccardo Piselli, and Karen Yeung, "How the EU can achieve legally trustworthy AI: A response to the European Commission's proposal for an Artificial Intelligence Act," http://dx.doi.org/10.2139/ssrn.3899991.

for consumers and collective rights for consumers organization to ensure an effective enforcement has been criticized.[103]

10.5 DARK PATTERNS AS A CASE STUDY

10.5.1 *The Concept of Dark Patterns*

The OECD Committee on Consumer Policy uses the following working definition of dark patterns:

> business practices employing elements of digital choice architecture, in particular in online user interfaces, that subvert or impair consumer autonomy, decision-making or choice. They often deceive, coerce or manipulate consumers and are likely to cause direct or indirect consumer detriment in various ways, though it may be difficult or impossible to measure such detriment in many instances.[104]

A universally accepted definition is lacking, but dark patterns can be described by their common features involving the use of hidden, subtle, and often manipulative designs or marketing tactics that exploit consumer biases, vulnerabilities, and preferences to benefit the business or provider of intermediary services that presents the information that may not align with the consumer's own preferences or best interest.[105] Examples of such marketing practices include (i) *false hierarchy* (the button for the business' desired outcome is more prominent or visually appealing than the others),[106] (ii) *hidden information*,[107] (iii) creating a sense of *false urgency*,[108] (iv) *forced continuity* or *roach motel* (making it significantly more difficult for consumers to cancel their subscription than it was to sign up or automatically renew the service without the user's express consent and repeatedly asking consumers to reconsider their choice).[109] All of these illustrations are practices closely related to the

[103] Natali Helberger, Hans-W. Micklitz, and Peter Rott, *The Regulatory Gap: Consumer Protection in the Digital Economy*, 2021, p. 36, www.beuc.eu/sites/default/files/publications/beuc-x-2021-116_the_regulatory_gap-consumer_protection_in_the_digital_economy.pdf.

[104] OECD, "Dark commercial patterns, OECD digital economy papers" (2022) No. 336, *OECD Publishing*, 8.

[105] Guidance UCPD 101; European Commission, Directorate-General for Justice and Consumers, Francesco Bogliacino, Alba Boluda, Francisco Lupiáñez-Villanueva et al., "Behavioural study on unfair commercial practices in the digital environment: dark patterns and manipulative personalization: final report" (2022) *Publications Office of the European Union*, https://data.europa.eu/doi/10.2838/859030, 6; Jamie Luguri and Lior Strahilevitz, "Shining a light on dark patterns" (2021) *Journal of Legal Analysis*, 44.

[106] Luguri and Strahilevitz, "Dark patterns" 55 and 58; Lupiáñez-Villanueva et al., "Behavioural study" 64.

[107] Luguri and Strahilevitz, "Dark patterns" 47; Lupiáñez-Villanueva et al., "Behavioural study" 105.

[108] For example, by claiming that a product or service is only available for a limited time, or communicating that the offer will pass to pressure the consumer to make a purchase, Guidance UCPD, 101; Luguri, "Dark patterns" 53 and 100.

[109] Luguri and Strahilevitz, "Dark patterns" 53, 55, and 58.

concept of choice architecture and hyper personalization discussed in Section 10.2 presenting choices in a non-neutral way.

Dark patterns may involve the use of personal data of consumers and the use of AI.[110] AI is an asset for modifying dark patterns to have a greater impact on consumers behavior in a subtle way. It allows business operators to examine which dark patterns work best, especially when personal data is involved, and dark patterns are adapted accordingly. Examples of the power of the combination of dark patterns and AI can be found in platforms encouraging consumers to become paying members by presenting this option in different ways and over different time periods.[111] Machine learning applications can analyze personal data to optimize dark patterns and find more innovative ways to convince consumers to buy a subscription. They can examine how many hours are spent a day watching videos, how many advertisements are being skipped and whether the app is closed when an ad is shown.[112] The ad play may be increased if the consumer refuses to become a paying member.[113] Such a process can be stretched over quite a long time, making the consumer believe it is its own decision to subscribe, without him feeling tricked.[114] In essence, the combination of AI, personal data and dark patterns, results in an increased ability to manipulate consumers.

10.5.2 *Overview of the Relevant Instruments of Consumer Protection against Dark Patterns*

The UCPD is a first instrument that offers a number of possible avenues to combat dark patterns. As mentioned, it covers a wide range of prohibited practices in a business to consumer context.[115] First, the general prohibition of unfair commercial practices of art. 5 UCPD that functions as a residual control mechanism can be invoked. It prohibits all practices that violate a trader's professional diligence obligation and that cause the average consumer to make a transactional decision that they would not otherwise have made.[116] This includes not only the decision to purchase or not purchase a product but also related decisions, such as visiting a website, or viewing content.[117] As mentioned, the standard of the "average" consumer (of the

[110] OECD, "Dark commercial patterns" 9.

[111] See, for example, referring to YouTube: Zakary Kinnaird, "Dark patterns powered by machine learning: An intelligent combination" (October 13, 2020) https://uxdesign.cc/dark-patterns-powered-by-machine-learning-an-intelligent-combination-f2804ed028ce, accessed February 3, 2023.

[112] Ibid.

[113] Ibid.

[114] Ibid.

[115] Article 2(d) UCPD refers to "any act, omission, course of conduct or representation, commercial communication including marketing, by a trader, directly connected with the promotion, sale or supply of a product to consumers."

[116] Art. 5 UCPD, Guidance UCPD 46.

[117] Guidance UCPD 31.

target group) is a normative standard that has (so far) been applied rather strictly, as rational behavior is the point of departure in the assessment.[118] The fact that the benchmark can be modulated to the target group does however offer some possibilities for a less strict standard in case of personalization, as the practice could then even be assessed from the perspective of a single targeted person.[119]

Article 5(3) UCPD, furthermore creates some possibilities to assess a practice from the perspective of a vulnerable consumer, but the narrow definition of vulnerability as mental or psychical disability, age or credulity is – as mentioned – not suitable for the digital age. Indeed, any consumer can be temporarily vulnerable due to contextual and psychological factors.[120] According to the European Commission, the UCPD provides a non-exhaustive list of characteristics that make a consumer "particularly susceptible" and therefore states that the concept of vulnerability should include these context-dependent vulnerabilities, such as interests, preferences, psychological profile, and even mood.[121] It will indeed be important to adopt such a broader interpretation to take into account the fact that all consumers can be potentially vulnerable in a digital context. The open norms of the UCPD might indeed be sufficiently flexible for such an interpretation,[122] but a clearer text in the directive – and not only (nonbinding) guidance of the Commission guidance – would be useful.

The more specific open norms prohibiting misleading and especially aggressive practices (arts. 6–9 UCPD) can also be invoked. But it is again uncertain how open concepts such as "*undue influence*" (art. 8 UCPD) must be interpreted in an AI context and to what extent the benchmark of the average consumer can be individualized. At what point does an increased exposure to advertising, tailored on past behavior, in order to convince a consumer to "choose" a paid subscription, amount to undue influence? More guidance on the interpretation of these open norms would be welcome.[123]

The blacklist in Annex I of the UCPD avoids the whole discussion on the interpretation of these benchmarks. That list prohibits specific practices that are considered unfair in all circumstances[124] and does not require an analysis of the potential effect on the average (or – exceptionally – vulnerable) consumer. The practices also do not require proof that the trader breached his professional diligence duty.[125] The list prohibits several online practices, including *disguised ads*,[126]

[118] See above, Section 3.3.
[119] See in any event in this sense, Guidance UCPD, point 4.2.7.
[120] Lupiáñez-Villanueva et al., "Behavioural study" 72.
[121] Guidance UCPD, points 2.6, 35.
[122] Lupiáñez-Villanueva et al., "Behavioural study" 72.
[123] Sartor, Digital services and artificial intelligence, 36–37.
[124] Annex 1 UCPD, currently 35 practices are listed.
[125] Case C-435/11 *CHS Tour Services GmbH* v *Team4 Travel GmbH* [2013] ECR I-00057, §45.
[126] Practice 11 Annex I UCPD.

false urgency (e.g., fake countdown timers),[127] *bait and switch*,[128] and *direct exhortations to children*.[129] However, these practices were not specifically formulated to be applied in an AI context and interpretational problems therefore also occur when applying the current list to dark patterns. Thus, it is for instance mentioned in the Commission guidance that "making repeated intrusions during normal interactions in order to get the consumer to do or accept something (i.e., nagging) *could* amount to a persistent and unwanted solicitation."[130] The same interpretational problem then rises: how much intrusion and pressure is exactly needed to make a practice a "persistent and unwanted solicitation"? Additional blacklisted (AI) practices would increase legal certainty and facilitate enforcement.

Finally, the recently added Article 7(4a) UCPD requires traders to provide consumers with general information about the main parameters that determine the ranking of search results and their relative importance. The effectiveness of this article in protecting consumers by informing them can be questioned, as transparency about the practices generated by an AI system collides with the black box problem. Sharing information about the input-*phase*, such as the data set and learning algorithm that were used, may to some extent mitigate the information asymmetry but it will not suffice as a means of protection.

While the UCPD has broad coverage for most types of unfair commercial practices, the case-by-case approach does not allow to effectively address all forms of deceptive techniques known as "dark patterns." For example, BEUC's report of 2022 highlights the lack of consumer protection for practices that use language and emotion to influence consumers to make choices or take specific actions, often through tactics such as shaming, also referred to as *confirmshaming*.[131] In addition, there is uncertainty about the responsibilities of traders under the professional diligence duty and whether certain practices are explicitly prohibited.[132] Insufficient enforcement by both public and private parties further weakens this instrument.[133]

A second piece of legislation that provides some protection against dark patterns is the DSA. The regulation refers to dark patterns as practices "that materially distort or impair, either purposefully or in effect, the ability of recipients of the service

[127] Practice 7 Annex I UCPD, Commission guidance, point 4.2.7.

[128] Practice 5 (bait) and 6 (bait and switch) Annex I UCPD. The provisions in essence prohibit making offers when the trader knows that he will probably not be able to meet the demand (bait advertising) or making offers at a specified price and then refusing to deliver the product (on time) with the intention of promoting a different product (bait and switch).

[129] Practice 28 Annex I UCPD.

[130] Practice 26 Annex I UCPD. Commission guidance, point 4.2.7.

[131] BEUC, "Dark Patterns and the EU consumer law acquis: Recommendations forbetter enforcement and reform" (February 7, 2022), www.beuc.eu/sites/default/files/publications/beuc-x-2022-013_dark_patters_paper.pdf, accessed December 23, 2022, 9; Lupiáñez-Villanueva et al., "Behavioural study" 66.

[132] Lupiáñez-Villanueva et al., "Behavioural study" 122.

[133] Ibid., 122.

to make autonomous and informed choices or decisions."[134] The DSA prohibits online platforms from designing, organizing, or operating their interfaces in a way that "deceives, manipulates, or otherwise materially distorts or impacts the ability of recipients of their services to make free and informed decisions"[135] in so far as those practices are not covered under the UCPD and GDPR.[136] Note that the important exception largely erodes consumer protection. Where the UCPD applies, and that includes all B2C practices, the vague standards of the UCPD will apply and not the more specific prohibition of dark patterns in the DSA. A cumulative application would have been preferable. The DSA inter alia targets exploitative design choices and practices as "forced continuity," that make it unreasonably difficult to discontinue purchases or to sign out from services.[137]

The AI Act contains two specific prohibitions on manipulation practices carried out through the use of AI systems that may cover dark patterns.[138] These bans prohibit the use of subliminal techniques to materially distort a person's behavior in a manner that causes or is likely to cause significant harm and the exploitation of vulnerabilities in specific groups of people to materially distort their behavior in a manner that causes or is likely to cause significant harm.[139] These prohibitions are similar to those in the UCPD, except that they are limited to practices carried out through the use of AI systems.[140] They furthermore have some limitations. The ban relating to the abuse of vulnerabilities only applies to certain explicitly listed vulnerabilities, such as age, disability or specific social or economic situation, yet the mentioned problem of digital vulnerability is not tackled. A further major limitation was fortunately omitted in the final text of the AI Act. Whereas in the text of the AI proposal, these provisions only applied in case of physical and mental harm – which will often not be present and may be difficult to prove[141] – the prohibitions of the final AI Act also apply to (significant) economic harm.

The AI Act is complementary to other existing regulations, including data protection, consumer protection, and digital service legislation.[142] Finally, taking into account the fact that this Regulation strongly focuses on high-risk AI and that there are not many private services that qualify as high risk, the additional protection for consumers from this regulation seems limited.

[134] Recital 67 DSA: "Practices that materially distort or impair, either purposefully or in effect, the ability of recipients of the service to make autonomous and informed choices or decisions."

[135] Art. 25(1) DSA.

[136] Recital 67 DSA.

[137] Recital 67 DSA.

[138] Art. 5 AI Act.

[139] Art 5 (a) and (b) AI Act.

[140] Lupiáñez-Villanueva et al., "Behavioural study" 83; Catalina Goanta, "Regulatory Siblings: The Unfair Commercial Practices Directive Roots of the AI ACT," in I. Graef & B. van der Sloot (ed.). *The Legal Consistency of Technology Regulation in Europe* (pp. 71–88). Oxford: Hart Publishing, 2024.

[141] See in this regard Rostam Josef Neuwirth, *The EU Artificial Intelligence Act Regulating Subliminal AI Systems* (Routledge, 2023).

[142] Recital 9 AI Act.

The Consumer Rights Directive with its transparency requirement for pre-contractual information[143] and its prohibition to use *pre-ticked boxes* implying additional payments might also provide some help.[144] However, the prohibition on pre-ticked boxes does not apply to certain sectors that are excluded from the directive, such as financial services.[145] The UCPD could however also be invoked to combat charging for additional services through default interface settings and that directive does apply to the financial sector.[146] The CRD does not regulate the conditions for contract termination, except for the right of withdrawal. An obligation for traders to insert a "withdrawal function" or "cancellation button" in contracts concluded by means of an online interface has recently been added to the CRD.[147] This function is meant to make it easier for consumers to terminate distance contracts, particularly subscriptions during the period of withdrawal. This has could be a useful tool to combat subscription traps.

10.6 CONCLUSION

AI poses major challenges to consumers and to consumer law and the traditional consumer law instruments are not well adapted to tackle these challenges. The mere provision of information on how AI operates will definitely not suffice to adequately protect consumers. The current instruments do allow to tackle some of the most blatant detrimental practices, but the application of the open norms in a digital context creates uncertainty and hinders effective enforcement, as our case study of dark patterns has shown. The use of AI in a business context creates a structural vulnerability for all consumers. This requires additional regulation to provide better protection, as well as additional efforts in raising awareness of the risks AI entails.

[143] Information provided to consumers before the conclusion of a contract in distance contracts must be presented in a clear and understandable manner, pursuant to Art. 8 (1) CRD; see also BEUC, "Dark Patterns," 9.

[144] Art. 33 CRD.

[145] Art. 3(3) (d) CRD.

[146] Guidance UCPD, point 4.2.7.

[147] The CRD was amended by Directive (EU) 2023/2673 of 22 November 2023 amending Directive 2011/83/EU as regards financial services contracts concluded at a distance and repealing Directive 2002/65/EC, OJ L, 2023/2673, 28.11.2023. This new article 11a must be transposed by 19 December 2025 and applied from 19 June 2026.

11

Artificial Intelligence and Intellectual Property Law

Jozefien Vanherpe

11.1 INTRODUCTION

This chapter reflects on the interaction between AI and Intellectual Property (IP) law. IP rights are exclusive rights vested in intangible assets that grant their owner a temporary monopoly as to the use thereof in a given territory. IP rights may be divided into industrial property and literary and artistic property. Industrial property rights protect creations that play a largely economic role and primarily include patents, trademarks, and design rights. The concept of literary and artistic property rights refers to copyright and related rights. Copyright offers the author(s) protection for literary and artistic works, while the three main related rights are granted to performing artists, producers, and broadcasting organizations.

The interface of AI and IP law has been the subject of much research already.[1] This chapter analyzes some of the relevant legal issues from a primarily civil law perspective, with a focus on the European Union (EU), and with the caveat that its limited length leaves little leeway for the nuance that this intricate, multifaceted topic demands. Section 11.2 treats the avenues open to innovators who seek to protect AI technology. Section 11.3 examines whether AI systems qualify as an author or inventor and who "owns" AI-powered content. Section 11.4 briefly notes the issues surrounding IP infringement by AI systems, the potential impact of AI on certain key concepts of IP law and the growing use of AI in IP practice.

[1] See, for example, Christian Hartmann, Jacqueline Allan, P. Bernt Hugenholtz, João Pedro Quintais, and Daniel Gervais, "Trends and developments in artificial intelligence. Challenges to the intellectual property rights framework," Brussels, 2020, https://bit.ly/3XgBPPa; Retó Hilty, Jyh-An Lee, and Kung-Chung Liu, *Artificial Intelligence and Intellectual Property* (Oxford University Press, 2021); Ryan Abbott (ed), *Research Handbook on Intellectual Property and Artificial Intelligence* (Edward Elgar Publishing, 2022); Larry A DiMatteo, Cristina Poncibò, and Michel Cannarsa (eds), *The Cambridge Handbook of Artificial Intelligence. Global Perspectives on Law and Ethics* (Cambridge University Press, 2022), pp. 87–160; Jozefien Vanherpe, "AI and IP: Great Expectations" in Jan De Bruyne and Cedric Vanleenhove (eds), *Artificial Intelligence and the Law* (2nd ed, Intersentia, 2023) pp. 233–267; Anke Moerland, "Intellectual property law and AI" in Ernest Lim and Phillip Morgan (eds), *The Cambridge Handbook of Private Law and Artificial Intelligence* (Cambridge University Press, 2024), 362–83.

11.2 PROTECTION OF AI TECHNOLOGY

Companies may protect innovation relating to AI technology through patent law and/or copyright law. Both avenues are treated in turn below.

11.2.1 *Protection under Patent Law*

Patent law seeks to reward investment into research and development in order to spur future innovation. It does so by providing patentees with a temporary right to exclude others from using a certain "invention," a technological improvement that takes the form of a product or a process (or both). This monopoly right is limited to 20 years following the patent application, subject to payment of the applicable annual fees.[2] It is also limited in scope: while patentees can bring both direct and indirect infringements of their patent(s) to an end, they must accept certain exceptions as a defense to their claims, including use for experimental purposes and noncommercial use.[3] In order to be eligible for a patent, the invention must satisfy a number of conditions.

First, certain exclusions apply. The list of excluded subject matter under the European Patent Convention (EPC)[4] includes ideas that are deemed too abstract, such as computer programs as such, methods for performing mental acts and mathematical methods.[5] Pure abstract algorithms, which are essential to AI systems, qualify as a mathematical method, and are thus ineligible for patent protection *as such*.[6] However, this does not exclude patent protection for computer-implemented inventions such as technology related to AI algorithms, especially given the lenient interpretation of the "as such" proviso in practice. If the invention has a technical effect beyond its implementation on a computer – a connection to a material object in the "real" world – patentability may yet arise.[7] This will for example be the case for a neural network used "in a heart monitoring apparatus for the purpose of identifying irregular heartbeats," as well as – in certain circumstances – methods for training AI systems.[8]

Further, a patentable invention must satisfy a number of substantive conditions: it must be novel and inventive as well as industrially applicable.[9] The novelty requirement implies that the invention may not have been made available to the public

2 Article 63 European Patent Convention (EPC).

3 The definition of "infringement" is left to national law, see Article 64(3) EPC.

4 See from a US perspective, https://tinyurl.com/37a763c3, accessed August 14, 2024.

5 Articles 52–53 EPC.

6 EPO, "Guidelines for Examination, Part G, Chapter II, 3.3.1," https://bit.ly/3SNGMyG, accessed August 14, 2024.

7 EBA Decision 10 March 2021 re patent application 03793825.5, G 0001/19, https://bit.ly/3108x9g, accessed August 14, 2024.

8 EPO, "Guidelines for Examination, Part G, Chapter II, 3.3.1," 2018, https://bit.ly/3BQb8W9, accessed August 14, 2024.

9 Articles 52 *juncto* 54–57 EPC.

at the date of filing of the patent application, indicated as the "state of the art."[10] The condition of inventive step requires the invention to not have been obvious to a theoretical person skilled in the art (PSA) on the basis of this state of the art.[11] Finally, the invention must be susceptible to use in an industrial context.[12] Both the novelty and industrial applicability requirements do not appear to pose any challenges specific to AI-related innovation.[13] However, the inventiveness analysis only takes account of the patent claim features that contribute to the "technical character" of the invention, to the solution of a technical problem. Conversely, nontechnical features (such as the abstract algorithm) are removed from the equation.[14]

The "patent bargain" between patentee and issuing government may lead to another obstacle. This implies that a prospective patentee must disclose their invention in a way that is sufficiently clear and complete for it to be carried out by a PSA, in return for patent protection.[15] This requirement of disclosure may be at odds with the apparent "black box" nature of many forms of AI technology, particularly in a deep learning context. This refers to a situation where we know which data were provided to the system (input A) and which result is reached (output B), but where it is unclear what exactly makes the AI system go from A to B.[16] Arguably, certain AI-related inventions cannot be explained in a sufficiently clear and complete manner, excluding the procurement of a patent therefor. However, experts will generally be able to disclose the AI system's structure, the applicable parameters and the basic principles to which it adheres.[17] It is plausible that patent offices will deem this to be sufficient. The risk of being excluded from patent protection constitutes an additional incentive to invest in so-called "explainable" and transparent AI.[18] The transparency requirements established by the EU AI Act also play a role in

10 Articles 54–55 EPC. In case priority is claimed, the relevant date is the priority date.

11 Article 56 EPC. In determining whether a certain invention involves inventive step (and is therefore not "obvious"), the EPO applies the so-called "problem-solution approach." This approach involves (1) determining the so-called "closest prior art," (2) establishing the "objective technical problem" in the state of the art, and (3) considering whether or not the claimed invention, starting from the closest prior art and the objective technical problem, would have been obvious to the skilled person ("could-would approach," see in more detail EPO, "Guidelines for Examination, Part G, Chapter VII.5," https://bit.ly/3GQL5ln, accessed August 14, 2024).

12 Article 57 EPC.

13 See however in relation to patent protection of AI-generated output below, Section 11.3.2.

14 EBA Decision 10 March 2021 re patent application 03793825.5, G 0001/19, in particular paras 106–138; Timo Minssen and Mateo Aboy, "The patentability of computer-implemented simulations and implications for computer-implemented inventions (CIIs)" (2021) *JIPLP*, 16: 633, 633–35.

15 Article 83 EPC.

16 Mizuki Hashiguchi, "The global artificial intelligence revolution challenges patent eligibility laws" (2017) *J Bus & Tech L*, 13: 1, 29–30.

17 Brian Higgins, "The role of explainable artificial intelligence in patent law" (2019) *Intell Prop & Tech LJ*, 31: 3, 7.

18 See, for example, Wojciech Samek et al. (eds), *Explainable AI: Interpreting, Explaining and Visualizing Deep Learning*, vol 11700 (Lecture Notes in Computer Science, Springer International Publishing, 2019).

this context.[19] Simultaneously, an overly strict assessment of the requirement of disclosure may push innovators toward trade secrets as an alternative way to protect AI-related innovation.[20]

It is often difficult to predict the outcome of the patenting process of AI-related innovation. This uncertainty does not seem to deter prospective patentees, as evidenced by the rising number of AI-related patent applications.[21] Since the 1950s, over 300,000 AI-related patent applications have been filed worldwide, with a sharp increase in the past decade: in 2019, it was already noted that more than half of these applications had been published since 2013.[22] It is to be expected that more recent numbers will confirm this evolving trend.

11.2.2 *Protection under Copyright Law*

AI-related innovation may also enjoy copyright protection. Copyright protection is generated automatically upon the creation of a literary and artistic work that constitutes a concrete and original expression by the author(s).[23] It offers exclusive exploitation rights as to protected works, such as the right of reproduction and the right of communication to the public (subject to a number of exceptions), as well as certain moral rights.[24] Copyright protection lasts until a minimum period of 50 years has passed following the death of the longest living author, a period that has been extended to 70 years in, for example, the EU Member States.[25]

[19] See Articles 11, 53 and Annexes IV, XI Regulation (EU) 2024/1689 of the European Parliament and of the Council of 13 June 2024 laying down harmonised rules on artificial intelligence and amending Regulations (EC) No 300/2008, (EU) No 167/2013, (EU) No 168/2013, (EU) 2018/858, (EU) 2018/1139 and (EU) 2019/2144 and Directives 2014/90/EU, (EU) 2016/797 and (EU) 2020/1828 [2024] OJ L1689/1 (hereinafter the "AI Act"). See on this topic, for example, Balint Gyevnar, Nick Ferguson and Burkhard Schafer, "Bridging the transparency gap: what can explainable AI learn from the AI Act?" (2023) DOI: 10.3233/FAIA230367. See also Thomas Gils, Frederic Heymans and Wannes Ooms, "Report: from policy to practice: prototyping the EU AI Act's transparency requirements" (2024), https://tinyurl.com/2s3w8jhp, accessed August 14, 2024.

[20] Cf. Katarina Foss-Solbrekk, "Three Routes to Protecting AI Systems and Their Algorithms under IP Law: The Good, the Bad and the Ugly" (2021) 16 *JIPLP* 247, 256–58.

[21] "WIPO Technology Trends 2019 – Artificial Intelligence," 2019, 14, https://bit.ly/3wlRQH5, accessed August 14, 2024.

[22] WIPO Technology Trends 2019, p. 13; "WIPO Technology Trends 2021, Assistive Technology," 2022, https://bit.ly/3EO8T7z, accessed August 14, 2024.

[23] Articles 2 and 5(2) Berne Convention.

[24] See, for example, Articles 6*bis*-14*ter* Berne Convention; Articles 2–4 Directive 2001/29/EC on the harmonisation of certain aspects of copyright and related rights in the information society [2001] OJ L167/10 (InfoSoc Directive). See on this topic Christophe Geiger, Franciska Schönherr, Irini Stamatoudi, Paul Torremans, and Stavroula Karapapa, "Chapter 11: the Information Society Directive," in Irini Stamatoudi and Paul Torremans (eds), *EU Copyright Law. A Commentary* (Edward Elgar Publishing, 2021), 279–380.

[25] Article 7 Berne Convention; Article 12 TRIPS Agreement; Article 1 Directive 2006/116/EC on the term of protection of copyright and certain related rights (codified version) [2006] OJ L 372/12 (Term Directive).

The validity conditions for copyright are the requirement of concrete form and the requirement of originality. First, copyright protection is not available to mere abstract ideas and principles; these must be expressed in a concrete way.[26] Second, the condition of originality implies that the work must be an intellectual creation of the author(s), reflecting their personality and expressing free and creative choices.[27] Applied to AI-related works in particular, the functional algorithm in its purest sense does not satisfy the first condition and is therefore not susceptible to copyright protection.[28] However, the object and source code of the computer program expressing this idea are sufficiently concrete, allowing for copyright protection once the condition of originality is fulfilled.[29] Given the low threshold set for originality in practice, software that implements AI technology is likely to receive automatic protection as a computer program under copyright law upon its creation.[30]

11.3 PROTECTION OF AI-ASSISTED AND AI-GENERATED OUTPUT

This section analyzes whether AI systems could – and, if not, should – claim authorship and/or inventorship in their output.[31] It then focuses on IP ownership as to such output.

11.3.1 *AI Authorship*

Can AI systems ever claim authorship? To answer this question, we must first ascertain whether "creative" machines already exist. Second, we discuss whether an AI system can be considered an author and, if not, whether it should be.

Certain AI systems available today can be used as a tool to create works that would satisfy the conditions for copyright protection if they had been solely created by humans. Many examples can be found in the music sector.[32] You may be reading

[26] Article 9(2) TRIPS Agreement. A common example of this requirement is that styles (such as Cubism) are not susceptible to copyright protection, while concrete expressions of such styles (such as a specific painting by Picasso in the Cubist style) may qualify for copyright protection, subject to the fulfilment of the condition of originality.

[27] C-5/08 *Infopaq* [2009] ECLI:EU:C:2009:465; C-393/09 *BSA* [2010] ECLI:EU:C:2010:816; C-145/10 *Painer* [2011] ECLI:EU:C:2011:798.

[28] C-406/10 *SAS Institute* [2012] ECLI:EU:C:2012:259.

[29] C-393/09 *BSA* [2010] ECLI:EU:C:2010:816.

[30] See Foss-Solbrekk, "Three Routes," pp. 249–253; Begoña Gonzalez Otero, "Machine learning models under the copyright microscope: Is EU copyright fit for purpose?" (2021) *GRUR International*, 70: 1043, 1–13.

[31] See re design law: Hasan Yılmaztekin, *Artificial Intelligence, Design Law and Fashion* (Routledge, 2023).

[32] See in detail Oleksandr Bulayenko, João Pedro Quintais, Daniel Gervais, and Joost Poort, "AI music outputs: Challenges to the copyright legal framework," 2022, https://ssrn.com/abstract=4072806, accessed August 14, 2024.

this chapter with AI-generated music playing, such as piano music by Google's "DeepMind" AI,[33] an album released by the "Auxuman"[34] algorithm, a soundscape created by the "Endel"[35] app or one of the unfinished symphonies of Franz Schubert or Ludwig van Beethoven as completed with the aid of an AI system.[36] If you would rather create music yourself, Sony's "Flow Machines" project may offer assistance by augmenting your creativity through its AI algorithm.[37] If you are bored with this text, which was written (solely) by a human author, you may instead start a conversation with "ChatGPT 4,"[38] read a novel[39] drafted by an AI algorithm or translate it using "DeepL."[40] AI-generated artwork is also available.[41] Most famously, Rembrandt van Rijn's paintings were fed to an AI algorithm that went on to create a 3D-printed painting in Rembrandt's style in 2016.[42] Since then, the use of AI in artwork has skyrocketed, with AI-powered image-generating applications such as "DALL-E 3"[43] and "Midjourney"[44] gaining exponential popularity.[45]

In most cases, there is still some human intervention, be it by a programmer, a person training the AI system through data input or somebody who modifies and/or selects output deemed "worthy" to disclose.[46] If such human(s) were to have created the work(s) without the intervention of an AI system, copyright protection would likely be available.

Copyright law requires the work at issue to show *authorship*; the personal stamp of the *author*. The author is considered to be a physical person, especially in the civil law tradition, where copyright protection is viewed as a natural right, granted to the author to protect emanations of their personality.[47] Creativity is viewed as a quintessentially human faculty, whereby a sentient being expresses their personality by

33 Video available at youtu.be/Y8UawLT4ito accessed August 14, 2024.

34 See www.auxuman.space accessed August 14, 2024.

35 See https://endel.io accessed August 14, 2024.

36 See https://bit.ly/3whiQHy and https://bit.ly/3wrGrFO accessed August 14, 2024.

37 See www.flow-machines.com accessed August 14, 2024.

38 See https://chat.openai.com accessed August 14, 2024.

39 See, for example, Thomas Hornigold, "The first novel written by AI is here – and it's as weird as you'd expect it to be," *Singularity Hub* (October 25, 2018), https://bit.ly/3mOs4rP, accessed August 14, 2024. See however Gary Smith, "The Great American Novel will not be written by a computer," *Mind Matters* (June 30, 2021), https://bit.ly/3HOUQRy.

40 See www.deepl.com, accessed August 14, 2024.

41 See, for example, https://aiartists.org/ai-timeline-art, accessed August 14, 2024.

42 See www.nextrembrandt.com, accessed August 14, 2024.

43 See https://openai.com/dall-e-3, accessed August 14, 2024.

44 See www.midjourney.com, accessed August 14, 2024.

45 See Pesala Bandara, "The best AI image generators in 2023" (*PetaPixel*, January 3, 2023), https://bit.ly/3Xxj1ej, accessed August 14, 2024; see also, for example, https://aiartists.org; www.artaigallery.com.

46 By way of example, users provide the DeepL translation app with relevant input and may manually modify the translated text.

47 See however also under US law, for example: US Copyright Office, "Copyright Registration Guidance: Works Containing Material Generated by Artificial Intelligence," 2023, 37 CFR Part 202, https://bit.ly/4dxQIEQ; US District Court for the District of Columbia 18 August 2023, 22-1564, https://bit.ly/4ckMr6l.

making free, deliberate choices.[48] This tenet pervades all aspects of copyright law. First, copyright laws grant initial ownership of copyright in a certain work to its author.[49] Further, the term of protection is calculated from the author's death. Also, certain provisions expressly seek to protect the author, such as those included in copyright contract law as well as the resale right applicable to original works of art. Moreover, particular copyright exceptions only apply if the author is acknowledged and/or if an equitable remuneration is paid to the author, such as the exception for private copies. The focus on the human author also explains the importance of the author's moral rights to disclosure, integrity, and attribution.[50] Such a system leaves no room for the authorship of a nonhuman entity.[51] If there is insufficient human input in the form of free and creative choices on the part of an author, if the AI crosses a certain threshold of autonomy, copyright protection is unavailable.[52] This anthropocentric view is unsurprising, since IP laws were largely drafted at a time when the concept of nonhuman "creators" belonged squarely in the realm of fiction.

However, the core of the issue is whether the abstract idea of originality *should* be held to include the creating behavior of an AI system. Account must hereby be taken of the broad range of potential AI activity and the ensuing distinction between AI-*assisted* and truly AI-*generated* content. At the one end of the spectrum, we may find AI systems that function as a tool to assist and/or enhance human creativity, where the AI itself acts as a mere executer.[53] We can compare this to the quill used by William Shakespeare.[54] Further down the line, there are many forms of AI-exhibited creativity that still result from creative choices made by a human, where the output flows directly from previously set parameters.[55] Such AI activity may still be viewed as pure execution. In such cases, copyright should be reserved to the human actor behind the machine.

48 Cf. Annemarie Bridy, "Coding creativity: Copyright and the artificially intelligent author" [2012] STLR 28, 4.

49 See, for example, Article 2(6) Berne Convention, which conceptualizes copyright as a form of protection for the *author* and their successors in title. An AI system *as such* is not a legal entity, which implies that it cannot be endowed with rights of any kind, including ownership rights. Notably, continental EU law does not have a rule similar to the "work-made-for-hire" doctrine that applies in the United States, which allows employers to be treated as the author of a work created by a human employee.

50 Annemarie Bridy, "The evolution of authorship: Work made by code" (2016) *Colum JL & Arts*, 39: 9, 401.

51 See, for example, Andres Guadamuz, "Do Androids dream of electric copyright? Comparative analysis of originality in artificial intelligence generated works" [2017] *IPQ* 169: 173–74.

52 Daniel Gervais, "The machine as author" (2020) *Iowa L Rev*, 105: 2053, 2062, 2098–101, 2106.

53 James Grimmelmann, "There's no such thing as a computer-authored work—And it's a good thing, too" (2016) *Colum JL & Arts*, 39: 403, 403, 406–08; Erica Fraser, "Computers as inventors – legal and policy implications of artificial intelligence on patent law" (2016) *SCRIPTed*, 13: 305, 305, 306; Samantha Fink Hedrick, "I 'Think,' therefore I create: Claiming copyright in the outputs of algorithms" (2019) *NYU Journal of Intell Prop & Ent Law*, 8: 324, 329.

54 Cf. Margot E Kaminski, "Authorship, disrupted: AI authors in copyright and first amendment law" (2017) *UCD L Rev*, 51: 589, 595.

55 Hedrick, "I 'Think,' therefore I create," 353, 358–60.

At the far end of the spectrum, we could find a hypothetical, more autonomous, "creative" AI, having independently created a work that exhibits the requisite creativity, which experts and nonexperts alike cannot distinguish from a work generated by a human. Even in such a case, it may be argued that there is no real act of "conception" in the AI system, given that every piece of AI-generated output is the result of prior human input.[56] Arguably, precisely this act, the *process* of creation, is the essence of creativity. As long as the human thought process cannot be formulated as an algorithm that may be implemented by a computer, this process will remain human, thus excluding AI authorship. However, the "prior input" argument also applies *mutatis mutandis* to humans, who create literary and artistic works while "standing on the shoulders of giants."[57] This could render the "act of conception" argument against AI authorship moot, as could choosing the end result and thus the originality of the output as a (functionalist) focal point instead of the creative process.[58] Additionally, it is argued that granting AI systems authorship may stimulate further creative efforts on the part of AI systems. This appears to be in line with the economic, utilitarian rationale of copyright.[59] However, copyright seeks to incentivize human creators, not AI systems.[60] Moreover, it is difficult to see how AI systems may respond to incentives in the absence of human consciousness.[61] Without convincing economic evidence, caution is advised against tearing down one of the fundamental principles of copyright law. The mere fact that we *can* create certain incentives does not in itself imply that we *should*. Further, if we were to allow AI authorship, we must be prepared for an upsurge in algorithmic creations, as well as the effects on human artistic freedom that this would entail.[62]

The risk of extending authorship to AI systems could be mitigated by instead establishing a related or *sui generis* right to AI-generated works and provide a limited

[56] See also Noam Shemtov, "A study on inventorship in inventions involving AI activity" (*European Patent Office*, 2019) 6, 20, 35. See for a more recent example Rhiannon Williams, "What happened when 20 comedians got AI to write their routines" (*MIT Technology Review* 17 June 2024), https://tinyurl.com/yxad3bse, accessed August 14, 2024.

[57] "If I have seen further, it is by standing upon the shoulders of Giants." – Sir Isaac Newton (1675).

[58] Cf. in relation to patent law Shemtov, "A study on inventorship in inventions involving AI activity," pp. 28–29; Ryan Abbott, "I think, therefore I invent: Creative computers and the future of patent law" (2016) *BC L Rev*, 57: 1079, 1082, 1099, 1108–11.

[59] Peter Blok, "The inventor's new tool: Artificial intelligence – how does it fit in the European patent system?" (2017) *EIPR*, 39: 69, 69, 72.

[60] Kaminski, "Authorship, disrupted," pp. 589, 599; Shlomit Yanisky-Ravid and Xiaoqiong (Jackie) Liu, "When artificial intelligence systems produce inventions: An alternative model for patent law at the 3A era" (2018) *Cardozo L Rev*, 39: 2215, 2243–46.

[61] Pamela Samuelson, "Allocating ownership rights in computer-generated works" (1986) *U Pitt L Rev*, 47: 1185, 1199; Hedrick, "I 'Think,' therefore I create," 334–336; Yanisky-Ravid and Liu, "When artificial intelligence systems produce inventions," pp. 2239–41; Garry A Gabison, "Who holds the right to exclude for machine work products?" [2020] *IPQ* 20, 20, 37.

[62] Cf. Gervais, "The machine as author," pp. 2060–2061.

degree of exclusivity in order to protect investments and incentivize research in this area. Such a right could be modelled in a similar way to the database right established by the EU in 1996.[63] This requires a substantial investment for protection to be available.[64]

11.3.2 *AI Inventorship*

We now turn to AI inventorship. By analogy to the previous section, the first question is whether "inventive" machines already exist. Such systems are much scarcer than AI systems engaged in creative endeavors.[65] However, progress on this front is undeniable.[66] The AI sector's primary allegedly inventive champion is "DABUS,"[67] labelled the "Creativity Machine" by its inventor, physicist Dr Stephen Thaler.[68] DABUS is a neural network-based system meant to generate "useful information" autonomously, thereby "simulating human creativity."[69] In 2018, a number of patent applications were filed for two of DABUS' inventions.[70] The prosecution files indicate DABUS as the inventor and clarify that Dr Thaler obtained the right to the inventions as its successor in title.[71] These patent applications offer a test case for the topic of AI inventorship.

Patent law requires inventors to be human. While relevant legislative provisions do not contain any explicit requirement in this sense, the inventor's need for physical personhood is implied in the law.[72] While the focus on the human *inventor* is much less pronounced than it is on the human *author*, a number of provisions would make no sense if we were to accept AI inventorship. First, many patent laws stipulate that the "inventor" is the first owner of an invention, except in an

[63] Directive 96/9/EC on the legal protection of databases [1996] OJ L77/20. See on this topic Estelle Derclaye, "Chapter 9: The database directive," in Irini Stamatoudi and Paul Torremans (eds), *EU Copyright Law. A commentary* (Edward Elgar Publishing, 2021), pp. 216–254.

[64] Article 7 Database Directive.

[65] See Dan Burk, "AI patents and the self-assembling machine" (2021) *Minn Law Rev Headnotes*, 105: 301; Daria Kim et al., "Ten assumptions about artificial intelligence that can mislead patent law analysis" [2021] SSRN Electronic Journal.

[66] See, for example, Robert Plotkin, *The Genie in the Machine; How Computer-Automated Inventing Is Revolutionizing Law and Business* (Stanford University Press, 2009).

[67] An acronym for "Device for the Autonomous Bootstrapping of Unified Sentience."

[68] See https://bit.ly/3qgbWSd; https://bit.ly/3CQNf26, accessed August 14, 2024.

[69] Dr Thaler has obtained several patents in relation to the technology behind DABUS. See Abbott, "I think, therefore I invent," 1083–1086.

[70] EP application with number 18275163.6 (EP 3 564 144 A1), filed on October 17, 2018 and EP application with number 18275174.3 (EP 3 563 896 A1), filed on November 7, 2018.

[71] See Legal Board of Appeal Decision December 21, 2021 re EP applications 18275163.6 and 18275174.3, J 0008/20, paras I–III, https://bit.ly/3WzzdNb, accessed August 14, 2024.

[72] See, for example, with regard to the priority right to a patent Article 4(A) Paris Convention for the Protection of Industrial Property, 20 March 1883, as amended. See also Yanisky-Ravid and Liu, "When artificial intelligence systems produce inventions," p. 2230; Eva Stanková, "Human inventorship in European patent law" (2021) *The Cambridge Law Journal*, 80: 338.

employment context, where the employer is deemed to be the first owner under the laws of some countries.[73] Since AI systems do not have legal personality (as of yet), they cannot have ownership rights, nor can they be an employee as such.[74] Given that those are the only two available options, AI systems cannot be considered "inventors" as the law currently stands, as confirmed in the DABUS case, not only by the Boards of Appeal of the European Patent Office in the DABUS case, but also by the UK Supreme Court and the German Federal Supreme Court.[75] Another argument against AI inventorship may be drawn from the inventor's right of attribution. Every inventor has the right to be mentioned as such and all patent applications must designate the inventor.[76] This moral right, which is meant to incentivize the inventor to innovate further, may become meaningless upon the extension of the concept of inventorship to AI systems.[77]

The second aspect of the discussion is whether there *should* be room for AI inventorship. The main argument in favor of this is that it would incentivize research and development in the field of AI.[78] However, in the absence of compelling empirical evidence, the incentive argument is not convincing, especially since AI systems as such are not susceptible to incentives and the cost of AI invention will likely decrease over time.[79] Another reason to accept AI inventorship would be to avoid humans incorrectly claiming inventorship. However, the as of yet instrumental nature of AI systems provides a counterargument.[80] Further, there is no AI-generated output without some form of prior human input. The resulting absence of an act of "conception," of the *process* of invention, excludes any extension of the scope of inventorship to nonhuman actors such as AI systems.[81] Again, however, the "prior input" argument also applies *mutatis mutandis* to humans. Also as to patent law, therefore, the "act of conception" argument against AI inventorship is susceptible to counterarguments.[82]

73 See Article 60 EPC.

74 Shemtov, "A study on inventorship in inventions involving AI activity," pp. 10–11, 20; Blok, "The inventor's new tool," pp. 71–72.

75 Legal Board of Appeal Decision 21 December 2021 re patent applications 18275163.6 and 18275174.3, Sections 4.1–4.4; UK Supreme Court 20 December 2023, UKSC 49, https://bit.ly/3YMYBBV, accessed August 14, 2024; German Federal Supreme Court 11 June 2024, case number X ZB 5/22, https://bit.ly/3YFkT8N, accessed August 14, 2024.

76 See Article 4*ter* Paris Convention. See also respectively Articles 62 and 81 *jo.* 90 and Rule 19.1 EPC. See also Shemtov, "A study on inventorship in inventions involving AI activity," p. 8.

77 Shemtov, "A study on inventorship in inventions involving AI activity," pp. 5, 23–25, 27.

78 Abbott, "I think, therefore I invent," pp. 1081–82, 1098–99, 1104; Alexandra George and Toby Walsh, "Artificial intelligence is breaking patent law" (2022) *Nature*, 605: 7911, 616. See, however, Rose Hughes, "Artificial intelligence is not breaking patent law: EPO publishes DABUS decision (J 8/20)" (*The IPKat*, July 11, 2022), https://bit.ly/3H8YMy6, accessed August 14, 2024.

79 Yanisky-Ravid and Liu, "When artificial intelligence systems produce inventions," p. 2239.

80 Blok, "The inventor's new tool," p. 73; Shemtov, "A study on inventorship in inventions involving AI activity," pp. 5, 17, 19.

81 Shemtov, "A study on inventorship in inventions involving AI activity," pp. 6, 20, 35.

82 Cf. Shemtov, "A study on inventorship in inventions involving AI activity," pp. 28–29; Abbott, "I think, therefore I invent," pp. 1082, 1099, 1108–11.

A final aspect is that allowing AI inventorship would entail an increased risk of both overlapping sets of patents indicated as "patent thickets," and the so-called "patent trolls," which are nonpracticing entities that maintain an aggressive patent enforcement strategy while not exploiting the patent(s) at issue themselves.[83]

11.3.3 *Ownership*

The next question is how ownership rights in AI-powered creations should be allocated.[84] As explained earlier, IP law does not allow AI systems to be recognized as either an author or an inventor. This begs the question whether the intervention of a creative and/or inventive AI excludes *any* kind of human authorship or inventorship (and thus ownership) as to the output at issue. It is submitted that it does not, as long as there is a physical person who commands the AI system and maintains the requisite level of control over its output.[85] In such a case, IP rights may fulfil their role of protecting the interests of creators as well as provide an indirect incentive for future creation and/or innovation.[86] However, if there is no sufficient causal relationship between the (in)actions of a human and the eventual end result, the argument in favor of a human author and/or inventor becomes untenable. What exactly constitutes "sufficient" control is tough to establish. A further layer of complexity is added by the black box nature of some AI systems: How can we determine whether a sufficient causal link exists between the human and the output, if it is impossible to find out exactly why this output was reached?[87] However, both copyright and patent protection may be available to works and/or inventions that result from coincidence or even dumb luck.[88] If we take a step back, both AI systems and serendipity may be considered as a factor outside the scope of human control. Given that Jackson Pollock may claim protection in his action paintings and given the role that chance plays in Pollock's creation process, can we really deny such protection to the person(s) behind "the next Rembrandt"?

In copyright jargon, we could say that for a human to be able to claim copyright in a work created through the intervention of AI, their "personal stamp" must be discernible in the end result. If we continue the above analogy, Pollock's paintings clearly reflect his personal choices as an artist. In patent law terms,

[83] See Blok, "The inventor's new tool," p. 73.

[84] IP ownership is (as of yet) primarily a matter of national law.

[85] Cf. Bridy, "Coding creativity," p. 20; Shemtov, "A study on inventorship in inventions involving AI activity," pp. 12–13, 19–20; Hedrick, "I 'think,' therefore I create," pp. 328–29, 332, 352. See, however, Tim W. Dornis, "Of 'authorless works' and 'inventions without inventor' – the muddy waters of 'AI autonomy' in intellectual property doctrine" (2021) *EIPR*, 43: 570.

[86] Hedrick, "I 'think,' therefore I create," pp. 337, 440.

[87] Cf. Hedrick, "I 'think,' therefore I create," pp. 367, 371–374.

[88] Grimmelmann, "There's no such thing as a computer-authored work," p. 413; Blok, "The inventor's new tool," p. 73; Shemtov, "A study on inventorship in inventions involving AI activity," p. 20. Patent protection is not available to "discoveries" as such (Article 52 EPC).

human inventorship may arise in case of a contribution that transcends the purely financial, abstract or administrative and that is aimed at conceiving the claimed invention – be it through input or output selection, algorithm design, or otherwise.[89] In an AI context, different categories of people may stake a claim in this regard.

First in line are the programmer(s),[90] designer(s),[91] and/or producer(s) of the AI system (hereinafter collectively referred to as "AI creators"). By creating the AI system itself, these actors play a substantive role in the production of AI-generated output.[92] However, the allocation of rights to the creator sits uneasily with the unpredictable nature of AI-generated output.[93] While the AI creator's choices define the AI system, they do not define the final form of the output.[94] This argument gains in strength the more autonomous the AI algorithm becomes.[95] Then again, a programmer who is somehow dissatisfied with the AI's initial output may tweak the AI's algorithm, thus manipulating and shaping further output, as well as curate the AI output based on their personal choices.[96] However, an economic argument against granting the AI creator rights in AI-generated output is that this may lead to "double-dipping." This would be the case if the creator also holds rights in patents granted as to the AI system or the copyright therein, or if the AI system is acquired by a third party for a fee and the output at issue postdates this transfer.[97] In both cases, the creator would obtain two separate sources of income for essentially the same thing. Moreover, enforcing the AI creator's ownership rights would be problematic if the AI system generates the output at issue after a third party has started using it. Indeed, knowing that ownership rights would be allocated to the creator, the user would have strong incentives not to report back on the (modalities of) creation of output.[98]

89 Shemtov, "A study on inventorship in inventions involving AI activity," pp. 19–21, 31; AIPPI resolution on inventorship of inventions made using artificial intelligence, October 14, 2020, https://bit.ly/3DRMOoN, accessed August 14, 2024.

90 Cf. Paul Sawers, "Chinese court rules AI-written article is protected by copyright," *Venture Beat* (January 10, 2020), https://bit.ly/3DW5SlD, accessed August 14, 2024.

91 See Mark Summerfield, "The impact of machine learning on patent law, Part 3: Who is the inventor of a machine-assisted invention?," *Patentology* (February 4, 2018), https://bit.ly/3xlHNlM, accessed August 14, 2024.

92 Samuelson, "Allocating ownership rights in computer-generated works," p. 1205; Shemtov, "A study on inventorship in inventions involving AI activity," p. 22; Gabison, "Who holds the right to exclude for machine work products?," p. 23.

93 Samuelson, "Allocating ownership rights in computer-generated works," p. 1209; Yanisky-Ravid and Liu, "When artificial intelligence systems produce inventions," pp. 2231–2232.

94 Bridy, "Coding creativity," p. 25.

95 Hedrick, "I 'think,' therefore I create," pp. 354, 362.

96 Cf. Hedrick, "I 'think,' therefore I create," pp. 338–339, 343, 354.

97 Samuelson, "Allocating ownership rights in computer-generated works," pp. 1207–1208, 1225; Yanisky-Ravid and Liu, "When artificial intelligence systems produce inventions", p. 2233; Shemtov, "A study on inventorship in inventions involving AI activity," p. 31.

98 Samuelson, "Allocating ownership rights in computer-generated works," p. 1208.

A similar claim to the AI system's creator may be made by the AI's trainer who feeds input to the AI system.[99] Alternatively, the user who has contributed substantially to the output at issue may claim ownership.[100] The list of stakeholders continues with the investor, the owner of the AI system and/or the data used to train the algorithm, the publisher of the work, the general public, and even the government. Moreover, some form of joint ownership may be envisaged.[101] However, this would entail other issues, such as an unnecessary fragmentation of ownership rights and difficulties in proving (the extent of) ownership claims.[102] It could even be argued that, in view of the ever-rising number of players involved, no individual entity can rightfully claim to have made a significant contribution "worthy" of IP ownership.[103]

As of yet, no solution to the ownership conundrum appears to be wholly satisfactory. The void left by this lingering uncertainty will likely be filled with contractual solutions.[104] Consequent to unequal bargaining power, instances of unfair ownership and licensing arrangements are to be expected.[105] A preferable solution could be to not allocate ownership in AI-generated output to anyone at all and instead allot such output to the public domain. Stakeholders could sufficiently protect their investment in AI-related innovation by relying on patent protection for the AI system itself, first-mover advantage, trade secret law, contractual arrangements, and technological protection measures, as well as general civil liability and the law of unfair competition.[106] However, there is a very pragmatic reason not to ban AI-generated output to the public domain, namely that it is increasingly difficult to distinguish output in the creation of which AI played a certain role from creations that were made solely by a human author.[107] This could be remedied by requiring aspiring IP owners to disclose the intervention of an AI-powered system in the creation and/or innovation process. However, the practical application of such a requirement remains problematic at present. The prospect of having a work be banished to the public domain would provide stakeholders seeking a return on investment with strong incentives to keep quiet

[99] Shemtov, "A study on inventorship in inventions involving AI activity," p. 31.

[100] Samuelson, "Allocating ownership rights in computer-generated works," pp. 1201–04; Hedrick, "I 'think,' therefore I create," p. 344; Gabison, "Who holds the right to exclude for machine work products?," p. 35; Tim Dornis, "Artificial intelligence and innovation: The end of patent law as we know it" (2020) *Yale J L & Tech*, 23: 97, 154–57.

[101] Shemtov, "A study on inventorship in inventions involving AI activity," pp. 6, 30.

[102] Samuelson, "Allocating ownership rights in computer-generated works," pp. 1221–24; Hedrick, "I 'think,' therefore I create," p. 348. See extensively Paulien Wymeersch, "Terms of use on the commercialisation of AI-produced images and copyright protection", (2024) *EIPR* pp. 374–381.

[103] Cf. Yanisky-Ravid and Liu, "When artificial intelligence systems produce inventions," p. 2235.

[104] Hedrick, "I 'Think,' therefore I create," p. 348.

[105] Cf. Abbott, "I think, therefore I invent," p. 1117; Hedrick, "I 'Think,' therefore I create," p. 347.

[106] Yanisky-Ravid and Liu, "When artificial intelligence systems produce inventions," pp. 2222, 2252–2256; Shemtov, "A study on inventorship in inventions involving AI activity," p. 24; Gabison, "Who holds the right to exclude for machine work products?," pp. 32–33, 39; Gervais, "The machine as author," p. 2060.

[107] See, for example, Jamie Grierson, "Photographer admits prize-winning image was AI-generated" (*The Guardian* April 17, 2023), https://bit.ly/4cq4xEd, accessed August 14, 2024.

on this point. This could invite misleading statements on authorship and/or inventorship of AI-generated output in the future.[108] Transparency obligations, such as the watermarking requirement imposed on providers of certain AI systems (including general-purpose AI models) under the EU AI Act, may bring us closer to a solution in this regard, likely combined with a "General-Purpose AI Code of Practice" that is to be drafted under the auspices of the AI Office at the EU level.[109]

11.4 MISCELLANEOUS TOPICS

In addition to the above, the interface between AI and IP has many other dimensions. Without any pretense of exhaustivity, this section treats some of them briefly, namely the issues surrounding IP infringement by AI systems, the potential impact of AI on certain key concepts of IP law and the growing use of AI in IP practice.

11.4.1 *IP Infringement*

First, in order to train an AI algorithm, a significant amount of data is often required. If (part of) the relevant training data is subject to IP protection, the reproduction and/or communication to the public thereof in principle requires authorization by the owner, subject to the applicability of relevant exceptions and limitations to copyright. The question thus arises whether actively scraping the internet for artists' work to reuse in the context of, for example, generative AI art tools constitutes an infringement. At the time of writing, several legal proceedings are pending on this question across the globe.[110] Importantly, the EU AI Act (1) confirms the applicability of text and data mining exceptions to the training of general-purpose AI models, subject to a potential opt-out on the part of rightholders; and (2) mandates the drawing up and public availability of "a sufficiently detailed summary about the content used for training of the general-purpose AI model."[111] Further, in order to ensure that authors, performers and other rightholders receive fair and appropriate

[108] Abbott, "I think, therefore I invent," pp. 1097–98; Higgins, "The role of explainable artificial intelligence in patent law," p. 29.

[109] See Article 50 AI Act; Thomas Gils, "A detailed analysis of Article 50 of the EU's Artificial Intelligence Act" (2024), https://ssrn.com/abstract=4865427, accessed August 14, 2024. See also https://tinyurl.com/m3bhr5a5, accessed August 14, 2024. For an extensive discussion of the AI Act, see also Chapter 12 of this book, authored by Nathalie A. Smuha and Karen Yeung, "The European Union's AI Act: beyond motherhood and apple pie?", 228–258.

[110] See for an overview https://tinyurl.com/j6wvr7ez, accessed August 14, 2024.

[111] Article 53(1)(c)–(d) AI Act. See also in particular Recitals 105, 107 AI Act. A template for such a "sufficiently detailed summary" is to be provided by the AI Office. See for a valiant attempt at operationalization of this requirement, https://tinyurl.com/yeu723r5, accessed August 14, 2024. See however extensively Tim W. Dornis and Sebastian Stober, "Urheberrecht und Training generativer KI-Modelle - technologische und juristische Grundlagen" (August 2024), https://ssrn.com/abstract_id=4946214, accessed 20 September 2024.

remuneration for the use of their content as training data, contractual solutions may be envisaged.[112]

Also after the training process, AI systems may infringe IP rights. By way of example, an AI program could create a song containing original elements of a preexisting work, thus infringing the reproduction right of the owner of the copyright in the musical work at issue. An inventive machine may develop a process and/or product that infringes a patent, or devise a sign that is confusingly similar to a registered trademark, or a product that falls within the scope of a protected (un)registered design. This in turn leads to further contentious matters, such as whether or not relevant exceptions and/or limitations (should) apply and whether fundamental rights such as freedom of expression may still play a role.[113]

11.4.2 *Impact of AI on Key Concepts of IP Law*

Next, the rise of AI may significantly affect a number of key concepts of IP law that are clearly tailored to humans, in addition to the concepts of "authorship" and "inventorship." First in line in this regard is the inventiveness standard under patent law, which centers around the so-called "person skilled in the art" (PSA).[114] This is a hypothetical person (or team) whose level of knowledge and skill depend on the field of technology.[115] If it is found that the PSA would have arrived at the invention, the invention will be deemed obvious and not patentable. If the use of inventive machines becomes commonplace in certain sectors of technology, the PSA standard will evolve into a PSA using such an inventive machine – and maybe even an inventive machine as such.[116] This would raise the bar for inventive step and ensuing patentability, since such a machine would be able to innovate based on the entirety of available prior art.[117] Taken to its logical extreme, this argument could shake the foundations of our patent system. Indeed, if the "artificially superintelligent" PSA is capable of an inventive step, everything becomes obvious, leaving no more room for patentable inventions.[118]

[112] See, for example, Martin Senftleben, "Generative AI and author remuneration" (2023) *IIC*, 54, 1535–60; Martin Senftleben, "AI Act and author remuneration – A model for other regions?" (2024), https://ssrn.com/abstract=4740268, accessed August 14, 2024.

[113] Camille Vermosen, "Copyright, liability and artificial intelligence: Who is responsible when an artificial intelligence system infringes copyright in the context of the EU?" (KU Leuven, 2017); Bridget Watson, "A mind of its own – direct infringement by users of artificial intelligence systems" (2017) *IDEA*, 58: 31; Alina Škiljić, "When art meets technology or vice versa: Key challenges at the crossroads of AI-generated artworks and copyright law" (2021) *IIC*, 52: 1338.

[114] Dornis, "Artificial intelligence and innovation," pp. 104, 124–134.

[115] EPO, "Guidelines for examination, Part G, Chapter VII.3," https://bit.ly/3xBzu5H, accessed August 14, 2024.

[116] Blok, "The inventor's new Tool," p. 72; Ryan Abbott, "Everything is obvious" (2018) 66 UCLA L Rev 2, 2, 5–6, 17, 34–37.

[117] Yanisky-Ravid and Liu, "When artificial intelligence systems produce inventions," pp. 2248–49.

[118] Abbott, "Everything is obvious," pp. 8–9, 31, 34, 37–38.

We therefore need to start thinking about alternatives and/or supplements to the current nonobviousness analysis – and maybe even to the patent regime as a way to incentivize innovation.[119]

Questions also arise in a trademark law context, such as how the increased intervention of AI in the online product suggestion and purchasing process may be reconciled with the anthropocentric conception of trademark law, as apparent from the use of criteria such as the "average consumer," "confusion," "imperfect recollection" – all of which are criteria that have a built-in margin for *human* error.[120]

11.4.3 *Use of AI in IP Practice*

Finally, the clear hesitancy of the IP community toward catering for additional incentive creation in the AI sphere by amending existing IP laws may be contrasted with apparent enthusiasm as to the use of AI in IP practice. Indeed, the increased (and still increasing) use of AI systems as a tool in the IP sector is striking. The ability of AI systems to process and analyze vast amounts of data quickly and efficiently offers a broad range of opportunities. First, the World Intellectual Property Organization (WIPO) has been mining the possibilities offered by AI with regard to the automatic categorization of patents and trademarks as well as prior art searches, machine translations, and formality checks.[121] Other IP offices are following suit.[122] Second, AI technology may be applied to the benefit of registrants. On a formal level, AI technology may be used to suggest relevant classes of goods and services for trademarks and/or designs. On a substantive level, AI technology may be used to aid in patent drafting and to screen registers for existing registrations to minimize risk. AI technology may assist in determining the similarity of trademarks and/or designs and even in evaluating prior art relating to patents.[123] AI-based IP

[119] Abbott, "Everything is obvious," pp. 48–50, 52.

[120] See Michael Grynberg, "AI and the 'death of trademark'" (2019) *Ky L J*, 108: 199–238; Anke Moerland and Conrado Freitas, "Artificial intelligence and trademark assessment" in Reto Hilty, Jyh-An Lee, and Kung-Chung Liu, *Artificial Intelligence and Intellectual Property* (Oxford University Press, 2021), 266–291; Marie-Christine Janssens and Viltė Kristina Dessers, "The artificially intelligent consumer in EU trademark law" in Veronika Fischer, Georg Nolte, Martin Senftleben, and Louisa Specht-Riemenschneider, *Gestaltung der Informationsordnung. Festschrift Commemorating the 65th Anniversary of Professor Thomas Dreier* (CH Beck, 2022), 143–160.

[121] See, for example, the tools and applications listed at https://bit.ly/3YPSlJV, including and WIPO's Vienna Classification Assistant https://bit.ly/3WQmCqj, accessed August 14, 2024.

[122] See, for example, the EUIPO https://bit.ly/30XlRRJ and the UKIPO https://bit.ly/3DOiNWX, accessed August 14, 2024.

[123] Re trademarks, see, for example, Brandstock https://bit.ly/30Voofc; CompuMark https://clarivate.com/compumark; Rocketeer https://bit.ly/311euZX; TrademarkNow www.trademarknow.com; and Corsearch https://corsearch.com, all accessed August 14, 2024. Re patents, see, for example, Rowan Patents https://rowanpatents.com, accessed August 14, 2024.

analytics and management software is also available.[124] Finally, AI-powered applications are used in the fight against counterfeit products.[125]

11.5 CONCLUSION

The analysis of the interface between AI and IP reveals a field of law and technology of increasing intricacy. As the term suggests, "intellectual" property law has traditionally catered for creations of the human mind. Technological evolutions in the field of AI have prompted challenges to this anthropocentric view. The most contentious questions are whether authorship and inventorship should be extended to AI systems and who, if anybody, should acquire ownership rights as to AI-generated content. Valid points may be raised on all sides of the argument. However, we should not unreservedly start tearing down the foundations of IP law for the mere sake of additional incentive creation.

In any case, regardless of the eventual (legislative) outcome, the cross-border exploitation of AI-assisted or -generated output and the pressing need for transparency of the legal framework require a harmonized solution based on a multistakeholder conversation, preferably on a global scale. Who knows, maybe one day an artificially super-intelligent computer will be able to find this solution in our stead. Awaiting such further hypothetical technological evolutions, however, the role of WIPO as a key interlocutor on AI and IP remains paramount, in tandem with the newly established AI Office at the EU level.[126]

[124] See, for example, Cipher https://cipher.ai; elementary IP https://elementaryip.com; IP Check-Up https://bit.ly/3E3Dxdr; Octimine www.octimine.com; and SHIP Global IP https://shipglobalip.com, all accessed August 14, 2024.

[125] See, for example, Visual-AI https://bit.ly/3HQtt9B, accessed August 14, 2024.

[126] The WIPO consultation process on AI and IP garnered over 250 substantive submissions, while the virtual WIPO seminars on AI and IP that WIPO has organized since 2019 attracted almost 9000 participants from all over the world. The submissions to the consultation process are available online at https://bit.ly/3GU9M09, accessed August 14, 2024. More information on the so-called 'WIPO Conversation on Intellectual Property and Frontier Technologies' is available online at https://bit.ly/3WOos8f, accessed August 14, 2024.

12

The European Union's AI Act

Beyond Motherhood and Apple Pie?

Nathalie A. Smuha and Karen Yeung[*]

12.1 INTRODUCTION

In spring 2024, the European Union formally adopted the "AI Act,"[1] purporting to create a comprehensive EU legal regime to regulate AI systems across sectors. In so doing, it signaled its commitment to the protection of core EU values against AI's adverse effects, to maintain a harmonized single market for AI in Europe and to benefit from a first mover advantage (the so-called "Brussels effect")[2] to establish itself as a leading global standard-setter for AI regulation. The AI Act reflects the EU's recognition that, left to its own devices, the market alone cannot protect the fundamental values upon which the European project is founded from unregulated AI applications.[3] Will the AI Act's implementation succeed in translating its noble aspirations into meaningful and effective protection of people whose everyday lives are already directly affected by these increasingly powerful systems? In this chapter, we critically examine the proposed conceptual vehicles and regulatory architecture upon which the AI Act relies to argue that there are good reasons for skepticism.

* Smuha primarily contributed to Sections 12.2 and 12.3, (drawing on Nathalie A. Smuha, *Algorithmic Rule by Law: How Algorithmic Regulation in the Public Sector Erodes the Rule of Law* (Cambridge University Press, 2025, Chapter 5.4), while Yeung contributed primarily to Section 12.4 (drawing extensively on a keynote speech delivered on September 12, 2022, ADM+S Centre Symposium, *Automated Societies*, RMIT, Melbourne, Australia. A recording is available at https://podcasters.spotify.com/pod/show/adms-centre/episodes/2022-ADMS-Symposium-Keynote-by-Professor-Karen-Yeung-e1nmp1r/a-a8gu1ph (accessed August 2, 2024)).

1 Regulation (EU) 2024/1689 of the European Parliament and of the Council of 13 June 2024 laying down harmonised rules on artificial intelligence and amending Regulations (EC) No 300/2008, (EU) No 167/2013, (EU) No 168/2013, (EU) 2018/858, (EU) 2018/1139 and (EU) 2019/2144 and Directives 2014/90/EU, (EU) 2016/797 and (EU) 2020/1828 (Artificial Intelligence Act), OJ L, 2024/1689, July 12, 2024.

2 Anu Bradford, *The Brussels Effect: How the European Union Rules the World* (Oxford University Press, 2020). See in this regard also Nathalie A. Smuha, "From a 'race to AI' to a 'race to AI regulation': regulatory competition for artificial intelligence," (2021) *Law, Innovation and Technology*, 13(1): 57–84.

3 See Karen Yeung, Andrew Howes, and Ganna Pogrebna, "AI governance by human rights–centered design, deliberation, and oversight: An end to ethics washing," in Markus D. Dubber, Frank Pasquale, and Sunit Das (eds), *The Oxford Handbook of Ethics of AI* (Oxford University Press, 2020), pp. 76–106.

Despite its laudable intentions, the Act may deliver far less than it promises in terms of safeguarding fundamental rights, democracy, and the rule of law. Although the Act appears to provide meaningful safeguards, many of its key operative provisions delegate critical regulatory tasks largely to AI providers themselves without adequate oversight or effective mechanisms for redress.

We begin in Section 12.2 with a brief history of the AI Act, including the influential documents that preceded and inspired it. Section 12.3 outlines the Act's core features, including its scope, its "risk-based" regulatory approach, and the corollary classification of AI systems into risk-categories. In Section 12.4, we critically assess the AI Act's enforcement architecture, including the role played by standardization organizations, before concluding in Section 12.5.

12.2 A BRIEF HISTORY OF THE AI ACT

Today, AI routinely attracts hyperbolic claims about its power and importance, with one EU institution even likening it to a *"fifth element after air, earth, water and fire."*[4] Although AI is not new,[5] its capabilities have radically improved in recent years, enhancing its potential to effect major societal transformation. For many years, regulators and policymakers largely regarded the technology as either wholly beneficial or at least benign. However, in 2015, the so-called "Tech Lash" marked a change in tone, as public anxiety about AI's potential adverse impacts grew.[6] The Cambridge Analytica scandal, involving the alleged manipulation of voters via political microtargeting, with troubling implications for democracy, was particularly important in galvanizing these concerns.[7] From then on, policy initiatives within the EU and elsewhere began to take a "harder" shape: eschewing reliance on industry self-regulation in the form of non-binding "ethics codes" and culminating in the EU's "legal turn," marked by the passage of the AI Act. To understand the Act, it is helpful to briefly trace its historical origins.

12.2.1 *The European AI Strategy*

The European Commission published a European strategy for AI in 2018, setting in train Europe's AI policy[8] to promote and increase AI investment and uptake across

[4] Statement by the European Parliament's Special Committee on Artificial Intelligence in a Digital Age (AIDA), "Draft report on artificial intelligence in a digital age" (European Parliament, 2021) (2020/2266(INI)) 9.

[5] See in this regard also Chapter 1 of this book by Wannes Meert, Tinne De Laet, and Luc De Raedt.

[6] The first use of this term is ascribed to Adrian Wooldridge in his *The Economist* article titled "The coming tech-lash," November 2013.

[7] See, for example, Jim Isaak and Mina J Hanna, "User data privacy: Facebook, Cambridge Analytica, and privacy protection" (2018) *Computer*, 51(8): 56-59.

[8] European Commission, Artificial Intelligence for Europe, COM (2018) 237 final, Brussels, April 25, 2018.

Europe in pursuit of its ambition to become a global AI powerhouse.[9] This strategy was formulated against a larger geopolitical backdrop in which the US and China were widely regarded as frontrunners, battling it out for first place in the "AI race" with Europe lagging significantly behind. Yet the growing Tech-Lash made it politically untenable for European policymakers to ignore public concerns. How, then, could they help European firms compete more effectively on the global stage while assuaging growing concerns that more needed to be done to protect democracy and the broader public interest? The response was to turn a perceived weakness into an opportunity by making a virtue of its political ideals and creating a unique "brand" of AI: infused with "European values" – charting a "third way," distinct from both the Chinese state-driven approach and the US' laissez-faire approach to AI governance.[10]

At that time, the Commission resisted calls for the introduction of new laws. In particular, in 2018 the long-awaited General Data Protection Regulation (GDPR) finally took effect,[11] introducing more stringent legal requirements for collecting and processing personal data. Not only did EU policymakers believe these would guard against AI-generated risks, but it was also politically unacceptable to position this new legal measure as outdated even as it was just starting to bite. By then, the digital tech industry was seizing the initiative, attempting to assuage rising anxieties about AI's adverse impacts by voluntarily promulgating a wide range of "Ethical Codes of Conduct" proudly proclaiming they would uphold. This coincided with, and concurrently nurtured, a burgeoning academic interest by humanities and social science scholars in the social implications of AI, often proceeding under the broad rubric of "AI Ethics." In keeping with industry's stern warning that legal regulation would stifle innovation and push Europe even further behind, the Commission decided to convene a High-Level Expert Group on AI (AI HLEG) to develop a set of *harmonized* Ethics Guidelines based on European values that would serve as "best practice" in Europe, for which compliance was entirely voluntary.

12.2.2 *The High-Level Expert Group on AI*

This 52 member group was duly convened, to much fanfare, selected through open competition and comprised of approximately 50% industry representatives, with the remaining 50% from academia and civil society organizations.[12] Following a public

9 Nathalie A. Smuha, "The EU approach to ethics guidelines for trustworthy artificial intelligence" (2019) *Computer Law Review International*, 20(4): 98.

10 See also Anu Bradford, *Digital Empires: The Global Battle to Regulate Technology* (Oxford University Press, 2023).

11 Regulation (EU) 2016/679 of the European Parliament and of the Council of 27 April 2016 on the protection of natural persons with regard to the processing of personal data and on the free movement of such data, and repealing Directive 95/46/EC, OJ L 119, May 4, 2016, pp. 1–88.

12 Both the composition and the mandate of the AI HLEG was criticized, mostly due to the larger representation of industry, and the fact that the Commission tasked the group with drafting voluntary

consultation, the group published its Ethics Guidelines for Trustworthy AI in April 2019,[13] coining "Trustworthy AI" as its overarching objective.[14] The Guidelines' core consists of seven requirements that AI practitioners should take into account throughout an AI system's lifecycle: (1) *human agency and oversight* (including the need for a fundamental rights impact assessment); (2) *technical robustness and safety* (including resilience to attack and security mechanisms, general safety, as well as accuracy, reliability and reproducibility requirements); (3) *privacy and data governance* (including not only respect for privacy, but also ensuring the quality and integrity of training and testing data); (4) *transparency* (including traceability, explainability, and clear communication); (5) *diversity, nondiscrimination and fairness* (including the avoidance of unfair bias, considerations of accessibility and universal design, and stakeholder participation); (6) *societal and environmental well-being* (including sustainability and fostering the "environmental friendliness" of AI systems, and considering their impact on society and democracy); and finally (7) *accountability* (including auditability, minimization, and reporting of negative impact, trade-offs, and redress mechanisms).[15]

The group was also mandated to deliver Policy Recommendations which were published in June 2019,[16] oriented toward Member States and EU Institutions.[17]

guidelines rather than asking its input on new binding rules. Yeung was one of these members. Smuha served as the group's coordinator from its initial formation until July 2019.

[13] High-Level Expert Group on AI, "Ethics Guidelines for Trustworthy AI," Brussels, April 8, 2019. The Guidelines were endorsed by the Commission in a Communication that was published the same day, encouraging AI developers and deployers to implement them in their organization. See European Commission, Building Trust in Human-Centric Artificial Intelligence, COM (2019) 168 final, Brussels, April 8, 2019.

[14] Trustworthy AI was defined as: (1) lawful, or complying with all applicable laws and regulations; (2) ethical, or ensuring adherence to ethical principles and values; and (3) robust since, even with good intentions, AI systems can still lead to unintentional harm. The AI HLEG was however careful in stating that the Guidelines only offered guidance on complying with the two latter components (*ethical* and *robust* AI), indicating the need for the EU to take additional steps to ensure that AI systems were also *lawful*. See in this regard also Nathalie A. Smuha, Emma Ahmed-Rengers, Adam Harkens, Wenlong Li, James MacLaren, Riccardo Piselli, and Karen Yeung, "*How the EU Can Achieve Legally Trustworthy AI: A Response to the European Commission's Proposal for an Artificial Intelligence Act*," Social Science Research Network, 2021, https://ssrn.com/abstract=3899991.

[15] The Guidelines also included an assessment list to operationalize these requirements in practice, and a list of critical concerns raised by AI systems that should be carefully considered (including, for example, the use of AI systems to identify and track individuals, covert AI systems, AI-enabled citizen scoring, lethal autonomous weapons, and longer-term concerns, covering what is today often referred to as "existential risks").

[16] High-Level Expert Group on AI, 'Policy and Investment Recommendations for Trustworthy AI' (European Commission, June 26, 2019), https://digital-strategy.ec.europa.eu/en/library/policy-and-investment-recommendations-trustworthy-artificial-intelligence.

[17] In addition, the group was also mandated to support the Commission with outreach through the European AI Alliance, a multi-stakeholder online platform seeking broader input on Europe's AI policy. See European Commission, Call for Applications for the Selection of Members of the High-Level Expert Group on Artificial Intelligence, March 9, 2018, https://digital-strategy.ec.europa.eu/en/news/call-high-level-expert-group-artificial-intelligence.

While attracting considerably less attention than the Ethics Guidelines, the Recommendations called for the adoption of new legal safeguards, recommending *"a risk-based approach to AI policy-making,"* taking into account *"both individual and societal risks,"*[18] to be complemented by *"a precautionary principle-based approach"* for *"AI applications that generate 'unacceptable' risks or pose threats of harm that are substantial."*[19] For the use of AI in the public sector, the group stated that adherence to the Guidelines should be mandatory.[20] For the private sector, the group asked the Commission to consider introducing obligations to conduct a "trustworthy AI" assessment (including a fundamental rights impact assessment) and stakeholder consultations; to comply with traceability, auditability, and ex-ante oversight requirements; and to ensure effective redress.[21] These Recommendations reflected a belief that nonbinding "ethics" guidelines were insufficient to ensure respect for fundamental rights, democracy, and the rule of law, and that legal reform was needed. Whether a catalyst or not, we will never know, for a few weeks later, the then President-elect of the Commission, Ursula von der Leyen, announced that she would *"put forward legislation for a coordinated European approach on the human and ethical implications of Artificial Intelligence."*[22]

12.2.3 *The White Paper on AI*

In February 2020, the Commission issued a White Paper on AI,[23] setting out a blueprint for new legislation to regulate AI *"based on European values,"*[24] identifying several legal gaps that needed to be addressed. Although it sought to adopt a risk-based approach to regulate AI, it identified only two categories of AI systems: high-risk and not-high-risk, with solely the former being subjected to new obligations inspired by the Guidelines' seven requirements for Trustworthy AI. The AI HLEG's recommendation to protect fundamental rights as well as democracy and the rule of law were largely overlooked, and its suggestion to adopt a precautionary approach in relation to "unacceptable harm" was ignored altogether.

On enforcement, the White Paper remained rather vague. It did, however, suggest that high-risk systems should be subjected to a prior conformity assessment by providers of AI systems, analogous to existing EU conformity assessment procedures for products governed by the New Legislative Framework (discussed later).[25]

[18] Policy and Investment Recommendations for Trustworthy AI (n 16), 26.

[19] Ibid., 38.

[20] Ibid., 20.

[21] Ibid., 40.

[22] Ibid., 13.

[23] European Commission, White Paper on Artificial Intelligence – A European approach to excellence and trust, Brussels, February 19, 2020, COM (2020) 65 final.

[24] See also the Explanatory Memorandum of the White Paper.

[25] The White Paper provides the examples of Decision No 768/2008/EC of the European Parliament and of the Council of 9 July 2008 on a common framework for the marketing of products, and repealing

In this way, AI systems were to be regulated in a similar fashion to other stand-alone products including toys, measuring instruments, radio equipment, low-voltage electrical equipment, medical devices, and fertilizers rather than embedded within a complex and inherently socio-technical system that may be infrastructural in nature. Accordingly, the basic thrust of the proposal appeared animated primarily by a light-touch market-based orientation aimed at establishing a harmonized and competitive European AI market in which the protection of fundamental rights, democracy, and the rule of law were secondary concerns.

12.2.4 *The Proposal for an AI Act*

Despite extensive criticism, this approach formed the foundation of the Commission's subsequent proposal for an AI Act published in April 2021.[26] Building on the White Paper, it adopted a "horizontal" approach, regulating "AI systems" in general rather than pursuing a sector-specific approach. The risk-categorization of AI systems was more refined (unacceptable risk, high risk, medium risk, and low risk), although criticisms persisted given that various highly problematic applications were omitted from the list of "high-risk" and "unacceptable" systems, and with unwarranted exceptions.[27] The conformity (self)assessment scheme was retained, firmly entrenching a product-safety approach to AI regulation, yet failing to confer any rights whatsoever for those subjected to AI systems; it only included obligations imposed on AI providers and (to a lesser extent) deployers.[28]

In December 2022, the Council of the European Union adopted its "general approach" on the Commission's proposal.[29] It sought to limit the regulation's scope by narrowing the definition of AI and introducing more exceptions (for example for national security and research), sought stronger EU coordination for the Act's enforcement; and proposed that AI systems listed as "high-risk" systems would not be automatically subjected to the Act's requirements. Instead, providers could self-assess whether their system is *truly* high-risk based on a number of criteria – thereby further diluting the already limited protection the proposal afforded. Finally, the Council took into account the popularization of Large Language Models (LLMs) and generative AI applications such as ChatGPT, which at that time were drawing

Council Decision 93/465/EEC, and to Regulation (EU) 2019/881 of the European Parliament and of the Council of 17 April 2019 on ENISA and on information and communications technology cybersecurity certification (the Cybersecurity Act).

26 Proposal for a Regulation laying down harmonized rules on artificial intelligence (Artificial Intelligence Act), COM (2021) 206 final, Brussels, April 21, 2021.

27 See also Smuha et al. (n 14), 28.

28 See ibid, 50.

29 Council of the European Union, General Approach, 2021/0106(COD) Brussels, 25 November 2022 (adopted December 6, 2022).

considerable public and political attention, and included modest provisions on General-Purpose AI models (GPAI).[30]

By the time the European Parliament formulated its own negotiating position in June 2023, generative AI was booming and called for more demanding restrictions. Additional requirements for the GPAI models that underpin generative AI were thus introduced, including risk-assessments and transparency obligations.[31] Contrary to the Council, the Parliament sought to widen some of the risk-categories; restore a broader definition of AI; strengthen transparency measures; introduce remedies for those subjected to AI systems; include stakeholder participation; and introduce mandatory fundamental rights impact assessments for high-risk systems. Yet it retained the Council's proposal to allow AI providers to self-assess whether their "high-risk" system could be excluded from that category, and hence from the legal duties that would otherwise apply.[32] It also sprinkled the Act with references to the "rule of law" and "democracy," yet these were little more than rhetorical flourishes given that it retained the underlying foundations of the original proposal's market-oriented product-safety approach.

12.3 SUBSTANTIVE FEATURES OF THE AI ACT

The adoption of the AI Act in spring 2024 marked the culmination of a series of initiatives that reflected significant policy choices which determined its form, content and contours. We now provide an overview of the Act's core features, which – for better or for worse – will shape the future of AI systems in Europe.

12.3.1 *Scope*

The AI Act aims to harmonize Member States' national legislation, to eliminate potential obstacles to trade on the internal AI market, and to protect citizens and society against AI's adverse effects, in that order of priority. Its main legal basis is Article 114 of the Treaty of the Functioning of the European Union (TFEU), which enables the establishment and functioning of the internal market. The inherent single-market orientation of this article limits the Act's scope and justification.[33] For this

[30] Essentially, it provided that GPAI systems used for high-risk purposes should be treated as such. However, instead of directly applying the high-risk requirements to such systems, the Council proposed that the Commission should adopt an implementing act to specify how they should be applied, based on a consultation and detailed impact assessment and taking into account their specific characteristics.

[31] European Parliament, Amendments adopted by the European Parliament on 14 June 2023 on the proposal for an Artificial Intelligence Act, COM (2021)0206 – C9-0146/2021 – 2021/0106(COD), Amendment 168.

[32] See also *infra* (n 61).

[33] See also Stephen Weatherill, "The limits of legislative harmonization ten years after tobacco advertising: How the court's case law has become a 'drafting guide'" (2011) *German Law Journal*, 12(3): 827–864.

reason, certain provisions on the use of AI-enabled biometric data processing by law enforcement are also based on Article 16 TFEU, which provides a legal basis to regulate matters related to the right to data protection.[34] Whether these legal bases are sufficient to regulate AI practices within the *public* sector or to achieve nonmarket-related aims remains uncertain, and could render the Act vulnerable to (partial) challenges for annulment on competence-related grounds.[35] In terms of scope, the regulation applies to providers who place on the market or put into service AI systems (or general purpose AI models) in the EU, regardless of where they are established; deployers of AI systems that have their place of establishment or location in the EU; and providers and deployers of AI systems that are established or located outside the EU, while the output produced by their AI system is used in the EU.[36]

The definition of AI for the purpose of the regulation has been a significant battleground,[37] with every EU institution proposing different definitions, each attracting criticism. Ultimately, the Commission's initial proposal to combine a broad AI definition in the regulation's main text with an amendable Annex that exhaustively enumerates the AI techniques covered by the Act was rejected. Instead, the legislators opted for a definition of AI which models that of the OECD, to promote international alignment: "a machine-based system designed to operate with varying levels of autonomy, that may exhibit adaptiveness after deployment and that, for explicit or implicit objectives, infers, from the input it receives, how to generate outputs such as predictions, content, recommendations, or decisions that can influence physical or virtual environments."[38]

AI systems used exclusively for military or defense purposes are excluded from the Act, as are systems used for "nonprofessional" purposes. So too are AI systems "solely" used for research and innovation, which leaves open a substantive gap in protection given the many problematic research projects that can adversely affect individuals yet do not fall within the remit of university ethics committees. The AI Act also foresees that Member States' competences in national security remain untouched, thus risking very weak protection of individuals in one of the potentially

[34] See Recital 3 of the AI Act.

[35] See in this regard also Nathalie A. Smuha, "The paramountcy of data protection law in the age of AI (Acts)," in Brendan Van Alsenoy, Julia Hodder, Fenneke Buskermolen, Miriam Čakurdová, Ilektra Makraki and Estelle Burgot (eds), *Twenty Years of Data Protection. What Next? – EDPS 20th Anniversary*, Luxembourg (2024), Publications Office of the European Union, 226–39.

[36] See in more details Article 2(1) of the AI Act.

[37] For a discussion of the importance of AI definitions, see also Bilel Benbouzid, Yannick Meneceur and Nathalie A. Smuha, "Four shades of AI regulation. A cartography of normative and definitional conflicts" (2022) *Réseaux*, 232–33(2–3), 29–64.

[38] Article 3(1) of the AI Act. The definition's emphasis on the system making inferences seems to exclude more traditional or rule-based AI systems from its scope, despite their significant potential for harm. Ultimately, it will be up to the courts to decide how this definition must be interpreted in case of a dispute.

most intrusive areas for which AI might be used.[39] Finally, the legislators also included certain exemptions for open-source AI models and systems,[40] and derogations for microenterprises.[41]

12.3.2 A *Risk-based Approach*

The AI Act adopts what the Commission describes as a "risk-based" approach: AI systems and/or practices are classified into a series of graded "tiers," with proportionately more demanding legal obligations that vary in accordance with the EU's perceptions of the severity of the risks they pose.[42] "Risks" are defined rather narrowly in terms of risks to "health, safety or fundamental rights." The Act's final risk categorization consists of five tiers: (1) systems that pose an "unacceptable" risk are prohibited; (2) systems deemed to pose a "high risk" are subjected to requirements akin to those listed in the Ethics Guidelines; (3) GPAI models are subjected to obligations that primarily focus on transparency, intellectual property protection, and the mitigation of "systemic risks"; (4) systems posing a limited risk must meet specified transparency requirements; and (5) systems that are not considered as posing significant risks do not attract new legal requirements.

12.3.2.1 Prohibited Practices

Article 5 of the AI Act prohibits several "AI practices," reflecting a view that they pose an unacceptable risk. These include the use of AI to manipulate human behavior in order to circumvent a person's free will[43] and to exploit the vulnerability of natural persons in light of their age, disability, or their social or economic situation.[44] It also includes the use of AI systems to make criminal risk assessments and predictions of natural

[39] More generally, yet less unusual, the legislator also carved out from the AI Act all areas that fall outside the scope of EU law.

[40] Article 2 of the AI Act provides that "this Regulation does not apply to AI systems released under free and open-source licences, unless they are placed on the market or put into service as high-risk AI systems or as an AI system that falls under Article 5 or 50" (covering respectively prohibited AI practices and systems requiring additional transparency measures). Moreover, Article 53 of the AI Act excludes providers of AI models that are released under a free and open-source licence from certain transparency requirements if the license "allows for the access, usage, modification, and distribution of the model" and if certain information (about the parameters including the weights, model architecture, and model usage) is made publicly available. The exclusion does not apply to general-purpose AI models with "systemic risks" though, which shall be discussed further below.

[41] For instance, Article 63 of the AI Act states that microenterprises can comply with certain elements of the quality management system required by Article 17 in "a simplified manner," for which "the Commission shall develop guidelines."

[42] See in this regard Karen Yeung and Sofia Ranchordas, *An Introduction to Law and Regulation*, 2nd ed. (Cambridge University Press, 2025), especially Chapter 9, Section 9.9.2.

[43] Article 5(1)(a) of the AI Act.

[44] Article 5(1)(b) of the AI Act.

persons without human involvement,[45] or to evaluate or classify people based on their social behavior or personal characteristics (social scoring), though only if it leads to detrimental or unfavorable treatment in social contexts that are either unrelated to the contexts in which the data was originally collected, or that is unjustified or disproportionate.[46] Also prohibited is the use of emotion recognition in the workplace and educational institutions,[47] thus permitting their use in other domains despite their deeply problematic nature.[48] The untargeted scraping of facial images from the internet or from CCTV footage to create facial recognition databases is likewise prohibited.[49] Furthermore, biometric categorization is not legally permissible to infer sensitive characteristics, such as political, religious, or philosophical beliefs, sexual orientation or race.[50]

Whether to prohibit the use of real-time remote biometric identification by law enforcement in public places was a lightning-rod for controversy. It was prohibited in the Commission's original proposal, but subject to three exceptions. The Parliament sought to make the prohibition unconditional, yet the exceptions were reinstated during the trilogue. The AI Act therefore allows law enforcement to use live facial recognition in public places, but only if a number of conditions are met: prior authorization must be obtained from a judicial authority or an independent administrative authority; and it is used either to conduct a targeted search of victims, to prevent a specific and imminent (terrorist) threat, or to localize or identify a person who is convicted or (even merely) suspected of having committed a specified serious crime.[51] These exceptions have been heavily criticized, despite the Act's safeguards. In particular, they pave the way for Member States to install and equip public places with facial recognition cameras which can then be configured for the purposes of remote biometric identification if the exceptional circumstances are met, thus expanding the possibility of function creep and the abuse of law enforcement authority.

12.3.2.2 High-Risk Systems

The Act identifies two categories of high-risk AI systems: (1) those that are (safety components of) products that are already subject to an existing ex ante conformity assessment (in light of exhaustively listed EU harmonizing legislation on health and safety in Annex I, for example, for toys, aviation, cars, medical devices or lifts) and (2) stand-alone

45 Article 5(1)(d) of the AI Act.
46 Article 5(1)(c) of the AI Act.
47 Article 5(1)(f) of the AI Act.
48 See also Smuha et al. (n 14) 27.
49 Article 5(1)(e) of the AI Act.
50 Article 5(1)(g) of the AI Act. The four latter practices were introduced by the European Parliament in its June 2023 negotiating mandate (along with other spurious practices that, unfortunately, did not survive the trilogue with the Commission and the Council).
51 Article 5(1)(h) of the AI Act.

high-risk AI systems, which are mainly of concern due to their adverse fundamental rights implications and exhaustively listed in Annex III, referring to eight domains in which AI systems can be used. These stand-alone high-risk systems are arguably the most important category of systems regulated under the AI Act (since those in Annex I are already regulated by specific legislation), and will hence be our main focus.

Only the AI applications that are explicitly listed under one of those eight domains headings are deemed high-risk (see Table 12.1). While the list of applications under each domain can be updated over time by the European Commission, the domain headings themselves cannot.[52] The domains include biometrics; critical infrastructure; educational and vocational training; employment, workers management and access to self-employment; access to and enjoyment of essential private services and essential public services and benefits; law enforcement; migration, asylum and border control management; and the administration of justice and democratic processes. Even if their system is listed in Annex III, AI providers can self-assess whether their system *truly* poses a significant risk to harm "*health, safety or fundamental rights*" and only then are they subjected to the high-risk requirements.[53]

High-risk systems must comply with "essential requirements" set out in Articles 8 to 15 of the AI Act (Chapter III, Section 2). These requirements pertain, inter alia, to:

- the establishment, implementation, documentation and maintenance of a risk-management system pursuant to Article 9;
- data quality and data governance measures regarding the datasets used for training, validation, and testing; ensuring the suitability, correctness and representativeness of data; and monitoring for bias pursuant to Article 10;
- technical documentation and (automated) logging capabilities for record-keeping, to help overcome the inherent opacity of software, pursuant to Articles 11 and 12;
- transparency provisions, focusing on information provided to enable deployers to interpret system output and use it appropriately as instructed through disclosure of, for example, the system's intended purpose, capabilities, and limitations, pursuant to Article 13;
- human oversight provisions requiring that the system can be effectively overseen by natural persons (e.g., through appropriate human–machine interface tools) so as to minimize risks, pursuant to Article 14;
- the need to ensure an appropriate level of accuracy, robustness, and cybersecurity and to ensure that the systems perform consistently in those respects throughout their lifecycle, pursuant to Article 15.

[52] Article 7 of the AI Act establishes a procedure for the Commission to amend Annex III through delegated acts. The domain headings can only be adapted by the EU legislator through a revision of the regulation itself.

[53] Article 6(3) of the AI Act. To avoid misuse of this provision, the AI Act states that such providers must justify why, despite being included in Annex III, their system does not pose a significant risk. Article 6 establishes a procedure for the European Commission to challenge their justification and to impose the high-risk requirements in case the justification is flawed.

TABLE 12.1 *High-risk AI systems listed in Annex III*

1. Biometric AI systems	• remote biometric identification systems (excluding biometric verification the sole purpose of which is to confirm that a specific natural person is the person he or she claims to be); • biometric categorisation according to sensitive or protected attributes or characteristics based on the inference of those attributes or characteristics; • emotion recognition systems.
2. Critical infrastructure	AI systems intended to be used as safety components in the management and operation of critical digital infrastructure, road traffic, or in the supply of water, gas, heating or electricity.
3. Education and vocational training	AI systems intended to be used: • to determine access or admission or to assign natural persons to educational and vocational training institutions at all levels • to evaluate learning outcomes, including when those outcomes are used to steer the learning process of natural persons in educational and vocational training institutions at all levels; • for the purpose of assessing the appropriate level of education that an individual will receive or will be able to access, in the context of or within educational and vocational training institutions at all levels; • for monitoring and detecting prohibited behaviour of students during tests in the context of or within educational and vocational training institutions at all levels.
4. Employment, workers management and access to self-employment	AI systems intended to be used: • for the recruitment or selection of natural persons, in particular to place targeted job advertisements, to analyse and filter job applications, and to evaluate candidates; • to make decisions affecting terms of work-related relationships, the promotion or termination of work-related contractual relationships, to allocate tasks based on individual behaviour or personal traits or characteristics or to monitor and evaluate the performance and behaviour of persons in such relationships.
5. Access to and enjoyment of essential private services and essential public services and benefits	AI systems intended to be used: • by public authorities or on behalf of public authorities to evaluate the eligibility of natural persons for essential public assistance benefits and services, including healthcare services, as well as to grant, reduce, revoke, or reclaim such benefits and services; • to evaluate the creditworthiness of natural persons or establish their credit score, with the exception of AI systems used for the purpose of detecting financial fraud; • for risk assessment and pricing in relation to natural persons in the case of life and health insurance;

(continued)

TABLE 12.1 *(continued)*

	• to evaluate and classify emergency calls by natural persons or to be used to dispatch, or to establish priority in the dispatching of, emergency first response services, including by police, firefighters and medical aid, as well as of emergency healthcare patient triage systems.
6. Law enforcement, in so far as their use is permitted under relevant Union or national law	AI systems intended to be used by or on behalf of law enforcement authorities, or by Union institutions, bodies, offices or agencies in support of law enforcement authorities or on their behalf: • to assess the risk of a natural person becoming the victim of criminal offences; • as polygraphs or similar tools; • to evaluate the reliability of evidence in the course of the investigation or prosecution of criminal offences; • for assessing the risk of a natural person offending or re-offending not solely on the basis of the profiling of natural persons as referred to in Article 3(4) of Directive (EU) 2016/680, or to assess personality traits and characteristics or past criminal behaviour of natural persons or groups; • for the profiling of natural persons as referred to in Article 3(4) of Directive (EU) 2016/680 in the course of the detection, investigation or prosecution of criminal offences.
7. Migration, asylum and border control management, in so far as their use is permitted under relevant Union or national law	AI systems intended to be used by or on behalf of competent public authorities or by Union institutions, bodies, offices or agencies: • to assess a risk, including a security risk, a risk of irregular migration, or a health risk, posed by a natural person who intends to enter or who has entered into the territory of a Member State; • to assist competent public authorities for the examination of applications for asylum, visa or residence permits and for associated complaints with regard to the eligibility of the natural persons applying for a status, including related assessments of the reliability of evidence; • in the context of migration, asylum or border control management, for the purpose of detecting, recognising or identifying natural persons, with the exception of the verification of travel documents.
8. Administration of justice and democratic processes	AI systems intended to be used: • by a judicial authority or on their behalf to assist a judicial authority in researching and interpreting facts and the law and in applying the law to a concrete set of facts, or to be used in a similar way in alternative dispute resolution; • for influencing the outcome of an election or referendum or the voting behaviour of natural persons in the exercise of their vote in elections or referenda. This does not include AI systems to the output of which natural persons are not directly exposed, such as tools used to organise, optimise or structure political campaigns from an administrative or logistical point of view.

Finally, Articles 16 and 17 require that high-risk AI providers[54] establish a "quality management system" that must include, among other things, the aforementioned risk management system imposed by Article 9 and a strategy for regulatory compliance, including compliance with conformity assessment procedures for the management of modifications for high-risk AI. These two systems – the risk management system and the quality management system – can be understood as the AI Act's pièce de resistance. While providers have the more general obligation to demonstrably ensure compliance with the "essential requirements," most of these requirements are concerned with technical functionality, and are expected to offer assurance that AI systems will function as stated and intended, that the software's functional performance will be reliable, consistent, "without bias," and in accordance with what providers claim about system design and performance metrics. To the extent that consistent software performance is a prerequisite for facilitating its "safe" and "rights-compliant" use, these are welcome requirements. They are, however, not primarily concerned, in a direct and unmediated manner, with guarding against the dangers ("risks") that the AI Act specifically states it is intended to protect against, notably potential dangers to health, safety and fundamental rights.

This is where the AI Act's characterization of the relevant "risks," which the Article 9 risk management system must identify, estimate and evaluate, is of importance. Article 9(2) refers to "*the known and reasonably foreseeable risks that the high-risk AI system can pose to health, safety or fundamental rights*" when used in accordance with its intended purpose and an estimate and evaluation of risks that may emerge under conditions of "*reasonably foreseeable misuse.*"[55] Risk management measures must be implemented such that any "*residual risk associated with each hazard*" and the "*relevant residual risk of the high-risk AI system*" is judged "*acceptable.*"[56] High-risk AI systems must be tested prior to being placed on the market to identify the "most appropriate" risk management measures and to ensure the systems "perform consistently for their intended purposes," in compliance with the requirements of Section 2 and in accordance with "appropriate" preliminarily defined metrics and probabilistic thresholds – all of which are to be further specified.

While, generally speaking, the imposition of new obligations is a positive development, their likely effectiveness is a matter of substantial concern. We wonder, for instance, whether it is at all *acceptable* to delegate the identification of risks and their evaluation as "acceptable" to AI providers, particularly given the fact that their assessment might differ very significantly from those who are the relevant risk-bearers

[54] Articles 23 to 27 also set out some obligations for importers, distributors and deployers of high-risk AI systems.

[55] Article 9(2)(a) and (b) of the AI Act.

[56] Article 9(5) of the AI Act.

and who are most likely to suffer adverse consequences if those risks ripen into harm or rights-violations. Furthermore, Article 9(3) is ambiguous: purporting to limit the risks that must be considered as part of the risk management system to "*those which may be reasonably mitigated or eliminated through the development or design of the high-risk AI system, or the provision of adequate technical information.*"[57] As observed elsewhere, this could be interpreted to mean that risks that *cannot* be mitigated through the high-risk system's development and design or by the provision of information can be ignored altogether,[58] although the underlying legislative intent, as stated in Article 2, suggests an alternative reading such that if those "unmitigatable risks" are unacceptable, the AI system cannot be lawfully placed on the market or put into service.[59]

Although the list-based approach to the classification of high-risk systems was intended to provide legal certainty, critics pointed out that it is inherently prone to problems of under and over-inclusiveness.[60] As a result, problematic AI systems that are not included in the list are bound to appear on the market, and might not be added to the Commission's future list-updates. In addition, allowing AI providers to self-assess whether their system actually poses a significant risk or not undermines the legal certainty allegedly offered by the Act's list-based approach.[61] Furthermore, under pressure from the European Parliament, high-risk AI *deployers* that are bodies governed by public law, or are private entities providing public services, must also carry out a "fundamental rights impact assessment" before the system is put into use.[62] However, the fact that an "automated tool" will be provided to facilitate compliance with this obligation "in a simplified manner" suggests that the regulation of these risks is likely to descend into a formalistic box-ticking exercise in which formal documentation takes precedence over its substantive content and real-world effects.[63] While some companies might adopt a more prudent approach, the effectiveness of the AI Act's protection mechanisms will ultimately depend on how its oversight and enforcement mechanisms will operate on-the-ground, which we believe, for reasons set out below, are unlikely to provide a muscular response.

57 Article 9(3) of the AI Act.

58 See Nathalie A. Smuha, *Algorithmic Rule by Law: How Algorithmic Regulation in the Public Sector Erodes the Rule of Law* (Cambridge University Press, 2025), Chapter 5.4.

59 Article 26(5) also states that: "*where deployers have reason to consider that the use of the high-risk AI system in accordance with the instructions may result in that AI system presenting a risk within the meaning of Article 79(1), they shall, without undue delay, inform the provider or distributor and the relevant market surveillance authority, and shall suspend the use of that system.*"

60 See Karen Yeung, "Response to European Commission White Paper," Social Science Research Network, 2020, https://ssrn.com/abstract=3626915; Nathalie A. Smuha et al., n (14).

61 That said, as noted in n (53), AI providers who self-assess their high-risk system as excluded from the Act's requirements will still need to justify their assessment and register their system in a newly established database, managed by the Commission. See Article 49(2) of the AI Act.

62 Article 27 of the AI Act.

63 Article 27(5) of the AI Act.

12.3.2.3 General-Purpose AI Models

The AI Act defines a general-purpose AI (GPAI) model as one that displays significant generality and is capable of competently performing a wide range of distinct tasks regardless of the way the model is placed on the market, and can be integrated into a variety of downstream systems or applications (GPAI systems).[64] The prime example of GPAI models are Large Language Models (LLMs) that converse in natural language and generate text (which, for instance, form the basis of Open AI's Chat-GPT or Google's Bard), yet there are also models that can generate images, videos, music or some combination thereof.

The primary obligations of GPAI model-providers are to draw up and maintain technical documentation, comply with EU copyright law and disseminate "sufficiently detailed" summaries about the content used for training models before they are placed on the market.[65] These minimum standards apply to all models, yet GPAI models that are classified as posing a "systemic risk" due to their "high impact capabilities" are subject to additional obligations. Those include duties to conduct model evaluations, adversarial testing, assess and mitigate systemic risks, report on serious incidents, and ensure an adequate level of cybersecurity.[66] Note, however, that providers of (systemic risk) GPAI models can conduct their own audits and evaluations, rather than rely on external independent third party audits. Nor is any public licensing scheme required.

More problematically, while the criteria to qualify GPAI models as posing a "systemic risk" are meant to capture their "*significant impact on the Union market due to their reach, or due to actual or reasonably foreseeable negative effects on public health, safety, public security, fundamental rights, or the society as a whole, that can be propagated at scale across the value chain*,"[67] the legislator opted to express these criteria in terms of a threshold pertaining to the size of the data on which the models are trained. Models trained with more than 10^{25} floating-point operations reach this threshold and are presumed to qualify as posing a systemic risk.[68] This threshold, though amendable, is rather arbitrary, as many existing models do not cross that threshold but are nevertheless capable of posing systemic risks. More generally, limiting "systemic risks" to those arising from GPAI models is difficult to justify, given that even traditional rule-based AI systems with far more limited capabilities can pose systemic risks.[69] Moreover, as Hacker has observed,[70] the industry is moving

64 Article 3(63) of the AI Act. It does exclude AI models used for research, development or prototyping activities before their placement on the market.

65 Article 53(1) of the AI Act.

66 Article 55(1) of the AI Act.

67 Article 3(65) of the AI Act.

68 Article 51(2) of the AI Act.

69 See in this regard also Smuha, n (58), Chapter 5.4.

70 See Philipp Hacker, "What's missing from the EU AI Act: Addressing the four key challenges of large language models," *VerfassungsBlog*, December 13, 2023, https://verfassungsblog.de/whats-missing-from-the-eu-ai-act/.

toward smaller yet more potent models, which means many more influential GPAI models may fall outside the Act, shifting the regulatory burden "to the downstream deployers."[71] Although these provisions can, in theory, be updated over time, their effectiveness and durability are open to doubt.[72]

12.3.2.4 Systems Requiring Additional Transparency

For a subset of AI applications, the EU legislator acknowledged that specific risks can arise, such as impersonation or deception, which stand apart from high-risk systems. Pursuant to Article 50 of the AI Act, these applications are subjected to additional transparency obligations, yet they might also fall within the high-risk designation. Four types of AI systems fall into this category. The first are systems intended to interact with natural persons, such as chatbots. To avoid people mistakenly believing they are interacting with a fellow human being, these systems must be developed in such a way that the natural person who is exposed to the system is informed thereof, in a timely, clear and intelligible manner (unless this is obvious from the circumstances and context of the use). An exception is made for AI systems authorized by law to detect, prevent, investigate, and prosecute criminal offences.

A similar obligation to provide transparency exists when people are subjected either to an emotion recognition system or a biometric categorization system (to the extent it is not prohibited by Article 5 of the AI Act). Deployers must inform people subjected to those systems of the system's operation and must, pursuant to data protection law, obtain their consent prior to the processing of their biometric and other personal data. Again, an exception is made for emotion recognition systems and biometric categorization systems that are permitted by law to detect, prevent, and investigate criminal offences.

Finally, providers of AI systems that generate synthetic audio, image, video or text must ensure that the system's outputs are marked in a machine-readable format and are detectable as artificially generated or manipulated.[73] Deployers of such systems should disclose that the content has been artificially generated or manipulated.[74] This provision was already present in the Commission's initial AI Act proposal, but

[71] If a GPAI system is deployed for the purpose of one of the high-risk applications listed in Annex III – and if it is self-assessed as posing a significant risk – it will need to comply with the standard requirements for high-risk systems as listed in Chapter III, Section 2.

[72] It should however be noted that the European Commission can also designate certain GPAI models as posing a systemic risk through a decision, either ex officio or based on a qualified alert by a scientific panel that the AI Act will set up for this purpose. It is also able to amend the thresholds through delegated acts. Moreover, at least in theory, also systems that do not fall under the specified threshold can be considered as posing a systemic risk if they show high impact capabilities evaluated on the basis of "appropriate technical tools and methodologies, including indicators and benchmarks," which the Commission can supplement over time.

[73] Article 50(2) of the AI Act.

[74] Article 50(4) of the AI Act.

it became far more relevant with the boom of generative AI, which "democratized" the creation of deep fakes, enabling them to be easily created by those without specialist skills. As regards AI systems that generate or manipulate text, which is published with *"the purpose of informing the public on matters of public interest,"* deployers must disclose that the text was artificially generated or manipulated, unless the AI-generated content underwent a process of human review or editorial control with editorial responsibility for its publication.[75] Here, too, exceptions exist. In each case, the disclosure measures must take into account the generally acknowledged state of the art, whereby the AI Act also refers to relevant harmonized standards,[76] to which we will return later.

12.3.2.5 Non-High-Risk Systems

All other AI systems that do not fall under one of the aforementioned risk-categories are effectively branded as "no risk" and do not attract new legal obligations. To the extent they fall under existing legal frameworks – for instance, when they process personal data – they must still comply with those frameworks. In addition, the AI Act provides that the European Commission, Member States and the AI Office (a supervisory entity that we discuss in the next section) should encourage and facilitate the drawing up of codes of conduct that are intended to foster the voluntary application of the high-risk requirements to those no-risk AI systems.[77]

12.3.3 *Supporting Innovation*

The White Paper on AI focused not only on the adoption of rules to *limit* AI-related risks, but also included a range of measures and policies to *boost* AI innovation in the EU. Clearly, the AI Act is a tool aimed primarily at achieving the former, but the EU still found it important to also emphasize its "pro-innovation" stance. Chapter VI of the AI Act therefore lists "measures in support of innovation," which fits into the EU's broader policy narrative which recognizes that regulation can facilitate innovation, and even provide a "competitive advantage" in the AI "race."[78] These measures mainly concern[79] the introduction of AI regulatory sandboxes, which are intended to offer a safe and controlled environment for AI providers to develop, test, and validate AI systems, including the facilitation of "real-world-testing." National authorities must oversee these sandboxes and help

75 Ibid.

76 Article 50(2) of the AI Act.

77 Articles 95 and following of the AI Act.

78 See European Commission, n (8), 2.

79 One could argue that the abovementioned derogations for open-source AI systems can likewise be seen as an innovation-boosting measure. See *supra*, n (41).

ensure that appropriate safeguards are in place, and that their experimentation occurs in compliance with the law. The AI Act mandates each Member State to establish at least one regulatory sandbox, which can also be established jointly with other Member States.[80] To avoid fragmentation, the AI Act further provides for the development of common rules for the sandboxes' implementation and a framework for cooperation between the relevant authorities that supervise them, to ensure their uniform implementation across the EU.[81]

Sandboxes must be made accessible especially to Small and Medium Enterprises (SMEs), thereby ensuring that they receive additional support and guidance to achieve regulatory compliance while retaining the ability to innovate. In fact, the AI Act explicitly recognizes the need to take into account the interests of "small-scale providers" and deployers of AI systems, particularly costs.[82] National authorities that oversee sandboxes are hence given various tasks, including increasing awareness on the regulation, promoting AI literacy, offering information and communication services to SMEs, start-ups, and deployers, and helping them identify methods that lower their compliance costs. Collectively, these measures are aimed to offset the fact that smaller companies will likely face heavier compliance and implementation burdens, especially compared to large tech companies that can afford an army of lawyers and consultants to implement the AI Act. It is also hoped that the sandboxes will help national authorities to improve their supervisory methods, develop better guidance, and identify possible future improvements of the legal framework.

12.4 MONITORING AND ENFORCEMENT

Our discussion has hitherto focused on the substantive dimensions of the Act. However, whether these provide effective protection of health, safety and fundamental rights will depend critically on the strength and operation of its monitoring and enforcement architecture, to which we now turn. We have already noted that the proposed regulatory enforcement framework underpinning the Commission's April 2021 blueprint was significantly flawed, yet these flaws remain unaltered in the final Act. As we shall see, the AI Act allocates considerable interpretative discretion to the industry itself, through a model which has been described by regulatory theorists as "meta-regulation." We also discuss the Act's approach to technical standards and the institutional framework for evaluating whether high-risk AI systems are in compliance with the Act, to argue that the regime as a whole fails to offer adequate protection against the adverse effects that it purports to counter.

80 Article 57(1) of the AI Act.
81 Article 58 of the AI Act.
82 See, for example, Article 34(2) of the AI Act.

12.4.1 *Legal Rules and Interpretative Discretion*

Many of the AI Act's core provisions are written in broad, open-ended language, leaving the meaning of key terms uncertain and unresolved. It will be here that the rubber will hit the road, for it is through the interpretation and application of the Act's operative provisions that it will be given meaning and be translated into on-the-ground practice.

For example, when seeking to apply the essential requirements applicable to high-risk systems, three terms used in Chapter III, Section 2 play a crucial role. First, the concept of "risk." Article 3 defines risk as "*the combination of the probability of an occurrence of harm and the severity of that harm*," reflecting conventional statistical risk assessment terminology. Although risks to health and safety is a relatively familiar and established concept in legal parlance and regulatory regimes, the Annex III high-risk systems are more likely to interfere with fundamental rights and may adversely affect democracy and the rule of law. But what, precisely, is meant by "risk to fundamental rights," and how should those risks be identified, evaluated and assessed? Secondly, even assuming that fundamental rights-related risks can be meaningfully assessed, how then is a software firm to adequately evaluate what constitutes a level of residual risk judged "acceptable"? And thirdly, what constitutes a "risk management system" that meets the requirements of Article 9?

The problem of interpretative discretion is not unique to the AI Act. All rules which take linguistic form, whether legally mandated or otherwise, must be interpreted before they can be applied to specific real-world circumstances. Yet how this discretion is exercised, and by whom, will be a product of the larger regulatory architecture in which those rules are embedded. The GDPR, for instance, contains a number of broadly defined "principles" which those who collect and process personal data must comply with. Both the European Data Protection Board (EDPB) and national level data protection authorities – as public regulators – issue "guidance" documents offering interpretative guidance about what the law requires. Compliance with this guidance (often called "soft law") does not guarantee compliance – for it does not bind courts when interpreting the law – but it nevertheless offers a valuable, and reasonably authoritative assistance to those seeking to comply with their legal obligations. This kind of guidance is open, published, transparent, and conventionally issued in draft form before-hand so that stakeholders and the public can provide feedback before it is issued in final form.[83]

In the AI Act, similar interpretative decisions will need to be made and, in theory, the Commission has a mandate to issue guidelines on the AI Act's practical implementation.[84] However, in contrast with the GDPR, the Act's adoption of the "New

[83] See Yeung and Ranchordas, n (42), Chapter 8.

[84] Article 96 of the AI Act. When issuing such guidelines, the Commission "*shall take due account of the generally acknowledged state of the art on AI, as well as of relevant harmonised standards and common*

Approach" to product-safety means that, in practice, providers of high-risk AI systems will likely adhere to technical standards produced by European Standardization Organizations on request from the Commission and which are expected to acquire the status of "harmonized standards" by publication of their titles in the EU's Official Journal.[85] As we explain below, the processes through which these standards are developed are difficult to characterize as democratic, transparent or based on open public participation.

12.4.2 *The AI Act as a Form of "Meta-Regulation"*

At first glance, the AI Act appears to adopt a public enforcement framework with both national and European public authorities playing a significant role. Each EU Member State must designate a national supervisory authority[86] to act as "market surveillance authority."[87] These authorities can investigate suspected incidents and infringements of the AI Act's requirements, and initiate recalls or withdrawals of AI systems from the market for non-compliance.[88] National authorities exchange best practices through a *European AI Board* comprised of Member States' representatives. The European Commission has also set up an AI Office to coordinate

specifications that are referred to in Articles 40 and 41, or of those harmonised standards or technical specifications that are set out pursuant to Union harmonisation law."

85 See Articles 40 and 41 of the AI Act. A harmonized standard is a European standard developed by a recognized European Standardization Organization and its creation is requested by the European Commission. The references of harmonized standards must be published in the Official Journal of the EU. See https://single-market-economy.ec.europa.eu/single-market/european-standards/harmonised-standards_en, accessed June 20, 2024.

86 Member States are free to establish a new entity for this purpose, or they can designate an existing authority. They can also assign this task to several existing authorities, as long as they designate one of those authorities as the main authority and contact point for practical purposes. See Article 70 of the AI Act.

87 Under the New Legislative Framework for product safety legislation, (national) market surveillance authorities have the task to monitor the market and, in case of doubt, to verify ex post whether the conformity assessment has correctly been carried out, and the CE mark duly affixed. This market surveillance authority can be a separate entity, or it can be the same authority that is also responsible for the supervision of the implementation of a regulation. As regards the regime of the AI Act, for all stand-alone high-risk systems, it provides that the national supervisory authority is also the market surveillance authority. For high-risk systems that are already covered by legal acts listed in Annex I (and that are hence already subject to a monitoring system, such as toys or medical devices), the competent authorities under those legal acts will remain the lead market surveillance authority, though cooperation is encouraged.

88 The supervisory authorities should act independently and impartially in performing their tasks and exercising their powers. These powers consist of e.g. requesting the technical documentation and records that providers of high-risk systems must create and – if they exhausted all other reasonable ways to verify the system's conformity, they can also request access to the system's training, validation and testing datasets, the trained and training model of the high-risk AI system, including its relevant model parameters. Pursuant to Article 74(13) of the AI Act, national supervisory authorities can exceptionally also obtain access to the source code of a high-risk AI system, upon a reasoned request. Any information must be treated as confidential, and with respect to intellectual property rights and trade secrets.

enforcement at the EU level.[89] Its main task is to monitor and enforce the requirements relating to GPAI models,[90] yet it also undertakes several other roles, including (a) guiding the evaluation and review of the AI Act over time,[91] (b) offering coordination support for joint investigations between the Commission and Member States when a high-risk system presents a serious risk across multiple Member States,[92] and (c) facilitating the drawing up of voluntary codes of conduct for systems that are not classified as high-risk.[93]

The AI Office will be advised by a *scientific panel of independent experts* to help it develop methodologies to evaluate the capabilities of GPAI models, to designate GPAI models as posing a systemic risk, and to monitor material safety risks that such models pose. An *advisory forum of stakeholders* (to counter earlier criticism that stakeholders were allocated no role whatsoever in the regulation) is also established under the Act, to provide both the Board and the Commission with technical expertise and advice. Finally, the Commission is tasked with establishing a public EU-wide database where providers (and a limited set of deployers) of stand-alone high-risk AI systems must register their systems to enhance transparency.[94]

In practice, however, these public authorities are twice-removed from where much of the *real-world* compliance activity and evaluation takes place. The AI Act's regulatory enforcement framework delegates many crucial functions (and thus considerable discretionary power) to the very actors whom the regime purports to regulate, and to other tech industry experts. The entire architecture of the AI Act is based on what regulatory governance scholars sometimes refer to as "meta-regulation" or "enforced self-regulation."[95] This is a regulatory technique in which legally binding obligations are imposed on regulated organizations, requiring them to establish and maintain internal control systems that meet broadly specified, outcome-based, binding legal objectives.

Meta-regulatory strategies rest on the basic idea that one size does not fit all, and that firms themselves are best placed to understand their own operations and systems and take the necessary action to avoid risks and dangers. The primary safeguards through which the AI Act is intended to work rely on the quality and risk management systems within the regulated organizations, in which these organizations

89 The establishment of the AI Office reflects the desire of both the European Parliament and the Council to have a stronger involvement at the EU level when it comes to implementing and enforcing the AI Act. Over time, the AI office could become a full-fledged European AI Agency.

90 Articles 53 and following of the AI Act. For those models, the AI Office will also contribute to fostering standards and testing practices and enforcing common rules in all member states.

91 Especially for those provisions that the Commission cannot adapt through a delegated act, but that can only be amended by the legislators (such as the domain headings under Annex III or the prohibited AI practices). See Article 112(11) of the AI Act.

92 Article 74(11) of the AI Act.

93 Article 95 of the AI Act.

94 Article 71 of the AI Act.

95 See Yeung and Ranchordas, n (42), Chapter 7 and literature cited therein.

retain considerable discretion to establish and maintain their own internal standards of control, provided that the Act's legally mandated objectives are met. The supervisory authorities oversee adherence to those internal standards, but they only play a secondary and reactionary role, which is triggered if there are grounds to suspect that regulated organizations are failing to discharge their legal obligations. While natural and legal persons have the right to lodge a complaint when they have grounds to consider that the AI Act was infringed,[96] supervisory authorities do not have any proactive role to ensure the requirements are met before high-risk AI systems are placed on the market or deployed.

This compliance architecture flows from the underlying foundations of the Act, which are rooted in the EU's "New Legislative Framework," adopted in 2008. Its aim was to improve the internal market for goods and strengthen the conditions for placing a wide range of products on the EU market.[97]

The AI Act largely leaves it to Annex III high-risk AI providers and deployers to self-assess their conformity with the AI Act's requirements (including, as discussed earlier, the judgment of what is deemed an "acceptable" residual risk). There is no routine or regular inspection and approval or licensing by a public authority. Instead, if they declare that they have self-assessed their AI system as compliant and duly lodge a declaration of conformity, providers can put their AI systems into service without any independent party verifying whether their assessment is indeed adequate (except for certain biometric systems).[98] Providers are, however, required to put in place a post-market monitoring system, which is intended to ensure that the possible risks emerging from AI systems that continue to "learn" or evolve once placed on the market or put into service can be better identified and addressed.[99] The role of

96 Article 85 of the AI Act. Article 86 also grants affected persons who are subjected to (most) high-risk AI systems listed in Annex III the 'right to an explanation', covering the "*right to obtain from the deployer clear and meaningful explanations of the role of the AI system in the decision-making procedure and the main elements of the decision taken.*" This right however only applies if the decision "*produces legal effects or similarly significantly affects that person in a way that they consider to have an adverse impact on their health, safety or fundamental rights,*" and national or Union law can provide exceptions to this right.

97 It refers to a package of measures intended to: improve market surveillance; establish a framework of rules for product safety; enhance the quality of and confidence in the conformity assessment of products through stronger and clearer rules on notification requirements of conformity assessment bodies; and clarify the meaning of CE markings to enhance their credibility. This package of measures consists of Regulation (EC) 765/2008, which sets out the requirements for accreditation and the market surveillance of products, Commission Decision 768/2008 on a common framework for the marketing of products, which is effectively a template for future product harmonisation legislation and Regulation (EU) 2019/1020 on market surveillance and compliance of products, which aims to govern the role of various economic operators (manufacturers, authorised representatives, importers) and standardizing their tasks with regard to the placing of products on the market.

98 See Article 43 of the AI Act.

99 High-risk AI providers and deployers must also have a system in place to report to the relevant authorities any serious incidents or breaches of national and Union law, and take appropriate corrective actions.

public regulators is therefore largely that of *ex post* oversight, unlike the European regulation of pharmaceuticals, reflecting the regulatory regime as permissive rather than precautionary. This embodies the basic regulatory philosophy underpinning the New Legislative Framework, which builds on the "New Approach" to technical standardization. Together, these are concerned first and foremost with strengthening single market integration, and hence with ensuring a single EU market for AI.

12.4.3 *The New Approach to Technical Standardization*

Under the EU's "Old Approach" to product safety standards, national authorities drew up detailed technical legislation, which was often unwieldy and usually motivated by a lack of confidence in the rigour of economic operators on issues of public health and safety. However, the "New Approach" framework introduced in 1985 sought instead to restrict the content of legislation to "essential requirements," leaving technical details to European Harmonized Standards[100] thereby laying the foundation for technical standards produced by European Standardization Organizations (ESOs) in support of Union harmonization legislation.[101]

The animating purpose of the "New Approach" to standardization was to open up European markets in industrial products without threatening the safety of European consumers, by allowing the entry of those products across European markets if and only if they meet the "essential [safety] requirements" set out in sector-specific European rules developed by one of the three ESOs: the European Committee for Standardization (CEN), the European Committee for Electrotechnical Standardization (CENELEC) and the European Telecommunications Standards Institute (ETSI).[102]

[100] The decision of the Court of Justice of the EU (CJEU) in *Cassis de Dijon* in 1979 was highly significant. The Court ruled that products lawfully manufactured or marketed in one Member State should in principle move freely throughout the Union where such products meet equivalent levels of protection to those imposed by the Member State of destination, and that barriers to free movement which result from differences in national legislation may only be accepted under specific circumstances, namely (1) the national measures are necessary to satisfy mandatory requirements (such as health, safety, consumer protection and environmental protection), (2) they serve a legitimate purpose which justifies overriding the principle of free movement of goods, and (3) they can be justified with regard to the legitimate purpose and are proportionate with the aims. See *Case 120/78 Cassis de Dijon* [1979] ECR 649 (*Rewe-Zentral v Bundesmonopolverwaltung für Branntwein*).

[101] Yet in practice, the framework did not create the necessary level of trust between Member States. Therefore, in 1989 and 1990, the "Global Approach" was adopted, which established general guidelines and detailed procedures for conformity assessment to cover a wide range of industrial and commercial products.

[102] See in this regard Jean-Pierre Galland, "Big Third-Party Certifiers and the Construction of Transnational Regulation" (2017) *The ANNALS of the American Academy of Political and Social Science*, 670(1), 263–279. This New Legislative Framework consists of a tripartite package of EU measures (1) EC Regulation No 765/2008 on accreditation and marketing surveillance (2) Decision No 768/2008/EC on establishing a common framework for the marketing of products (3) EC Regulation

Under this approach, producers can choose to *either* interpret the relevant EU Directive themselves *or* to rely on "harmonized (European) standards" drawn up by one of the ESOs. This meta-regulatory approach combines compulsory regulation (under EU secondary legislation) and "voluntary" standards, made by ESOs. Central to this approach is that conformity of products with "essential safety requirements" is checked and certified by *producers themselves* who make a declaration of conformity and affix the CE mark to their products to indicate this, thereby allowing the product to be marketed and sold across the whole of the EU. However, for some "sensitive products," conformity assessments must be carried out by an independent third-party "notified body" to certify conformity and issue a declaration of conformity. This approach was taken by the Commission in its initial AI Act proposal, and neither the Parliament nor the Council has sought to depart from it. By virtue of its reliance on the "New Approach," the AI Act lays tremendous power in the hands of private, technical bodies who are entrusted with the task of setting technical standards intended to operationalize the "essential requirements" stipulated in the AI Act.[103]

In particular, providers of Annex III high-risk AI systems that fall under the AI Act's requirements have three options. First, they can self-assess the compliance of their AI systems with the essential requirements (which the AI Act refers to as the conformity assessment procedure based on internal control, set out in Annex VI). Under this option, whenever the requirements are vague, organizations need to use their own judgment and discretion to interpret and apply them, which – given considerable uncertainty about what they require in practice – exposes them to potential legal risks (including substantial penalties) if they fail to meet the requirements.

Second, organizations can rely on a conformity assessment by a "notified body,"[104] which they can commission to undertake the conformity assessment. These bodies are independent yet nevertheless "private" organizations that verify the conformity of AI systems based on an assessment of the quality management system and the technical documentation (a procedure set out in Annex VII). AI providers pay for these certification services, with a flourishing "market for certification" emerging in response. To carry out the tasks of a notified body, it must meet the requirements of Article 31 of the AI Act, which are mainly concerned with ensuring that they possess the necessary competences, a high degree of professional integrity, and that they are independent from and impartial to the organizations they assess to avoid conflicts of interest. Pursuant to the AI Act, only providers of biometric identification systems

No 764/2008 to strengthen the internal market for a wide range of other products not subject to EU harmonisation.

[103] See Commission Implementing Decision of 22 May 2023 on a standardisation request to the European Committee for Standardisation and the European Committee for Electrotechnical Standardisation in support of Union policy on artificial intelligence, Brussels, 22 May 2023, C(2023) 3215 final.

[104] This is because an organization that seeks to act as an independent third-party certifier first needs to receive accreditation from a national notifying authority which evaluates and monitors that these third-party certifiers meet certain quality and independence standards.

must currently undergo an assessment by a notification body. All others can opt for the first option (though in the future, other sensitive systems may also be obliged to obtain approval via third-party conformity assessment).

Third, AI providers can choose to follow voluntary standards currently under development by CEN/CENELEC following acceptance of the Commission's standardization request which are intended, once drafted, to become "harmonized standards" following citation in the Official Journal of the European Commission. This would mean that AI providers and deployers could choose to follow these harmonized standards and thereby benefit from a legal *presumption of conformity* with the AI Act's requirements. Although the presumption of compliance is rebuttable, it places the burden of proving non-compliance on those claiming that the AI Act's requirements were not met, thus considerably reducing the risk that the AI provider will be found to be in breach of the Act's essential requirements. If no harmonized standards are forthcoming, the Commission can adopt "common specifications" in respect of the requirements for high-risk systems and GPAI models, which likewise, will confer a presumption of conformity.[105]

Thus, although harmonized standards produced by ESOs are formally voluntary, providers are strongly incentivized to follow them (or, in their absence, to follow the common specifications) rather than carrying the burden of demonstrating that their own specifications meet the law's essential requirements. This means that harmonized standards are likely to become binding *de facto*, and will therefore in practice determine the nature and level of protection provided under the AI Act. The overwhelming majority of providers of Annex III high-risk systems can self-assess their own internal controls, sign and lodge a conformity assessment declaration, affix a CE mark to their software, and then notify the Commission's public register.

12.4.4 *Why Technical Standardization Falls Short in the AI Act's Context*

Importantly, however, several studies have found that products that have been self-certified by producers are considerably more likely to fail to meet the certified standard. For example, Larson and Jordan[106] compared toy safety recalls in the US, within a toy safety regime requiring independent third-party verification, and the EU's toy self-certification regime which relies on self-assessment and found stark differences. Over a two-year period, toy safety recalls in the EU were 9 to 20 times more frequent than those in the US. Their findings align with earlier policy studies finding that self-assessment models consistently produce substantially higher rates of worker injury compared with those involving independent third-party evaluation. Based on these studies, Larson and Jordon conclude that transnational product

[105] Article 41 of the AI Act.

[106] Derek B. Larson and Sara R. Jordan, "Playing it safe: toy safety and conformity and assessment in Europe and the US" (2018) *International Review of Administrative Sciences*, 85(4), 763–79.

safety regulatory systems that rely on the self-assessment of conformity with safety standards fail to keep products off the market, which do not comply with those standards.

What is more, even third-party certification under the EU's New Approach has shown itself to be weak and ineffective, as evidenced by the failure of the EU's Medical Device regime which prevailed before its more recent reform. This was vividly illustrated by the PIP breast implants scandal in which approximately 40,000 women in France, and possibly 10 times more in Europe and worldwide, were implanted with breast implants that were filled with industrial grade silicon, rather than the compulsory medical grade standard required under EU law.[107] This occurred despite the fact that the implants had been certified as "CE compliant" by a reputable German notified body, which was possible because, under the relevant directive,[108] breast implant producers could choose between different methods of inspection. PIP had chosen the "full quality assurance system," whereby the certifiers' job was to audit PIP's quality management system without having to inspect the breast implants themselves. In short, the New Approach has succeeded in fostering flourishing markets for certification services – but evidence suggests that it cannot be relied on systematically to deliver trustworthy products and services that protect individuals from harm to their health and safety.

Particularly troubling is the New Approach's reliance on testing the *quality of internal document keeping and management systems*, rather than an inspection and evaluation of the service or product itself.[109] As critical accounting scholar Mike Power has observed, the process of "rendering auditable" through measurable procedures and performance – is a test of "the quality of internal systems rather than the quality of the product or service itself specified in standards."[110] As Hopkins emphasizes in his analysis of the core features that a robust "safety case" approach must meet, "*without scrutiny by an independent regulator, a safety case may not be worth the paper it is written on.*"[111] The AI Act, however, does not impose any external

[107] See in this regard also Victoria Martindale and Andre Menache, "The PIP scandal: an analysis of the process of quality control that failed to safeguard women from the health risks" (2013) *Journal of the Royal Society of Medicine*, 106(5), 173–77.

[108] Council Directive 93/42/EEC of 14 June 1993 concerning medical devices, OJ L 169, July 12, 1993, 1–43.

[109] This is borne out in Laura Silva-Cataneda, "A forest of evidence: Third-party certification and multiple forms of proof – a case study on oil palm plantations in Indonesia" (2012) *Agriculture and Human Values*, 29(3): 361–70. In her study, she found that in practice, auditors regard the company's documents as the ultimate form of evidence. Villagers who disagree with the company may point to localized and personalized markers but not to documents, and this is regarded by the auditors as a "lack of evidence." Hence, in contrast to the company's documentary arsenal, auditors' unwillingness to recognize the validity of evidence other than in documentary while disregarding the local knowledge of local communities exacerbated the power imbalance between them.

[110] See Michael Power, *The Audit Society: Rituals of Verification* (Oxford University Press, 1997), p. 84.

[111] As Hopkins clarifies, under a safety case regime, when regulators make site visits, "rather than inspecting to ensure that hardware is working, or that documents are up to date, they must audit against the

auditing requirements. For Annex III high-risk AI systems, the compliance evaluation remains primarily limited to verification that there is requisite documentation in place. Accordingly, we are skeptical of the effectiveness of the CE marking regime for delivering meaningful and effective protections for those affected by rights-critical products and services regulated under the Act.[112]

What, then, are the prospects that the technical standards which the Commission has tasked CEN/CENELEC to produce will translate into practice the Act's noble aspirations to protect fundamental rights, health, safety and uphold the rule of law? We believe there are several reasons to worry. Technical standardization processes may appear "neutral" as they focus on mundane technical tasks, conducted in a highly specialized vernacular, yet these activities are in fact highly political. As Lawrence Busch puts it: "Standards are intimately associated with power."[113] Moreover, these standards will not be publicly available. Rather, they are protected by copyright and thus only available on payment.[114] If an AI provider self-certifies its compliance with an ESO-produced harmonized standard, that will constitute "deemed compliance" with the Act. But, if, in fact, that provider has made no attempt to comply with the standard, no-one will be any the wiser unless and until action is taken by a market surveillance authority to evaluate that AI system for compliance, which it cannot do unless it has "sufficient reasons to consider an AI system to present a risk."[115]

In addition, technical standardization bodies have conventionally been dominated by private sector actors who have had both the capacity to develop particular technologies and can leverage their market share to advocate for the standardization of the technology in line with their own products and organizational processes.

safety case, to ensure that the *specified controls are functioning* as intended." See Andrew Hopkins, "Explaining the 'safety case,'" Working Paper 87, Australian National University, April 2012, p. 6.

[112] The EU is currently struggling to implement a wide-ranging change in how medical devices are regulated – from the 1993 Medical Device Directive (MDD) to the 2017 Medical Device Regulation (MDR). Phased introduction of the MDR was due to be completed by May 2020, but was extended until this year due to COVID-19 pressures. This new regulatory framework is designed to ensure more thorough testing of devices before they can be used on patients, requiring clinical investigation and more rigorous monitoring of performance of devices once on the market. The MDR's implementation, however, has not gone smoothly.

[113] Lawrence Bush, *Standards: Recipes for Realities* (The MIT Press, 2011), p. 13.

[114] However, in *Public.Resource.Org, Inc., Right to Know CLG vs. European Commission* (C-588/21 P) the CJEU ruled that the Commission must indeed grant access to the four requested harmonized standards on the basis that harmonized standards form part of EU law and that the rule of law requires that access to harmonized standards must be freely available without charge. There is thus an overriding public interest in free access to the harmonized standards.

[115] See Article 79(2) of the AI Act. Supervisory authorities (in their capacity of market surveillance authorities) are empowered to have access to documentation, datasets and code upon reasoned request, together with other "appropriate technical means and tools enabling remote access" and datasets. However, only if the documentation is "insufficient to ascertain whether a breach of obligations under EU law intended to protect fundamental rights has occurred" can the MSA organize the testing of the high-risk system through technical means (see Article 77(3) of the AI Act).

Standards committees tend to be stacked with people from large corporations with vested interests and extensive resources. As Joanna Bryson has pithily put it, "even when technical standards for software are useful they are ripe for regulatory capture."[116] Nor are they subject to democratic mechanisms of public oversight and accountability that apply to conventional law-making bodies. Neither the Parliament nor the Member States have a binding veto over harmonized standards, and even the Commission has only limited powers to influence their content, at the point of determining whether the standard produced in response to its request meets the essential requirements set out in the Act, but otherwise the standard is essentially immune from judicial review.[117]

Criticisms of the lack of the democratic legitimacy of these organizations has led to moves to open up their standard-setting process to "multi-stakeholder" dialogue, with civil society organizations seeking to get more involved.[118] In practice, however, these moves are deeply inadequate, as civil society struggles to obtain technical parity with their better-resourced counterparts from the business and technology communities. Stakeholder organizations also face various de facto obstacles to use the CEN/CENELEC participatory mechanisms effectively. Most NGOs have no experience in standardization and many lack EU level representation. Moreover, active participation is costly and highly time-consuming.[119]

Equally if not more worrying is the fact that these "technical" standard-setting bodies are populated by experts primarily from engineering and computer science, who typically have little knowledge or expertise in matters related to fundamental rights, democracy, and the rule of law. Nor are they likely to be familiar with the analytical reasoning that is well established in human rights jurisprudence to determine what constitutes an interference with a fundamental right and whether it may be justified as necessary in a democratic society.[120] Without a significant cadre of human rights lawyers to assist them, we are deeply skeptical of the competence

[116] Joanna J. Bryson, "Belgian and Flemish policy makers' guide to AI regulation," KCDS-CiTiP Fellow Lectures Series: Towards an AI Regulator?, Leuven, October 11, 2022.

[117] Although the CJEU decided in the *James Elliot* case that it has jurisdiction to interpret harmonized standards in preliminary ruling procedures, according to Ebers (2022), it is unlikely that the Court would be willing to rule on the validity of a harmonized standard, either in an annulment action (per Article 264 TFEU) or a preliminary ruling procedure (per Article 267 TFEU). And even if it were, the CJEU is unlikely to review and invalidate its substantive content – its jurisdiction would be limited to reviewing whether the Commission made an error in making the decision to publish a harmonized standard in the official journal. See Martin Ebers, "Standardizing AI: The case of the European Commission's proposal for an 'Artificial Intelligence Act,'" in L. A. DiMatteo, C. Poncibò, and M. Cannarsa (eds.), *The Cambridge Handbook of Artificial Intelligence: Global Perspectives on Law and Ethics* (Cambridge University Press, 2022), pp. 321–344.

[118] See for example the ANEC and BEUC standardization project: https://anec.eu/projects/ai-standards, accessed June 20, 2024.

[119] CENELEC/CEN standardization committees are dispersed across all corners of Europe, yet most of the meetings now tend to take place online.

[120] Our experiences when piloting the AI HLEG's Trustworthy AI Assessment List showed an across-the-board lack of understanding of what a fundamental rights impact assessment entails, with the majority

and ability of ESOs to translate the notion of "risks to fundamental rights" into tractable technical standards that can be relied upon to facilitate the protection of fundamental rights.[121]

Furthermore, unlike risks to safety generated by chemicals, machinery, or industrial waste, all of which can be materially observed and measured, fundamental rights are, in effect, political constructs. These rights are accorded special legal protection so that an evaluation of alleged interference requires close attention to the nature and scope of the relevant right and the specific, localized context in which a particular right is allegedly infringed. We therefore seriously doubt whether fundamental rights can *ever* be translated into generalized technical standards that can be precisely measured in quantitative terms, and in a manner that faithfully reflects what they are and how they have been interpreted under the European Charter on Fundamental Rights and the European Convention on Human Rights.

Moreover, the CENELEC rules nevertheless state that any harmonized standard must contain "objectively verifiable requirements and test methods,"[122] which does not alleviate our difficulties in trying to conceive of how "risks to fundamental rights" can be subject to quantitative "metrics" and translated into technical standards such that the "residual risk" can be assessed as "acceptable." Taken together, this leaves us rather pessimistic about the capacity and prospects for ESOs (even assuming a well-intentioned technical committee) to produce technical standards that will, if duly followed, provide the high level of protection to European values that the Act claims to aspire to, and which will constitute "deemed compliance" with the regulation. And if, as expected, providers of high-risk AI systems will choose to be guided by the technical standards produced by ESOs, this means that the "real" standard-setting for high-risk systems will take place within those organizations, with little public scrutiny or independent evaluation.

12.5 CONCLUSION

In this chapter, we have recounted the European Union's path toward a new legal framework to regulate AI systems, beginning in 2018 with the European AI strategy and the establishment of a High-Level Expert Group on AI, culminating in the AI Act of 2024. Since most of the AI Act's provisions will only apply two years after its entry into force,[123] we will not be in a position to acquire evidence of its effectiveness until the end of 2026. By then, both those regulated by the Act, and the supervisory

of respondents mystified by the requirement to consider the impact of their AI system on fundamental rights in the first place.

[121] But see recent efforts by Equinet, "Equality-compliant artificial intelligence: Equinet's plans for 2024", available at https://equineteurope.org/latest-developments-in-ai-equality/ (accessed June 20, 2024).

[122] See in this regard the CENELEC Internal Regulations, Part 3.

[123] See Article 113 of the AI Act, which also lists some exceptions.

actors at national and EU level will need to ramp up their oversight and monitoring capabilities. However, by that time, new AI applications may have found their way to the EU market, which – due to the AI Act's list-based approach – will not fall within the Act, or which the Act may fail to guard against. In addition, since the AI Act aspires a maximum market harmonization for AI systems across Member States, any gaps are in principle *not* addressable through national legislation.

We believe that Europe can rightfully be proud of its acknowledgement that the development and use of AI systems requires mandatory legal obligations, given the individual, collective and societal harms they can engender,[124] and we applaud its aspirations to offer a protective legal framework. What remains to be seen is whether the AI Act will in practice deliver on its laudable objectives, or whether it provides a veneer of legal protection without delivering meaningful safeguards in practice. This depends, crucially, on how its noble aspirations are *operationalized* on the ground, particularly through the institutional mechanism and concepts through which the Act is intended to work.

Based on our analysis, it is difficult to conclude that the AI Act offers much more than "motherhood and apple pie." In other words, although it purports to champion noble principles that command widespread consensus, notably "European values" including the protection of democracy, fundamental rights, and the rule of law, whether it succeeds in giving concrete expression to those principles in its implementation and operation remains to be seen. In our view, given the regulatory approach and enforcement architecture through which it is intended to operate, these principles are likely to remain primarily aspirational.

What we do expect to see, however, is the emergence of flourishing new markets for service-providers across Europe offering various "solutions" intended to satisfy the Act's requirements (including the need for high-risk AI system providers and deployers to establish and maintain a suitable "risk management system" and "quality management system" that purport to comply with the technical standards developed by CEN/CENELEC). Accordingly, we believe it is likely that existing legal frameworks – such as the General Data Protection Regulation, the EU Charter of Fundamental Rights, and the European Convention on Human Rights – will prove even more important and instrumental in seeking to address the erosion and interference with foundational European values as ever more tasks are increasingly delegated to AI systems.

[124] See also Karen Yeung, "Responsibility and AI – A Study of the Implications of Advanced Digital Technologies (Including AI Systems) for the Concept of Responsibility within a Human Rights Framework," Council of Europe, 2019, DGI (2019)05; Nathalie A. Smuha, "Beyond the individual: governing AI's societal harm," *Internet Policy Review*, 10(3), 2021.

PART III

AI across Sectors

13

Artificial Intelligence and Education

Different Perceptions and Ethical Directions

Inge Molenaar, Duuk Baten, Imre Bárd[*], *and Marthe Stevens*

13.1 INTRODUCTION

Recently there has been much discussion about AI in all application domains, especially in the field of education.[1] Since the introduction of ChatGPT, a storm has swept through the educational landscape.[2] The awareness that AI will impact education has now reached the general public. For instance, teachers are confronted with AI in their daily practices when students, from late primary education to university, find their way to generative AI as an easy help to support homework, write essays, and make assessments.[3] In this way, generative AI comes into schools through the backdoor, and educational professionals struggle to respond meaningfully. This stands in stark contrast with the instructional design approach and responsible research and innovation trajectories, in which applications of technology and AI are carefully designed for use in education, relevant stakeholders are included in the development process, and diverse societal and ethical implications are assessed.[4] In this chapter, we argue that these recent developments further increased the need for ethical approaches that stimulate the responsible use of AI in education.

Although AI in education has been a scientific field for over 35 years,[5] policy-oriented developments and ethical approaches directly focused on AI and education are more recent. Following the development of general guidelines for developing

[*] At the time of writing this chapter, Imre Bárd was also a part-time Trust and Safety contractor at OpenAI.

[1] Wayne Holmes and Ilkka Tuomi, "State of the art and practice in AI in education" (2022) *European Journal of Education*, 57: 542; Inge Molenaar, "Towards hybrid human-AI learning technologies" (2022) *European Journal of Education*, 57: 632.

[2] Enkelejda Kasneci et al., "ChatGPT for good? On opportunities and challenges of large language models for education" (2023) *Learning and Individual Differences*, 103: 102274.

[3] Cindy Gordon, "How are educators reacting to Chat GPT?" (*Forbes*), www.forbes.com/sites/cindygordon/2023/04/30/how-are-educators-reacting-to-chat-gpt/, accessed August 4, 2023.

[4] Jack Stilgoe, Richard Owen, and Phil Macnaghten, "Developing a framework for responsible innovation" (2013) *Research Policy*, 42: 1568; Molenaar, "Towards hybrid human-AI learning technologies" (n 1).

[5] "International AIED Society," https://iaied.org/about, accessed August 4, 2023.

and using AI,[6] the first international event on AI in education with a policy and ethics perspective was organized by UNESCO in 2019.[7] The resulting statement, the Beijing consensus,[8] was followed up by numerous NGO initiatives to support governments toward policy for responsible use of AI in education. Examples are the *OECD Digital Education Outlook 2021: Pushing the frontiers with AI, Blockchain and robots*[9] and the European Commission's *Ethical guidelines on using artificial intelligence (AI) and data in teaching and learning for educators*.[10]

In this chapter, we discuss why AI in education is a special application domain and outline different perspectives on AI in education. We will provide examples of various specific-purpose AI applications used in the educational sector and generic-purpose AI solutions moving into schools (Section 13.2). Next, we will outline ethical guidelines and discuss the social impact of AI in education (Section 13.3), elaborating on initial steps taken in the Beijing consensus and ethical guidelines for AI and data use in education from the European Union. Finally, we describe concrete examples from the Netherlands, where the *Dutch value compass for digital transformation* and the *National Education Lab AI (NOLAI)* serve as an illustration of how a collaborative research-practice center can facilitate proactive ethical discussions and support the responsible use of AI in education (Section 13.4), and conclude (Section 13.5).

13.2 AI IN EDUCATION: A SPECIAL APPLICATION DOMAIN OF AI

It has been argued that AI in education is a special application area of AI.[11] To explain why the use of AI in education is unique, we build on the distinction between the *replacement* and *augmentation* perspectives on the role of AI in education.[12] In many application areas of AI, the replacement perspective is most dominant

[6] Anna Jobin, Marcello Ienca, and Effy Vayena, "The global landscape of AI ethics guidelines" (2019) *Nature Machine Intelligence*, 1: 389.

[7] Fengchun Miao and Wayne Holmes, "International forum on AI and the futures of education, developing competencies for the AI era, December 7–8, 2020: Synthesis Report" (UNESCO, 2021), https://unesdoc.unesco.org/ark:/48223/pf0000377251, accessed August 3, 2023.

[8] UNESCO, "Beijing consensus on artificial intelligence and education – UNESCO Digital Library," https://unesdoc.unesco.org/ark:/48223/pf0000368303, accessed August 4, 2023.

[9] "OECD digital education outlook 2021 – Pushing the frontiers with AI, blockchain, and robots," https://digital-education-outlook.oecd.org/, accessed August 4, 2023.

[10] European Union, "Ethical guidelines on the use of artificial intelligence (AI) and data in teaching and learning for educators – Publications Office of the European Union," https://op.europa.eu/en/publication-detail/-/publication/d81a0d54-5348-11ed-92ed-01aa75ed71a1/language-en, accessed August 4, 2023.

[11] Ryan S. Baker, "Artificial intelligence in education: Bringing it all together" (OECD, 2021), www.oecd-ilibrary.org/education/oecd-digital-education-outlook-2021_f54ea644-en, accessed August 4, 2023; Inge Molenaar, "Personalisation of learning: Towards hybrid human-AI learning technologies" (OECD, 2021), www.oecd-ilibrary.org/education/oecd-digital-education-outlook-2021_2cc25e37-en, accessed August 4, 2023.

[12] R. Luckin and W. Holmes, "Intelligence unleashed: An argument for AI in education" (UCL Knowledge Lab, 2016) Report www.pearson.com/content/dam/corporate/global/pearson-dot-com/files/innovation/Intelligence-Unleashed-Publication.pdf, accessed August 4, 2023.

and considered appropriate. This means that the focus is on replacing human behavior with AI systems. For example, the application of AI in the self-driving car explicitly aims to offload driving from humans to AI. In contrast, AI in education aims to optimize human learning and teaching.[13] It is important to note that humans and artificial intelligence have different strengths.[14] While AI systems are good at quickly analyzing and interpreting large amounts of data, humans excel at social interaction, creativity, and problem-solving. The augmentation perspective strives for a meaningful combination of human and artificial intelligence.

Current AI systems cannot make broad judgments and considerations as humans do: they merely recognize patterns and use those to optimize learning outcomes or mirror human behavior. In addition, the function of education is broader than the development of knowledge and skills; general development, socialization, and human functioning are critical aspects.[15] With a restricted focus on optimizing learning outcomes, there is a considerable risk that these broader education functions will be lost out of sight.[16] Consequently, it is important to ensure that critical processes for human learning and teaching are not offloaded to AI. For example, adaptive learning technologies (ALTs) can take over human regulation, that is, control and monitoring of learning, in optimizing the allocation of problems to learners.[17] Similarly, automated forms of feedback may reduce social interaction between learners and teachers.[18] Hence, it is important to understand how the application of AI in education offloads elements from human learning and teaching.[19]

This notion of offloading can also help us understand the storm that the introduction of ChatGPT has created in educational institutions around the world. Students bypass the intended learning process when they use generative AI for homework. Homework is designed to help students engage in cognitive processing activities to integrate new knowledge into their mental models and develop a more elaborate understanding of the world.[20] Hence, students using generative AI for homework brings considerable risks of offloading and reduced learning. At the same time,

13 Inge Molenaar, "The concept of hybrid human-AI regulation: exemplifying how to support young learners' self-regulated learning" (2022) *Computers and Education: Artificial Intelligence*, 3: 100070.

14 Zeynep Akata et al., "A research agenda for hybrid intelligence: Augmenting human intellect with collaborative, adaptive, responsible, and explainable artificial intelligence" (2020) *Computer*, 53: 18.

15 Gert Biesta, "Risking ourselves in education: Qualification, socialization, and subjectification revisited" (2020) *Educational Theory*, 70: 89.

16 Neil Selwyn, "Should robots replace teachers?: AI and the future of education," 145.

17 Inge Molenaar, Anne Horvers, and Ryan S. Baker, "What can moment-by-moment learning curves tell about students' self-regulated learning?" (2021) *Learning and Instruction*, 72: 101206.

18 Cultuur en Wetenschap Ministerie van Onderwijs, "Inzet van intelligente technologie – Advies – Onderwijsraad" (September 28, 2022), www.onderwijsraad.nl/publicaties/adviezen/2022/09/28/inzet-van-intelligente-technologie, accessed August 4, 2023.

19 Molenaar, "Towards hybrid human-AI learning technologies" (n 1).

20 Jeroen J. G. Van Merriënboer, and Paul A. Kirschner, *Ten Steps to Complex Learning: A Systematic Approach to Four-Component Instructional Design* (Routledge, 2017).

combining generative AI with effective pedagogics may provide new education opportunities.[21] For example, dynamic assessment in combination with collaborative writing, where the students write a paragraph and generative AI writes the next paragraph, can help students develop new writing skills while still ensuring students' conscious processing and engagement with the instructional materials offered and challenging them to make a cognitive effort to learn. Despite these good examples, many questions about implementing AI that augments human learning and teachers remain. Therefore, it is important to understand how AI offloads human learning and teaching. A careful analysis of the pedagogical and didactical arrangements can ensure that we do not offload critical processes for learning or teaching.

13.2.1 *Understanding Offloading in Education*

In order to better analyze how AI is offloading human learning and teaching, two different models can be used.[22] First, the Detect-Diagnose-Act Framework distinguishes three mechanisms underlying the functioning of AI in education (see Figure 13.1). In *detect*, the data that AI uses to understand student learning or teacher teaching are made explicit. The constructs AI analyses to understand the learning or teaching process are outlined in the *diagnosis*. Finally, *act* describes how the diagnostic information is translated into didactic pedagogical action. For example, an ALT for mathematical learning uses the learners' answers to questions as input to diagnose a learner's knowledge of a specific mathematical topic.[23] This insight is used to adjust the difficulty level of problems provided to the learner and to determine how a learner should continue to practice this topic. Below, we provide an example of how this can look like in practice under "Case 1."

From the teaching perspective, the task of adjusting problems to students' individual needs is offloaded to ALT. The technology and the teachers share the task of determining when a learner has reached sufficient mastery. Although these technologies support teachers,[24] it is important to ensure that teachers stay in control. From the learner's perspective, the need to monitor and control learning is reduced as the technology supports learning by adjusting the problem's difficulty, which decreases

[21] Mike Sharples, "Towards social generative AI for education: Theory, practices and ethics" (2023) *Learning: Research and Practice*, 9(2): 159–167.

[22] Molenaar, "Personalisation of learning" (n 11).

[23] Inge Molenaar and Annemarie van Schaik, "A methodology to investigate the usage of educational technologies on tablets in schools," (2017) *Tablets in Schule und Unterricht*.

[24] Carolien A. N. Knoop-van Campen, Alyssa Wise, and Inge Molenaar, "The equalizing effect of teacher dashboards on feedback in K-12 classrooms" (2021) *Interactive Learning Environments*, 31(6): 3447–3463; Anouschka van Leeuwen et al., "How teacher characteristics relate to how teachers use dashboards: Results from two case studies in K-12" (2021) *Journal of Learning Analytics*, 8(2): 6–21.

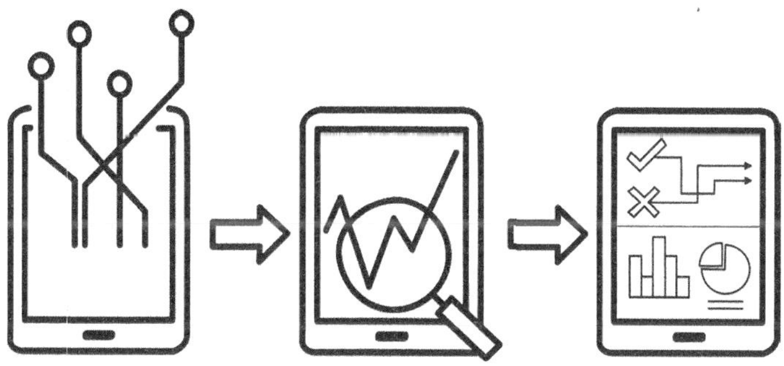

FIGURE 13.1 Detect-Diagnose-Act Framework[25]

the need for learners to self-regulate their learning and may affect the development of these skills.[26]

In this way, the Detect-Diagnose-Act Framework helps analyze offloading by AI, illustrating how particular AI solutions function in educational arrangements. At the same time, this model only describes the AI's roles and largely ignores the roles of learners and teachers. Here *the six levels of the automation model* can be used to understand the division of control between AI, learners, and teachers in education. This model distinguishes six levels of automation in which the degree of control gradually transfers from the teacher to the AI system. The model starts with full teacher control and ends with full automation or AI control (see Figure 13.2). Hence the model goes from no offloading to AI to full offloading.

This model includes elements from the detect-diagnose-act framework. The input lines at the bottom represent detection and data collection in intelligent technologies. The data forms the basis for the AI system to diagnose meaningful constructs for learning and teaching, as described earlier. Hence, more data and different data streams are required for further automation. The diagnostic information is consequently transformed into different pedagogical didactical actions that can be taken in response. The main focus of this model is to make explicit which actors, that is, teachers, learners, or the AI system, perform those actions. This largely determines the position of an educational arrangement with AI on the model.

This model has distinct levels of automation at which AI can execute actions.

First, the AI system can provide information and *describe* student behavior without taking over any control (*teacher assistance level*). The information provided is known

[25] Molenaar, "Personalisation of learning" (n 11).
[26] Molenaar, "The concept of hybrid human-AI regulation" (n 13).

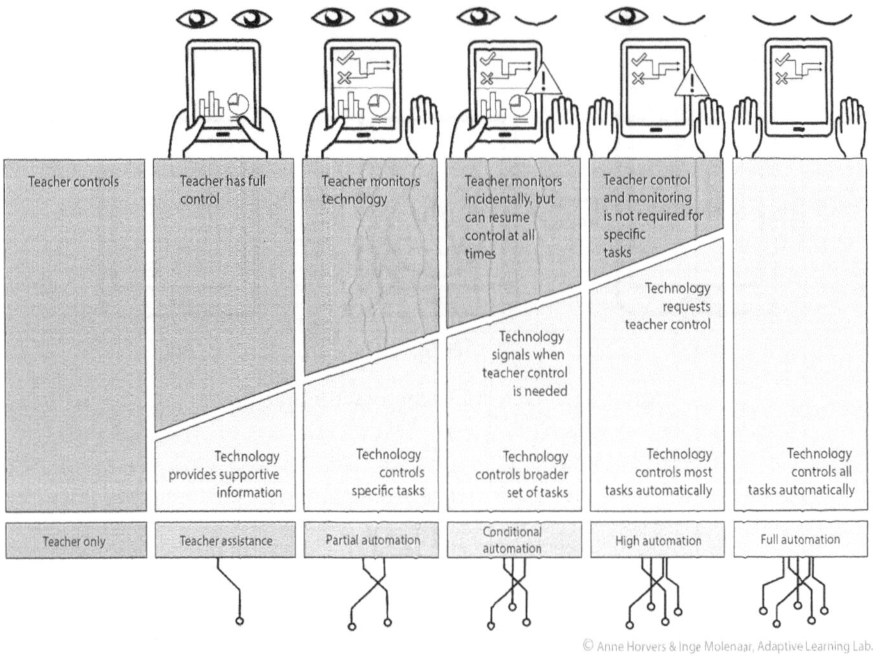

FIGURE 13.2 Six Levels of Automation Model[27]

to impact teacher behavior.[28] It can be communicated in different forms describing, guiding, and even recommending particular actions.[29] Second, the AI system can *enact* simple actions during learning. These actions typically are at three levels: the *step* level providing feedback within a problem, the *task* level adjusting the task to the student's needs, or the *curriculum* level optimizing the order of learning topics. In this *partial automation* level, AI only takes over tasks at one particular level, either enacting step, task, or curriculum adaptivity in interaction with the learner. In Case 1, an example of task adaption is outlined. In *conditional automation*, multiple tasks are taken over by AI, which can be a combination of different levels of adaptivity. With the transition of tasks to the AI system, the importance of the interface between the system and the teacher increases. For teachers to orchestrate the learning scenarios in the classroom, AI must inform the teacher adequately about the actions taken. Hence coordination between AI and humans becomes more critical. In *high automation*, control transfers primarily to AI and teachers step in only for specific tasks. Teacher actions are needed in case AI does not oversee the learning context. Here AI steers learning to a large extent. Finally, in *full automation*, the system autonomously supports learning and teaching without human control.

[27] Molenaar, "Personalisation of learning" (n 11).

[28] Carolien Knoop-Van Campen and Inge Molenaar, "How teachers integrate dashboards into their feedback practices" (2020) *Frontline Learning Research*, 8: 37.

[29] Van Leeuwen et al. (n 24).

This model is functional for describing the augmentation perspective of AI in education, positioning the current role of AI in education, and discussing the future development of the role of AI in education. It can also help foster the discussion about the envisioned role of AI in education, in which it should be made explicit that the goal is not to reach full automation. Successful augmentation requires an ongoing interaction between humans and AI, and the interface between humans and AI is critical.[30] The *Detect-Diagnose-Act Framework* and the *Six Levels of Automation Model* help to understand offloading by AI in specific educational arrangements and analyze the implications of AI in education more broadly. These insights can help teachers and educational professionals understand different applications of AI in the educational domain, allow scientists from different disciplines to compare use cases and discuss implications, and enable companies to position their products in the EdTech market.

CASE 1 Adaptive Learning Technologies

Adaptive Learning Technologies (ALT) and Intelligent Tutoring Systems (ITS) have become increasingly prevalent in European primary and secondary schools. These technologies personalize learning for students in foundational mathematics, grammar, and spelling skills. Using tablets and computers allows rich data on student performance to be captured during practice sessions. For instance, the Snappet technology,[31] widely used in the Netherlands, is typically employed in combination with the pedagogical direct instruction model. In this approach, the teacher activates prior knowledge through examples and explains today's learning goal to the students. Smartboard materials support this direct instruction phase, and students work on adaptively selected problems during the individual practice phase. This practice is tailored to the needs of each student, with the technology providing direct feedback during the process. Teacher-facing dashboards give educators the information they need to make informed decisions about providing feedback and additional instruction. They can also optimize the balance between digital and face-to-face lesson components.

The current generation of ALTs uses data on student performance to adapt problems to learners' predicted knowledge levels and to provide additional information on their progress in teachers' dashboards. These technologies enable more efficient teaching of foundational skills, and free time to focus on more complex problem-solving, self-regulation, and creativity. Adaptive learning technologies offer advantages, including advanced personalization of practice materials tailored to each

[30] Akata et al. (n 14).
[31] "Homepage" (*Snappet*), https://snappet.nl/, accessed August 4, 2023.

student's needs and the ability for teachers to devote more time to tasks beyond the reach of technology, such as providing elaborate feedback or helping students who need additional instruction. This case represents an example of partial automation, in which the teacher and the ALT work closely together. The functions of the ALT are to describe, diagnose, and advise the teacher through the dashboards based on ongoing student activities and, in specific cases, to select student problems. Teachers continue to control most organizational tasks in this learning scenario and remain responsible for monitoring the functioning of the technology, in which teacher dashboards play an important role. ALTs are one example of AI in education, below we provide an overview applications.

13.2.2 *Applications of AI in Education*

Generally, applications of AI in education can be divided into student-faced, teacher-faced, and administrative AI solutions, depending on the actor/stakeholder they support.[32] Below the most commonly used AI systems of each type are shortly outlined.

13.2.2.1 Student-Facing AI in Education

AI for learners is directed at human learners to support learning and make it more efficient, effective, or enjoyable. A large range of ALTs and intelligent tutor systems (ITS) adjusts to the needs of individual learners.[33] These technologies mostly show three levels of adaptivity: step, task, and curriculum adaptivity. In step adaptivity, the learner receives feedback or support within a particular learning task, for example, elaborative feedback on a mistake made in solving math equations providing automatic formative assessment. Task adaptivity aims to give students a task that fits their progress or interest. For example, when a learner is making progress, the next problem selected can be more difficult than when a learner is not making progress. Finally, curriculum adaptivity is directed at supporting learners' trajectories and selecting fitting next learning goals or topics to address. Intelligent Tutoring Systems often combine multiple levels of adaptivity[34] and have been shown to improve students' learning.[35] Most adaptive technologies focus on analyzing students' knowledge; these systems often do not measure other important learning constructs such as self-regulated learning, motivation, and emotion. Case 2 provides an example of how to develop systems that also consider these broader learning characteristics. New developments are chatbots for learning with a more dialogic character, dialogue-based

[32] Holmes and Tuomi (n 1).

[33] Vincent Aleven et al., "Instruction based on adaptive learning technologies" (2016) *Handbook of Research on Learning and Instruction*.

[34] Kurt VanLehn, "The relative effectiveness of human tutoring, intelligent tutoring systems, and other tutoring systems" (2011) *Educational Psychologist*, 46: 197.

[35] James A. Kulik and J. D. Fletcher, "Effectiveness of intelligent tutoring systems: A meta-analytic review" (2016) *Review of Educational Research*, 86: 42.

tutoring systems, exploratory learning environments with games, learning network orchestrators, simulations, and virtual reality.[36]

13.2.2.2 Teacher-Facing AI in Education

Teacher-facing AI applications are mostly systems that help teachers to optimize their instruction methods. The best-known solutions are teacher dashboards that have been shown to impact teacher feedback practices during lessons. Teachers provide different feedback,[37] allocate it to different students,[38] and reduce inequality.[39] Classroom orchestration can also help teachers when teaching classes to make changes based on how students respond to their teaching.[40] Automatic summative assessment systems directly assess students' work. More recently, double-teaching solutions and teaching assistants have provided teachers with instructional support in their classrooms.[41] Finally, classroom monitoring systems[42] and plagiarism detection are helping teachers ensure academic integrity and maintain a fair learning environment in their classrooms.

13.2.2.3 Administrative AI in Education

Administrative AI solutions are directed at helping schools to enact education in an efficient matter. Here, AI is used for administrative purposes such as financial planning, course planning, and making schedules.[43] Quality control is another application that uses predictive analytics of how students develop, both for admission and to identify at-risk students.[44] Finally, e-proctoring monitors students during exams.[45]

36 Holmes and Tuomi (n 1).

37 I. Molenaar and C. Knoop-van Campen, "How teachers make dashboard information actionable" (2018) *IEEE Transactions on Learning Technologies*.

38 Knoop-Van Campen and Molenaar (n 28).

39 Kenneth Holstein et al., "The classroom as a dashboard: Co-designing wearable cognitive augmentation for K-12 teachers," *ACM International Conference Proceeding Series* (2018), https://dl.acm.org/doi/abs/10.1145/3170358.3170377?casa_token=dn-UmbWKvosAAAAA:mfruhjvvLGSfKtF5fZUUd5km5WypTmZAPsLE2vXLt4CXTWtMyYMl-TvebU-POtCQsJe_x1Vjh8c, accessed March 3, 2020.

40 Pierre Dillenbourg, "Classroom analytics: Zooming out from a pupil to a classroom" (OECD, 2021), www.oecd-ilibrary.org/education/oecd-digital-education-outlook-2021_336f4ebf-en, accessed August 4, 2023.

41 Alex Guilherme, "AI and education: The importance of teacher and student relations" (2019) *AI and Society*, 34: 47.

42 Qui X. Lieu, Dieu T. T. Do, and Jaehong Lee, "An adaptive hybrid evolutionary firefly algorithm for shape and size optimization of truss structures with frequency constraints" (2018) *Computers & Structures*, 195: 99.

43 Kirsty Kitto et al., "Towards skills-based curriculum analytics: Can we automate the recognition of prior learning?," *ACM International Conference Proceeding Series* (Association for Computing Machinery, 2020).

44 Alex J. Bowers, "Early warning systems and indicators of dropping out of upper secondary school: The emerging role of digital technologies" (OECD, 2021), www.oecd-ilibrary.org/education/oecd-digital-education-outlook-2021_c8e57e15-en, accessed August 4, 2023.

45 Aditya Nigam et al., "A systematic review on AI-based proctoring systems: Past, present and future" (2021) *Education and Information Technologies*, 26: 6421.

CASE 2 Student-Facing Dashboards for Self-Regulated Learning

Recent advancements in learning technologies have expanded the focus of personalized education beyond learner knowledge and skills to include self-regulated learning, metacognitive skills, monitoring and controlling learning activities, motivation, and emotion. Research shows that self-regulated learning, motivation, and emotion play a vital role in learning. Incorporating self-regulated learning in personalized education can improve current and future learning outcomes.

The Learning Path App[46] is an example of this development. The app uses ALT's log data to detect self-regulated learning processes during learning. The moment-by-moment learning algorithm was developed to visualize the probability that a learner has learned a specific skill at a specific time. The algorithm provides insight to learners on how accurately they worked (monitoring) and when they need to adjust their approach (control). Personalized dashboards were developed for students to provide feedback, changing the role of learner-facing dashboards from discussing *what* learners learned to also incorporating *how* learners learned.

Results indicate that learners with access to dashboards improved control and monitoring of learning and achieved higher learning outcomes and monitoring accuracy. Widening the indicators that are tracked and increasing the scope of diagnosis can further personalize learning and advance our ability to accurately understand a learner's current state and improve the prediction of future development. This supports better approaches toward the personalization of learning that incorporate more diverse learner characteristics and a better understanding of the learner's environment.[47]

The above-illustrated perspectives on the use of AI in education offers insights into how AI can offload human learning, how that affects the roles of teachers and learners and which different AI solutions exist. Still, many challenges and questions remain, and many initiatives have been taken to steer the development of AI in education in a desirable direction. The next section will reflect on those policy, governance, and ethical initiatives, starting with a cursory view of the AI ethics discourse developed over the past decade. We then concentrate on the specific realm of education, discussing major ethical frameworks chronologically. The section concludes with a closer look at the Netherlands' pioneering role in addressing the ethical dimensions of digital applications in education.

46 "Leerpaden – Apps op Google Play," https://play.google.com/store/apps/details?id=com.leerpaden.rickdijkstra.iprogress20&hl=nl, accessed August 4, 2023.

47 S. H. E. Dijkstra, M. Hinne, E. Segers, & I. Molenaar. "Clustering children's learning behaviour to identify self-regulated learning support needs" (2023) *Computers in Human Behavior*, 145, 107754.

13.3 TOWARD THE DEVELOPMENT OF RESPONSIBLE AI FOR EDUCATION

13.3.1 *Overview of AI Ethics Frameworks*

The mid-2010s saw a surge in AI ethics discussions, spurred by rapid advances in deep learning and growing controversies surrounding the technology's implications. More specifically, the years between 2016 and 2019 have seen the proliferation of AI ethics guidelines issued by technology companies, NGOs, think tanks, international organizations, and research institutions.[48] Jobin et al.[49] analyzed 84 published sets of ethical principles for AI, which they concluded converged on five areas: transparency, justice and fairness, non-maleficence, responsibility, and privacy. Similarly, a comparative analysis by Fjeld et al.[50] identified an emerging normative core comprised of 8 key themes: privacy, accountability, safety and security, transparency and explainability, fairness and nondiscrimination, human control of technology, professional responsibility, and the promotion of human values. While this convergence may be seen as a sign of maturation and a key step for the development of binding rules and laws, a review by Blair Attard-Frost et al.[51] revealed a disproportionate emphasis on principles intended for the governance of algorithms and technologies and little attention to the ethics of business practices and the political economies within which AI technologies are embedded. These latter aspects are of key importance in the context of education, given that the adoption of AI in schools can accelerate the commodification of education and further embed large private tech companies into the provision of public goods.[52]

In recent years the AI ethics discussion gradually moved from the enumeration of key values toward efforts to translate abstract principles into real-world practices. However, this is wrought with several difficulties, and the field is currently exploring various approaches.[53] For example, at the time of writing, the OECD's Policy Observatory catalogues[54] over 500 procedural, educational, and technical tools intended to support trustworthy and responsible AI development. However, there is currently little evidence about this uptake and impact. A 2021 review of AI

[48] "AI ethics guidelines global inventory by AlgorithmWatch" (*AI Ethics Guidelines Global Inventory*), https://inventory.algorithmwatch.org, accessed August 4, 2023.

[49] Jobin, Ienca, and Vayena (n 6).

[50] Jessica Fjeld et al., "Principled artificial intelligence: Mapping consensus in ethical and rights-based approaches to principles for AI" (2020) *SSRN Electronic Journal*, https://papers.ssrn.com/abstract=3518482, accessed August 3, 2023.

[51] Blair Attard-Frost et al., "The ethics of AI business practices: a review of 47 AI ethics guidelines" (2023) *AI and Ethics*, 3: 2.

[52] Niels Kerssens and José van Dijck, "The platformization of primary education in the Netherlands" (2021) *Learning, Media and Technology*, 46: 250.

[53] Jessica Morley et al., "From what to how: An initial review of publicly available AI ethics tools, methods and research to translate principles into practices" (2020) *Science and Engineering Ethics*, 26: 2141.

[54] "OECD AI policy observatory," https://oecd.ai/fr/, accessed August 4, 2023.

impact assessments and audits concluded that most approaches suffered from a lack of stakeholder participation, failed to utilize the full range of possible techniques and that internal self-assessment methods exhibited scarce external verification or transparency mechanisms.[55]

Finally, in addition to developments in AI ethics, there has been increasing regulatory attention in several jurisdictions, including the EU,[56] the UK,[57] the United States,[58] and China, along with calls for international harmonization. The European Union adopted the world's first comprehensive regulation, the AI Act, in July 2024, which enshrines several previously voluntary ethical principles into law. As a result, schools will need to implement a comprehensive AI governance strategy to adequately deal with transparency, data protection and risk assessment requirements. The law also classifies certain uses of AI in education as high risk, including systems that determine access to educational institutions, determine the appropriate education level for students, evaluate learning outcomes, or monitor students for prohibited behaviour during tests. These use-cases are subject to additional regulatory requirements.[59]

Still, AI represents a uniquely difficult technology for lawmakers to regulate.[60] Given the pace, potential scale, and complexity of AI's societal impacts, ethical frameworks, guidelines, and tools for responsible technology development will likely continue to evolve alongside regulatory efforts.

13.3.2 *Ethics of AI in Education*

When AI is applied in the domain of education, it may substitute, augment, modify, or redefine existing educational practices.[61] Consequently, the ethics of AI in education should not just be based on an ethics of AI, but also based on an ethics of

55 Jacqui Ayling and Adriane Chapman, "Putting AI ethics to work: Are the tools fit for purpose?" (2021) *AI and Ethics*, 2(3): 405.

56 Proposal for a Regulation of the European Parliament and of the Council Laying Down Harmonised Rules on Artificial Intelligence (Artificial Intelligence Act) and Amending Certain Union Legislative Acts 2021.

57 "A pro-innovation approach to AI regulation" (*GOV.UK*), www.gov.uk/government/publications/ai-regulation-a-pro-innovation-approach/white-paper, accessed August 4, 2023.

58 "Oversight of A.I.: Rules for artificial intelligence" (2023) U.S. Senate Committee on the Judiciary, www.judiciary.senate.gov/committee-activity/hearings/oversight-of-ai-rules-for-artificial-intelligence, accessed August 4, 2023.

59 Clara Hawking, "The EU AI Act, for Schools" (2024) LinkedIn https://media.licdn.com/dms/document/media/D4D1FAQHbIET4k7CRKA/feedshare-document-pdf-analyzed/0/1721386685072?e=1723680000&v=beta&t=mMr1FocvwoqiptNP-rjrOm5888BbHeZ8fvUAfOVaXBQ, accessed August 2, 2024.

60 Richard Wheeler and Fiona Carroll, "An explainable AI solution: Exploring extended reality as a way to make artificial intelligence more transparent and trustworthy" (2023) *Springer Proceedings in Complexity* 255.

61 Erica R. Hamilton, Joshua M. Rosenberg and Mete Akcaoglu, "The Substitution Augmentation Modification Redefinition (SAMR) Model: A critical review and suggestions for its use" (2016) *TechTrends* 60.

education.[62] Aiken and Epstein set the stage for ethics in AI education back in 2000. They advocated for focusing on human needs rather than letting technology dictate decisions.[63] They considered a multidimensional view of humans, looking at ethical, social, intellectual, and other aspects. This laid the groundwork for today's human-centered AI ethos.[64] Aiken and Epstein's guidelines emphasized positive, adaptive AI that supported diverse learning approaches and cultures, respected teachers and underscored the human role in education. However, principles we commonly see in AI ethics guidelines today, such as transparency, explainability, and avoiding bias, are notably absent, as these emerged later due to the rise of data-driven deep learning systems. Despite the changes in AI technologies, Aiken and Epstein's principles still remind us to prioritize human-centered educational values in AI development and align well with the augmentation perspective on AI in education.

13.3.2.1 Framework of the Institute for Ethical AI in Education

Discussions about the ethics of AI in education were further galvanized in the late 2010s as part of the broader engagement with the risks and opportunities of machine learning systems. The Institute for Ethical AI in Education in the UK developed a framework[65] iteratively based on extensive consultations with stakeholders, including policymakers, academics, philosophers and ethicists, industry experts, educators, and young people. The framework acknowledges the necessity of wider educational reform to ensure that AI can benefit all learners while expressing the hope that AI might help *"combat many of the deep-rooted problems facing education systems and learners themselves: from a narrow and shallow curriculum to entrenched social immobility. AI could allow societies to move away from an outdated assessment system, and it could also enable high-quality, affordable lifelong learning to become universally available."* (The Institute for Ethical AI in Education, 2021: 4)[66]

The framework recognized the power of public institutions in setting high-quality standards for product development and was therefore intended for those making procurement and application decisions related to AI systems in education. The framework advanced nine overall objectives that AI systems must adhere to: AI in education should focus on achieving well-defined educational goals beneficial to learners, support the assessment of a broader range of talents, and increase organizational capacity while respecting human relationships. It should promote equity and learner autonomy and

[62] Holmes and Tuomi (n 1).

[63] Robert M. Aiken and Richard G. Epstein, "Ethical guidelines for AI in education: Starting a conversation" (2000) *International Journal of Artificial Intelligence in Education*, 11: 163.

[64] Ben Shneiderman, "Human-centered AI" (2022) Human-centered AI 1; Raphael Koster et al., "Human-centred mechanism design with democratic AI" (2022) *Nature Human Behaviour*, 6(10):1398.

[65] "The institute for ethical AI in education" (*University of Buckingham*), www.buckingham.ac.uk/research/research-in-applied-computing/the-institute-for-ethical-ai-in-education/, accessed August 4, 2023.

[66] Ibid.

uphold privacy. Human oversight and accountability must be maintained, educators and learners should understand AI implications, and ethical design principles should be followed by those creating AI resources. Many of these principles track broader values articulated in AI ethics guidelines – such as autonomy, privacy, and transparency – but we also find education-specific values. These high-level objectives were further specified into a list of criteria and a checklist of concrete questions to guide pre-procurement, procurement, implementation, and monitoring and evaluation phases.[67]

13.3.2.2 The UNESCO 2019 Beijing Consensus

At a global level, UNESCO's 2019 Beijing Consensus[68,69] was a major accomplishment toward defining the requirements for the sustainable development of educational AI technologies. The drafting committee consisted of selected members from the electoral world districts who were invited to focus on the 2030 agenda for sustainable development with specific attention to Sustainable Development Goal 4 to ensure high-quality education for all learners. In different sessions, a broad range of topics around AI and education were discussed: from AI for learning to learning in an AI era, as well as societal consequences and labor market impacts. It was also explicitly recognized that demands differ depending on the broader socioeconomic characteristics of member countries.

The Beijing Consensus emphasized the utilization and scaling of intelligent ALTs for foundational skills, such as math and language learning, while highlighting the need for developing unique human competencies such as problem-solving, creativity, and the regulation of learning processes in an AI era. Ensuring teacher professional development and using formative assessment was crucial for effective AI implementation, and governments were encouraged to harness AI for optimizing educational policies and understanding system effectiveness. The consensus accentuates the importance of lifelong learning, AI literacy skills, and inclusivity for all demographics. Ethical considerations were emphasized as important and included equitable and inclusive use of AI, addressing the needs of vulnerable groups such as minorities and students with learning impairments or disabilities. The consensus also highlighted the importance of ensuring gender equity and maintaining auditable transparency in data use. Finally, attention was also placed on evidence-based AI applications and establishing novel regulatory frameworks.

Overall, there was a strong agreement on the human-centred approach to AI in education, whereby teachers were considered the central focus, and AI

[67] Ibid.

[68] "Beijing consensus on artificial intelligence and education – UNESCO digital library" (n 8); F. Miao and W. Holmes, "Artificial intelligence and education. Guidance for policy-makers" (United Nations Educational, Scientific and Cultural Organization (UNESCO) 2021) Report, https://unesdoc.unesco.org/ark:/48223/pf0000376709, accessed August 4, 2023.

[69] Author Inge Molenaar was a member of the expert panel that produced the Beijing Consensus.

in education should always be human-controlled. Following up on the Beijing Consensus, UNESCO issued guidance on AI and education intended for policymakers to support the achievement of SDG4 to "ensure inclusive and equitable quality education and promote lifelong learning opportunities for all".[70] The document reaffirmed the principles of the Beijing Consensus. It emphasized that for AI to be best exploited for the common good, it should be used to reimagine teaching and learning rather than just automating often outmoded existing practices. This involves adopting a system-wide vision for AI in education that puts teachers and learners in the center. Importantly, the document recognized that getting AI right in the context of education requires an integrated approach that involves interdisciplinary planning, fostering ethical and inclusive AI use, developing a comprehensive plan for AI in educational management and teaching, conducting pilot testing and evaluations, and encouraging local AI innovations in the field of education.[71]

13.3.2.3 European Commission's Ethical Guidelines on the Use of AI and Data in Teaching and Learning for Educators

The European Union is one of the main actors in the discussion around AI ethics, governance, and regulation. This started with the European Commission's establishment of a High-Level Expert Group on AI in 2018, which drafted a set of Ethics Guidelines with seven key requirements for trustworthy AI: human agency and oversight, transparency, diversity, nondiscrimination and fairness, societal and environmental well-being, privacy and data governance, technical robustness and safety, and accountability.[72] The European Commission's Digital Education Action Plan[73] specifically describes the development of "ethical guidelines on the use of AI and data in teaching and learning for educators" (in priority 1, action 6). To achieve this action, it set up a European Expert Group for this specific purpose, resulting in guidelines on the use of AI and data in teaching and learning for educators, published in 2022.[74,75]

[70] F. Miao and W. Holmes, "Artificial intelligence and education. Guidance for policy-makers" (United Nations Educational, Scientific and Cultural Organization (UNESCO) 2021) Report, https://unesdoc.unesco.org/ark:/48223/pf0000376709, accessed August 4, 2023, page 5. See also Beijing consensus on artificial intelligence and education – UNESCO digital library (n 8).

[71] Miao and Holmes (n 70).

[72] "Ethics guidelines for trustworthy AI | Shaping Europe's digital future" (April 8, 2019), https://digital-strategy.ec.europa.eu/en/library/ethics-guidelines-trustworthy-ai, accessed August 4, 2023; Nathalie A. Smuha, "The EU approach to ethics guidelines for trustworthy artificial intelligence" (2019) *Computer Law Review International*, 20: 97.

[73] "Digital education action plan (2021–2027) | European education area," https://education.ec.europa.eu/focus-topics/digital-education/action-plan, accessed August 3, 2023.

[74] "Ethical guidelines on the use of artificial intelligence (AI) and data in teaching and learning for educators – Publications office of the EU" (n 10).

[75] Authors Inge Molenaar and Duuk Baten were involved as invited members of the European Expert Group.

The guidelines consist of four main elements: a description of the EU policy and regulatory context, examples of AI and data use in education, ethical considerations and requirements, and guidance for teachers and school leaders. The background report specifically mentions how the ethics of AI and the ethics of education are deeply related and highlights the importance of interpreting the ethical dilemmas and challenges of AI in education in the context of educational practices.[76] The guidelines are based on Biesta's three key objectives of education: qualification, socialization, and subjectification.[77] From an ethical perspective, the guidelines focus on four interrelated dimensions of ethics: *human agency*, *fairness*, *humanity*, and *justified choice*. These are seen as guiding the choices around using AI systems in education.[78]

The guidelines also have a strong basis in the requirements set by the European Commission's High-Level Expert Group on AI, and rearticulate the abovementioned seven key requirements for trustworthy AI in the context of education. Using these requirements as a scaffolding, the document offers guiding questions for schools and educators as a starting point for reflection and constructive dialogue among various stakeholders about using AI systems in educational practices. In line with this, the guidelines describe the competencies necessary to successfully implement and use AI systems in education. The existing European Framework for the Digital Competence of Educators (DigCompEdu)[79] provides a basis for developing the integral skills and capacities necessary within the educational system.

A critical note here would be to wonder whether educators and schools are equipped to ask and answer these questions, some of which require extensive technical understanding as well as access to elaborate system documentation; think of "*Are the appropriate oversight mechanisms in place for data collection, storage, processing, minimisation and use?*" and "*Are there monitoring systems in place to prevent overconfidence in or overreliance on the AI system?*"[80] Dealing with these questions around the application of AI in education is not an easy feat and requires extensive collaboration among educators, schools, and public institutions. This is why the guidelines proposed that schools adequately prepare for the effective use of AI and recommended raising awareness around the challenges. Such reflective action will require additional resources to be committed to supporting schools or new organizations to address these issues together with teachers and schools. Hence, NGOs have raised awareness of the need to implement ethical guidelines and have requested national governments to act accordingly. In the next section, we turn to the example of the Netherlands to show how this can be organized at a national level.

76 Ibid., p.7.

77 Gert J. J. Biesta, "Good education in an age of measurement: Ethics, politics, democracy." 159.

78 "Ethical guidelines on the use of artificial intelligence (AI) and data in teaching and learning for educators – publications office of the EU" (n 10) 18.

79 Ibid., p. 18

80 Ibid., pp. 19–21.

13.4 THE DUTCH EXPERIENCE: A NATIONAL AMBITION TOWARD VALUE-DRIVEN EDUCATIONAL INNOVATION

13.4.1 *The Value Compass for the Digital Transformation of Education*

Within the Netherlands, there has been an increasing discussion of the impact of digital technologies on education. This has been symbolized by a call for action in a national newspaper by the rector magnifici of all Dutch public universities,[81] warning about the influence of large tech corporations on the public educational system and calling for the higher education sector to take responsibility for its public values. This can be seen as the start of a national discussion on prioritizing educational values in public education, which was reflected in a subsequent advisory report on public values in education by the Dutch Association of Universities (UNL).[82] Public values are the values that ground and give meaning to our interactions, societal institutions and political structures.[83] Public values are not fixed, but are the result of continuous societal and political processes.[84] And the public interests they represent are of such importance that they need to be safeguarded within the public sector.[85] The underlying thought is that the digitalization of public services needs to be guided by "fundamental public values such as privacy, autonomy, equity and equality."[86]

As technologies become more pervasive in educational institutions, we see, on the one hand, how these technologies start to shape educational practices and, on the other hand, how the dependency on existing software providers can become problematic. AI applications in education only compound those challenges, raising questions about how the roles of students and teachers change and which new responsibilities emerge for educational institutions.[87] To facilitate navigating the influence of digital technologies in education, Kennisnet,[88] SURF,[89] and the Rathenau Institute[90] developed a Value Compass as a reference framework for public values in education (see Figure 13.3).[91]

81 "Digitalisering bedreigt onze universiteit. Het is tijd om een grens te trekken" (*de Volkskrant*, December 22, 2019), www.volkskrant.nl/columns-opinie/digitalisering-bedreigt-onze-universiteit-het-is-tijd-om-een-grens-te-trekken~bff87dc9/, accessed August 6, 2023.

82 "Advisory report on public values in education," www.universiteitenvannederland.nl/files/documenten/Advisory%20report%20on%20public%20values%20in%20education_EN_vnov22.pdf, accessed August 4, 2023.

83 "Value lines" (iHub Radboud University) https://ihub.ru.nl/valuelines/, accessed August 2, 2024.

84 José Van Dijck, Thomas Poell, and Martijn De Waal, *De Platformsamenleving: Strijd Om Publieke Waarden in Een Online Wereld* (Amsterdam University Press, 2016).

85 Wat dan weer komt van: WRR (2000). Het borgen van publiek belang. Den Haag: Sdu Uitgevers.

86 Rinie van Est et al., "Valuable digitalisation: How local government can play the 'technology game' in the public's interest."

87 John Walker and Duuk Baten, "Promises of AI in education" (Zenodo, 2022), https://zenodo.org/record/6874315, accessed August 4, 2023.

88 "Laat ict werken voor het onderwijs" (*Kennisnet*, July 4, 2023), www.kennisnet.nl/, accessed August 4, 2023.

89 "SURF is de ict-coöperatie van onderwijs en onderzoek | SURF.nl," www.surf.nl/, accessed August 4, 2023.

90 "Onderzoek en debat over de impact van wetenschap, technologie en innovatie op ons leven | Rathenau Instituut," www.rathenau.nl/nl, accessed August 4, 2023.

91 "Value compass for digital transformation of education," www.surf.nl/files/2022-01/surf-value-compass-english.pdf, accessed August 4, 2023.

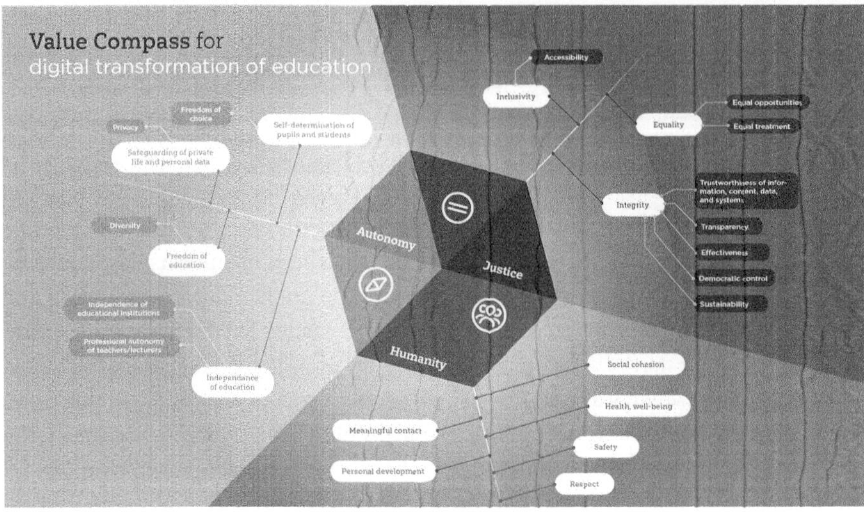

FIGURE 13.3 The value compass[92]

This common language aims to elicit a discussion that transcends functionalities, costs and benefits toward formulating shared ambitions for a future of digital education.

The value compass emphasizes three core values as central to educational practices: autonomy, justice, and humanity. These values are loosely defined as constellations of other values, such as privacy (autonomy), inclusivity (justice), and well-being (humanity). Here autonomy is seen as the ability "to live under your own laws" for diverse educational stakeholders, the students and teachers, and the institutions themselves.[93] Justice is defined as collected values that mainly describe the importance of treating others in terms of themselves and treating them equally in an inclusive manner.[94] The human aspect of education is central to the value of humanity, consisting of the meaningful contact, respect, safety, and well-being necessary to value the unique aspects of each student.[95] The framework was developed through deliberative engagement with sector stakeholders, including a published beta version for public consultation, as can be read in the Rathenau report[96] which describes in more detail how this compass of values was developed. Working from a previous list of seven key themes and questions around the digital transformation of the public sector,[97] the value compass conceptualizes themes such as *power*

92 Ibid., p. 7.
93 Ibid., p. 5.
94 Ibid., p. 6.
95 Ibid., pp. 142–147.
96 "Naar hoogwaardig digitaal onderwijs | Rathenau Instituut," www.rathenau.nl/nl/digitalisering/naar-hoogwaardig-digitaal-onderwijs, accessed August 4, 2023.
97 L. Kool et al., *Urgent Upgrade: Protect Public Values in Our Digitized Society* (Rathenau Instituut, 2017), www.rathenau.nl/en/file/33578/download?token=FA8OpJuY, accessed August 4, 2023.

relations and *control over technology* into values such as autonomy. The three main values of autonomy, justice, and humanity can be seen as equally important, with underlying instrumental values that allow the operationalization of these values.

The Value Compass is not a normative framework for digital transformation but a basis for considering educational values in decision-making.[98] The value compass is used for deliberative workshops, for example, a workshop of SURF with the national student bodies ISO and LSVB on the ethics of using online proctoring in examinations.[99] Here the values in the value compass helped guide the discussion through all relevant perspectives. A more normative approach can be achieved through value hierarchies, where one conceptualizes values into norms and design requirements to guide choices in digital transformation.[100] For example, Kennisnet conceptualized the value of inclusivity for a digital learning system into the norm "accessible for all students," which led to the design requirement of "meets web accessibility requirements." These requirements can then be taken into account within the development or procurement processes. Through a lens of public values, educational institutions can proactively structure the digital transformation by "weighing values," using them as a guide in shaping considerations and priorities.[101] By looking at the design, procurement, and use of new technologies through the lens of these values, the education sector can become an active participant in the digitalization of education.[102]

13.4.2 *The NOLAI as an Approach to Drive Responsible Use of AI in Education*

To finalize this chapter, we introduce the example of the National Education Lab AI (NOLAI)[103] in the Netherlands, which pursues an embedded ethics approach to iteratively develop, prototype, implement, evaluate and scale responsible AI technologies for primary and secondary education.

NOLAI is an innovative research initiative at the Faculty of Social Sciences of Radboud University in the Netherlands in collaboration with several strategic partners[104] and the Dutch Growth Fund.[105] NOLAI's main goal is to develop intelligent

98 "Value compass for digital transformation of education" (n 91). P.41.

99 "Publieke waarden in de praktijk: met het Ethiekkompas in gesprek over online proctoring | SURF Communities" (April 4, 2022), https://communities.surf.nl/publieke-waarden/artikel/publieke-waarden-in-de-praktijk-met-het-ethiekkompas-in-gesprek-over, accessed August 4, 2023.

100 Ibo Van de Poel, "Translating values into design requirements" (2013) Philosophy and engineering: Reflections on practice, principles and process 253.

101 Kennisnet. (2020). "Weighing values: An ethical perspective on digitalisation in education." Kennisnet (Authors: Pijpers, R., Bomas, E., Dondorp, L., and Ligthart, J.) – www.kennisnet.nl/app/uploads/Kennisnet-Waardenwegen-ENG.pdf, accessed August 4, 2023.

102 "Value compass for digital transformation of education" (n 91). P.3.

103 "NOLAI | National Education Lab AI," www.ru.nl/en/nolai, accessed August 4, 2023.

104 www.nolai.nl

105 Ministerie van Economische Zaken en Klimaat, "Home – Nationaal Groeifonds" (June 30, 2023), www.nationaalgroeifonds.nl/, accessed August 4, 2023.

technologies that improve the quality of primary and secondary education. The institute aims to achieve this goal by developing innovative prototypes that use AI and promoting the responsible use of AI in education. This is done in two programs: the co-creation program and the scientific program. The co-creation program develops innovative prototypes and applications of AI in co-creation with schools, scientists, and businesses. The scientific program develops knowledge in five focus areas: teacher professionalization, technology for AI in education, sustainable data, pedagogy & didactics and embedded ethics.

NOLAI's main activities are developing state-of-the-art applications of AI in education and investigating their use NOLAI's activities start with dialogues with schools to explore their needs for using AI to improve education and literature reviews that, map current knowledge. After, NOLAI brings scientists and educational practitioners together to develop AI prototypes, explore current applications of AI technologies and ambitions for the future with businesses. An example of a co-creation project by NOLAI is the visualization of student data collected across different learning management, ALTs, and summative assessment systems. This project is a collaboration between three schools, an ALT company, an assessment company, and pedagogical and AI scientists. The collaborative and interdisciplinary approach ensures the connection between educational practice, science, and business development.

NOLAI stimulates the responsible development of AI in education. NOLAI has a dedicated Data and Privacy Officer who helps the co-creation projects comply with relevant privacy and data protection regulations. Also, all projects need approval from institutional ethical committees that monitor the ethical conduct of the research being conducted. In addition, as there are many open questions about the ethical issues that will emerge throughout the development and implementation of AI in education, NOLAI strives to further the discussions around the responsible use of AI in education in the Netherlands with its embedded ethics approach.

Embedded ethics approaches have most famously been developed in computer science education, where it is referred to as an approach for teaching ethics in computer science curricula and aims to incorporate ethics into the entire engineering process in an integrated, interdisciplinary, and collaborative way.[106] As such, embedded ethics is aptly seen as an ongoing process of anticipating, identifying, and addressing ethical features of technological innovations by helping developers to integrate ethical awareness and critical reasoning in their technical projects, thereby benefitting individuals and society at large.[107]

The embedded ethics approach developed within NOLAI complements such existing approaches with for example, insights from the "ethics parallel research"

[106] Hannah Bleher and Matthias Braun, "Reflections on putting AI ethics into practice: How three AI ethics approaches conceptualize theory and practice" (2023) *Science and Engineering Ethics*, 29.

[107] Daniel W. Tigard and others, "Toward best practices in embedded ethics: Suggestions for interdisciplinary technology development" (2023) *Robotics and Autonomous Systems*, 167: 104467.

approach that has been developed to provide ethical guidance parallel to the development process of emerging biomedical innovations.[108] This last approach has many similarities with the embedded ethics approaches as it can also be characterized by focusing on bottom-up, inductive ethical dilemmas and stimulating ethical reflexivity and awareness. An important difference is that the ethics parallel research approach argues for the inclusion of a wider variety of stakeholders in the deliberation process (beyond engineers and ethicists) and is less focused on the design of technology but also its broader sociopolitical implications.

This means that for the embedded ethics approach within NOLAI, ethicists will closely collaborate with various stakeholders in co-creation projects, including technologists, company representatives, scientists, and educational professionals. As the co-creation projects develop and mature, the ethicists aim to provide ethical support and develop sustainable processes to advance responsible innovation, navigating the "messy" reality of the co-creation projects and the ethical questions, complex dilemmas, and practices that emerge. This means they will advise stakeholders and support them with anticipating, identifying, and addressing moral dilemmas iteratively and continuously.

In addition to ethical literature and theory, ethicists within NOLAI will conduct empirical research within the co-creation projects to inform and advance their ethical support. Through various qualitative research studies, including participant observations, focus groups, and surveys, the ethicists will study the effects and implications of introducing AI systems in education. For example, they will study students' and teachers' moral beliefs, intuitions, and reasoning using AI systems within NOLAI. These findings can help align the AI systems with students' and teachers' needs and wishes. In another study, ethicists will use qualitative research methods to explore value conflicts that emerge when AI systems are introduced in classrooms and how these conflicting values are balanced in practice. The findings help formulate "best practices" regarding implementing AI systems in education.

As a last step, the ethicists within NOLAI will use the insights gained from their participation in the co-creation projects and the results of their empirical studies to inform more abstract ethical debates about AI in education. The diversity and large amounts of co-creation within NOLAI provide an exceptional opportunity to help answer complex ethics questions outlined in this chapter.

13.5 CONCLUSION

In this chapter, we explained that education is a special application domain of AI that optimizes human learning and teaching. The replacement and augmentation perspectives were contrasted, and we emphasized the importance of human

[108] Karin R. Jongsma and Annelien L. Bredenoord, "Ethics Parallel Research: An Approach for (Early) Ethical Guidance of Biomedical Innovation" (2020) *BMC Medical Ethics*, 21.

learners and teachers staying in control over AI. We outlined a variety of AI applications used in education, covering student-faced, teacher-faced, and administrative-oriented systems. AI in education is about carefully designing learning and teaching in a way that technologies augment human learning. As we have recently witnessed the increasing presence of generative AI, developments outside educators' control raise questions and impact the educational system.[109]

Subsequently, we discussed the ethical and social impacts of AI in education. We outlined how ethics in AI and education developed, describing general AI ethics developments, the Beijing consensus based on UNESCO's conference on AI in Education in 2019, and the recent European Commission's ethical guidelines on the use of AI and data in teaching and learning for educators. Finally, we outlined the example of the Netherlands with the Dutch value compass and the embedded ethics approach of NOLAI, as concrete illustrations of how AI ethics can be embedded in the educational context.

One of the central distinguishing features of ethical frameworks for AI in education has been to prioritize decision-making aligned with ethical values and sound pedagogical objectives. This call has been echoed in numerous frameworks ever since Aiken and Epstein[110] first put AI and education on the agenda, and has been reaffirmed by UNESCO's and the EU's guidelines. Efforts to combine pedagogical and didactical values with generic ethical values in a way that ensures a sound approach to ethics in education are still in their infancy. This also requires the understanding and navigation of potential misalignments in interests between stakeholders, including students, parents, teachers, schools, companies, and policymakers.[111] As Selwyn[112] notes, the ethics of AI is not a clear-cut case of solving technological challenges or doing the right thing intuitively but requires an ongoing, morally reflective process.[113]

[109] Walker and Baten (n 87).

[110] Aiken and Epstein (n 63).

[111] Miao and Holmes (n 70); Wayne Holmes and Kaska Porayska-Pomsta, *The Ethics of Artificial Intelligence in Education : Practices, Challenges, and Debates*, www.routledge.com/The-Ethics-of-Artificial-Intelligence-in-Education-Practices-Challenges/Holmes-Porayska-Pomsta/p/book/9780367349721, accessed August 3, 2023.

[112] Neil Selwyn, "AI, education and ethics – starting a conversation."

[113] Holmes and Porayska-Pomsta (n 111).

14

Artificial Intelligence and Media*

Lidia Dutkiewicz, Noémie Krack, Aleksandra Kuczerawy, and Peggy Valcke

14.1 INTRODUCTION

Media companies can benefit from artificial intelligence (AI)[1] technologies to increase productivity and explore new possibilities for producing, distributing, and reusing content. This chapter demonstrates the potential of the use of AI in media.[2] It takes a selective approach to showcase a variety of applications in the following areas: Can ChatGPT write news articles? How can media organizations use AI to recommend public interest content? Can AI spot disinformation and instead promote *trustworthy* news? These are just a few opportunities offered by AI at the different stages of news content production, distribution, and reuse (Section 14.2). However, the use of AI in media also brings societal and ethical risks, as well as legal challenges. The right to freedom of expression, media pluralism and media freedom, the right to nondiscrimination, and the right to data protection are among the affected rights. This chapter will therefore also show how the EU legal framework (e.g., the Digital Services Act,[3] the AI Act,[4] and the European Media Freedom

* This chapter received funding from EU Horizon 2020 programme grants: n° 951962 MediaFutures and n° 951911 AI4Media and from FWO grants: nr. 1214321N and ALGEPI (FWOAL1088).

[1] For the definition of AI, see Chapter 1 of this book.

[2] This chapter takes a narrower understanding of media, focusing on traditional mass media outlets such as news media, public service media, as well as media archives. However, because of the impact which social media algorithmic content moderation practices have on media content distribution and editorial decision-making, they will also be covered in this chapter. For a broad understanding of the use of AI in the audiovisual sector, see, for example, Rehm, "The Use of Artificial Intelligence in the Audiovisual Sector: Concomitant Expertise for INI Report: Research for CULT Committee" (European Parliament, Directorate-General for Internal Policies of the Union), https://data.europa.eu/doi/10.2861/294829.

[3] Regulation (EU) 2022/2065 of the European Parliament and of the Council of October 19, 2022 on a Single Market for Digital Services and amending Directive 2000/31/EC (Digital Services Act) 2022 (OJ L 277/1).

[4] Regulation (EU) 2024/1689 of the European Parliament and of the Council of 13 June 2024 laying down harmonised rules on artificial intelligence and amending Regulations (EC) No 300/2008, (EU) No 167/2013, (EU) No 168/2013, (EU) 2018/858, (EU) 2018/1139 and (EU) 2019/2144 and Directives 2014/90/EU, (EU) 2016/797 and (EU) 2020/1828 (Artificial Intelligence Act) 2024 (OJ L 2024/1689).

Act[5]) tries to mitigate some of the risks to fundamental rights posed by the development and the use of AI in media (Section 14.3). Section 14.4 offers conclusions.

14.2 OPPORTUNITIES OF AI APPLICATIONS IN MEDIA[6]

14.2.1 *AI in Media Content Gathering and Production*

Beckett's survey of journalism and AI presents an impressive list of possible AI uses in day-to-day journalistic practice.[7] At the beginning of the news-creating process, AI can help gather material, sift through social media, recognize genders and ages in images, or automatically add tags for newspaper articles with topics or keywords.[8]

AI is also used in story discovery to identify trends or spot stories that could otherwise be hard to grasp by the human eye and to discover new angles, voices, and content. To illustrate, already in 2014, Reuters News Tracer project used natural language processing techniques to decide which topics are *newsworthy*.[9] It detected the bombing of hospitals in Aleppo and the terror attacks in Nice and Brussels before they were reported by other media.[10] Another tool, the Topics Compass, developed under EU-funded Horizon 2020 ReTV project, allows an editorial team to track media discourse about a given topic coming from news agencies, blogs, and social media platforms and to visualize its popularity.[11]

AI has also been proven useful in investigative journalism to assist journalists in tasks that could not be done by humans alone or would have taken a considerable amount of time. To illustrate, in a cross-border Panama Papers investigation, the International Consortium of Investigative Journalists used an open-source data mining tool to sift through 11.5 million whistleblowers' documents.[12]

Once journalists have gathered information on potential stories, they can use AI for the production of news items: text, images, and videos. Media companies such

5 Regulation (EU) 2024/1083 of the European Parliament and of the Council of 11 April 2024 establishing a common framework for media services in the internal market and amending Directive 2010/13/EU (European Media Freedom Act) 2024 (OJ L 2024/1083).

6 For a broad overview, see, for example, Filareti Tsalakanidou, "AI technologies and applications in media: State of play, foresight, and research directions" (2022) *AI4Media*, www.ai4media.eu/wp-content/uploads/2022/03/AI4Media_D2.3_Roadmap_final.pdf.

7 Beckett, "New powers, new responsibilities. A global survey of journalism and artificial intelligence" (*Blogs LSE*, November 18, 2019), https://blogs.lse.ac.uk/polis/2019/11/18/new-powers-new-responsibilities/, accessed March 18, 2023.

8 Ibid.

9 Stray, "The age of the cyborg" (*Columbia Journalism Review*, November 30, 2016), www.cjr.org/analysis/cyborg_virtual_reality_reuters_tracer.php, accessed March 18, 2023.

10 Ibid.

11 See, for example, ReTV, https://retv-project.eu/news-discourse-monitoring/.

12 Guevara, "How Artificial Intelligence Can Help Us Crack More Panama Papers Stories" (*International Consortium of Investigative Journalists*, March 25, 2019), www.icij.org/inside-icij/2019/03/how-artificial-intelligence-can-help-us-crack-more-panama-papers-stories/, accessed March 18, 2023.

as the Associated Press, *Forbes*, and *The New York Times* have started to automate news content.[13] Terms like *robot journalism, automated journalism*, and *algorithmic journalism* have been used interchangeably to describe this phenomenon.[14] In addition, generative AI tools such as ChatGPT,[15] Midjourney,[16] or DALL-E[17] are being used to illustrate news stories, simplify text for different audiences, summarize documents, or writing potential headlines.[18]

14.2.2 *AI in Media Content Distribution*[19]

Media organizations can also use AI for providing personalized recommendations. Simply put, "recommendation systems are tools designed to sift through the vast quantities of data available online and use algorithms to guide users toward a narrower selection of material, according to a set of criteria chosen by their developers."[20]

In recent years, online news media (e.g., online newspapers' websites and apps) started engaging in *news recommendation* practices.[21] Recommendation systems curate users' news feed by automatically (de)prioritizing items to be displayed in user interfaces, thus deciding which ones are visible (to whom) and in what order.[22]

The 2022 Ada Lovelace report[23] provides an informative in-depth snapshot of the BBC's development and use of recommendation systems, which gives insights into the role of recommendations in public service media (PSM).[24] As pointed out by

[13] Graefe, "Guide to Automated Journalism" (2016) *Columbia Journalism Review* www.cjr.org/tow_center_reports/guide_to_automated_journalism.php.

[14] Although they do not have the same meaning. See, for example, Graefe, Guide to automated journalism, p. 3; Monti, "Automated journalism and freedom of information: Ethical and juridical problems related to AI in the press field" (2018) *Opinion Juris in Comparatione, Studies in Comparative and National law* 1; Dörr, "Mapping the field of algorithmic journalism" (2015) *Digital Journalism*.

[15] See OpenAI, "Introducing ChatGPT," https://openai.com/blog/chatgpt, accessed April 5, 2023.

[16] "Midjourney," www.midjourney.com/home/?callbackUrl=%2Fapp%2F, accessed April 5, 2023.

[17] OpenAI, "DALL-E2," https://openai.com/product/dall-e-2, accessed April 5, 2023.

[18] See also Generative AI in the Newsroom, https://generative-ai-newsroom.com/, accessed April 5, 2023.

[19] This section focuses on recommendation systems. Note that in this chapter, the terms "recommendation systems" and "recommender systems" are used interchangeably. For the broader discussion about AI and media content distribution, see, for example, Carlson, "Order versus access: news search engines and the challenge to traditional journalistic roles" (2007) *Media, Culture & Society*, 29(6): 1014–1030.

[20] Ada Lovelace Institute "Inform, educate, entertain … and recommend? Exploring the use and ethics of recommendation systems in public service media" (2022), www.adalovelaceinstitute.org/report/inform-educate-entertain-recommend/.

[21] Vermeulen "The Algorithmic State of Mind: A Human Rights Frame for Governing News Recommendation" (2022) (Ghent University, Faculty of Law and Criminology).

[22] Ibid.

[23] Ada Lovelace Institute, "*Inform, educate, entertain … and recommend?(…)*," p. 4.

[24] See also PEACH, "Relevant content to the people, crafted by broadcasters for broadcasters. Personalisation and Recommendation Ecosystem for the digital transformation," https://peach.ebu.io/, accessed April 5, 2023.

the authors, developing recommendation systems for PSM requires an interrogation of the organizations' role in democratic societies in the digital age, that is, how to translate the public service values[25] into the objectives for the use of recommendation systems that serve the public interest. The report concludes that the PSM had internalized a set of normative values around recommendation systems: Rather than maximizing engagement, they want to broaden their reach to a more diverse set of audiences.[26] This is a considerable difference between the public and private sectors. Many user-generated content platforms rank information based on how likely a user is to interact with a post (comment on it, like it, reshare it) or to spend more time using the service.[27]

Research shows that social media platforms are using a mix of commercial criteria, but also vague public interest considerations in their content prioritization measures.[28] Importantly, prioritization of some content demotes other.[29] As a way of example, Facebook explicitly says it will not recommend *content that is associated with low-quality publishing*, including news that it is unclear about its provenance.[30] In fact, online platforms use a whole arsenal of techniques to (de)amplify the visibility or reach of some content.[31] To illustrate, in an aftermath of Russian aggression on Ukraine, platforms announced they would *restrict access* to RT and Sputnik media outlets.[32] Others have also been adding labels and started reducing the visibility of content from Russian state-affiliated media websites even before the EU-imposed sanctions.[33]

[25] Public service media organizations are legally mandated to operate with a particular set of public interest values. The EBU has codified the public service mission into six core values: universality, independence, excellence, diversity, accountability, and innovation, and member organizations commit to strive to uphold these in practice. See EBU, "Empowering society, a declaration on the core values of public service media," www.ebu.ch/files/live/sites/ebu/files/Publications/EBU-Empowering-Society_EN.pdf.

[26] Ada Lovelace Institute, "*Inform, educate, entertain … and recommend?(…)*," p. 4.

[27] See, for example, Mosseri, "Shedding More Light on How Instagram Works" AboutInstagram.com (June 8, 2021), https://about.instagram.com/blog/announcements/shedding-more-light-on-how-instagram-works, accessed March 22, 2023.

[28] CMPF-CiTiP-IViR-SMIT, Study on Media Plurality and Diversity Online, CNECT/2020/OP/0099, May 2022, https://digital-strategy.ec.europa.eu/en/library/study-media-plurality-and-diversity-online, accessed April 5.

[29] Keller uses the term "demote" to cover any form of deamplification, including decreasing content's algorithmic ranking or excluding it from features like recommendations. Keller, "Amplification and Its Discontents." *Knight First Amendment Institute at Columbia University* (June 8, 2021), https://knightcolumbia.org/content/amplification-and-its-discontents, accessed March 19, 2023.

[30] Facebook, "What are recommendations on Facebook?" *Facebook Help Center*, www.facebook.com/help/1257205004624246, accessed April 5, 2023.

[31] See, for example, Goldman, "Content Moderation Remedies" (2021) *Mich. Tech. L. Rev.*, 28: 1.

[32] Kayali, "Facebook's Parent Company Restricts EU Access to Russia's RT, Sputnik" *Politico* (February 28, 2022), www.politico.eu/article/facebook-parent-company-restricts-eu-access-to-russia-rt-sputnik/, accessed April 5, 2023.

[33] Culliford "Twitter Will Label, Reduce Visibility of Tweets Linking to Russian State Media" Reuters (February 28, 2022), www.reuters.com/technology/twitter-will-label-reduce-visibility-tweets-linking-russian-state-media-2022-02-28/, accessed January 17, 2023.

Overall, by selecting and (de)prioritizing news content and deciding on its visibility, online platforms take on some of the functions so far reserved to traditional media.[34] Ranking functions and optimization metrics in recommendation systems have become powerful determinants of access to media and news content.[35] This has consequences for both the fundamental right to freedom of expression and media freedom (see Section 14.3).

14.2.3 *AI in Fact-Checking*

Another important AI potential in media is fact-checking. The main elements of automated fact-checking are: (1) identification of false or questionable claims circulating online; (2) verification of such claims, and (3) (real-time) correction (e.g., flagging).[36]

To illustrate, platforms such as DALIL help fact-checkers spot questionable claims which then require subsequent verification.[37] Then, to verify the identified content, the AI(-enhanced) tools can perform a reverse image search, detect bot accounts and deep fakes, assess source credibility, check nonfactual statements (claims) made on social media or analyze the relationships between accounts.[38] WeVerify plug-in is a highly successful tool which offers a variety of verification and analysis features in one platform to fact-check and analyze images, video, and text.[39] Some advanced processing and analytics methods can also be used to analyze different types of content and apply a trustworthiness scoring to online articles.[40]

The verified mis- or disinformation can then be flagged to the end user by adding warnings and providing more context to content rated by fact-checkers. Some platforms have also been labeling content containing *synthetic and manipulated media*.[41]

34 Council of Europe, “Guidance Note on the Prioritisation of Public Interest Content Online adopted by the Steering Committee for Media and Information Society (CDMSI) at its 20th plenary meeting, December 1–3, 2021,” https://rm.coe.int/cdmsi-2021-009-guidance-note-on-the-prioritisation-of-pi-content-e-ado/1680a524c4, accessed April 5, 2023.

35 Ibid.

36 Graves, “Understanding the promise and limits of automated fact-checking” (*Reuters Institute for the Study of Journalism*, February 2018), https://reutersinstitute.politics.ox.ac.uk/sites/default/files/2018-02/graves_factsheet_180226%20FINAL.pdf, accessed April 4, 2023.

37 EU Neighbours South, “AI-driven platform launched to accelerate Arabic language fact-checking” (January 2, 2023), https://south.euneighbours.eu/news/ai-driven-platform-launched-to-accelerate-arabic-language-fact-checking/, accessed April 4, 2023.

38 DW Innovation, “AI for Content Verification I: Status Quo and Current Limitations” (*DW Innovation* October 24, 2022), https://innovation.dw.com/articles/ai-for-content-verification-i-status-quo-and-current-limitations, accessed April 4, 2023.

39 See WeVerify, weverify.eu/verification-plugin/, accessed April 5, 2023.

40 Nucci et al., “Artificial Intelligence against Disinformation: The FANDANGO Practical Case (short paper)” (International Forum on Digital and Democracy (IFDaD), Venice, Italy, 2020).

41 Twitter, “Synthetic and manipulated media policy,” *Twitter Help Centre*, https://help.twitter.com/en/rules-and-policies/manipulated-media, accessed April 5, 2023.

Countering disinformation with the use of AI is a growing research area. The future solutions based on natural language processing, machine learning, or knowledge representation are expected to deal with different content types (audio, video, images, and text) across different languages.[42] Collaborative tools that enable users to work together to find, organize, and verify user-generated content are also on the rise.[43]

14.2.4 *AI in Content Moderation*

AI in content moderation is a broad topic. Algorithmic (commercial) content moderation can be defined as "systems that classify user-generated content based on either matching or prediction, leading to a decision and governance outcome (e.g., removal, geoblocking, and account takedown)."[44] This section focuses on the instances where AI is used either by media organizations to moderate the discussion on their own sites (i.e., in the comments section) or by social media platforms to moderate posts of media organizations and journalists.

14.2.4.1 Comment Moderation

For both editorial and commercial reasons, many online news websites have a dedicated space under their articles (a comment section), which provides a forum for public discourse and aims to engage readers with the content. Empirical research shows that a significant proportion of online comments are *uncivil* (featuring a disrespectful tone, mean-spirited, disparaging remarks and profanity),[45] and encompass stereotypes, homophobic, racist, sexist, and xenophobic terms that may amount to hate speech.[46] The rise of incivility in online news comments negatively affects people's perceptions of news article quality and increases hostility.[47] "Don't read the comments" has become a mantra throughout the media.[48] The amount of hateful and racist comments, together with high costs – both economic and psychological – of human moderators, has prompted news sites to change their practices.

[42] See, for example, vera.ai, www.veraai.eu/home, accessed April 5, 2023.

[43] See Truly Media, www.truly.media, accessed April 5, 2023. See also AI4Media, "UC1: AI for Social Media and Against Disinformation," *AI4Media*, www.ai4media.eu/uc1-ai-for-social-media-and-against-disinformation/, accessed April 4, 2023.

[44] Gorwa, Binns, and Katzenbach, "Algorithmic content moderation: Technical and political challenges in the automation of platform governance" (2020) *Big Data & Society*, 7.

[45] Coe, Kenski, and Rains "Online and uncivil? Patterns and determinants of incivility in newspaper website comments" (2014) *Journal of Communication*, 64: 658.

[46] Che, *Online Incivility and Public Debate: Nasty Talk* (Springer International Publishing AG, 2017).

[47] Kathleen Searles, Sophie Spencer, and Adaobi Duru, "Don't read the comments: The effects of abusive comments on perceptions of women authors' credibility" *Information, Communication & Society*, 23(7).

[48] Gardiner, "'It's a terrible way to go to work': What 70 million readers' comments on the Guardian revealed about hostility to women and minorities online" (2018) *Feminist Media Studies*, 18(4): 592–608.

Some introduced AI systems to support their moderation processes. To illustrate, both the New York Times[49] and the Washington Post[50] use machine learning to prioritize comments which are then evaluated by human moderators or to automatically approve or delete abusive comments. Similarly, STANDARD Community (part of the Austrian newspaper DerSTANDARD) has developed an automated system to prefilter problematic content, as well as a set of preemptive moderation techniques, including forum design changes to prevent problematic content from being posted in the first place.[51]

Others, like Reuters or CNN, have removed their comment sections completely.[52] Apart from abusive and hateful language, the reason was that many users were increasingly commenting on media organizations' social media profiles (e.g., on Facebook), and not on media organizations' websites.[53] This, however, did not remove the problem of hateful speech. To the contrary, it amplified it.[54]

14.2.4.2 Content Moderation

Online intermediary services (e.g., online platforms such as social media) can, and sometimes have to, moderate content which users post on their platforms. In the EU, to avoid liability for illegal content hosted on their platforms, online intermediaries must remove or disable access to such content when the illegal character of the content becomes known. Other content moderation decisions are performed by platforms voluntarily, based on platforms' community standards, that is, private rules drafted and enforced by the platforms (referred to as *private ordering*).[55] Platforms can therefore remove users' content which they do not want to host according to their terms and conditions, even if the content is not illegal. This includes legal editorial content of media organizations (see Section 14.3.4).

[49] Traub, "Why Humans, Not Machines, Make the Tough Calls on Comments" *The New York Times* (October 26, 2021), www.nytimes.com/2021/10/26/insider/why-humans-not-machines-make-the-tough-calls-on-comments.html, accessed April 5, 2023.

[50] WashPostPR, "The Washington Post leverages artificial intelligence in comment moderation" *The Washington Post* (June 22, 2017), www.washingtonpost.com/pr/wp/2017/06/22/the-washington-post-leverages-artificial-intelligence-in-comment-moderation/, accessed April 5, 2023.

[51] Wagner, Kübler, Pírková, Gsenger, and Ferro "Reimagining content moderation and safeguarding fundamental rights. A study on community-led platforms" *The Greens/EFA in the European Parliament* (May 3, 2021), www.greens-efa.eu/files/assets/docs/alternative_content_web.pdf, accessed April 4, 2023.

[52] Liu and McLeod, "Pathways to news commenting and the removal of the comment system on news websites" (2021) *Journalism*, 22(4): 867–881.

[53] Ibid.

[54] United Nations, "Hate Speech: Turning the tide" *UN News, Global perspective Human stories* (January 30, 2023), https://news.un.org/en/story/2023/01/1132617, accessed April 5, 2023; Munn, "Angry by design: Toxic communication and technical architectures." (2020) *Humanities and Social Sciences Communications*, 7: 53.

[55] Belli and Venturini, "Private ordering and the rise of terms of service as cyber-regulation" (2016) *Internet Policy Review*, 5(4).

Given the amounts of content uploaded on the Internet every day, it has become impossible to identify and remove illegal or unwanted content using only traditional human moderation.[56] Many platforms have therefore turned to AI-based content moderation. Such automation can be used as proactive detection of potentially problematic content prior to its publication or as a reactive moderation after it has been flagged by other users or automated processes.[57] Besides deleting content and suspending users, platforms use a whole arsenal of tools to reduce the visibility or reach of some content, such as age barriers, geo-blocking, labeling content as fact-checked or adding a *graphic content* label to problematic content before or as users encounter it.[58]

Algorithmic moderation systems help classify user-generated content based on either matching or prediction techniques.[59] These techniques present a number of technical limitations.[60] Moreover, speech evaluation is highly context dependent, requiring an understanding of cultural, linguistic, and political nuances as well underlying facts. As a result, AI is frequently inaccurate; there is growing empirical evidence of platforms' over-removal of content coming from individuals and media organizations (see Section 14.3.4).[61]

14.3 LEGAL AND ETHICAL CHALLENGES OF AI APPLICATIONS IN MEDIA

This section identifies the legal and ethical challenges of AI in media across various stages of the media value chain described earlier. The section also shows how these challenges may be mitigated by the EU legal framework.[62]

56 Llansó et al., "Artificial Intelligence, Content Moderation, and Freedom of Expression" (Working Papers from the Transatlantic High Level Working Group on Content Moderation Online and Freedom of Expression, 2020), www.ivir.nl/publicaties/download/AI-Llanso-Van-Hobken-Feb-2020.pdf, accessed April 5, 2023.

57 Cambridge Consultants, "Use of AI in online content moderation" (Report produced on behalf of Ofcom 2019), www.cambridgeconsultants.com/sites/default/files/uploaded-pdfs/Use%20of%20AI%20in%20online%20content%20moderation.pdf, accessed April 5, 2023.

58 Goldman, "Content moderation remedies" (2021) *Michigan Technology Law Review*, 28(1): 1–59.

59 Gorwa, Binns, and Katzenbach, "*Algorithmic content moderation: Technical and political challenges in the automation of platform governance*," p. 6.

60 Llansó et al., *Artificial Intelligence, Content Moderation, and Freedom of Expression*.

61 Keller and Leerssen, "Facts and Where to Find Them: Empirical Research on Internet Platforms and Content Moderation" in Persily and Tucker (eds), *Social Media and Democracy: The State of the Field, Prospects for Reform (SSRC Anxieties of Democracy* (Cambridge University Press), 220–251.

62 The issues of attribution of responsibility for automated content between the journalist, editor, media organization, and AI system providers, as well as liability regarding AI systems, fall outside of the scope of this chapter. See Chapter 6 AI and Responsibility and Chapter 8 AI and Liability Law for more information. The challenges related to how to assign authorship or copyright to an automated article are also left out. See Chapter 12 AI and IP Law.

14.3.1 *Lack of Data Availability*

Lack of data availability is a cross-cutting theme, with serious consequences for the media sector. Datasets are often inaccessible or expensive to gather and data journalists rely on private actors, such as data brokers which have already collected such data.[63] This concentrated control over the data influences how editorial decision-making is automated (see Section 14.3.6).

Data availability is also of paramount importance for news verification and fact-checking activities. Access to social media data is vital to analyze and mitigate the harms resulting from disinformation, political microtargeting, or the effect of social media on elections or children's well-being.[64] This is because it enables journalists and researchers to hold platforms accountable for the working of their AI systems. Equally, access to, for example, social media data is important for media organizations that are developing their own AI solutions – particularly in countries where it can be difficult to gain access to large quantities of data in the local language.[65]

Access to platforms' data for researchers is currently mainly governed by contractual agreements, platforms' own terms of service, and public application programming interfaces (APIs). Application programming interfaces access can be restricted or eliminated at any time and for any reason.[66] The UN Special Rapporteur on the promotion and protection of the right to freedom of opinion and expression stressed a lack of transparency and access to data as "the major failings of companies across almost all the concerns in relation to disinformation and misinformation."[67]

A key challenge for research access frameworks is to comply with the General Data Protection Regulation (GDPR).[68] Despite a specific derogation for scientific

[63] van Drunen and Fechner, "Safeguarding Editorial Independence in an Automated Media System: The Relationship between Law and Journalistic Perspectivess" (2022) *Digital Journalism*.

[64] Pasquetto et al., "Tackling misinformation: What researchers could do with social media data" (2020) *Harvard Kennedy School Misinformation Review*, 1(8): 01–14; Ausloos, Leerssen, and ten Thije, "Operationalizing Research Access in Platform Governance: What to Learn from Other Industries?" *Algorithm Watch* (June 25, 2020), www.ivir.nl/publicaties/download/GoverningPlatforms_IViR_study_June2020-AlgorithmWatch-2020-06-24.pdf, accessed March 23, 2023.

[65] Bocyte, Krack, Dutkiewicz, Schjøtt Hansen, 'Blog series: More policies and initiatives need to support responsible AI practices in the media' Medium (July 29, 2024), medium.com/ai-media-observatory/blog-series-more-policies-and-initiatives-need-to-support-responsible-ai-practices-in-the-media-2a42d271d1e1, accessed July 29, 2024.

[66] See, for example, "We research misinformation on Facebook. It just disabled our accounts" *The New York Times* (August 10, 2021), www.nytimes.com/2021/08/10/opinion/facebook-misinformation.html?referringSource=articleShare, accessed April 5, 2023; Nicolas Kayser-Bril, "AlgorithmWatch forced to shut down Instagram monitoring project after threats from Facebook" *Algorithm Watch* (August 13, 2021), https://algorithmwatch.org/en/instagram-research-shut-down-by-facebook/, accessed April 5, 2023.

[67] Khan, "Disinformation and freedom of opinion and expression: report of the Special Rapporteur on the Promotion and Protection of the Right to Freedom of Opinion and Expression" (April 13, 2021).

[68] Regulation (EU) 2016/679 of the European Parliament and of the Council of April 27, 2016, on the protection of natural persons with regard to the processing of personal data and on the free movement

research purposes (art. 89), the GDPR lacks clarity regarding how platforms might share data with researchers (e.g., on what legal grounds).[69] To mitigate this uncertainty, various policy and regulatory initiatives aim to clarify how platforms may provide access to data to researchers in a GDPR-compliant manner.[70] In addition, there have been calls for a legally binding mechanism that provides independent researchers with access to different types of platform data.[71]

The Digital Services Act (DSA) requires providers of very large online platforms (VLOPs) and very large online search engines (VLOSEs) to grant *vetted researchers* access to data, subject to certain conditions.[72] Data can be provided "for the sole purpose" of conducting research that contributes to the detection, identification and understanding of systemic risks and to the assessment of the adequacy, efficiency and impacts of the risk mitigation measures (art. 40(4)). Vetted researchers must meet certain criteria and procedural requirements in the application process. Importantly, they must be affiliated to a research organization or a not-for-profit body, organization or association (art. 40(12)). Arguably, this excludes unaffiliated media practitioners, such as freelance journalists or bloggers. Many details about researchers' access to data through the DSA will be decided in delegated acts that have yet to be adopted (art. 14(13)).

Moreover, under the Digital Markets Act,[73] the so-called *gatekeepers* will have to provide advertisers and publishers with access to the advertising data and allow business users to access the data generated in the context of the use of the core platform service (art. 6(1) and art. 6(8)).

Furthermore, the European strategy for data[74] aims at creating a single market for data by establishing common European data spaces to make more data available

of such data, and repealing Directive 95/46/EC (General Data Protection Regulation) [2016] OJ L119. See also Chapter 9 AI and Privacy Law.

69 Dutkiewicz "From the DSA to Media Data Space: the possible solutions for the access to platforms' data to tackle disinformation" *European Law Blog* (October 19, 2021), https://europeanlawblog.eu/2021/10/19/from-the-dsa-to-media-data-space-the-possible-solutions-for-the-access-to-platforms-data-to-tackle-disinformation/, accessed March 13, 2023.

70 See, for instance, the European Digital Media Observatory, "Report of the European Digital Media Observatory's Working Group on Platform-to-Researcher Data Access" (May 31, 2022), https://edmoprod.wpengine.com/wp-content/uploads/2022/02/Report-of-the-European-Digital-Media-Observatorys-Working-Group-on-Platform-to-Researcher-Data-Access-2022.pdf, accessed April 4, 2023.

71 Vermuelen, "The Keys to the Kingdom." *Knight First Amendment Institute* (July 27, 2021), https://knightcolumbia.org/content/the-keys-to-the-kingdom, accessed March 20, 2023.

72 Digital Services Act, art. 40. See also Albert, "A guide to the EU's new rules for researcher access to platform data" *Algorithm Watch* (December 7, 2022), https://algorithmwatch.org/en/dsa-data-access-explained/, accessed April 5, 2023.

73 Regulation (EU) 2022/1925 of the European Parliament and of the Council of September 14, 2022 on contestable and fair markets in the digital sector and amending Directives (EU) 2019/1937 and (EU) 2020/1828 (Digital Markets Act) [2022] OJ L265.

74 European Commission, Communication from the Commission to the European Parliament, the Council, the European Economic and Social Committee and the Committee of the Regions, A European strategy for data [COM/2020/66 final].

for use in the economy and society. The Data Governance Act[75] and the Data Act proposal[76] seek to strengthen mechanisms to increase data availability and harness the potential of industrial data, respectively. Lastly, the European Commission announced the creation of a dedicated media data space.[77] The media data space initiative, financed through the Horizon Europe and Digital Europe Programmes,[78] aims to support both PSM and commercial media operators to pool their content and customer data to develop innovative solutions.

14.3.2 *Data Quality and Bias in Training Datasets*

Another, closely related, consideration is data quality. There is a growing literature on the quality and representation issues with training, testing, and validation data, especially those in publicly available datasets and databases.[79] Moreover, generative AI raises controversies regarding the GDPR compliance of the training data[80] and brings a broader question of *extraction fairness*, defined as "legal and moral concerns regarding the large-scale exploitation of training data without the knowledge, authorization, acknowledgement or compensation of their creators."[81]

The quality of training data and data annotation is crucial, for example, for hate speech and abusive language detection in comments. A 2022 report by the EU Agency for Fundamental Rights shows how tools that automatically detect or *predict* potential online hatred can produce biased results.[82] The predictions frequently overreact to various identity terms (i.e., words indicating group identities like ethnic

75 Regulation (EU) 2022/868 of the European Parliament and of the Council of May 30, 2022 on European data governance and amending Regulation (EU) 2018/1724 (Data Governance Act) OJ L152.

76 European Commission, Proposal for a Regulation of the European Parliament and of the Council on harmonised rules on fair access to and use of data (Data Act) [COM/2022/68 final].

77 European Commission, Communication from the Commission to the European Parliament, the Council, the European Economic and Social Committee and the Committee of the Regions, Europe's Media in the Digital Decade: An Action Plan to Support Recovery and Transformation (December 3, 2020, COM/2020/784 final).

78 In particular the Cloud Data and TEF Call (DIGITAL-2022-CLOUD-AI-03).

79 See, for example, Inioluwa Deborah Raji, Timnit Gebru, Margaret Mitchell, Joy Buolamwini, Joonseok Lee, and Emily Denton, "Saving Face: Investigating the Ethical Concerns of Facial Recognition Auditing" in *Proceedings of the AAAI/ACM Conference on AI, Ethics, and Society* (AIES '20). Association for Computing Machinery, New York, NY, USA, 145–151; Osonde Osoba and William Welser IV, "An Intelligence in Our Image: The Risks of Bias and Errors in Artificial Intelligence" (RAND Corporation, 2017).

80 See, for instance, "Artificial intelligence: Stop to ChatGPT by the Italian SA Personal data is collected unlawfully, no age verification system is in place for children" (March 31, 2023), www.garanteprivacy.it/home/docweb/-/docweb-display/docweb/9870847#english, accessed April 5, 2023.

81 Helberger and Diakopoulos, "ChatGPT and the AI Act" (2023) *Internet Policy Review*, 12(1). For AI and fairness, see Chapter 5 of this book.

82 European Union Agency for Fundamental Rights, "Bias in Algorithms – Artificial Intelligence and Discrimination" (Publications Office of the European Union, 2022).

origin or religion), flagging text that is not actually offensive.[83] Research shows that social media content moderation algorithms have difficulty differentiating hate speech from discussion about race and often silence marginalized groups such as racial and ethnic minorities.[84] At the same time, underrepresentation of certain groups in a training dataset may result in them experiencing more abusive language than other groups.

There are blurred lines between what constitutes *hateful, harmful,* and *offensive* speech, and these notions are context dependent and culturally specific. Many instances of hate speech cannot be identified and distinguished from innocent messages by looking at single words or combinations of them.[85] Such contextual differentiation, between, for example, satirical and offensive uses of a word proves challenging for an AI system. This is an important technical limitation that may lead to over- and under-removal of content. Both can interfere with a range of fundamental rights such as the right to freedom of expression[86] (see Section 14.3.4), the right to data protection, as well as the right to nondiscrimination.

The consequence of using unreliable data could be the spread of misinformation[87] as illustrated by inaccurate responses to news queries from search engines using generative AI. Research into Bing's generative AI accuracy for news queries shows that there are detail errors and attribution errors, and the system also sometimes asserts the opposite of the truth.[88] This, together with the lack of media literacy, may cause an automation bias, that is, the uncritical trust in information provided by the automated system despite the information being actually incorrect.

83 Ibid.

84 Oliver L. Haimson, Daniel Delmonaco, Peipei Nie, and Andrea Wegner, "Disproportionate Removals and Difering Content Moderation Experiences for Conservative, Transgender, and Black Social Media Users: Marginalization and Moderation Gray Areas" (2021) Proc. ACM Hum.-Comput. Interact. 5, CSCW2, Article 466.

85 Policy Department for Citizens' Rights and Constitutional Affairs Directorate-General for Internal Policies, "The impact of algorithms for online content filtering or moderation 'Upload filters'" (Study Requested by the JURI Committee, September 2020).

86 See, for example, Helberger, van Drunen, Eskens, Bastian, and Moeller, "A freedom of expression perspective on AI in the media – with a special focus on editorial decision making on social media platforms and in the news media" (2020) *European Journal of Law and Technology*, 11(3); Krack, Beudels, Valcke, and Kuczerawy, "AI in the Belgian Media Landscape. When Fundamental Risks Meet Regulatory Complexities," *Artificial Intelligence and the Law*, vol 13 (2nd rev ed., Jan De Bruyne and Cedric Vanleenhove (eds), *Intersentia*, 2023).

87 Misinformation, as opposed to disinformation is not deliberate. The EU defines it as "false or misleading content shared without harmful intent though the effects can be still harmful," see "Tackling online disinformation" *European Commission* (June 29, 2022), https://digital-strategy.ec.europa.eu/en/policies/online-disinformation, accessed April 5, 2023.

88 Diakopoulos, "Can We Trust Search Engines with Generative AI? A Closer Look at Bing's Accuracy for News Queries" *Medium* (February 17, 2023), https://medium.com/@ndiakopoulos/can-we-trust-search-engines-with-generative-ai-a-closer-look-at-bings-accuracy-for-news-queries-179467806bcc, accessed April 5, 2023.

14.3.3 *Transparency*

Transparency can mean many different things. Broadly speaking, it should enable people to understand how an AI system is developed, is trained, how it operates, and how it is deployed so that they can make more informed choices.[89] This section focuses on three aspects of transparency of AI in media.[90]

The *first* aspect relates to *internal transparency*, which describes the need for journalists and other non-technical groups inside media organizations to have sufficient knowledge around the AI systems they use.[91] The importance of closing the intelligibility gap around AI within a media organization is necessary for an understanding of how AI systems work to use them responsibly.[92] The AI Act requires providers and deployers of AI systems including media organizations to ensure, to their best extent, a sufficient level of AI literacy of their staff and other persons dealing with the operations and use of AI systems on their behalf (art. 4).[93]

The *second* aspect concerns *external transparency*, which refers to transparency practices directed toward the audience to make them aware of the use of AI. The AI Act requires providers of AI systems, such as OpenAI, to make it clear to users that they are interacting with an AI system, unless this is obvious from the circumstances and the context of use (art. 50(1)).[94] As a rule, they must also mark generative AI outputs (synthetic audio, image, video or text content) as AI-generated or manipulated (art. 50(2)). For now it remains unclear what forms of transparency will be sufficient and whether they will be meaningful to the audience. Transparency requirements also apply to those who use AI systems that generate

89 "Transparency and explainability (Principle 1.3)" *OECD*, https://oecd.ai/en/dashboards/ai-principles/P7, accessed April 5, 2023.

90 Drawing on the distinction made by Cools and Koliska. See: Hannes Cools, Michael Koliska, "News Automation and Algorithmic Transparency in the Newsroom: The Case of the Washington Post" (2024) *Journalism Studies* 25(6): 662–80.

91 Schjøtt Hansen, Bocyte, Krack, Dutkiewicz, "Blog series: AI regulation is overlooking the need for third-party transparency in the media sector," *Medium* (July 15, 2024), medium.com/ai-media-observatory/blog-series-ai-regulation-is-overlooking-the-need-for-third-party-transparency-in-the-media-sector-df843118c1fa, accessed July 31, 2024.

92 Jones Bronwyn, Rhianne Jones, and Ewa Luger, "AI 'Everywhere and Nowhere': Addressing the AI Intelligibility Problem in Public Service Journalism" (2022) *Digital Journalism*, 10 (10): 1731–55. doi: 10.1080/21670811.2022.2145328.

93 The AI Act does not provide details on whether and how (media) organizations will be supported in this work. It has been pointed out that supporting AI literacy in media organizations is highly resource-intensive and takes a lot of translational work. See, for example, DW Innovation, "AI in Media Tools: How to Increase User Trust and Support AI Governance" (June 21, 2024), innovation.dw.com/articles/ai-media-tools-user-trust, accessed July 31, 2024.

94 What "interaction" means in this context is unclear, but it could cover applications such as chatbots, newsbots, recommender systems, and automated writing systems. See: Helberger and Diakopoulos, "The European AI Act and How It Matters for Research into AI in Media and Journalism" (2022) *Digital Journalism*.

or manipulate images, audio or video content constituting a deep fake (art. 50(4) para 1). However, if the content is part of an evidently artistic, creative or satirical work, the disclosure should not hamper the display or enjoyment of the work. Moreover, deployers of an AI-generated or manipulated text which is published with the purpose of informing the public on matters of public interest shall disclose that the text has been artificially generated or manipulated. There is an important exception for the media sector. If the AI-generated text has undergone a process of human review or editorial control within an organisation that holds editorial responsibility for the content (such as a publisher), disclosure is no longer necessary. This provision raises questions as to what will count as a *human review* or *editorial control* and who can be said to hold *editorial responsibility*.[95] Moreover, research shows that audiences want media organisations to be transparent and provide labels when using AI.[96]

In addition to the AI Act, the DSA presents multiple layers of transparency obligations for the benefit of users that differ depending on the type of service concerned.[97] In particular, it requires transparency on whether AI is used in content moderation. All intermediary services must publish in their terms and conditions, in a "clear and unambiguous language," a description of the tools used for content moderation, including AI systems that either automate or support content moderation practices (art. 14). In practice, this means that users must know why, when, and how online content is being moderated, including with the use of AI, and when human review is in place.

The DSA also regulates recommender system transparency. As mentioned earlier, recommender systems can have a significant impact on the ability of recipients to retrieve and interact with information online. Consequently, providers of online platforms are expected to set out in their terms and conditions in plain and intelligible language the main parameters used in their recommender systems and the options for users to modify or influence them (art. 27). The main parameters shall explain why certain information is suggested, and include, at least, the criteria that are most significant in determining the information suggested, and the reasons for the relative importance of those parameters. There are additional requirements

95 Schjøtt Hansen, Bocyte, Krack, Dutkiewicz, 'Blog series: AI regulation is overlooking the need for third-party transparency in the media sector' *Medium* (July 15, 2024), medium.com/ai-media-observatory/blog-series-ai-regulation-is-overlooking-the-need-for-third-party-transparency-in-the-media-sector-df843118c1fa, accessed July 31, 2024.

96 Fletcher, Kleis Nielsen, 'What does the public in six countries think of generative AI in news?' (May 28, 2024), reutersinstitute.politics.ox.ac.uk/what-does-public-six-countries-think-generative-ai-news#header–6, accessed July 31, 2024.

97 Other transparency requirements include, for example, an obligation for VLOPs and VLOSEs to explain the design, the logic, the functioning and the testing of their algorithmic systems, including their recommender systems as well as transparency of online advertising. See Digital Services Act art. 40(3) and art. 26, respectively. See also Krack, Beudels, Valcke and Kuczerawy, *AI in the Belgian Media Landscape. When Fundamental Risks Meet Regulatory Complexities.*

imposed on the providers of VLOPs and VLOSEs to provide at least one option for their recommendation systems which is not based on profiling.

There are also further obligations for VLOPs and VLOSEs to perform an assessment of any systemic risks stemming from the design, functioning, or use of their services, including algorithmic systems (art. 34(1)). This risk assessment shall include the assessment of any actual or foreseeable negative effects on the exercise of fundamental rights, including the right to freedom of expression and the freedom and pluralism of the media (art. 34(1)(b)). When conducting risk assessments, VLOPs and VLOSEs shall consider, in particular, whether the design of their recommender systems and their content moderation systems influence any of the systemic risks. If so, they must put in place mitigation measures, such as testing and adapting their algorithms (art. 35).

Lastly, intermediary services (excluding micro and small enterprises) must publish, at least once a year, transparency reports on their content moderation activities, including a qualitative description, a specification of the precise purposes, indicators of the accuracy and the possible rate of error of the automated means (art. 15). Extra transparency reporting obligations apply to VLOPs (art. 42).

The *third* aspect concerns *third-party transparency*, which refers to the importance of having insights into how AI systems provided by third-party providers have been trained on and how they work.[98]

In both the DSA and the AI Act, there are no explicit provisions that make such information widely available.[99]

14.3.4 *Risks for the Right to Freedom of Expression*

Article 10 of the European Convention of Human Rights (ECHR), as well as Article 11 of the Charter of Fundamental Rights of the European Union (CFR),[100] guarantees the right to freedom of expression to everyone. The European Court of Human Rights (ECtHR) has interpreted the scope of Article 10 ECHR through an extensive body of case law. The right to freedom of expression includes the right to impart information, as well as the right to receive it. It protects the rights of individuals, companies, and organizations, with a special role reserved for media organizations and journalists. It is their task to inform the public about matters of public interest

[98] Schjøtt Hansen, Bocyte, Krack, Dutkiewicz, "Blog series: AI regulation is overlooking the need for third-party transparency in the media sector" *Medium* (July 15, 2024), medium.com/ai-media-observatory/blog-series-ai-regulation-is-overlooking-the-need-for-third-party-transparency-in-the-media-sector-df843118c1fa, accessed July 31, 2024.

[99] In the AI Act, requirements to provide some information about the training datasets and documentation around the capabilities and limitations of AI models only apply to general-purpose AI models or high-risk AI systems (see Recitals 66-67, Article 53, and Annex XII AI Act).

[100] According to CFR art. 52(3), the meaning and scope of rights in both instruments shall be the same.

and current events and to play the role of the public watchdog.[101] The right applies offline and on the Internet.[102]

One of the main risks for freedom of expression associated with algorithmic content moderation is over-blocking, meaning the unjustified removal or blocking of content or the suspension or termination of user accounts. In 2012, the Court of Justice of the EU held that a filtering system for copyright violations could undermine freedom of information since it might not distinguish adequately between lawful and unlawful content, which could lead to the blocking of lawful communications.[103] This concern is equally valid outside the copyright context. The technical limitations of AI systems, together with regulatory pressure from States who increasingly request intermediaries to take down certain categories of content, often based on vague definitions, incentivize platforms to follow a "if in doubt, take it down" approach.[104] There is, indeed, growing empirical evidence of platforms' over-removal of content.[105] To illustrate, social media platforms have deleted hundreds of posts condemning the eviction of Palestinians from the Sheikh Jarrah neighborhood of Jerusalem[106] or restricted access to information about abortion.[107] Both examples are a consequence of the algorithmic content moderation systems either not being able to recognize context or not knowing underlying facts and legal nuances. Such automated removals, even if unintentional and subsequently revoked, potentially limit both the right to impart information (of users who post content online) and the right to receive information (of third parties who do not get to see the deleted content).

On the other hand, the under-blocking of certain online content may also have a negative impact on the right to freedom of expression. Not acting against illegal

[101] Satakunnan Markkinapörssi Oy and Satamedia Oy v. Finland, App no 931/13 (ECtHR June 27, 2017); Von Hannover v. Germany (no 2.), Apps nos 40660/08 and 60641/08) (ECtHR February 7, 2012).

[102] See, for example, Council of Europe, "Recommendation of the Committee of Ministers to member States on a Guide to human rights for Internet users" (adopted by the Committee of Ministers on April 16, 2014 at the 1197th meeting of the Ministers' Deputies).

[103] Case C-360/10 *Belgische Vereniging van Auteurs, Componisten en Uitgevers CVBA (SABAM) v Netlog NV* [2012], para 50.

[104] Keller, "Empirical Evidence of Over-Removal by Internet Companies under Intermediary Liability Laws: An Updated List" *CIS Blog* (February 8, 2021), https://cyberlaw.stanford.edu/blog/2021/02/empirical-evidence-over-removal-internet-companies-under-intermediary-liability-laws, accessed April 4, 2023.

[105] Keller and Leerssen, *Facts and Where to Find Them: Empirical Research on Internet Platforms and Content Moderation*.

[106] "Sheikh Jarrah: Facebook and Twitter silencing protests, deleting evidence" *Article 19* (May 10, 2021), www.article19.org/resources/sheikh-jarrah-facebook-and-twitter-silencing-protests-deleting-evidence/, accessed April 4, 2023; "Israel/Palestine: Facebook Censors Discussion of Rights Issues" *Human Rights Watch* (October 8, 2021), www.hrw.org/news/2021/10/08/israel/palestine-facebook-censors-discussion-rights-issues, accessed April 4, 2023.

[107] Kuczerawy and Dutkiewicz, "Accessing Information about Abortion: The Role of Online Platforms under the EU Digital Services Act" *VerfBlog* (July 28, 2022), https://verfassungsblog.de/accessing-information-about-abortion/, accessed March 28, 2023.

content and some forms of legal but harmful content (i.e., hate speech) may lead people (especially marginalized communities) to express themselves less freely or withdraw from participating in the online discourse.

In addition, in the context of fact-checking, AI cannot yet analyze entire, complex disinformation narratives and detect all uses of synthetic media manipulation.[108] Thus, an overreliance on AI systems to verify the trustworthiness of the news may prove detrimental to the right to freedom of expression.

To mitigate these risks, the DSA provides certain procedural safeguards. It does not force intermediary services to moderate content, but requires that any restrictions imposed on users' content based on terms and conditions are applied and enforced "in a diligent, objective and proportionate manner," with "due regard to the rights and legitimate interests of all parties involved" (art. 14(4)). Not only do they have to take *due regard* to fundamental rights in cases of content removal, but also when restricting the availability, visibility, and accessibility of information. What *due regard* means in this context will be defined in courts. Moreover, the DSA requires intermediary services to balance their freedom to conduct a business with other rights such as users' freedom of expression. Online platforms also have to provide a statement of reasons as to why the content has been removed or the account has been blocked and implement an internal complaint-handling system that enables users to lodge complaints (art. 21). Another procedural option is the out-of-court dispute settlement or a judicial remedy.[109]

A novelty foreseen by the DSA is an obligation for VLOPs and VLOSEs to mitigate systemic risks such as actual or foreseeable negative effects for the exercise of fundamental rights, in particular freedom of expression and information, including the freedom and pluralism of the media, enshrined in Article 11 of the CFR, and foreseeable negative effects on civic discourse (art. 34).

News personalization from the freedom of expression perspective looks paradoxical at first glance. As Eskens points out, "news personalisation may enhance the right to receive information, but it may also hinder or downplay the right to receive information and the autonomy with which news users exercise their right to receive information."[110] Given that content prioritization practices have a potential for promoting trustworthy and reliable news, it can be argued that platforms should be required to ensure online access to content of general public interest. The Council of Europe, for instance, suggested that States should act to make public interest content more prominent, including by introducing new obligations for platforms and intermediaries, and also impose minimum standards such as transparency.[111] Legal

[108] DW Innovation, "AI for Content Verification I: Status Quo and Current Limitations," p. 7.

[109] See also Kuczerawy, "Remedying Overremoval: The Three-Tiered Approach of the DSA," *VerfBlog* (November 3, 2022), https://verfassungsblog.de/remedying-overremoval/, accessed April 5, 2023.

[110] Eskens, "The fundamental rights of news users: The legal groundwork for a personalised online news environment" (PhD Thesis University of Amsterdam, 2021).

[111] Council of Europe, "Guidance Note on the Prioritisation of Public Interest Content Online," p. 7.

scholars have proposed *exposure diversity* as a design principle for recommender systems[112] or the development of "diversity-enhancing public service algorithms."[113] But who should decide what content is trustworthy or authoritative, and based on what criteria? Are algorithmic systems of private platforms equipped enough to quantify normative values such as *newsworthiness*? What safeguards would prevent States from forcing platforms to prioritize State-approved-only information or government propaganda? Besides, many of the problems with content diversity are at least to some extent user-driven – users themselves, under their right to freedom of expression, determine what kind of content they upload and share.[114] Legally imposed public interest content recommendations could limit users' autonomy in their news selection by paternalistically censoring the range of information that is available to them. While there are no such obligations in the DSA, some legislative proposals at the national level are currently reviewing such options.[115]

14.3.5 *Threats to Media Freedom and Pluralism Online*

Freedom and pluralism of the media are pillars of liberal democracies. They are also covered by Art. 10 ECHR and Art. 11 CFR. The ECtHR found that *new electronic media*, such as an online news outlet, are also entitled to the protection of the right to media freedom.[116] Moreover, the so-called positive obligations doctrine imposes an obligation on States to protect editorial independence from private parties, such as social media.[117]

Social media platforms have on multiple occasions erased content coming from media organizations, including public broadcasters, and journalists. This is often illustrated by the controversy that arose around Facebook's decision to delete a post by a Norwegian journalist, which featured the well-known Vietnam War photo of a nude young girl fleeing a napalm attack.[118] Similarly, users sharing an article from The Guardian showing Aboriginal men in chains were banned from Facebook on

[112] Helberger, Karppinen, and D'Acunto, "Exposure diversity as a design principle for recommender systems" (2018) *Information, Communication & Society*, 21(2): 191–207.

[113] Vermeulen, "Access Diversity through Online News Media and Public Service Algorithms. An Analysis of News Recommendation in Light of Article 10 ECHR" in James Meese and Sara Bannerman (eds), *The Algorithmic Distribution of News : Policy Responses* (Cham: Palgrave Macmillan, 2022), pp. 269–287.

[114] Helberger, Pierson, and Poell, "Governing online platforms: From contested to cooperative responsibility" (2017) *The Information Society*.

[115] See, for example, the UK Draft Online Safety Bill presented to Parliament by the Minister of State for Digital and Culture by Command of Her Majesty May 2021.

[116] OOO Regnum v. Russia, App no 22649/08 (ECtHR, September 8, 2020).

[117] van Drunen and Fechner, "*Safeguarding Editorial Independence in an Automated Media System: The Relationship Between Law and Journalistic Perspectives.*"

[118] Scott and Isaac, "Facebook Restores Iconic Vietnam War Photo It Censored for Nudity" *The New York Times* (September 9, 2016), www.nytimes.com/2016/09/10/technology/facebook-vietnam-war-photo-nudity.html, accessed April 4, 2023.

the grounds of posting nudity.[119] Other examples include videos of activists and local news outlets that documented the war crimes of the regime of Bashar al-Assad in Syria[120] or a Swedish journalist's material reporting sexual violence against minors.[121] This is due to technical limitations of the algorithmic content moderation tools and their inability to distinguish educational, awareness raising or journalistic material from other content.

In order to prevent removals of content coming from media organizations, a so-called *media exemption*[122] was proposed during the discussions of the DSA proposal, aiming to ensure that the media would be informed and have the possibility to challenge any content moderation measure before its implementation. The amendments were not included in the final text of the DSA. There is no special protection or any obligation of prior notice to media organizations in the DSA. Media organizations and journalists can invoke the same procedural rights that apply to all users of online platforms. One can also imagine that mass-scale algorithmic takedowns of media content, suspension or termination of journalists' accounts by VLOPs could amount to a *systemic risk* in a form of a negative effect on the exercise of the freedom and pluralism of the media.[123] However, what qualifies as *systemic*, and when a threshold of systemic risk to freedom and pluralism of the media is reached, remains undefined.

Recognizing media service providers' role in the distribution of information and in the exercise of the right to receive and impart information online, the European Media Freedom Act (EMFA) grants media service providers special procedural rights vis-à-vis VLOPs. Where a VLOP considers that content provided by recognized media service providers[124] is incompatible with its terms and conditions, it

[119] Tylor, "Facebook blocks and bans users for sharing Guardian article showing Aboriginal men in chains" *The Guardian* (June 15, 2020), www.theguardian.com/technology/2020/jun/15/facebook-blocks-bans-users-sharing-guardian-article-showing-aboriginal-men-in-chains, accessed April 4, 2023. Note that a spokeswoman for Facebook apologized for the mistake and that the post was restored.

[120] Alimardani and Elswah, "*Digital Orientalism: #SaveSheikhJarrah and Arabic Content Moderation*"; see also Hadi Al Khatib and Dia Kayyali "YouTube Is Erasing History" *The New York Times* (October 23, 2019), www.nytimes.com/2019/10/23/opinion/syria-youtube-content-moderation.html, accessed April 5, 2023.

[121] Oversight Board decision 2021-016-FB-FBR.

[122] Amendments 511 and 513 to Recital 38 and Article 12 of the Digital Services Act proposal (January 15, 2022). Note that the term "media exemption" is contested; other terms like "non-interference principle" are used interchangeably. See, for example, EBU. "The Digital Services Act must safeguard freedom of expression online" (January 18, 2022), www.ebu.ch/files/live/sites/ebu/files/News/Position_Papers/open/2022/220118-DSA-media-statment-final.pdf, accessed April 4, 2023.

[123] Buijs "The Digital Services Act and the implications for news media and journalistic content (Part 1)" *DSA Observatory* (September 29, 2022), https://dsa-observatory.eu/2022/09/29/digital-services-act-implications-for-news-media-journalistic-content-part-1/, accessed April 5, 2023.

[124] EMFA grants this and other procedural rights to media who declare that they are media service providers and meet the conditions of art. 18(1) EMFA. Interestingly, one of the conditions is a declaration that a media service provider does not provide AI-generated content without subjecting it to

should "duly consider media freedom and media pluralism" in accordance with the DSA and provide, as early as possible, the necessary explanations to media service providers in a statement of reasons as referred to in the DSA and the P2B Regulation (recital 50, art. 18). In what has been coined as a *non-interference principle*[125], VLOPs should provide the media service provider concerned, prior to the suspension or restriction of visibility taking effect, with an opportunity to reply to the statement of reasons within 24 hours of receiving it.[126] Where, following or in the absence of a reply, a VLOP takes the decision to suspend or restrict visibility, it shall inform the media service provider concerned without undue delay. Moreover, media service providers' complaints under the DSA and the P2B Regulation shall be processed and decided upon with priority and without undue delay. Importantly, EMFA's Article 18 does not apply where VLOPs suspend or restrict the visibility of content in compliance with their obligations to protect minors, to take measures against illegal content or in order to assess and mitigate systemic risks.[127]

Next to media freedom, media pluralism and diversity of media content are equally essential for the functioning of a democratic society and are the corollaries of the fundamental right to freedom of expression and information.[128] Media pluralism is recognized as one of the core values of the European Union.[129]

In recent years, concerns over the decline of media diversity and pluralism have increased.[130] Online platforms "have acquired increasing control over the flow, availability, findability and accessibility of information and other content online."[131] Considering platforms' advertising-driven business model based on a profit maximization, they have more incentives to increase the visibility of content that would keep users more engaged. It can be argued that not only does this fail to promote

human review or editorial control (art. 18(1)(e)). At the same time, VLOPs have the right to reject such self-declarations where they consider that those conditions are not met.

125 Papaevangelou, "The Non-Interference Principle": Debating Online Platforms' Treatment of Editorial Content in the EU's Digital Services Act'. *European Journal of Communication*, 2023.

126 A shorter timeframe could apply in the event of a crisis as defined in Article 36(2) of the DSA in order to take into account, in particular, an urgent need to moderate the relevant content in such exceptional circumstances.

127 See Articles 28, 34 and 35 DSA.

128 Committee of Ministers, "Recommendation CM/Rec(2007)2 on media pluralism and diversity of media content" January 31, 2007. See also the similar Committee of Ministers, "Recommendation No. R (99) 1 on measures to promote media pluralism" adopted on January 19, 1999.

129 CFR, art. 11; Treaty on European Union Articles 2 and 6.

130 Mathias A. Färdigh, "Monitoring media pluralism in the digital era: Application of the Media Pluralism Monitor in the European Union, Albania, Montenegro, the Republic of North Macedonia, Serbia and Turkey in the year 2021. Country report: Sweden" Centre for Media Pluralism and Media Freedom (CMPF); Media Pluralism Monitor (MPM); 2022. Parcu, "New digital threats to media pluralism in the information age" (2020) *Competition and Regulation in Network Industries*, 21(2): 91–109; CMPF-CiTiP-IViR-SMIT, "*Study on Media Plurality and Diversity Online.*"

131 Committee of Ministers, "Recommendation CM/Rec(2018)(1)[1] of the Committee of Ministers to member States on media pluralism and transparency of media ownership" March 7, 2018.

diversity, but it strongly reduces it.[132] The reduction of plurality and diversity of news content resulting from platforms' content curation policies may limit users' access to information. It also negatively affects society as a whole, since the availability and accessibility of diverse information is a prerequisite for citizens to form and express their opinions and participate in the democratic discourse in an informed way.[133]

14.3.6 *Threats to Media Independence*

The growing dependence on automation in news production and distribution has a profound impact on editorial independence as well as on the organizational and business choices of media organizations. One way in which automation could potentially challenge editorial independence is media reliance on non-media actors such as engineers, data providers, and technology companies that develop or fund the development of the datasets or algorithms used to automate editorial decision-making.[134]

(News) media organizations depend more and more on platforms to distribute their content. The phenomena of *platformed publishing* refers to the situation where news organizations have no or little control over the distribution mechanisms decided by the platforms.[135] Moreover, media organizations optimize news content to make it *algorithm ready*, for example, by producing popular content which is attractive for the platforms' recommender systems.[136] The entire news cycle, from production, distribution, to consumption of news "is (re)organized around platforms, their rules and logic and thus influenced and mediated by them."[137] Individuals and newsrooms, therefore, depend structurally on platforms, which affects the functioning and power allocation within the media ecosystem.[138]

Moreover, platforms provide essential technical infrastructure (e.g., cloud computing and storage), access to AI models, or stand-alone software.[139] This increases the potential for so-called *infrastructure capture*[140] and risks shifting even more

[132] Stasi, "Ensuring Pluralism in Social Media Markets: Some Suggestions" (2020) Working Paper, EUI RSCAS, 2020/05, Centre for Media Pluralism and Media Freedom.

[133] Council of Europe, Commissioner for Human Rights, "Media Pluralism and Human Rights, Issue Discussion paper," (2011), https://rm.coe.int/16806da515, accessed April 5, 2023; *Lingens* v. *Austria* App no 9815/82 (EctHR July 8, 1986); *Castells* v. *Spain*, App No 11798/85 (EctHR April 23, 1992).

[134] Van Drunen and Fechner, "*Safeguarding Editorial Independence in an Automated Media System: The Relationship between Law and Journalistic Perspectives.*"

[135] Nielsen and Ganter, "The power of platforms" *Reuters Institute* (April 29, 2022), https://reutersinstitute.politics.ox.ac.uk/news/power-platforms, accessed April 5, 2023.

[136] Seipp, Helberger, de Vreese, and Ausloos, "Dealing with Opinion Power in the Platform World: Why We Really Have to Rethink Media Concentration Law" (2023) *Digital Journalism*.

[137] Ibid.

[138] Ibid.

[139] Simon, "Uneasy Bedfellows: AI in the News, Platform Companies and the Issue of Journalistic Autonomy" (2022) *Digital Journalism*, 10(10): 1832–1854.

[140] Nechushtai, "Could Digital Platforms Capture the Media through Infrastructure?" (2018) *Journalism* 19(8): 1043–1058.

control to platform companies, at the expense of the media organizations autonomy and independence.

The relationship between AI, media, and platforms, raises broader questions about the underlying political, economic, and technological power structures and platforms' opinion power.[141] To answer these challenges, legal scholars have called for rethinking media concentration rules[142] and media law in general.[143] However, the considerations about opinion power of platforms, values, and media independence are somehow missing from the current EU regulatory initiatives. The EMFA rightly points out that providers of video-sharing platforms and VLOPs "play a key role in the organisation of content, including by automated means or by means of algorithms," and some "have started to exercise editorial control over a section or sections of their services" (recital 11). While it does mention "the formation of public opinion" as relevant parameter in the assessment of media market concentrations (art. 21), it does not provide a solution to address the concerns about the dependency between platforms' AI capacities and media organizations.[144]

14.4 CONCLUSIONS

AI will continue to transform media in ways we can only imagine. Will news articles be written by fully automated systems? Will the proliferation of synthetic media content dramatically change the way we perceive information? Or will virtual reality experiences and new forms of interactive storytelling replace traditional (public interest) media content? As AI technology continues to advance, it is essential that the EU legal framework keeps pace with these developments to ensure that the use of AI in media is responsible, ethical, and beneficial to society as a whole. After all, information is a public good and media companies cannot be treated as any other businesses.[145]

The DSA takes an important step in providing procedural safeguards to mitigate risks for the right to freedom of expression and freedom of the media posed by online platforms' content moderation practices. It recognizes that the way VLOPs

[141] Helberger, "The Political Power of Platforms: How Current Attempts to Regulate Misinformation Amplify Opinion Power" (2020) *Digital Journalism*, 8(6): 842–854; see also Orla Lynskey, "Regulating 'Platform Power'" (2017) LSE Legal Studies Working Paper No. 1/2017.

[142] See, for example, Helberger, "*The Political Power of Platforms: How Current Attempts to Regulate Misinformation Amplify Opinion Power*"; Seipp, Helberger, de Vreese and Ausloos, "*Dealing with Opinion Power in the Platform World: Why We Really Have to Rethink Media Concentration Law.*"

[143] Tambini, "A theory of media freedom" (2021) *Journal of Media Law*, 13(2): 135–152.

[144] Other than art. 18 EMFA, mentioned earlier, which is limited in scope.

[145] See the speech of Ursula Von der Leyen (President of the European Commission) for the release of the MFA: European Commission, "European Media Freedom Act" (2022), https://commission.europa.eu/strategy-and-policy/priorities-2019-2024/new-push-european-democracy/european-democracy-action-plan/european-media-freedom-act_en, accessed April 5, 2023. See also Explanatory Memorandum of the European Commission, Proposal for a Regulation of the European Parliament and of the Council establishing a common framework for media services in the internal market (European Media Freedom Act) and amending Directive 2010/13/EU 2022 [COM(2022) 457 final].

and VLOSEs moderate content may cause systemic risks to the freedom and pluralism of the media and negatively affect civic discourse. The EMFA also aims to strengthen the position of media organizations vis-à-vis online platforms. However, it remains to be seen how effective a 24-hour *non-interference* rule will be given the high threshold of who counts as a *media service provider* and which content falls within the scope of Art. 18 EMFA.

Many of the AI applications in (social) media, such as recommender systems, news bots, or the use of AI to generate or manipulate content are likely to be covered by the AI Act. A strong focus on external transparency both in the AI Act and in the DSA can be seen as a positive step to ensure that users become more aware of the extensive use of AI in (social) media.

However, many aspects of the use of AI in and by media such as the intelligibility gap, societal risks raised by AI (including worker displacement and environmental costs), as well as reliance of tech companies for access to high-quality media content to develop AI systems,[146] remain only limitedly addressed. Media organizations' dependency on social media platforms recommender systems and algorithmic content moderation as well as power imbalances in access to AI infrastructure should also be tackled by the European legal framework.

It is equally important to facilitate and stimulate responsible research and development of AI in the media sector, particularly in local and small media organizations, to avoid the AI divide. In this regard, it is worth mentioning that the Council of Europe's Committee of Experts on Increasing Resilience of the Media adopted Guidelines on the responsible implementation of AI systems in journalism.[147] The Guidelines offer practical guidance to news media organizations, States, tech providers and platforms that disseminate news, on how AI systems should be used to support the production of journalism. The Guidelines also include a checklist for media organizations to guide the procurement process of AI systems by offering questions that could help in scrutinizing the fairness of a procurement contract with an external provider (Annex 1).

Now the time has come to see how these regulations are enforced and whether they will enable a digital level playing field. To this end, policymakers, industry stakeholders, and legal professionals must work together to address the legal and ethical implications of AI in media and promote a fair and transparent use of AI.

[146] For an overview of how the media sector is responding to content crawling for model training, see Bocyte, Dutkiewicz, "How is the Media Sector Responding to Content Crawling for Model Training" *Medium* (June 18, 2024), medium.com/ai-media-observatory/how-is-the-media-sector-responding-to-content-crawling-for-model-training-9812ac2916d8, accessed August 1, 2024.

[147] Committee of Experts on Increasing Resilience of the Media (MSI-RES), *Council of Europe* (November 30, 2023), rm.coe.int/cdmsi-2023-014-guidelines-on-the-responsible-implementation-of-artific/1680adb4c6, accessed August 1, 2024.

15

AI and Healthcare Data

Griet Verhenneman

15.1 INTRODUCTION

A strict regulatory trajectory must be followed to introduce artificial intelligence in healthcare. Each stage in the development and improvement of AI for healthcare is characterized by its own regulatory framework. Let us consider AI-assisted cancer detection in medical images. Typically, the development and testing of the algorithms indicating suspicious zones requires setting up one or more clinical trials. During the clinical research stage, regulations such as the Clinical Trials Regulation apply.[1] When the results are good, the AI-assisted cancer detection software may be deployed in products such as MRI scanners. At that moment, the use of AI-assisted cancer detection software becomes standard-of-care and (national) regulatory frameworks on patients' rights must be considered. However, after the introduction of the AI-assisted cancer detection software to the market, post-market rules will require further follow-up of product safety. These regulatory instruments are just a few examples. Other identified risks, such as violations of medical secrecy or fundamental rights to the protection of private life and personal data, have led regulators to include specific rights and obligations in regulatory initiatives on the processing of personal data (such as the General Data Protection Regulation, hereinafter "GDPR"),[2] trustworthy artificial intelligence (such as the AI Act),[3] fair governance of personal and nonpersonal data (such as the Data Governance Act)[4]

[1] Regulation (EU) 536/2014 of the European Parliament and of the Council of April 16, 2014 on clinical trials on medicinal products for human use, and repealing Directive 2001/20/EC 2014.

[2] Regulation (EU) 2016/679 of the European Parliament and of the Council of April 27, 2016, on the protection of natural persons with regard to the processing of personal data and on the free movement of such data, and repealing Directive 95/46/EC (General Data Protection Regulation) 2016.

[3] Regulation (EU) 2024/1689 of the European Parliament and the Council of June 23, 2024, laying down harmonised rules on artificial intelligence and amending Regulation (EC) No 300/2008, (EU) No 167/2013, (EU) No 168/2013, (EU) 2018/858, (EU) 2018/1139 and (EU) 2019/2144 and Directives 2014/90/EU, (EU) 2016/797 and (EU) 2020/1828 (Artificial Intelligence Act).

[4] Regulation (EU) 2022/868 of the European Parliament and of the Council of May 30, 2022 on European data governance and amending Regulation (EU) 2018/1724 (Data Governance Act) 2022.

and the proposal for a Regulation on a European Health Data Space (hereinafter "EHDS").[5]

The safety of therapies, medical devices, and software is a concern everyone shares, whether or not they include AI. After all, people's lives may be at stake. Previously, incidents with more classic types of medical devices, such as metal-on-metal hip replacements[6] and PIP breast implants,[7] have led regulators to adapt the safety monitoring processes and adopt the Medical Devices Regulation and In Vitro Medical Devices Regulation.[8] When updated in 2017, these regulatory frameworks not only considered "physical" medical devices but clarified the requirements also for software as a medical device.[9] Following the increased uptake of machine learning methods and the introduction of decision-supporting and automated decision-making software in healthcare, regulators deemed it necessary to act more firmly and sharpen regulatory oversight also with respect to software as a medical device.

Throughout the development and deployment of AI in healthcare, the collection and use of data is a connecting theme. The availability of data is a condition for the development of AI. It should arrest our attention that data availability is also a regulatory requirement, especially in the healthcare sector. The collection of data to establish sufficient evidence, for example, on product safety, is not only a requirement for the development of AI but also for the permanent availability of AI-driven products on the market. Initiatives such as the Medical Devices Regulation and the AI Act have indeed enacted obligations to collect data for the purpose of establishing (evidence of) the safety of therapies, devices, and procedures.

5 Proposal for a Regulation of the European Parliament and of the Council on the European Health Data Space, COM(2022) 197 final, May 3, 2022.

6 Metal-on-metal hip replacements are all-metal implants whereby a metal ball replaces the femur, and a metal cup is created in the hip bone to keep the ball in place. When moving, the ball's metal surface touches the cup's metal surface, causing friction. Investigations by, amongst others, the BMJ and BBC Newsnight had raised concerns over metal hip implants causing people to be exposed to dangerously high levels of toxic metals. Despite the risks being known and documented since 2008, metal-on-metal hip implants continued to be used without having to pass any clinical trials. See www.bmj.com/press-releases/2012/02/28/joint-bmj-bbc-newsnight-investigation-raises-new-concerns-over-metal-hip-i.

7 The PIP breast implant was a silicon gel-based breast implant used for breast augmentation or reconstruction. The company developing the implant, Poly Implant Prothèse, had used an industrial-grade silicone that later proved to cause health risks. Gaps in the approval process had made it possible for the silicone to be used for ten years after the first indications of health risks. See Victoria Martindale and Andre Menache, "The PIP scandal: An analysis of the process of quality control that failed to safeguard women from the health risks" (2013) *Journal of the Royal Society of Medicine*, 106: 173. This case is also discussed in Chapter 12 of this Handbook, authored by Nathalie A. Smuha and Karen Yeung.

8 Regulation (EU) 2017/745 of the European Parliament and of the Council of April 5, 2017 on medical devices, amending Directive 2001/83/EC, Regulation (EC) No 178/2002; and Regulation (EC) No 1223/2009 and repealing Council Directives 90/385/EEC and 93/42/EEC 2017; Regulation (EU) 2017/746 of the European Parliament and of the Council of April 5, 2017 on in vitro diagnostic medical devices and repealing Directive 98/79/EC and Commission Decision 2010/227/EU 2017.

9 Article 2(1) and Recital 17 Medical Device Regulation provide that the software may be qualified as a medical device depending on its intended purpose.

Even though the collection of data is imposed as a legal obligation, the processing of personal data must be compliant with the GDPR. Especially in healthcare applications, AI typically requires the processing of special-category data. The GDPR considers personal data as special-category data when, due to their nature, the processing may present a higher risk to the data subject. In principle, the processing of special-category data is prohibited, while exemptions to that prohibition are specified.[10] Data concerning the health of a natural person is qualified as special-category data. Often health-related data are collected in the real world from individual data subjects.[11] Regulatory instruments such as the AI Act or the proposal for a Regulation on the EHDS explicitly mention that they shall be without prejudice to other Union legal acts, including the GDPR.[12]

Since the (re-)use of personal health-related data is key to the functioning and development of artificial intelligence for healthcare, this chapter focuses on the role of data custodians in the healthcare context. After a brief introduction to real-world data, the chapter first discusses how law distinguishes data ownership from data custodianship. How is patient autonomy embedded in the GDPR and when do patients have the right to agree or disagree via opt-in or opt-out mechanisms? Next, the chapter discusses the reuse of health-related data and more specifically how they can be shared for AI in healthcare. Federated learning is discussed as an example of a technical measure that can be adopted to enhance privacy. Transparency is discussed as an example of an organizational measure. Anonymization and pseudonymization are introduced as minimum measures to always consider before sharing health-related data for reuse.

15.2 PRE-AI: THE REQUEST FOR HEALTH-RELATED DATA

Whether private or public, hospitals and other healthcare organizations experience increasing requests to share the health-related data they collected in the "real world." "Real-world data" are relied on to produce "real-world evidence," which is subsequently relied on to support the development and evaluation of drugs, medical devices, healthcare protocols, machine learning, and AI.

Real-world data (hereinafter RWD) are collected through routine healthcare provision. Corrigan-Curay, Sacks, and Woodcock define RWD as "*data relating to patient health status or the delivery of health care routinely collected from a variety of sources, such as the [Electronic Health Record] and administrative data.*"[13]

[10] Article 9, 1. of the GDPR specifies the prohibition of processing special-category personal data. Article 9, 2. of the GDPR explains that the prohibition does not apply if one of the listed exemptions can be referred to.

[11] The data are typically subject to Article 9 General Data Protection Regulation.

[12] Article 2, 7. AI Act; Article 1, 4. proposal for a Regulation on EHDS.

[13] Jacqueline Corrigan-Curay, Leonard Sacks, and Janet Woodcock, "Real-world evidence and real-world data for evaluating drug safety and effectiveness" (2018) *The Journal of the American Medical Association*, 320: 867.

The data are, in other words, collected while healthcare organizations interact with their patients following a request from the patient. RWD result from anamneses, medicinal and non-medicinal therapies, medical imaging, laboratory tests, applied research taking place in the hospital, medical devices monitoring patient parameters, and, for example, claims and billing data. Real-world evidence (hereinafter RWE) is evidence generated through the use of RWD to complement existing knowledge regarding the usage and potential benefits or risks of a therapy, medicinal product, or device.[14]

Typically healthcare providers use an electronic health record (hereinafter EHR) to collect health-related data per patient. The EHR allows healthcare providers, working solo or in a team, to access data about their patients to follow up on patient care. However, an EHR is typically not set up to satisfy data-sharing requests for a purpose other than providing healthcare. The EHR's functionalities are chosen and developed to allow a high-quality level of care, on a continuous basis, for an individual patient. These functionalities are not necessarily the same functionalities that are needed to create reliable and trustworthy AI.

First of all, AI needs structured data. Today, most EHRs contain structured data to a certain level, but apart from structured data, most EHRs also contain a high level of natural language text. This text needs interpretation before it can be translated to structured databases suitable to feed AI applications. Even today existing AI-supported tools for deciphering natural language text were once fed with structured data on, for example, medical diagnoses, medication therapies, medication components,... as well as street names, and first and second names, for instance. The need for universal coding languages, such as the standards developed by HL7, has been long-expressed in medical informatics.[15]

Secondly, AI does, in general, not need patient names. Inevitably, an EHR, however, must allow direct identification of patients. When considering safety risks in healthcare, the misidentification of a patient would be regarded as a severe failure. Therefore, internationally recognized accreditation schemes for healthcare organizations will oblige healthcare practitioners to check multiple identifiers to uniquely identify the patient before any intervention. When EHR data are used for secondary purposes, such as the development of AI, data protection requirements will encourage the removal of patient identifiers (entirely or to the extent possible).[16]

[14] Anuradha Ramamoorthy and Shiew-Mei Huang, "What does it take to transform real-world data into real-world evidence?" (2019) *Clinical Pharmacology & Therapeutics*, 106: 10.

[15] Health Level Seven International (HL7) is an organization that develops standards to allow global health data interoperability. For more information, see www.hl7.org/about/index.cfm?ref=nav; D. M. López and B. Blobel, "Architectural approaches for HL7-based health information systems implementation" (2010) *Methods of Information in Medicine*, 49: 196.

[16] This idea is capsulated in the data minimization principle and described as a technical measure to protect data from unlawful use. See, for example, Articles 5, 1. (b), 32 and 89 GDPR.

Therefore, data holders increasingly prepare the datasets they primarily collected for the provision of healthcare to allow secondary use. While doing so, data holders will "process" personal health-related data in the sense of Article 4 (2) of the GDPR. Consequently, they must consider the principles, rights, and obligations imposed by the GDPR. They must do so when preparing data for secondary purposes they define themselves and when preparing data following instructions of a third party requesting data. In the following paragraphs, it will be explained that data holders must consider technical and organizational measures to protect personal data at that moment.

15.3 DATA OWNER- OR CUSTODIANSHIP?

Especially in discussions with laypeople, it is sometimes suggested that patients own their data. However, in the legal debate on personal and nonpersonal data, the idea of regulating the value of data in terms of ownership has been abandoned largely.[17]

First, while it is correct that individual-level health-related data are available only after patients have presented themselves, it is incorrect to assume that only patients contribute to the emergence of health-related data. Many others contribute knowledge and interpretations. Physicians, for example, build on the anamneses and add their knowledge to order tests, conclude about the diagnosis, and suggest prescriptions. Nurses observe the patient while at the hospital and while they register measurements, frequencies, and amounts. Lab technicians receive samples, run tests, and return inferred information about the sample. All of those actions generate relevant data too.

Second, from a legal perspective, it should be stressed that ownership is a right *in rem*.[18] Considering data ownership would imply that an exclusive right would rest on the data. If we were to consider the patient as the owner of their health-related data, we would have to acknowledge an exclusive right to decide who can have, hold, modify, or destroy the data (and who cannot). EU law does not support such a legal status for data. On the contrary, when considering personal data, it should be stressed that a salient characteristic of the GDPR is the balance it seeks between the individual's rights and society's interests. The fundamental right to the protection of personal data is not and has never been an absolute right. Ducuing indicates that

[17] See, for example, Kathleen Liddell, David A. Simon, and Anneke Lucassen, "Patient data ownership: Who owns your health?" (2021) *Journal of Law and the Biosciences*, 8: lsab023; Gianclaudio Malgieri, "'User-provided personal content' in the EU: Digital currency between data protection and intellectual property" (2018) *International Review of Law, Computers & Technology*. 32: 118.

[18] The European Union Intellectual Property Office describes a "right in rem" also as a "real right" or a right that reflects the absolute right to recover, possess and enjoy a specific object. Rights in rem are directed toward an object rather than a person and therefore differ from rights "in personam." See EUIPO Trade mark guidelines, Part E, Section 15.3, Chapter 2: Licenses, rights in rem, levies of execution, insolvency proceedings, entitlement proceedings or similar proceedings, ed. 2023.

more recent regulatory initiatives (such as the Data Governance Act) present "traces" of data ownership to organize the commodification and the economic value of data as a resource. The "traces," Ducuing concludes, seem to suggest a somewhat functional approach in which, through a mixture of legal sources, including ownership and the GDPR, one aims to regulate data as an economic resource.[19]

Instead, it is essential to consider data custodianship. The custodian must demonstrate a high level of knowledge and awareness about potential risks for data subjects, especially when they are in a vulnerable position, such as patients. Data custodians should be aware of and accept the responsibility connected to their role as a guardian of personal data. In healthcare organizations, the pressure is high to see to the protection of health-related data kept in an EHR and to ensure attention for the patient as the data subject behind valuable datasets, and rightfully so. Not more than patients, data custodians should consider EHR data as "their" data in terms of ownership. They are expected to consider the conditions for data sharing carefully, but they should not hinder sharing when the request is legitimate and lawful.

15.3.1 *Custodianship and Patient Autonomy*

When considering patient autonomy as a concept reflecting individuality,[20] the question arises how the GDPR allows the data subject to decide autonomously about the reuse of personal data for the development or functioning of AI. While, as explained earlier, data protection is not enacted as an absolute right, patients can decide autonomously about the processing of their data unless the law provides otherwise. In general terms, Article 8 of the European Convention on Human Rights and Article 52 of the Charter of Fundamental Rights of the European Union provide that limitations to the fundamental rights to the respect for private life and the protection of personal data shall be allowed only when necessary in a democratic society and meeting the objectives of general interest or the protection of rights and freedoms of others. A cumulative reading of Articles 6 and 9 of the GDPR can establish a more concrete interpretation of this general principle. Together, Articles 6 and 9 of the GDPR provide the limitative list of situations in which the (secondary)

[19] Charlotte Ducuing, "What can we still learn from data ownership? The traces of ownership in the regulation of data as an economic resource" (ELI Digital Law SIG Seminar, online, June 1, 2022).

[20] John Stuart Mill adopted the concept of individuality as a characteristic of the self-determining and self-ruling subject reflecting authentic subjective preferences. Many refer to the work of John Stuart Mill when discussing the patient as an autonomous individual. See, for example, Thomas Nys, Yvonne Denier, and Toon Vandevelde, *Autonomy & Paternalism: Reflections on the Theory of Health Care* (Peeter Publishers, 2007). For a more extensive discussion on the role of autonomy in relation to the processing of health-related data see also Griet Verhenneman, *The Patient, Data Protection and Changing Healthcare Models: The Impact of e-Health on Informed Consent, Anonymisation and Purpose Limitation* (Intersentia, 2021), www.cambridge.org/core/books/patient-data-protection-and-changing-healthcare-models/5B12AE59BE02759D9762B14C768E5FD5, accessed February 19, 2023, 137–140.

use of personal health-related data is allowed without the patient's consent.[21] In these situations, the data subject's wish is considered to not necessarily prevail over the interests of other parties or society. Examples include the collection of health-related data for the treatment of a patient. Depending on specifications in Member State law, the collection can be based on Article 6, 1. (b) "performance of a contract to which the data subject is party" or 6, 1. (c) "legal obligation to which the data controller is subject" on the one hand, and Article 9, 2. (h) "necessary for the provision of health" on the other hand.[22] A national cancer screening program is another example. In this case, the data collection is typically enacted in Member State law, causing Article 6, 1. (e) "performance of a task in the public interest" to apply in combination with Article 9, 2. (h) "necessary for purposes of preventive medicine."

Another situation in which the data subject's individual wishes do not prevail over society's interest concerns scientific research. By default, data can be reused for scientific research. The data subject's consent (opt-in) is not required, and when in the public interest, the data subject does not even enjoy a right to opt out.[23] First of all, Article 5, 1. (b) of the GDPR provides a specification of the purpose limitation principle indicating that "*further processing for [...] scientific [...] research purposes [...] shall, in accordance with article 89 (1), not be considered to be incompatible with the initial purpose.*" Additionally, Article 9, 2. (j) provides that contrary to the general prohibition to process health-related data, the processing is allowed when necessary for the purpose of scientific research. The application of Article 6.4 of the GDPR to the secondary use of personal data has raised some discussions, but not in a research context. Read together with Recital 50, Article 6.4. of the GDPR indicates that a new legal basis is not required when the secondary processing can be compatible with the primary processing. A combined reading of Article 6.4. and Article 5, 1. (b) has convinced many[24] that a new legal basis is indeed not required when the purpose of the secondary processing is scientific research.[25]

[21] On the need for a legal basis to process personal data, see also Chapter 7 of this book, authored by Pierre Dewitte.

[22] Some Member States qualify the patient–doctor relationship as contractual. Some Member States impose a legal obligation for the healthcare practitioner to keep a(n) electronic health record for each patient.

[23] Article 21, 6. GDPR.

[24] Dutch Data Protection Authority "Adviesverzoek onderzoek oversterfte," February 13, 2022, available online: www.autoriteitpersoonsgegevens.nl/sites/default/files/atoms/files/advies_ap_onderzoek_oversterfte.pdf; Request for advice European Data Protection Board, "Guidelines 03/2020 on the processing of data concerning health for the purpose of scientific research in the context of the COVID-19 outbreak" (2020) 03/2020 6; Evelien De Sutter et al., "Rethinking informed consent in the time of COVID-19: An exploratory survey" (2022) 9 Frontiers in Medicine 995688; G. Verhenneman et al., "How GDPR enhances transparency and fosters pseudonymisation in academic medical research" (2020) *European Journal of Health Law*, 27: 35.

[25] About other types of secondary use (such as post-market monitoring of a medical device, market authorization applications, and reimbursement dossiers submitted to national health programs), the application of especially Recital 50 seems to be somewhat more contested. See Mahsa Shabani and

It should, however, be noted that notwithstanding the intention of the GDPR to achieve a higher level of harmonization, one specific provision should not be overlooked when discussing patient autonomy in relation to health-related data. Article 9, 4. of the GDPR foresees that Member States may introduce further restrictions on the processing of health-related, genetic, and biometric data.[26] Building on this provision, some Member States have introduced the obligation to obtain informed consent from the individual as an additional measure to empower patients.[27]

15.3.2 *Informed Consent for Data Processing*

When the purpose for which data are shared cannot be covered by a legal basis available in Article 6 and an additional safeguard as laid down in Article 9 of the GDPR, the (valid) informed consent of the patient should be sought prior to the secondary processing. In that case, the requested informed consent should reflect patient autonomy. The conditions for valid informed consent, as laid down in Articles 4 (11) and 7 of the GDPR, indicate that the concept of informed consent was developed as an instrument for individuals to express their wishes and be empowered. These articles stress that consent must be freely given, specific, informed, and reflect an unambiguous indication of the data subject's wishes. The controller shall be able to demonstrate that the data subject has consented and shall respect the fact that consent can be withdrawn at any time, with no motivation required.

These requirements may sound obvious, but they are challenging to fulfill in practice. In particular, the fact that for informed consent to be freely given a valid alternative for not providing consent for the processing of personal data should be available is often an issue.[28] Typically, data processing is a consequence of a service, product, or project,... especially in the context of AI. I cannot agree to participate in a data-driven research project to develop AI for medical imaging without allowing my MRI scan to be processed. I cannot use an AI-supported meal app that provides personalized dietary suggestions while not allowing data about my eating habits to be shared. I cannot use an AI-driven screening app for skin cancer without allowing

Sami Yilmaz, "Lawfulness in secondary use of health data: Interplay between three regulatory frameworks of GDPR, DGA & EHDS" (2022) *Technology and Regulation*, 2022: 128.

[26] Article 9, 4. GDPR.

[27] These conclusions are based on the work done on the secondary use of personal data for research purposes by a consortium led by MILIEU, with contributions from UNamur (CRIDS/NaDI), KULeuven (CiTIP), University of Leiden (eLaw) and Vrije Universiteit Amsterdam (CLI). The authors of the study are Teodora Lalova, Els Kindt, Eleftherios Chelioudakis, Griet Verhenneman, Antoine Delforge and Jean Herverg. National-level input was provided by Carla Barbosa, Elisabetta Biasin, Gauthier Chassang, Eleftherios Chelioudakis, Athena Christofi, Agnes Csonta, Antoine Delforge, Ivo Emanuilov, Danaja Fabcic, Nenad Georgiev, Dara Hallinan, Erik Kamenjasevic, Linda de Keyser, Karolina La Fors, Teodora Lalova, Zuzana Lukacova, Sjaak Nouwt, Domenico Orlando, Anastasia Siapka, Griet Verhenneman, and Katerina Yordanova.

[28] See, for example, reservations expressed by the European Data Protection Supervisor, "A preliminary opinion on data protection and scientific research" (2020) 19–21.

a picture of my skin to be uploaded. In this case, it should be questioned whether data can be reused or shared for secondary purposes based on informed consent.

15.4 SHARING DATA FOR AI IN HEALTHCARE

"Data have evolved from being a scarce resource, difficult to gather, managed in a centralized way and costly to store, transmit and process, to becoming an abundant resource created in a decentralized way (by individuals or sensors) easy to replicate, and to communicate or broadcast on a global scale."[29] This is how the European Union Agency for Cybersecurity (ENISA) introduces her report on how to ensure privacy-preserving data sharing. The quote is illustrative not only for the naturalness with which we think about keeping data for secondary use but also for the seemingly infinite number of initiatives that can benefit from the reuse of data, including personal data. In that sense, sharing health-related data differs significantly from sharing human bodily material. While the number of projects that can benefit from one sample of bodily material is, per definition, limited to, for example, the number of cuts that can be made, the reuse of data only ends when the data itself have become irrelevant.

It is essential to stress that facilitating data sharing is also a specific intent of regulators. Policy documents on FAIR data,[30] open science initiatives, and the proposal for a European Health Data Space are just a few examples hereof. *"Sharing data is already starting to become the norm and not the exception in data processing,"* ENISA continues.[31] Even in the GDPR itself, it is stated that: *"The free movement of personal data within the Union shall be neither restricted nor prohibited for reasons connected with the protection of natural persons with regard to the processing of personal data."*[32] Although frustrations over the rigidity of the GDPR sometimes seem to gain the upper hand, also in discussions on the secondary use of data, the goal of the Regulation is thus not to hamper but to facilitate the processing of personal data.

During the COVID-19 pandemic, several authors stressed this fundamental assumption also in relation to health-related data. Albeit specific requirements must be met, the processing of personal health-related data is not necessarily not allowed.[33] Two weeks after the outbreak, the European Data Protection Board, for example, issued a statement indicating that *"data protection rules (such as the GDPR) do not*

[29] ENISA, "Engineering personal data sharing" (2023) Report/Study www.enisa.europa.eu/publications/engineering-personal-data-sharing, accessed February 22, 2023.

[30] "FAIR" stands for Findable, Accessible, Interoperable and Reusable. The FAIR Data Principles are used as a guideline for those wishing to enhance the reusability of the data.

[31] Ibid.

[32] Article 1 GDPR.

[33] Marcello Ienca and Effy Vayena, "On the responsible use of digital data to tackle the COVID-19 pandemic" (2020) *Nature Medicine*, 26: 463.

hinder measures taken in the fight against the coronavirus pandemic."[34] Several possible exemptions that would allow the processing of health-related data in the fight against COVID-19 were stressed and explained. The European Data Protection Board (EDPB) pointed at the purpose limitation and transparency principle and the importance of adopting security measures and confidentiality policies as core principles that should be considered, even in an international emergency.

To meet these principles, so-called data protection- or privacy-enhancing measures must be considered. Different privacy-enhancing techniques can be applied to the data flows and infrastructures. At the operational level of a healthcare organization, suggestions for privacy-preserving techniques profiles such as data protection officers, compliance officers, or the chief information security officer typically suggest the implementation of measures. "*It used to be the case that if you did nothing at all, you would have privacy [...]. Now, you need to take conscious, deliberate, intentional actions to attain any level of privacy. [...] This is why Privacy Enhancing Technologies (PETs) exist,*" writes Adams referring to technical measures that can be implemented to better protect data about individuals.[35] Examples of such PETs include pseudonymization through polymorphic encryption[36] and federated learning, but next to technical measures, organizational measures such as transparency must also be considered.

The following sections illustrate the impact and necessity of privacy-enhancing measures in health-related scenarios. Anonymization and pseudonymization are discussed first. They are considered minimum measures to consider before reusing personal data. However, because anonymous data are considered out of the material scope of the GDPR while pseudonymous data are considered in scope, it is essential to understand the difference between them. Next, by discussing two other examples of privacy-enhancing techniques, one technical and one organizational, it is illustrated how anticipating the technical and the organizational aspects of a data flow help to ensure the robust protection of personal data as an "abundant resource."

15.4.1 *Anonymization and Pseudonymization*

In the GDPR, a preference for the use of anonymized data over pseudonymized and non-pseudonymized data is expressed, for example, in the data minimization principle, as a security measure and in relation to scientific research.[37] The use of

[34] Andrea Jelinek, "Statement by the EDPB chair on the processing of personal data in the context of the COVID-19 outbreak" (2020), https://edpb.europa.eu/news/news/2020/statement-edpb-chair-processing-personal-data-context-covid-19-outbreak_en.

[35] Carlisle Adams, *Introduction to Privacy Enhancing Technologies: A Classification-Based Approach to Understanding PETs* (Springer International Publishing, 2021), https://link.springer.com/10.1007/978-3-030-81043-6, accessed February 21, 2023. p. 2.

[36] ENISA (n 29) 13.

[37] Articles 5, 1. (c); 32 and 89 GDPR in particular.

anonymized data is considered to present a sufficiently low risk for the data subject's fundamental rights to allow the processing without any further measures, and is hence excluded from the GDPR's requirements.[38] Pseudonymized data, however, fall under the GDPR because the data can still be attributed to an individual data subject.[39]

In healthcare and other data-intensive sectors, for data not to fall under the definition of personal data, as provided in Article 4(1) of the GDPR, is increasingly difficult due to enhanced data availability and data linkability.[40] Data availability relates to the number of data kept about individuals. Data are not only kept in EHRs but spread over many other datasets held by public and private organizations. Data linkability relates to the ease with which data from different datasets can be combined. Machine learning and other types of AI have a distinct impact in this sense as they facilitate this process.

Requirements on open science,[41] explainability,[42] and citizen empowerment[43] stimulate data holders to increase the level of data availability and linkability. To create innovations this is a great assumption, but there is another side to the coin. A higher level of data availability and linkability requires data holders, such as healthcare organizations, to increasingly qualify data as pseudonymous rather than anonymous.

Influential studies continue to show limitations in anonymization techniques in relation to patient data. Schwarz et al., for example, reidentified patients based on de-identified MRI head scans, which were released for research purposes. Schwarz's research team showed that in 83% of the cases, face-recognition software matched

[38] Art 4(1) and Recital 26 GDPR.

[39] Art 4(5) GDPR.

[40] For a detailed analysis of the qualification of health-related data as personal data under Article 4(1) of the GDPR, see Griet Verhenneman, *The Patient, Data Protection and Changing Healthcare Models: The Impact of e-Health on Informed Consent, Anonymisation and Purpose Limitation* (Intersentia, 2021), www.cambridge.org/core/books/patient-data-protection-and-changing-healthcare-models/5B12AE59BE02759D9762B14C768E5FD5, accessed February 19, 2023.

[41] Open science is considered the standard working method for all European Union research and innovation funding programs. Beneficiaries must make their data available, including source data, as open as possible. See European Union, Unit Research, and Innovation, "Open Science" (2019), available at: https://research-and-innovation.ec.europa.eu/system/files/2019-12/ec_rtd_factsheet-open-science_2019.pdf.

[42] Explainability refers to the idea that technology, such as AI, should not be a black box but allow transparency and traceability to enable humans to understand the decisions made through artificial intelligence. See Andreas Holzinger et al., "Causability and explainability of artificial intelligence in medicine" (2019) *WIREs Data Mining and Knowledge Discovery*, 9: e1312.

[43] Especially, while not exclusively, in the context of genomic research, the idea of returning results of scientific research to individual study participants has been suggested as an essential requirement for achieving justice, beneficence, and respect for persons. To allow the return of results, the participant must remain re-identifiable, for example, by attaching a unique code to the human bodily samples obtained for research purposes. See Emmanuelle Lévesque, Yann Joly, and Jacques Simard, "Return of research results: general principles and international perspectives" (2011) *The Journal of Law, Medicine & Ethics*, 39: 583.

an MRI with a publicly available picture. In 95% of the cases, the image of the actual patient was amongst the five selected public profiles.[44] Studies such as Schwarz's led to the development of "defacing techniques," a privacy-enhancing measure to hinder the reidentification of head scans.[45] However, is the hindrance caused by the defacing technique sufficient for the scan to qualify as nonpersonal data?

To answer that question, it is important to stress that the scope of the GDPR is not delineated based on the presence of certain specific identifiers in a particular dataset. Contrary to, for example, the US Health Insurance Portability and Accountability Act (HIPAA),[46] which provides that individually identifiable information can be de-identified by removing the listed identifiers (exhaustive account) from the dataset, the GDPR requires a more complex assessment. The possibility for the controller or another person to single out a data subject building on the information in the dataset *and any additional information* that can be obtained using all the means reasonably likely must be evaluated. When considering the MRI image, this means that account must be taken of the MRI image with defacing techniques applied, pictures available on the internet, *and* the original MRI available in the EHR even when this image is not available to the data controller.[47]

15.4.2 *Federated Learning, an Example of a Privacy-Enhancing Technical Measure*

Federated analysis allows for building knowledge from data kept in different local sources (such as various EHRs in hospitals, public health databases in countries, or potentially even individual health "pods" kept by citizens[48]) while avoiding the transfer of individual-level data.[49] Hence, federated analysis is presented as a solution to avoid the centralization of (personal) health-related data for secondary use.

Imagine building an AI model for cancer detection through MRI images: In a nonfederated scenario, the MRI images are requested through multiple participating hospitals, pseudonymized, and subsequently collected in a central, project-specific database. The algorithm is trained on the central database. In a federated scenario, however, the MRI images are not pooled in a central database. Instead, they remain with the local hospital. The algorithmic model, carrying out analytical tasks, visits the local databases ("nodes") and executes tasks on the locally stored

44 Christopher G. Schwarz et al., "Identification of anonymous MRI research participants with face-recognition software" (2019) *The New England Journal of Medicine*, 381: 1684.

45 Elizabeth EL Buimer et al., "De-identification procedures for magnetic resonance images and the impact on structural brain measures at different ages" (2021) *Human Brain Mapping*, 42: 3643.

46 Health Insurance Portability and Accountability Act [HIPAA] of 1996, Pub. L. No. 104–191.

47 Article 29 Working Party Opinion 05/2014 on Anonymisation Techniques, April 10, 2014, 9.

48 Hemant Ghayvat et al., "SHARIF: Solid pod-based secured healthcare information storage and exchange solution in internet of things" (2022) *IEEE Transactions on Industrial Informatics*, 18: 5609.

49 Felix Nikolaus Wirth et al., "Privacy-preserving data sharing infrastructures for medical research: systematization and comparison" (2021) *BMC Medical Informatics and Decision Making*, 21: 242.

MRI images.[50] Subsequently, aggregated results (the conclusions) are shared with a central node for merging and meta-analysis. On the condition of a small cell risk analysis,[51] these results can often be considered nonpersonal data because individual patients can no longer be singled out.

Avoiding centralization is particularly interesting because it can reduce the risk of illicit data usage. The control on the secondary use remains with the data holder: A data custodian (such as a hospital), the individual (such as a patient), or perhaps, as suggested in Article 17 et seq of the Data Governance Act, a recognized data altruism organization.[52] Unlike organizational measures, such as contractual arrangements on the purpose of the processing, federated learning thus allows the data holder to manage the processing independently.

The implementation of federated learning should, however, not trigger the assumption that the processing operations are not covered by the material scope of the GDPR. Federated learning does not avoid the processing of personal data for a secondary purpose. It merely avoids the transfer of personal data. In other words: the processing takes place locally, but data are reused for a purpose different from the purpose for which they were initially collected. Consequently, GDPR requirements must be complied with, including the need for a legal basis.

Following Article 4 (7) of the GDPR, the party defining the purpose and (at least the essential) means of the secondary use should be considered the data controller. Generally, the requestor, not the requestee, defines the purpose and means of the secondary processing. Therefore the requestor is considered the data controller.[53] The location of the data processing (locally or centrally) is irrelevant. Who has access to the data is equally irrelevant.[54] Consequently, although a data transfer

[50] Oya Beyan et al., "Distributed analytics on sensitive medical data: The personal health train" (2020) *Data Intelligence*, 2: 96; J. Simm et al., "Splitting chemical structure data sets for federated privacy-preserving machine learning" (2021) *Journal of Cheminformatics*, 13: 96; A. Ardeshirdavani et al., NGS-logistics: Federated analysis of NGS sequence variants across multiple locations (2014), *Genome Medicine*, 6: 17.

[51] Depending on the level of specificity in the number of individuals that are included in the aggregation, aggregated data may still allow the extraction of personal data. Hence, when considering the data that are shared with the central node as anonymous one should first assess in how far individuals can still be singled out. See also N. Truong et al., "Privacy preservation in federated learning: An insightful survey from the GDPR perspective" (2021) *Computers & Security*, 110: 102402.

[52] Article 18 Data Governance Act defines the tasks of a data altruism organization.

[53] Nevertheless, the qualification of the requestee as a joint controller is a possibility we must consider. Should the requestee and the requestor determine the secondary purpose of the processing together, they will be qualified as joint-controllers. This may be the case when the parties are setting up a research project together and determining the project's scope, research questions, work packages, and tasks within the work packages. See Brendan Van Alsenoy, *Data Protection Law in the EU: Roles, Responsibilities and Liability* (Intersentia 2019) 331–334, https://intersentia.be/nl/data-protection-law-in-the-eu-roles-responsibilities-and-liability-48825.html, accessed February 24, 2023.

[54] Parties may be qualified as data controller even if they do not have access to the data, the European Court of Justice confirmed, see *Tietosuojavaltuutettu (Supreme Administrative Court Finland) vs Jehovan todistajat – uskonnollinen yhdyskunta (Jehovah's witnesses)* [2018] European Court of Justice (Grand Chamber) EU:C:2018:551.

agreement may be avoided when sharing merely anonymous data with the central node, a data processing agreement (or joined controller agreement) must be in place before reusing the data.[55]

15.4.3 *Transparency, an Example of a Privacy-Enhancing Organizational Measure*

The importance of transparency cannot be overestimated. As indicated by the EDPB in the adopted Article 29 Working Party Guidelines on transparency under the GDPR: "*transparency is a long established feature [...] engendering trust in the processes which affect the citizen by enabling them to understand, and if necessary, challenge those processed.*"[56] The transparency principle entails an overarching obligation to ensure fairness and accountability. Therefore, data controllers must provide clear information that allows data subjects to have correct expectations.

The transparency obligation is a general obligation isolated from any information obligations that may follow from informed consent as a legal basis. Whichever legal basis is most suitable and whether it concerns primary or secondary use, the data controller is responsible for providing transparent information actively (following Articles 13 and 14 GDPR) and passively (following a data subject access request under Article 15 GDPR). This includes the obligation to inform about (intentions to) reuse.[57]

Today data controllers often focus on the availability of general information on websites, in brochures, and in privacy notices, to comply with their transparency obligation. Unfortunately, these general information channels often prove insufficient to enable data subjects to really understand for which purposes and by whom data *about them* is used. They feel insufficiently empowered to hold the data controller accountable or to exercise control over their personal data. If other patients' rights such as the right not to know, can be respected, wouldn't it make sense to create personalized overviews of secondary data processing operations in an era where personalization is a buzzword? These overviews could be provided through consumer interfaces such as client accounts, personalized profiles, or billing platforms. In healthcare, it is no longer uncommon for healthcare providers to provide patients with a direct view of their medical records through an app or website. A patient-tailored overview of secondary use could be included in this patient viewer.

[55] Following respectively Article 28 or 26 GDPR.

[56] Article 29 Working Party, "Guidelines on Transparency under Regulation 2016/679" (2018) WP260 rev. 01 4.

[57] Article 13, 3. and Article 14, 4. explicitly foresee the obligation to inform about the processing of data for "a purpose other than that for which the data were obtained," while Article 13, 1. (e), Article 14, 1. (e) and Article 15, 1. (c) oblige controllers to inform the data subject about "recipients or categories of recipients to whom the personal data have been disclosed." See also EDPB, Document on response to the request from the European Commission for clarifications on the consistent application of the GDPR, focusing on health research, adopted February 2, 2021, 9.

As a side note, it must be mentioned that the EDPB announced further clarifications on the scope of the exceptions to the obligation to actively inform data subjects individually.[58] Article 14, 5. (b) of the GDPR acknowledges that when data were not obtained directly from the data subject, it may occur that "*the provision of information proves impossible or would involve a disproportionate effort.*"[59] In earlier interpretations, the limitations of this exception were stressed explaining It that the data controller must demonstrate either impossibility or a disproportionate effort. In demonstrating why Article 14, 5. (b) should apply, data controllers must mention the factors that prevent them from providing the information and illustrate the impact and effects for the data subject when not provided with the information in the case of disproportionate effort.[60]

15.5 CONCLUSIONS

In Belgium, the seven university hospitals developed a methodology to see to their responsibility as the guardian of health-related data. While not exclusively intended to address the requests for the reuse of data for AI, it was noted that requests for secondary use have an "*increasing variability in purpose, scope and nature*" and include "*the support of evidence-based medicine and value-driven healthcare strategies, the development of medical devices, including those relying on machine learning and artificial intelligence.*"[61] The initiative of the Belgian university hospitals is just one illustration of the need for legal and ethical guidelines on the use of health-related data for AI. As indicated by the Belgian hospitals, the goal is "*to keep hospitals and healthcare practitioners from accepting illegitimate proposals [for the secondary use of real-world data].*"[62] The same intention can also be found in regulatory initiatives such as the Act on AI and the Proposal for a Regulation on the European Health Data Space.

Any initiative for future regulations or guidelines will build on the provisions already included in Europe's General Data Protection Regulation. Even with the need to clarify specific provisions and harmonize various interpretations of these provisions, the GDPR lays down the principles that must be considered when collecting data for AI.

58 EDPB, "Document on response to the request from the European Commission for clarifications on the consistent application of the GDPR, focusing on health research, adopted February 2, 2021, 9."

59 Article 29 Working Party (n 56) 30–31

60 Article 29 Working Party Guidelines on transparency under Regulation 2016/679, as adopted on 29, November 2017 and last revised and adopted on April 11, 2018 and as adopted by the EDPB during its first plenary meeting on May 25, 2018, 28–29.

61 Raad Universitaire Ziekenhuizen België, "Common position establishing a framework for secondary use of real-world data (routinely) collected in hospitals," adopted July 7, 2022, available online at: www.univ-hospitals.be/common-position-establishing-a-framework-for-secondary-use-of-real-world-data-routinely-collected-in-hospitals/

62 Ibid.

Within the healthcare domain, the data necessary for the development and use of AI are unlikely to be qualified as anonymous data. Most likely, they will fall under the definition of pseudonymized data as provided in Article 4 (5) of the GDPR. Notwithstanding the general prohibition to process health-related data pursuant to Article 9, 1. of the GDPR, the processing of health-related data can be justified when the interests of society or other parties prevail over the interests of the individual data subject or when informed consent reflects the data subject's wish. Additionally, all other data protection principles, such as transparency, must be respected.

Despite the numerous current and future challenges arising from regulatory instruments applicable to data custodians and data users and ongoing ethical discussions, the key message should not be that we should refrain from using health-related data for AI. Rather, we should never forget that behind the data are flesh-and-blood people who deserve protection through the implementation of organizational and technical measures.

16

Artificial Intelligence and Financial Services

Katja Langenbucher

16.1 INTRODUCTION

"Information processing," "decision-making," and "achievement of specific goals." These are among the key elements defining artificial intelligence (AI) in a JRC Technical Report of the European Commission.[1] Information processing is understood as "collecting and interpreting inputs (in the form of data)," decision-making as "taking actions, performance of tasks (…) with certain level of autonomy," and achievement of specific goals as "the ultimate reason of AI systems."[2] All these elements play a key role in financial services. Against this background, it is unsurprising that AI has started to fundamentally change many aspects of finance.

The actors that are active in the financial world process vast amounts of information, starting from customer data and account movements over market trading data to credit underwriting or money-laundering checks. As the earlier definition suggests, it is one thing to collect and store these data, and yet another challenge to interpret and make sense of them. Artificial intelligence helps with both, for example by checking databases or crawling the internet in search of relevant information, by sorting it according to predefined categories, or by finding its own sorting parameter. In this way, AI provides input to decision-making of financial institutions, of financial intermediaries such as a broker or investment adviser, and of regulatory agencies, monitoring financial institutions and markets such as the US SEC or the European Central Bank.

Today, decision-making based on AI preparatory work often involves human actors. However, the spectrum of tasks that can be wholly or partly performed by AI is growing. Some of these tasks are repetitive chores such as a chatbot used in customer communication or a robo-advisor suggesting how to best invest. Others

1 Samoili Sofia et al., *AI Watch. Defining Artificial Intelligence. Towards an Operational Definition and Taxonomy of Artificial Intelligence* (JRC Publications Repository, 2020) 8, https://publications.jrc.ec.europa.eu/repository/handle/JRC118163, accessed July 22, 2024 (with further references on each element, a fourth element listed in the report (but less salient for financial services) is the perception of the environment).

2 Ibid.

require enormous speed, for instance, high-frequency algorithmic trading of financial instruments, reacting in split seconds to new market information.[3]

AI involves a goal or a "definition of success"[4] which it is trained to optimize. A regulatory agency tasked with monitoring insider trading might employ an AI system to search market data for suspicious trades. The agency predefines what it understands as suspicious, for instance, large sales right before bad news is released to the market, and supervises what the AI system finds, to make sure it gets it right. With more sophisticated AI, regulators train the AI system to learn what a suspicious trade is. The Italian Consob, together with a group of researchers, has explored unsupervised machine learning of this type, allowing it to "provide an indication on whether the trading behavior of an investor or a group of investors is anomalous or not, thus supporting the monitoring and surveillance processes by the competent Authority and the assessment of the conduct."[5]

There is a broad range of ethical issues when employing AI in financial services. Many of these are not entirely novel concerns, but AI might make the risks they entail more likely to happen. As the OECD has noted in a report on AI, a tactic called "tacit collusion" to the detriment of market competition might become easier.[6]

> In a tacitly collusive context, the non-competitive outcome is achieved by each participant deciding its own profit-maximizing strategy independently of its competitors. (...) The dynamic adaptive capacity of self-learning and deep learning AI models can therefore raise the risk that the model recognizes the mutual interdependencies and adapts to their behavior and actions of other market participants or other AI models, possibly reaching a collusive outcome without any human intervention and perhaps without even being aware of it.[7]

Cyber security threats count among these risks:

> While the deployment of AI does not open up possibilities of new cyber breaches, it could exacerbate pre-existing ones by, *inter alia*, linking falsified data and cyber breaches, creating new attacks which can alter the functioning of the algorithm through the introduction of falsified data into models or the alteration of existing ones.[8]

3 Jasmina Arifovic, Xuezhong He, and Lijian Wei, "High frequency trading in FinTech age: AI with speed" (2019), https://papers.ssrn.com/sol3/Papers.cfm?abstract_id=2771153, accessed July 22, 2024.

4 Cathy O' Neil, *Weapons of Math Destruction: How Big Data Increases Inequality and Threatens Democracy* (Penguin Books, 2016) 21.

5 Consob et al., "A machine learning approach to support decision in insider trading detection" (December 5, 2022), www.consob.it/documents/1912911/1933915/FinTech_11.pdf/eebb010d-e5e8-9f75-9e77-b2a1407e418f, accessed July 22, 2024.

6 OECD, "Artificial intelligence, machine learning and big data in finance, opportunities, challenges and implications for policy makers" (2021) 40, www.oecd-ilibrary.org/docserver/98e761e7-en.pdf?expires=1721652654&id=id&accname=guest&checksum=0F3E9BBBAD171D31FCB2E11F4BE3D33C, accessed July 22, 2024.

7 Ibid.

8 Ibid., 38.

The same goes for data protection. This has long been identified as a core policy concern in the digitalized world.[9] Black box algorithms compound the problem when consumers are not only uncertain that data are collected but do not know what an AI system will make of the information it processes:

> These systems run historical data through an algorithm, which then comes up with a prediction or course of action. Yet often we don't know how such a system reaches its conclusion. It might work correctly, or it might have a technical error inside of it. It might even reproduce some form of bias, like racism, without the designers even realising it.[10]

For financial services, the complicated interplay between data protection, biases of AI models, and big data available to be processed at low cost is of particular concern. The EU has selected credit scoring and creditworthiness assessments of natural persons as a "high-risk AI system," facing strict compliance requirements.[11] Additionally, the (reformed) Consumer Credit Directive[12] engages with consumer rights whenever an AI system produces a score.

In what follows, this chapter takes AI scoring and creditworthiness assessments as an example of how AI is employed in financial services (Section 16.2), for the ethical challenges this raises (Section 16.3), and for the legal tools that attempt to adequately balance advantages and challenges of this technique (Section 16.4). It closes with a look at scoring beyond the credit situation (Section 16.5).

16.2 AN ILLUSTRATION: AI-BASED CREDITWORTHINESS EVALUATIONS AND CREDIT SCORING[13]

A financial institution that hands out a loan and prices interest rates must first conduct an assessment of the borrower's credit risk. This is an evident business rationale and is required by several laws. Some of these have the overall stability of the

9 Shoshana Zuboff, *The Age of Surveillance Capitalism: The Fight for a Human Future at the New Frontier of Power* (Public Affairs, 2019).

10 Tom Cassauwers, "Opening the 'black box' of artificial intelligence" *Horizon* (December 1, 2020), https://ec.europa.eu/research-and-innovation/en/horizon-magazine/opening-black-box-artificial-intelligence, accessed July 22, 2024.

11 Regulation (EU) 2024/1689 of the European Parlament and of the Council laying down harmonised rules on artificial intelligence of June 13, 2024 (Artificial Intelligence Act, AI Act) and amending Regulations (EC) No 300/2008, (EU) No 167/2013, (EU) No 168/2013, (EU) 2018/858, (EU) 2018/1139 and (EU) 2019/2144 and Directives 2014/90/EU, (EU) 2016/797 and (EU) 2020/1828, Art. 6(2), Annex III No. 5(b).

12 Directive (EU) 2023/2225 of the European Parliament and of the Council of October 18, 2023 on credit agreements for consumers and repealing Directive 2008/48/EC (Directive (EU) 2023/2225).

13 In what follows, I draw on a working paper of mine: Katja Langenbucher, "Consumer Credit in The Age of AI – Beyond Anti-Discrimination Law" ECGI Law Working Paper N° 663/2022 (November 2022), www.ecgi.global/working-paper/consumer-credit-age-ai—beyond-anti-discrimination-law, accessed July 22, 2024. In the following text, I sometimes include literal quotes from my working paper. For better readability, I do not use quotation marks.

financial system in mind. To reduce risk, they attempt to ensure that financial institutions have clearly established procedures to hand out credit and monitor credit portfolios.[14] Other laws focus on both, financial stability, and the creditor. Following the financial crisis of 2008, irresponsible lending practices on mortgage markets had been identified as a potential source of the crisis.[15] Reacting to this concern, EU legislators aimed at restoring consumer confidence.[16] After the pandemic, and fueled by concerns about increasing digitalization, the Proposal for a Consumer Credit Directive explicitly stresses that the assessment of the creditworthiness of the borrower will be done "in the interest of the consumer, to prevent irresponsible lending practices and overindebtedness."[17]

16.2.1 *Traditional Methods to Predict Credit Default Risk*

When going about an evaluation, the lender faces uncertainty about an applicant's credit default risk. In the parlance of economics, he must rely on observable variables to reconstruct hidden fundamental information.[18] Sociologists add the role of trust in social relations to explain the denial or success of a loan application.[19] The potential borrower will provide some information himself, for instance on existing obligations, income, or assets. To reduce uncertainty, the lender will often require additional input. Historically, a variable as qualitative and vague as "character" was "considered the foundation of consumer creditworthiness."[20] Starting in the 1930s, lenders profited from advances in statistics which allowed to correlate attributes of

[14] Directive 2013/36/EU of the European Parliament and of the Council of June 26, 2013, on access to the activity of credit institutions and the prudential supervision of credit institutions and investment firms, amending Directive 2002/87/EC and repealing Directives 2006/48/EC and 2006/49/EC [2013] OJ L176/38, Art. 79.

[15] Directive 2014/17/EU of the European Parliament and of the Council of February 4, 2014, on credit agreements for consumers relating to residential immovable property and amending Directives 2008/48/EC and Regulation (EU) No 1093/2010 [2014] OJ L60/34, Recital (4).

[16] Directive 2014/17/EU, Recitals (3), (5), Arts. 18, 20.

[17] Commission, COM(2021)347 final, Art. 18(1).

[18] Robert Bartlett et al., "Consumer-lending discrimination in the FinTech era" (2022) *Journal of Financial Economics*, 143: 30; Dagobert Brito and Peter Hartley, "Consumer rationality and credit cards" (1995) *Journal of Political Economy*, 103: 400; Christine Parlour and Uday Rajan, "Competition in loan contracts" (2001) *The American Economic Review*, 91: 1311; Joseph Stiglitz and Andrew Weiss, "Credit rationing in markets with imperfect information" (1981) *The American Economic Review*, 71: 393; see Alya Guseva and Akos Rona-Tas, "Uncertainty, risk, and trust: Russian and American credit card markets compared" (2001) *American Sociological Review*, 66: 623 on uncertainty and institutions which allow for reducing uncertainty to measurable risk.

[19] Akos Rona-Tas and Alya Guseva, "Consumer credit in comparative perspective" (2018) *Annual Review of Sociology*, 44: 55; Guseva and Rona-Tas (n 18).

[20] Josh Lauer, *Creditworthy: a history of consumer surveillance and financial identity in America* (Columbia University Press, 2017) 199ff on the five variables used by the mail-order firm Spiegel in the 1930s; tracing the historical development: Danielle Citron and Frank Pasquale, "The scored society: Due process for automated predictions" (2014) *Washington Law Review* 89(1): 8ff.

individual loan applicants with high or low credit default risk.[21] Depending on the country, the relevant characteristics "can include a wide variety of socioeconomic, demographic, and other attributes or only those related to credit histories."[22] Being a white, middle-aged man with a stable job and living in wholly owned property usually predicted a lower credit-default risk than being a young man living in a shared flat, an unmarried woman, or a person of color without a stable job.

The exercise requires two main ingredients: mathematical tools and access to data. The former serves to form statistical buckets of similarly situated persons and to correlate individual attributes of loan applicants with attributes that were in the past found to be relevant predictors of credit default risk. The latter was initially provided by lenders compiling their own data, for instance on credit history with the bank, loan amounts, or in- and outgoing payments. Later, credit registries spawned that are, until today, a key source of data.[23] The type of data a credit registry collects is highly standardized, but varies across countries. Examples are utilities data, late payments, number of credit cards used, collection procedures, or insolvency proceedings.[24] Using the available input data, the probability of credit default risk is often expressed in a standardized credit score.[25]

16.2.2 *AI-Based Methods to Predict Credit Default Risk*

Over the last decade, both ingredients,[26] mathematical tools and access to data, have changed radically. Digitization across many areas of life leaves digital footprints of consumers. Collecting and processing these "big data" allows us to refine statistical output that can now work with large amounts of information, far beyond what traditional credit registries hold. Artificial intelligence in the form of machine learning helps to correlate variables, interprets results, sometimes learns from these, and, in that way, finds ever more complex patterns across input data.[27]

"All data is credit data"[28] is an often-quoted remark, hinting at the potential to use unanticipated attributes and characteristics toward a prediction of credit

[21] Rona-Tas and Guseva (n 19) 61; Lauer (n 20) 210ff.

[22] Rona-Tas and Guseva (n 19) 62.

[23] Ibid., 61–62; see WorldBank, "Doing business project on the public credit registry coverage," https://data.worldbank.org/indicator/IC.CRD.PUBL.ZS, accessed July 22, 2024, showing an enormous increase of data collection.

[24] World Bank Group, "Credit scoring approaches guidelines" (2019) 10, https://thedocs.worldbank.org/en/doc/935891585869698451-0130022020/original/CREDITSCORINGAPPROACHESGUIDELINESFINALWEB.pdf, accessed July 22, 2024.

[25] Rona-Tas and Guseva (n 19) 62; as an overview, see the World Bank Group (n 24).

[26] See Section 16.2.1.

[27] World Bank Group (n 24) 16–17.

[28] See Quentin Hardy, "Just the facts. Yes, all of them." *The New York Times* (March 25, 2012), https://archive.nytimes.com/query.nytimes.com/gst/fullpage-9A0CE7DD153CF936A15750C0A9649D8B63.html, accessed July 22, 2024; discussion at Emily Rosamond, "'All data is credit data,' reputation, regulation and character in the entrepreneurial imaginary" (2016) *Paragrana*, 25: 112.

default risk. This starts with an applicant's online payment history or performance on a lending platform but does not stop there.[29] Age or sex, job or college education, ZIP code, income, or ethnic background can all be relevant predictors. Depending on a jurisdiction's privacy laws, more variables can be scrutinized. Such "alternative data" include, for instance, preferred shopping places, social media friends, political party affiliation, number of typos in text messages, brand of smartphone, speed in clicking through a captcha exercise, daily work-out time, or performance in a psychometric assessment. All these are potential sources for correlations, the AI system will detect between individual data points, and the goal it is optimizing. An example of an optimization goal (which is also called "definition of success"[30]) is credit default. An AI system working with this definition of success is useful for a lender who wishes to price his loan according to the probability of default. The system will find various correlations between the big data input variables and the optimization goal. Some correlations might be unsurprising, such as a high steady income and low default. Others will be more unexpected. The German company Kreditech illustrates this. It learned that an important variable its AI system found was a specific type of font on an applicant's electronic devices.[31] A research study provides another illustration by concluding that:

> customers without a financial application installed on their phones are about 25% more likely to default than those with such an app installed. (…) In contrast, those with a mobile loan application are 26% more likely to default.[32]

16.2.3 *Inclusion Through AI-Based Methods*

A score that an AI model develops based on alternative data can provide access to finance for persons who have found this difficult in the past, due to their unusual profile. A recent immigrant will often not be able to provide a utility payment or a credit history in his new country of residence. However, this "thin-file applicant" might have relevant alternative data of the type described earlier to support his creditworthiness assessment.

[29] For the following examples, see Langenbucher (n 13) 3.

[30] O'Neil (n 4) 21.

[31] See Katja Langenbucher and Patrick Corcoran, "Responsible AI credit scoring – a lesson from Upstart.com" (2022) *European Company and Financial Law Review*, 5(141): 165ff on this example. The reason for this unanticipated correlation – as they later figured out – was that this unusual font was used by an online gambling site, see Sachverständigenrat für Verbraucherfragen, "Consumer-friendly scoring" (2018) 62, https://fragdenstaat.de/dokumente/238777-report-consumer-friendly-scoring/, accessed July 22, 2024.

[32] Sumit Agarwal et al., "Financial inclusion and alternate credit scoring: role of big data and machine learning in FinTech" (2021) 4, https://papers.ssrn.com/sol3/papers.cfm?abstract_id=3507827, accessed July 22, 2024.

Several empirical studies have found that AI-based credit scoring broadens financial access for some thin-file applicants.[33] One important source of data are mobile phones. "The type of apps installed or information from call log patterns," so the authors of one study find, "outperforms a traditional model that relies on credit score."[34] Another study, working with an e-commerce company, produced good predictions using only ten digital footprint variables.[35] The authors find, for example, that the difference in default rates between customers using an Apple and customers using an Android device is equivalent to the difference in default rates between a median credit score and the 80th percentile of the credit score.[36] Yet another illustration is provided by the US online lending company Upstart.[37] Upstart claims to outperform traditional scoring as to all borrowers, specifically as to those with traditionally low credit scores. A study on this company shows that:

> more than 30% of borrowers with credit scores of less than 680 funded by Upstart over our sample period would have been rejected by the traditional model. We further find that this fraction declines as credit score increases, that is the mismatch between the traditional and the Upstart model is magnified among low-credit score borrower.[38]

A US regulatory agency, the Consumer Financial Protection Bureau, investigated Upstart's business model and confirmed that, in the aggregate, applicants with low credit scores were approved twice as frequently by Upstart if compared with a hypothetical lender.[39]

16.3 ETHICAL CONCERNS AROUND AI-BASED METHODS TO PREDICT CREDIT DEFAULT RISK

16.3.1 *Algorithmic Discrimination*

The US lender Upstart illustrates not only how AI can further inclusion. Additionally, it provides an example of AI models producing unequal output across groups of loan applicants. Among those who profit, persons facing historical or current

[33] Tetyana Balyuk, "FinTech lending and bank credit access for consumers" (2021), https://papers.ssrn.com/sol3/papers.cfm?abstract_id=2802220, accessed July 22, 2024; Bartlett et al. (n 18) 55.

[34] Agarwal et al. (n 32) 26.

[35] Tobias Berg et al., "On the rise of FinTechs – credit scoring using digital footprints" (2018) *NBER* Working Paper 24551, 2.

[36] Berg et al. (n 35) 3.

[37] Langenbucher and Corcoran (n 31); Marco Di Maggio, Dimuthu Ratnadiwakara, and Don Carmichael, "Invisible primes: FinTech lending with alternative data" (2022) 2, https://papers.ssrn.com/sol3/papers.cfm?abstract_id=3937438, accessed July 22, 2024.

[38] Di Maggio et al. (n 37) 4.

[39] Patrick Alexander Fickling and Paul Watkins, "An update on credit access and the Bureau's first no-action letter" (2019), www.consumerfinance.gov/about-us/blog/update-credit-access-and-no-action-letter/, accessed July 22, 2024.

discrimination are underrepresented. A well-documented example concerns a report from a US NGO which ran a mystery shopping exercise with Upstart.[40] It involved three loan applicants that were identical to college degree, job, and yearly income, but had attended different colleges: New York University, Howard University, which is a historically Black college, and New Mexico State University, a Hispanic-serving institution. Holding all other inputs constant, the authors of the study found that a hypothetical applicant who attended Howard or New Mexico State University would pay significantly higher origination fees and interest rates over the life of their loans than an applicant who attended NYU.

One explanation for these findings points to the AI system predicting credit default in a world of (past and current) discrimination where Black and Hispanic applicants face thresholds that otherwise similarly situated borrowers do not. Along those lines, the unequal output reflects real differences in credit default risk.

Alternatively (or additionally), the AI system's result might be skewed by a variety of algorithmic biases.[41] In this case, its credit score or creditworthiness assessment paints a picture that does not correctly reflect actual differences. Historical bias provides one example. A machine-learning system is trained based on past data, involving borrowers, their characteristics, behavior, and payment history.[42] Based on such data, the AI system learns which individual attributes (or bundles of attributes) are good predictors of credit default. If certain groups, for example unmarried women, have in the past faced cultural or legal obstacles in certain countries, the AI system learns that being an unmarried woman is a negative signal. It will weigh this input variable accordingly. In this way, an attribute that would have lowered a credit score in the past will lower it today, even if the underlying discriminatory situation has been overcome (as is partly the case for unmarried women). Majority bias is another example.[43] The AI system builds its model by attributing weight to input variables.

40 Student Borrower Protection Center, "Educational redlining" (2020), https://protectborrowers.org/wp-content/uploads/2020/02/Education-Redlining-Report.pdf, accessed July 22, 2024, methodology described at 16.

41 For a critical discussion, see Laura Blattner and Scott Nelson, "How costly is noise? Data and disparities in consumer credit" (2021), www.researchgate.net/publication/351656623_How_Costly_is_Noise_Data_and_Disparities_in_Consumer_Credit, accessed July 22, 2024; Citron and Pasquale (n 20); Margot Kaminski, "Binary governance: Lessons from the GDPR's approach to algorithmic accountability" (2019) *Southern California Law Review*, 92: 1529, 1538; O'Neil (n 4); from the perspective of sociology: Jenna Burrell and Marion Fourcade, "The society of algorithms" (2021) *Annual Review of Sociology*, 47: 213, 224; Dan L. Burk, "Algorithmic legal metrics" (2021) *Notre Dame Law Review*, 96: 1147, 1163; Barbara Kiviat, "The art of deciding with data: evidence from how employers translate credit reports into hiring decisions" (2019) *Socio-Economic Review*, 17: 283; Ead, "The moral limits of predictive practices: The case of credit-based insurance scores" (2019) *Socio-Economic Review* 84: 1134; Pauline Kim, "AI and inequality," in Kristin Johnson and Carla Reyes (eds), *The Cambridge Handbook on Artificial Intelligence and the Law* (forthcoming), https://papers.ssrn.com/sol3/papers.cfm?abstract_id=3938578, accessed July 22, 2024.

42 See Section 16.2.2.

43 Solon Barocas and Andrew Selbst, "Big data's disparate impact" (2016) *California Law Review*, 104: 671, 689; Talia Gillis, "The input fallacy" (2022) *Minnesota Law Review*, 106: 1175–1261; Jennifer Graham,

What it finds for most candidates that were successful in the past will be accorded considerable weight, for instance, stability as to place of residence. Candidates who score badly in that respect because their job requires them to move often will face a risk premium. It is important to understand that the machine-learning system finds correlations only and does not attempt to establish causation. An individual might have very good reasons for moving houses often, he might even hold a high-paying job that requires him to do so. The AI system will still count this as a negative attribute if the majority of past candidates did not move often.

Another empirical study suggests that there can be yet further factors at play. Researchers explored data on the US Government Sponsored Enterprises Fannie Mae and Freddie Mac.[44] These offer mortgage-backed lenders a guarantee against credit risk, charging a fee that depends only on the borrower's credit score and the loan-to-value ratio. Against that background, one would assume that for candidates with identical scores and LTV ratios, interest rates must be identical. This was not what the study found. Hispanic and Black borrowers faced markups of 7.9 basis points for purchase mortgages and 3.6 basis points for refinance mortgages. The "morally neutral" AI system might have understood this as a promising strategy to meet the goal of maximizing profit for the lender. Instead, the lender might have himself formulated the AI's definition of success as identifying applicants who were open to predatory pricing, for instance because they urgently needed a loan or were financially less literate than other borrowers.[45]

16.3.2 *Opaque Surveillance*

Let us revisit the lender who faced uncertainty as to potential borrowers. Today, he uses credit scores and creditworthiness assessments that rely on a limited list of input variables. Usually, their relevance for credit default risk is obvious, and advanced statistics allows for good predictions. For the applicant, this entails the upside that he will typically know which attributes are important to be considered a good credit risk.[46] Against that background, one would expect that an unobservable

"Risk of discrimination in AI systems, evaluating the effectiveness of current legal safeguards in tackling algorithmic discrimination" in Alison Lui and Nicholas Ryder (eds), *FinTech, Artificial Intelligence and the Law* (Routledge, 2021), p. 211; Katja Langenbucher, "Responsible A.I. credit scoring – a legal Framework" (2020) *European Business Law Review* 31: 527; Burk (n 41); Antje von Ungern-Sternberg, "Diskriminierungsschutz bei algorithmischen Entscheidungen" in Anna Katharina Mangold and Mehrdad Payandeh (eds), *Handbuch Antidiskriminierungsrecht* (Mohr Siebeck, 2022) nt 15ff.

44 Bartlett et al. (n 18) 31.

45 Ibid., 32: "The fact that the relation between the rate differential and either credit score or realized default is minor suggests the income and LTV results may instead reflect something else, such as the correlation between income, financial sophistication, and a propensity to shop for rates"; similarly Gillis (n 43) 1188 ("personalized pricing"); Christophe Hurlin, Christophe Pérignon, and Sébastien Saurin, "The Fairness of credit scoring models" (2021), https://papers.ssrn.com/sol3/papers.cfm?abstract_id=3785882, accessed July 22, 2024: "lack of fairness."

46 But see Rona-Tas and Guseva (n 19) 62: "they act as disciplining devices."

and hardly quantifiable variable such as "character"[47] loses significance. With AI-based scoring, this might change, if the seemingly objective machine lends new credibility to such concepts. The researchers who used mobile phone data for credit scoring interpreted their findings as a strategy to access "aspects of individuals behavior" that "has implications for the likelihood of default."[48] The authors of the e-commerce study[49] explicitly suggest that the variables they investigated provide a "proxy for income, character and reputation."[50]

A borrower whose credit application is assessed by an algorithm might feel compelled to give access to his personal data unless he is prepared to accept a lower credit rating. At the same time, he does not necessarily know which elements of the data he hands over will be relevant. Credit applicants today often know what is important for obtaining credit and have legal rights to be informed about a denial.[51] Under an AI black box model, not even the lender is necessarily aware of what drives the credit score his AI system produces.[52] If he does, his incentives to inform the applicant are often small. This is especially likely if the lender feels he found a variable that is a powerful predictor but at the same can be manipulated by the applicant. Consider, for instance, a finance or a dating app on his phone, one helping, the other hurting his credit score, while both apps are easily installed/uninstalled.

AI scoring of this type places consumers in a difficult spot. They are likely to worry about a "world of conformity"[53] where they "fear to express their individual personality online" and "constantly consider their digital footprints."[54] They might feel that they are exposed to arbitrary decisions that they do not understand and that are sometimes unexplainable even to the person using the algorithm.[55] Economists have predicted that consumers might try to randomly change their online behavior in the hope for a better score.[56] Manipulation along those lines will work better for some variables (such as regularly charging a mobile device) than for others (such as changing mobile phone brand or refraining from impulse shopping).[57] One strategy is to mimic the profile of an attractive borrower. This suggests side effects to the overall usefulness of AI scoring. If it is costless to mimic an attractive borrower, an

47 See Section 16.2.1.
48 Agarwal et al. (n 32) 3.
49 See Section 16.2.3.
50 Berg et al. (n 35) 3.
51 See, for example, Section 202.9(a)(2)(i), (b)(2) of US Regulation B, implementing the Equal Credit Opportunity Act.
52 Fickling and Watkins (n 39) 8; Burrell and Fourcade (n 41) 226.
53 Berg et al. (n 35) 26.
54 Ibid., 6; Burk (n 41).
55 Fickling and Watkins (n 39) 18; Burrell and Fourcade (n 41) 226.
56 Berg et al. (n 35) 25 referencing the Lucas Critique, see Robert Lucas, "Econometric policy evaluation: A critique" (1976) *Carnegie-Rochester Conference Series on Public Policy*, 1: 19.
57 Berg et al. (n 35) 25–26.

uninformative pooling equilibrium evolves: All senders choose the same signals.[58] Firm behavior might adapt as well.[59] A firm whose products signal low creditworthiness could try to conceal its products' digital footprint. Commercial services may develop, offering such services or making consumers' digital footprint look better. Along similar lines, the US CFPB fears that the chances to change credit standing through behavior may become a random exercise.[60] While the applicant today receives meaningful information about (many of) the variables which are relevant for his score, with opaque AI modelling, this is not guaranteed any more.

16.4 LEGAL TOOLS REGULATING DISCRIMINATION AND SURVEILLANCE FOR AI-BASED CREDIT SCORING AND CREDITWORTHINESS EVALUATION

Using AI for scoring and underwriting decisions does not raise entirely novel concerns. However, it compounds some of the well-known risks or shines an unanticipated light on existing strategies to deal with these challenges.

16.4.1 *Anti-Discrimination Laws Faced with AI*

Is unequal output across groups of applicants, for instance as to sex or race, necessarily a cause for concern? Arguably, the answer depends on the context and the goal pursued by the lender.

Under the assumption that the AI model presents an unbiased picture of reality, an economist would find nothing wrong with unequal output if it tracked features that are relevant to the lender's business strategy. Any creditor must distinguish between applicants for a loan,[61] and score and rank them, usually according to credit default risk. This produces statistical discrimination that reflects the state of the world. Prohibiting unequal output entirely would force the lender to underwrite credit default risk he does not wish to take on.[62]

By contrast, if the assumption of the AI system reflecting an unbiased picture of the world does not hold, the unequal output can be a signal for potential inefficiencies.

58 Ibid., 26. A higher cost for mimicking, those authors explain, results in a separating equilibrium with a highly informative digital footprint. They illustrate this with the example of Pentaquark, who rejects loans from applicants who "write a lot about their souls on Facebook, as these persons are usually too concerned about what will happen in thirty years, but not the fine print of today's life."

59 Ibid., 26–27.

60 Fickling and Watkins (n 39) 17; see on further concerns, such as "gaming the system"; Burk (n 41) 1187ff; Citron and Pasquale (n 20) 29ff; Langenbucher (n 43).

61 See Section 16.2.1.

62 Further side effects can hurt the borrower (if he ends up unable to repay and gets into financial difficulties), other borrowers (if the lender raises interest rates to finance the credit risk, he is forced to accept) and the economy as a whole (if unsustainable loans lead to a credit bubble and to market instability).

An AI model's flawed output, for example due to historical or majority bias,[63] leads to opportunity cost if it produces too many false negatives: Candidates that would be a good credit risk but are flagged as a bad credit risk. In this case, the lender should have granted a loan, but he refused, based on the flawed AI system. If, by contrast, the model triggers too many false positives, it can skew the lender's portfolio risk. The lender has underwritten more contracts than his business model would have suggested to.

A lawyer has a more complicated answer to the question mentioned earlier.[64] Depending on the situation, unequal output can violate anti-discrimination laws. A clear case is presented by a lender who denies a loan *because of* a specific attribute – sex, race, religion, ethnicity, or similar protected characteristics. If this is the case (and the plaintiff can prove it), the lender is liable for damages.[65] The test prong *because of* is met, if the protected characteristic was one reason toward the decision.

Direct discrimination[66] in this form is not a risk that is unique to AI-based decision-making. Quite to the contrary, many point out that a well-trained, *objective* AI system will overcome human biases and discriminatory intentions.[67] However, if a lender pursues discriminatory motives or intentionally seeks members of protected communities because they are more vulnerable to predatory pricing, AI systems compound the risks plaintiffs face. This has to do with the AI system's potential to help the lender "mask" his true preferences.[68] Masking behavior can be successful because anti-discrimination law needs a hook, as it were, in the lender's decision-making process. The plaintiff must establish that he was discriminated against because of a protected characteristic, such as race or sex. A discriminatory lender can try to circumvent this legal rule by training its AI system to find variables that correlate narrowly with a protected characteristic. Eventually, circumventing the law will not be a valid strategy for the lender. However, the applicant might find it very hard to prove that this was the lender's motive, especially in jurisdictions that do not offer pre-trial discovery.[69]

63 See Section 16.3.1.

64 See in detail Langenbucher (n 13).

65 Michael Heese, "Offene Preisdiskriminierung und zivilrechtliches Benachteiligungsverbot, Eine Zwischenbilanz" (2012) *Neue Juristische Wochenschrift* 572, 575–576. On punitive damages see, for example, US 15 U.S.C. § 1691e(b).

66 The US terminology is: "disparate treatment."

67 Cass Sunstein, "Algorithms, correcting biases" (2019) *Social Research: An International Quarterly*, 86: 499.

68 Barocas and Selbst (n 43) 699, use the term "masking"; for German law, see Florian Rödl and Andreas Leidinger, "Diskriminierungsschutz im Zivilrechtsverkehr" In Anna Katharina Mangold and Mehrdad Payandeh (eds), *Handbuch Antidiskriminierungsrecht* (Mohr Siebeck, 2022), nt 57 ("cover-up").

69 Such as the EU, see Geoffrey C. Hazard Jr., "Civil procedure rules for European courts" (2016) *Judicature*, 100: 58.

The disproportionate output of an AI system does not always go back to business strategies that imply direct discrimination.[70] One of the most characteristic features of algorithm-based credit risk assessments is to find unanticipated correlations between big data variables and the optimization goal.[71] What happens if it turns out that a neutral attribute, for instance the installation of a finance app on a smartphone, triggers disproportionate results across sex? Unless a lender intentionally circumvents the rule to not discriminate against women, this is not a case of direct discrimination.[72] Instead, we potentially face indirect discrimination.[73] Under this doctrine, a facially neutral attribute that consistently leads to less favorable output for protected communities becomes "suspicious," as it were. Plaintiffs must establish a correlation between the suspicious attribute and the unequal output. Defendants will be asked to provide justificatory reasons for using the attribute, in spite of the troubling correlation.[74] In a credit underwriting context, the business rationale of the lender is a paradigm justificatory reason. The plaintiff might counter that there are equally powerful predictors with less or no discriminatory potential. However, the plaintiff will often fail to even establish the very first test prong, namely to identify the suspicious attribute. The more sophisticated the AI system and the larger the big data pool, the more likely it is that the AI system will deliver the same result without access to the suspicious variable. The reason for this is *redundant encoding*: The information encoded in the suspicious variable can be found in many other variables.[75]

16.4.2 *AI Biases and Quality Control in the EU Artificial Intelligence Act*

The EU AI Act[76] starts from the assumption that AI credit underwriting can lead to discriminatory output:

> In addition, AI systems used to evaluate the credit score or creditworthiness of natural persons (…) may lead to discrimination of persons or groups and perpetuate historical patterns of discrimination, such as that based on racial or ethnic origins, gender, disabilities, age or sexual orientation, or create new forms of discriminatory impacts.[77]

70 US: "disparate treatment."
71 See Section 16.2.2.
72 US: "disparate treatment."
73 US: "disparate impact"; in more detail: Langenbucher (n 13).
74 See Deborah Hellman, "Measuring algorithmic fairness" (2020) *Virginia Law Review*, 106: 811, 852 on the US Supreme Court distinguishing between a defendant relying on a neutral variable "because of" or "in spite of" the foreseeable consequences.
75 Von Ungern-Sternberg (n 43) nt 27.
76 See Chapter 12.
77 AI Act, Recital (58).

However, the remedy the AI Act proposes is not to adjust anti-discrimination law. Instead, it proposes a strategy of product regulation. Artificial intelligence systems employed in the loan context "should be classified as high-risk AI systems, since they determine those persons' access to financial resources or essential services such as housing, electricity, and telecommunication services."[78]

Employing a high-risk AI system entails mandatory compliance checks as to monitoring, testing, and documentation with an eye on both software and data.[79] Article 9 of the Act has the software part in mind. It requires identifying risks to fundamental rights and developing appropriate risk management measures. Ideally, the design or development of the high-risk AI system eliminates or reduces these risks. If they cannot be eliminated, they must be mitigated and controlled.[80] Article 10 addresses training data which might lead to the biases mentioned earlier.[81] According to Article 14 of the proposal, high-risk AI systems must be "designed and developed in such a way (...) that they can be effectively overseen by natural persons."[82] Supervisory agencies are in charge of enforcing compliance with the AI Act. For credit institutions, the competent banking regulator is entrusted with this task. Nonbank entities, for instance credit scoring agencies, will be supervised by a different body in charge of AI.[83] Both supervisors must deal with the challenge of quantifying a fundamental rights violation (which includes balancing borrower's rights against competing rights) to produce a workable benchmark for risk management.

16.4.3 *Privacy and Retail-Borrower Protection Laws Faced with AI*

Private enforcement via litigation is not included in the AI Act.[84] Against this background, the following section looks at privacy and retail-borrower protection laws that provide such tools. Privacy law aims at keeping personal data private and subjecting its use by third parties to certain requirements. Retail-borrower protection laws cover many aspects of a transaction between borrower and lender. These include rights that are especially useful in the context of algorithmic credit evaluations, for example a right to be informed about a denial of credit.

78 Ibid., Recital (58), Annex III No 5(b) lists credit-scoring and underwriting algorithms if they concern natural persons.

79 Overview at Katja Langenbucher, "AI credit scoring and evaluation of creditworthiness – a test case for the EU proposal for an AI Act" (2022) *ECB Legal Conference* 362, 367, www.ecb.europa.eu/pub/pdf/other/ecb.ecblegalconferenceproceedings202204~c2e5739756.en.pdf, accessed July 22, 2024.

80 AI Act, Art. 9(5).

81 Section 16.3.1, see AI Act, Art. 10(2) lit g on examining the system "in view of possible biases."

82 AI Act, Art. 14(1), on human oversight, see Langenbucher (n 79) 372.

83 Critical on this distinction Langenbucher (n 79) 375ff.

84 Critical ibid., 381ff.

16.4.3.1 Credit Reporting and Data Privacy

Big data access is a key ingredient of algorithm-based credit underwriting.[85] At the same time, data collected from online sources are often unreliable and prone to misunderstandings. If an AI model is trained on flawed or misleading data, its output will likely not fully reflect actual credit default risk. However, this might not be immediately visible to the lender who uses the model. Even worse, automation bias, the tendency to over-rely on what was produced by automated models and disregard conflicting human judgments,[86] might induce the lender to go ahead with the decision prepared by the algorithm.

In many countries, credit reporting bureaus have traditionally filled the role of collecting data, some run by private companies, some by the government.[87] Those bureaus have their proprietary procedures to verify information. Additionally, there are legal rights for borrowers to correct false entries in credit registries. Illustrative for such rights is the US Fair Credit Reporting Act. It entitles credit applicants to access information a credit reporting agency holds on them and provides rights to rectify incorrect information.[88] However, one requirement is that the entity collecting big data qualifies as a credit reporting agency under the Act.[89] While some big data aggregators have stepped forward to embrace this responsibility, others claim they are mere "conduits," performing mechanical tasks when sending the data to FinTech platforms.[90]

EU law does not face this doctrinal difficulty. The prime EU data protection law is the General Data Protection Regulation (GDPR) that covers any processing of personal data under Article 2 of GDPR. For processing to be lawful, it must qualify for a justificatory reason under Article 6 GDPR. The data controller must provide information, *inter alia* on the purpose of data collection and processing pursuant to Article 13 GDPR. If sensitive data are concerned, additional requirements follow Article 9. However, in practice, GDPR requirements are often met by a standard tick-the-box-exercise whenever data are collected. Arguably, this entails rationally apathetic, rather than well-informed consumers.[91] When a data aggregator furnishes

[85] See Section 16.2.1.

[86] Definition (in a clinical context) by Kate Goddard, Abdul Roudsari, and Jeremy C. Wyatt, "Automation bias: A systematic review of frequency, effect mediators, and mitigators" (2012) *Journal of the American Medical Informatics Association*, 19: 121.

[87] International overview at Rona-Tas and Guseva, (n 19) 61ff.

[88] Langenbucher and Corcoran (n 31) 162.

[89] For a second concern see Section 16.4.3.2.

[90] Federal Trade Commission, "40 years of experience with the Fair Credit Reporting Act" (Report) (2011) 29, www.ftc.gov/sites/default/files/documents/reports/40-years-experience-fair-credit-reporting-act-ftc-staff-report-summary-interpretations/110720fcrareport.pdf, accessed July 22, 2024; see for a narrow reading of the LexisNexis product "Accurint" which was not considered delivering "credit reports": Pauline Kim and Erika Hanson, "People Analytics and the Regulation of Information under the Fair Credit Reporting Act" (2016) 61 *Saint Louis University Law Journal* 17, 28–29.

[91] Langenbucher (n 43) 535–536.

data he lawfully collected to the lender or to a scoring bureau, there is no additional notice required.[92] This foregoes the potential to incentivize consumers to react in the face of a particularly salient use of their data.

16.4.3.2 Credit Scoring, Creditworthiness Evaluation, and Retail Borrower Rights

If collecting big data is the first important element of AI-based credit underwriting,[93] the way in which an algorithm assesses the applicant is the second cornerstone. The uneasy feeling of facing unknown variables, which drive scores and evaluations in opaque ways, might be mitigated if applicants receive meaningful explanations about which data were used and how the algorithm arrived at the output it generated.

US law provides two legal tools to that end. One rule was mentioned in the previous section.[94] It requires the lender to disclose that he used a credit report. In that way, it allows the applicant to verify the information in the credit report. In the old world of traditional credit reporting and scoring, based on a short list of input variables, this is an appropriate tool. It remains to be seen how this right to access information will perform if the input data are collected across a vast amount of big data sources. The second rule gives consumers a right to a statement of specific reasons for adverse action on a credit application.[95] The underlying rationale is to enable the applicant to make sure no discriminatory reasons underlie the denial of credit. In the current environment, US regulators have already struggled to incentivize lenders to provide more than highly standardized information.[96] With algorithmic scoring, this information is even harder to provide if the algorithm moves from a simple machine-learning device to more sophisticated black box or neural network models.

The EU GDPR includes no rule to specifically target the scoring or underwriting situation. General rules concern "decisions based solely on automated processing" and vest the consumer with a right to get "meaningful information about the logic involved" and "to obtain human intervention, to express his or her point of view and to contest the decision."[97] At the time of writing, a case was pending before the European Court of Justice to assess what these rules entail as to credit scoring.[98]

92 See Regulation (EU) 2016/679 of the European Parliament and of the Council of April 27, 2016, on the protection of natural persons with regard to the processing of personal data and on the free movement of such data, and repealing Directive 95/46/EC (General Data Protection Regulation) [2016] OJ L119/1, Art. 13(1), (2) referencing the "time when personal data are obtained." According to Art. 13(3), this is different if "the controller intends to further process the personal data for a purpose other than that for which the personal data were collected."

93 Section 16.4.3.1.

94 Section 16.4.3.1.

95 Section 202.9(a)(2)(i), (b)(2) of Regulation B, implementing the Equal Credit Opportunities Act.

96 For details on the official interpretation of that rule, see Consumer Financial Protection Bureau, www.consumerfinance.gov/rules-policy/regulations/1002/9/#9-b-2-Interp-2, accessed July 22, 2024.

97 See Regulation (EU) 2016/679, Art. 13(2) lit f, Art. 15(1) lit h, Art. 22.

98 The case was decided on 7 December 2023, see ECLI:EU:C:2023:957.

In contrast with the GDPR, the EU Consumer Credit Directive directly engages with algorithmic decision-making in the underwriting context.[99] It includes a right to inform the consumer whose credit application is denied if the "application is rejected on the basis of a consultation of a database."[100] However, it refrains from requiring specific reasons for the lender's decision. Art. 18 includes more detailed access, namely a right to "request a clear and comprehensible explanation of the assessment of creditworthiness, including on the logic and risks involved in the automated processing of personal data as well as its significance and effects on the decision."[101] What such information would look like in practice, and whether it could be produced for more sophisticated algorithms, remains to be seen. The same concern applies to a different strategy proposed by the Directive. It entirely prohibits the use of alternative data gathered from social networks and certain types of sensitive data.[102] Arguably, redundant encoding[103] can make this a toothless rule if the same information is stored in a variety of different variables.

16.5 LOOKING AHEAD – FROM CREDIT SCORING TO SOCIAL SCORING

Scoring consumers to assess their creditworthiness is an enormously important use of the novel combination that big data and AI bring about. Chances are that scoring will not stop there but extend to more areas of social life, involving novel forms of social control.[104] When considering high-risk areas, the EU AI Act not only has "access to essential private and public services and benefits"[105] in mind. The lawmakers have set their eyes on social scoring as well, which they understand as an "evaluation or classification of natural persons or groups of persons over a certain period of time based on their social behavior or known, inferred or predicted personal or personality characteristics."[106] Social scoring of this type is prohibited if it occurs out of the context in which the data were collected or leads to unjustified treatment.[107] However, the success of a substantive rule depends on efficient means of enforcement. Faced with the velocity of digital innovation, it is doubtful that either public or private enforcement tools can keep pace.

[99] Directive (EU) 2023/2225 (n 12).
[100] Directive (EU) 2023/2225, Art. 19(6).
[101] Directive (EU) 2023/2225, Art. 18(8) lit a.
[102] Directive (EU) 2023/2225, Art. 19(5).
[103] See Section 16.4.1.
[104] AI Act, Recital (28).
[105] AI Act, Recital (58).
[106] AI Act, Art. 5(1) lit c.
[107] AI Act, Art. 5(1) lit c.

17

Artificial Intelligence and Labor Law

Aída Ponce Del Castillo and Simon Taes

17.1 INTRODUCTION

Technological systems are crucial elements in every organization and sector of the economy. With digitalization being a Megatrend, and the "platformization" of business models becoming more prevalent, workplaces are being transformed at the source, from the way a business is first conceived, to how work is organized and how individual workers perform their jobs. These transformations, which are often driven by Artificial Intelligence (AI) systems, impact work relations, work organization, working conditions, and – more generally – jobs and workers at all levels.

The agreements that employers and workers achieve can shape technological change in an organization. The connection between technological change and innovation on the one hand, and labor law on the other, needs to be addressed beyond possible conflictual considerations. Labor law is composed of a set of legal rules applicable to individual and collective relations that arise between (private) employers and those who work under their instruction in exchange for a certain remuneration.

The objective of this chapter is to shed light on the intersection between the role of AI in the work sphere and labor law, and to signal several issues that require a legal response. After Section 17.1, Section 17.2 of this chapter provides a general overview of the goal and function of labor law. Section 17.3 illustrates some of the main applications of AI systems in workplaces and addresses the ethical and legal concerns they raise. Section 17.4 discusses some essential labor law rights and concepts, including the role of Social Partners. Section 17.5 focuses on AI-related legislation that also applies to the context of employment, and assesses the extent to which it addresses the identified concerns. Finally, with a foresight perspective in mind, Section 17.6 reflects on a number of issues that require further attention by lawmakers.

17.2 SCOPE AND GOALS OF LABOR LAW

The application of AI systems in workplaces brings many legal questions and challenges for the relationship between employers and workers. For this reason, it is necessary to first understand the characteristics of this relationship from a legal point of view. Considering that the regulation of employment relationships belongs to the domain of labor law, it is also pivotal to comprehend the meaning of this legal domain and the purposes it aims to achieve.

There are many different types of work relationships, each of which can be covered by various types of contractual agreements. Therefore, in legal terms, it can be rather complicated to define the "typical" employment relationship between an employer and workers. Considering this difficulty, an employment relationship is hence often assessed by its characteristics or indicators, which will determine whether or not a genuine employment relationship exists. This is demonstrated by Recommendation no. 198 of the International Labour Organization (ILO) regarding the employment relationship, published in 2006. The Recommendation suggests specific indicators to identify the existence of such relationship, including:

(a) *the fact that the work: is carried out according to the instructions and under the control of another party; involves the integration of the worker in the organization of the enterprise; is performed solely or mainly for the benefit of another person; must be carried out personally by the worker; is carried out within specific working hours or at a workplace specified or agreed by the party requesting the work; is of a particular duration and has a certain continuity; requires the worker's availability; or involves the provision of tools, materials and machinery by the party requesting the work;*
(b) *periodic payment of remuneration to the worker; the fact that such remuneration constitutes the worker's sole or principal source of income; provision of payment in kind, such as food, lodging or transport; recognition of entitlements such as weekly rest and annual holidays; payment by the party requesting the work for travel undertaken by the worker in order to carry out the work; or absence of financial risk for the worker* (emphasis added).[1]

These indicators emphasize that the employment relationship is predominantly characterized by work that is carried out under the control of another person in return for remuneration. These characteristics of the employment relationship also come forth in the case law of the Court of Justice of the European Union (CJEU). In its famous case Lawrie Blum, the Court explicitly states that "*the essential feature of an employment relationship, however, is that for a certain period of time a person performs services for and under the direction of another person in return for which he receives remuneration.*"[2] Although national legislation may apply different criteria to

[1] International Labour Organisation Recommendation no. 198 [2006] on the Employment Relationship.

[2] Case 66/85 *Deborah Lawrie-Blum v Land Baden-Württemberg* [1986] ECR 2121, ECLI:EU:C:1986:284, para 17.

establish these elements, the employment relationship is mainly characterized by work, subordination of the worker to the employer and remuneration.

In other words, this perspective on the employment relationship implies an imbalance between the subordinate worker and the authority of the employer. Based on this authority, the employer has the right to direct or give instructions to workers, to control or monitor their performance in the workplace and to discipline or, in case of misconduct, impose sanctions on them.

Considering this power asymmetry, one of the goals of labor law is to address the unequal bargaining position between the parties to the employment relationship.[3] This means that labor law aims to strike a balance between the interests of employers and workers,[4] both at the individual and at the collective level.

At the collective level, labor law aims to create a framework for social dialogue between workers' representatives, employers, and governments. This framework promotes democracy in workplaces, the redistribution of resources and economic efficiency.[5] Therefore, labor law includes workers' right to organize, to bargain collectively, and to strike.[6] In this regard, labor law also enables activities that are a form of economic cooperation.[7] For this reason, it provides information and consultation rights to workers' representatives and acknowledges the right to negotiate collective bargaining agreements regarding economic and social policy or working conditions (see Section 17.4). These collective agreements may be considered as a set of rules that are able to limit the arbitrariness of being subjected to the complete control of the employer and, therefore, as a means to balance the interests of workers and employers.[8]

At the individual level, labor law not only establishes minimal standards for working conditions but also encompasses provisions that protect the personal integrity and self-development of workers.[9] This implies that labor law includes on the one hand regulation about working conditions (such as working times, occupational safety and health and remuneration). On the other hand, it addresses the human dignity of workers and protects their human rights in the workplaces, such as the protection of their private life. More generally, labor law also pursues the protection and promotion of human autonomy and social justice.[10]

3 International Labour Organisation Recommendation no. 198 [2006] on the Employment Relationship, preamble.

4 Frank Hendrickx, "Foundations and functions of contemporary labour law" (2012) *European Labour Law Journal*, 3: 122.

5 Guy Davidov, "Collective bargaining laws: Purpose and scope" (2004) *International Journal of Comparative Labour Law and Industrial Relations*, 20: 83.

6 Davidov, Collective Bargaining Laws: Purpose and Scope 82.

7 Davidov, Collective Bargaining Laws: Purpose and Scope 82.

8 Davidov, Collective Bargaining Laws: Purpose and Scope 85.

9 Frank Hendrickx, "Foundations and functions of contemporary labour law" (2012) *European Labour Law Journal*, 3: 123.

10 Guy Davidov, "Articulating labour law's goals: Why and how" (2012) *European Labour Law Journal*, 3: 148.

17.3 MAJOR USES OF AI IN THE EMPLOYMENT CONTEXT

AI is increasingly introduced in workplaces, for an increasing number of tasks. It is found in almost every sector of the economy, from agriculture to education, healthcare, manufacturing, public services, retail and services, or transport – all of which have implications for the underlying employment relationships in those sectors. Initially, AI adoption primarily affected low- and middle-skilled workers, whose tasks tend to be routine. However, it is extending to high-skilled workers who perform cognitive tasks.[11] AI find applications in many different work contexts, including automation and robotics, especially of repetitive tasks; but also predictive analytics; virtual assistant systems for scheduling or handling customer enquiries; human resources management, screening and recruitment processes; quality control of products and services; predictive maintenance and monitoring of workers.[12] Moreover, emerging applications of AI, such as generative AI, are gaining traction. Research forecasts that two-thirds of occupations could be partially automated by AI systems.[13] Labor law is especially concerned with the use of AI applications that assist in decision-making about workers and their working conditions. This particular use of AI is referred to as the phenomenon of algorithmic management, which deserves to be addressed more in-depth.

17.3.1 *The Specific Case of Algorithmic Management: Automated Decision-Making and Monitoring Systems*

One of the most prominent uses of AI systems in the context of employment concerns the management of workers. It can be broadly understood as the use of data-driven tools that collect and analyze an extensive amount of data on workers in order to allocate tasks to them, to evaluate their performance, or to discipline them.[14] Taking a more granular view, algorithmic management can be defined as

[11] Artificial Intelligence and Employment. New evidence from occupations most exposed to AI (2021) OECD Policy brief on the future of work, www.oecd.org/future-of-work/reports-and-data/AI-Employment-brief-2021.pdf, accessed May 29, 2023.

[12] Aleksandr Christenko, Vaida Jankauskaitė, Agnė Paliokaitė, Egidius Leon van den Broek et al., "Artificial intelligence for worker management: an overview" (2022) EU OSHA, https://osha.europa.eu/en/publications/artificial-intelligence-worker-management-overview? accessed May 29, 2023; OECD, "Panel discussion: the impact of AI on the labour market" International conference AI in work, innovation, productivity and skills (2021), https://oecd.ai/en/work-innovation-productivity-skills/key-themes/labour-markets, accessed May 29, 2023.

[13] Goldman Sachs Research, "Generative AI could raise global GDP by 7%" (2023), www.goldmansachs.com/intelligence/pages/generative-ai-could-raise-global-gdp-by-7-percent.html? accessed May 29, 2023.

[14] Katherine Kellogg, Melisa Valentine, and Angele Christin, "Algorithms at work: The new contested terrain of control" (2020) *Academy of Management Annals*, 14: 368.

> automated or semi-automated computing processes that perform one or more of the following functions: (1) workforce planning and work task allocation, (2) dynamic piece rate pay setting per task, (3) controlling workers by monitoring, steering, surveilling or rating their work and the time they need to perform specific tasks, nudging their behavior, (4) measuring actual worker performance against predicted time and/or effort required to complete task and providing recommendations on how to improve worker performance and (5) penalizing workers, for example, through termination or suspension of their accounts. Metrics might include estimated time, customer rating or worker's rating of customer.[15]

There is a genuine risk that the deployment of such tools occurs to the detriment of workers' social protection, allowing discrimination and the worsening of their working conditions.

Algorithmic management is a concept that has first been used in the mid-2000s, mainly in the context of delivery platforms in the USA. It started as a relatively "unseen" practice, but its wider adoption is happening incrementally and has now spread to many sectors of the economy.[16] Even though most algorithmic management tools are commercialized outside the European Union (EU), they are often also implemented in companies and organizations established within the EU or elsewhere in the world.

Algorithmic management can take different forms, with many examples found in recruitment processes to screen or analyze the CVs of job candidates, or to "assess" facial expressions during video interviews. It is however also used to assess the job performance of workers, by tracking and analyzing their physical work.[17] For instance, wearable devices are now used in warehouses, call centers, and other workplaces to produce metrics on productivity and create rankings of workers' performance.[18] Other wearables used for safety purposes integrate sensors to measure physical distancing, to detect a potential harmful environment on a specific site, or to measure physiological parameters of individual workers and observe their health conditions and well-being.[19] Algorithmic systems also exist that direct workers by specifying the tasks they have to carry out, including the order and timeframe in which this needs

[15] Aida Ponce Del Castillo, and Diego Naranjo, Regulating algorithmic management. An assessment of the EC's draft Directive on improving working conditions in platform work. *ETUI Policy Brief*, 2022, 08, https://etui.org/publications/regulating-algorithmic-management, accessed January 20, 2023.

[16] Sara Baiocco, Enrique Fernández-Macías, Uma Rani and Annarosa Pesole, "The algorithmic management of work and its implications in different contexts" (2022) *JRC Working Papers Series on Labour, Education and Technology* 2.

[17] Valerio De Stefano and Simon Taes, "Algorithmic management and collective bargaining" (2022) 29: *Transfer* 3.

[18] Alex Wood, "Algorithmic management: Consequences for work organisation and working conditions" (2021) *JRC Working Papers Series on Labour, Education and Technology* 7.

[19] Fan Wu, Taiyang Wu, and Mehmet Rasit Yuce, "Design and implementation of a wearable sensor network system for IoT-connected safety and health applications" (2019) *IEEE 5th World Forum on Internet of Things (WF-IoT)* 87–90.

to be done.[20] Other tools can track and evaluate teams at individual levels, collecting metrics to measure their level of interaction[21] or to nudge workers' behavior. This algorithmic management practice already permeates sectors such as transport and logistics, with the objective of optimizing delivery services, but other sectors are following suit.

Finally, algorithmic management is at the heart of digital labor platforms, where it is used to process customer feedback or to analyze and evaluate workers. This is especially the case for transport-oriented platforms, which use algorithmic systems to manage drivers.[22] These workers receive their assignments based on, among others, their location and profile, and they are then provided with directions to pick up customers or deliver orders.

17.3.2 *Challenges of Algorithmic Management*

These examples demonstrate that AI systems are already present in workplaces and raise numerous questions for labor law.[23] Adopting an interdisciplinary approach, this section offers a non-exhaustive mapping of the most relevant issues that require attention, touching upon elements that relate not only to labor law provisions, but also privacy and data protection rules, fundamental rights, and computer science practices.

Large processing of data. The first issue to point out, is that algorithmic management relies on the complex processing of large amounts of personal data, which allows for the "*quantification of workers.*"[24] Two important questions that need to be addressed in this context are: Why are personal (and potentially also sensitive) data collected? And for what purposes are such data used? After all, someone must explicitly take the decision of collecting and using data, and such decisions needs to be accounted for. As noted earlier, when algorithmic management systems are used to assess workers' performance, this can enable the analysis or monitoring of processes that would go beyond the supervision of a human manager. In other words, algorithmic management not only leads to monitoring workers to extents unthinkable in the past, but also to the collection and processing of data to analyze and make decisions about workers' jobs and

[20] Kellogg, Valentine and Christin, "Algorithms at work: The new contested terrain of control" 368.

[21] Alan Hern, "Microsoft productivity score feature criticised as workplace surveillance" *The Guardian* (November 26, 2020) accessed January 23, 2023.

[22] Rachel Aleks, Michael Maffie and Tina Saksida, "Collective bargaining in the digitized workplace" Dionne Pohler (ed), *Reimagining the Governance of Work and Employment* (Labor and Employment Relations Association, 2020) 91.

[23] For more information on the issues related to algorithmic management, see Valerio De Stefano and Simon Taes, "Algorithmic management and collective bargaining" (2022) *Transfer* 29: 5–7.

[24] Phoebe Moore and Andrew Robinson, "The quantified self: What counts in the neoliberal workplace" (2016) *New Media & Society*, 18: 2774–2792.

their working conditions in a far more intrusive manner. Although algorithms themselves are used to implement certain rules,[25] the actual decision-making is not yet fully in the hands these systems. Indeed, behind AI systems, there are human beings who set rules and parameters for data collection and for decision-making. Accordingly, before such systems are implemented in workplaces, important concerns about responsibility and accountability for these systems and their impact on workers need to be addressed.

Transparency of AI systems. A second issue relates to the transparency of the systems' architecture, operations, and opacity around the purpose of the systems. To determine whether algorithmic management systems process personal data lawfully, it is important that their operations can be verified. This is also important to assess whether they are affected by certain biases – which can lead to the discrimination of vulnerable groups of workers – or whether they showcase other failures due to poor data quality, inaccuracy or errors. Some cases have already evidenced that bias in learning systems resulted in discriminatory outcomes. For example, Amazon introduced a recruiting Machine Learning based algorithm to sort out and select talented applicants on the basis of selected features of their CV. However, the algorithm considered male candidates as more talented, because it had been trained on the basis of data that reflected the male dominance across the tech industry.[26] Therefore, besides risks of privacy violations, the lack of transparency about how data is collected and processed may, among others, put workers in a position where they will not be treated equally and, hence, be deprived of job opportunities on the basis of discriminatory criteria.

Privacy and data protection rights. A third issue relates to the effective protection of workers' right to privacy and data protection when working alongside AI systems. Article 22 of the General Data Protection Regulation (GDPR)[27] gives data subjects "*the right not to be subject to a decision based solely on automated processing, including profiling, which produces legal effects concerning him or her or similarly significantly affects him or her.*" However, the scope of application of this article seems to be interpreted rather restrictively.

Three legal proceedings were brought before the District Court of Amsterdam by the App Drivers and Couriers Union, a platform workers union, claiming violations of the EU GDPR: a first case, *Uber drivers* v. *Uber*, on transparency requests and

[25] Sara Baiocco, Enrique Fernández-Macías, Uma Rani, and Annarosa Pesole, "The Algorithmic Management of work and its implications in different contexts."

[26] Roberto Iriondo, "Amazon Scraps Secret AI Recruiting Engine that Showed Biases Against Women, Carnegie Mellon University" (October 11, 2028), www.ml.cmu.edu/news/news-archive/2016-2020/2018/october/amazon-scraps-secret-artificial-intelligence-recruiting-engine-that-showed-biases-against-women.html, accessed January 23, 2023.

[27] General Data Protection Regulation. EU Regulation 2016/679, https://eur-lex.europa.eu/eli/reg/2016/679/oj, accessed May 12, 2023.

access to personal data[28]; a second case, *Uber drivers* v. *Uber*, on deactivation of drivers accounts and termination of their contract[29]; and a third case, *Ola drivers* v. *Ola Cabs*, on transparency requests by drivers and access to their data.[30]

The App Drivers and Couriers Union relied inter alia on Articles 15 of the GDPR to gain access to all their personal data processed by the platforms, including the use of drivers' monitoring systems such as Uber's Real Time ID and Ola's Guardian system. On the basis of Article 22 of the GDPR, the drivers also asked to receive information on the platforms' algorithmic systems that make decisions about them, including the deactivation of their accounts, known as "robo-firing."

However, in judgments pronounced on March 11, 2021, the Amsterdam District Court rejected most of the drivers' claims, as it found that Article 22 did not apply to these algorithmic systems. The platforms had demonstrated that staff members intervened during the decision-making process and that the decisions did not significantly affect the drivers, thus rendering the protection of Article 22 inapplicable.

Moreover, the App Drivers and Couriers Union appealed to receive access to their personal data and to receive explanation about how automated decisions were made. The Court of Appeal in Amsterdam on April 4, 2023[31] decided positively in their favour. The court ruled that Uber had to provide access to the personal data related to profile, tags, reports per journey, individual ratings, upfront pricing-system, information regarding recipients of personal data, a category from the Guidance note, and information about automated individual decision-making. It also ruled that profiling and management assessments are personal data and they must be disclosed. Regarding the (automated) decisions, the court found that they were taken fully automatically, and that there was insufficient evidence of human intervention which affected drivers significantly, partly because they affect their income without the access to the App. The court rejected Uber's argument of drivers taking collective action to seek access to their data, amounted to an abuse of data protection rights. It confirmed the right of third parties, including trade unions, to establish a gig workers data trust.[32] On the third judgment related to Ola Cars, the court ruled that data access requests fell within the scope of Article 15 of the GDPR. It ordered Ola Cars to disclose information to workers on automated decision-making relating to work allocation and fares.

[28] *Uber drivers* v. *Uber*. Amsterdam District Court [2021] C / 13/687315 / HA RK 20-207 on transparency request under the GDPR.

[29] *Uber drivers* v. *Uber*. Amsterdam District Court [2021] C / 13/692003 / HA RK 20-302 on deactivation of drivers' accounts.

[30] *Ola drivers* v. *Ola cars*. Amsterdam District Court [2021] C / 13/689705 / HA RK 20-258 on transparency request under the GDPR.

[31] *App Drivers & Couriers Union* v. *Uber & Ola* [Amsterdam, 2023] ECLI:NL:GHAMS:2023:793.

[32] De Rechtspraak "Uber and Ola-Cabs need to better inform London taxi drivers about automated decisions" (2023), www.rechtspraak.nl/Organisatie-en-contact/Organisatie/Gerechtshoven/Gerechtshof-Amsterdam/Nieuws/Paginas/Uber-en-Ola-Cabs-moeten-Londense-taxichauffeurs-beter-informeren-over-automatische-besluiten.aspx, accessed May 12, 2023.

Despite the more successful appeal, these cases demonstrate that the provisions and principles of the GDPR may be difficult to exercise vis-à-vis employers, in concrete to access request to data, transparency of the operation and logic of algorithmic management systems or other AI tools. In the context of employment, it is important to note that the employer, as a controller, must fulfill their obligations. These obligations include ensuring the protection of the data subject and being accountable for all personal data processed related to workers. It sheds light into how is crucial to provide additional information regarding the intended or future processing, on how automated decision-making may impact workers and on the limits of profiling. It is hence fair to question whether the workers' fundamental right to privacy is sufficiently safeguarded when their behavior and performance in the workplace is reduced or transformed to mere numbers and digits on the parameters or criteria applied in AI tools or algorithmic systems. The European Court of Human Rights (ECtHR) has given a broad interpretation to Article 8 of the European Convention on Human Rights, whereby the right to respect for private and family life also includes the right *"to develop one's physical and social identity"*[33] and *"to establish and develop relationships with other human beings."*[34] Therefore, it would be paramount to provide further clarification on how these rights can actually be protected when AI applications are used at work.

Technostress. A fourth issue is the use of algorithmic management to influence (nudge) and control workers' behavior,[35] which may have consequences to occupational safety, health or well-being. The primary promise of AI in this domain is its ability to ability to enhance the accurate prediction of potential accidents. AI applications are increasingly integrated into equipment, industrial machines, drones, robots or self-driving vehicles. They can also be embedded in systems associated with personal protective equipment, such as bracelets, wearables, exoskeletons, sensors, and other hardware.

However, it is important to recognize that these systems rely on personal and sensitive data and on an increasingly digitized working environment, thereby posing risk significantly impacting workers' occupational health, safety and well-being. Additionally, complications may arise from other factors, such as when operators or managers have incomplete understanding of the data and its analysis. In broad terms, the key concerns arising within this context can be categorized into two dimensions: physical and psychosocial.

[33] *Denisov v Ukraine* App no 76639/11 (ECtHR September 25, 2018), ECLI:CE:ECHR:2018:0925 JUD007663911, para 95.

[34] *Niemietz v Germany* App no 13710/88 (ECtHR December 16, 1992), ECLI:CE:ECHR:1992:1216 JUD001371088, para 29.

[35] Alex J Wood, Mark Graham, Vili Lehdonvirta, and Isis Hjorth "Good gig, bad gig: Autonomy and algorithmic control in the global gig economy" (2019) *Work, Employment and Society*, 33(1): 56–75. W Alec Cram, Martin Wiener, Monideepa Tarafdar, & Alexander Benlian "Examining the impact of algorithmic control on Uber drivers' technostress" (2022) *Journal of Management Information Systems*, 39(2): 426–453.

When it comes to workers' physical safety, there can occur various types of risks, for example, a risk that the AI-driven machine, robot or partly automated vehicle can wrongly process or analyze the data it collects, thereby leading to an erroneous output or acting unexpectedly, resulting in an injury or accident. Similar risks exist when there are errors or inaccuracies in the dataset, when the system's parameters are not properly tuned or optimized, or when the system's accuracy – and hence the accuracy of its predictions – is faulty.[36] Risk assessment is crucial to identify the possible sources, mitigate or eliminate possible harms.

In relation to the psychosocial and well-being aspects, workers may experience high stress levels when they are aware that their behavior, location, performance, and even emotions, are being monitored and analyzed. In this context, the issue of technostress becomes relevant. The term was coined in 1984 and scholars describe this phenomenon as "*any negative impact on attitudes, thoughts, behaviors, or body physiology that is caused either directly or indirectly by technology*."[37] It combines five common technostressors: techno-overload, techno-invasion, techno-complexity, techno-insecurity, and techno-uncertainty. Technostress has become increasingly significant in the workplace, particularly when workers have to rely on information and communication technologies (ICTs) and AI-driven applications to carry out their tasks.[38]

Technostress may impact workers' psychophysical health and work-life, the consequences can be seen on the short- and long-term on somatic, cognitive–emotional, and behavioural levels,[39] for example, causing psychophysical distress and depleting both emotional and cognitive resources in the individual directly or indirectly.[40] These consequences can extend beyond the individual level, affecting the organizational and societal environments, because of the "always-on" culture and nature of work-related to ICT arrangements, that "create an unbridgeable gap between how an individual is expected to behave during family time and job requests as mediated through ICTs."[41]

36 Sobhan Sarkar, Sammangi Vinay, Rahul Raj, Jhareshwar Maiti, and Pabitra Mitra, "Application of optimized machine learning techniques for prediction of occupational accidents" (2019) *Computers & Operations Research*, 106: 210–224.

37 Bram Tombeur, *De smartphone en technostress* (Wolters Kluwer, 2018) 10; Jan Popma, *The Janus face of the "New Ways of Work": Rise, risks and regulation of nomadic work* (European Trade Union Institute, 2013) 10.

38 Giorgia Bondanini, Gabriele Giorgi, Antonio Ariza-Montes, Alejandro Vega-Muñoz, A., and Paola Andreucci-Annunziata. "Technostress dark side of technology in the workplace: A scientometric analysis" (2020) *International Journal of Environmental Research and Public Health*, 17(21): 8013.

39 Elisabeth Rohwer, Joelle-Cathrin Flöther, Volker Harth & Stefanie Mache "Overcoming the 'dark side' of technology – A scoping review on preventing and coping with work-related technostress" (2022) *International Journal of Environmental Research and Public Health*, 16(6): 3625.

40 Valentina Sommovigo, Chiara Bernuzzi, Georgia Libera Finstad, Ilaria Setti, Paola Gabanelli, Gabriele Giorgi, & Elena Fiabane, "How and when may technostress impact workers' psychophysical health and work-family interface? A study during the COVID-19 pandemic in Italy" (2023) *International Journal of Environmental Research and Public Health*, 20(2): 1266.

41 Sommovigo, Bernuzzi, and Finstad, "How and when may technostress impact workers' psychophysical health and work-family interface?" 15.

Finally, algorithmic management can also be used to reward and discipline workers, to elicit cooperation or to enforce compliance.[42] The automated deactivation of riders' accounts, whether temporarily or permanently, has for instance become a common practice. Some digital labor platforms reward high rated drivers by enabling them access to rides that are financially more attractive, and by giving them priority in queues at popular places (such as airports).[43] In this way, digital platforms "enforce" compliance by providing workers access to higher remuneration when they show certain behavior. There are also examples regarding algorithmic disciplining processes that lead to the discipline of workers. For instance, there is some evidence that in the hospitality sector algorithmic evaluations based on online reviews may result in dismissing staff members, when they do not meet the expected targets.[44] These uses contribute to precarious working conditions.

Considering the earlier mentioned concerns, one can raise the question how they should best be managed and how the risks should be prevented and mitigated? As companies have a legal responsibility to improve workers health by preventing excessive work-related technostress, it is recommended to apply specific prevention policies and other appropriate measures to remove risk factors and mitigate the potential negative effects associated with this practice.[45] Policies and strategies can be centered on the user, the technological environment, organizational environment, and social environment.[46]

More concretely, this involves establishing an ICT environment that meets job-specific requirements to reduce the frequency, duration, and/or intensity of technostressors; tailoring the use of ICTs to the needs of workers; providing transparency over how work-related data collected by technology is processed and used; providing transparency regarding which technologies are used for which purpose; and conducting impact assessments on the possible risks and consequences of AI systems prior to their implementation.[47] Further, a robust legislative framework is essential to address the identified issues of concern and to respond in a preventive and adequate manner. This may include the prohibition of some of these practices to the extent they are not compatible with workers' fundamental rights. Overall, given the goals of labor law, it may well be required that a new balance between workers' and employers' interests must be sought in light of the increasing

[42] Kellogg, Valentine, and Christin, "Algorithms at work: The new contested terrain of control" 380.

[43] *FNV v Uber BV*, Court Amsterdam District Court [2021], 8937120 CV EXPL 20–22882, ECLI:NL:RBAMS:2021:5029, para 29.

[44] Wood, "Algorithmic management: Consequences for work organisation and working conditions" 9.

[45] Rohwer, Flöther, and Harth "Overcoming the 'dark side' of technology" 17.

[46] Katharina Pflügner "Technostress management at the workplace: A systematic literature review" (2022) *Wirtschaftsinformatik 2022 Proceedings* 2.

[47] Michelle Berger, Ricarda Schäfer, Marco Schmidt, Christian Regal, and Gener Gimpel "How to prevent technostress at the digital workplace: A Delphi study" (2023) *Journal of Business Economics*, 1: 63.

application of AI in workplaces. Yet before turning to new legislative initiatives on AI that are relevant for the sphere of work, we discuss some of the key rights and concepts of labor law.

17.4 ESSENTIAL RIGHTS AND CONCEPTS IN LABOR LAW

17.4.1 *Information, Consultation, and Participation*

Both international and European law recognize the rights to information, consultation, and participation as three essential rights of labor law. At the international level, reference can be made to Convention 158 of the ILO, which states that workers' representatives must be consulted "*on measures to be taken to avert or to minimize the terminations and measures to mitigate the adverse effects of any terminations on the workers concerned such as finding alternative employment.*"[48]

ILO Recommendation 166 also refers to consultations on major changes in the undertaking:

> When the employer contemplates the introduction of major changes in production, programme, organisation, structure or technology that are likely to entail terminations, the employer should consult the workers' representatives concerned as early as possible on, inter alia, the introduction of such changes, the effects they are likely to have and the measures for averting or mitigating the adverse effects of such changes.[49]

Whereas the provisions of the earlier mentioned Convention must be implemented in the national legislation upon (voluntary) ratification by ILO Member States, the provisions of the Recommendation are not obligatory but rather contain reference standards for Member States on which they are encouraged to base their labor policies and legislation.[50]

In the EU, these labor law rights are enshrined in the Charter of Fundamental Rights of the European Union (CFR). Article 27 of the CFR states that "*workers or their representatives must, at the appropriate levels, be guaranteed information and consultation in good time in the cases and under the conditions provided for by Community law and national laws and practices.*"

Moreover, there are more than fifteen EU directives dealing with the right to information and consultation. The most important directives in this regard are: (1) the Directive on European Works Councils[51]; (2) the Directive on Employee

[48] International Labour Organisation Convention no. 158 on the Termination of Employment [1982], Article 13.

[49] International Labour Organisation Recommendation no. 166 on the Termination of Employment [1982], para. 20.

[50] Jean-Michel Servais *International Labour Law* (Wolters Kluwer, 2022) 58 and 81.

[51] Directive 2009/38/EC of May 6, 2009 on the establishment of a European Works Council or a procedure in Community-scale undertakings and Community-scale groups of undertakings for the purposes of informing and consulting employees [2009] OJ L122/28.

Involvement in the European Company,[52] (3) the European Framework Directive on Information and Consultation, which sets the minimum requirement for workers' right to information, consultation, and participation[53] and the (4) Directive relating to collective redundancies[54].

Whenever technological changes are introduced in European multinational companies, the Directive on European Works Councils applies. Point 1(a) of Annex I of the Directive states that "*the information and consultation of the European Works Council shall relate in particular to [...] substantial changes concerning organisation, introduction of new working methods or production processes to negotiate about the impact of the introduction of new processes [...].*" European Works Councils (EWC) are the information and consultation bodies that bring together both management and workers representatives from the European countries in which a given multinational company has operations. In the EWC, the representatives of central management inform and consult the workers' delegation, and they can negotiate a variety of topics and company decisions that have an impact at a transnational level.[55] Collectively, this body of legislation aims at providing workers and employers with strong social protection, in order to improve living and working conditions and to protect social cohesion.[56] It should also be added that various of these rights are protected through national legislation too.

17.4.2 *Social Dialogue*

Another essential component of the labor law acquis concerns *Social Dialogue*. This refers to the specific role of social partners, meaning the recognized organizations representing the two sides of the industry, the employers and employees. The social partners usually comprise employers' organizations and trade unions respectively.

Social Dialogue is a unique instrument of governance and cooperation. At international level, the ILO is the only tripartite United Nations agency that brings together governments, employers and workers of 187 member States. The ILO

[52] Council Directive 2001/86/EC of October 8, 2001, supplementing the Statute for a European company with regard to the involvement of employees [2001] OJ L 294/22.

[53] European Parliament and Council Directive 2002/14/EC of March 11, 2002, establishing a general framework for informing and consulting employees in the European Community – Joint declaration of the European Parliament, the Council, and the Commission on employee representation [2002] OJ L 80/29. ETUI, "Worker participation issues in EU," www.worker-participation.eu/EU-Framework-for-I-C-P/Information-and-Consultation/Fragmented-legislation-to-be-harmonised, accessed November 25, 2022.

[54] Council Directive 98/59/EC of July 20, 1998, on the approximation of the laws of the Member States relating to collective redundancies [1998] OJ L 225/16.

[55] ETUI. European Works Councils, www.worker-participation.eu/European-Works-Councils, accessed January 23, 2022.

[56] European Commission. Labour law. Employment, Social Affairs & Inclusion. Labour law – Employment, Social Affairs & Inclusion – European Commission (europa.eu), accessed January 20, 2023.

defines Social Dialogue as "*all types of negotiation, consultation or simply exchange of information between, or among, representatives of governments, employers and workers, on issues of common interest relating to economic and social policy.*" Social Dialogue can take numerous forms and the ILO recognizes the following[57]:

- "*Negotiation, consultation and information exchange between and among governments, employers' and workers' organizations;*
- *Collective bargaining between employers/employers' organizations and workers' organizations;*
- *Dispute prevention and resolution; and*
- *Other approaches such as workplace cooperation, international framework agreements and social dialogue in the context of regional economic communities.*"

In Europe, social dialogue encompasses bi-partite dialogue between employer organizations and trade unions. Importantly, the Treaty on the Functioning of the European Union (TFEU) recognizes and promotes the role of the social partners in the EU, who can contribute to policy-making and design and implement national reforms in the social and employment areas, both at national and European level. Their involvement in policymaking has been acknowledged in Guideline 7 of Council Decision 2018/1215 for the employment policies of the Member States, as well as in Principle 8 of the European Pillar of Social Rights.[58] Some recent examples of social dialogue themes are education, skills and training, the circular economy, climate change, telework, and the right to disconnect.[59]

The European Social Dialogue can also be tripartite and involve public authorities. It then refers to discussions, consultations, negotiations and joint actions involving European Social Partners, who are organizations working at EU level and taking part in consultations and negotiating agreements.[60] Tripartite social dialogue contributes to the construction of EU economic and social policies, and has a role in strengthening democracy, social justice and a productive and competitive economy. The association of employers, workers organizations and governments, in the design and implementation of economic and social policies, allows for a balanced consensus in such policies and the taking into account of the interests of all the parties involved.[61]

57 ILO, Social Dialogue and Tripartism www.ilo.org/global/topics/workers-and-employers-organizations-tripartism-and-social-dialogue/lang--en/index.htm, accessed November 27, 2023.

58 EUROFOUND "Social Partners," www.eurofound.europa.eu/topic/social-partners, (December 20, 2022) accessed January 23, 2022.

59 EU Social Dialogue Resource Centre, https://resourcecentre.etuc.org/eu-social-dialogue, accessed November 25, 2022.

60 European Commission. "Social Dialogue," https://ec.europa.eu/social/main.jsp?catId=329&langId=en, accessed January 21, 2023.

61 Junko Ishikawa, "*Key features of national social dialogue: A social dialogue resource book.*" Vol. 11. (International Labour Office, 2003).

17.4.3 *The Autonomous Framework Agreement on Digitalization*

Social partners conduct bi-partite negotiations at inter-sectoral, sectoral or company level, which can result in autonomous agreements. Articles 154 and 155 of the TFEU provide a legal basis to negotiate Framework Agreements, which are contractually binding on social partners and their members.

In the field of digitalization, one of the core agreements that European social partners have negotiated and signed in 2000 concerns the "Autonomous Framework Agreement on Digitalization."[62] This agreement is the result of challenging negotiations between the European Trade Union Confederation (ETUC), BusinessEurope, the European Centre of Employers and Enterprises providing Public Services and Services of general interest (CEEP) and the Association of Crafts and SMEs in Europe (SMEunited). It represents a shared commitment of the European cross-sectoral social partners to optimize the benefits and deal with the challenges of digitalization in the world of work.

The rationale of the Agreement is that digital technologies impact four interrelated dimensions: work content (skills), work organization (employment terms and conditions, work-life balance), working conditions (work environment, health and safety, physical and mental demands, well-being, climate, comfort, work equipment) and work relations (relations or interpersonal relations that can impact the performance and the well-being of the workers). To manage the interrelationship of these dimensions, the Agreement specifies that in addition, four issues need to be considered:

a) digital skills and securing employment: The challenge is to determine which digital skills and process changes are necessary, thereby allowing adequate training measures to be organized, and to foster digital transformation strategies in support of employment;
b) modalities of connecting and disconnecting from technology applications;
c) artificial intelligence, including the guarantee of the human-in-control principle; and
d) respect of human dignity and worker surveillance.[63]

European Social Partners recognize that AI systems have a valuable potential to increase the productivity of the enterprise, the well-being of the workforce and a better allocation of tasks between humans, between different parts of the enterprise, and between machines and humans. However, they also indicate that it is "*important to make sure that AI systems and solutions do not jeopardize but augment human*

[62] European Social Partners. "Autonomous Framework Agreement on Digitalisation," www.etuc.org/en/document/eu-social-partners-agreement-digitalisation, (June 2020) accessed November 25, 2022.

[63] Aida Ponce del Castillo, "Europe's digital agenda. People-centric, data-centric or both," in Bart Vanhercke and Slavina Spasova (eds), *Social policy in the European Union: state of play 2021. Re-emerging social ambitions as the EU recovers from the pandemic*, (ETUI OSE, 2022).

involvement and capacities at work."[64] They also stress that AI systems should be designed and operated in order to comply with legislation (including the GDPR), guarantee privacy rights and ensure the dignity of the individual worker.

In the Agreement, the European Social Partners also referred to the concept of "Trustworthy AI" which they aspire to implement, and defined it – based on the Ethics Guidelines of the Commission's High-Level Expert Group on AI[65] – as a concept that should meet three criteria:

- it should be lawful, fair, transparent, safe, and secure, complying with all applicable laws and regulations as well as fundamental rights and non-discrimination rules,
- it should follow agreed ethical standards, ensuring adherence to EU Fundamental/human rights, equality and other ethical principles and,
- it should be robust and sustainable, both from a technical and social perspective since, even with good intentions, AI systems can cause unintentional harm[66]

These criteria should be met throughout the AI system's entire life cycle and must be respected whenever AI systems are deployed in the world of work. The Agreement also acknowledges that there can be tensions between different principles, such as respect for human autonomy, prevention of harm, fairness and explicability of decision-making, and states that these tensions should be addressed. However, it does not provide mechanisms to do so.

By virtue of the Framework Agreement, social partners have taken the responsibility to implement the measures described therein at the national, sectoral, and enterprise level in all EU Member States. While, during the first year of the Agreement, their commitment focused on translating and disseminating its content, the second year is dedicated to the actual implementation of its measures.

17.5 LEGISLATIVE INITIATIVES ON AI THAT ARE PIVOTAL FOR LABOR LAW

The rule of law, democratic participation in policymaking and the respect of fundamental and social rights are essential in the labor context. With the increased presence of AI systems in workplaces and the risks they create, laws are needed that are up to the task of protecting these values. It is argued that relying on a multiplicity of ethical guidelines, codes of conduct or other similar voluntary initiatives to govern AI systems cannot sufficiently guarantee adequate workers' protection. Instead, enforceable rules are necessary, that also establish compensation mechanisms in

64 European Social Partners. "Autonomous Framework Agreement on Digitalisation" 11.

65 High-Level Expert Group on AI (2018) "Ethics Guidelines for Trustworthy AI," https://digital-strategy.ec.europa.eu/en/library/ethics-guidelines-trustworthy-ai, (April 8, 2019) accessed May 12, 2023.

66 European Social Partners. "Autonomous Framework Agreement on Digitalisation" 11.

case workers' rights are infringed. It is worth exploring the EU's AI package in relation to the employment context.

17.5.1 *The AI Act*

In April 2021, the European Commission put forward a regulatory package on AI,[67] with at its core the Regulation laying down harmonized rules on AI, hereafter referred to as the AI Act, published in the Official Journal of the EU on July 12, 2024.[68] According to the European Commission, a legal framework on AI was needed "*to foster the development, use and uptake of AI in the internal market that at the same time meets a high level of protection of public interests, such as health and safety and the protection of fundamental rights, including democracy, the rule of law and environmental protection.*" The claim to be putting fundamental rights at the heart of its approach, has been the object of criticism.[69]

It should be noted that the AI Act is modeled after product market regulation, typically used for technical safety standards. Therefore it is not specifically designed to address social issues and does not provide workers with specific rights. To address social issues, another legal basis could have been added to the text. However, whichever legal basis, Recital 9 recognizes that it "should be without prejudice to existing Union law, in particular on data protection, consumer protection, fundamental rights, employment, and protection of workers," and should not affect Union law on social policy and national labor law. Similarly, Article 2(11) emphasizes that the AI Act does not preclude the Union or Member States from maintaining or introducing laws, regulations, administrative provisions or collective agreements more favourable to workers. However, the disregard for labor-related issues may in fact diminish the legal protection currently afforded by labor law, posing a significant risk to be addressed.[70]

[67] The EC's AI package also included a Communication on Fostering a European approach to Artificial Intelligence and a review of the Coordinated Plan on AI with EU Member States. EU Commission "A European approach to artificial intelligence," https://digital-strategy.ec.europa.eu/en/policies/european-approach-artificial-intelligence, accessed May 12, 2023.

[68] Regulation (EU) 2024/1689 of the European Parliament and of the Council of 13 June 2024 laying down harmonised rules on artificial intelligence and amending Regulations (EC) No 300/2008, (EU) No 167/2013, (EU) No 168/2013, (EU) 2018/858, (EU) 2018/1139 and (EU) 2019/2144 and Directives 2014/90/EU, (EU) 2016/797 and (EU) 2020/1828 (Artificial Intelligence Act), https://eur-lex.europa.eu/eli/reg/2024/1689/oj, accessed July 23, 2024.

[69] See Chapter 12 of this book. See also Nathalie Smuha et al., "How the EU can achieve legally trustworthy AI," available at *SSRN* 3899991 (2021); Michael Veale and Frederik Zuiderveen Borgesius, "Demystifying the draft EU artificial intelligence act" (2021) *Computer Law Review International*, 22.

[70] Aida Ponce Del Castillo "The AI regulation: entering an AI regulatory winter? Why an ad hoc directive on AI in employment is required" (2021) *ETUI Policy Brief* 06; Jeremias Adams-Prassl "Regulating algorithms at work: Lessons for a 'European approach to artificial intelligence" (2022) *European Labour Law Journal*, 13(1), 30–50; Valerio De Stefano, "The EU Proposed Regulation on AI: a threat to labour protection?" (2021) Global Workplace Law and Policy.

The EU Commission has recognized that the use of discriminatory AI systems in employment might violate many fundamental rights and lead to broader "*societal consequences, reinforcing existing or creating new forms of structural discrimination and exclusion.*"[71] Therefore, Annex III of the AI Act lists high-risks AI systems related to the employment sphere. Point 3 refers to systems relating to *education and vocational training*, Point 4 refers to systems that relate to *employment, workers management, and access to self-employment*. Are mentioned in particular: "*AI systems intended to be used for the recruitment or selection of natural persons, in particular to place targeted job advertisements, to analyse and filter job applications, and to evaluate candidates*" and "*AI systems intended to be used to make decisions affecting terms of work-related relationships, the promotion or termination of work-related contractual relationships, to allocate tasks based on individual behaviour or personal traits or characteristics or to monitor and evaluate the performance and behaviour of persons in such relationships.*" As discussed in Chapter 12 of this book, high-risk AI systems are subjected to certain mandatory requirements.

In addition to regulating high-risks systems, the AI Act prohibits certain practices. In the context of work, Article 5(f) prohibits the use of AI systems "*to infer emotions of a natural person in the areas of workplace and education institutions, except where the use of the AI system is intended to be put in place or into the market for medical or safety reasons.*" Recital 44 states that such systems can "*lead to discriminatory outcomes*" and "*be intrusive to the rights and freedoms of the concerned persons*," particularly considering the imbalance of power in the context of work or education combined with the intrusive nature of these systems. However, the prohibition does not apply to AI systems placed on the market strictly for medical or safety reasons, such as systems intended for therapeutical use. This exception allows the use of AI systems under the guise of medical or safety reasons, while the actual motive may be different.

Connected to this, it should be noted that the notion of "emotion recognition system" "*does not include physical states, such as pain or fatigue, including, for example, systems used in detecting the state of fatigue of professional pilots or drivers for the purpose of preventing accidents*" (Recital 18). Fatigue or pain are not considered as emotions and thus not subject to the prohibition established by Article 5(f).

Most of the burden to comply with the AI Act falls on providers. However, from a workplace perspective, very few employers are providers; the majority are deployers. It is therefore key for workers and their representatives to keep a close eye on how deployers comply, notably with their *ex ante* obligation to inform (or to inform and consult) workers or their representatives, under Union or national law, before putting into service or using a high-risk AI system at the workplace (Article 26(7)). If the conditions for those obligations in other legal instruments are not fulfilled, it

[71] EU Commission "Impact Assessment accompanying the proposal for a regulation laying down harmonised rules on artificial intelligence" (2021), https://digital-strategy.ec.europa.eu/en/library/impact-assessment-regulation-artificial-intelligence, accessed January 20, 2023.

still remains necessary to ensure that workers and their representatives are informed on the planned deployment of high-risk AI systems at the workplace (Recital 92).

Pursuant to Article 26 (and Annex VIII), deployers also have to comply with other specific obligations when deploying high-risk systems. These include transparency and information obligations to enable appropriate human oversight of high-risk systems (Articles 13 and 14), as well as disclosure obligations for the use of certain systems (Article 50). To secure that the provision of information (and consultation) occurs effectively, the AI Act encourages providers and deployers to ensure a sufficient level of AI literacy of their staff and other persons dealing with the operation and use of AI systems on their behalf (Article 4).

Finally, the AI Act addresses the role of trade unions in the context of stakeholder involvement and training. It emphasizes their involvement in the development and deployment of AI systems and voluntary codes of conduct (Recital 165). As social partners, they are not involved in the AI Office (Article 64), but they do have a role in the Advisory Forum established to advise and provide technical expertise to the European Artificial Intelligence Board and the Commission (Recital 150 and Article 67(2)).

17.5.2 *The AI Liability Directive*

The rules on AI could not have been complete without a liability regime. The EC's AI Liability Directive[72] proposes a strict liability regime for non-contractual fault-based civil claims for damages arising from random events or incidents caused by an AI system, between entities not bound by a contract. The proposed directive is complementary to the AI Act and hence, focuses on high-risk AI systems considered products, whereby an injured person has to prove that an AI system caused damage. The key liable economic operator is the provider or user. The burden of proof for the injured person can be eased if certain conditions are met, in order to obtain compensation under national law. However, it is uncertain whether and how the AI liability directive applies to labor law. Three situations could arise. First, in cases where an AI system is involved in firing workers, the AI Liability Directive does not apply most likely due to the existence of an employment contract. Second, in cases where AI systems are used for recruitment services, the proposed directive does not apply because the AI system "only provided information or advice which was taken into account by the relevant human actor," as Recital 15 states. Finally, in cases where a worker has suffered harm involving an AI system, the directive will probably not apply due to the contractual nature of these damages. However, other (safety) obligations in labor law may apply and the employer could be held liable on the basis of these obligations.

[72] EU Commission "Proposal for a Directive on adapting non contractual civil liability rules to artificial intelligence" (2022), https://commission.europa.eu/document/f9acodaf-baa3-4371-a760-810414ce4823_en, accessed May 29, 2023.

Finally, the AI liability directive is welcome as a first attempt to provide a harmonized regime to liability challenges that arise in an AI-context. It includes novel provisions, one of them being the disclosure of information, which could be potentially useful for deployers of AI systems. However, it remains unclear whether and how individuals can utilize the information disclosed effectively.[73] The proposed directive also provides a rebuttable presumption of a causal link between the fault of the user of a high-risk AI system and the output of this AI system, when this user does not comply its obligations to use or monitor the AI system in accordance with the accompanying instructions.[74] Despite its potential to substantially facilitate the proof of damages for workers, this presumption will not apply for many applications of work-related AI systems due to the contractual nature of the claims for these damages.

17.5.3 *The New Machinery Regulation*

Another piece of the "AI Package" concerns the new Regulation on Machinery 2023/1230, replacing Machinery Directive 2006/42/EC.[75] This directive was based on the principles of the so-called "New Approach to Technical Harmonization and Standards."[76] It set a range of minimum health and safety requirements that machinery must fulfill to be placed on the market and the conformity assessment through which it can be demonstrated that the machine indeed fulfils them. Machines that meet these requirements are said to have a "presumption of conformity." Given the role that machinery plays in many work environments, the directive was key to ensure workers' safety, mainly in the industrial and manufacturing sectors.

An evaluation study conducted by the European Commission in 2018 identified a number of issues with the directive, and found that it required more efficiency. The study concluded that a new version of the legislation was needed, ideally in the form of a regulation, to facilitate the homogenous application of and alignment with horizontal rules on essential health and safety requirements to guarantee that all pieces

[73] Orian Dheu, Jan De Bruyne, and Charlotte Ducuing. "The European Commission's Approach to Extra-Contractual Liability and AI–A First Analysis and Evaluation of the Two Proposals" (2022) available at SSRN accessed June 19, 2023.

[74] EU Commission "Proposal for a Regulation of the European Parliament and of the Council on machinery products" (2021) (Article 4.3), https://ec.europa.eu/docsroom/documents/45508, accessed May 12, 2023.

[75] Regulation (EU) 2023/1230 of the European Parliament and of the Council of 14 June 2023 on machinery and repealing Directive 2006/42/EC of the European Parliament and of the Council and Council Directive 73/361/EEC, https://eur-lex.europa.eu/eli/reg/2023/1230/oj, accessed August 2, 2024.

[76] The "New Approach" is a legislative technique that aims at preventing barriers to trade in the EU. It limits the adoption of rules to essential safety requirements with which products must conform to be put on the market. European Standardization Organizations (ESOs) have the task of drawing up the technical specifications and/or Harmonized Standards needed to meet the Essential Requirements. Although Harmonized Standards are not mandatory, products manufactured in conformity with them, are presumed to be in conformity with the Essential Requirements. CEN/CENELEC, https://boss.cen.eu/reference-material/guidancedoc/pages/newapproach/, accessed May 12, 2023.

of industrial machinery (interchangeable equipment, safety components or lifting accessories) are safe to use at work.

Beyond an update of the directive's provisions, the new Machinery Regulation also proposes Essential Health and Safety Requirements (EHSRs) listed in Annex III that address the latest developments in digital technology, including the integration of AI systems and Internet of Things (IoT) into machinery equipment and the collaboration between human and robots. The EU Commission's underlying rationale is that although the risks of AI systems are regulated by the AI Act, the entire machinery needs to be safe, considering the interactions between the machinery components, including AI systems. The EU Commission states that "*machines are becoming more powerful, autonomous and some look almost like humans, which requires adapting the EHSRs related to the contact between the human and the machinery*."[77] The regulation provides specifically that:

(a) For evolving machines: in the risk assessments, manufacturers will need to include those risks appearing after the machinery is placed on the market due to its evolving and autonomous behaviour;
(b) On ergonomics: under the intended conditions of use, the discomfort, fatigue and physical and psychological stress faced by the operator shall be reduced to the minimum possible, taking into account ergonomic principles;
(c) Regarding risks related to moving parts and psychological stress: the prevention of risks "shall be adapted to human-machine coexistence, in a shared space without direct collaboration, and human-machine interaction."

The new Regulation also addresses "*the risks related to 'moving parts' (accidents in human-robot collaboration), cyber-safety aspects in the connected machinery, and software updates after the placing on the market of the machinery product which might change functionality*."[78] The Regulation was published in the Official Journal of the EU on June 29, 2023, but it will only become applicable from January 2027 onwards.

17.5.4 *The Directive on Improving Working Conditions in Platform Work*

A third important EU legislative initiative concerns the directive on Improving Working Conditions in Platform Work.[79] This directive is the first piece of EU

[77] EU Commission "Explanatory Memorandum of the proposal for a Regulation on Machinery Products," Brussels, 21.4.2021, COM(2021) 202 final, https://eur-lex.europa.eu/legal-content/EN/TXT/HTML/?uri=CELEX:52021PC0202, accessed August 2, 2024.

[78] Mari Tuominen and Solène Festor, "Revising the Machinery Directive. Briefing. Initial Appraisal of a European Commission Impact Assessment" (2020) European Parliament. www.europarl.europa.eu/RegData/etudes/BRIE/2021/694208/EPRS_BRI(2021)694208_EN.pdf, accessed January 20, 2023.

[79] EU Commission "Provisional agreement for a directive of the European Parliament and of the Council on improving working conditions in platform work," https://data.consilium.europa.eu/doc/document/ST-7212-2024-ADD-1/en/pdf), accessed July 22, 2024.

labor law that regulates automated monitoring and decision-making systems. In the European Commission's view, platform work is developing rapidly, raising new challenges relating to working conditions, algorithmic management, access to social protection and benefits, and collective representation and bargaining. These concerns were more visible during the pandemic, given the increased reliance on platform work in this period.

The work that led to the directive was a two-phase consultation of the European Social Partners, through which the European Commission identified four specific challenges: (1) the employment status of platform workers, (2) the algorithm-based business model of the platforms, (3) the cross-border nature of platform work, and (4) the existence of regulatory gaps at EU level. Nicolas Schmit, Commissioner for Jobs and Social Rights, made an important statement referring to the role of social partners in this field: "*We cannot lose sight of the basic principles of our European social model (...) and social partners' views on this will be key in finding a balanced initiative for platform work in the EU.*"[80] Therefore, the Commission decided to propose a new directive that could help address these concerns.

The directive has two main goals: (1) to improve the working conditions of platform workers by facilitating the correct determination of their employment status through a rebuttable legal presumption, (2) to improve the protection of the personal data of platform workers by improving transparency and accountability in the use of automated monitoring and decision-making systems. The directive includes an innovative chapter on algorithmic management, with hybrid labor and data protection provisions. Article 7, in particular, limits the processing of personal data, notably biometrics data, or data related to the emotional or psychological state of workers. Article 7 not only applies to automated monitoring systems and automated decision-making systems, but also to automated systems *supporting* or taking decisions that affect persons performing platform work in any manner.

As the processing of workers' data by automated monitoring and decision-making systems is likely to result in a high risk to workers' rights, platforms must carry out a Data Protection Impact Assessment, following GDPR requirements (Article 8). They also must respect transparency and information obligations, in relation to the systems they use to take or support decisions that affect workers and their working conditions (Article 9). They must ensure human oversight (Article 10), with the involvement of workers' representatives, of the impact of individual decisions taken or supported by their systems. Finally, workers have the right to obtain an

[80] EU Commission "Protecting people working through platforms: Commission launches a first-stage consultation of the social partners" Press release, https://ec.europa.eu/commission/presscorner/api/files/document/print/en/ip_21_686/IP_21_686_EN.pdf (February 24, 2021) accessed January 20, 2023.

explanation from the platform for any decision taken or supported by their systems, as well as the right to review it (Article 11). In relation to health and safety, platforms must evaluate the risks of automated monitoring or decision-making systems, in particular possible work-related accidents, as well as psychosocial and ergonomic risks. They may not use automated monitoring or decision-making systems in any manner that puts undue pressure on workers or puts at risk their safety and their physical and mental health (Article 12).

17.5.5 *International Initiatives*

The EU is not the only jurisdiction that is taking legislative action on AI. Several international organizations worked simultaneously in this sphere, and their outcomes will impact the labor law context. In 2024, the OECD revised the "*Principles for responsible stewardship of trustworthy AI.*" Initially adopted in 2019,[81] the Principle related to "transparency and explainability" mentions the need for AI actors "*to commit to transparency and responsible disclosure regarding AI systems,*" and "*to make stakeholders aware of their interactions with AI systems, including in the workplace.*"[82] At the same time, the Council of Europe, through its *ad hoc* Committee on Artificial Intelligence (CAHAI), and its successor the Committee on AI (CAI), adopted an international legally binding convention. The "Framework Convention on Artificial Intelligence, Human Rights, Democracy and the rule of law" aims to set "*minimum standards for AI development*" based on the Council of Europe's standards of human rights, democracy and the rule of law.[83] Similarly to the AI Act, the Council of Europe's convention deals with AI systems according to a risk-based assessment, and imposes new obligations based on the level of risk posed by the systems. It does not make reference to labour issues. At the United Nations, the ILO has the intention to develop a Policy Observatory on AI and Work in the Digital Economy, and to analyse the implications of shifts in AI regulation for decent work.[84] These are but a few of the initiatives that international organizations are establishing in this context.

Table 17.1 maps the key legal sources that are relevant for the use of AI systems in the workplace.

[81] OECD "Recommendation of the Council on Artificial Intelligence," https://legalinstruments.oecd.org/en/instruments/OECD-LEGAL-0449 (May 3, 2024), accessed July 22, 2024.

[82] OECD Recommendation of the Council on Artificial Intelligence (2024).

[83] Council of Europe, Committee on Artificial Intelligence. Framework Convention on Artificial Intelligence, Human Rights, Democracy and the Rule of Law, https://rm.coe.int/cai-2023-01-revised-zero-draft-framework-convention-public/1680aa193f, accessed (May 17, 2024) accessed July 22, 2024.

[84] ILO "Proposal for an ILO Policy Observatory on Work in the Digital Economy," www.ilo.org/global/research/events-courses/WCMS_857701/lang--en/index.htm#:~:text=Our%20proposal%20for%20the%20%27ILO,in%20the%20global%20digital%20economy, accessed May 12, 2023.

TABLE 17.1 *Key legislative instruments on AI for labor*

International level	EU level	National level
ILO Convention 153 ILO Convention 158 ILO Convention 166 European Convention on Human Rights	Treaty on the Functioning of the EU EU social acquis relating to employment and industrial relations: – Directive establishing a general framework for informing and consulting employees – Directive on employee involvement in the European Company – Framework Directive on occupational safety and health, and 5 individual Directives, addressing particular workplace environments or risks, including the OSH Strategic Framework 2021 – Directive on transparent and predictable working conditions – Directive on Work-Life Balance – Directive on Working Time – Machinery Regulation European Framework Agreements European Court of Justice case law	National law Collective agreements
AI-related initiatives that can impact work and employment		
OECD AI Principles Council of Europe on AI and Human Rights, Democracy and the Rule of Law	AI Act Upcoming AI Liability Directive Data Act Digital Services Act Digital Markets Act GDPR Regulation on promoting fairness and transparency for business users of online intermediation services (Platform to Business Regulation) Directive on improving working conditions in platform work	National AI strategies

Authors' own elaboration

17.6 FORESIGHT PERSPECTIVE: LABOR-RELATED AI ISSUES THAT REMAIN TO BE ADDRESSED

Aside from the fact that the AI Act takes a product safety approach, its list of high-risk systems does not comprehensibly address the full spectrum of problematic uses of AI systems in the context of employment. Likewise, the protection that will be afforded by the Platform Work Directive only applies to workers in digital labor platforms, even though automated monitoring and decision-making systems can pose threats to workers also in non-platform contexts. Many legal gaps hence remain. Increasingly confronted with the use of AI systems, the world of work faces a multitude of open questions. These are reinforced by the relationship of subordination and the power imbalance that is typical of the employment context. The broader effect of AI systems on the world of work hence remains to be seen. Here below, we discuss a few aspects that require a further and multidisciplinary analysis, and provide some recommendations.

a) **Preserving autonomy in human–machine interactions**: Many AI systems converge in a diversity of forms and layers in workplaces. Worker autonomy entails ensuring that workers are "in the loop," in fully or semi-automated decision-making. This is particularly important when joint (human–machine) problem-solving takes place. To ensure that workers' autonomy is maintained, employers must ensure that the use of AI systems respects workers' agency. The tacit knowledge that each individual worker develops, through years of experience and learning, should not be taken away from them and transferred to the machine – whether it be a cooperative robot or a piece of software. Rather than using digital technologies to streamline and rationalize work processes, as has been the trend in recent years, with the corresponding reduction in worker agency, new technologies should be used to support the active involvement of workers, thereby promoting and strengthening their autonomy and agency.
b) **Informing about the purpose of AI systems at work**: In an occupational setting, having access to the code behind an algorithm is not useful per se. What matters to workers is understanding the overall architecture of the AI model, the intended purpose; the context of use, how they are embedded in a system or layers of systems in the workplace; how they are exposed to or which personal data is collected from them. The GDPR covers these aspects to some extent in relation to the transparency of processing of data, data access, and the right to explanation in automated decision-making. Article 11 of the AI Act provides that technical documentation of high-risk AI systems should be drawn up containing comprehensive information, related to the intended purpose, how the system interacts with other systems, the forms of the AI systems, a basic description of the user interface, among other listed in the Annex IV of the AI Act. Workers representatives need to have access to this documentation. Further action is needed to make sure their involvement in the oversight or evaluation, and in providing the guidance of how to exercise workers' rights. Consultation rights should be exercised when AI systems process workers personal data.
c) **Ensuring the exercise of the right to explanation for automated decisions**: As demonstrated by the example in Section 17.3.2, automated decision-making systems can impact workers in various ways: incorrect performance

assessment, the allocation of tasks based on the analysis of reputational data, or profiling. Additionally, these systems can exhibit biases in multiple aspects (e.g., in the design, data, infrastructure, or model misuse), all of which influence the outcomes. In such situations, the right to explanation becomes indispensable for workers. Drawing upon Articles 13–15 and Recital 71 of the GDPR and on Chapter III on algorithmic management the Platform Work Directive, it is imperative to establish legal provisions that enable workers from all sectors to exercise this right, while ensuring that employers establish adequate accountability measures. In practical terms, this entails provisions that clarify when automated decisions should be prohibited or restricted, as well as provisions related to obtaining information about the categories of such decisions. Also, legal clarifications should be introduced to facilitate: (a) understanding the significance and consequences of an automated decision in a given work context, that is simultaneously understandable, meaningful, and actionable (GDPR Art 12); and (b) mechanisms to challenge the decision with the employer or competent authority

d) **Developing AI risk assessments together with workers' representatives**: AI systems are often invisible due to their virtual nature. This means that identifying AI-related risks is not always an easy task. The possible risks are related to security and safety issues, physical and ergonomic hazards; errors, misuse of AI systems, or unintended or unanticipated harmful outcomes; bias, discrimination and loss of autonomy. These risks can impact various dimensions of workforce their fundamental rights, health, privacy and safety, encompassing both physical, well-being and psychosocial aspects. They can further exacerbate discrimination, manipulation, inequalities, and labor market disparities. The magnitude and severity of these risks depend on the affected population. Beyond their obligations to comply with occupational health and safety provisions, employers are also required to conduct both data and technology risk assessments, and a proportionality assessment, before the deployment of AI systems. This requires a workplace assessment of possible hazards that should address issues about health, cybersecurity, psychosocial, privacy and safety, as well as specific associated threats. The development of such risk assessment frameworks should build upon the long-standing tradition of occupational safety and health risk assessments. Workers' representatives should be systematically involved in the development of such frameworks, and have a role in characterizing the types and level of risk arising from the use of AI systems. They should also help identify proportionate mitigation measures, throughout the AI systems' life cycle.

e) **Setting limits to worker surveillance:** The ever-increasing market offer of data-driven technologies and AI solutions tends to encourage companies to use these tools to exercise power over workers beyond the employment relation. Traditional workplace monitoring is being surpassed by more intrusive forms of surveillance, using data related to workers' physiology, behavior, biometrics and emotions, or political opinions. Consequently, companies can deploy tools that process workers' data for various purposes, some of which may infringe GDPR. As a result, workers face significant risks to their privacy and data protection rights. As noted earlier, the provisions of the GDPR are particularly relevant for the context of employment where the worker is in an unbalanced relationship *vis a vis* the employer and where sensitive data should not be processed and where "informed consent" in the employment context is not be a lawful legal ground for data processing. Therefore, given the power asymmetry, intrusive AI-based surveillance practices need to be clearly prohibited and only be allowed highly exceptionally, while ensuring the right of workers to exercise the control of their personal data. Moreover, general prevention policies should prevail over automated forms of prevention.

f) **Ensuring that workers become AI literate**: Acquiring technical skills and using them "at work," although necessary, is not enough and mostly serves the interests of one's employer. Becoming "AI literate" means being able to understand critically the role of AI systems and their impact on one's work and occupation, and being able to anticipate how it will transform one's career and role. There is scope here for a new role for workers' representatives expanding their responsibilities to include the role of "data representatives." This would involve identifying and highlighting digitally related risks and interactions, assessing the possible impacts of largely invisible technologies, and developing methods to preserve tacit knowledge and agency when working alongside AI systems. Workers' representatives, along with social partners more generally, should also play a role in making workers more AI literate. This can be achieved through an increased exercise of information and consultation rights, and through other educational activities.

17.7 CONCLUSION

Labor law deals with the relationship between workers and employers, and tries to address the imbalance between the parties involved in this relationship. Artificial Intelligence, one of the most disruptive technologies of our time, is increasingly used by companies, at all levels and in all sectors, with an impact on the employment relationship. As discussed in this chapter, AI applications impact workers, collectively and individually, in unprecedented ways. This creates new realities and new risks, from workers' surveillance to problematic algorithmic management practices, which can increase the imbalance in the employment relationship and further tip it in favor of employers.

In such an uncertain and changing reality, labor law can help to address some of the risks, such as the erosion of workers autonomy and agency, possible discriminatory practices, and the opacity of algorithmic decisions. Labor law experts should also maintain an inter-disciplinary focus, draw on insights from other disciplines in order to address other connected aspects: Workers' data protection and privacy, human rights impact assessments, the increased reliance on standards and technical specifications, and so on. With the addition of a foresight perspective, labor law will not only be in a better position to address the impact of AI systems on labor, it will also better anticipate the impact on the world of work of other technologies that will emerge in the future.

18

Legal, Ethical, and Social Issues of AI and Law Enforcement in Europe

The Case of Predictive Policing

Rosamunde Van Brakel

18.1 INTRODUCTION

Artificial intelligence (AI)[1] increasingly plays a role within law enforcement. According to Hartzog et al., "*[w]e are entering a new era when large portions of the law enforcement process may be automated … with little to no human oversight or intervention.*"[2] The expansion of law enforcement use of AI in recent years can be related to three societal developments: austerity measures and a push toward using more cost-effective means; a growing perception that law enforcement should adopt a preventive or preemptive stance, with an emphasis on anticipating harm; and, finally an increase in the volume and complexity of available data, requiring sophisticated processing tools, also referred to as Big Data.[3]

AI is seen as providing innumerable opportunities for law enforcement. According to the European Parliament, AI will contribute "*to the improvement of the working methods of police and judicial authorities, as well as to a more effective fight against certain forms of crime, in particular financial crime, money laundering and terrorist financing, sexual abuse and the exploitation of children online, as well as certain types of cybercrime, and thus to the safety and security of EU citizens.*"[4] Some of the main current applications include predictive policing (see further), traffic control

[1] For an overview of AI as a technology, see Chapter 1 of this book.

[2] Woodrow Hartzog, Gregory Conti, John Nelson, and Lisa A. Shay, "Inefficiently automated law enforcement" (2016) *Michigan State Law Review* 2015: 1763–1796.

[3] Alexander Babuta en Marion Oswald, "Machine learning predictive algorithms and the policing of future crimes: governance and oversight," in *Policing and Artificial Intelligence*, ed John L. M. McDaniel and Ken Pease (London: Routledge, 2021), 214–236; Rosamunde Van Brakel, pre-emptive big data surveillance and its (dis)empowering consequences: the case of predictive policing, in Bart van der Sloot, Dennis Broeders, and Erik Schrijvers (eds) *Exploring the Boundaries of Big Data* (Amsterdam University Press, 2016), 117–141.

[4] European Parliament, European Parliament resolution of October 6, 2021 on artificial intelligence in criminal law and its use by the police and judicial authorities in criminal matters, www.europarl.europa.eu/doceo/document/TA-9-2021-0405_EN.html

(automated license plate detection and vehicle identification),[5] cybercrime detection (analysis of money flows via the dark web/ detection of online child abuse),[6] and smart camera surveillance (facial recognition and anomaly detection).[7]

The goal of this chapter is to introduce one type of AI used for law enforcement: predictive policing and discuss the main concerns this raises. I first examine how predictive policing emerged in Europe and discuss its (perceived) effectiveness (Section 18.2). Next, I unpack, respectively, the legal, ethical, and social issues raised by predictive policing, covering aspects relating to its efficacy, governance, and organizational use and the impact on citizens and society (Section 18.3). Finally, I provide some concluding remarks (Section 18.4).

18.2 PREDICTIVE POLICING IN EUROPE

18.2.1 *The Emergence of Predictive Policing in Europe*

The origins of predictive policing can be found in the police strategy "Intelligence-led policing", which emerged in the 1990s in Europe.[8] Intelligence-led policing can be seen as "*a business model and managerial philosophy where data analysis and crime intelligence are pivotal to an objective, decision-making framework that facilitates crime and problem reduction, disruption and prevention through both strategic management and effective enforcement strategies that target prolific and serious offenders.*"[9] One of the developments within intelligence-led policing was prospective hotspot policing, which focused on developing prospective maps. Using knowledge of crime events, recorded crime data can be analyzed to generate an ever-changing prospective risk surface.[10] This then led to the development of one of the first predictive policing applications in the United Kingdom,

[5] Kirstie Ball, "Search and identify: Automatic Number Plate Recognition in Europe" in Kirstie Ball and William Webster (eds), *Surveillance and Democracy in Europe* (London: Routledge, 2019); Francesco Ragazzi, Elif Kuskonmaz, Ildikó Plájás, Ruben van de Ven, and Ben Wagner *Biometric and behavioural mass surveillance in EU member states: report for the Greens/EFA in the European Parliament* (Greens/EFA, 2021), https://scholarlypublications.universiteitleiden.nl/handle/1887/3256585.

[6] Stephan Raaijmakers, "Artificial Intelligence for law enforcement: challenges and opportunities" (2019) *IEEE Security & Privacy* 17(5): 74–77.

[7] Rosamunde Van Brakel, "Democratic oversight of algorithmic police surveillance in Belgium" (2021a) *Surveillance & Society*, 19(2): 228–240; Peter Fussey and Darragh Murray, *Independent Report on the London Metropolitan Police Service's Trial of Live Facial Recognition Technology*. (Human Rights and Big Data Project, University of Essex July 2019), https://repository.essex.ac.uk/24946/1/London-Met-Police-Trial-of-Facial-Recognition-Tech-Report-2.pdf.

[8] Mike Maguire, "Policing by risks and targets: some dimensions and implications of intelligence-led crime control" (2000) *Policing and Society*, 9: 315–336; Paul De Hert, Wim Huisman and T. Vis (2005) "Intelligence Led Policing ontleed" (2005) *Tijdschrift voor Criminologie* 4(48): 365–376.

[9] Jerry H. Ratcliffe, *Intelligence-Led Policing* (Portland, OR: Willan, 2008).

[10] Kate. J. Bowers, Shane D. Johnson, and Ken Pease, "Prospective hot-spotting: the future of crime-mapping?" (2004) *British Journal of Criminology*, 44(5): 641–658.

known as ProMap.[11] Early in the twenty-first century, the rise of the use of predictive machine learning led to what is now known as predictive policing.

Predictive policing refers to "any policing strategy or tactic that develops and uses information and advanced analysis to inform forward-thinking crime prevention."[12] It is a strategy that can be situated in a broader preemptive policing model. Preemptive policing is specifically geared to gather knowledge about what will happen in the future with the goal to intervene before it is too late.[13] The idea behind predictive policing is that crime is predictable and that societal phenomena are, in one way or another, statistically and algorithmically calculable.[14]

Although already being implemented since the beginning of the twenty-first century in the United States (US), Law Enforcement Agencies in Europe are increasingly experimenting with and applying predictive policing applications. Two types can be identified: predictive mapping and predictive identification.[15] According to Ratcliffe, predictive mapping refers to "*the use of historical data to create a spatiotemporal forecast of areas of criminality or crime hot spots that will be the basis for police resource allocation decisions with the expectation that having officers at the proposed place and time will deter or detect criminal activity*."[16] Some law enforcement agencies use or have used software developed by (American) technology companies such as PredPol in the UK and Palantir in Denmark, while in other countries, law enforcers have been developing their own software. Examples are the Criminality Awareness System (CAS) in the Netherlands, PRECOBS in Germany, and a predictive policing algorithm developed in Belgium by criminology researchers in cooperation with the police.[17] Predictive mapping applications have in most cases focused on predicting the likelihood that a certain area is more prone to burglaries and adjusting patrol management according to the predictions.

[11] Shane D. Johnson, Kate J. Bowers, Dan J. Birks, and Ken Pease, "Predictive mapping of crime by Promap: accuracy, units of analysis and the environmental backcloth," in David Weisburd, Wim Bernasco, and Gerben J. N. Bruinsma (eds), *Putting Crime in Its Place* (Dordrecht: Springer, 2009), 171–198.

[12] Craig D. Uchida (2009) "Predictive policing," in *Encyclopedia of Criminology and Criminal Justice* (Dordrecht: Springer, 2009), 3871–3880.

[13] Rosamunde van Brakel and Paul De Hert "Policing, surveillance and law in a pre-crime society: understanding the consequences of technology based strategies" (2011) *Cahiers Politiestudies/ Journal of Police Studies*, 20(3): 163–192; Lyria Bennett Moses and Janet Chan "Algorithmic prediction in policing: assumptions, evaluation, and accountability" (2018) *Policing and Society*, 28(7): 806–822.

[14] Simon Egbert and Susann Krasmann (2019) "Predictive policing: not yet, but soon preemptive?" *Policing and Society*, 30(8): 905–919.

[15] Van Brakel, 2016, see note 3.

[16] Jerry H. Ratcliffe, "What is the future … of predictive policing?" *Translational Criminology* (Spring 2014): 4.

[17] Rosamunde Van Brakel, "Rethinking predictive policing towards a holistic framework of democratic algorithmic surveillance," in Marc Schuilenberg and Rik Peeters (eds), *The Algorithmic Society: Technology, Power, and Knowledge* (London: Routledge, 2021b) 104–118.

Predictive identification has the goal to predict who is a potential offender, the identity of offenders, criminal behavior, and who will be a victim of crime.[18] These types of technologies build upon a long history of using risk assessments in criminal justice settings.[19] The difference is that the risk profiles are now often generated from patterns in the data instead of coming from scientific research.[20] This type of predictive policing has been mainly applied in Europe in the context of predicting the likelihood of future crime (recidivism). However, other examples can be found in the use of video surveillance that deploys behavior and gait recognition. There are also developments in lie and emotion detection,[21] the prediction of radicalization on social media,[22] passenger profiling, and the detection of money laundering.[23] A recent example can be found in the Netherlands where Amsterdam police uses what is known as the Top400. The Top400 targets 400 young "high potentials" in Amsterdam between twelve and twenty-four years old "that have not committed serious offences but whose behavior is considered a nuisance to the city."[24] In the context of the Top400, the ProKid+ algorithm has been used to detect children up to sixteen years old that could become "a risk" and might cause future crime related problems. When on the list, youngsters receive intensive counseling and they and their families are under constant police surveillance.[25]

18.2.2 *Effectiveness of Predictive Policing*

Evaluations of the effectiveness of predictive policing in preventing crime have, so far, been inconclusive due to a lack of evidence.[26] In addition, not all evaluations

[18] Van Brakel, 2016, see note 3.

[19] Van Brakel, 2021b, see note 17.

[20] Rosamunde Van Brakel, *Taming the Future? A Rhizomatice Analysis of Pre-emptive Surveillance of Children* unpublished PhD thesis (Vrije Universiteit Brussel, 2018).

[21] Javier Sánchez-Monedero and Lina Dencik, "The politics of deceptive borders: 'biomarkers of deceit' and the case of iBorderCtrl" (2022) *Information, Communication and Society*, 25(3): 413–430.

[22] Miriam Hernandez and Harith Alani, "Artificial intelligence and online extremism: challenges and opportunities" in John McDaniel and Ken Pease (eds), *Predictive Policing and Artificial Intelligence* (London: Routledge, 2021).

[23] Plixavra Vogiatzoglou, "Mass surveillance, predictive policing and the implementation of the CJEU and ECtHR requirement of objectivity" (2019) *The European Journal of Law and Technology*, 10(1): 1–18.

[24] Fieke Jansen, *Top400: A Top-Down Crime Prevention Strategy in Amsterdam*. Report, Project Interest Litigation Project, The Netherlands (November 2022): 5.

[25] Rosamunde Van Brakel and Lander Govaerts, "Exploring the impact of algorithmic policing on social justice: Developing a framework for rhizomatic harm in the pre-crime society" *Theoretical Criminology*, OnlineFirst, https://doi.org/10.1177/13624806241246267.

[26] For an overview of evaluations conducted in the US, see Van Brakel, 2021b, note 17. While writing this ` an evaluation was conducted by investigative journalists of the use of Geolitica software (previously Predpol). They examined 23,631 predictions generated by Geolitica between February 25 to December 18, 2018, for the Plainfield Police Department (PD). They noted that: "*each prediction we analyzed from the company's algorithm indicated that one type of crime was likely to occur*

have been conducted in a reliable way, and with general falling crime rates, it is hard to show that fall in crime is the result of the technology. Moreover, it is difficult to evaluate the technology's effectiveness in preventing crime as algorithms identify correlations, not causality.

For instance, the Dutch Police Academy concluded in their evaluation of the CAS system that it does seem to prevent crime but that it does have a positive effect on management.[27] The evaluation study conducted by the Max Planck Institute in Freiburg of a PRECOBS pilot-project in Baden-Württemberg concluded that it remains difficult to judge whether the PRECOBS software is able to contribute toward a reduction in home burglaries and a turnaround in case development. The criminality-reducing effects were only moderate and crime rates could not be clearly minimized by predictive policing on its own.[28] In Italy, reliability of 70 percent was found for the predictive algorithm of KEYCRIME which predicted which specific areas in Milan would become a crime hotspot.[29] In their overview of recent challenges and developments, Hardyns and Rummens did not find significant effects of predictive policing and argue that more research is needed to assess the effectiveness of current methods.[30]

Apart from inconclusive evaluations, several police forces stopped using the software altogether. For instance, the use of PredPol by Kent Police was discontinued in 2019 and the German police forces of Karlsruhe and Stuttgart decided to stop using PRECOBS software because there was insufficient crime data to make reliable predictions.[31] Furthermore, amid public outcry about the use of PredPol, the Los Angeles Police Department in the US stopped using the software, yet at the same time it launched a new initiative: "data-informed community-focused policing

in a location not patrolled by Plainfield PD. In the end, the success rate was less than half a percent. Fewer than 100 of the predictions lined up with a crime in the predicted category that was also later reported to police." See Aaron Sankin and Surya Mattu, Predictive Policing Software Terrible At Predicting Crimes, *The Markup* (October 2, 2023), https://themarkup.org/prediction-bias/2023/10/02/predictive-policing-software-terrible-at-predicting-crimes.

27 Bas Mali, Carla Bronkhorst-Giesen and Mariëlle Den Hengst. *Predictive policing: Lessen voor de toekomst, Politieacademie* (2017) www.politieacademie.nl/kennisenonderzoek/kennis/mediatheek/PDF/93263.PDF.

28 Dominik Gerstner, Predictive policing in the context of residential Burglary: an empirical illustration on the basis of a pilot project in Baden-Württemberg, Germany (2018) *European Journal of Security Research*, 3: 115–138.

29 Bogolomov, Andrey, Lepri, Bruno, Staiano, Jacopo, Oliver, Nuria, Pianesi, Fabio and Pentland, Alex, Once Upon a Crime: Towards Crime Prediction from Demographics and Mobile Data, ACM International Conference on Multimodal Interaction (ICMI, 2014).

30 Hardyns Wim and Rummens Anneleen, Predictive policing as a new tool for law enforcement? Recent developments and challenges (2017) *European Journal of Criminal Policy and Research*, 24: 201–218.

31 Nils Mayer, Strobl entscheidet sich gegen Precobs, Stuttgarter Nachrichten (September 3, 2019), www.stuttgarter-nachrichten.de/inhalt.aus-fuer-die-einbruchvorhersage-softwarestrobl-entscheidet-sich-gegen-precobs.19a18735-9c8f-4f1a-bf1b-80b6a3ad0142.html.

(DICFP)."[32] The goal of this initiative is to establish a deeper relationship between community members and police, and to address some of the concerns the public had with previous policing programs. However, critics have raised questions about the initiative's similarities with the use of PredPol.[33] Similar to PredPol, the data that is fed into the system is biased and often generated through *feedback loops*. Feedback loops refers to a phenomenon identified in research that police are repeatedly sent back to the same neighborhoods regardless of the true crime rate.[34]

Regarding *predictive identification*, almost no official evaluations have been conducted. Increasingly, investigative journalists and human rights organizations are showing that there is significant bias in these systems.[35] Moreover, issues that have been raised with the effectiveness of actuarial risk assessment methods before it was digitalized, such as the (un)reliability of the risk factor research that underscores the applied theories of crime, are not solved by implementing algorithmic decision-making.[36] As to the use of *predictive analytics* in this area, the effectiveness of these systems likewise remains unclear. An assessment of a predictive model used by Los Angeles' children's services, which was promoted as highly effective in practice, "produced a false alarm 96 percent of the time."[37]

In general, the effectiveness concerns that were already identified for (prospective) hot-spot policing on the one hand and traditional risk assessments on the other, prior to the implementation of AI systems, did not disappear. With regards to predictive mapping spatial displacement, which is when crime moves to a different area after implementing a control measure such as CCTV or increased police presence is but one example.[38] It should also be noted that the long-term impacts of predictive policing on individuals and society are unclear and longitudinal research assessing

[32] Michel R. Moore, Data-Informed Community-Focused Policing in the Los Angeles Police Department (2018) https://lapdonlinestrgeacc.blob.core.usgovcloudapi.net/lapdonlinemedia/2021/12/data-informed-guidebook-042020.pdf (2019).

[33] Johana Bhuiyan, LAPD ended predictive policing programs amid public outcry. A new effort shares many of their flaws *The Guardian* (November 8, 2021), www.theguardian.com/us-news/2021/nov/07/lapd-predictive-policing-surveillance-reform.

[34] Danielle Ensign, Sorelle Friedler, Scott Neville, Carlos Sheidegger, and Suresh Venkatasubramanian, Runaway feedback loops in predictive policing (2018) *Conference on Fairness, Accountability, and Transparency. Proceedings of Machine Learning Research*, 81: 1–12.

[35] Julia Angwin, Jeff Larson, Surya Mattu, Lauren Kirchner, Machine Bias, *ProPublica* (2016) www.propublica.org/article/machine-bias-risk-assessments-in-criminal-sentencing; Liberty *Policing by Machine*, Predictive policing and the threat to our rights (2019), www.libertyhumanrights.org.uk/issue/policing-by-machine/.

[36] Van Brakel, 2018, see note 20; Babuta and Oswald, 2020, see note 3. See also SyRI judgement in the Netherlands, ECLI:NL:RBDHA:2020:1878, https://uitspraken.rechtspraak.nl/#!/details?id=ECLI:NL:RBDHA:2020:1878.

[37] Christopher E. Church and Amanda J. Fairchild, In search of a silver bullet: child welfare's embrace of predictive analytics (2017) *Juvenile & Family Court Journal*, 68(1): 71.

[38] David Weisburd, Laura A. Wyckoff, Justin Ready, John E. Eck., Joshua C. Hinkle, and Frank Gajewski, Does crime just move around the corner? A controlled study of spatial displacement and diffusion of crime control benefits (2006) *Criminology*, 44(3): 549–592.

this is not conducted. Finally, as demonstrated by the earlier overview, it is unclear if the adoption of predictive mapping will reduce overall crime, and whether it will be able to do so for different types of crime.[39]

18.3 A LEGAL, ETHICAL, AND POLICY ANALYSIS OF PREDICTIVE POLICING

18.3.1 *Legal Issues*

The European Union regulation on AI, published by the European Commission in 2024, provides numerous safeguards depending on how much risk a certain AI application poses to fundamental rights.[40] As Chapter 12 of this book more extensively explains, the AI Act classifies AI systems into several categories, including low or limited risk (not subject to further rules), medium/opacity risk (with new transparency obligations), high risk (with a broad set of conformity assessment requirements), and unacceptable risk (which are prohibited).

In its amendments published in June 2023, the European Parliament clearly opted for stricter safeguards by removing exceptions for law enforcement's use of real-time remote biometric identification systems, and prohibiting some applications that the Commission had previously classified as high risk, such as predictive policing, and more specifically predictive identification applications used in criminal justice.[41] However, ultimately, the final text provides extensive exceptions for law enforcement when it comes to real-time remote biometric identification systems[42] and does not prohibit place-based predictive policing. It does prohibit predictive identification in so far the risk assessments are solely based on the "profiling of a natural person or on assessing their personality traits and characteristics."[43] It remains to be seen to what extent the interpretation, implementation, and enforcement of the regulation will provide sufficient democratic safeguards to protect the fundamental rights of citizens.

In addition to the AI regulation, the use of AI for law enforcement purposes is also regulated by the transposition into national laws of member states of the Law

[39] David Weisburd and Cody W. Telup, Hot spots policing: what we know and what we need to know (2014) *Journal of Contemporary Criminal Justice*, 30(2): 200–220.

[40] Regulation (EU) 2024/1689 of the European Parliament and of the Council of 13 June 2024 laying down harmonised rules on artificial intelligence and amending Regulations (EC) No 300/2008, (EU) No 167/2013, (EU) No 168/2013, (EU) 2018/858, (EU) 2018/1139 and (EU) 2019/2144 and Directives 2014/90/EU, (EU) 2016/797 and (EU) 2020/1828 (Artificial Intelligence Act).

[41] Amendment 224, Article 5(1d a). Amendments adopted by the European Parliament on June 14, 2023 on the proposal for a regulation of the European Parliament and of the Council on laying down harmonised rules on artificial intelligence (Artificial Intelligence Act) and amending certain union legislative acts (COM(2021)0206 – C9-0146/2021 – 2021/0106(COD)).

[42] Article 5(1h) Artificial Intelligence Act.

[43] Article 5(1d) Artificial Intelligence Act.

Enforcement Directive (LED).[44] The application of this directive concerns the processing of personal data by competent authorities for the prevention, investigation, detection, and prosecution of criminal offenses or the execution of criminal penalties.[45] It does not apply in the context of national security, to EU institutions, agencies, or bodies such as Europol, and it only applies to processing of personal data wholly or partly by automated means. The directive came about primarily out of the need felt by law enforcement agencies, including in response to terrorist attacks in the US and Europe in the first decades of the twenty-first century, to exchange data between member states. The directive, therefore, aims to strike a balance between law enforcement needs and the protection of fundamental rights.[46]

The focus of the directive is on "personal data." This is defined as "any information relating to an identified or identifiable natural person ('data subject')."[47] An identifiable natural person is one who can be "identified, directly or indirectly, in particular by reference to an identifier such as a name, an identification number, location data, an online identifier or to one or more factors specific to the physical, physiological, genetic, mental, economic, cultural, or social identity of that natural person."[48] Already in 2007 the European advisory body, the Data Protection Working Party Article 29 (WP29),[49] proposed a very broad interpretation of personal data: "any information" includes not only objective and subjective information, but even false information. It does not just concern private or sensitive information.[50] Information can be associated with an individual in three ways: (1) content (when it is about a particular person); (2) purpose (when data is used to evaluate, treat, or influence an individual's status or behavior in a certain way) and (3) result (when it is likely to have an impact on the rights and interests of a particular person taking into account all the circumstances of a particular case).[51]

It is often questioned, especially by law enforcement agencies themselves, if predictive mapping applications process "personal data." Lynskey argues that based

[44] Directive (EU) 2016/680 of the European Parliament and of the Council of April 27, 2016 on the protection of natural persons with regard to the processing of personal data by competent authorities for the purposes of the prevention, investigation, detection, or prosecution of criminal offences or the execution of criminal penalties, and on the free movement of such data, and repealing Council Framework Decision 2008/977/JHA (Law Enforcement Directive).

[45] Article (1), Law Enforcement Directive.

[46] Paul De Hert and Vagelis Papakonstantinou The new police and criminal justice data protection directive (2016) *New Journal of Criminal Law*, 7(1): 7–19.

[47] Article (3)1, Law Enforcement Directive.

[48] Art. 3(1) Law Enforcement Directive.

[49] The Article 29 Data Protection Working Party (Art 29 WP) was established by Directive 95/46/EC. It dealt with issues relating to the protection of privacy and personal data until May 25, 2018 when the GDPR entered into force. From then on, the European Data Protection Board (EDPB) took over its role.

[50] The Article 29 Data Protection Working Party Opinion on the concept of Personal Data 01248/07/EN WP 136 2007 See also Case C-434/16, Nowak v. Data Protection Commissioner EU:C:2017:994.

[51] Orla Lynskey, Criminal justice profiling and EU data protection law: precarious protection from predictive policing, *International Journal of Law in Context* (June 2019): 162–176.

on the advice of WG 29 and case law, it is possible to conclude that data processing in predictive mapping involves the processing of personal data.[52] The data processed are potentially linked to the data subject because of the purpose (to treat people in a certain way) or the effect (impact on those identified in the hotspots). Regarding predictive identification, it is clearer that personal data are processed, both when it comes to the input data (as the content concerns the data subject) and the output data (as the purpose and effect of the data are used to influence the prospects of an identified individual). In practice, however, interpretations diverge. For instance, in the case of the CAS system in the Netherlands, the Dutch law enforcement authority nevertheless concluded that it is not processing personal data and, therefore, that the data protection regulation does not apply to the system's use.[53] This example shows that lack of clear guidance and specific regulation when it comes to the use of AI by law enforcement raises questions about the effectiveness of the current legislative safeguards for these applications.

18.3.2 *Ethical and Social Issues*

Predictive policing raises several ethical and social issues. These issues are dependent on what type of technology is implemented and the way the technologies are governed.[54] They can not only impact the effectiveness and efficacy of the technology, but they can also cause harm.[55] Below, I respectively discuss concerns pertaining to efficacy, governance, organization, and individual and social harms.

18.3.2.1 Efficacy

Several issues can be identified as regards the efficacy of predictive policing and of the use of AI by law enforcement more generally. Efficacy refers to the capacity to produce a desired result (in the case of predictive policing, a reduction in crime). First, law enforcement and technology companies often claim that the accuracy of the system's prediction is high. However, these claims of "predictive accuracy" are often mistaken for efficacy, whereas the level of accuracy does not say anything about the system's impact on crime reduction, making it difficult for a police force to assess a tool's real-world benefits.[56] Second, the way the AI system is designed and purposed

[52] Lynskey, 2019, see note 52.

[53] Interview conducted with representative Amsterdam police in the context of the WRR Big Data, privacy and security project (2015), www.wrr.nl/adviesprojecten/big-data-privacy-en-veiligheid.

[54] Van Brakel, 2018, see note 20; Rosamunde Van Brakel, Hartmut Arden, Elisabeth Aston, Sharda Murria, and Zjelko Kerras, "The possibilities and pitfalls of the use of accountability technologies in the governance of police stops" in Elizabeth Aston, Sofie De Kimpe, Janos Fazekas, Genevieve Lennon and Mike Rowe (eds) *Governing Police Stops Across Europe* (Palgrave MacMillan, 2023).

[55] van Brakel, 2021b, see note 17; Van Brakel and Govaerts 2024, see note 25.

[56] Babuta and Oswald, 2020, see note 3.

is largely driven by data science and technology companies, with comparatively little focus on the underlying conceptual framework, criminological theory, or legal requirements.[57] Third, specifically with regards to predictive policing, runaway feedback loops are a significant issue (see previous text).[58] Fourth, lack of transparency in the way algorithms are designed and implemented, the exact data, formulas, and procedures carried out by the software developers and the way the AI system works ("the black box"[59]) makes it harder to evaluate its operation. It also makes it more difficult for independent researchers to replicate methods using different data.[60] Fifth, the role of technology companies can also have an impact on efficacy.

A first example arises when law enforcement authorities work with software developed by (non-EU) technology companies. Such companies often foresee a vendor lock in the software, which implies that law enforcement is not able to adjust or tweak the software themselves and are dependent on the companies for any changes. A second example is that cultural differences and/or translation issues can arise when buying software from other countries. For instance, in Denmark, a hospital invested in a digital hospital management system, EPIC, developed by an American company.[61] The software was translated into Danish using Google Translate and this led to significant errors. This was not merely a translation issue. In fact, the "design of the system was so hard-coded in U.S. medical culture that it couldn't be disentangled," hence making it problematic for use in a Danish context.[62] A third example is that technology companies can also have an impact on how predictive policing is regulated. To provide another example from Denmark: The Danish government recently adjusted its police law to enable the use of an intelligence-led policing platform developed by Palantir.[63] Finally, a lack of academic rigor can be identified in this field. Since there are not many publications by researchers evaluating and testing predictive policing applications, there is still little reliable evidence on whether it works.[64] The lack of scientific evidence raises questions about the legitimacy and

57 Ibid.

58 Ensign, Friedler, Neville, Sheidegger, and Venkatasubramanian, 2018, see note 34.

59 Frank Pasquale, *The Black Box Society: The Secret Algorithms That Control Money and Information* (Boston MA: Harvard University Press, 2015).

60 Van Brakel, 2016, see note 3; Rachel B. Santos, Critic: Predictive policing: where's the evidence? In David Weisburd and Anthony A. Braga (eds) *Police innovation: contrasting perspectives* (Cambridge University Press, 2019): 366–396.

61 See the website of EPIC: https://open.epic.com/CountrySpecific/Denmark.

62 Morten Hertzum, Gunnar Ellingsun and Åsa Cajander, Implementing large-scale electronic health records: experiences from implementations of Epic in Denmark and Finland, *International Journal of Medical Informatics*, 167.

63 See nr 671 af 08/06/2017 Lov om ændring af lov om politiets virksomhed og toldloven. EDRI New legal framework for predictive policing in Denmark, https://edri.org/our-work/new-legal-framework-for-predictive-policing-in-denmark/.

64 National Academies Sciences, Engineering, Medicine, Law Enforcement Use of Predictive Policing Approaches: A Workshop, June 24-25, 2024, www.nationalacademies.org/event/42513_06-2024_law-enforcement-use-of-predictive-policing-approaches-a-workshop-public-session; Santos, 2019, see note 59.

proportionality of the application of predictive policing. When law enforcement deploys technology that poses an intrusion of fundamental rights law, law enforcement needs to demonstrate the necessity for the application in a democratic society and proportionality. However, considering the earlier discussion, that there is insufficient proof to show the efficacy and effectiveness of the technology the question arises if the fundamental rights test can be conducted in a reliable way and if the implementation of such technologies is justifiable.

18.3.2.2 Social Issues

There is increasing scientific evidence that AI applications and the poor-quality data the algorithms are trained on are riddled with error and bias.[65] They raise social and ethical concerns beyond undermining privacy and causing individual harm such as discrimination, stigmatization and social harms,[66] but they also can have an impact on society.[67] Predictive policing is a form of surveillance. Research in surveillance studies has shown that digital (police) surveillance potentially leads to several unintended consequences that go beyond a violation of individual privacy. For instance, surveillance can lead to social sorting cumulative disadvantage, discrimination, and chilling effects, but also fear, humiliation, and trauma.[68] Importantly, the harms raised by AI-driven predictive policing are also increasingly becoming cumulative through the significant increase of the more general implementation of surveillance in society.[69]

65 Van Brakel, 2016, see note 3; Kristen Lum and William Isaac, To predict and serve? (2016) *Significance Magazine Royal Statistical Society*, 13(5): 14–19, Andrew G. Ferguson, *The Rise of Big Data Policing* (New York: NYU Press, 2017); Patrick Williams and Erik Kind, Data-driven policing: The hardwiring of discriminatory policing practices across Europe. Report, ENAR (March 2019); Rashida Richardson, Jason Schultz and Kate Crawford, Dirty data, bad predictions: how civil rights violations impact police data, predictive policing systems, and justice (2019) *New York University Law Review*, 94: 192–233; Babuta and Oswald, 2020, see note 3.

66 Van Brakel, 2016, see note 3; Mali, Bronkhorst-Giesen and Den Hengst, 2017; Ferguson, 2017; Santos, 2019, see note 59; Egbert, Simon and Krasmann, Susanne, Predictive policing: not yet, but soon preemptive? (2019) *Policing & Society*, 30(8): 905–919; Fussey and Murray, 2019, see note 7; Van Brakel and Govaerts, 2024, see note 25.

67 Nathalie A. Smuha, "Beyond the individual: governing AI's societal harm" (2021) *Internet Policy Review*, 10(3): https://policyreview.info/articles/analysis/beyond-individual-governing-ais-societal-harm; Van Brakel 2022, see note 72.

68 David Lyon (ed.), *Surveillance as Social Sorting: Privacy, Risk and Automated Discrimination* (London: Routledge, 2003); Gandy Jr., O. H. (2009) *Coming to Terms With Chance: Engaging Rational Discrimination and Cumulative Disadvantage*, London: Ashgate; Jonathon W. Penny, Understanding Chilling Effects (2022) *Minnesota Law Review*: 1451–1530; Daragh Murray Pete Fussey, Kuda Hove, Wairagala Wakabi, Paul Kimumwe, Otto Saki, and Amy Stevens, The chilling effects of surveillance and human Rights: insights from qualitative research in Uganda and Zimbabwe (2023) *Journal of Human Rights Practice*: 1–16; John Gilliom, *Overseers of the Poor: Surveillance, Resistance, and the Limits of Privacy* (Chicago University Press, 2001).

69 Thomas Mitchener-Nissen, Failure to collectively assess security surveillance technologies will inevitably lead to an absolute surveillance society (2014) *Surveillance & Society*, 12(1): 73–88.

More specifically, in the United Kingdom, a recent study concluded that national guidance is urgently needed to oversee the use of data-driven technology by law enforcement amid concerns that it could lead to discrimination.[70] In the US an example of harms of predictive policing can be found in a lawsuit that has been filed against Pasco County Sheriff's Office (PCSO) in Florida.[71] This concerns a predictive policing application which, without notice to parents and guardians, places hundreds of students on a secret list, created using an algorithmic risk assessment identifying those who they believe are most likely to commit future crimes. When children are on the list, they are subject to persistent and intrusive monitoring. The criteria used to target children for the program are believed to have a greater impact on Black and Brown children.[72] Similarly, in the Netherlands a mother of a teenage boy, who was taken up in the Top400 list (see earlier content), states that as the result of police harassment she feels "like a prisoner, watched and monitored at every turn, and I broke down mentally and physically, ending up on cardiac monitoring."[73]

When law enforcement's use of AI systems leads to these harms, this will also have an impact on police legitimacy. As was already mentioned when discussing hot-spot policing, intensive police interventions may erode citizen trust in the police and lead to fear through over-policing, and thus lead to the opposite result of what the technology is intended for.[74]

18.3.2.3 Governance

AI has been heralded as a disruptive technology. It puts current governance frameworks under pressure and is believed to transform society in the same way as electricity.[75] It is therefore no surprise that several concerns arise around the governance structure of this disruptive technology when it is used to drive predictive policing. First, there is a lack of clear guidance and codes of practice outlining appropriate constraints on how law enforcement should trial predictive algorithmic

70 Babuta & Oswald, 2020, see note 3.

71 CAIR Florida, Inc vs Christopher Nocco, Sherrif of Pasco County, 13 09 2022, www.splcenter.org/sites/default/files/petition_-_pages_1_to_144.pdf. Another lawsuit is in process against the Sherrif for another type of predictive policing program as well: Case: Taylor v. Nocco 8:21-cv-00555 | U.S. District Court for the Middle District of Florida, https://clearinghouse.net/case/18194/.

72 The Southern Poverty Law Centre Civil Rights Groups sue for public records linke dot Pasco County's predictive policing program (September 14, 2022) www.splcenter.org/presscenter/civil-rights-groups-sue-public-records-linked-pasco-countys-predictive-policing-program.

73 Diana Sardjoe, My sons were profiled by a racist predictive policing system – the AI Act must prohibit these systems, *Medium* (September 28, 2022), https://medium.com/@FairTrials/my-sons-were-profiled-by-a-racist-predictive-policing-system-the-ai-act-must-prohibit-these-b2ea66a9a763.

74 Dennis P Rosenbaum, The limits of hot spots policing. *Police Innovation: Contrasting Perspectives*: 245–263 (Cambridge University Press, 2006).

75 Shana Lynch, Why AI is the new electricity? www.gsb.stanford.edu/insights/andrew-ng-why-ai-new-electricity, *Insights by Stanford Business* (March 11, 2017).

tools[76] and implement them in practice.[77] Second, there is a lack of quality standards for evaluations of these systems.[78] Whenever evaluations do take place, there is still a lack of attention to data protection and social justice issues, which also impact evidence-based policy that is based on such evaluations.[79] Third, there is a lack of expertise within law enforcement and oversight bodies,[80] which raises issues about how effective the oversight over these systems really is.

Finally, even when predictive machine learning does not process personal data or where it is compliant with the LED, there are still other concerns as we discussed earlier. These social and ethical concerns need to be addressed through innovative oversight mechanisms that go beyond judicial oversight.[81] Current oversight mechanisms are geared to compliance with data protection law, they do not address ethical or social issues discussed earlier (Van Brakel, 2021a).

New types of oversight bodies could be inspired by adding a relational ethics perspective to the current rational perspective. Governance structures must also involve citizens, and they should specifically engage with targeted and vulnerable communities when making policy decisions about implementing AI.[82] An example of a step in the right direction is the establishment of the Ethics Committee by the Westmidlands Police.[83] The committee evaluates pilot projects and implementation of new technologies by the police. What is positive about the committee is that it works in a transparent way publishing the reports fully on the website of the committee and the members of the committee are diverse. Members include representatives from the police, civil society, and community and academic experts in law, criminology, social science, and data science. However, to be successful and sustainable, such initiatives should also ensure that people are sufficiently compensated for their time and work, and this they not merely rely on volunteers and goodwill of the members.[84]

[76] Babuta and Oswald, 2019, see note 3.

[77] Van Brakel, 2021b, see note 17.

[78] Ibid

[79] Ibid.; Ralph B. Taylor and Jerry H. Ratcliffe, Was the pope to blame? Statistical powerlessness and the predictive policing of micro-scale randomized control trials (2020) *Criminology & Public Policy*, 19(3): 965–996; Robin Khalfa and Wim Hardyns, De evaluatie van big data policing: krijtlijnen voor het opzetten van een geschikt experimenteel evaluatiemodel (2023) *Cahiers Politiestudies Big Data*, 66: 179–208.

[80] Van Brakel, 2021b, see note 17; Hielke Heijmans and Rosamunde van Brakel, 2023. Article 44 in Eleni Kosta and Franziska Boehm (2023) *The Law Enforcement Directive. A Commentary*. Oxford University Press.

[81] Van Brakel, 2021a, see note 7; 2022; Elizabeth Aston (2023) *Independent Advisory Group on Emerging Technologies in Policing Final Report*. Scottish Government.

[82] Abeba Birhane, "Algorithmic injustice: a relational ethics approach" (2021) *Patterns*, 2(2): 1–9; Rosamunde Van Brakel, De controle op het gebruik van algoritmische surveillance onder druk? Een exploratie door de lens van de relationele ethiek (2022) *Tijdschrift voor Mensenrechten*, 1: 23–28.

[83] West-Midlands Police Ethics Committee, www.westmidlands-pcc.gov.uk/ethics-committee.

[84] Van Brakel, 2021b, see note 17.

18.3.2.4 Organizational Issues

The implementation of AI in policing by law enforcement also raises several organizational issues. The LED foresees a right to obtain human intervention when an impactful decision is taken solely by automated means.[85] This has been referred to as a "human in the loop,"[86] which is a safeguard to protect the data subject *against "a decision evaluating personal aspects relating to him or her which is based solely on automated processing and which produces harm."*[87] However, in practice, this legal provision raises several challenges.

First, the directive does not specify what this "human in the loop" should look like or in what way the human should engage with the loop (on the loop, in the loop, or outside of the loop).[88] According to advice of the Article 29 Working Party, it is necessary to make sure that *"the human intervention must be carried out by someone who has the appropriate authority and capability to change the decision and who will review all the relevant data including the additional elements provided by the data subject."*[89]

According to Methani et al., meaningful human control refers to control frameworks in which humans, not machines, remain in control of critical decisions.[90] This means that, when it comes to AI, the notion of human oversight should extend beyond mere technical human control over a deployed system: It also includes the responsibility that lays in the development and deployment process, which entirely consists of human decisions and is therefore part of human control. The concept of meaningful human control should, in addition to mere oversight, also include design and governance layers into what it means to have effective control. However, these aspects are currently insufficiently taken into consideration, and guidance on how law enforcement must deal with this is lacking. Questions remain, therefore, how law enforcement officers need to be in the loop to make sure this safeguard is effective.

Second, not everybody is enthusiastic about new technologies. Resistance against surveillance is hence important to consider when implementing AI in law enforcement and evaluating its effectiveness. Research by Sandhu and Fussey on predictive

85 Article 11 LED.

86 Article 11 LED.

87 Recital 38 LED.

88 "Human on the loop" means that the human is part of every decision in the cycle of the system, "human in the loop" means that the human is a supervisor that controls the decisions and might intervene, and "human outside of the loop" means that the human is pushed entirely out of the control loop, allowing the system to independently execute its task. See for a more elaborate discussion, Leila Methnani, L., Andrea Aler Tubella, Virginia Dignum and Andreas Theodorou, Let Me Take Over: Variable Autonomy for Meaningful Human Control (2021) *Frontiers in Artificial Intelligence*, www.frontiersin.org/articles/10.3389/frai.2021.737072/full.

89 Article 29 Data Protection Working Party, Guidelines on Automated individual decision-making and Profiling for the purposes of Regulation 2016/679 (October 3, 2017): 10.

90 Methnani, Tubella, Dignum and Theodorou, 2021, note 79.

policing has shown that many police officers have a skeptical attitude toward and reluctance to use predictive technologies.[91] A third implementation issue concerns automation bias, whereby a person will favor automatically generated decisions over a manually generated decision.[92] This is what Fussey et al. have called deference to the algorithm, when evaluating Live Facial Recognition Technology piloted by the London Metropolitan Police.[93] It also involves potential de-skilling, which implies that by relying on automated processes, people loose certain types of skills and/or expertise.[94] Of course, not everyone will respond to the use of such systems in the same way. However, this risk is something that needs to be taken seriously by both law enforcement agencies and by policymakers. At the same time, Terpstra et al. have suggested that as policing is becoming more dependent on abstract police information systems, professional knowledge, and discretion are becoming devalued, which may have negative impacts on officers' sense of organizational justice and self-legitimacy.[95]

18.4 CONCLUSION

In this chapter, I discussed predictive policing in Europe and its main legal, ethical, and social issues. Law enforcement will become increasingly dependent on AI in the coming years, especially if it is considered to be superior to traditional policing methods, and cheaper than hiring more officers. Current models of regulating, organizing, and explaining policing are based on models of human decision-making. However, as more policing will be performed by machines, we will urgently need changes to those assumptions and rules.[96] Hence, the challenge lies not only in rethinking regulation but also in rethinking policy and soft law, and exploring what role other modalities can play. Consideration must be given to how the technology is designed, how its users and those affected by it can be made more aware of its impact and be involved in its design, and how the political economy affects this impact. Current policy tools and judicial oversight mechanisms are not sufficient to address the broad range of concerns that were identified in this chapter. Because the harm that AI can cause can be individual, collective, and social, and

[91] Ajay Sandhu and Peter Fussey, The "uberization of policing"? How police negotiate and operationalise predictive policing technology (2020) *Policing & Society*, 31(1): 66–81.

[92] Linda J Skitka, Kathleen L. Mosier, and Mark Burdick, Does automation bias decision-making? (1999) *International Journal of Human-Computer Studies*, 51(5): 991–1006.

[93] Peter Fussey, Bethan Davies, and Martin Innes, Assisted facial recognition and the reinvention of suspicion and discretion in digital policing (2021) *The British Journal of Criminology*, 61(2): 325–344.

[94] Elizabeth Joh, The consequences of automating and deskilling the police (2019) *UCLA Law Review*, 67: 133–164.

[95] Jan Terpstra, Nicholas R. Fyfe, and Renze Salet, The Abstract Police: a conceptual exploration of unintended changes of police organisations (2019) *The Police Journal: Theory, Practice and Principles*, 92(4): 339–359.

[96] Joh, 2019.

often stems from an interaction of an existing practice with technology, an individualistic approach with a narrow technological focus, is not adequate.[97]

While some of the earlier mentioned issues and challenges are dealt with by the upcoming AI regulation, as shown, it remains to be seen to which extent these safeguards will be taken up and be duly applicable in the context of law enforcement. Like the way regulation of data processing by law enforcement is always striving to find a balance between law enforcement goals and fundamental rights, the proposed AI regulation aims to find a balance between on the one hand corporate and law enforcement needs and on the other protecting fundamental rights. However, to address the social and ethical issues of AI, it is necessary to shift the focus in governance from the compulsion to show "balance" by always referring to AI's alleged potential for good by acknowledging that the social benefits are still speculative while the harms have been empirically demonstrated.[98]

Considering, on the one hand, the minimal evidence of the impact of predictive policing on crime reduction, and on the other hand, significant risks for social justice and human rights, should we not rethink the way AI is being used by law enforcement? Can it at all be used in a way that is legitimate, does not raise the identified social and ethical issues and is useful for police forces and society? Simultaneously, the question arises if the money that is invested in predictive policing applications should not be invested instead in tackling causes of crime and in problem-oriented responses, such as mentor programs, youth sports programs, and community policing, as they can be a more effective way to prevent crime.[99]

As Virginia Dignum nicely puts it: "AI is not a magic wand that gives their users omniscience or the ability to accomplish anything."[100] To implement AI for law enforcement purposes in a responsible and democratic way, it will hence be essential that law enforcement officials and officers take a more nuanced and critical view about using AI for their work.

97 Van Brakel, 2021a, see note 7; Jonas Breuer, Rob Heyman, and Rosamunde Van Brakel, Vulnerable data protection as privilege – factors to increase meaning of GDPR in vulnerable groups (2022) *Frontiers in Sustainable Cities*, 4, www.frontiersin.org/articles/10.3389/frsc.2022.977623/full; Van Brakel and Govaerts, 2024, see note 25.

98 Dan McQuillian, We come to bury ChatGPT not to praise it, www.danmcquillan.org/chatgpt.html.

99 Van Brakel, 2016, see note 3; Litska Strikwerda, Predictive policing: the risks associated with risk assessment *The Police Journal: Theory* (2021) *Practice and Principles*, 94(3): 422–436. See also work on best practices by the International Center for the Prevention of Crime and the Policing Project, www.unodc.org/unodc/en/commissions/CCPCJ/PNI/institutes-ICPC.html.

100 Virginia Dignum, *Responsible Artificial Intelligence: How to Develop and Use AI in a Responsible Way* (Dordrecht: Springer, 2019).

19

The Use of Algorithmic Systems by Public Administrations

Practices, Challenges and Governance Frameworks

Nathalie A. Smuha

19.1 INTRODUCTION

Public administrations play a unique role in our societies. As an instrument of the state, they are responsible for the execution of laws, the implementation of public policies, and the management of public programs – both at the national and the local level. A large part of their tasks consists of taking administrative acts, which can have an individual or a general scope.[1] These decisions affect individual, collective and societal interests, and can have a significant impact on the everyday lives of natural and legal persons.[2] Increasingly, public administrations rely on algorithmic systems – including artificial intelligence (AI) systems – in their decision-making processes.[3] This practice has also been referred to as "algorithmic regulation," since it essentially comes down to regulating[4] natural and legal persons through algorithmic applications.[5] Today, most of these applications are still primarily used to *inform*

[1] The Council of Europe's Committee of Ministers has defined administrative acts as comprising (a) legal acts, of both individual and general application, (b) physical acts of the administration taken in the exercise of public authority which may affect the rights or interests of natural or legal persons; and (c) situations of refusal to act or an omission to do so in cases where a public authority is under an obligation to act. See Committee of Ministers, "Recommendation Rec (2004) 20 of the Committee of Ministers to Member States on Judicial Review of Administrative Acts."

[2] See Nathalie A. Smuha, "Beyond the individual: Governing AI's societal harm" (2021) *Internet Policy Review*, 10(3): 1–33. See also Karen Yeung, "Why worry about decision-making by machine?" in Karen Yeung and Martin Lodge (eds), Algorithmic Regulation (Oxford University Press, 2019), 21–48.

[3] See also Weslei Gomes de Sousa, Elis Regina Pereira de Melo, Paulo Henrique De Souza Bermejo, Rafael Araújo Sousa Farias, and Adalmir Oliveira Gomes, "How and where is artificial intelligence in the public sector going? A literature review and research agenda" (2019) *Government Information Quarterly*, 36(4): 101392; Jamie Berryhill, Kévin Kok Heang, Rob Clogher, and Keegan McBride, "Hello, World: Artificial intelligence and its use in the public sector," *OECD Working Papers on Public Governance*, No. 36, OECD Publishing, Paris, 2019.

[4] Drawing on Julia Black, regulation is broadly understood as a means of managing risk or influencing behaviour in order to achieve a pre-specified goal. See Julia Black, "Learning from regulatory disasters," *24 LSE Law, Society and Economy Working Papers* 3, 2014.

[5] See Nathalie A. Smuha, *Algorithmic Rule by Law: How Algorithmic Regulation in the Public Sector Erodes the Rule of Law* (Cambridge University Press, 2025), 4. This term has also been used in a broader sense. For a useful overview, see Lena Ulbricht and Karen Yeung, "Algorithmic regulation:

rather than to *adopt* administrative acts. This is, however, rapidly changing, as ever more acts – as well as sub-decisions that underpin those acts – are being outsourced to algorithmic systems.

Algorithmic regulation can offer numerous advantages to public administrations,[6] many of which center around faster information retrieval and data processing, which in turn can lead to efficiency gains and better service provision. For this reason, algorithmic regulation is sometimes also heralded as a tool to enhance human rights, democracy and the rule of law, as it could help ensure that the execution and implementation of legal rules occurs in a more efficient manner, and that the rights of natural and legal persons are better protected. At the same time, the proclaimed benefits of algorithmic regulation do not always materialize in practice, and even when they do, they are rarely evenly distributed. Numerous examples exist of algorithmic regulation deployed by public administrations in a way that – often unintendedly – ran counter to the values of liberal democracy.[7] These values should however also be protected when the state decides to rely on algorithmic systems. In this chapter, I will therefore focus on the deployment of algorithmic regulation by public administrations, and explore some of the ethical and legal challenges that may arise in this context.

I start by setting out a brief history of public administrations' reliance on automation and algorithmic systems (Section 19.2). Subsequently, I explore some applications of algorithmic regulation that have been implemented by public administrations across several public sector domains (Section 19.3). I then respectively discuss some of the horizontal and sectoral challenges that reliance on algorithmic regulation brings forth, which require being addressed to ensure that core liberal democratic values remain protected (Section 19.4). Finally, I move toward an analysis of the legal framework that governs the use algorithmic regulation by public administrations, with a particular focus on the European Union (Section 19.5), before concluding (Section 19.6).

19.2 ALGORITHMIC REGULATION IN CONTEXT

Public administrations have existed since antiquity, yet in many jurisdictions, the nineteenth century brought a significant transformation both in terms of their size and their professionalization. The expansion of their competences and tasks – which

A maturing concept for investigating regulation of and through algorithms" (2022) *Regulation & Governance*, 16(1): 3–22.

6 See Chapter 1 of this Handbook for an extensive discussion of artificial intelligence as a research domain.

7 See for example, Virginia Eubanks, *Automating Inequality – How High-Tech Tools Profile, Police and Punish the Poor* (New York, Picador, 2019); Fabio Chiusi, Sarah Fischer, Nicolas Kayser-Bril and Matthias Spielkamp (eds), Automating Society Report 2020, AlgorithmWatch and Bertelsmann Stiftung, 2020, https://automatingsociety.algorithmwatch.org; Calo, Ryan, and Danielle Keats Citron, "The automated administrative state: A crisis of legitimacy" (2021) *Emory Law Journal* 70(4): 797–845.

was also propelled by the growth of welfare programs – was accompanied by a demand for more specialized expertise, as well as a process of rationalization and streamlining of public decision-making processes. This, in turn, also required more data collection and analysis based on which administrative acts could subsequently be taken.[8] In this regard, Peeters and Widlak pointed out that: "*as state tasks expanded, especially in welfare states, so did the number of registrations and their importance. Knowing your citizens has never been more important as when you try to decide who is eligible to student grants, social security, health care, social housing, or pensions.*"[9] The increase in the number of decisions to be taken also necessitated a rethinking of organizational information processes in order to secure the continued efficiency of public administrations. Unsurprisingly, the adoption of modern information and communication technologies (ICT) was strongly aligned with this purpose.[10]

Public administrations' embrace of ICT technologies is hence nothing new, and algorithmic regulation is an inherent part of this development. From the 1980s onwards, the uptake of such tools was further spurred by the New Public Management (NPM) movement, "*a collection of ideas that have as their main focus the importation of private sector tools, such as efficiency, private sector approaches, privatization and outsourcing, market-based mechanisms, and performance indicator into the public service.*"[11] While these ideas have not been immune from criticism and were found outdated already by the early 2000s,[12] they were quite influential and further entrenched the belief that public administrations could rely on (commercial) digital applications to attain their goals more efficiently – thereby, however, problematically elevating "efficiency" to a prime consideration, sometimes to the detriment of other important (public) interests and values.[13] Gradually, the uptake of ICT technologies also transformed the administrative

8 See in this regard also Smuha, n (5), 83.

9 Rik Peeters and Arjan Widlak, "The digital cage: Administrative exclusion through information architecture – The case of the Dutch civil registry's master data management system" (2018) *Government Information Quarterly*, 35(2): 175–183.

10 Arre Zuurmond therefore points out that "*bureaucracy and informatisation seem to go hand in hand.*" See Arre Zuurmond, *De Infocratie: Een Theoretische En Empirische Heroriëntatie Op Weber's Idealtype in Het Informatietijdperk* (Phaedrus, 1994), 2.

11 Rónán Kennedy, "The Rule of Law and Algorithmic Governance" in Woodrow Barfield (ed), *The Cambridge Handbook of the Law of Algorithms* (Cambridge University Press, 2020), 211. See also E. H. Klijn, New Public Management and Governance: A Comparison, in D. Levi-Faur (ed.), *The Oxford Handbook of Governance* (Oxford University Press, 2012) 209.

12 See in this regard Karen Yeung, "The new public analytics as an emerging paradigm in public sector administration" (2022) *Tilburg Law Review* 27(2): 4. In this regard, she also refers to Christopher Hood, "Public Management, New" in N. J Smeltser and P. B Bates (eds) *International Encyclopedia of the Social & Behavioral Sciences*, Volume 12 (Oxford: Elsevier, 2001), 12553–12556.

13 See also Patrick Dunleavy, Helen Margetts, Simon Bastow, Jane Tinkler, "New public management is dead-long live digital-era governance" (2005) *Journal of Public Administration Research and Theory*, 16(3): 467–494.

apparatus from "street-level" to "system-level" bureaucracies, as pointed out by Bovens and Zouridis.[14] They note that:

> Insofar as the implementing officials are directly in contact with citizens, these contacts always run through or in the presence of a computer screen. Public servants can no longer freely take to the streets, they are always connected to the organization by the computer. Client data must be filled in with the help of fixed templates in electronic forms. Knowledge-management systems and digital decision trees have strongly reduced the scope of administrative discretion. Many decisions are no longer made at the street level by the worker handling the case; rather, they have been programmed into the computer in the design of the software.[15]

Over time, the trend of informatization and automatization persisted, while the technologies used for this purpose became ever more sophisticated. Rather than relying primarily on rule-based systems and decision-trees, in the last few years, public administrations also increasingly started turning to data-driven automated analysis, often in a way that likewise seems to "*mimic or borrow from the success of commercial techniques*," a trend that Karen Yeung conceptualized as New Public Analytics (NPA), to highlight its (dis)continuity with NPM.[16] These data-driven technologies are typically based on advanced statistics and machine learning, and can be used to make probabilistic inferences and predictions.

Today, a large number of countries in the world adopted an "AI strategy," which virtually always includes a section with policy initiatives to bolster the uptake of AI systems in the public sector. Often, these strategies focus on maximizing AI's benefits, which in public administrations translates to a more efficient provision of citizen services, a speedier allocation of rights and benefits, and a reduction of backlogs and waiting times – or more generally: doing more with less.

This aspiration should not be seen separate from the difficult economic situation in which many countries found themselves after respectively the global financial crisis of 2008 and the COVID-19 pandemic which broke out in 2020. These developments, along with a more political tendency to limit public spending, forced many public administrations to cut costs. Indeed, as noted by Yeung, "*the pursuit of austerity policies that have seriously reduced public sector budgets has prompted*

[14] See Mark Bovens and Stavros Zouridis, "From street-level to system-level bureaucracies: How information and communication technology is transforming administrative discretion and constitutional control" (2002) *Public Administration Review*, 62(2): 174–184. They rely on Lipsky's conceptualization of public-service workers as "street-level bureaucrats," by virtue of the fact that they interact directly with individual citizens (hence "street-level"), and have considerable discretion when taking decisions. See Michael Lipsky, *Street-level Bureaucracy: Dilemmas of the Individual in Public Service* (New York, NY: Russell Sage Foundation, 1980).

[15] Bovens and Zouridis, n (14), 177. See in this regard also Justin B. Bullock, "Artificial intelligence, discretion, and bureaucracy" (2019) *The American Review of Public Administration*, 49(7): 751–761.

[16] See Yeung, n (12), 7.

growing interest in automation to reduce labour costs while increasing efficiency and productivity."[17] Unfortunately, as the next section will show, this eagerness has sometimes also led to problematic implementations of algorithmic regulation, with significant adverse consequences to those who were subjected to such systems, and without generating the benefits that were promised by the system's developers.

19.3 ALGORITHMIC REGULATION IN PRACTICE

Public administrations take a wide array of administrative acts on a daily basis. These acts or decisions are as diverse as allocating social welfare benefits, identifying tax fraud, imposing administrative fines, collecting taxes, granting travel visas, procuring goods and services, and handing out licenses and permits. Algorithmic regulation is gradually being deployed in all of these areas, in ever more creative and far-reaching ways. Evidently, the uptake of such applications significantly differs from one country to the other, and even from one ministry or municipality to the other – also in the European Union. While some are rolling out fancy facial recognition systems, others are still struggling with putting in place basic infrastructures that will enable digital technologies to operate in the first place. To concretize the variety of applications for which algorithmic regulation is deployed, and especially some of the risks they entail, let me offer a few examples.

Under French tax laws, properties with a pool must be declared to the government, as they increase a property's value and are hence subjected to higher taxes.[18] Many property owners however do not declare their pools, in contravention with the law. Therefore, in October 2021, nine French regions trialed an AI application developed by Capgemini (a French IT and consulting company) and Google, which analyzes areal images of properties and applies object recognition technology to assess whether the properties showcase non-declared pools.[19] The application's development was said to cost around €26 million.[20] According to several media outlets in 2022, more than 20,000 "hidden pools" were discovered by the tax authorities, contributing to about €10 million in revenues.[21] Later that year, the French authorities decided to roll out the application across the country, hoping this would lead to

[17] See Yeung, n (12), 6.

[18] Environmental considerations play a role here too, as many French regions adopted policies to reduce water consumption given its scarcity, while private swimming pools require considerable water.

[19] James Vincent, "French government uses AI to spot undeclared swimming pools – and tax them," *The Verge*, August 30, 2022, www.theverge.com/2022/8/30/23328442/france-ai-swimming-pool-tax-aerial-photos.

[20] Hannah Thompson, "France's way of tracking undeclared pools is unfair, says report," *The Connexion*, January 23, 2024, www.connexionfrance.com/article/Practical/Money/France-s-way-of-tracking-undeclared-pools-is-unfair-says-report.

[21] See for example, Kim Willsher, "French tax officials use AI to spot 20,000 undeclared pools," *The Guardian*, August 29, 2022, www.theguardian.com/world/2022/aug/29/french-tax-officials-use-ai-to-spot-20000-undeclared-pools; Undeclared pools in France uncovered by AI technology, *BBC News*, August 29, 2022, www.bbc.com/news/world-europe-62717599

€40 million additional tax earnings. By 2024, it was reported that more than 120,000 undeclared pools had been identified, thus allegedly reaching this target.[22]

That said, claims have also been made that the application has a margin of error of 30%, "*mistaking solar panels for swimming pools*" and "*failing to pick up taxable extensions hidden under trees or in the shadows of a property*."[23] Furthermore, in addition to questions that arose around the right to privacy, in November 2023, the French Court of Audit ("Cour des Comptes") published a report in which it found that the application's use constitutes a form of unequal treatment of French citizens, as it is not deployed in France's overseas territories and in Corsica, but only in the mainland. Accordingly, not all French taxpayers are subjected to the same scrutiny, which constitutes an inequality.[24] Interestingly, in the same report, the Court of Audit also questioned the deployment of automated tax evasion detection techniques more generally, stating that insufficient evidence of their effectiveness exists[25] – a recurring theme in the context of algorithmic regulation.

For another example, let me turn to the Netherlands, where the government was forced to resign in 2021 following the so-called "childcare benefits scandal."[26] Since the early 2010s, the Dutch tax authorities have been deploying an algorithmic system to help determine the risk of fraud by recipients of childcare benefits. Due to the unduly harsh legal rules of the Dutch system at the time, even a suspicion of fraud or involuntary error could lead to a penalty, whereby all the received benefits were retroactively claimed back by the government, leading thousands of families to accumulate (at times wrongfully attributed) debts they could not afford to pay off.[27] This not only caused depressions and suicides, but – due to ensuing poverty and a risk of neglect – some children were subsequently also taken away from their parents into foster care.[28] Only years later, the system was found to be in breach with privacy legislation, as well as reliant on discriminatory risk indicators.[29] People with

[22] Thompson, n (20).

[23] Willsher, n (21). At this stage, the application is hence merely used to suggest tax authorities which taxpayers must be further scrutinized.

[24] Cour des Comptes, "La Détection de la Fraude Fiscale des Particuliers – Une incontestable modernization des méthodes, des résultats encore insuffisants," November 2023, www.ccomptes.fr/sites/default/files/2023-11/20231115-Detection-fraude-fiscale-des-particuliers.pdf.

[25] Ibid., 42.

[26] John Henley, "Dutch government resigns over child benefits scandal," *The Guardian*, January 15, 2021, www.theguardian.com/world/2021/jan/15/dutch-government-resigns-over-child-benefits-scandal.

[27] Tweede Kamer der Staten-Generaal (Dutch Parliament), "Verslag – Parlementaire ondervragingscommissie Kinderopvangtoeslag: Ongekend onrecht," December 2020, www.tweedekamer.nl/sites/default/files/atoms/files/20201217_eindverslag_parlementaire_ondervragingscommissie_kinderopvangtoeslag.pdf.

[28] Melissa Heikkilä, "Dutch scandal serves as a warning for Europe over risks of using algorithms," *Politico*, March 29, 2022, www.politico.eu/article/dutch-scandal-serves-as-a-warning-for-europe-over-risks-of-using-algorithms/.

[29] Autoriteit Persoonsgegevens (Dutch Data Protection Authority), Belastingdienst/Toeslagen: De verwerking van de nationaliteit van aanvragers van kinderopvangtoeslag, July 2020, 2018–22445, https://autoriteitpersoonsgegevens.nl/uploads/imported/onderzoek_belastingdienst_kinderopvangtoeslag.pdf.

a second nationality and single mothers were, for instance, more likely to be identified as potential fraudsters, and hence subjected to higher scrutiny. However, by the time this breach was established, the damage was done, often irreparably so.[30]

Algorithmic regulation is also finding its way into other public sector domains. During the COVID-19 pandemic in 2020, the UK, for instance, decided to deploy an algorithmic system to allocate students' A-level grades after exams had been canceled in schools.[31] One potential solution was to rely on teachers' predictions of what the final grade would have been had the exam gone through. Yet given the observation that teachers tend to inflate grades and that this should hence not be the only factor to consider, the government suggested using an algorithmic system instead, claiming it would provide a "fairer" result. It decided to outsource students' grading to an algorithmic tool that determined its output not only based on teachers' predictions but also based on previous exam results and the overall grade distribution of a school over the last three years. When almost 40% of the students ultimately received lower grades than they anticipated, this led to a public outcry, as well as public scrutiny of the system.[32] In addition to concerns around the system's low accuracy and the way it penalized students in schools with a historically lower performance, the system was also deployed in a biased manner. If a school had fifteen students or less for a particular subject, more weight was given to the teacher's estimate – which the government already acknowledged was likely "too high." This policy choice ended up benefitting students attending private schools in particular, as they typically have fewer students per subject, thus also raising concerns of discrimination.

Finally, let me provide an example from the United States, where the Idaho Department of Health and Welfare decided to roll out an algorithmic system in 2011 in the context of a Medicaid program for persons with a disability. Such persons were eligible for a personalized benefits budget depending on their needs, and the system was used to calculate this budget with the aim of enhancing the program's efficiency. However, it turned out to have several flaws: Some people who had developed more substantial needs contradictorily saw their budget shrinking, without any sound explanation or justification.[33] As a consequence, highly vulnerable

[30] See also the Australian example discussed in Terry Carney Ao, "The new digital future for welfare: Debts without legal proofs or moral authority?" (2018) *UNSW Law Journal Forum*, 1: 1–16.

[31] Will Bedingfield, "Everything that went wrong with the botched A-levels algorithm," *Wired UK*, August 10, 2020, www.wired.co.uk/article/alevel-exam-algorithm.

[32] Daan Kolkman, "'F**k the algorithm'?: What the world can learn from the UK's A-level grading fiasco," *LSE Impact Blog*, August 26, 2020, https://blogs.lse.ac.uk/impactofsocialsciences/2020/08/26/fk-the-algorithm-what-the-world-can-learn-from-the-uks-a-level-grading-fiasco/.

[33] See David Restrepo-Amariles, 'Algorithmic Decision Systems: Automation and Machine Learning in the Public Administration' in Woodrow Barfield (ed), *The Cambridge Handbook of the Law of Algorithms* (Cambridge University Press, 2020), 289.

individuals were wrongfully denied the help they required. Similar systems were also deployed in other states, which in the worst case even led to the death of disabled persons who did not receive the care they depended on.[34] Since the problematic decisions of Idaho's algorithmic system were not reversed and the people concerned felt unheard, they were forced to span a class action before Idaho's District Court, thus bringing to the surface a number of the system's deficiencies, which were tied to its lack of transparency and model and data validation.[35] Ultimately, the Court found that the tool's use amounted to a breach of due process rights and was hence unconstitutional.[36]

These examples, while taken from various public sector areas, show at least two similarities. First, the implementation of algorithmic regulation in each of these cases started from the desire to enhance public services' efficiency, whether it concerns detecting tax evasion, uncovering benefits fraud, or allocating healthcare benefits. Second, they also showcase the adverse consequences that can ensue when such systems are used to implement (problematic) policies at scale, without consideration for the risks they entail when developed and deployed irresponsibly. In what follows, drawing on these examples, let me unpack in more detail some of the challenges that public administrations must consider when relying on algorithmic regulation.

19.4 CHALLENGES FOR THE RESPONSIBLE USE OF ALGORITHMIC REGULATION

Over the past decade, a rich academic literature developed around the ethical, legal and societal concerns associated with algorithmic systems, and particularly with AI. Many of AI's risks manifest themselves horizontally, in virtually all domains in which the technology is used. Others are more sector-specific and depend on the particular context or domain. As noted earlier, public authorities play a different role in society than private actors do, as they are tasked with upholding and promoting the *public* interest. Since public administrations are responsible for the fulfilment of numerous rights that are essential for people's well-being, the automation of problematic government policies can have vast adverse consequences. In what follows, I respectively discuss how algorithmic regulation can affect fundamental rights like privacy and non-discrimination (Section 19.4.1), the rule of law (Section 19.4.2), a sense of responsibility (Section 19.4.3), and the exercise of public power (Section 19.4.4).

34 Erin McCormick, "What happened when a 'wildly irrational' algorithm made crucial healthcare decisions," *The Guardian*, July 2, 2021, www.theguardian.com/us-news/2021/jul/02/algorithm-crucial-healthcare-decisions.

35 See Restrepo-Amariles, n (33), 289. See also a discussion of this case in Smuha, n (5), 55.

36 K.W. v. Armstrong, 180 F. Supp. 3d 703 (D. Idaho, 2016) (No. 1:12-cv-00022-BLW).

19.4.1 *Impacting Fundamental Rights*

One of the most common challenges arising from use of algorithmic regulation is its impact on fundamental rights, and most notably the right to privacy and data protection.[37] The performance of algorithmic systems hinges on the availability, collection and processing of high volumes of (personal) data, especially when used to enable scaled decision-making about individuals. Such data collection can have vastly intrusive effects on people's lives and can potentially be used in ways that undermine their agency.[38]

In the worst case, the irresponsible implementation of algorithmic regulation not only breaches privacy legislation (such as in the Dutch case discussed earlier), but can also lead to the mass-surveillance of citizens, in the name of efficiency. Unjustified intrusions into people's private lives can also affect the value of democracy, especially when data is gathered about potential individuals or groups that are not favored by the government. Moreover, privacy is often instrumental to secure other fundamental rights, such as the right to free speech and the right to human dignity, which are hence also at stake.[39] Yet given the financial investments that public administrations undertake when they decide to develop, procure or implement algorithmic regulation, and given the path dependencies this brings along, administrations are only incentivized to gather ever more data. A balance must hence be found between the government's desire to exercise its tasks with more efficiency, and the protection of people's private lives.

Another important concern relates to the way in which algorithmic systems can affect the right to non-discrimination.[40] Human beings have a range of biases and prejudices, which can at times be unjust or discriminatory, for instance when they echo societal stereotypes, historical inequalities, or other (often unconscious) problematic influences. Since algorithmic systems are designed and developed by human beings, their output can reproduce these unjust human biases, thus mirroring and potentially even exacerbating discriminatory practices.[41] The earlier

[37] See in this regard also Chapter 7 of this Book: Pierre Dewitte, 'AI meets the GDPR: Navigating the impact of data protection on AI systems' in Nathalie A. Smuha (ed), *The Cambridge Handbook of the Law, Ethics and Policy of Artificial Intelligence* (Cambridge University Press, 2025).

[38] See also Carissa Véliz, *Privacy is Power: Why and How You Should Take Back Control of Your Data* (Penguin, 2020).

[39] See also for example, Ruth Gavison, "Privacy and the limits of law" (1980) *Yale Law Journal*, 89(3): 421–471, 455; Bart van der Sloot, "Privacy as human flourishing: Could a shift towards virtue ethics strengthen privacy protection in the age of Big Data?," *Journal of Intellectual Property, Information Technology and Electronic Commerce Law* 5(3), 2014, 230–244, 231; See also more generally Orla Lynskey, *The Foundations of EU Data Protection Law* (Oxford University Press, 2015).

[40] See in this regard also Chapter 4 of this Book: Laurens Naudts and Anton Vedder, "Fairness and Artificial Intelligence" in Nathalie A. Smuha (ed), *The Cambridge Handbook of the Law, Ethics and Policy of Artificial Intelligence* (Cambridge University Press, 2025).

[41] See also Mireille Hildebrandt, "The Issue of Bias: The Framing Powers of Machine Learning," in Marcello Pelillo and Teresa Scantamburlo (eds), *Machines We Trust: Perspectives on Dependable AI* (The MIT Press, 2021).

illustrations of algorithmic regulation have shown that this risk is not hypothetical. In the Dutch example, inequalities found their way into the system's parameters and dataset during the development phase, thus adversely affecting certain groups of the population. In France and in the UK, the algorithmic system was deployed in an unequal manner and hence exposed individuals to its impact in an uneven way.

At a much more banal level, it is also possible that flaws or errors seep into the development and deployment process of algorithmic regulation – whether through erroneous human input or invalid correlations and inferences drawn by the system. This risk, and the problematic consequences ensuing therefrom, was illustrated by the benefits-allocation system deployed in the US, yet many other examples exist.[42] More generally, the fact that public administrations are responsible for the allocation of basic socio-economic rights also renders these rights vulnerable when their implementation is wholly or partly outsourced to a flawed or biased system.

Evidently, public administrations can also adversely affect people's rights without the use of algorithmic systems. Yet their reliance on powerful tools that enable data processing at a much wider scale and higher speed, coupled with the opacity of the internal processes of these systems and the recurrent lack of transparency about their deployment not only aggravate these risks, but also makes it more difficult to discover them. Adding a layer of digitalization to public services can certainly provide benefits of scale, but it is also precisely this scale-element that renders it so risky when implemented without considering these concerns.

19.4.2 *Eroding the Rule of Law*

Algorithmic regulation also raises a number of challenges to the rule of law. In essence, the rule of law comes down to the idea that nobody stands above the law, and that citizens and government officials alike are subjected to legal rules.[43] It embodies the notion that, rather than being governed by the arbitrary whims of "men" (who, as Aristotle already pointed out, are susceptible to arbitrary passions that undermine rational thinking),[44] people should be governed by "laws," which are based on reason and offer predictability. The rule of law is a broad term that has been defined

[42] See in this regard also the examples provided by Eubanks, n (7).

[43] See for example, AV Dicey, *Introduction to the Study of the Law of the Constitution [1885]*, 10e ed., (Macmillan, 1968); Friedrich A Hayek, *The Road to Serfdom [1944]* (Institute of Economic Affairs, 2005); Joseph Raz, "The Rule of Law and Its Virtue," *The Authority of Law: Essays on Law and Morality* (Oxford University Press, 1979).

[44] In Aristotle's words *"he who bids the law rule may be deemed to bid God and Reason alone rule, but he who bids man rule adds an element of the beast; for desire is a wild beast, and passion perverts the minds of rulers, even when they are the best of men,"* see Aristotle, *Politics* (Benjamin Jowett tr, Batoche Books, 1999), 77.

in countless ways,[45] yet the Council of Europe's Venice Commission[46] provided a helpful conceptualization for the European legal order by breaking it down into several principles (which were subsequently taken over by the European Union).[47] Under this conceptualization, the rule of law encompasses six principles: (1) the principle of legality; (2) the principle legal certainty; (3) the prohibition of arbitrariness of executive power; (4) equality before the law; (5) effective judicial protection, with access to justice and a review of government action by independent and impartial courts, also as regards human rights; and (6) the separation of powers.[48]

Under this conceptualization, the rule of law is hence understood not only as requiring *procedural* safeguards, but also *substantive* ones.[49] Indeed, it is not enough to merely apply the law in an efficient and procedurally agreed upon manner. Otherwise, the law could simply be used as a (powerful) instrument to enforce illiberal and authoritarian policies – a practice that has been denoted as rule *by* law instead.[50] Rather, the law and its application should also protect and comply with substantive values, and particularly respect for human rights and democracy. Accordingly, whenever public administrations want to exercise their powers, they are constrained by these rule of law-principles, which ensure that the law plays a protective role in society.[51]

At first glance, algorithmic regulation seems rather innocuous from a rule of law-perspective, and could even be seen as potentially advancing its principles to a greater extent. By eliminating civil servants' discretion from the picture, along with their potentially inconsistent or arbitrary decision-making, algorithmic regulation could arguably catalyze Aristotle's aspiration of being ruled by *law* instead of *men*. However, on closer inspection, this unqualified relationship between the rule of law and the rule of men is too simplistic: just like laws are created, applied and interpreted by human beings, so are algorithmic systems inherently dependent on

45 For this reason, it has also been described as an "essentially contested concept," see Jeremy Waldron, "The Rule of Law as an Essentially Contested Concept," in Jens Meierhenrich and Martin Loughlin (eds), *The Cambridge Companion to the Rule of Law. Cambridge Companions to Law* (Cambridge University Press, 2021), 121–136.

46 European Commission for democracy through law (Venice Commission), The Rule of Law Checklist, Venice, March 11–12, 2016, www.venice.coe.int/webforms/documents/default.aspx?pdffile=CDL-AD(2016)007-e.

47 See, for example, the EU's Conditionality Regulation which establishes a mechanism to protect the EU's budget against rule of law-infringements by Member States: Regulation 2020/2092 of the European Parliament and of the Council of 16 December 2020 on a general regime of conditionality for the protection of the Union budget 2020, OJ L 433I, 22.12.2020, 1–10.

48 For an analysis of these principles in the context of the public sector, see Smuha n (5), chapter 3.2.

49 See in this regard also Paul Craig, "Formal and substantive conceptions of the rule of law: An analytical framework" (1997) *Public Law*, 467–487.

50 See for example, Brian Tamanaha, "*On the Rule of Law: History, Politics, Theory*" (Cambridge University Press, 2004); Jeremy Waldron, "The Rule of Law," *The Stanford Encyclopedia of Philosophy*, in Edward N. Zalta and Uri Nodelman (eds.) (Fall 2023), https://plato.stanford.edu/archives/fall2023/entries/rule-of-law/.

51 See also, Geranne Lautenbach "The Rule of Law Concept" in *The Concept of the Rule of Law and the European Court of Human Rights* (Oxford University Press, 2013), 18–69.

the human beings that design, develop and deploy them.[52] There are hence several distinctive challenges to the ideal of the rule of law when public administrations rely on algorithmic systems,[53] of which an important one relates to the very act of implementing the law in an automated manner.

Automating the law's application through algorithmic regulation requires a "translation process" from text-based laws and policies to digital code. To a greater or lesser extent, text-based provisions are inevitably open to different (and contestable) interpretations, sometimes inadvertently, sometimes purposely. It is often precisely this very openness of the law that enables it to play its protective role, by facilitating its tailored interpretation to the specific situation at hand. Indeed, laws typically consists of (overly) general rules set forth by the legislator, which must subsequently be interpreted and applied to concrete cases. However, once automated, the law becomes more rigid, as a particular interpretation must be codified or optimized for. There is thus a risk that this translation process changes the nature of the law in a problematic manner. The translation may, for instance, occur in a way that is too legalistic, that incorporates biases and inequalities, that deviates from the intent of the legislator and unwarrantedly bolsters the power of the executive, that undermines the predictability and congruence of the law's application, that erodes essential rights and liberties or limits their scope, or that leaves individuals unable to contest the chosen interpretation and subject it to judicial review.

This risk not only undermines the rule of law's principles, but also erodes the constraints they place on government power, to the detriment of other liberal democratic values. In other words, algorithmic regulation could turn into a powerful tool to enforce rule *by* law. While this risk is not limited to the algorithmic context, the automated application of the law could be a highly efficient tool to erode the very protection the law is meant to afford, on a broader scale than ever before – a threat I conceptualized as *algorithmic rule by law*.[54] Bearing in mind the inherent malleability of software, and the additional level of opacity it introduces, it is thus essential to remain vigilant and put the necessary safeguards in place to ensure public administrations do not sacrifice efficiency over human rights, democracy and the rule of law.

19.4.3 *Delegating Responsibility*

Despite the push of the NPM movement to reconceptualize public administrations as "service providers" toward "customers," citizens are more than just customers. A far more inherent power imbalance is at play between governments and individuals as, unlike in private settings, the latter cannot easily "shop" at another service provider when for example, their social welfare benefits are wrongfully denied. As Sofia

[52] See in this regard also *infra*, Sections 19.4.3 and 19.4.4.

[53] For an extensive overview, see Smuha n (5).

[54] Nathalie A. Smuha, *Algorithmic Rule By Law: How Algorithmic Regulation in the Public Sector Erodes the Rule of Law* (Cambridge University Press, 2025).

Ranchordas and Luisa Scarcella pointed out, this power asymmetry can also exacerbate citizens vulnerabilities, and even instigate dehumanizing effects.[55] This risk can be spurred by the datafication process that accompanies the use of algorithmic regulation,[56] as it inevitably reduces individuals to numbers in a quite literal sense, thus diminishing their individuality and potentially even their human dignity. Yet it is far easier to overlook one's responsibility for the well-being of a number than for the well-being of an individual human being.

One of the distinctive elements of algorithmic regulation concerns the elimination of the need for direct personal interactions between individuals and civil servants, as such interactions can instead be mediated through algorithmic systems. At the same time, this time-saving feature can also make it more difficult for citizens to interact with another human being that understands their needs and concerns, and that can rectify any erroneous information that public administrations may have (which is a common difficulty with networked databases).[57] It can also render it more challenging for individuals to receive a clear explanation of the decisions affecting them, or to voice their concerns when problematic administrative acts are taken about them. In other words: it might be far more difficult for them to be heard, and to be acknowledged in their human individuality.[58]

In this regard, it is also important to consider the role of discretion, "*a power which leaves an administrative authority some degree of latitude as regards the decision to be taken, enabling it to choose from among several legally admissible decisions the one which it finds to be the most appropriate.*"[59] Civil servants use this discretion when they decide how to apply general rules to specific cases in the most appropriate way, in line with the rule of law. However, when public administrations rely on algorithmic regulation, this typically reduces discretion at the level of individual officials. Instead of officials exercising their judgment in specific cases, it is the *system* that will "apply" the law to a given case and take or suggest a decision.[60] Even

55 Sofia Ranchordás and Luisa Scarcella, "Automated government for vulnerable citizens: intermediating rights" (2021) *William & Mary Bill of Rights Journal*, 30(2): 371–418.

56 See also Heather Broomfield and Lisa Reutter, "In search of the citizen in the datafication of public administration" (2022) *Big Data & Society* 9(1): 3.

57 As thoroughly explored by Marlies van Eck in her dissertation, this can be especially problematic when erroneous data from one administration is used to inform the decision of another administration – see *Geautomatiseerde ketenbesluiten & rechtsbescherming: Een onderzoek naar de praktijk van geautomatiseerde ketenbesluiten over een financieel belang in relatie tot rechtsbescherming*, Tilburg Law School, 2021, https://pure.uvt.nl/ws/portalfiles/portal/20399771/Van_Eck_Geautomatiseerde_ketenbesluiten.pdf.

58 See in this regard also Nathalie A. Smuha, 'The Human Condition in An Algorithmized World: A Critique through the Lens of twentieth-Century Jewish Thinkers and the Concepts of Rationality, Alterity and History', KU Leuven Institute of Philosophy, *SSRN*, 2021, http://dx.doi.org/10.2139/ssrn.4093683.

59 See Committee of Ministers of the Council of Europe, "Recommendation No. R (80) 2 of the Committee of Ministers Concerning the Exercise of Discretionary Powers by Administrative Authorities," Strasbourg, 1980.

60 See also Justin B Bullock, "Artificial intelligence, discretion, and bureaucracy" (2019) *The American Review of Public Administration* 49(7): 751–761; David Freeman Engstrom, Daniel E. Ho, Catherine M. Sharkey, and Mariano-Florentino Cuéllar. "Government by Algorithm: Artificial Intelligence in Federal Administrative Agencies" *Administrative Conference of the United States*, 2020,

when the system merely offers a suggestion, officials will often be strongly incentivized to follow it for reasons of efficiency and the system's perceived authority. Indeed, if they would want to deviate from the system's suggestion, they typically need to provide a justification for this deviation, which not only requires time but also space for critical judgment to go against the system's centralized and allegedly more commanding suggestion.[61]

Civil servants might also feel that, by relying on the system's outcomes, they can delegate or at least share responsibility for the decision they take.[62] Especially when they do not see or talk with the individual concerned, the distance often renders it easier and more convenient to delegate a decision to an algorithmic system, though that could also lead to an (at least psychological) delegation of responsibility for that decision, and thus for the potential adverse consequences in case it is wrong or unjust. This can, in turn, increase the likelihood of negligence, nurture a lack of concern for citizens' interests and how they are impacted, and more generally diminish the procedural legitimacy of decisions taken by public administrations. Prior to the implementation of algorithmic regulation, it is hence important to anticipate and mitigate this challenge.

19.4.4 *Delegating Public Power*

At the same time, it must be pointed out that administrative discretion does not disappear when algorithmic regulation is deployed. While it is significantly reduced at the level of individual civil servants, it is instead transferred to the level of the designers and developers of the algorithmic systems, who through their seemingly technical choices in fact shape the system's highly normative outcomes.[63] A related problem is the fact that these designers and developers are typically *not* the civil servants who have the necessary experience and training to adopt administrative acts, who have expertise on how a specific law should be applied, and who must abide by the public sector's deontological standards. Rather, these algorithmic systems are often developed by data scientists and engineers working for private companies. This

[61] For a more nuanced perspective of an empirical study aiming to mimic automated decision-making in bureaucratic context, see Saar Alon-Barkat and Madalina Busuioc, "Human–AI Interactions in Public Sector Decision Making: 'Automation Bias' and 'Selective Adherence' to Algorithmic Advice" (2023) *Journal of Public Administration Research and Theory* 33(1), 153–169. See however also Albert Meijer, Lukas Lorenz, Martijn Wessels, "Algorithmization of bureaucratic organizations: Using a practice lens to study how context shapes predictive policing systems" (2021) *Public Administration Review*, 81(5): 837–846.

[62] See in this regard Albert Meijer, Lukas Lorenz, Martijn Wessels, n (56), See also Matthew M. Young, Justin B. Bullock, and Jesse D. Lecy, "Artificial discretion as a tool of governance: A framework for understanding the impact of artificial intelligence on public administration" (2019) *Perspectives on Public Management and Governance*, 2(4): 301–313.

[63] See in this regard Smuha n (5), 211–212. See also Reuben Binns, "Human judgment in algorithmic loops: Individual justice and automated decision-making" (2022) *Regulation & Governance*, 16: 197.

raises questions about the influence of the private sector on public decision-making, given the normative relevance of the systems they develop for this purpose. The less a public administration can count on in-house infrastructure and knowledge about how algorithmic systems work and what their capabilities and limitations are, the more this can lead to a problematic dependency on actors that are driven by non-public values.[64] The use of algorithmic regulation should however never lead to the unwarranted delegation of public powers to private actors.

The COVID-19 pandemic, for instance, made many public administrations aware of the fact that they were utterly dependent on private actors to set up and use digital infrastructures for their day-to-day operations (many of which had to move entirely to the digital realm) and for their management of the pandemic itself (for instance through contact tracing apps).[65] This also contributed to concerns around "digital sovereignty," or a nation's ability to autonomously decide on its relationship with (providers of) digital technology.[66] As discussed elsewhere, digital sovereignty implies the exercise of control over two entwined elements, namely: (1) the normative values that underly the technology, and (2) the physical and socio-technical digital infrastructure that enables the technology.[67] Sovereignty over both of these elements is essential to ensure that the core values which public administrations ought to protect – including human rights, democracy and the rule of law – are safeguarded also when they deploy algorithmic regulation.

19.5 GOVERNING ALGORITHMIC REGULATION

This brings me to the penultimate section of this chapter: how is algorithmic regulation governed to ensure that these challenges are tackled and that the necessary safeguards are in place? Let me start by jettisoning the misconception that no regulation currently applies to the use of these new technologies. Over the centuries, a rich body of law was developed to oblige public administrations and civil servants to act in line with a set of rules that limit their power, thus seeking to rebalance the inherent power asymmetry between governments and individuals. These rules did not seize applying once public administrations started relying on algorithmic regulation. Rather, they offer protection independently of how governments take administrative decisions, and thus play an important role in digital contexts too.

[64] See in this regard also Linnet Taylor, "Public actors without public values: Legitimacy, domination and the regulation of the technology sector" (2021) *Philosophy & Technology*, 34: 897–922.

[65] See for example, Luciano Floridi, "The fight for digital sovereignty: What it is, and why it matters, especially for the EU" (2020) *Philosophy & Technology* 33: 369–378.

[66] See also Julia Pohle and Thorsten Thiel, "Digital sovereignty" (2020) *Internet Policy Review*, 9; Benjamin Cedric Larsen, "The Geopolitics of AI and the Rise of Digital Sovereignty," *Brookings*, December 8, 2022, www.brookings.edu/articles/the-geopolitics-of-ai-and-the-rise-of-digital-sovereignty/.

[67] Nathalie A. Smuha, "*Digital Sovereignty in the European Union: Five Challenges from a Normative Perspective*" (SSRN 2023), http://dx.doi.org/10.2139/ssrn.4501591.

19.5.1 *Constitutional Law and Administrative Law*

The most primary of these rules are enshrined in national constitutions and set out the competences that governments have when exercising their powers, as well as the limitations of such powers. Fundamental rights and freedoms – such as the right to equality and nondiscrimination, freedom of speech and association, the right to privacy, and the right to a fair trial – are typically part of constitution-level norms, either directly or through (international) human rights treaties. This enables (constitutional) courts to review public administrations' actions in light of these limitations and safeguards. To carry out judicial review, it should not matter whether the administration's actions were taken solely by human civil servants or with the help of algorithmic systems.

A more detailed set of rules can be found in the realm of administrative law. While this area of law emerged as a scientific study in Europe around the nineteenth century, as a body of law its was already established prior to that time in several countries.[68] In essence, administrative law sets out the contours of the space of action of public administrations, drawing on constitutional norms and principles. It can thus be seen as limiting but also legitimizing and empowering administrations and the discretion they exercise when implementing the rules established by the legislative branch of power.[69] While each country has its own administrative law rules, some commonalities can be identified, as these rules are closely associated with the rule of law principles mentioned earlier.[70] They have sometimes also been conceptualized under the concept of "good governance" or "good administration."[71] In what follows, let me discuss some of the principles that the Council of Europe's Committee of Ministers laid down in its "Code of Good Administration" ("the Code").[72]

The first concerns the *principle of lawfulness*, which broadly corresponds to the concept of "legality."[73] It states that public authorities must act in accordance with the law (including domestic, supranational and international law), and cannot take any arbitrary measures, also when exercising discretion. This means they must have a legal basis to act, in accordance with the rules that define their powers and

68 See Giacinto della Cananea, *The Common Core of European Administrative Laws* (Brill Nijhoff, 2023), 2.

69 Christine B. Harrington and Lief H. Carter, *Administrative Law and Politics: Cases and Comments* (Sage, 2014), 25.

70 See Section 19.4.2 above.

71 See, for instance, Henk Addink, *Good Governance: Concept and Context* (Oxford University Press, 2019).

72 The Code was an appendix to Recommendation CM/Rec(2007)7 of the Council of Europe's Committee of Ministers to member states on good administration, adopted by the Committee of Ministers on June 20, 2007 at the 999bis meeting of the Ministers' Deputies.

73 Article 2 of the Code. See also Franz Merli, "Principle of Legality and the Hierarchy of Norms," in Werner Schroeder (ed), *Strengthening the Rule of Law in Europe: From a Common Concept to Mechanisms of Implementation* (Oxford: Hart Publishing, 2016), 37–45.

procedures, and they can only use the powers conferred upon them for the purpose delimited in those rules. The interpretation of how this principle must be complied with in practice differs from state to state, but given the intrusiveness of algorithmic systems, many countries in Europe provide that outsourcing certain tasks to such systems requires a specific legal basis. Accordingly, the legislative branch will typically need to set out the conditions under which public administrations can rely on algorithmic regulation. Additionally, public administrations have the obligations to ensure that – when they deploy algorithmic regulation – this occurs in full compliance with existing legislation, including the protection of human rights.

The *principle of equality* is likewise mentioned in the Code and provides that public administrations must treat persons who are in the same situation in the same way.[74] Any difference in treatment must be objectively justified – and merely claiming that an algorithmic system makes unintended discriminatory distinctions would not be a sufficient justification. Linked thereto is the *principle of impartiality*, which the Code conceptualizes as ensuring that public administrations act objectively, having regard only to "relevant matters" when they adopt administrative acts, and that they should not act in a "biased manner."[75] Individual public officials, too, must carry out their duties in an impartial manner, irrespective of their personal beliefs and interests. Applied to the context of algorithmic regulation, these principles hence require public administrations to ensure preemptively that the tools they deploy do not provide biased outcomes, and do not take into account elements that are not relevant for the administrative act in question. The latter point is especially interesting, since data-driven systems typically function by correlating different information points that may not necessarily have a causal link with the matter at hand. Importantly, respect for these principles must also be ensured when administrations *procure* algorithmic applications; they cannot escape this obligation by outsourcing the system's development, but remain responsible to respect these principles also when they make use of (privately developed) systems.[76] Public administrations must hence exercise a certain standard of care before they take specific actions, which arguably also extends to the action of implementing algorithmic regulation.

The Code's *principle of proportionality* is also of relevance: measures affecting the rights or interests of individuals should only be taken where necessary "*and to the extent required to achieve the aim pursued.*"[77] This principle is particularly

[74] See Article 3 of the Code.

[75] See Article 4 of the Code.

[76] The *principle of due diligence*, acknowledged in many administrative law systems, plays an important role in this regard too. Under Belgian law, public administrations must for instance abide by the due diligence principle pursuant to the (binding) "general principles of good administration." See for example, Kaat Leus, "Het Zorgvuldigheidsbeginsel" in Ingrid Opdebeek and Marnix Vandamme (eds), *Beginselen van Behoorlijk Bestuur* (Die Keure, 2006).

[77] See Article 5 of the Code.

important whenever civil servants exercise discretion, as it also states they must maintain "*a proper balance between any adverse effects which their decision has on the rights or interests of private persons and the purpose they pursue*," without these measures being excessive.[78] Given the problematic examples of algorithmic regulation discussed earlier, the proportionality principle plays an important role in the algorithmic context, especially when discretion is shifted away from individual civil servants who are able to balance different rights and interests, toward (designers of) algorithmic systems that rely primarily on pre-codified rules or optimization functions.

The Code also includes the *principle of participation*, which emerged more recently.[79] This principle is closely connected to the notion of (deliberative) democracy and embodies the idea that public administrations should offer individuals the opportunity to participate in the preparation and implementation of administrative decisions which affect their rights or interests. As I argued elsewhere, one could claim that participation should not only extend to administrations' decision-making processes based on algorithmic regulation, but also to the very choice taken by public administrations to implement algorithmic regulation in the first place.[80]

Finally, I should point out the *principle of transparency*, which states that public administrations must ensure that individuals are informed, by appropriate means, of their actions and decisions.[81] This may also include the publication of official documents and should in any case encompass respect for the rights of access to official documents according to the rules relating to personal data protection. A debate exists about the extent to which this principle applies to algorithmic systems used by public administrations, in so far as the source code of these algorithms (or at least their parameters) can be said to constitute information that falls under such access rights.[82]

This brings me to the observation that existing administrative law rules undoubtedly apply when public administrations use algorithmic systems, yet the enforcement of such rules is often rendered more difficult in this context precisely due to the nature and features of such systems, and civil servants' unfamiliarity with the particular challenges they pose. Partly for this reason, more specific legal rules have been developed to protect individuals when their personal data is processed in an automated way, and when they are subjected to AI systems – two domains I will discuss next.

78 Ibid.

79 See Article 8 of the Code.

80 See also Smuha, n (5), 228.

81 See Article 10 of the Code.

82 See, for example, Henrik Palmer Olsen, Thomas Troels Hildebrandt, Cornelius Wiesener, Matthias Smed Larsen, and Asbjørn William Ammitzbøll Flügge, "The right to transparency in public governance: Freedom of information and the use of artificial intelligence by public agencies," *Digital Government: Research and Practice*, 5(1): 2024, 1–15.

19.5.2 *Data Protection Law*

In the EU legal order, the right to privacy and personal data protection is enshrined respectively in Articles 7 and 8 of the Charter of Fundamental Rights of the EU (CFR) and in Article 8 of the European Convention on Human Rights. These fundamental rights were further concretized in other legal instruments. At the level of the Council of Europe, Convention 108 for the protection of individuals with regard to the processing of personal data was already opened for signatures in 1981, being the first legally binding international instrument in the field of data protection (later modernized through Convention 108+ in 2018).[83] Unsurprisingly, the Council of Europe's 2007 Code of Good Administration also included the *principle of respect for privacy*.[84] At the level of the European Union, the most well-known legal instrument in this field is the General Data Protection Regulation or GDPR,[85] which was largely inspired by Convention 108 and on which I will focus in what follows in a very succinct way, as it establishes directly invokable rights and obligations in EU Member States.[86]

The GDPR imposes obligations on private and public entities alike, and hence also applies to all personal data processing activities of public administrations (though a separate regime exists for the processing of data by law enforcement authorities in the context of criminal investigations).[87] Its protective provisions are especially relevant in the context of algorithmic regulation, which almost by definition implies the *processing* of *personal data*.[88] Public administrations must, pursuant

83 This Convention was ratified by fifty-five states, including also non-member States of the Council of Europe.

84 See Article 9 of the Code of Good Administration.

85 Regulation (EU) 2016/679 of the European Parliament and of the Council of April 27, 2016, on the protection of natural persons with regard to the processing of personal data and on the free movement of such data, and repealing *Directive 95/46/EC, OJ L 119, 4.5.2016*, 1–88.

86 The GDPR is a revision of an earlier EU directive dating from 1995, which already contained several safeguards against the processing of individuals' personal data. See Directive 95/46/EC of the European Parliament and of the Council of October 24, 1995, on the protection of individuals with regard to the processing of personal data and on the free movement of such data, *OJ L* 281, 23.11.1995, 31–50.

87 This is known as the Law Enforcement Directive or LDR. See Directive 2016/680 of the European Parliament and of the Council of April 27, 2016 on the protection of natural persons with regard to the processing of personal data by competent authorities for the purposes of the prevention, investigation, detection or prosecution of criminal offenses or the execution of criminal penalties, and on the free movement of such data, and repealing Council Framework Decision 2008/977/JHA, OJ L 119, 4.5.2016, 89–131.

88 Article 4(1) of the GDPR defines personal data as '*any information relating to an identified or identifiable natural person ('data subject'); an identifiable natural person is one who can be identified, directly or indirectly, in particular by reference to an identifier such as a name, an identification number, location data, an online identifier or to one or more factors specific to the physical, physiological, genetic, mental, economic, cultural or social identity of that natural person*'. Processing is also broadly defined (in Article 4(2)), as '*any operation or set of operations performed on personal data or on sets of personal data, whether or not by automated means*' (which, to illustrate, can include the collection, recording,

to Article 6 of the GDPR, be able to justify each data processing activity through a legal basis that confers them such power, whether this be the data subject's consent, the protection of the vital interests of a person, or the performance of a task carried out in the public interest or in the exercise of official authority vested in the data controller.[89] In case a public administration seeks to rely on the latter ground, the legal basis must be laid down further in Union law or in domestic law which sets out the processing's purpose, meets an objective of public interest and is proportionate to the legitimate aim pursued.[90]

The GDPR also mandates that administrations processing personal data do so in line with several principles, including the need to process data in a lawful, fair and transparent manner; to ensure it is collected only for specified, explicit and legitimate purposes, in a way that is adequate, relevant and limited to what is necessary in relation to such purposes; to ensure the data is accurate, kept up to date, and not stored for longer than necessary; and to ensure the data is processed with appropriate security measures, including protection against unlawful processing, accidental loss or damage.[91] Finally, administrations are not only responsible to make sure these principles are respected, but they must also be able to *demonstrate* compliance with them to foster accountability.[92]

In addition to these obligations, data subjects also have certain rights regarding their personal data, including the right to information about which data is being processed and in what way, as well as the right to rectify or erase such data.[93] Moreover, at any time, Article 21 of the GDPR grants data subjects a right to object to the automated processing of their personal data based on "*the performance of a task carried out in the public interest or in the exercise of official authority*" on grounds relating to their particular situation. Administrations must demonstrate compelling legitimate grounds for the data processing which override the interests, rights and freedoms of the data subject (or for the establishment, exercise or defense of legal claims). Pursuant to Article 22 of the GDPR, data subjects also have a right not to be subject to a decision based solely on automated processing if it produces legal effects concerning them or similarly significantly affects them – which comes down to a general prohibition on such decision-making, subject to the exceptions listed in the article.[94]

organization, structuring, storage, adaptation or alteration, retrieval, consultation, use, disclosure by transmission, dissemination or otherwise making available, alignment or combination, restriction, erasure or destruction of data). See in this regard also Chapter 7 of this Book.

89 Article 6 GDPR also refers to a number of other potential legal bases, yet public administrations would need to be able to provide a justification for their applicability.

90 See Article 6(3) GDPR.

91 See Article 5(1) GDPR.

92 See Article 5(2) GDPR.

93 See in particular Articles 12 to 22 GDPR.

94 See Article 22 GDPR.

The question of how much human intervention is needed to disqualify as "solely" automated processing is still not satisfactorily answered, though the European Data Protection Board (formerly the "Article 29 Data Protection Working Party")[95] issued interpretative guidelines in this respect.[96] The Guidelines for instance clarify that this provision cannot be avoided *"by fabricating human involvement. For example, if someone routinely applies automatically generated profiles to individuals without any actual influence on the result, this would still be a decision based solely on automated processing."*[97] Indeed, to qualify as human involvement, the public administration should ensure that *"any oversight of the decision is meaningful, rather than just a token gesture. It should be carried out by someone who has the authority and competence to change the decision. As part of the analysis, they should consider all the relevant data."*[98] Of course, to meaningfully exercise their right to object to automated decision-making, individuals must first be made aware of the fact that a public administration is taking an automated decision which concerns them (though administrations would have an information obligation in this respect under the GDPR).[99]

19.5.3 *AI Law*

While data protection law provides important safeguards to counter the risks of algorithmic regulation,[100] the GDPR's entry into force also revealed that many legal gaps still remain. From 2020 onwards, these gaps were also more explicitly recognized by policymakers in Europe,[101] such as the Council of Europe's Ad Hoc Committee

[95] This organization was set up under Article 29 of Directive 95/46/EC, the predecessor of the GDPR, and is now called the European Data Protection Board. It is an independent European advisory body on data protection and privacy.

[96] Article 29 Working Party, 'Guidelines on Automated individual decision-making and Profiling for the purposes of Regulation 2016/679,' October 3, 2017 (revised and adopted on February 6, 2018), WP251rev.01. See in this regard also Lorenzo Gugliotta, "Towards a right to explanation for automated (and AI-based) decisions? Anticipating the upcoming judgment in C-634/21 OQ v SCHUFA," *The Law, Ethics and Policy of AI Blog*, November 28, 2023, www.law.kuleuven.be/ai-summer-school/blogpost/Blogposts/SCHUFA-right-to-explanation.

[97] Article 29 Working Party, n (99), 21.

[98] Ibid.

[99] See in this regard chapter 3 of the GDPR, which sets out the rights of data subjects, and particularly articles 13(2)(f) and 14(2)(f).

[100] For a discussion of the interaction between the data protection framework and the AI Act, and the remaining importance of the former, see also Nathalie A. Smuha, "The paramountcy of data protection law in the age of AI (Acts)," *Two decades of personal data protectin. What's next? EDPS 20th Anniversary*, Luxembourg: Publications Office of the European Union, 2024.

[101] Also in other parts of the world, legislators started considering the adoption of new legislation to counter AI's risks. Consider, in this regard, Canada's proposed Artificial Intelligence and Data Act (tabled in June 2022), the US' Executive Order on the Safe, Secure, and Trustworthy Development and Use of AI (issued in October 2023), and China's regulation of inter alia recommendation algorithms and generative AI systems (adopted in March 2022 and May 2023, respectively).

on AI (in its Feasibility Study on a legal framework on AI),[102] and the European Commission (in its White Paper on Artificial Intelligence[103] and the work of its High-Level Expert Group on Artificial Intelligence[104]). The realization that existing legal rules were insufficient to protect people's rights against AI's risks, and that the promulgation of nonbinding AI ethics guidelines did not provide a satisfactory solution either, prompted new legislative initiatives. At the level of the Council of Europe, in Spring 2022, negotiations were launched to adopt a new international "Framework Convention on Artificial Intelligence, Human Rights, Democracy and the Rule of Law," finalized in Spring 2024.[105] At the level of the EU, the Commission proposed a new regulation laying down harmonized rules on AI in Spring 2021 – referred to as "the AI Act" – which after lengthy negotiations was adopted by the European Parliament and the Council in Spring 2024 as well.[106] Since the former is very succinct and abstract, and still needs to be converted into national legislation by the States who wish to sign it, I will briefly focus on the latter.

As discussed more extensively in Chapter 12 of this book, the AI Act establishes mandatory requirements for AI systems that pose risks to people's "health, safety and fundamental rights" and introduces prohibitions for several AI practices that are deemed incompatible with EU values.[107] Being a regulation rather than a directive, the AI Act has binding legal force in every EU Member State without the need for any national transposition rules. Yet a first question to ask is whether algorithmic regulation by public administration falls under the scope of the AI Act. Rather

[102] See Council of Europe Ad Hoc Committee on Artificial Intelligence (CAHAI), "Feasibility Study," Council of Europe, CAHAI(2020)23, https://rm.coe.int/cahai-2020-23-final-eng-feasibility-study-/1680a0c6da, 21–25. This formed the basis of the subsequent negotiations by the CAHAI's successor (the CAI or Committee on AI) for a new Convention on Artificial Intelligence, Human Rights, Democracy and the Rule of Law.

[103] European Commission, White Paper on Artificial Intelligence – A European approach to excellence and trust, COM(2020) 65 final, Brussels, February 19, 2020.

[104] Before proposing the AI Act, the European Commission set up a High-Level Expert Group on AI with the task of drafting '*Ethics Guidelines for Trustworthy AI*' (published in April 2019), which later inspired the Act's proposal. The non-binding nature of this initiative was however criticized, and also the Expert Group itself noted in its '*Policy Recommendations for Trustworthy AI*' (published in June 2019) that binding rules were needed for AI systems that can adversely affect fundamental rights. See in this regard also Nathalie A. Smuha, "The EU Approach to Ethics Guidelines for Trustworthy Artificial Intelligence: A continuous journey towards an appropriate governance framework for AI," *Computer Law Review International* 4 (2019), 97–106.

[105] Council of Europe Framework Convention on Artificial Intelligence and Human Rights, Democracy and the Rule of Law [Vilnius, 5.IX.2024], https://rm.coe.int/1680afae3c.

[106] Regulation (EU) 2024/1689 of the European Parliament and of the Council of 13 June 2024 laying down harmonised rules on artificial intelligence and amending Regulations (EC) No 300/2008, (EU) No 167/2013, (EU) No 168/2013, (EU) 2018/858, (EU) 2018/1139 and (EU) 2019/2144 and Directives 2014/90/EU, (EU) 2016/797 and (EU) 2020/1828 (Artificial Intelligence Act).

[107] Since the AI Act is extensively discussed in Chapter 12 of this book, the discussion in this section focuses primarily on its applicability in the context of public administrations. See Nathalie A. Smuha and Karen Yeung, "The European Union's AI Act: Beyond Motherhood and Apple Pie?" in *The Cambridge Handbook of the Law, Ethics and Policy of Artificial Intelligence* (Cambridge University Press, 2025).

than focusing on algorithmic systems, the AI Act applies to "AI," which it defines as a "*machine-based system designed to operate with varying levels of autonomy and that may exhibit adaptiveness after deployment and that, for explicit or implicit objectives, infers, from the input it receives, how to generate outputs such as predictions, content, recommendations, or decisions that can influence physical or virtual environments.*"[108] In the recitals, the EU legislator made it clear that this does not encompass "simpler traditional software systems or programming approaches" or "systems that are based on the rules defined solely by natural persons to automatically execute operations." This means that some applications of algorithmic regulation might not be captured by the AI Act, despite their potentially harmful consequences, merely because they are considered too "traditional" – which would be an unfortunate gap.[109] That said, public administrations are increasingly jumping on the machine learning hype (often without a proper assessment of whether this is also more useful for the purpose they envisage), so it can be expected that ever more applications of algorithmic regulation will fall under the AI Act's scope.

It is, however, not enough to merely fall under the scope of the regulation to also be subjected to its restrictive provisions. Taking a risk-based approach, the AI Act sets out five categories: (1) prohibited systems; (2) high-risk systems; (3) general purpose AI models; (4) systems requiring transparency measures; and (5) low-risk systems. The most relevant categories for the purpose of this chapter are the first two, since they pertain most frequently to the public sector.

The first category contains a list of several AI practices that are considered to pose an unacceptable level of risk to fundamental rights, and that are hence prohibited. For instance, AI systems cannot be used to deduce or infer people's race, political opinions, trade union membership, religious or philosophical beliefs, sex life or sexual orientation based on their biometric data (so-called biometric categorization).[110] Public and private organizations are also banned from engaging in social scoring of individuals or groups based on their social behavior or based on known, inferred or predicted personality characteristics, if this scoring leads to their unfavorable treatment in unrelated contexts, or to a disproportionate detrimental treatment.[111] Fully automated risk assessments of natural persons to predict the risk they commit a

[108] See Article 3(1) of the AI Act.

[109] See Recital 12 of the AI Act, which focuses particularly on the capability of making "inferences." According to this recital, the relevant techniques that enable this include machine learning approaches that learn from data how to achieve certain objectives; and logic- and knowledge-based approaches that infer from encoded knowledge or symbolic representation of the task to be solved. Yet the capacity of an AI system to infer goes "beyond basic data processing, enable learning, reasoning or modeling." It remains to be seen how a distinction will be drawn between "basic" modeling and more advanced applications.

[110] See Article 5(1)(g) of the AI Act. An exception is foreseen for the labelling or filtering of lawfully acquired biometric datasets, such as images, based on biometric data or categorizing of biometric data in the area of law enforcement, which does not fall under this prohibition.

[111] See Article 5(1)(c) of the AI Act.

criminal offence based solely on their profiling is also prohibited,[112] as is law enforcement's use of real time facial recognition in public places, unless one of three exceptions apply and safeguards are foreseen.[113]

The second category encompasses AI systems that are considered to pose a high risk to the health, safety and fundamental rights of individuals. Either they are already covered by existing product safety legislation (listed in Annex I) or they fall under the list of stand-alone high-risk systems (listed in Annex III). Many algorithmic regulation applications used by public administrations (to the extent they fall under the regulation's "AI" definition) are included in Annex III, such as the use of AI systems to "*evaluate the eligibility of natural persons for essential public assistance benefits and services, including healthcare services, as well as to grant, reduce, revoke, or reclaim such benefits and services.*"[114] Annex III also lists several applications used by law enforcement and by migration and border control administrations, including the use of AI to assist in asylum application decisions, to profile individuals in the detection of criminal offenses, or to serve as a polygraph.

Before being put into service, high-risk systems must undergo a conformity assessment to ensure they respect the requirements listed in Articles 9–15 of the AI Act, taking into account the systems' "*intended purpose*" and the "*generally acknowledged state of the art on AI.*"[115] That said, for virtually all high-risk AI systems public administrations can carry out this assessment themselves,[116] meaning there is no prior licensing or approval scheme before these systems are used.[117] Concretely, high-risk systems must be subjected to a risk-management process ("*understood as a continuous iterative process planned and run throughout the entire lifecycle of a high-risk AI system*") that allows the identification of reasonably foreseeable risks the system can pose to "*health, safety or fundamental rights when the high-risk AI system is used in accordance with its intended purpose,*" on the basis of which "*appropriate and targeted risk management measures*" must be taken.[118] High-risk systems are

[112] See Article 5(1)(d) of the AI Act.

[113] See Article 5(1)(h) of the AI Act These exceptions pertain to the search for victims of a crime, the prevention of an imminent threat to the life or safety of individuals, and the localization or suspects of specific crimes.

[114] Annex III, point 5(a) of the AI Act.

[115] Article 8(1) of the AI Act.

[116] The only exception to this self-assessment are high-risk AI systems listed under point 1 of Annex III (biometrics), for which the conformity assessment must be undertaken by a notified authority. The systems currently falling under this exception are: (a) remote biometric identification systems (unless it concerns biometric verification the sole purpose of which is to confirm that a natural person is who they claim to be); (b) AI systems used for biometric categorisation, according to sensitive or protected attributes or characteristics based on the inference of those attributes or characteristics; and (c) AI systems used for emotion recognition.

[117] They can also rely on technical specifications and standards which are being developed to facilitate compliance with the requirements (see Article 40 and following of the AI Act). Compliance with harmonized standards offers a presumption of conformity with the high-risk requirements.

[118] Article 9 of the AI Act.

also subject to data governance obligations for the training, validation and testing of systems, which include considerations regarding the relevant design choices of the model, the formulation of assumptions with respect to the information the data are supposed to represent, an assessment of the data availability and suitability and potential gaps, as well as the examination and mitigation of possible biases.[119]

Besides obligations that pertain to their accuracy, robustness and cybersecurity,[120] high-risk systems must also technically allow for the automatic recording of events for recordkeeping purposes[121] and set up a technical documentation of their compliance with those requirements, which national supervisory authorities can inspect if need be.[122] They must additionally be designed in a way that enables them to be overseen by natural persons. Such human oversight is meant to act as a supplementary safeguard to prevent or minimize risks (all the while taking into account the risk of so-called automation bias)[123] and to enable the system's user to decide *not* to use the system or to reverse its output.[124] In the context of public administrations, civil servants should hence always have the possibility to deviate from the system's suggested decision – though, as discussed earlier, this not only depends on a legal provision, but also requires an organizational environment that enables them to do so in practice.

As to the systems' transparency, providers of high-risk systems must present deployers of their systems with the necessary information to "*interpret the system's output and use it appropriately*."[125] This means that civil servants who procure AI systems should in principle receive information about the system's "*characteristics, capabilities and limitations of performance*."[126] Note, however, that this information need not be shared with those who are subjected to (and potentially negatively affected by) the system, but only to the system's users. The only information about high-risk systems that must be made publicly available is enumerated in Annex VIII of the AI Act and must be registered in the new "EU database for high-risk systems listed in Annex III," which the European Commission must set up as per Article 71 of the AI Act. The most useful information that AI providers must register is "*a description of the intended purpose of the AI system and of the components and functions supported through this AI system*," as well as "*a basic and concise description of the information used by the system (data, inputs) and its operating logic*." Whenever a high-risk system is used by a public sector deployer, the system's use must also be registered in the database, including a summary of "*the findings of the fundamental rights impact*

[119] Article 10 of the AI Act.
[120] Article 15 of the AI Act.
[121] Article 12 of the AI Act.
[122] Article 11 of the AI Act.
[123] See, for example, Linda J. Skitka, Kathleen Mosier, and Mark D. Burdick, "Accountability and automation bias," *International Journal of Human-Computer Studies*, 52(4), 2000, 701–717.
[124] Article 14 of the AI Act.
[125] Article 13 of the AI Act.
[126] Article 13(3)(b) of the AI Act.

assessment" which such deployers must conduct pursuant to Article 27 of the AI Act, and a summary of the data protection impact assessment they must carry out pursuant to Article 35 of the GDPR or Article 27 LED. The new EU database might hence become a valuable source for individuals seeking more information about public administrations' use of algorithmic regulation, especially with a view of challenging it in case there are concerns about breaches of their rights.

At the same time, there are many shortcomings in the protection the AI Act intends to afford, which are discussed in more detail in Chapter 12 of this book.[127] Particularly in the context of algorithmic regulation, many concerns remain unaddressed. The AI Act barely mentions the rule of law and has nothing to say about the normative influence that private actors can have on the public sphere through the procurement of algorithmic regulation tools. It also does not ensure that citizens get a say about whether certain algorithmic regulation applications should be used by public administrations in the first place, and its overly restrictive scope means it does not cover many harmful applications of algorithmic regulation, especially when based on more traditional systems. The AI Act also has many carve-outs which undermine its protection: AI systems deployed for research or for national security fall outside its scope, which risks constituting a significant gap. In addition, the safeguards against the use of live facial recognition (or biometric identification more generally) in public places only apply in the context of law enforcement and do not include borders, which leaves migrants – who already find themselves in a very vulnerable position – even more vulnerable.[128]

One could also argue that, by virtue of AI Act, the use of certain problematic applications is actually legitimized, since they can now be rubberstamped by claiming conformity with the AI Act's rules. This also led some people to criticize the AI Act an instrument of "deregulation," by potentially undermining safeguards drawn from other legal domains.[129] Finally, the AI Act's list-based approach – which exhaustively lists the systems that fall within its different categories – also means that some important applications are not covered, as the lists are underinclusive.[130] Combined with the fact that providers of high-risk systems can largely self-assess their system's

[127] See Chapter 12 of this Book: Nathalie A. Smuha and Karen Yeung, "The European Union's AI Act: beyond motherhood and apple pie?" in Nathalie A. Smuha (ed.), *The Cambridge Handbook on the Law, Ethics and Policy of AI* (Cambridge University Press, 2025).

[128] See also Petra Molnar, "EU's AI Act Falls Short on Protecting Rights at Borders," *Just Security*, December 20, 2023, www.justsecurity.org/90763/eus-ai-act-falls-short-on-protecting-rights-at-borders/.

[129] See for example, Aída Ponce Del Castillo, "The AI Act: Deregulation in Disguise," *Social Europe*, December 11, 2023, www.socialeurope.eu/the-ai-act-deregulation-in-disguise. See also Michael Veale and Frederik Zuiderveen Borgesius, "Demystifying the Draft EU Artificial Intelligence Act – Analysing the good, the bad, and the unclear elements of the proposed approach," *Computer Law Review International*, 22(4), 2021, 97–112.

[130] The Annexes of the AI Act can however be updated over time through the procedures laid down therein. As regards the high-risk systems listed in Annex III, Article 7 for instance sets out the conditions under which the European Commission can adopt a delegated act to add, modify, or eliminate AI applications from the list.

conformity with the requirements, and the fact that they can even self-assess whether their system is truly high-risk,[131] the regulation leaves a lot of leeway to the very actors against which it allegedly seeks to protect individuals.[132]

That said, the AI Act does provide a number of new safeguards that can be invoked to counter some risks posed by public administrations' use of AI. Moreover, the fact that it establishes a novel public enforcement mechanism both at the national and the European level also provides a strong signal that the EU takes AI's challenges seriously. The AI Act should hence be seen as part of a broader legal framework that also includes other protective provisions, and that is complementary to the legal domains set out above. Its relationship with existing legislation is also clarified in the AI Act itself, which for instance states that it "*does not seek to affect the application of existing Union law governing the processing of personal data,*"[133] and that "*where an AI practice infringes other Union law*" it can still be prohibited regardless of its inclusion in the exhaustive list of prohibitions of Article 5.[134] Accordingly, one should look beyond the AI Act's provisions to hold public administrations to account when they choose to rely on algorithmic regulation. Rather, the AI Act should be invoked along with provisions of constitutional law, administrative law and data protection law (as well as other relevant legal domains) to provide stronger protection against the challenges discussed in this chapter.

19.6 CONCLUSIONS

Algorithmic regulation has found its way to virtually all areas of the public sector. While the level of its uptake strongly varies from one country to another, and from one administration to another, it is being used for ever more impactful decisions – a trend that will undoubtedly continue. In the previous sections, along with setting out the reasons for this uptake, I also discussed some of the challenges that public administrations must consider when fully or partly delegating their tasks – and especially administrative acts – to algorithmic systems.

Drawing on existing practices from France, the UK, the Netherlands and the US, I showed that algorithmic regulation can raise legitimate concerns around the risk of biased decision-making, unwarranted privacy intrusions, and errors that can lead

131 See Article 6(3) of the AI Act, which states that "*an AI system referred to in Annex III shall not be considered to be high-risk where it does not pose a significant risk of harm to the health, safety or fundamental rights of natural persons, including by not materially influencing the outcome of decision making.*" Accordingly, even if an AI system is specifically listed in the Annex of high-risk systems, the requirements attached thereto can still be avoided if the system's provider believes it does not pose a significant risk of harm. In that case, the provider must however still register the system, and be ready to provide a justification for the exclusion.

132 See Chapter 12 of this Book, n (132). See also Smuha n (5), 291.

133 Recital 10 of the AI Act.

134 Article 5(8) of the AI Act. One could however question what such "other Union law" refers to, given that the AI Act supposedly already includes protective provisions for health, safety and fundamental rights.

to wide-scaled harm given the essential role that public administrations fulfil in society. Whether through traditional techniques or advanced machine learning applications, the automated execution and implementation of laws and policies implies a transformation from natural language to code, which has normative implications that can also affect the rule of law. As the earlier illustrations have shown, these risks also exist in countries that are committed to protect human rights, democracy and the rule of law, which makes it even more important for them to ensure they maintain sovereignty over the way in which (algorithmically driven) public decision-making occurs. Furthermore, we must stay vigilant that the delegation of administrative decision-making to algorithmic systems does not simultaneously lead to a delegation of responsibility and a neglect of citizens' rights and interests, in the name of efficiency.

Public administrations are already bound by an array of legal norms that can contribute to countering those risks, including safeguards from constitutional law, administrative law, data protection law, or AI-specific law. Yet even when invoked in a strategic and complementary way, these legal protection mechanisms will never be perfect. And while it is sensible to strive for their improvement and to develop further guidance for practitioners on how existing legal norms should be applied to the algorithmic context, one should also be careful not to treat the law as a panacea for all the challenges raised by technology. Beyond legal compliance, it is essential that public administrations also invest in education and literacy efforts among their civil servants, that they provide them with the necessary conditions to exercise their critical judgment, and that they prevent the delegation of public power – especially when this happens without democratic deliberation and accountability. It is only by taking these considerations seriously and adopting adequate measures prior to the implementation of algorithmic regulation that public administrations can continue fulfilling their vital role in liberal democracies with the help of algorithmic systems.

20

Artificial Intelligence and Armed Conflicts

Katerina Yordanova[*]

20.1 INTRODUCTION

War has been an integral part of human history since the dawn of time. It evolved together with human society and influenced its development in a tremendous manner. Military historians and political scientists established numerous systems in an attempt to better classify and analyze military endeavors, taking into account global political trends, the evolution of the means and tactics of war, and local geographical and cultural specifics.[1] Nevertheless, armed conflicts of all kinds have been persistently disrupting human lives, leaving individuals with little to no remedy against various infringements of their human rights.[2] While rules such as the distinction between combatants and civilians have been around for centuries, their application was dependent on factors such as the personal honor of the individual soldier,[3] or whether the enemy was considered as belonging to a "civilized nation."[4]

The modern development of international humanitarian law (IHL), which started during the second half of the nineteenth century, initially did not change much vis-à-vis the means of response and remedy individuals had over violation of their rights during armed conflicts. A treaty-based framework was established, largely based on customary rules. Despite its wide scope, the framework was

* The present research was conducted in the framework of Cybersecurity Initiative Flanders – Strategic Research Program and Imec.

1 See, for example, Max Boot, *Savage Wars of Peace: Small Wars and the Rise of American Power* (Basic Books, 2014); Mary Kaldor, *New and Old Wars: Organized Violence in a Global Era, 3rd ed* (Stanford University Press, 2013).

2 The term here is used in the broadest sense, without prejudice to the modern-day framework of human rights developed post-Second World War.

3 Jean-Marie Henckaerts and Louise Doswald-Beck, *Customary International Humanitarian Law. Volume I. Rules* (Cambridge University Press, 2009), p. xxxi.

4 Sven Lindqvist, *"Exterminate All the Brutes": One Man's Odyssey into the Heart of Darkness and the Origins of European Genocide* (The New Press, 1997); James Sloan, "Civilized Nations" *Max Planck Encyclopedia of Public International Law* (April 2011), https://opil-ouplaw-com.kuleuven.e-bronnen.be/display/10.1093/law:epil/9780199231690/law-9780199231690-e1748, accessed December 28, 2022.

founded on the deep humanist ideals of just one man to relieve the unnecessary suffering of fellow human beings elevating their protection as a main consideration for all parties involved in an armed conflict. International humanitarian law evolved dramatically during the twentieth century in response to the numerous wars that caused huge casualties and unimaginable destruction all over the world, directly related to the rapid change of military strategies and the utilization of new weapons. This tendency of IHL "lagging behind"[5] the contemporary challenges of the day is often characterized as one of its biggest weaknesses. However, this "weakness" permeates the entire legal system, as it became particularly evident in the last decades with the booming development of new technologies, and especially disruptive ones[6] such as blockchain, the internet of things (IoT), and artificial intelligence (AI).

Examples such as the drastic changes in the regulation of technologies used in the financial sector after the Financial Crisis of 2008 and the general abandonment of the laissez-faire approach toward them come to show that law in general struggles to adapt to technological progress and that the traditional reactive approach[7] is not always sufficient to ensure legal certainty and fairness in society. In the context of IHL, this problem becomes even more pressing due to its focus on the preservation of human life and the prevention of unnecessary suffering.

AI is largely recognized as a disruptive technology with the biggest current and potential future impact on armed conflicts. In this context, the media often uses AI and lethal autonomous weapons systems (LAWS) as synonyms, but in reality, LAWS is just one application in which AI is utilized for military and paramilitary purposes.

The purpose of the present chapter is to provide the reader with a brief overview of the main uses of AI in armed conflicts with a specific focus on LAWS, and the main societal concerns this raises. For this purpose, the chapter will first provide an overview of IHL, so as to supply the reader with general knowledge about its principles and development. This, in turn, will hopefully allow for a better understanding of the legal and ethical challenges that society currently faces regarding the use of AI in armed conflicts. Finally, the chapter also attempts to pose some provocative questions on AI's use in this context, in light of contemporary events and global policy development in this area.

5 James D. Fry, "Contextualized Legal Reviews for the Methods and Means of Warfare: Cave Combat and International Humanitarian Law" (2006) *Columbia Journal of Transnational Law*, 44(453): 466.

6 Disruptive technologies do not have a commonly accepted definition, but they are often characterized by their refinement, ground-breaking nature, and ability to create new industries. The term was first used by Clayton M. Christensen and later explored in Clayton M. Christensen, "The Innovator's Dilemma: When New Technologies Cause Great Firms to Fail" (1997) Harvard Business Review Press.

7 A "reactive approach" of the law implies that, traditionally, legal norms are adopted and amended as a response or reaction toward new relations in society or significant changes in already existing ones.

20.2 INTERNATIONAL HUMANITARIAN LAW

20.2.1 *Brief Introduction to the History of IHL*

The term *armed conflict*, which stands central to IHL, has a distinctive meaning in international law. The most commonly referred definition[8] is the one provided by the International Criminal Tribunal for the Former Yugoslavia which describes it as existing "whenever there is a resort to armed force between States or protracted armed violence between governmental authorities and organized armed groups or between such groups within a state."[9] The definition itself shows the armed conflicts are typically divided into those having an international and a non-international dimension.[10] For the sake of simplifying the scope of the present chapter, it will focus on the usage of AI solely in international armed conflicts. As a matter of fact, international armed conflicts were the only subject of regulation before the Second World War[11] which once again demonstrates the reactive nature of IHL.

IHL is considered to be born in the second half of the nineteenth century after the infamous battle of Solferino on June 24, 1859.[12] The battle resulted in the victory of the allied French Army of Napoleon III and the Piedmont-Sardinian Army commanded by Victor Emmanuel II over the Austrian Army under Emperor Franz Joseph I. It was documented that over 300,000 soldiers participated in the fifteen-hour massacre from which 6,000 died and more than 35,000 were wounded or went missing.[13] A detailed testimonial regarding the fallout of the battle and the suffering of both combatants and civilians was given by the Swiss national Henry Dunant, who happened to be in the area and witnessed the gruesome picture of the battlefield, later described in his book named *A Memory of Solferino*.[14] Henry Dunant dedicated his life and work to the creation of an impartial organization tasked with caring for the wounded in armed conflicts and providing humanitarian relief. It became a reality on February 17, 1863, when the International Committee of the Red Cross (ICRC) was established in Geneva. This event,

[8] See cases such as Prosecutor v. Charles Ghankay Taylor, SCSL-03-1-T, Special Court for Sierra Leone, May 18, 2012, para. 506, The Prosecutor v. Thomas Lubanga Dyilo, ICC-01/04-01/06-2842, International Criminal Court, April 05, 2012.

[9] *Prosecutor* v. *Dusko Tadic Appeal* Judgement (1999) International Criminal Tribunal for the former Yugoslavia (ICTY), IT-94-1-A.

[10] Non-international armed conflicts are usually perceived as every armed conflict that is not qualified as international.

[11] Yoram Dinstein, *Non-International Armed Conflicts in International Law 2nd Edition* (Cambridge University Press, 2021), 3.

[12] ICRC, "What are the origins of International Humanitarian Law?" (August 2017) *ICRC Blog*, https://blogs.icrc.org/ilot/2017/08/07/origins-international-humanitarian-law/ accessed June 5, 2023.

[13] International Committee of the Red Cross, "Solferino and the International Committee of the Red Cross" (June 2010) *ICRC Feature*, www.icrc.org/en/doc/resources/documents/feature/2010/solferino-feature-240609.htm, accessed December 28, 2022.

[14] Original title: *Un souvenir de Solferino*, self-published in 1962.

while significant, was just the beginning of the rapid development of modern IHL. In 1864, the Geneva Convention for the Amelioration of the Condition of the Wounded in Armies in the Field was adopted, becoming the first international treaty regulating armed conflicts in a universal manner, opened for all States to join.[15] That instrument, and the following Geneva conventions, established three key obligations for the parties: (1) providing medical assistance to the wounded regardless of their nationality, (2) respecting the neutrality of the medical personnel and establishments, and (3) recognizing and respecting the sign of the Red Cross on white background.

These first steps predefine the characteristics of modern IHL as part of the body of international law that governs the relations between states. Its subsequent development also broadens its scope to protecting "persons who are not or are no longer taking part in hostilities, the sick and wounded, prisoners and civilians, and to define the rights and obligations of the parties to a conflict in the conduct of hostilities."[16] In addition, IHL evolved to serve as a guarantee for preserving humanity even on the battlefield by attempting to ease the suffering of the combatants. This development in the role of IHL occurred early on due to the rapid uptake of new weapons. In particular, the invention of the *dum-dum bullet*[17] in 1863 inspired the adoption of the first international treaty concerning weaponry (namely the St. Petersburg Declaration Renouncing the Use, in Time of War, of Explosive Projectiles under 400 gm weight, in 1868).[18] It is a pivotal instrument for IHL not only because it was the first of its kind but also because it recognized the customary character of the rule according to which using arms, projectiles, and materials that cause unnecessary suffering is prohibited.[19] This line of work was continued through the Hague Conventions from 1899 and 1907, governing the "laws of war" as opposed to the Geneva Conventions that focus on the right to receive relief.

The First World War indicated the end of this period of development of IHL, bringing forward the concept of total war, new weapons (including weapons of

[15] Bilateral treaties protecting war victims existed before 1864, but they were often breached and circumvented. Moreover, they were concluded and enforced only regarding a specific armed conflict.

[16] International Committee of the Red Cross, "War and international humanitarian law" (October 2010) *ICRC Overview*, www.icrc.org/en/doc/war-and-law/overview-war-and-law.htm, accessed December 28, 2022.

[17] The expanding bullet or the dum-dum bullet was invented by the Russian military and as the name shows it expands when it comes into contact with a hard surface. Even though it was initially created in order to deal more effectively with ammunition wagons, it was soon modified to expand when coming into contact with soft services as well, thus causing serious wounds to human beings Edward M. Spiers, "The use of the Dum Dum bullet in colonial warfare" The Journal of Imperial and Commonwealth History, vol. 4, issue 1, p. 3.

[18] Orlin Borisov, *Public International Law* (2008), Nova Zvezda, 712.

[19] Luc Reydams and Jan Wouters, "A la guerre comme à la guerre: patterns of armed conflict, humanitarian law responses and new challenges" in Jan Wouters, Philip De Man, and Nele Verlinden (eds), *Armed Conflicts and the Law* (Intersentia, 2016), 6.

mass destruction such as poison gas), and the anonymization of combat.[20] These novel technologies and the effects they had on people, as well as the outcome of the campaigns and individual battles, naturally resulted in the adoption of further legal instruments in response of the new treats to the already established law of war.[21] In addition, the Geneva Convention was overhauled by the 1929 Convention for the Amelioration of the Condition of the Wounded and Sick in Armies in the Field which further reflected the influence of the new technologies establishing, for example, protection of medical aircraft.

The Second World War brought another set of challenges for IHL besides the tremendously high percentage of civil causalities compared to the First World War.[22] The concept of total war which transforms the economies of the states into war economies fogged the distinction between civilians and combatants and also between civilian and military objects, which is one of the key principles of IHL. Other contributing factors were the civilian groups targeted by the Nazi ideology and the coercive warfare used by the Allied powers.[23]

The immediate response to the horrors of the biggest war in human history was the establishment of the United Nations and the International Military Tribunals of Nuremberg and Tokyo. In addition, four new conventions amended and reinforced the IHL framework. The 1949 Geneva Conventions on the sick and wounded on land; on the wounded, sick, and shipwrecked members of the armed forces at sea; on prisoners of war; and on civilian victims (complemented by the Additional Protocols from 1977) codified and cemented the core principles of the modern-day IHL, the way we know it at present days.

The second half of the twentieth century, and in particular the Cold War period and the Decolonization, contributed mostly to the development of the IHL rules regarding non-international armed conflicts. Nevertheless, the tendency of adopting treaties in response to technological advancement continued. Certain core legal instruments on arms control were adopted during that time, such as the Treaty on the Non-Proliferation of Nuclear Weapons from 1968,[24] the Biological Weapons Convention from 1972,[25] and the Chemical Weapons

[20] Ibid., 7–8.

[21] See, for example, The Protocol for the Prohibition of the Use of Asphyxiating, Poisonous or Other Gases, and of Bacteriological Methods of Warfare from 1925, Geneva Conference for the Supervision of the International Traffic in Arms.

[22] The percentage of civil casualties directly cause by the Second World War is close to 50 percent compared to 5 percent during the First World War, see Orlin Borisov, Public International Law, p. 670.

[23] Reydams and Wouters, *A la guerre comme à la guerre*, p. 11.

[24] Unlike biological and chemical weapons, nuclear weapons have not been formally banned, but regulatory efforts were concentrated on their nonproliferation. The Treaty on the Prohibition of Nuclear Weapons from 2017 is unfortunately lacking effectiveness due to the absence of the states that actually own nuclear weapons among the signatory states. Therefore, one can hardly talk about a ban on nuclear weapons in practice, despite the existence of the instrument in theory.

[25] The Convention on the Prohibition of the Development, Production and Stockpiling of Bacteriological (Biological) and Toxin Weapons and on their Destruction (1972) United Nations General Assembly.

Convention from 1993.[26] Another important legal treaty, directly connected to the regulation of new technologies used as weapons, concerns the Convention on Certain Conventional Weapons (CCW) from 1980.[27] This Convention will be further discussed in Section 20.3.

The global tendencies of the twenty-first century signaled the decreasing political will of nation-states to enter into binding multilateral agreements beyond trade and finance due to their lack of effectiveness.[28] This is extremely worrisome not only because of its effect on the international legal order, but also due to the consequences it has on the ambition of making law anticipatory rather than reactionary, especially in the context of new weapons such as LAWS. Therefore, the principles of IHL which have already been established during the last century and a half, need to be taken into account when interpreting the existing body of law applicable vis-à-vis technologies such as AI, regardless of the capacity it is used for in military context. The next section offers an exposition of these principles which should provide the reader with a better understanding of the IHL challenges created by AI.

20.2.2 *Principles of IHL*

To understand the effect of AI on IHL, six core principles of IHL need to be unpacked, as they serve both as an interpretative and guiding tool for the technology's use in this area. This section will briefly discuss each principle in turn.

20.2.2.1 Distinction between Civilians and Combatants

The principle that a distinction should be made between civilians and combatants is extremely important in armed conflicts, as it could mean the difference between life and death for an individual. In essence, the principle requires belligerents to distinguish at all times between people who can be attacked lawfully and people who cannot be attacked and should instead be protected.[29] This principle reflects the idea that armed conflicts represent limited conflicts between the armed forces of certain

[26] Convention on the Prohibition of the Development, Production, Stockpiling and Use of Chemical Weapons and on their Destruction (1992) Conference of Disarmament and General Assembly of United Nations.

[27] Convention on Prohibitions or Restrictions on the Use of Certain Conventional Weapons Which May Be Deemed to Be Excessively Injurious or to Have Indiscriminate Effects (1981) United Nations Conference on Prohibitions or Restrictions of the Use of Certain Conventional Weapons Which May Be Deemed Excessively Injurious or to Have Indiscriminate Effects and the General Assembly of United Nations.

[28] Steven J. Hoffman, Prativa Baral et al., "International treaties have mostly failed to produce their intended effects" (2022) *Proceedings of the National Academy of Sciences (PNAS)*, 119(32).

[29] Nils Melzer, "The principle of distinction between civilians and combatants" in Andrew Clapham and Paola Gaeta (eds), *The Oxford Handbook of International Law in Armed Conflict* (Oxford University Press, 2014), 297.

States and not between their populations. The only legitimate goal is hence to weaken the military forces of the opposing State.[30] The importance of the principle of distinction as a cornerstone of IHL was reaffirmed by the International Law Commission[31] which argued it should be considered as a rule of *jus cogens*. This term is used to describe peremptory norms of international law from which no derogation is allowed. While the scope of *jus cogens* norms is subject to a continuing debate,[32] the fact that the principle of distinction is regarded as such a norm has a lot of merit.[33]

While the principle of distinction between civilians and combatants sounds very clear and easy to follow, in reality, it is not always easy to apply. On the one hand, the changing nature of armed conflicts blurs the differences between the two categories and shifts the traditional battlefield into urban areas. On the other hand, many functions previously carried out by military personnel are currently being outsourced to private contractors and to government personnel sometimes located in different locations. Involving technologies such as AI either in attacking (e.g., LAWS) or defensive (e.g., in cybersecurity) capability further complicates the distinction between civilians and combatants[34] and brings uncertainty, potentially increasing the risk of civilians being targeted erroneously or arbitrarily.

20.2.2.2 Prohibition to Attack Those Hors De Combat

The principle of prohibition to attack those *hors de combat* shows some similarities with the principle of distinction between civilians and combatants, mainly because one needs to be able to properly identify those *hors de combat*. The term originates from the French language and literally means "out of combat." Article 41 from Additional Protocol I to the Geneva Conventions from 1949 stipulates that a person "who is recognized or who, in the circumstances, should be recognized to be hors de combat shall not be made the object of attack." Paragraph 2 provides additional defining criteria, including the person to be in the power of an adverse Party, in case that person clearly expresses an intention to surrender. This also covers persons who

30 Jean Simon Pictet, *Development and Principles of International Humanitarian Law* (Martinus Nijho Publishers, 1985), 62.

31 International Law Commission, "Report on State Responsibility" (Yearbook of the International Law Commission, 2001) vol II, Part Two, 113.

32 Ulf Linderfalk, "The effect of jus cogens norms: whoever opened pandora's box, did you ever think about the consequences?" (2007) *European Journal of International Law*, 18(5): 853–871. Andrea Bianchi, "Human rights and the magic of jus cogens" (2008) *European Journal of International Law*, 19(3): 491–508.

33 International Court of Justice, "Legality of the threat or use of nuclear weapons opinion" (July 8, 1996) *Advisory Opinion*: § 78.

34 The distinction between civilians and combatants could be complicated by AI systems due to a number of factors including, for instance, bias in the data used to train the systems; the unclear status of the people who develop, deploy, and maintain such systems who are usually contractors and employees of private companies; and the subjective psychological element which often compromises mechanisms such as human oversight and authority due to situations resembling the Milgram experiment.

have been rendered unconscious or who are otherwise incapacitated by wounds or sickness, and, therefore, are incapable of defending themselves, as long as they do not conduct any hostile acts or try to escape. These additional criteria are important because they expand the scope of the protection of the principle not only to individuals who are explicitly recognized as *hors de combat* in all situations but also to those who should be recognized as *hors de combat* in a given moment of time based on the specific circumstances.[35]

While the principle was historically easy to apply nowadays, it raises several issues. First and foremost, the changing nature of the various armed conflicts makes determining the status of *hors de combat* dependent on the context. Steven Umbrello and Nathan Gabriel Wood provide an interesting example involving poorly armed adversary soldiers who do not have any means to meaningfully engage a tank but do not surrender or fall under another condition described in Additional Protocol I. The authors, however, argue that the customary understanding of the principle involves "powerless" as well as "defenseless" as characteristics that define an individual as being *hors de combat.*[36]

Another possible issue stems from the utilization of autonomous and semi-autonomous weapons. The contextual dependency mentioned earlier makes the application of the principle complicated from a technical point of view. For example, the dominating approach to machine learning e.g., in language modeling, relies on calculating statistical probabilities.[37] State-of-the-art models have no contextual or semantic understanding, and this makes them susceptible to so-called "hallucinations."[38] Reliance on such models to assess whether a person is conducting any hostile acts or is trying to escape is therefore a risk, and an unreliable undertaking. In addition, despite the advances in mitigating the risks of adversarial attacks, computer vision applications remain vulnerable to evasion attacks with adversarial examples that do not require sophisticated skills on the part of the attacker.[39] In addition, any kind of identification is susceptible to unfair bias that could be extremely hard to overcome in military context due to the lack of availability of datasets that are domain specific and reflecting physical traits of combatants (e.g., skin color and uniforms).[40]

[35] Steven Umbrello and Nathan Gabriel Wood, "Autonomous Weapons Systems and the Contextual Nature of Hors de Combat Status" (2021) *Information*, 12(5): 216.

[36] Ibid.

[37] Daniel Jurafsky and James H. Martin, *Speech and Language Processing* (2022) Third Edition draft, 31 https://web.stanford.edu/~jurafsky/slp3/ed3book.pdf, accessed June 5, 2023.

[38] Open AI, "GPT-4 Technical Report" (2023), arxiv Cornell University, 10 https://arxiv.org/abs/2303.08774, accessed June 5, 2023.

[39] Naveed Akhtar, Ajmal Mian, Navid Kardan, and Mubarak Shah, "Advances in adversarial attacks and defenses in computer vision: a survey" (2021) arxiv Cornell University: 24–25 https://arxiv.org/abs/2108.00401v2

[40] Marcus Comiter, "Attacking artificial intelligence. AI's security vulnerability and what policymakers can do about it" (August 2019) *Harvard Kennedy School for Science and International Affairs, Belfer Center*, 37, www.belfercenter.org/sites/default/files/2019-08/AttackingAI/AttackingAI.pdf accessed June 5, 2023.

20.2.2.3 Prohibition to Inflict Unnecessary Suffering

The principle of prohibition to inflict unnecessary suffering was one of the cornerstones of IHL, as demonstrated by the fact that it was implemented in one of the first IHL legal instruments adopted internationally, namely the St. Petersburg Declaration.[41] This principle is also the key rationale behind important treaties such as the CCW that bans and limits a number of weapons inflicting unnecessary suffering, such as laser weapons and incendiary weapons.[42]

The principle has a customary character,[43] but it is nevertheless codified in written law, primarily in Article 35, paragraph 2 of Additional Protocol I to the Geneva Conventions. This article contains a general prohibition for States to employ "weapons, projectiles, and material and methods of warfare of a nature to cause superfluous injury or unnecessary suffering." This formulation of the rule is derived from the principle of humanity which is explained in Section 20.2.2.6.[44] While States agree that the only legitimate military goal is weakening the military of the adversary state, this goal needs to be achieved without unnecessary suffering. In other words, combatants are not prohibited of being killed during an armed conflict, but if it is to be done, it needs to be done "humanely." This notion, however, could be subject to discussion, due to the questionable coexistence of killing and humanely in one sentence in military context. The meaning of the terms "unnecessary" and "superfluous" is also problematic from the standpoint of employing LAWS which need to be designed, created, and used in accordance with this principle, as well as the rest of the rules of IHL. This is so because concepts such as "unnecessary" and "superfluous" suffering are not susceptible to mathematical formalization.

20.2.2.4 Military Necessity

The principle of military necessity[45] was already briefly touched upon in the previous sections due to its relation to the other principles of IHL. The Hague

41 St. Petersburg Declaration Renouncing the Use, in Time of War, of Explosive Projectiles under 400 Grammes Weight, consideration 4.

42 Protocols III and IV to the CCW.

43 Henri Meyrowitz, "The principle of superfluous injury or unnecessary suffering: from the Declaration of St. Petersburg of 1868 to Additional Protocol 1 of 1977" (1994) *International Review of the Red Cross (1961–1997)*, 34(299): 101.

44 Theodor Meron, "The Martens Clause, principles of humanity, and dictates of public conscience" (2000) *The American Journal of International Law*, 94(1): p. 87.

45 It is important to mention that military necessity as principle of IHL should not be confused with the state of necessity usually related to state responsibility, as a circumstance precluding the wrongfulness of an act that would otherwise be considered wrongful under international law, see Article 25 of "Articles on Responsibility of States for Internationally Wrongful Acts" in "Report of the International Law Commission on the Work of its 53rd Session" (April 23–June 1, and July 2–August 10, 2001) UN Doc A/56/10.

Regulations from 1899 and 1907[46] refer to the principle by proclaiming that "[t]he right of belligerents to adopt means of injuring the enemy is not unlimited."[47] This rule shows the collision between military necessity and humanitarian considerations, which results in limiting the former, sometimes even through the creation of new norms, for example the prohibition of destruction of cultural property.[48] As a result of this collision, the principle covers the range of justified and thus allowed use of armed force and violence by a State in order to achieve specific legitimate military objectives, as long as it stays within the limits of the principle of proportionality.

This principle is probably technically the hardest one to abide by when deploying autonomous technologies in military context. This could be explained by the fact that the military necessity is a justification for disregarding the principle of distinction under the circumstances provided in Articles 51 and 52 from Additional Protocol I. Both articles concern defining and protecting civilians in armed conflicts except in the cases when they take direct part in the hostilities. Article 52 also prohibits attacking objectives that are not military objectives, although it acknowledges that civilian objects could become military "when, 'by their nature, location, purpose or use,' such objects 'make an effective contribution to military action' and their total or partial destruction, capture or neutralization, in the circumstances ruling at the time, offers a definite military advantage."[49] Evidently, performing such assessments is of paramount importance and in the author's opinion requires meaningful human oversight in order to avoid fatal mistakes.

20.2.2.5 Proportionality

The principle of proportionality in IHL prohibits attacks that may lead to "incidental loss of civilian life, injury to civilians, damage to civilian objects, or a combination thereof, which would be excessive in relation to the concrete and direct military advantage anticipated."[50] The main issues that doctrine and practice have been facing regarding this principle are related to defining military advantage,[51]

46 Convention Respecting the Laws and Customs of War on Land annex Article 22 and Convention with Respect to the Laws and Customs of War on Land annex Article 22.

47 Regulations concerning the Laws and Customs of War on Land annexed to Hague Convention IV (adopted October 18, 1907, entered into force January 26, 1910) (1907) 205 CTS 227 (Hague Regulations), Art. 22.

48 Nobuo Hayashi, "Hayashi, Nobuo, Requirements of Military Necessity in International Humanitarian Law and International Criminal Law" (2010) *Boston University International Law Journal*, 28(1): 48.

49 Michael N. Schmitt, "Military necessity and humanity in International Humanitarian Law: preserving the delicate balance" in *Essays on Law and War at the Fault Lines* (Springer, 2012), 96.

50 Article 51(5)(b) from Additional Protocol I to the Geneva Conventions.

51 Robin Geiss, "The Principle of Proportionality: 'Force Protection' as a military advantage" (2012) *Israel Law Review*, 45(1): 71–89.

incidental harm,[52] and excessiveness[53] – all three of these terms being heavily context reliant.

Furthermore, the comparison between the "military advantage" on the one hand and the "excessiveness" on the other hand when performed by a machine learning algorithm (for example by an autonomous military drone such as the STM Kargu-2)[54], requires weighting exercise represented in a computational format. This means that certain values are to be assigned to the categories, which is extremely difficult not only from a technical but also from a legal and ethical perspective.[55] For instance, using autonomous drones designed to destroy military equipment is considered a military advantage. However, doing so in densely populated areas could lead to significant collateral damage, including loss of human life. In this scenario, it is extremely hard if not impossible to assign numerical value and assess whether destroying one piece of military equipment constitutes such a military advantage that it is proportionate to killing two civilians in the blast.

20.2.2.6 The Principle of Humanity

Finally, the principle of humanity underlies every other principle of IHL. It could be defined as a prohibition of inflicting "all suffering, injury or destruction not necessary for achieving the legitimate purpose of a conflict"[56] that aims to protect combatants from unnecessary suffering. It also protects those *hors de combat*.[57] Customary by nature, the principle was first codified in the St. Petersburg Declaration, pointing out that "laws of humanity" are the reason behind the prohibition of arms which "uselessly aggravate the sufferings of disabled men, or render

[52] Eliav Lieblich, "Beyond life and limb: exploring incidental mental harm under International Humanitarian Law" in Derek Jinks, Jackson Maogoto, and Solon Solomon (eds) *Applying International Humanitarian Law in Judicial and Quasi-Judicial Bodies* (T.M.C. Asser Press, 2014), 159–187.

[53] Jason Wright, "'Excessive' ambiguity: analysing and refining the proportionality standard" (2012) *International Review of the Red Cross*, 94(886): 819–854.

[54] For the technical characteristics of the STM Kargu-2 and its capabilities, see www.stm.com.tr/en/kargu-autonomous-tactical-multi-rotor-attack-uav; Hitoshi Nasu, "The Kargu-2 autonomous attack drone: legal & ethical dimensions" (June 2021) Lieber Institute Blog, https://lieber.westpoint.edu/kargu-2-autonomous-attack-drone-legal-ethical/ accessed June 5, 2023.

[55] Tomasz Zurek, Taylor Woodcock, Magdalena Pacholska, and Tom van Engers, "Computational modelling of the proportionality analysis under International Humanitarian Law for military decision-support systems" (January 14, 2022) *SSRN* https://ssrn.com/abstract=4008946 accessed January 6, 2023.

[56] The definition is proposed by the ICRC in ICRC, "What is IHL?" (September 2015) *ICRC blog*, www.icrc.org/en/document/what-ihl, accessed June 7, 2023. However, the discussion on the content and the applicability of the principle is still ongoing, see Kjetil Larsen, Camilla Guldahl Cooper, & Gro Nystuen (Eds.), "Searching for a 'Principle of Humanity' in International Humanitarian Law" (2012) Cambridge University Press.

[57] Geoffrey S Corn, "Humanity, Principle of" Max Planck Encyclopedia of Public International Law (July 2013) https://opil-ouplaw-com.kuleuven.e-bronnen.be/display/10.1093/law:epil/9780199231690/law-9780199231690-e1810, accessed January 6, 2023.

their death inevitable."[58] The principle of humanity also further balances military necessity, which is reflected in most IHL instruments. This balancing function is best described by the so-called Martens Clause in the Preamble to the Hague Conventions on the Laws and Customs of War on Land from 1899. The idea of the clause named after the diplomat Friedrich Martens is very simple. In essence, it attempts to fill a possible gap in the legislation by providing that, in the situation of an armed conflict in the absence of a legal norm, belligerents are still bound by the laws of humanity and the requirements of public conscience.

This principle is rather vague and open to interpretation, evident by the attempts to apply it in numerous contexts, from the deployment of LAWS to nuclear weapons.[59] Furthermore, it is one of the most challenging principles from an ethical and philosophical point of view. The principle of humanity requires an almost Schrödinger-like state of mind in which the enemy on the battlefield which is to be killed is also regarded as a fellow human being. This paradox makes the practical application of the principle a very hard task not only by humans but even more so by autonomous systems used in a military context, which more often than not reflect human bias.

20.3 USING AI IN ARMED CONFLICTS

The present chapter already sporadically touched upon several legal, ethical, and technical problems raised by applying the principles of IHL to AI systems used for military purposes. This next section is going to concentrate on the different applications for which AI systems are used, which includes LAWS or so-called "killer-robots" without being limited thereto. It also discusses the possible regulatory framework and challenges before the full-scale adoption of such systems.

20.3.1 *Lethal Autonomous Weapons Systems*

LAWS have been in the spotlight for several years already due to the blooming of the tech industry and in particular the huge investments and reliance on AI systems. Naturally, realizing the capabilities of AI in everyday life poses the question of how it can be used in military setting. Combining technological development with justified ethical concerns and the catchy phrase "killer robots" served as a great source of inspiration for media and entertainment, with the unfortunate result of shifting the focus of the discussion from people and their behavior to the regulation of inanimate objects.

[58] St. Petersburg Declaration Renouncing the Use, in Time of War, of Explosive Projectiles under 400 Grammes Weight, consideration 5.

[59] Theodor Mero, "The Martens Clause, principles of humanity, and dictates of public conscience" (2017) *American Journal of International Law*, 94(1): 78–89.

There are a number of problematic points related to the discussion about LAWS that prevent policymakers and other relevant stakeholders to move away from speculation and concentrate instead on the real dangers and immediate issues caused by using AI in armed conflicts.

First, despite the concept of LAWS being around for quite a while, we still lack a universal definition of what constitutes a lethal autonomous weapon.[60] A definition is extremely important because "autonomy" is a scaled feature. Therefore, the answer to the question of whether a system is truly autonomous depends on where on the curve the definition positions LAWS. A similar issue appeared during the ongoing process of creating legislation on AI in several jurisdictions,[61] such as the AI Act in the EU, discussed in Chapter 12 of this Book.

Defining LAWS has been a key task for the High Contracting Parties and Signatories of the CCW, through the Group of Governmental Experts on emerging technologies in the area of LAWS (GGE on LAWS). However, their efforts to adopt a universal definition currently remain fruitless.[62] Hence, the lack of a universal definition is filled by a plethora of more regional definitions serving various purposes. For example, the United States Department of Defense characterizes fully autonomous weapons systems as systems that "once activated, can select and engage targets without further intervention by a human operator."[63]

The European Parliament, by comparison, adopted another definition through a resolution referring to LAWS as "weapon systems without meaningful human control over the critical functions of selecting and attacking individual targets."[64] The two definitions, although similar, reveal some important differences. The definition provided by the European Parliament is based on the absence of *meaningful* human oversight, while the US definition only speaks about control. Additionally, Directive 3000.09[65] also defines semi-autonomous systems, highlighting the scale-based nature of autonomy, while the resolution of the European Parliament does

[60] UNIDIR, "The Weaponization of Increasingly Autonomous Technologies: Concerns, Characteristics and Definitional Approaches" (2017) *UNIDIR Resources*, https://unidir.org/publication/weaponization-increasingly-autonomous-technologies-concerns-characteristics-and, accessed January 3, 2023.

[61] Jonas Schuett, "Defining the scope of AI regulations" (August 22, 2021) *Law, Innovation and Technology, Legal Priorities Project Working Paper Series No. 9*; Katerina Yordanova, "The EU AI Act – Balancing Human Rights and Innovation Through Regulatory Sandboxes and Standardization" (2022) *Competition Policy International*, www.competitionpolicyinternational.com/the-eu-ai-act-balancing-human-rights-and-innovation-through-regulatory-sandboxes-and-standardization/, accessed January 7, 2023.

[62] Ann-Katrien Oimann, "The responsibility gap and LAWS: a critical mapping of the debate" (2023) *Philosophy & Technology*, 36(3): 4.

[63] US Department of Defense, "Directive 3000.09 Autonomy in Weapon Systems" (November 21, 2012) www.esd.whs.mil/portals/54/documents/dd/issuances/dodd/300009p.pdf, accessed January 7, 2023.

[64] European Parliament resolution of September 12, 2018 on autonomous weapon systems (2018/2752(RSP)), www.europarl.europa.eu/doceo/document/TA-8-2018-0341_EN.html, accessed January 7, 2023.

[65] USA Department of Defense Directive 3000.09, "Autonomy in Weapon Systems," November 21, 2012.

not mention them at all. The discrepancy between just these two examples of LAWS definitions demonstrates that a number of weapons systems might fall in or out of the scope of norms that should regulate LAWS based on the criteria applied by a certain State, which leads to uncertainty.

A second problematic point in the LAWS discussion is the speculative nature of their capabilities and deployment. While the general consensus is that the deployment of killer robots is a highly undesirable prospect for both ethical and legal reasons, such as the alleged breach of the principle of humanity[66] and compromised human dignity,[67] those arguments are based on what we imagine LAWS to be. Military technology has always been surrounded by a very high level of confidentiality, and this is also the case when it comes to LAWS. Until recently, their nature could only be speculated on based on more general knowledge about AI advances and robotic applications outside their military application. The first officially recognized use of LAWS was established by the UN Security Council's Panel of Experts on Libya regarding an incident from March 2020. During that incident, a Turkish STM Kargu-2 drone, referred to as a lethal autonomous weapon, "hunted down and remotely engaged" logistic convoys and retreating forces in Libya.[68] The drone was described as being "programmed to attack targets without requiring data connectivity between the operator and the munition: in effect, a true 'fire, forget and find' capability."[69] There is little to no information, however, regarding the measure taken to ensure compatibility of the drone with the norms and principles of international law.

The UN's recognition of the use of autonomous drones in Libya reignited the public debate on the international rules applicable to LAWS. It also strengthened the calls for a total ban on killer robots, unfortunately without the participation of countries like the USA, Russia, Turkey, and others having the necessary resources for the research and development of autonomous weapons.

Nevertheless, relevant stakeholders such as states, NGOs, companies, and even individuals with high standing in society[70] did take some significant steps in two directions. First, they launched campaigns promoting a total ban on LAWS[71] and

[66] Elvira Rosert and Frank Sauer, "Prohibiting autonomous weapons: put human dignity first" (2019) *Global Policy*, 10(3): 373.

[67] Amanda Sharkey, "Autonomous weapons systems, killer robots and human dignity" (2019) *Ethics and Information Technologies*, 21(2): 87.

[68] UN Security Council's Panel of Experts on Libya, "Final report of the Panel of Experts on Libya established pursuant to Security Council resolution 1973 (2011)" (March 8, 2021) S/2021/229.

[69] Ibid.

[70] Ian Sample, "Thousands of leading AI researchers sign pledge against killer robots" (2018) *The Guardian*, www.theguardian.com/science/2018/jul/18/thousands-of-scientists-pledge-not-to-help-build-killer-ai-robots, accessed January 13, 2023.

[71] Human Rights Watch, "Stopping killer robots. Country positions on banning fully autonomous weapons and retaining human control" (2020) *Human Rights Watch Website*, www.hrw.org/report/2020/08/10/stopping-killer-robots/country-positions-banning-fully-autonomous-weapons-and, accessed January 13, 2023.

second, they started developing and applying rules that govern the existing LAWS in accordance with IHL.[72]

The first initiative, even though remaining popular in civil society, does not currently show any significant development on a global scale.[73] The second one has a better success rate, being built around the application of the CCW, which was deemed to be the most suitable instrument to attempt to regulate LAWS. It is so because of its purpose to ban or restrict the use of specific types of weapons that are considered to cause unnecessary or unjustifiable suffering to combatants or to affect civilians indiscriminately. In addition, the structure of the Convention allows flexibility in dealing with new types of weapons, such as for example blinding laser weapons.[74]

Therefore, this particular forum was considered as best placed to discuss the technological development of LAWS and the legal and customary rules applicable to them,[75] as well as to codify the results of this discussion. The GGE on LAWS adopted the eleven guiding principles in the 2019 Meeting of the High Contracting Parties to the CCW.[76] The eleven guiding principles first and foremost address the need for LAWS to comply with IHL (guiding principle 1), as well as the human responsibility for the use of LAWS (guiding principle 2). This was important not only because of the ongoing trend of personification of machines[77] but also because of the existing debate regarding the so-called "responsibility gap" created by LAWS.[78] This is further supported by guiding principle 7, which forbids anthropomorphizing LAWS. The guiding principles also elaborate on the need for human–machine interaction, accountability mechanisms, and a sound balance between military necessity and humanitarian considerations.

[72] An example of that is the established GGE, under the mandate of the CCW Meeting of High Contracting Parties and their ongoing work, including the eleven guiding principles on LAWS.

[73] James Dawes, "UN fails to agree on 'killer robot' ban as nations pour billions into autonomous weapons research" (December 2021) *The Conversation*, https://theconversation.com/un-fails-to-agree-on-killer-robot-ban-as-nations-pour-billions-into-autonomous-weapons-research-173616, accessed January 13, 2023.

[74] Protocol IV of CCW adopted on October 13, 1995 during the First Review Conference of the States parties to the convention, entered into force July 30, 1998.

[75] In particular, see Additional Protocol I to the Geneva Conventions, Article 36 providing that "[i]n the study, development, acquisition or adoption of a new weapon, means or method of warfare, a High Contracting Party is under an obligation to determine whether its employment would, in some or all circumstances, be prohibited by this Protocol or by any other rule of international law applicable to the High Contracting Party."

[76] Meeting of the High Contracting Parties to the Convention on Prohibitions or Restrictions on the Use of Certain Conventional Weapons Which May Be Deemed to Be Excessively Injurious or to Have Indiscriminate Effects, "Final Report" (December 13, 2019) CCW/MSP/2019/9, https://documents-dds-ny.un.org/doc/UNDOC/GEN/G19/343/64/PDF/G1934364.pdf?OpenElement, accessed January 13, 2023.

[77] Ugo Pagallo, "Vital, Sophia, and Co., The quest for the legal personhood of robots" (2018) *Information*, 9: 230.

[78] Oimann, *The Responsibility Gap and LAWS: A Critical Mapping of the Debate*, p. 7.

Despite the guiding principles showing some progress and common ground among States Parties to the CCW on the subject of LAWS, they are not a binding legal instrument and are not a lot to show after eight years of work on the side of the GGE. Indeed, the formulated principles could become useful by demonstrating convergence on elements of customary international law such as *opinion juris*[79] or serving as a starting point for a new protocol to the CCW. Currently, however, neither of those appear to be on the agenda.

20.3.2 *Other Applications of Autonomous Systems in Armed Conflicts*

As discussed previously, the precise extent of the use and development of LAWS remain mostly confined to speculations. While weapons with a certain degree of autonomy such as unmanned aerial vehicles are currently used in many armed conflicts, truly autonomous weapons remain a rarity. However, outside the context of LAWS, the more general use of AI systems in armed conflicts and for military purposes is becoming the new normal.

AI remains a great tool for supporting decision-making in the military, assisting personnel with going through large quantities of data and analyzing it, and making the "right" judgment regarding transport, logistics, communications, and others.

Furthermore, AI has many applications in data gathering, including as a surveillance tool, although such AI products may fall under the category of dual-use items.[80] Other possible utilizations of AI systems are applications for predictive maintenance of military equipment,[81] unarmed vehicles such as ambulances, supply trucks or drones,[82] and medical aid.[83] While for some of these purposes of IHL might still be a consideration, such as for example the special regime of medical vehicles, other uses might raise more fundamental concerns when aspiring conformity with human rights law. A typical example is dual-use technologies used for

[79] In public international law, *opinio juris sive necessitates* refers to the second element needed for the establishment of a binding customary rule, namely the belief of a State that it is *bound* by a certain rule or obligation.

[80] Dual-use items are goods designed for civilian use, which also have military utilization. Usually, such goods are subject to a special export control regime. In EU, this regime is established by Regulation (EU) 2021/821. For more information, see Machiko Kanetake, "Dual-Use Export Control: Security and Human Rights Challenges to Multilateralism" in Marc Bungenberg, Markus Krajewski, Christian J. Tams, Jörg Philipp Terhechte, and Andreas R. Ziegler (eds), *European Yearbook of International Economic Law 2020* (Springer, 2021).

[81] For example, ALIS is an AI tool used to predictively maintain F-35 fighter jets.

[82] Millicent Abadicio, "Artificial intelligence for military logistics – current applications" (2019) *EMERJ website* https://emerj.com/ai-sector-overviews/artificial-intelligence-military-logistics/ accessed January 13, 2023.

[83] Ajinkya Jadhav, "Developing AI in combat healthcare" (2021) *CLAWS* www.claws.in/developing-ai-in-combat-healthcare/ accessed January 13, 2023.

surveillance of individuals, which violate their right to privacy and often other rights too, without a plausible justification based on military necessity.[84]

Finally, AI is increasingly used in cyberwarfare, both for its attack and defense capabilities.[85] Typically, this involves the spreading of viruses and malware, data theft, distributed denial-of-service attacks, but also disinformation campaigns.[86] AI systems can enhance these activities, as well as help to circumvent defenses on the way. AI is, however, not only used for defense purposes beyond military infrastructure but also to protect civilian objects and infrastructure that is more susceptible to cyberattacks due to being part of IoT.[87]

While cyberwarfare has not been explicitly mentioned by IHL instruments, this does not mean that it falls outside its scope. On the contrary, the potential (and often the intent) of cyberattacks to be indiscriminate is a considerable reason for applying IHL to cyberwarfare in full force, especially when AI systems are involved given their ability to further increase the scale of the attack.

20.4 CONCLUSION

All around the world, regulators are thinking about the changing power of AI in every aspect of our lives. Although some are calling for the adoption of stricter rules that would not allow something to be done just because we have the technology to do it, others support a more innovation-friendly, liberal approach to AI regulation, which would assist the industry and allow a more rapid development of AI in the tech sector. While both positions have their merit, when it comes to using AI in the military context, the stakes change dramatically.

The potential of AI in armed conflicts goes in two directions. It can save resources and lives more efficiently by supporting humans to make the "right" decisions or avoid unnecessary causalities or it could assist in killing people more efficiently. During a war, those might be the two sides of the same coin. Therefore, we need to ensure that IHL is embedded in the design, development, and use of AI systems to the best extent possible.

84 For a more in-depth discussion on dual-use AI, see Ilaria Carrozza, Nicholas Marsh & Gregory M. Reichberg, "Dual-use AI technology in China, the US and the EU: strategic implications for the balance of power" (2022) *PRIO Paper*. Oslo: PRIO, www.prio.org/publications/13150, accessed June 10, 2023.

85 For a more in-depth discussion, see Maria Taddeo, Tom McCutcheon, and Luciano Floridi, "Trusting artificial intelligence in cybersecurity is a double-edged sword" (2019) *Nature Machine Intelligence*, 12(1): 557–560.

86 Rod Thornton and Marina Miron, "Towards the 'third revolution in military affairs'. The Russian military's use of AI-enabled cyber warfare" (2020) *The 165 RUSI Journal*, 165(3): 12–21.

87 Petri Vähäkainu, Martti Lehto, Antti Kariluoto, and Anniina Ojalainen, "Artificial intelligence in protecting smart building's cloud service infrastructure from cyberattacks" in Hamid Jahankhani, Stefan Kendzierskyj, Nishan Chelvachandran, and Jaime Ibarra (eds) (Springer, 2020) *Cyber Defence in the Age of AI, Smart Societies and Augmented Humanity*, 289–319.

Even if killer robots would be successfully banned, that is not a guarantee that they would not be used anyway. Furthermore, as demonstrated, AI has many more applications on the battlefield, all of which need to be in accordance with the basic considerations of humanity during an armed conflict. Bringing military AI systems under the scope of IHL would give us at least some hope that, while we cannot stop AI from being used in wars, maybe we can change the ratio of its use as a weapon for killing, toward its use as a shield for protection.

Concluding Remarks

Nathalie A. Smuha

The central aim of this book was to provide an accessible and comprehensive overview of the legal, ethical and policy implications of artificial intelligence and algorithmic systems more broadly. As the various chapters in this book have shown, these technologies have a significant and growing impact on all domains of our lives, which makes it increasingly important to map, understand, and assess the challenges and opportunities they raise. This calls for an interdisciplinary approach, which is why this book brought together contributions from different disciplines with the goal of advancing our understanding of AI's societal impact, as well as examining how the current legal framework deals with this impact, and where it falls short in protecting the core values of our societies. To conclude this book, I first wish to take a step back and highlight some of themes that were common across its chapters. Second, I want to draw attention to a few gaps that require further exploration in the future.

An important thread across this book was the observation that AI and algorithmic systems do not exist in a legal vacuum. In particular, Parts II and III of the book provided an overview of the prevailing normative landscape, looking at both cross-cutting legal areas and sectoral domains. While this resulted in a description of a patchwork of rules that apply to the technology's development and use, sometimes even with tensions or inconsistencies across domains, it simultaneously showcased the possibility of mobilizing existing legal norms toward better protection against AI's adverse effects. Arguably, this possibility is too easily overlooked in today's public debate, as all eyes are on the European Union's new AI Act. Laws that were enacted prior to the advent of AI may not be perfectly tailored to its idiosyncrasies and the way in which it causes harm, yet they still have an important role to play, and should be invoked and enforced to make most out of their protective provisions.

At the same time, practically all authors identified certain shortcomings in the legal framework, especially when it comes to the protection of individual rights. In some instances, the substantive gaps within the – often convoluted – existing legal patchwork were the culprit, while in other instances, the authors instead hinted at a lack of enforcement of existing rules, which is no less of a concern. The new

AI Act is frequently invoked as an attempt to address the former, but it is not free from criticism either, and the effectiveness of its enforcement mechanism over the longer term is far from evident in light of the questionable regulatory architecture it adopted. While this does not mean that we should despair at the state of Europe's legal framework for AI – there is, in fact, much to be hopeful about in light of the EU's (albeit imperfect) attempt to protect human rights against AI's risks – it does underline the fact that we should not put all our hope on new or better legislation, or on legislation altogether. The AI Act has its limits, and other regulatory frameworks can complement its provisions, but they have their limits too. No law is perfect, as it is always a compromise solution that must meet the political reality, and that has inherent tensions between the demands of generality and specificity, and between predictability and flexibility.

Rather than losing faith in the power of the law altogether, this should instead incite us to also consider how law complements and interacts with solutions outside the legal realm. Several contributions for instance made the case for more AI literacy and education, responsibility-taking, awareness raising, public deliberation, and the encouragement of critical engagement more generally. Part I of this book has also shown how philosophical and ethical reflections on AI can inspire, inform and contribute to those aims, as well as strengthening the normative underpinnings of the existing laws. Indeed, the study of other disciplines – covering not only ethics and philosophy, but also sociology, anthropology, psychology, economics, cognitive science, and many others – are prerequisites for any sound critique and improvement of the normative framework that governs AI as a technology, its impact on society, and especially the human action involved in it.

In addition, they can also enable us to reflect on our approach to AI more generally, and the ease with which we seem to be ready to relinquish our agency in setting out the role and functions we want this technology to have in our society. The idea that AI overcomes us, and that all we can do as a society is run behind the facts and try to come up with some imperfect legal rules to control it, is both erroneous and dangerous, as it unwittingly deprives us from our individual, collective and societal self-determination vis-à-vis technology, which remains a human-made and human-caused object. Reclaiming this agency is important, but it requires a more nuanced understanding and debate about AI's short and long-term societal effects, to which this book aspired to contribute.

There are, however, also some themes that fall outside the scope of this book, and that require further exploration in light of their importance for the AI governance debate. Let me point out two in particular. The first pertains to the jurisdictional area of attention. Indeed, when examining AI through the lens of law, ethics and policy, and assessing whether new or updated norms and theories are warranted, it is important to ask at which jurisdictional level those updates should take place. This book is heavily Europe-focused, and primarily analyses the normative framework of AI in the EU legal order. In this regard, this book is not an exception, as many contributions in the sphere of AI governance have a markedly Western perspective. In fact, most AI ethics guidelines originate from the US and Europe,[1] despite the fact that these jurisdictions represent less than 20% of the world population.

Admittedly, the EU was the first to adopt a cross-sectoral AI-specific regulation, and could hence arguably offer important insights for the AI governance debate (though other jurisdictions, such as China in particular, already adopted domain-specific AI rules prior to the AI Act's adoption). It is, however, rather evident that governance solutions which might (theoretically) work for Europe, will not necessarily work in other parts of the world – nor should we assume this to be the case. As noted elsewhere, *"the economic, social, legal and political situation of countries strongly differ. Hence, the manner in which countries will be affected by AI – both in positive and negative ways – will inevitably differ as well."*[2]

Already today, it is extremely clear that the benefits of AI are unevenly distributed not only within states, but also among states. Nevertheless, voices of the global majority are still given less space and weight, despite the alleged "universality" of the global AI governance discussion, and despite the (direct and indirect) extraterritorial reach of the EU's standards.[3] While this book does not pretend to adopt a universal perspective to the challenges that AI raises, it remains important to acknowledge the virtues as well as the limitations of examining those challenges from a European lens, and to assert the importance for readers to complement contributions like this book with the study of works that illuminate perspectives beyond the Global North.

The second aspect that this book does not discuss, but that may be useful to reflect upon, pertains to the role of international organizations in the governance of AI. Not only national and supranational entities (such as the EU), but also international organizations have increasingly been awarded with a mandate to develop policies (and even laws) to guide AI-related human behavior toward one that is "ethical" and "trustworthy." Some of these developments are briefly touched upon in this book's contribution – from the Council of Europe's new Convention on AI, human rights, democracy and the rule of law, to the UN's attempts at governing lethal autonomous weapons, and UNESCO's role in the ethics of AI in education. However, a systematic analysis of the practical and political impact of those organizations in governing AI, and the way in which they succeed or fail at fostering (more universal and potentially inclusive) norms to protect societal values, would be an important complementary contribution to consider in this context.

[1] Anna Jobin, Marcello Ienca, and Effy Vayena, "The global landscape of AI ethics guidelines" (2019) *Nature Machine Intelligence*, 1: 391.

[2] Nathalie A. Smuha, "From a 'race to AI' to a 'race to AI Regulation': Regulatory competition for artificial intelligence" (2021) *Law, Innovation and Technology*, 13(1): 81.

[3] Often referred to as the so-called "Brussels effect." See Anu Bradford, *The Brussels Effect: How the European Union Rules the World* (Oxford University Press, 2020).

Finally, let me close with a remark that may sound obvious, but which has important repercussions that merit being pointed out nevertheless. AI as a technological phenomenon is continuously in flux, and so are the law, ethics and policy that relate to it. And while we can to some extent identify and anticipate the various risks and harms that are associated with its irresponsible development and use, there are undoubtedly also problems as well as benefits that we do not yet grasp or that we cannot yet predict. The launch of AI governance debates and initiatives at several jurisdictional levels can certainly be helpful in discovering, framing and analyzing the concerns we wish to address and the advantages we wish to gain, but we must equally be mindful of the fact that there is much information we do not have, and that there are also unknown unknowns, especially over the longer term.

It is therefore essential that we clarify, especially for ourselves, which values we wish to hold on to amidst the potential changes that societies might undergo, whether impelled by technology or by other developments – and it is precisely there that law, ethics and policy play a vital role. This role will, however, only come to fruition in its fullest force when imbued with the openness to keep on listening to and learning from other disciplines and jurisdictions, and when accompanied by an appropriate level of (regulatory) humbleness.